GENDER AND NARRATIVE IN THE *MAHĀBHĀRATA*

The Sanskrit *Mahābhārata* is one of the most important texts to emerge from the Indian cultural tradition. At almost 75,000 verses it is the longest poem in the world, and throughout Indian history it has been hugely influential in shaping gender and social norms. In the context of ancient India, it is the definitive cultural narrative in the construction of masculine, feminine and alternative gender roles.

This book brings together many of the most respected scholars in the field of *Mahābhārata* studies, as well as some of its most promising young scholars. By focusing specifically on gender constructions, some of the most innovative aspects of the *Mahābhārata* are highlighted. Whilst taking account of feminist scholarship, the contributors see the *Mahābhārata* as providing an opportunity to frame discussion of gender in literature not just in terms of the socio-historical roles of men and women. Instead they analyse the text in terms of the wider poetic and philosophical possibilities thrown up by the semiotics of gendering. Consequently, the book bridges a gap in text-critical methodology between the traditional philological approach and more recent trends in gender and literary theory. It will be appreciated by readers interested in South Asian Studies, Hinduism, Religious Studies and Gender Studies.

Simon Brodbeck and **Brian Black** are researchers in the Department of the Study of Religions at the School of Oriental and African Studies, University of London. Brodbeck is the author of several scholarly articles on aspects of the *Mahābhārata*; Black is the author of *The Character of the Self in Ancient India: priests, kings, and women in the early Upaniṣads*.

ROUTLEDGE HINDU STUDIES SERIES

Series Editor: Gavin Flood, University of Stirling
Former Series Editor: Francis X. Clooney, SJ, Harvard University

OCHS

The Routledge Hindu Studies Series, in association with the Oxford Centre for Hindu Studies, intends the publication of constructive Hindu theological, philosophical and ethical projects aimed at bringing Hindu traditions into dialogue with contemporary trends in scholarship and contemporary society. The series invites original, high-quality, research-level work on religion, culture and society of Hindus living in India and abroad. Proposals for annotated translations of important primary sources and studies in the history of the Hindu religious traditions will also be considered.

EPISTEMOLOGIES AND THE LIMITATIONS OF PHILOSOPHICAL INQUIRY
Doctrine in Mādhva Vedānta
Deepak Sarma

A HINDU CRITIQUE OF BUDDHIST EPISTEMOLOGY
Kumārila on Perception
The 'Determination of Perception' Chapter of Kumārilabhaṭṭa's *Ślokavārttika*
Translation and Commentary
John Taber

ŚAṂKARA'S ADVAITA VEDANTA
A Way of Teaching
Jacqueline Hirst

ATTENDING KṚṢṆA'S IMAGE
Caitanya Vaiṣṇava Mūrti-sevā as Devotional Truth
Kenneth Russell Valpey

ADVAITA VEDĀNTA AND VAIṢṆAVISM
The Philosophy of Madhusūdana Sarasvatī
Sanjukta Gupta

CLASSICAL SĀṂKHYA AND YOGA
An Indian Metaphysics of Experience
Mikel Burley

SELF-SURRENDER (PRAPATTI) TO GOD IN ŚRĪVAIṢṆAVISM
Tamil Cats and Sanskrit Monkeys
Srilata Raman

THE CAITANYA VAIṢṆAVA VEDĀNTA OF JĪVA GOSVĀMĪ
When Knowledge Meets Devotion
Ravi M. Gupta

GENDER AND NARRATIVE IN THE *MAHĀBHĀRATA*
Edited by Simon Brodbeck and Brian Black

GENDER AND NARRATIVE IN THE *MAHĀBHĀRATA*

Edited by Simon Brodbeck and Brian Black

Routledge
Taylor & Francis Group
LONDON AND NEW YORK

First published 2007
by Routledge
2 Park Square, Milton Park, Abingdon, Oxon OX14 4RN

Simultaneously published in the USA and Canada
by Routledge
270 Madison Ave, New York, NY 10016

Routledge is an imprint of the Taylor & Francis Group, an informa business

Transferred to Digital Printing 2009

Typeset in Times New Roman by
RefineCatch Limited, Bungay, Suffolk

British Library Cataloguing in Publication Data
A catalogue record for this book is available from the British Library

Library of Congress Cataloging in Publication Data
Gender and narrative in the Mahabharata / edited by Simon Brodbeck and Brian Black.
p. cm.—(Routledge Hindu studies series)
Listen but do not grieve : grief, paternity, and time in the laments of Dhrtarastra / Emily T. Hudson—Eavesdropping on the Epic : female listeners in the Mahabharata / Brian Black— Arguments of a queen : Draupadi's views on kingship / Angelika Malinar – How do you conduct yourself? : gender and the construction of a dialogical self in the Mahabharata / Laurie L. Patton—Among friends : marriage, women, and some little birds / Alf Hiltebeitel—Gendered soteriology : marriage and the karmayoga / Simon Brodbeck—Bhisma as matchmaker / Nick Allen – Bhisma beyond Freud : Bhisma in the Mahabharata / James L. Fitzgerald—"Show you are a man!" : transsexuality and gender bending in the characters of Arjuna/Brhannada and Amba/Sikhandin(i) / Andrea Custodi—Krsna's son Samba : faked gender and other ambiguities on the background of lunar and solar myth / Georg von Simson – Paradigms of the good in the Mahabharata : Suka and Sulabha in quagmires of ethics / Arti Dhand.
Includes bibliographical references and index.
1. Mahabharata–Criticism, interpretation, etc. 2. Gender identity in literature. I. Brodbeck, Simon, 1970– II. Black, Brian, 1970–
BL1138.27.G43 2007
294.5′923048—dc22

ISBN10: 0–415–41540–3 (hbk)
ISBN10: 0–415–54471–8 (pbk)
ISBN10: 0–203–02964–X (ebk)

ISBN13: 978–0–415–41540–8 (hbk)
ISBN13: 978–0–415–54471–9 (pbk)
ISBN13: 978–0–203–02964–0 (ebk)

TO THE MEMORY OF JULIA LESLIE,
A WONDERFUL WOMAN, COLLEAGUE
AND SCHOLAR

CONTENTS

NOTES ON CONTRIBUTORS

Until his retirement in 2001, **Nick Allen** was for twenty-five years Lecturer/Reader in the Social Anthropology of South Asia at the Institute of Social and Cultural Anthropology at Oxford, and a Fellow of Wolfson College. His D.Phil., based on twenty months' fieldwork in East Nepal, focused on the mythology and oral traditions of a Tibeto-Burman 'tribal' community. Apart from Himalayan comparativism, he has published on the origin and macro-history of kinship systems and on the French tradition in sociological thought (see his *Categories and Classifications*, 2000). However, in recent years his main research interest has been in Indo-European cultural comparativism, and in particular in the idea of a common origin lying behind Sanskrit and ancient Greek epic traditions.

Brian Black received his B.A. in philosophy at the University of California at San Diego, and his M.A. and Ph.D. in the study of religions at the School of Oriental and African Studies (SOAS), University of London, where he is currently a researcher. His primary scholarly interests are the Upaniṣads, the *Mahābhārata* and the Buddhist Nikāyas. He has taught a number of courses on the texts and philosophies of Hinduism and Buddhism at both SOAS and Birkbeck College. He is author of the book *The Character of the Self in Ancient India: priests, kings, and women in the early Upaniṣads*.

Simon Pearse Brodbeck was born in Lancaster and studied at Clare College, Cambridge, King's College, London, and the School of Oriental and African Studies, London, where he obtained his doctorate with a thesis on the philosophy of the *Bhagavadgītā*. He taught in the Asian Studies Department at the University of Edinburgh, before returning to London to work on the Arts and Humanities Research Council *Mahābhārata* research project which led to this book. He has written papers on religious experience, on various aspects of the *Bhagavadgītā* and *Mahābhārata*, and on the philosophy of cricket. His current projects are studies of the *Mahābhārata*'s patrilineal ideology and of its ring-compositional structures.

Andrea Custodi received her doctorate from the George Washington University's Human Sciences Program, with concentrations in South Asian religious studies, Lacanian psychonanalysis, and feminist theory. Her dissertation, 'Dharma and desire: Lacan and the left half of the *Mahābhārata*', brings this interdisciplinary focus to bear on themes of gender, sexuality, and subjectivity in the epic, and seeks to apply Lacanian theoretical innovations to psychoanalytic discourse on the subcontinent. Dr Custodi is currently Executive Director of the South India Term Abroad (SITA) Program, a consortium of U.S. colleges and universities that conducts an undergraduate academic and cultural immersion program in Tamil Nadu.

Arti Dhand is Assistant Professor at the Department and Centre for the Study of Religion, University of Toronto. She is the author of *Woman as Fire, Woman as Sage: sexual ideology in the Mahābhārata* (State University of New York Press, in press). She has also written several articles dealing with the ethics of gender and violence in the Hindu epics.

James L. Fitzgerald is Professor of Religious Studies at the University of Tennessee. He studied for his Ph.D. at the University of Chicago under the supervision of J.A.B. van Buitenen, and is now the editor and principal translator of the ongoing University of Chicago Press translation of the Poona Critical Edition of the *Mahābhārata*, which was interrupted by van Buitenen's death in 1980, but which continued in 2004 with the publication of *The Mahābhārata*, vol. 7: *The Book of the Women; The Book of Peace, part 1*. In addition to his translation work, Fitzgerald has authored a number of ground-breaking scholarly articles on the *Mahābhārata*, most notably 'India's fifth Veda: the *Mahābhārata*'s presentation of itself' (1985, 1991) and 'The Rāma Jāmadagnya "thread" of the *Mahābhārata*: a new survey of Rāma Jāmadagnya in the Pune text' (2002).

Alf Hiltebeitel is Professor of Religion, History, and Human Sciences at the George Washington University. His research has focused on the *Mahābhārata* and the *Rāmāyaṇa*, regional Indian folk epics, and the cult of the goddess Draupadī. Influenced by the French scholars Georges Dumézil and Madeleine Biardeau (whose work he has translated), he has authored a great many articles on India's epics, and two books on the *Mahābhārata*: *The Ritual of Battle: Krishna in the Mahābhārata* (1976) and *Rethinking the Mahābhārata: a reader's guide to the education of the dharma king* (2001). He is a co-editor of *Is the Goddess a Feminist? The politics of South Asian goddesses* (2002, with Kathleen Erndl). His work continues to focus on the classical period and the Tamil Draupadī cult. He is currently working on a book titled *Dharma*, and on various essays on the epics following up his *Rethinking the Mahābhārata*.

Emily T. Hudson received her M.A. in the History of Religions from the

University of Chicago and her Ph.D. from the Graduate Division of Religion at Emory University. Currently she is a Lecturer on South Asian Religions at Harvard Divinity School. Situating herself methodologically at the crossroads of religious ethics, the history of religions, and religion and literature, she has research interests in Sanskrit literature and literary theory, Greek epic and tragedy, and comparative religious ethics. She is the author of 'Heaven's riddles or the hell trick: theodicy and narrative strategies in the *Mahābhārata*' (2006).

Angelika Malinar is Lecturer in Hinduism at the School of Oriental and African Studies, University of London. She is the author of *Rājavidyā: Das königliche Wissen um Herrschaft und Verzicht. Studien zur Bhagavadgītā* (1996), editor of *Time in India: concepts and practices* (2006) and co-editor of *Charisma and Canon: essays on the religious history of the Indian subcontinent* (2003). Since completing her habilitation on the concept of *prakṛti* in Sāṃkhya philosophy, she has taught at the Universities of Tübingen and Berlin. She has conducted several collaborative research projects that have resulted in major publications, for instance on the *Nārāyaṇīya* section of the *Mahābhārata*, on Hindu monastic institutions in Orissa, and on the relationship between religious and aesthetic experience in Hinduism.

Laurie L. Patton is Winship Distinguished Research Professor in the Humanities at Emory University. Her scholarly interests include the interpretation of early Indian ritual and narrative, comparative mythology, literary theory in the study of religion, and women and Hinduism in contemporary India. She is the author of *Bringing the Gods to Mind: poetry and performance in early Indian sacrifice* (2005) and *Myth as Argument: the Bṛhaddevatā as canonical commentary* (1996); the editor of *Jewels of Authority: women and textual tradition in Hindu India* (2002) and *Authority, Anxiety, and Canon: essays in Vedic interpretation* (1994); and the co-editor of *The Indo-Aryan Controversy: evidence and inference in Indian history* (2005, with Edwin Bryant) and *Myth and Method* (1996, with Wendy Doniger). Her translation of the *Bhagavadgītā* is in press with Penguin Books. She is also the author of a volume of poetry: *Fire's Goal: poems from the Hindu year* (2003). She is currently at work on a book, *Grandmother Language*, focusing on the status of women and Sanskrit in contemporary India.

Georg von Simson studied Indology and Classical Philology in Mainz and Göttingen, and was Professor of Indian Languages and Literature at the University of Oslo (Norway) from 1977 to 2003. He lives after his retirement in Göttingen (Germany). Apart from Buddhist Sanskrit (language and literature), one of his main fields of interest is the *Mahābhārata*, its text transmission, the (mythic) time structure of its plot and the epic's underlying myth in general. He pays particular attention to myths that are based on the experience of the seasons of the year (calendar myths) and of astral phenomena. His publications include *Einführung in die Indologie: Stand, Methoden, Aufgaben* (1979, 2nd edn 1993, co-editor and co-author with Heinz Bechert), 'Die zeitmythische Struktur des Mahābhārata' (1994), and 'Characterizing by contrast: the case of the Buddha and Devadatta, Bhīṣma and Karṇa' (2003).

PREFACE

The Routledge Hindu Studies Series, published in collaboration with the Oxford Centre for Hindu Studies, intends primarily the publication of constructive Hindu theological, philosophical, and ethical projects. The focus is on issues and concerns of relevance to readers interested in Hindu traditions in particular, yet also in the context of a wider range of related religious concerns that matter in today's world. The Series seeks to promote excellent scholarship and, in relation to it, an open and critical conversation among scholars and the wider audience of interested readers. Though contemporary in its purpose, the Series recognizes the importance of retrieving the classic texts and ideas, beliefs and practices, of Hindu traditions, so that the great intellectuals of these traditions may as it were become conversation partners in the conversations of today.

The study of the Hindu epic literature has developed in recent years with philological studies showing the layering and development of this corpus and more accurate dating allowing the texts to be placed in historical context. Not only philological work but hermenutical work also needs to be done and the texts re-interpreted in the light of concerns of new generations and new locations. In this book on the *Mahābhārata*, Simon Brodbeck and Brian Black have significantly developed the study of the text. Assuming philological rigour, the contributors attempt to go beyond philology in raising questions of contemporary relevance, particularly about narrative and gender. The authors have shown in some detail for the first time how complex narrative structures and embeddings are used in the epic. They have also shown how the text deals with issues such as gender in a complex way by bringing to bear on it questions of contemporary, social relevance. Not only is this book a contribution to Indology, it is an important contribution to gender studies and other cultural studies. Indeed, any general accounts of gender or theories of text that do not take into account the Indian material are of limited value and this book will need to be read by cultural theorists in other areas. The authors are to be congratulated on producing a very significant contribution to the study of the Indian epics.

Gavin Flood
Series Editor

ACKNOWLEDGEMENTS

The editors would like to acknowledge the support of the Arts and Humanities Research Council (formerly a part of the British Academy), which funded the research project at the School of Oriental and African Studies from which this volume proceeds. The project, *Epic Constructions: gender, myth and society in the Mahābhārata*, was conceived by the late Julia Leslie, whose formative input and interest we will never forget. Since Julia's death, we have been glad of the support of the Centre for Gender and Religions Research, particularly through Brian Bocking's overall supervision of the project and Sîan Hawthorne's technical assistance. We are grateful to all those who contributed to the *Epic Constructions* conference in July 2005, and most especially to the contributors to this book, who have indulged and accommodated our spotted and inconstant visions with unerring good humour. We are grateful also to our respective families and numerous colleagues who have rendered assistance too various to be detailed here; to the Brooklyn Museum who gave their kind permission for the use of the cover picture; and to the staff at Routledge for sharing our enthusiasm for the volume.

FAMILY TREE

Many characters are omitted. Brahmins are in bold; gods, *apsarās* and rivers are in italics; '♀' denotes female; '=' denotes marriage; arrow denotes impregnation; '*' indicates intervening generations.

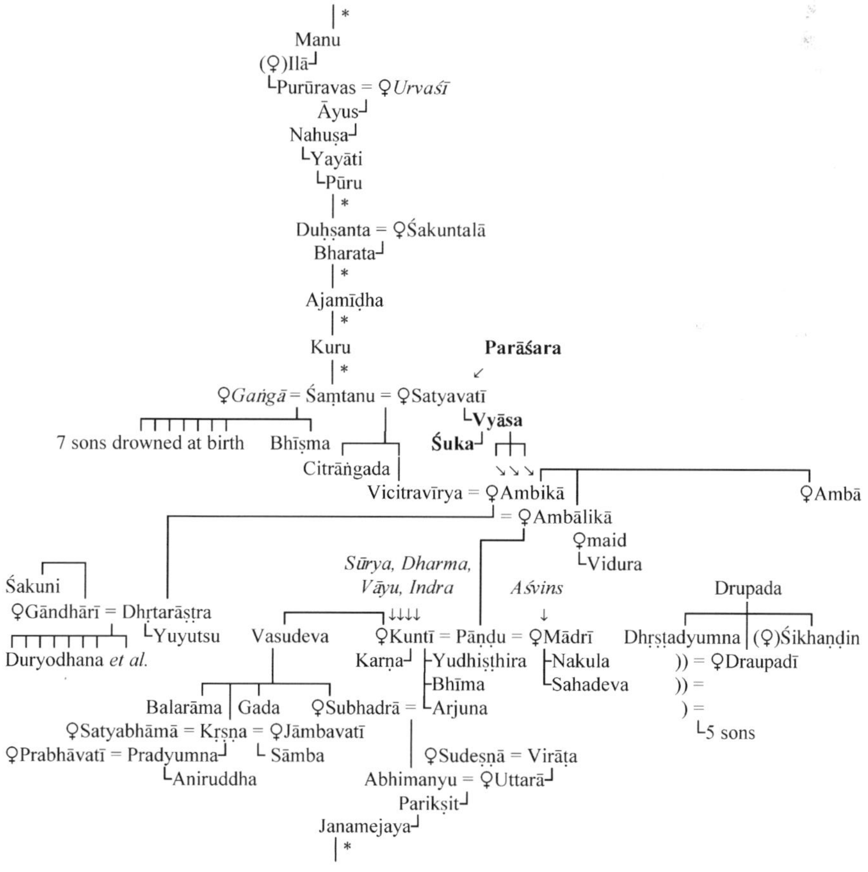

1

INTRODUCTION

Simon Brodbeck and Brian Black

This introduction is intended to contextualize the book as effectively as is briefly possible, bearing in mind that different readers will be approaching it from different directions and with different backgrounds. It contains indicative sections on the *Mahābhārata*, and on Gender Studies and its interface with the text, before turning to consider the structure and layout of the rest of the book.

The *Mahābhārata*

The *Mahābhārata* is a long narrative text in Sanskrit which tells the story of the five Pāṇḍava brothers before, during and after the war at Kurukṣetra (Kuru's Field or the Field of the Kurus, near present-day Delhi and the Yamuna-Ganges doab) between the Pāṇḍavas (and their allies) and their 100 paternal cousins (and their allies) over the kingship of their ancestral realm. The '*mahā*' in the title indicates the text's size and importance,[1] and the '*bhārata*' indicates that these two sets of cousins, descendants of King Kuru, are also descendants of King Bharata, whose name is now interchangeable with that of India itself (see Family Tree). As this suggests, the *Mahābhārata*, along with the Sanskrit *Rāmāyaṇa* (the Career of Rāma, with which it is often grouped for study as a Sanskrit 'epic'), is something of a national text; it has recently been called 'the quintessence of every thing that is Indian' (Sanyal 2006: 197). The eighteen Kurukṣetra armies are drawn from – and the Pāṇḍavas' various pilgrimages take them wandering over – most of the subcontinent, and versions of the *Mahābhārata* story recur throughout India in a wide variety of literary, performative, ritual, and political contexts.[2] The precise relationships between these various *Mahābhārata* traditions and the Sanskrit *Mahābhārata* are in many cases difficult to determine, but they will not concern us in this book, which focuses tightly upon the old Sanskrit text. More specifically, it focuses upon the text as presented by the Poona Critical Edition[3] (Sukthankar *et al.* 1933–66), which was prepared by minutely comparing as many existing Sanskrit *Mahābhārata* manuscripts as could conveniently be found, and by thus producing a 'reconstituted text' consisting of broadly that material (nearly 75,000 verses) which the many manuscripts were found to have in common, supplemented by a critical apparatus of footnotes and appendices representing the additional material (occurring in some or even most of the manuscripts) which was presumed to have accumulated over time in the various manuscript traditions. All the *Mahābhārata* references in this book are to the Critical Edition unless otherwise stated.

The 'reconstituted text', it is supposed, may approximate an ancient *Mahābhārata* (there has been much discussion of this supposition and of the procedural details of the Poona project,[4] and various scholars have suggested textual amendations): exactly how ancient is a matter of considerable debate, but few would suggest a date later than the sixth century CE, and many would place it – or parts of it, certainly – a number of centuries earlier. This 'reconstituted text', which has also been published in free-standing form (Dandekar 1971–5), has yet to be entirely translated into English, the efforts of Johannes van Buitenen for Chicago University Press having been interrupted by his death in 1979 and only recently taken up by James Fitzgerald and his team.[5] In the meantime, although the Sanskrit text of the Critical Edition is now also available on the world-wide web (J.D. Smith 1999a), the most widely used English *Mahābhārata* is the 'Roy Edition' (Ganguli 1970, first published 1883–96, also now online),[6] which readers may correlate with the Critical Edition references given in this book (and elsewhere) by using the concordance in the Appendix.

The *Mahābhārata* comprises eighteen books (*parvans*) of varying proportions. Its main story follows the Pāṇḍavas from their birth, childhood, and polyandrous marriage to Draupadī,[7] through their deepening breach with their cousins, through the eighteen-day Kurukṣetra war (in which all 100 cousins are killed) and its aftermath, to their deaths and even to their afterlives. This Pāṇḍava narrative is not told at a fixed pace; it is punctuated and embellished along the way by the many sub-stories and diverse teachings which the characters within the narrative tell to each other. These sub-stories are a vital aspect of the *Mahābhārata*; they are often called *upākhyāna*s, though many names are used (Hiltebeitel 2005a: 464–76). They are fitted carefully by their tellers to their hearers, at once diverting and pedagogical, and the characters develop and grow partly by means of them. Some are tales of Bhārata ancestors; some are situated teachings of one kind or another; some are back-stories of characters who also figure in the main Pāṇḍava story (some of whom we meet also in other texts); some are stories of gods and demons, or notable brahmins or snakes or kings of yore; yet their motifs tend to be of a piece with the *Mahābhārata* as a whole. In parallel to their effect upon the characters who hear them, they seem also to provide a kind of interpretive commentary applied by the authors and available directly to the text's audience. Otherwise unconnected stories or episodes from widely separated points in the text can be juxtaposed and compared by the redeployment of names or distinctive motifs. And the Pāṇḍava narrative, despite its sheer extent, is in the final analysis a sub-story itself, for it is presented in the *Mahābhārata* as told by Vaiśaṃpāyana to King Janamejaya, great-grandson of the Pāṇḍavas, on the occasion of his (Janamejaya's) snake sacrifice (*sarpasatra*), and as heard there by Ugraśravas and re-told, along with the story of the snake sacrifice and one or two others, to Śaunaka and other brahmins assembled for a protracted ritual *satra* in the forest of Naimiṣa. In every case the narratives are formally presented as dynamic interactions between the teller and the told; and the told may intervene repeatedly to direct the teller or to ask for details or commentary. This telescoping technique of nested narrative frames stretching into and out of the Pāṇḍava story, as well as giving the text an intra-commentarial property, allows the 'authorial voice' to remain obscured behind a sequence of inverted commas; and it is this, in part, which makes the *Mahābhārata* such an intriguing text to explore and interpret. The text highlights the question of its own authorial voice by containing a putative author as a character within several levels of its own narrative: Kṛṣṇa Dvaipāyana Vyāsa is the great-uncle of the Pāṇḍavas and their father's biological father; he appears at many points in their story to give them advice and assistance of various kinds; and he later puts the story together for posterity, teaching it to several of his pupils and witnessing Vaiśaṃpāyana's performance of it in person at Janamejaya's snake sacrifice.[8]

Broadly speaking, the *Mahābhārata*'s most obvious principal concerns are the problems and possibilities of government, most explicitly at the level of society, but also ranging beyond the human into the cosmic level involving various gods, as well as focusing more tightly within the household and ultimately within the individual. Social government pivots around the figure of the king, who should be of the *kṣatriya varṇa*, the class of warrior-aristocrats, which is said primordially to have been created from the chest or arms of the cosmic man.[9] The necessity for a king is stated very clearly by the *Mahābhārata* at various junctures (e.g. 12.59; 12.67–71), and the question of who is to be king in the Kuru capital Hāstinapura brings out issues of primogenitive birthright and of behavioural fitness. On the first issue, Dhṛtarāṣṭra, older brother of Pāṇḍu, was incapable of fully discharging the kingly function because he was blind, so the two effectively took it in turns, superintended by their uncle Bhīṣma; but both of the eldest cousins in the next generation, Dhṛtarāṣṭra's son Duryodhana and Pāṇḍu's son Yudhiṣṭhira, are about the same age. Before their story is told in full, we are given tales of odd behaviour in many previous generations of the royal line (Bhīṣma, for example, abdicated his primogenitive claim to the throne and vowed life-long celibacy in order that his aged father might marry again), and there is a sense in which irregularities of dynastic succession are something of a family tradition.

Here follows a summary of the Pāṇḍava story as told in the text's eighteen books.[10] When Pāṇḍu dies in the Himālaya and his five sons are brought by their mother Kuntī to grow up with their cousins at Hāstinapura, it becomes clear that Duryodhana is aggressively jealous of his role as favoured prince, and the Pāṇḍavas leave Hāstinapura with Kuntī, survive an assassination attempt, and marry Draupadī. Dhṛtarāṣṭra partitions the ancestral kingdom at Bhīṣma's suggestion, the Pāṇḍavas building themselves a new city at Indraprastha in the provinces (Book 1, *Ādiparvan*, The Book of the Beginning). In Book 2 (*Sabhāparvan*, The Book of the Assembly Hall) the Pāṇḍavas gain *kṣatriya* popularity and allies when Yudhiṣṭhira, the eldest Pāṇḍava, has the *rājasūya* ritual performed, but Duryodhana fiercely resents them and, ganging up with his best friend Karṇa, his maternal uncle Śakuni, and his brother Duḥśāsana, he coerces his blind father into presiding over a dice match at which Yudhiṣṭhira bets and loses his wealth and kingdom, his brothers, himself, and Draupadī. Draupadī, who is brought into the hall, suggests that Yudhiṣṭhira's betting and losing of her should be null and void, because at that point he had already bet and lost himself; but she is verbally and physically insulted. The drama escalates and Dhṛtarāṣṭra annuls the match; but after Duryodhana's remonstrations he agrees to another, at which the Pāṇḍavas lose their wealth and kingdom and are sent into exile with Draupadī. The exile is for twelve years (Book 3, *Āraṇyakaparvan* or *Vanaparvan*, The Book of the Forest), plus one year in disguise (Book 4, *Virāṭaparvan*, The Book of Virāṭa). Having served the term of exile, the return of the Pāṇḍavas' kingdom is refused, and they prepare for war (Book 5, *Udyogaparvan*, The Book of the Effort). In the war – famously prefaced by the *Bhagavadgītā* (*Mahābhārata* 6.23–40) – the Pāṇḍavas' seven armies are outnumbered by their cousins' eleven, and in order to triumph they are driven to fight ruthlessly and mercilessly by their strategic consultant Kṛṣṇa Vāsudeva, felling four successive generals of Duryodhana's forces: their 'grandfather'/great-uncle Bhīṣma (Book 6, *Bhīṣmaparvan*, The Book of Bhīṣma); their martial arts tutor Droṇa (Book 7, *Droṇaparvan*, The Book of Droṇa); Duryodhana's friend Karṇa, who unknown to them is their own elder brother, Kuntī's abandoned pre-marital son (Book 8, *Karṇaparvan*, The Book of Karṇa); and their maternal uncle Śalya, plus Duryodhana himself (Book 9, *Śalyaparvan*, The Book of Śalya). Aśvatthāman, Droṇa's son, butchers most of the remaining warriors in their beds to avenge his father's death, and is banished in return (Book 10, *Sauptikaparvan*, The Book of the Sleepers). Book 11 (*Strīparvan*, The Book of the Women) illustrates, in the immediate aftermath of the battle, the extent and human implications of the war for the non-combatant relatives. Yudhiṣṭhira's first wish now is to retire to the forest and let his brother Arjuna be king, but he is persuaded to take up the throne, and is instructed at length in matters of kingship and salvation by Bhīṣma before the latter, mortally wounded previously on the tenth day of the battle, finally dies (Book 12, *Śāntiparvan*, The Book of Peace, and Book 13, *Anuśāsanaparvan*, The Book of Instructions). Yudhiṣṭhira then has the *aśvamedha* ritual performed to expiate his war crimes and consolidate his rule over the reunited ancestral kingdom (Book 14, *Āśvamedhikaparvan*, The Book of the Horse Sacrifice). Years later Dhṛtarāṣṭra and the elder generation retire to the forest and pass away (Book 15, *Āśramavāsikaparvan*, The Book of the Residence in the Hermitage); Kṛṣṇa Vāsudeva's warrior relatives kill themselves off in a drunken brawl (Book 16, *Mausalaparvan*, The Book of the Pestle); and the Pāṇḍavas retire and die (Book 17, *Mahāprasthānikaparvan*, The Book of the Great Journey), meeting up with Duryodhana in the hereafter (Book 18, *Svargārohaṇaparvan*, The Book of the Ascent to Heaven).

In a contrast of various *kṣatriya* masculinities, Yudhiṣṭhira's virtuous abstraction, Bhīma Pāṇḍava's passionate but good-hearted brawniness, Arjuna Pāṇḍava's cool heroism, and Duryodhana's uncompromising and ambivalent manners (sometimes noble, sometimes shocking, at once traditional and unworkable) are nicely juxtaposed within one generation. Yudhiṣṭhira plays the public role of the proper, righteous king (he is also called Dharmarāja, which can mean exactly that), but this role depends also upon his brothers, most specifically Bhīma, who kills every one of the 100 cousins, and Arjuna, who disposes of most of Duryodhana's other allies and whose grandson Parikṣit becomes the family heir. The context of the Pāṇḍava story's recital is Parikṣit's son Janamejaya's snake sacrifice (see *Mahābhārata* 1.3–53, where Janamejaya begins to massacre all snakes to avenge his father's death but is eventually dissuaded, aborting the attempt): this is doubly appropriate because not only is the story recited a story of Janamejaya's ancestors, but it is also a story of the *kṣatriya* king's delicate and ambivalent relationship to violence – state violence on the one hand, and the violence of the unruly on the other.[11]

Heavenly and ethereal hosts assemble from afar to witness the Kurukṣetra war, which is described in bright detail as a wondrous marvel. The extent of the destruction is astonishing (1,660,020,000 warriors die, according to Yudhiṣṭhira's count at 11.26.9–10, and an additional 24,165 go missing), and both before and after the heat of battle the Pāṇḍava story is suffused by sorrow and confusion over the event. Yudhiṣṭhira, Dhṛtarāṣṭra, and his wife Gāndhārī lament prominently.[12] Blame is apportioned variously by the survivors and non-combatants; Vyāsa (amongst others) often suggests that no one but Time (*kāla*) is ultimately responsible, and there is a persistent rumour that Kṛṣṇa Vāsudeva, who instigates the various ruses by which the outnumbered Pāṇḍava armies triumph and who at *Bhagavadgītā* 11.32 tells Arjuna that he himself is Time, might hold the key. Vaiśaṃpāyana prefaces his narration of the Pāṇḍava story with the revelation that its various principal characters were earthly incarnations of *deva*s and *asura*s (gods and demons): the *asura*s infiltrated the ranks of human kings and caused great distress to the lady Earth, so a heavenly mission was organized, culminating in the Kurukṣetra showdown. On this view, the war was the hidden business of the gods led by Indra and Viṣṇu-Nārāyaṇa (see Fitzgerald 2004b); and as

Alf Hiltebeitel has shown (1976: 60–76; 1984; 1991b), four of the characters who most effectively drive the Pāṇḍava narrative towards its outcome go by the name 'Kṛṣṇa/ā' (Dark One: Kṛṣṇa Vāsudeva, Kṛṣṇā Draupadī, Kṛṣṇa Dvaipāyana Vyāsa, and Arjuna). The war's participants and their associates on the whole are ignorant of this higher dimension, but are nonetheless exercised by various theories of the relative influence of *daiva* (the business of the gods, whatever it may be) and *puruṣakāra* (autonomous human action).[13]

Although the *Mahābhārata* generically resembles the *Rāmāyaṇa* in many respects, and both are written in similar Sanskrit (see Oberlies 2003), traditionally the former is usually classed as *itihāsa*,[14] the latter as (the first) *kāvya*. The *Mahābhārata* seems to have the more robust intent (see Fitzgerald 1991), featuring a greater wealth of didactic matter within its narrative, and it considers itself to be comprehensive on all matters pertaining to the four *puruṣārtha*s (*dharma*, *artha*, *kāma*, and *mokṣa* – briefly: propriety, profit, pleasure, and liberation),[15] maximally purifying to hear or dwell upon, and no less in fact than the fifth Veda, widely accessible in contrast to its predecessors. This claim places it in a definite relation to the Sanskrit past – its debt to Vedic cosmological, sacrificial, and social-hierarchical narrative idioms is clear throughout – but the opening up of the discourse to a wider cosmopolitan public beyond the *dvija* ('twice-born', that is, well-born and Vedically educated) elites may be correlated with a new socio-political context after the rise of the kingdom of Magadha (most famously under the imperial Mauryas Candragupta and his grandson Aśoka), and of Buddhism and other non-Vedic religious movements (see Thapar 2002: 98–325; Kulke and Rothermund 1998: 41–91). Although the *Mahābhārata*'s treatment of 'Buddhism' and 'Jainism' is rather cryptic,[16] the text clearly indicates a new religious vision (see John Brockington 1998: 232–312; Sutton 2000), which incorporates glorious heavens as well as the possibility of complete escape from all rebirths, and which, while not sustainedly antagonistic to the tradition of renunciation, primarily depends upon the disinterested and transfigured performance of social and cosmic obligations – the *karmayoga* expounded by Kṛṣṇa in the *Bhagavadgītā* – in a spirit of *bhakti*, that is, loyalty or reverential service. In this the text embodies what Greg Bailey has called 'a blending of ideologies' (1985: 11), these ideologies being those of *pravṛtti* (the business of mundane, generative effort, of social and cosmic maintenance) and *nivṛtti* (the contrasting stopping or running-down of the wheel, particularly the wheel of individual rebirth). The text features certain religious activities which are comparatively invisible in Vedic literature, such as the visiting of *tīrtha*s (holy places, usually bathing places) and the pursuit of asceticism and yogic discipline, sometimes with the comment (e.g. 3.80.34–40; see also 12.192–3) that such activities are cheaper and more efficacious than the commissioning of a *yajña* (Vedic ritual sacrifice). But while the *Mahābhārata* incorporates important elements of Vaiṣṇava and Śaiva mythology and presents both Viṣṇu and Śiva as suitable objects of exclusive devotion, its explicitly religious material appears in service to the Pāṇḍava story: it has the *Harivaṃśa*, which focuses on Kṛṣṇa Vāsudeva's family and his divine exploits as a youngster, as its *khila* or appendix.[17] Although these exploits are alluded to within the Pāṇḍava story, they are not narrated there.

The Sanskrit *Mahābhārata* has been attracting scholarly attention for at least a thousand years: Śaṅkarācārya and other medieval Vedānta theologians produced famous commentaries on the *Bhagavadgītā*, and Nīlakaṇṭha in the seventeenth century wrote a commentary on the entire *Mahābhārata* (Kinjawadekar 1929–36). The study of the text within 'Western' universities (see John Brockington 1998: 41–81) followed upon the British economic interest in India and contemporary developments in comparative philology, including the 1786 announcement by William 'Oriental' Jones of a close genetic kinship between Sanskrit, Greek, Latin, Gothic, Celtic, and Persian. Much of the ensuing work on the *Mahābhārata* exists only in German;[18] the first sustained scholarly writings on it in English were those of E. Washburn Hopkins at the end of the nineteenth century and the beginning of the twentieth. Hopkins rejected the 'synthetic' approach of Joseph Dahlmann, who suggested that the *Mahābhārata* was the product of a single author-redactor, and instead suggested, in line with the 'analytic' scholarly majority, that the text developed over a period of some several centuries, an old narrative core having been successively revised to fit with the changing times, and augmented by subtales and didactic passages – a view which is encouraged by the intra-textually diachronic re-presentation of the Pāṇḍava story at Janamejaya's snake sacrifice several generations after the Kurukṣetra war, and then at Śaunaka's gathering in the Naimiṣa Forest.

Before we turn in the next section to the study of gender, the remainder of this section will briefly mention some other recent (post-1990) trends in *Mahābhārata* scholarship insofar as they bear upon the studies included in this book. The early difference of views over the composition of the text (the 'synthetic'/'analytic' disjunction) has had an enormous influence within *Mahābhārata* scholarship right down to the present day, and may seem to encompass not just how the text came to be, but also what it actually is and what kinds of methodology do and do not spring to mind for its study. For although in one sense there is no difference between Dahlmann's *Mahābhārata* (the product of a single genius) and Hopkins's (the product of centuries of accumulation) – both are the same *Mahābhārata* – nonetheless Dahlmann's text seems suited to holistic literary analysis, and Hopkins's to analysis in terms of the diachronic development of Indian ideas, but not necessarily *vice versa*.[19] The dominance of the 'analytic' approach for most of the twentieth century[20] is consonant with the normative stance of academic Indology, which has been closely aligned to the discipline of history (historical linguistics, historical anthropology, history of religions, history of philosophy); nonetheless we write today in the ongoing wake of a vibrant critique of the 'analytic' approach, and in the realization that the Sanskrit *Mahābhārata*, notwithstanding its internal variety and inconvenient bulk, is a natural inclusion in any broad category of world literature. Hiltebeitel has suggested, building on the work of Sheldon Pollock on the *Rāmāyaṇa* and responding to various famous scholarly dismissals of the *Mahābhārata*'s literary merits, that 'the largest inadequacy in *Mahābhārata* scholarship . . . is simply the failure to appreciate the epic as a work of literature' (1999b: 156); he has followed this with suggestive essays in such appreciation, accompanied by a conception of the text's written composition over a few generations (2001a; 2004b), and scholars are increasingly taking advantage of the new interpretive possibilities his lead opens up (Brodbeck and Black 2006: 3). We must bear in mind that although any theory of the text's composition does inevitably encourage certain types of textual analysis over others, any and all such theories,[21] howsoever accepted they may or may not be, remain immensely speculative when compared to the fact of the text itself.

As noted above, it is common for the *Mahābhārata* to be studied in terms of the diachronic development of Indian ideas (Proudfoot 1979; Ježić 1986), and here questions of the mutual influence of texts come to the fore. Apart from the intuitive tendency to study the *Mahābhārata* in concert with the *Rāmāyaṇa* (John Brockington 1998; Hiltebeitel 1994; 2005a; Shulman 1991), many recent studies address some aspect of the *Mahābhārata*'s relationship with the Vedic literature which is commonly thought to predate it, and/or the Dharmaśāstra and/or Purāṇa literature which is commonly thought to overlap and postdate it.[22] One strand of scholarship addresses the text in terms of a broad 'Indo-European' tradition through its demonstrable connections with old heroic literature from, most commonly, Greece and north-western Europe; but the wider field of 'comparative epic' is as yet little charted, perhaps largely because of the polyglossia required.[23]

One of the most distinctive and persistent themes in the text is that of repeated, large-scale, but inconclusive human destruction; the business at Kurukṣetra is just one in a series of various near-genocides, as explored by Chris Minkowski (1991) in the context of the snakes, by Alf Hiltebeitel (1999b) in the context of the Bhārgava brahmins, and by Jim Fitzgerald (2002a) in the context of Rāma Jāmadagnya (who killed all *kṣatriya*s twenty-one times, but they kept coming back). This theme, which is also evident as reported by commercial and independent media throughout the world today, certainly strengthens the *Mahābhārata*'s claim to contemporary relevance. Also, as many scholars each in their various ways have shown,[24] this theme is very much tied up with the idea of 'sacrifice' (*yajña*) in the Vedic philosophy of ritual, which is difficult to interpret on the basis of the surviving Vedic texts because many of these were intended only for the use of certain of the ritual's specialized officiants.

With regard to the historicity of the events portrayed in the *Mahābhārata*, we do not and cannot know enough to say how true the story might be.[25] The sense in which a story such as the Pāṇḍava story could possibly be true is difficult to gauge. With its apparently magical realism (pots as mothers, gods as fathers, etc.), some might wish to 'demythologize' it before asking the question; but plausibility is in the eye of the beholder. In any case, we cannot say how accurate the narrative transmissions within the text would be (Ugraśravas repeating what Vaiśaṃpāyana has said, and so on). But wherever individual persons inferred from a range of data (royal inscriptions, the accounts of foreign visitors, other genres of text, etc.) have come to be regarded as historical figures reasonably predating the text, it is reasonable to ask whether any *Mahābhārata* character might be some more or less precise or caricatured representation of them, even if at such a distance in the past this is effectively a process of comparing one caricature with another. The past few years have seen several attempts to understand Yudhiṣṭhira and/or Arjuna Pāṇḍava in juxtaposition and counterpoint with Aśoka 'Beloved-of-the-gods' Maurya, who according to his inscriptions championed the cause of '*dhamma*', i.e. *dharma* (albeit with more sympathy for its 'Buddhist' than its Vedic varieties), and was painfully responsible for a large massacre in eastern India.[26] There have also been attempts historically to locate the cultural provenance of the Pāṇḍavas ('*pāṇḍu*' means 'pale'; Parpola 1984; 2002). But explorations of the text's 'socio-cultural milieu' (Pande 1990; Moorthy 1990; John Brockington 1998: 159–231) vary in terms of the extent to which they assume that the society depicted within the text reflects the society within which the text was created; and, as we shall see, this is a particular problem when considering questions of gender.

The vast majority of recent *Mahābhārata* studies have approached the text selectively; that is to say, they have not focused on the text as a whole (understandable, with a text of such proportions), but on some specific aspect of it. There are recurring lines of attack, which often appear in combination: to focus on one specific character or group of characters,[27] or one specific *parvan*, or some other demarcated textual unit or units,[28] or one specific narrative moment or episode or type of episode,[29] or one or a group of related ideas, usually signalled by certain verbal formulae.[30] These micro-studies are invaluable and as they continue to be produced they will and do make it more and more possible for sound holistic theories to be ventured and assessed.

Micro-studies concentrating on individual *Mahābhārata* characters have been particularly well placed to explore gender-related issues, a trend in the scholarship that has become more and more commonplace in recent years. There have been numerous article-length studies focusing on one or more female characters,[31] many of which come from a feminist perspective, highlighting the epic's androcentric assumptions, its gendered stereotyping, and the ways in which female characters are represented in a male-authored text. There have also been a handful of studies on male characters in the *Mahābhārata* that explicitly address issues of masculinity and sexuality.[32]

Building on the renewed appreciation of the text's literary merits, one of the most dynamic trends in recent *Mahābhārata* scholarship has been a focus on organizational features of the text's composition. Current speculations include the suggestions that the text is modelled on the Vedic ritual in terms of its structure and function (Minkowski 1989; Hegarty 2006); that the text features symmetrical ring-compositions and to some extent maps its various 'divisions into eighteen' – the eighteen-book text, the eighteen-day war, and various eighteen-chapter sections – onto each other (Dennis Hudson 2001; Tubb 2002; Brodbeck 2006); that the text features interlinking and interconnected sets of stories that are strung together by means of their sequential placement (Thomas 2006a); and that aspects of the narrative and some of the characters are modelled carefully upon the solar and lunar cycles (von Simson 1994; 1999; and Chapter 11 below). There has also been important work on the text's poetic style and metrical form.[33]

Gender and narrative in the *Mahābhārata*

While individual chapters within this book build on various studies and insights representing the vast array of research on the *Mahābhārata*, the book as a whole focuses particularly on the themes of gender and of textual and narrative construction, offering a number of speculations on the various ways in which these themes are intertwined. It is well known that Gender Studies has become an increasingly fashionable field during the past decade, but our motive in addressing issues of gender is not to subject the *Mahābhārata* to the most recent trend in Western scholarship, nor is it to be unnecessarily probative. Rather, this focus grows out of an increasing awareness that gender is of fundamental importance throughout the *Mahābhārata*. Indeed, one could say that, along with *dharma* and *varṇa*, gender is one of the most central and most contested issues in the text, and, as the following chapters will demonstrate, discussions regarding gender operate on a number of different levels and are manifested in multiple ways without the text providing one consistent and definitive view.

Although this book approaches the *Mahābhārata* with questions about gender in mind, it does not locate itself specifically within the field of Gender Studies, and we do not claim that there is one theoretical foundation upon which all the chapters rest. In fact, although this section of the Introduction situates the *Mahābhārata* and the book in relation to some prevailing ideas within the field, few of the following chapters engage with the work of Gender Studies scholars directly. Rather, we have encouraged *Mahābhārata* scholars to undertake research on gender issues and gender constructions within the text. By gathering and framing the results,[34] this book attempts to bring scholars of Gender Studies and Literary Criticism into contact with the more traditional philologically oriented discipline of *Mahābhārata* Studies, and *vice versa*. The *Mahābhārata* is one of the definitive cultural narratives in the construction of masculine and feminine gender roles in ancient India, and its numerous tellings and retellings have helped shape Indian gender and social norms ever since. The epic not only frames discussions of gender in terms of the social roles of men, women, and other gendered identities, but also in terms of the artistic employment of symbols, tropes, and metaphors that may or may not have any direct connection to males and females and pre-existing masculinities and femininities outside the text. Although we claim to explore gender in the context of the *Mahābhārata* in new ways, this contribution is one small part of an ongoing dialogue exploring gender in India's grandest text. We hope the material collected here will inspire further explorations on similar issues by *Mahābhārata* specialists and Gender Studies scholars alike.

What is gender?

In their recent survey of Gender Studies, David Glover and Cora Kaplan have commented upon the ubiquitous use of the word 'gender' in scholarly discourse: ' "Gender" is now one of the busiest, most restless terms in the English language, a word that crops up everywhere, yet whose uses seem to be forever changing, always on the move, producing new and often surprising inflections of meaning' (2000: ix). Although the word 'gender' has featured in the English language since the days of Chaucer (ibid.: x), its contemporary connotations are quite new. Since the writings of feminist scholars in the 1970s and 1980s, the word 'gender' has frequently been used in tandem with the word 'sex' in a similar oppositional relationship as that between 'culture' and 'nature'. Whereas 'sex' is understood as a biological identity, 'gender' has been employed to refer to a social identity; 'sex' is what makes a human being male or female, but 'gender' is what makes someone masculine or feminine. Accordingly, sex is understood as universal, while gender is culturally specific.

This distinction has been important in the work of a number of feminist writers because it is a way of acknowledging anatomical differences between women and men, while arguing that valuations based on these differences are cultural, and therefore capable of changing. Kate Millet, for example, has argued that gender distinctions not only pertain to different kinds of behaviour for men and women, but also could be seen as cultural differences: 'male and female are really two cultures and their life experiences are utterly different' (1972: 31). Gayle Rubin has also generally accepted this nature/nurture explanation of sex and gender, defining what she calls the 'sex/gender system' as 'the set of arrangements by which a society transforms biological sexuality into products of human activity, and in which these transformed sexual needs are satisfied' (1996: 106).

This tension between sex and gender has also been at play in the trajectory of feminist scholarship influenced by psychoanalysis. Whereas Sigmund

Freud's theories of the Oedipus and Electra complexes, which placed much emphasis on anatomical differences between the sexes, have been interpreted by many as propounding a biological determinism, theorists such as Jacques Lacan have reworked some of Freud's ideas in ways that de-emphasize their biological implications. Lacan focused on the symbolic and linguistic implications of anatomical differences between the sexes, associating masculinity with the symbol of the phallus, rather than with the physical penis. As such, for Lacan maleness is not merely a physical identity, but a cultural one too.

> [The phallus] is the embodiment of the male status, to which men accede and in which certain rights inhere – among them a right to a woman. It is an expression of the transmission of male dominance. It passes through women and settles upon men.
>
> (Rubin 1996: 131)

With the emergence of the field of Gender Studies, scholars have questioned the neat divide between sex and gender. Michel Foucault's work (1979) on the history of sexuality, in particular, challenged the notion of 'sex' as a biological fact, claiming that sex does not have an existence prior to its conceptualization in discourse, and concluding that sex is not easily reduced to a biological category and thus should be viewed as a social practice. For feminists and scholars of Gender Studies, one of the most important implications of Foucault's work is that both 'gender' and 'sex' are cultural categories. Glover and Kaplan conclude:

> Sex and gender are therefore intimately related, but not because one is 'natural' while the other represents its transformation into 'culture'. Rather, *both* are inescapably cultural categories that refer to ways of describing and understanding human bodies and human relationships, our relationships to our selves and to others. Sex and gender necessarily overlap, sometimes confusingly so.
>
> (2000: xxvi)

In recent years, Gender Studies scholars have paid less attention to the distinction between sex and gender, instead focusing on the complex ways in which class and race, as well as economic and political systems, contribute towards the shaping and defining of gendered identities. Judith Butler has been one of the most influential scholars in theorizing gender in these ways. In her groundbreaking work *Gender Trouble: feminism and the subversion of identity* Butler sees gender as a symbolic form of 'public action', an effect produced by regularly repeated speech and behaviour:

> [G]ender is an identity tenuously constituted in time, instituted in an exterior space through a *stylized repetition of acts*. The effect of

> gender is produced through the stylization of the body and, hence, must be understood as the mundane way in which bodily gestures, movements, and styles of various kinds constitute the illusion of an abiding gendered self. This formulation moves the conception of gender off the ground of a substantial model of identity to one that requires a conception of gender as a constituted *social temporality*.
>
> (1999: 179)

Accordingly, gender is not an essence, nor does it constitute a stable identity. Rather, gendered identities are tenuous and provisional, and can never be demonstrated once and for all; they exist, as Butler emphasizes, only insofar as they are performed and re-performed. This is not to say that gender is therefore a matter of choice. Gendered identities might be unstable, subtly and constantly changing, but this does not mean that individuals can completely control their gender. Any given culture has a set of expectations and rewards, reinscribed through institutions, social practices and political structures, for how men and women should speak, act and internalize their identities.

So, what then, is gender? Do these recent theories assist our understanding of gender, or do they merely complicate the picture to the point where we no longer know what we are talking about? If we are looking for a hard and fast definition, then obviously such theories make gender less understandable and less accessible. However, even if both gender and sex are cultural, with no ontological distinction between them, this does not mean that the words have the same connotations. There is still a tendency to use the word 'gender' to refer to social roles and behaviour; whereas 'sex', even if not biologically determined, tends to refer more to anatomy, reproduction, and coitus. While mindful of the theorists who continue to challenge even a tentative binary opposition between sex and gender, it is important to point out that this book is about gender more than it is about sex: it is more concerned with social and cultural representations than with intercourse and reproduction. Treating gender as something to be queried, as an identity that is always fragile and conditional, we hope that we can open up a number of fruitful avenues of exploration into the *Mahābhārata*.

Gender and narrative

One of the reasons why we have chosen to examine gender in conjunction with narrative is to shift focus away from attempts to reconstruct a historical reality. This is not to deny that the *Mahābhārata* is historically situated and that its production as a text is indelibly connected to real social and political events that took place in ancient India. Indeed, as a number of Gender Studies scholars have argued, gender cannot be discussed in a social vacuum, but needs to be considered in tandem with political, economic, and religious structures. However, due to the complexity of the *Mahābhārata* and the probability that it contains material composed in different historical periods – not to mention a variety of regions and political regimes – it is very difficult to establish concrete connections between the text and the social worlds from which it might have emerged, particularly since those social worlds are not directly accessible and must be reconstructed in the first place largely on the basis of texts. Thus, while discussing gender as it intersects with social factors such as *dharma*, *varṇa*, marriage practices, family relations, and soteriological paths, it is important to emphasize that the world of the *Mahābhārata* is a literary world, and not a direct reflection or representation of the ever-evasive 'reality' of ancient India.[35]

Furthermore, any discussion about gender in a literary product like the *Mahābhārata* must necessarily address much more than the degree to which the text represents real life. Gender roles in narrative literature are not merely reflections of or instructions for the real world; they are always also artistic and metaphorical literary devices, and sometimes gendered symbolism in the text gives added meaning at a textual level without necessarily referring to a social reality. For example, at the most basic level, gender exists grammatically in Sanskrit, as it does in many languages, dividing nouns into masculine, feminine, and neuter. Although the gender of an object is often quite arbitrary and may not reflect anything natural or essential about it, for poets and philosophers the gender of words can be employed to enrich ideas of opposition and complementarity, particularly when common nouns or abstract ideas are anthropomorphized. One of the most well-known examples from ancient Indian sources is the rich imagery surrounding the philosophical principles of *puruṣa* and *prakṛti*. In the Sāṃkhya philosophical school the masculine word *puruṣa* refers to consciousness, while the feminine word *prakṛti* represents primordial nature. Although often used in technical ways that do not necessarily bring attention to the gender of the words, *puruṣa* and *prakṛti* can represent an oppositional relationship between a masculine principle, associated with inaction and detachment, and a feminine principle, representing activity and passion. Similar characterizations are also present in the depiction of male and female characters in a number of stories in the *Mahābhārata*.

Another prominent example of gendered symbolism in the *Mahābhārata* appears in theories and mythologies about kingship, which conceive the physical extent of the kingdom as the goddess Earth, and the king as her husband and protector (Hara 1973). Several other far-reaching examples will be discussed in the chapters that follow; here it is enough to state that although the mechanics of gender within the text obviously bear some relation to actual ancient Indian social realities, this relationship is very obscure and indirect.

By focusing on narrative we also hope to bring attention to the artistic and literary merits of the *Mahābhārata*. Regardless of the length of its compositional period, there are a number of aspects of the text's organization and structure that suggest it was woven together purposefully and creatively. As such, it is not sufficient to explain contradictions and discontinuities in terms of the encyclopedic nature of the text or in terms of contemporary cultural and ideological developments. This tendency can be particularly distortive when considering issues of gender. To illustrate this point, let us briefly review some debates about the *Mahābhārata*'s female characters and the position of women in ancient India.

One of the first studies directly to address gender-related issues in the South Asian context was A.S. Altekar's *The Position of Women in Hindu Civilization* (1938, second edition 1959).[36] Focusing on the status of women, Altekar argued that women in ancient India were highly regarded as compared with those in other ancient societies such as Greece and Rome, but that 'from about the beginning of the Christian era, Hindu society began to assume a patronising attitude towards women' (1959: 333). 'Women once enjoyed considerable freedom and privileges in spheres of family, religion and public life; but as centuries rolled on, the situation went on changing adversely' (ibid.: 335). Recently, a number of scholars have questioned Altekar's claims and methods, bringing attention to the inadequacy of making sweeping historical generalizations from a few select examples from brahmanical sources. Yet, as Uma Chakravarti has commented, despite the shortcomings of Altekar's model, it continues to 'influence and even dominate historical writing':

> [Altekar's] picture of the idyllic condition of women in the Vedic Age . . . is a picture which now pervades the collective consciousness of the upper castes in India and has virtually crippled the emergence of a more analytically rigorous study of gender relations in ancient India.
>
> (1999: 80)

Indeed, a number of studies of female characters in the *Mahābhārata* have assumed the 'Altekarian paradigm', reading the depiction of women in the text as chronicling their declining status in ancient India. Pradip Bhattacharya, for example, claims to see 'an abrupt decline in the status of woman which takes place as Draupadī replaces Kuntī as the central female character in the epic' (1995: 73). Similarly,[37] Nancy Falk has attempted to explain the contrasting behaviours of Draupadī, from devoted wife to outspoken critic of her husband, in terms of the chronological layers of the text:

> The passages about ideal wifehood are probably more recent than the memories of Draupadī herself. She is a throwback; her stories

> come from a time when women were more highly respected than in the days of the meek and submissive wifely models.
>
> (1977: 91–2)

Although it is possible that chronology is a factor in these cases, both explanations fail to explore the complex literary and artistic reasons why gendered roles and identities are portrayed the way that they are. Despite the fact that the text often makes totalizing remarks about 'women', the narrative and its discussions about *dharma* complicate this view, suggesting that there is not a monolithic *strīdharma* for all women in all situations, but rather that expectations for modes of speech and behaviour depend on whether one is a wife or widow, daughter or mother, sister or friend, renunciate or queen. As such, the different portrayals of Draupadī and Kuntī could easily be discussed in terms of their different roles as wife and mother, or the different roles of their particular characters within the unfolding of the narrative.

This brings us to another reason for our focus on narrative, which is to highlight the *Mahābhārata*'s main story and sub-tales rather than its didactic sections. In addition to its various teachings on the specifics of spiritual progress and of regal and martial comportment, the *Mahābhārata* has several sections that are similar in style and content to the Dharmaśāstras, with hundreds of verses of the *Mānava Dharmaśāstra* (also known as *Manusmṛti*, and variously translated as *The Laws of Manu* and *The Law Code of Manu*) also appearing in the epic. Much of this material, with its emphasis on marriage, sexual relations, and daily rituals, as well as sections specifically pertaining to the rites of women and rules of conduct between men and women, supplies fertile ground for the examination of gender. However, rather than concentrating on these prescriptive codes and explicit statements concerning gender identities and relationships, in this book we are primarily interested in how gender plays itself out in the characters, the unfolding of the story, the social world within the narrative, and the structure and symbology of the text as a whole.

Literary characters: females and males, femininities and masculinities

On the level of characterization, the text features literary personae who flesh out normative paradigms for both women and men. The ideal woman is often portrayed in terms of the *pativratā*, the wife who is religiously devoted to her husband. One of the most well-known *Mahābhārata* examples of the *pativratā* is Sāvitrī, who, by means of cunning, perseverance, and eloquence, outwits Death to save her husband. Another example is Gāndhārī, who makes loyalty to her husband her highest aim (*pativrataparāyaṇā*) by wilfully blindfolding herself when she marries the blind Dhṛtarāṣṭra, resolving that 'she would not experience more than her husband could' (1.103.13, tr. van

Buitenen).[38] The ideal of the *pativratā* is perhaps best articulated by Draupadī, as she instructs Satyabhāmā in how to be a successful wife: 'My Law rests on my husband, as, I think, it eternally does with women. He is the God, he is the path, nothing else' (3.222.35, tr. van Buitenen).

Masculinities and femininities are relational identities and are not best understood in isolation. If the *pativratā* is the text's principal explicit model of femininity, it is complemented by the advocacy of a masculinity whereby men are virile husbands and fearless warriors. After all, the *Mahābhārata* is often considered a heroic text, even 'manly' (van Buitenen 1978: 168). Leonard Zwilling and Michael Sweet have commented upon the close connection between masculinity and virility as articulated in Vedic sources: 'From the outset, we see that vedic society was strongly patriarchal in character and placed an extremely high value on male potency, procreative ability being one of the means by which a man could achieve high social status' (2000: 101). The *Mahābhārata* shares this association between masculinity and procreation, characterizing the ideal male as a married householder who has sons. An attribute that is often put forth as an ideal characteristic of the married householder is that of *rakṣaṇa*, or protection (of his wife and family); and this applies especially to the king, the 'householder' of the whole realm, whose protection must extend to all corners and all dharmic citizens, and whose success in this endeavour is indicated by the realm's productivity.

Additionally, there is a strong connection between masculinity and fighting, and many characters are repeatedly[39] obliged to demonstrate their manhood through their participation in battle. Most of the prominent female characters act in ways that reinforce this model of masculinity, actively encouraging their husbands and/or sons to fight. Draupadī tells Yudhiṣṭhira that a man is one who can take advantage of the weakness of others (3.33.53). Kuntī recounts the story of Vidurā, who instructed her son not to refrain from battle: 'Don't smolder – blaze up! Attack with a vengeance and slay the enemies . . . One is a man to the extent of his truculence and unforgivingness. The forgiving man, the meek man is neither woman nor man' (5.131.29–30, tr. van Buitenen).

Indeed, through violent self-assertion a *kṣatriya* man becomes worthy of delightful female company, be this the company of the *apsarā*s (heavenly nymphs) who entertain all those fallen nobly in battle, or the company of Śrī (Prosperity, Fortune), the paradigmatic symbolic consort of the king (Hara 1996–7). Śrī, who in some ways resembles the courtesan (*gaṇikā*) as depicted in the *Kāmasūtra*, chooses the man who pleases her most (this is the difference between victory and defeat), and features as a temporary and fickle consort, not as a childbearer. This is in sharp contrast with Earth, who is patient and longsuffering and whose role, once married to (i.e. conquered by) the king, is to be devoted and productive. A number of *Mahābhārata* heroines – including Draupadī, Gaṅgā, Śakuntalā, Damayantī, and Sāvitrī – are compared to Śrī, emphasizing their mobility, activity, and independence.

Like Śrī, these particular heroines all choose their husbands, indicating that they represent the royal power that is responsible for their husbands assuming the throne.

The *pativratā* and Śrī are two of the more prominent paradigms of femininity in the *Mahābhārata*. Both paradigms present women as important complements to their husbands' success. Both are restrictive, only representing women in relation to their menfolk; but in terms of the behaviour of female characters, there is a sense in which neither paradigm is complete in itself – situational considerations can sometimes cause a woman to shift from one to another. Many *pativratā*s are found sometimes to step out of that role. As Stephanie Jamison observes,

> In story after story women see what needs to be done, take command, and order the bewildered, hand-wringing male participants into their supporting roles – and the enterprise fails only when one of these ninnies messes up his part of the woman's plan.
>
> (1996: 15)

The conundrum for Jamison, as well as others, is how to make sense of texts which offer stories of 'resourceful, energetic, and verbally and dharmically accomplished women' (ibid.: 15), but which at the same time contain scores of 'misogynist maxims' (ibid.: 12–14). King Duḥṣanta, for example, tells Śakuntalā, who claims that her child is his, that women are liars (1.68.72); Nārada warns Yudhiṣṭhira against trusting women or telling them secrets (2.5.73; see also 5.39.59); and Bhīṣma tells Yudhiṣṭhira that women will only be sexually faithful if restrained by men (13.38.18, 23). As Jamison explains, these contrasting portrayals of women 'do not seem to inhabit the same conceptual planet' (1996: 15).

Thus the *Mahābhārata*'s mainstream portrayals of female norms are repeatedly questioned, challenged, and subverted by the speech and behaviour of characters who do not conform to these models, and even by that of characters who usually do. Similarly, a number of central male characters do not consistently fulfil their roles in siring offspring or in protecting their wives. One of the most important ways in which concerns over masculinity are woven into the narrative is through the concern over progeny, with the recurring motif of the king who, for one reason or another, cannot sire a male heir. A solution that appears on several occasions in the *Mahābhārata* is the practice of *niyoga*, which refers to a woman procreating with an appointed male other than her husband, for the purpose of carrying on the family line.[40] One of the results of this practice in the *Mahābhārata* is that many of the central male characters are not biologically connected to their fathers. In terms of protection, the model of the responsible *kṣatriya* householder stands in dynamic contrast to the renunciant or quietist ideal popularized in particular by early Jains and Buddhists: from this perspective, which in the *Mahābhārata* is not limited to brahmins but is voiced by some of the central *kṣatriya* characters, the *dharma* of *kṣatriyas* is cruel to others and antithetical to spiritual progress. Here we see a stark opposition between the ideals of *pravṛtti* and *nivṛtti*.

These examples illustrate the instability and contextuality of even the most mainstream portrayals of femininity and masculinity in the *Mahābhārata*. Furthermore, some philosophical passages, most notably Sulabhā's debate with Janaka (12.308), put forth positions that question altogether the validity of gender distinctions. So how are we to understand these conflicting portrayals of women and men? One of the advantages of using a hermeneutic of gender to understand female and male characters in the *Mahābhārata* is that this allows us to avoid conceptualizing 'women' and 'men' as essentializing categories, and to focus instead on the different interacting models of female and male behaviour, and the different methods by which these various ideals are expressed.

Gender-bending characters

Another way in which normative gender roles are subverted and challenged is through the *Mahābhārata*'s several gender-bending characters. The notion of a third sex, or of a gendered identity that is neither male nor female, appears in a number of sources from ancient India. As Zwilling and Sweet have noted, a 'three-sex model was an important feature of the ancient Indian world view' (2000: 99), with ambiguous categories such as *napuṃsaka*[41] and *klība*[42] appearing in late Vedic texts. Zwilling and Sweet suggest that at first these concepts denoted a condition of defective masculinity that was the result of magic or misfortune, but that by the post-Vedic period a third-sex concept was in place. This meant that the third sex was no longer considered merely the result of a curse or a physical accident, but could be considered 'innate or congenital'. Zwilling and Sweet conclude that 'in general the third sex is a residual category, comprising a wide variety of non-normative biological, gender role and socio-behavioural traits' (ibid.: 123).

Despite the recognition of a third biological category in other sources, however, the gender bending that takes place in the *Mahābhārata* does not necessarily constitute a third sex, nor does it necessarily challenge the binary framework. First of all, the most well-known cases of gender bending are instances of transsexualism – changing from a man to a woman, or from a woman to a man – rather than the assumption of a third-sex identity. Moreover, the gender transformations that take place in the *Mahābhārata* are often only temporary. Arjuna's appearance as an effeminate dance instructor in the *Virāṭaparvan* is only a temporary disguise (see Chapter 10); Ambā, reborn as Śikhaṇḍinī,[43] makes a deal with a *yakṣa* to switch sexes only for a limited time; and Sāmba masquerades as a woman only briefly.[44] These episodes seem more likely to be playful narrative tropes than examples or justifications of an alternative lifestyle. In other words, these episodes do not challenge the foundations of sexual dimorphism or the social practices that reinforce this binary model. As Zwilling and Sweet have illustrated,

> the third sex is defined in opposition to the two other, more basic and privileged sexes. Those without unequivocal masculinity or femininity – either because they lack reproductive capacity or mix gender behaviour or physical characteristics – will fall into the residual third or liminal category. Therefore, the third sex could not exist on its own, but only as it participates in a negation or combination of male and female traits.
>
> (2000: 123)

Despite being a residual category, containing aspects of both masculinity and femininity, gender ambiguity in the *Mahābhārata* is often employed more in relation to notions of masculinity. This is illustrated when male characters taunt their enemies to show they are men, with the label 'eunuch' (*klība*) repeatedly employed to describe a man who refrains from battle. Female characters also reinforce this notion of masculinity by employing similar taunts. Draupadī, for example, likens Yudhiṣṭhira to a eunuch and then suggests that he is a *kṣatriya* 'without the rod of rule' (*nādaṇḍa*, tr. Fitzgerald) (12.14.13–14).[45]

However, in one case in particular an episode of gender bending offers reflections upon the limitations of being a woman in the *Mahābhārata*'s male-dominated social world. Ambā is captured by Bhīṣma as a prospective wife for his brother; still in love with her previous boyfriend Śālva, she is released by Bhīṣma; but now neither Śālva nor Bhīṣma will have her back. Consequently she is 'totally disgusted with being a woman' (*strībhāve parinirviṇṇā*, 5.188.6), and she cannot exact revenge upon Bhīṣma until she has become a man. As Goldman comments, she is no longer able to be a virgin or a wife and thus she has 'no socially viable alternative to the death she chooses. It is this that gives rise to her strange vow to inflict upon the author of her dilemma the consequences of his theft of her womanhood' (1993: 392). Madhusraba Dasgupta explores Ambā's character by comparing her fate with that of her sisters, Ambikā and Ambālikā, whose 'total submission' affords them sons, prestige and a place in heaven; by contrast, 'Ambā's resistance disrupted the social norm and brought her nothing but trouble and unhappiness . . . For all her singleminded efforts, Ambā did not, after all, have the satisfaction of exacting revenge on her own' (2000: 51–2).

Gender and dharma

As mentioned above, one of the crucial positions shared by a number of feminists and Gender Studies scholars is that gendered and sexual identities do not appear in a vacuum, but are intertwined with social institutions and practices. As such, gender is not a fixed or isolated aspect of one's identity, but intersects and interacts in complex ways with one's class, race, education, religion, family, etc., and with the exigencies of particular situations. Similarly, a number of characters in the *Mahābhārata*, notably Yudhiṣṭhira, Arjuna, and Draupadī, manifest different modes of gendered behaviour at different moments in the narrative. Indeed, part of the depth of these particular characters is that they negotiate between contrasting gender norms. Yudhiṣṭhira oscillates between being passive and aggressive, between contemplating the life of an ascetic and fulfilling his role as king. Arjuna is both the virile lover and the effeminate dance instructor; he has sexual relations with several women, but his most profound bond is his friendship with Kṛṣṇa.[46] Draupadī is both the outspoken critic and the ideal *pativratā*; she is active and passive, articulate speaker and symbolic listener. It is well documented that many of the pivotal episodes that face these characters – such as Yudhiṣṭhira's staking of Draupadī at the *Sabhāparvan* dice match, Arjuna's *Bhagavadgītā* indecision about fighting, and Yudhiṣṭhira's reflections prior to assuming the throne after the war – revolve around issues of *dharma*. However, less attention has been paid to the gendered dimensions of *dharma* – that is, the degree to which the dharmic ambiguities of these and other characters are issues of gender. One way that *dharma* combines with gender is by demarcating clear behavioural differences between men and women. As Custodi points out in her chapter in this book, 'a lack of clear distinction between the sexes has inauspicious resonances' throughout the *Mahābhārata*. Yet interactions between male and female characters, as Falk suggests, often provide a narrative opportunity to question *dharma*: 'the epic frequently develops its representations of ambiguities in the *dharma* in the context of conflicts between males and females' (1977: 105). Episodes which feature male and female characters in debate with each other, as well as situations where a character appears out of step with their typical gendered identity, serve to illustrate that *dharma* in the *Mahābhārata* is provisional and contextual. It is universal in the sense that it applies to everyone, yet its application and its particular form depend upon a person's class (*varṇadharma*), region (*deśadharma*), and family (*kuladharma*), as well as their gender.

By implication, gender roles can change according to particular social and political situations. In the *Śāntiparvan* Bhīṣma teaches Yudhiṣṭhira that desperate times call for desperate measures, that in times of distress the normal *dharma* rules do not necessarily apply. The rules for these extreme situations are called *āpaddharma*.

> The basic notion of *āpaddharma* involves behavior that is an exception to a requirement of dharma, a deviation from a particular rule that may still be regarded as a secondary form of the rule. Such exceptions are admissible because circumstances demanded the

> deviation for one reason or another, and the deviation can be handled as a mere exception according to one interpretive understanding or another.
>
> (Fitzgerald 2004a: 153)

Although there is only one section in the text – the *Āpaddharmaparvan*[47] – that addresses the *dharma* for extreme circumstances in detail, Fitzgerald points out that 'there is a fairly widespread sense in the *MBh* that good people can do things during such times that would normally be considered wrong (*adharma*) and yet incur no permanent bad karma' (2004a: 154).

Keeping this in mind, part of what can justify or explain the sometimes aggressive and outspoken behaviour of female characters such as Śakuntalā (at 1.68–9) and Draupadī (at e.g. 2.60–2; 3.28–33) is that *āpaddharma* applies to gender as well.[48] Despite the fact that these two arguably break the rules of mainstream *strīdharma* (the '*dharma* of women'), they both act according to higher *dharma*s: Śakuntalā, despite arguing in front of an all-male assembly and criticizing the king, can be seen as doing the right thing in terms of continuing the family line or preserving the truth; similarly, Draupadī's outspoken criticism of her husband after he has bet and lost her at dice can be seen in terms of the greater good of preserving the honour of her family, or, at a cosmic level, of saving the Earth. Indeed, Draupadī seems well aware of the principles of *āpaddharma* in her effort to convince Yudhiṣṭhira to reclaim his kingdom: 'the actual ways to success are declared to be various, as they depend on various times and conditions' (3.33.55, tr. van Buitenen).

Yet, despite the allowances of *āpaddharma* in opening up the possibilities for acceptable speech and behaviour, gender roles remain less flexible in matters of *mokṣadharma*, the rules for attaining final spiritual emancipation. According to mainstream brahmanical ideology, both men and women should marry and produce male offspring, in order to guarantee a place in heaven. As noted above, however, the tension between the *pravṛtti* and *nivṛtti* ideals is a theme running throughout the *Mahābhārata*. Whereas marriage continues to be expected for *kṣatriya* men, brahmin men – even those who, like Vyāsa, are not renouncers – do not necessarily have to marry to maintain their status and achieve their soteriological goals. Yet even as *nivṛtti* ideas opened up more possibilities for some men, both brahmin and *kṣatriya* women were supposed to marry, and a woman's soteriological goals continued to be linked with her connections to men. Even Subhrū – an exceptional female renouncer who practised asceticism her entire life – needed to be married, if just for one night, in order to go to heaven (9.51). In light of this story, one wonders about the fate of the unmarried renounceress Sulabhā *after* her debate with Janaka.

Gender and textual construction

Another significant factor in the development of ideas of gender in the *Mahābhārata* is the dialogical structure of the text. The *Mahābhārata* is presented as a series of nested conversations, many of which are consciously presented as lenses through which other conversations at other narrative levels might be reinterpreted. This particular arrangement might seem to reinscribe social and gender hierarchies, as the text brings attention to the authority of the narrators and the transformative possibilities for listeners. The text's many *upākhyāna*s (subsidiary stories embedded and told within the main story) tend to be told by authoritative males; only one *upākhyāna* is narrated by a female character. And as the dialogical structure of the text brings attention to the teller of stories, it also highlights those who listen, thus pointing to the text's projected audience and highlighting the gendered dimension of the *Mahābhārata*'s reception. The text's internal listeners are usually men whose need to listen is also a need to know how to be better men, that is, how to negotiate their own specific masculinity; but as Brian Black and Alf Hiltebeitel point out in their chapters in this book, some female characters, particularly Draupadī and Gāndhārī, also figure as prominent listeners.

The dialogical structure of the text has some other important literary implications. Although there are many female characters who make crucial speeches within the Pāṇḍava story, all those speeches are presented by the *Mahābhārata* as re-composed by Vyāsa (the text's putative author), and re-presented by his disciple Vaiśaṃpāyana, and then re-presented again by Ugraśravas, and then re-presented again by the text's actual authors (who narrate to us the story of Ugraśravas's narration). So as far as the female voices within the text are concerned, we are dealing with a multi-layered ventriloquism whereby such voices are filtered through a battery of nominally male subject-positions. Although in recent decades the question of gendered ventriloquism has been an important topic on the interface of Gender Studies and Literary Criticism, the *Mahābhārata* might appear to provide, by way of its multiple and nested framings, its own explicit theorization of this process – and to do so in a form which operates irrespective of whether or not the gender of the text's actual authors is known or indeed knowable.

Although the text would look very different with a female narrator in the outer frame, nonetheless the compounded maleness of its narratorial voice is by no means undifferentiated. The main actors in the central drama are *kṣatriya*s, Vaiśaṃpāyana and Vyāsa are brahmins, and the outer narrator Ugraśravas is a *sūta* (a low-class court factotum, often translated – in both cases potentially misleadingly – as 'bard' or 'charioteer'), narrating for the entertainment of a brahmin and his guests; so overall we have a superimposition of various narratorial identities. The effect of this is to splinter or diffuse the agency of the narration as a whole, in a way which seems to mirror the splintering and diffusion of agency for the actions in the central drama – which is parcelled out variously to the characters themselves (in the context of their unique and accidental experiences), or to their deeper identities as reborn *deva*s and *asura*s, or to their actions in past lives, or to *prakṛti* the substrate of all psycho-physical phenomenality, or to Kṛṣṇa, or Time. But if this narratorial diffusion presents a multivocal impression, as if the specific idiosyncracies of each narratorial position have been averaged out into something approximating to a view from nowhere, it is nonetheless a view from a decidedly male nowhere.

This book and beyond

Continuing our introductory guide to the sense and purpose of the book, the present section presents a kind of *parvasaṃgraha* – a prospectus and summary of the following chapters – as well as an explanation of the order in which we have arranged them, and an indication of the specific thematic linkages between them.

Placed first is a chapter by Emily Hudson which focuses on the intriguing and little-studied character of Dhṛtarāṣṭra, as revealed through his conversations with Saṃjaya, his sidekick and reporter. One reason this chapter comes first is because its first section explores a passage from the first chapter of the *Mahābhārata*, a flashforward presenting Dhṛtarāṣṭra's lament – his response to hearing the news of the death of his son Duryodhana – uttered at the conclusion of the war. Hudson discusses the literary effect of the placement of this lament, and its contextualization within a dialogue between Dhṛtarāṣṭra and Saṃjaya which probes the extent to which Dhṛtarāṣṭra himself might be responsible for the bloodshed. The text's narrative technique is discussed also in terms of the structure of the four 'battle books' at the heart of the text, which likewise play with the order of narrative presentation and filter the battlefield events through the suffering and philosophizing of the same two dialogue partners. The chapter calls out some of the *Mahābhārata*'s central issues – principally the issues of personal agency and the ripening of deeds into consequences through time – and discusses them in relation to the interaction of various narrative frames. The topic of father–son relationships – here the relationship between Dhṛtarāṣṭra and Duryodhana – is a prominent gendered theme in the *Mahābhārata* and will be explored again in several later chapters.

Taking up some of the same issues as Hudson, Brian Black's chapter examines the ways in which the *Mahābhārata*'s narrative presentation gives an indication of potential female audiences both inside and outside the text. Black suggests that the text's authors intended it for a mixed audience, and he does this through a study of the text's various *phalaśruti*s – passages which claim that hearing the text or certain portions of it results in specific benefits for the hearers – and by focusing on the women who listen to the many stories and teachings within the text. With a particular focus upon the characters of Draupadī and Dhṛtarāṣṭra's wife Gāndhārī, Black shows that the dialogues which frame the text's subsidiary discourses highlight the characters who hear them and the effects that this hearing has upon them: 'the frame dialogues give us a social context for the transmission of knowledge'. Although the king emerges as the paradigmatic listener and the person whose edification is paramount, the pairing of the *yajamāna* (ritual patron) and his wife in Vedic ritual texts, and of the king and queen in the court, indicates that the queen is also an important listener, even if her presence is not highlighted to the same degree. Black tracks the silent presence of Gāndhārī and Draupadī listening to discourses in the proximity of their husbands, and shows how this education furnishes them with the means of making their own authoritative statements and active interventions as the plot unfolds.

The final third of Black's chapter prepares us for the next several chapters, which constitute a cluster centred largely on the character of Draupadī; she is viewed most obviously in terms of her partnership with the Pāṇḍavas, her marital family, and in dealing with the issue of marriage this cluster forms a wider unity with the chapters that follow – in which marriage (or its absence) continues to be an important theme in the story of several male characters, notably Bhīṣma.

Angelika Malinar focuses tightly upon one specific dialogue between Draupadī and her eldest husband Yudhiṣṭhira, which takes place near the beginning of their years in exile, not long after Draupadī has been humiliated at the dicing match, and which explores their options and their possible next move. Malinar takes us through this dialogue point by point, carefully laying out the steps of the argument. She discusses the exchange in terms of the representative and performative dimension of royalty – that is, the need for the king and queen to embody and demonstrate the core values by which their society and realm is organized. Prior to the losses at dice, the relationship between Yudhiṣṭhira and Draupadī was dependent upon their social status, but since they are now no longer king and queen, their gendered roles stand in need of re-negotiation on both sides. In tracing the trajectory of this debate, Malinar emphasizes that the gender roles of the two parties are relational and cannot be understood independently of each other or of their social context; and although the dialogue does succeed in setting the couple's relationship on an even keel once more, 'no typical "female" argument can be identified'.

Laurie Patton's chapter also concentrates in some detail upon specific dialogues involving Draupadī: her exchange with Kṛṣṇa's wife Satyabhāmā towards the end of the period in exile, and her exchange with Queen Sudeṣṇā, the wife of King Virāṭa in whose household the Pāṇḍavas live during their year in disguise. Drawing upon recent theoretical developments in the fields of gender and psychology – most particularly in the work of Judith Butler and Hubert Hermans – Patton demonstrates that the gender ideology of the text is multifaceted, and that its characters are 'constructed through dialogue itself'. When in conversation with Satyabhāmā, Draupadī describes her attentiveness to her husbands in the manner of the stereotypical *pativratā* (a woman whose vow is to her Lord). In analysing this speech, however, Patton shows that '*pativratā* is a two-way street': Draupadī is highly conscious of the power dynamics within households, not least the power that she herself holds, and her words invoke a wide variety of female gender roles. This multiple performative emphasis is also brought out in the conversation between Draupadī (disguised as a maidservant) and Sudeṣṇā, in which Draupadī negotiates her employment in the palace and her relationship with the queen: 'Sudeṣṇā is patron, friend, and rival, all in one single relationship.'

The next chapter, by Alf Hiltebeitel, focuses on the *Mahābhārata*'s substories and the role they play in the development of the text's principal characters – here, most saliently, Draupadī. After showing that the suffering women in the text tend to blame their misfortunes on their unknown deeds in past lives, Hiltebeitel deals in some detail with two stories which address issues of friendship and marriage, particularly in the context of marital difficulties and the misbehaviour of husbands. Both stories feature birds: in the first, the story of a family of Śārṅgaka birds, a couple are estranged and then re-united; in the second, the story of 'Adorable' and King Brahmadatta, a couple split up for good. The chapter then turns to the *Mahābhārata*'s main story in light of these, dwelling on an amusing and risqué episode in Book 14 of the text, and exploring most particularly the close friendship between Draupadī (also called Kṛṣṇā, 'Dark Lady') and Kṛṣṇa, but also the relationships between Draupadī and Arjuna and between Arjuna and Kṛṣṇa. Arjuna and Kṛṣṇa are well known (to the text's audience at least) as the deities Nara and Nārāyaṇa, and through attention to some Upanishadic verses Hiltebeitel suggests that Draupadī also has a parallel divine identity which transcends her identification with the goddess Śrī: she is primal substance, the material cause of all phenomena.

The book now leaves the specific character of Draupadī behind; but Simon Brodbeck's chapter takes up the suggestion that the previous chapter finished with, and explores the possibility that the *Mahābhārata*'s many stories depicting problematic male–female dynamics may be understood, at least in part, as soteriological allegories. The goal of *mokṣa* – complete and final incorporeal salvation, the deliverance of an approximately male soul from an approximately female world of embodiment – is achieved as if mimetically in early Indian narrative traditions, involving as it does the man's renunciation of his wife and family. The *Mahābhārata* problematizes this renunciative soteriology, and Kṛṣṇa in the *Bhagavadgītā* suggests that salvation may be achieved without renunciation; Brodbeck shows that the text's narratives also reflect this philosophical development, with men tempted or attempting to renounce their wives but eventually achieving success without doing so. In order to set up this analogy, Brodbeck explores a persistent Vedic and post-Vedic cosmogony in which the world is the product of a union of gendered poles; he then surveys the biography of Yudhiṣṭhira (who is notoriously ambivalent with respect to his wife and his royal responsibilities), showing that the gendered ideal of *rakṣaṇa* – husbandly and kingly protection, the male counterpoint to *pativratā* – is crucially consonant with Kṛṣṇa's new non-renunciative soteriology, the *karmayoga*.

The book now features a cluster of chapters concentrating in different ways on the figure of Bhīṣma. Nick Allen's treatment concerns the celibate Bhīṣma's role of organizing marriages for many of his patrilineal relatives, and seeks to determine 'whether Bhīṣma's matchmaking presents any patterning or structure'. Allen locates his work within the field of cultural comparativism, and begins by reviewing George Dumézil's work on this topic and its dependence on a tri-functional Indo-European classificatory ideology according to which specific types of marriage (for example, and as differentiated in the *Mahābhārata* and the Dharmaśāstras) may be connected with specific functions. He then explains how his own work has led to the refinement of this schema into a five-functional model (briefly, *transcendence*; *1 the sacred*; *2 force*; *3 fertility*; *exclusion*). Paying attention to minute narrative details in the text, Allen assigns the marriages organized by Bhīṣma to their respective functions and finds a pattern of descending functional values (*3*, *2*, *1*) in successive generations and of ascending functional values (*1*, *2*, *3*) in successive marriages within the same generation. He then shows how Bhīṣma's first and last marriages (the first one was arranged in a previous life) frame this chiasmic unit with marriages representing the *transcendence* and *exclusion* functions. The analysis is reinforced through brief discussion of an Eddic poem, the *Rígsþula*, which shows a similar pattern in which a central character promotes fertility associated with descending functions in successive generations; and the chapter ends by reflecting on the implications of such Indo-European correlations for the study of the *Mahābhārata*.

James Fitzgerald's chapter is the first instalment of a larger study of Bhīṣma that he is undertaking and will continue elsewhere. The chapter begins with the scene where Bhīṣma dies some months after being felled and fatally wounded in the battle, and is lamented by his mother Gaṅgā; it then moves back in time to the battlefield scene at Kurukṣetra and Arjuna Pāṇḍava's terrible deed (fear of which is the main narrative cause of the *Bhagavadgītā*) of killing his most venerable patrilineal elder – a deed achieved with the vital assistance of Śikhaṇḍin. Fitzgerald discusses Robert Goldman's Freudian and Oedipal interpretation of the scene and its characters, and its ramifications elsewhere in *Mahābhārata* episodes where Bhīṣma fights against his 'father-figure' Rāma Jāmadagnya and where Arjuna is killed by his son Babhruvāhana (only to be revived). Fitzgerald discusses William Sax's interpretation of the latter episode as dramatized in present-day

Himalayan village ritual, and argues that Freudian-psychoanalytical theory might profitably be used in order to explain the *Mahābhārata* story. He then sets out the basis of an approach to this and other narrative material which will 'push past the bounds of the classical Oedipal triangle', and which, following the lead of Gananath Obeyesekere in particular, will understand 'the psychodynamics of family relations' in a sense not limited by Freud's Eurocentric model of the nuclear family. This approach seeks to locate 'representations of cathected objects of family relations' within the realm and pallette of narrative poetry, and to explore them in their interaction with other structured conceptual elements within the narrative.

Andrea Custodi's chapter continues the use of psychoanalytical theoretical perspectives to illuminate the *Mahābhārata* narrative, and is informed in particular by the work of Jacques Lacan. It is the first in a pair of chapters which address characters whose gender is ambiguous or variable, and which advert back to the story of Bhīṣma in contrasting ways. Custodi begins by highlighting the frequency with which *kṣatriya* warriors are called upon to demonstrate their manhood, and links this with the 'instability inherent in phallic subjectivity'. Noting the prevalence of gender play in the *Mahābhārata*, she proceeds to discuss two of its gender-bending characters. The virile warrior Arjuna successfully disguises himself during the year in Virāṭa's kingdom as Bṛhannaḍā, a dance teacher of definitively defective masculinity; Custodi explores the implications of Arjuna's feminization in a variety of contexts, utilizing the work of Wendy Doniger, Hiltebeitel, and Goldman. She then turns to Ambā/Śikhaṇḍinī/Śikhaṇḍin, whose story, stretched over two lifetimes, involves her change of sex in order to take fatal revenge on Bhīṣma, the man who once wronged and disgraced her by abducting her for marriage and then dismissing her unwed. The ambiguity of this cathartic tale is discussed, and the female-to-male sex change is viewed in light of its homicidal intent: Custodi remarks that 'this current of feminine vengeance . . . is an important strand of femininity in the *Mahābhārata*', and 'drives the major events of the epic'. In her conclusion she critiques Goldman's Oedipal analysis of epic stories, and shows how a Lacanian approach can help us to understand the male desire to be female in a new light.

Georg von Simson's chapter continues the specific focus on gender bending and, in common with recent chapters, deals with deep metaphors. He addresses the minor character of Sāmba, a cross-dressing son of Kṛṣṇa whose antics (he pretends to be pregnant) result in the self-destruction of the Vṛṣṇi clan in Book 16 of the *Mahābhārata*. Von Simson probes Sāmba's origins (he is given as a blessing by Śiva and Umā) and name – both of which demonstrate his essentially androgynous character – and explores the imagery of the Book 16 episode in light of its Vedic resonances in order to suggest that Sāmba represents the new-moon period of the lunar cycle, and that his oddness as a male is an integral part of this representation. A series of further considerations are introduced in order to support this theory: von

Simson connects other Vṛṣṇi heroes with other sections of the lunar cycle, and marshals evidence from the *Harivaṃśa*, various Purāṇas, and the drama *Nāgānanda* as well as the *Mahābhārata*, laying out the lunar symbolism. Solar symbolism is intertwined with this, since the new (dark) moon occurs when the sun and moon are close together in the sky (as viewed from earth). In the *Mahābhārata* Śiva and Umā grant the births not only of Sāmba but also of Bhīṣma's nemesis Śikhaṇḍin – born female, later a male – and, drawing on his previous studies of the *Mahābhārata*'s calendrical mythology, von Simson links these characters with specific stages at opposite extremities of the annual cycle.

The final chapter, by Arti Dhand, returns us to the issue of soteriology raised by Brodbeck's chapter, and to the issue of ethical responsibility raised by Hudson's at the start. It details and discusses two minor characters in the text: the author Vyāsa's son Śuka, who abandons his father in favour of spiritual progress, and the female mendicant Sulabhā who maintains, against King Janaka, that spiritual emancipation is impossible for one still living as a householder. Both of these characters, Śuka and Sulabhā, are presented by their narrators as having achieved *mokṣa*, which would imply the transcendence of all worldly values; but, as Dhand shows by probing their stories in terms of issues of gender and social class, in both cases 'the *brahmavādin*'s acts are yet circumscribed by social biases to which s/he pays a muted ideological deference'. Dhand pays particular attention to Śuka's apparently cruel treatment of his father, which seems intended to illustrate the degree of aloofness required for spiritual progress; but, assessing the stories in ethical terms, she shows that these two 'Paradigms of the Good', in their very aloofness, abdicate their moral responsibility towards their fellow humans. This soteriologically oriented aloofness is also visible in the *karmayoga*, whereby the aspirant must perform his or her received social duties without attachment and, crucially, without assessing their moral quality. In concluding Dhand recommends that, if the Hindu epics are to be used as authoritative source texts for present-day traditions, they should first be thoroughly ethically scrutinized.

* * *

A word or two may be in order here to consolidate the progress made by this book and to sketch some likely lines of further study. In addition to the themes of gender and narrative, the chapters in this book are joined together by a shared appreciation of the integrity of the text and by a set of questions regarding how its composition is related to its potential meanings or messages: how is the text organized and presented? How do particular scenes unfold? What is the relationship between the parts and the whole? How and to what effect does the text employ metaphors? What do particular stories teach? Although there remain competing theories as to how, when, and by whom the *Mahābhārata* was composed and/or compiled, the chapters in this book approach the text with a sensitivity to its literary techniques and narrative strategies.

Since within the general topic of 'gender and the *Mahābhārata*' the contributors have been free to choose what to write about, we may comment on the subjects they chose and those they did not, even bearing in mind the *Mahābhārata*'s claim to be about everything. Throughout the chapters two main narrative axes are clear: the focus on Draupadī, and the focus upon Bhīṣma, particularly as regards his interactions with Ambā/Śikhaṇḍin and Arjuna. But in the case of Draupadī, her experiences during the dicing scene are treated only in passing. Some other gender topics are not dealt with directly: although attention is paid to male–female, female–female and male–male friendships, and to male–female enmities, there is less said about female–female enmities (such as those of Kadrū and Vinatā at 1.14ff. and Devayānī and Śarmiṣṭhā at 1.73–80), and about male–male ones. With the exception of the relationship between Bhīṣma and Arjuna, the subject of same-sex violence, in many ways the central issue of the *Mahābhārata* – particularly as it might involve King Janamejaya as he hears about his warring ancestors – is not looked squarely in the face here. This is a recurring tendency in *Mahābhārata* studies (begun perhaps by Dhṛtarāṣṭra, as we shall shortly see), to look away from the dazzling mayhem at the text's centre, the magnificently hideous flowering that stands and falls between seed and bitter fruit. Nonetheless, same-sex fighting is a gendered business. In the case of Arjuna and Bhīṣma that is highlighted in this book, the conflict, being intrafamilial and intergenerational, inevitably invokes the double genders of human reproduction. Where same-sex fighters are not related, gender is nonetheless central, since whatever gender the fighters might be, they tend to be fighting over something of the *other* gender. The female–female feuds just mentioned may be seen as variants on a theme of 'co-wife' rivalry; and, as mentioned by several of our chapters, whenever *kṣatriya*s face up in battle the female is present as Śrī, Earth and *apsarā* – that is, as stake, ground, spur, and prize.

In this connection it is worth noting that certain types of exploration of the issue of male–male antagonism in the *Mahābhārata* might yield insights concerning the traditional mode of operation of institutional academies (involving a mannered, agonistic, and originally male-on-male dynamic,[49] and the narrative extremes of charlatan and colleague); concerning these academies' relations with each other (in competition for funding and well-schooled students); and concerning their operation and that of their members within nation states which move with countless casualties on an international field (again in a similar mannered and basically male-on-male[50] dynamic, involving the narrative extremes of misguided but merciless psychopath and inalienable ally). However, this book's focus falls predominantly within the various dimensions of family life. In this context the issues involved in being a father, mother, son, daughter, husband, or wife are of obvious human interest. Indeed, there is much more to be said with regard to the *Mahābhārata*'s treatment of family life, of parenting in general, and of the father–son relationship in particular: after all, the gender roles and constraints explored in the Dharmaśāstras and in both Sanskrit epics seem predicated on the possibility of intergenerational patrilineal continuity.

There is much that is not in this book, but we hope that what is here will help inspire an appreciation of the *Mahābhārata* as one of the most complex and profound works in the history of the world's literatures. In terms of methodology the book demonstrates a range of approaches, any one or any combination of which might be taken up and applied to a wider study of gender in the *Mahābhārata*, and in other narrative texts too, from ancient India and/or elsewhere and/or also from more recent times. Indeed, since our lives begin and end in narratives in so many different ways, there might be principles of 'gender and narrative' emergent from these studies of the *Mahābhārata* which could enable us to reassess and come to new terms with the ways we think about and are led to think about ourselves, and each different other and kind of other, the wider objects – human, living, physical, textual, or abstract – of our professional and non-professional activity and discourse.

Notes

1 Huberman has suggested that the '*mahā*' may be allied with the text's tendency 'to refuse to be circumscribed by any singular perspective' – that is, its being 'consciously and blatantly intertextual' (1996: 151, 152).
2 See, for example, Sax 2002; Saklani and Negi 2005; K.S. Singh 1993; Hiltebeitel 1988; 1991a; 1999a; Miller 1991; Sullivan and Unni 1995; 2001; Lothspeich 2006; Pai and Kadam 1989; Chopra and Chopra 1988–90; Dandekar 1990: 151–289; Narang 1995: 250–89.
3 Throughout this book the Poona text is referred to simply as the 'Critical Edition'.
4 See Sukthankar 1933: lxxv–xcii, cii–civ; Biardeau 1968; 1970; Dunham 1991; van der Veer 1999; Bigger 2002; Brodbeck 2006.
5 See van Buitenen 1973; 1975; 1978; 1981; Fitzgerald 2002b; 2004a.
6 There is also a complete English *Mahābhārata* translated by M.N. Dutt, recently reprinted with parallel Sanskrit text (Dutt 2001). The Clay Sanskrit Library have begun also to publish a bilingual version, based on the 'Vulgate' *Mahābhārata*, i.e. the text which was commented upon by Nīlakaṇṭha (see Kinjawadekar 1929–36): at the time of writing only two Clay *Mahābhārata* volumes have appeared (W.J. Johnson 2005; Meiland 2005), but many more are in process.
7 On ancient Indian polyandry, see S.D. Singh 1988.
8 For recent work on Vyāsa, see Sullivan 1990; J.L. Mehta 1990; Hiltebeitel 2001a: 32–91, 278–322.
9 For the origins of the four *varṇa*s – *brāhmaṇa* (brahmin), *kṣatriya*, *vaiśya* and *śūdra* – from his mouth, arms, thighs, and feet, see *Ṛgveda* 10.90.11–12; *Mānava Dharmaśāstra* 1.31. The royal privilege of *kṣatriya*s is delicately explored by the text, most particularly through the 'low-born' characters of Karṇa, Vidura, and Ekalavya. On 'ethnicity', see Goldman 1996 (also Mehendale 1984); on 'race', John Brockington 1995.

10 For longer book-by-book summaries of the *Mahābhārata* narrative, see W.J. Johnson 1998: 87–103; *Mahābhārata* 1.2.70–234.
11 On this relationship as set in historical context, see Fitzgerald 2004a: 100–42; on *kṣatriya* belligerence, see Hara 1974; on the textual construction of the *kṣatriya* role, see Hiltebeitel 2004a.
12 See especially Book 11 and the beginning of Book 12, and Chapter Two. On the text's humanistic depth, see Bailey 1983a; 1993.
13 On this conundrum, see Chakravarty 1955; Bharadwaj 1992; Hill 2001; Woods 2001; Vassilkov 1999.
14 On the text's own use of the term, see Tokunaga 2005.
15 On the *puruṣārtha*s, see Biardeau 1989; Krishan 1989; Flood 1997; Halbfass 2000; Davis 2005.
16 See Lindtner 1995; Bailey 2004; 2005b; Szczurek 2005a; Hiltebeitel 2005b; Söhnen-Thieme 2005; Bedekar 1968; Bronkhorst 1993: 31–77.
17 On the *Harivaṃśa*, see Matchett 1996; Couture 1996; John Brockington 1998: 313–44; Koskikallio 2005: 297–433.
18 Important nineteenth-century figures include Christian Lassen, the Adolf Holtzmanns elder and younger, Albrecht Weber, Alfred Ludwig, and Joseph Dahlmann.
19 Perhaps the best example of an approach which accommodates both of these poles is that of Fitzgerald, who combines the proposal of successive redactions with a keen eye for the dynamics and internal logic of the resulting text (2004a: xvi; 2002a).
20 See again John Brockington 1998: 41–81, also 524–5. This approach may explain the text's apparent internal inconsistencies: see Mehendale 1995b; 2001.
21 One of the more interesting recent theories locates the *Mahābhārata*'s genesis in the context of interactions at *tīrtha*s between different types of textual performers (Vassilkov 2002).
22 See e.g. Lidova 2002–3; Feller 2004; Olivelle 1993: 131–60; Brinkhaus 2000; Biardeau 1997; Magnone 2000.
23 See Hiltebeitel 1976; 1982; Jamison 1994; 1999; Allen 1996; 1999; 2002; West 2005–6; Hughes 1992; Vassilkov 2001. It is to be hoped that this field does not get too bogged down by the theorization or critique of vaguely indicative terms such as 'epic' and 'Indo-European'.
24 See Feller 1999; Minkowski 2001; Reich 2001; 2005a; 2005b; Tieken 2004.
25 For a sensitive challenge to the mutual opposition of the categories 'myth' and 'history', see Hirst 1998 ('story is about self-perception and identity', p. 109); see also Thapar 1976; 1986. Madeleine Biardeau says of Vyāsa, 'his mythic characterisation does not exclude his historical reality; it simply keeps it out of reach' (1968: 118).
26 See Selvanayagam 1992; Sutton 1997; Fitzgerald 2004a: 100–42. On Aśoka, see Thapar 1961; Strong 1983. John Brockington has also related the *Mahābhārata*'s story of Jarāsaṃdha to the decline of the Mauryas (2002: 78–86).
27 On Indra, see John Brockington 2001; on Satyavatī, Ghosh 2000; on Bhīṣma, Harzer 2005; on Bhīma, Gitomer 1991; on Arjuna, Pelissero 2002; on the Pāṇḍavas and Draupadī, Goldman 1995; on Kṛṣṇa, Matilal 1991; More 1995; on Duryodhana, Gitomer 1992; on Karṇa, Jarow 1999; McGrath 2004; on Śuka, Shulman 1993: 108–32.
28 As well as its primary division into eighteen books (*parvans*), the *Mahābhārata* also performs a self-inventory in terms of 100 *upaparvans* ('minor books', 1.2.34–71), and internally refers to various *upākhyāna*s (subtales), *saṃvāda*s (dialogues), and other types of sub-text. On the *Dyūtaparvan* (2.43–65), see Söhnen-Thieme 1999; on the *Nala-Upākhyāna* (3.50–78), J.D. Smith 1992; Shulman 1994; von Simson 2005; on the *Udyogaparvan*, Greer 2005; on the *Bhagavadgītā*,

Malinar 1996; John Brockington 1997; Szczurek 2002; 2005b; on the *Mokṣadharmaparvan*, John Brockington 2000; on the *Nārāyaṇīya* (12.321–39), Schreiner 1997; on the *Āśvamedhikaparvan*, Reich 2005a.

29 On the role of curses, see Ramankutty 1999; on 'epic parthenogenesis', M.C. Smith 1991; on the Ekalavya episode (1.123), Shankar 1994; on the dicing scene, Mary Brockington 2001; 2003; on the Pāṇḍavas' exiles, Parkhill 1995; on Karṇa's rejection of his natal family, Adarkar 2005a; Chapple 2005; on the conduct of the war, Mehendale 1995a; on the horse sacrifice, Koskikallio 1995; on a variety of episodes, Dange 1997; 2001; 2002.

30 On *dharma*, see Hara 1999; Bailey 2005a; Sutton 2005; Fitzgerald 2004c; on *yoga*, John Brockington 2003; on *sāṃkhya*, John Brockington 1999; on *sāṃkhya* and *yoga*, Schreiner 1999a; on the *yuga*s, González-Reimann 2002; on *asakta karman* (non-attached action), Appelbaum 1990; Brodbeck 2004; in press b; on *ānṛśaṃsya* (non-cruelty), Lath 1990; Hiltebeitel 2001a: 177–214; on *devana* and *daiva*, Shulman 1992; on *tejas*, Magnone 2003; Whitaker 2000; 2002.

31 On Draupadī, see Falk 1977; on Sāvitrī, see Vidyut Aklujkar 1991; for a comparison of Draupadī and Sītā, see Sally Sutherland 1989; on epic women in general, see Bhattacharya 1995; on Sulabhā, see Vanita 2003.

32 On Janaka, see Piantelli 2002; on Arjuna, see Pelissero 2002; for a psychoanalytic perspective on male characters, see Goldman 1978.

33 On style (broadly conceived), see Ramanujan 1991; Vassilkov 1995; 2001; J.D. Smith 1999b; Huberman 1996; Shulman 1991; Cosi 2005; on metre, Sharma 2000; Fitzgerald 2005.

34 Most of the chapters were first embodied as oral presentations at the *Epic Constructions* conference, SOAS, University of London, 7–9 July 2005.

35 With regard to future explorations on the topic of gender relations in the epics, John Brockington has written that 'one limitation that will have to be borne in mind is the interests of the authors and audience, which means that as with aspects related to social groups the picture given in the epics may well not be realistic' (1998: 520).

36 Johann Jakob Meyer had by then already produced his exhaustive work *Sexual Life in Ancient India* (1930), which is based upon the *Mahābhārata* and the *Rāmāyaṇa*.

37 Other examples include Shah 1995; 2002. Altekar's work is often deemed to have been overdetermined by nationalist discourse, but more generally it may easily be co-opted and exaggerated by those who would argue for 'prehistoric matriarchy', an approach which has found favour in some feminist circles (see Eller 2000), and which may to some extent be suggested by explicit statements of *Mahābhārata* characters (e.g. at 1.113.4–20).

38 Aklujkar notes that many of the paradigmatic *pativratā*s are 'knowingly or unknowingly' treated unjustly by their husbands, and with the exception of Draupadī a common characteristic of the *pativratā* is silent suffering. The *pativratā*s 'are somewhat passive women, who endure ordeals and yet come out virtuous and devoted towards their husbands' (Aklujkar 1991: 328). For further discussion of *pativratā* see Aklujkar 2000.

39 The iterative nature of such demonstrations well illustrates Butler's idea of 'performativity' (see above).

40 According to Arti Dhand, *niyoga* is employed when a woman's husband is 'deceased, infertile, or otherwise incapacitated' (2004: 38). According to Gail Sutherland, brahmins are the ideal candidates for *niyoga* because of their purity and their cosmological equivalence to the source of creation: 'To reassert Brāhmans as the true means of propagation is tantamount to inaugurating a new golden age' (1990: 93).

41 The etymological meaning of *napuṃsaka* is 'not a male', but it came to mean 'neither man nor woman'. According to Zwilling and Sweet, however, '*napuṃsaka* was a polysemous term, carrying connotations of lack of procreative/generative ability, androgyny, hermaphroditism and castration' (2000: 104). Goldman describes Arjuna's manifestation as a *napuṃsaka* as 'a feminized transvestite of ambiguous sex and feminized gender' (1993: 380).

42 Originally *klība* meant 'impotent man'; however, the word 'came to be associated with certain qualities which changed [its] referent from the category of sexually defective males to that of beings of equivocal sexuality' (Zwilling and Sweet 2000: 105).

43 As Ruth Vanita observes, women are rarely reborn as men, but are more likely to be reborn as virtuous women. And when a man changes into a woman 'the change is much more ambiguous' (2000: 18).

44 Other cases of sexual transformation include Ilā (1.70.16) and King Bhaṅgāśvana (13.12). See Goldman 1993: 379–82.

45 Lacan's theory of the phallus has interesting implications when considering the *daṇḍa*, which Goldman describes as 'the unambiguous phallic rod of sovereignty' (1993: 382). In the story of King Bhaṅgāśvana, for example, the king realizes that s/he is not fit to rule after Indra has changed her/him into a woman (ibid.: 381–2).

46 As Ruth Vanita comments, although both are married to women, '[t]he two men's state is comfortably integrated into their love for one another, which is repeatedly stated to be primary' (2000: 4).

47 *Mahābhārata* 12.129–67, on which see Bowles 2004.

48 Similarly, Dhand has argued that *niyoga* 'belongs best within the category of practices excused by *āpaddharma . . . niyoga* represents an apparent violation of the ethic of sexual fidelity to one's husband. It is excused, however, because the circumstances under which it is performed are exceptional and the need for the survival of the lineage supercedes the mores of sexual chastity' (2004: 39).

49 For this point we are gratefully indebted to Sîan Hawthorne (personal communication, August 2006).

50 Casualties of one kind or another are of all genders unavoidably, but this can seem to be something of an embarrassment; human death-dealing, by Bhīṣma's *dharma*, is supposed to be male on male.

2

LISTEN BUT DO NOT GRIEVE

Grief, paternity, and time in the laments of Dhṛtarāṣṭra

Emily T. Hudson

> The angry Duryodhana is the great tree, Karṇa its trunk, Śakuni the branches, Duḥśāsana the abundant blossoms and fruits, and the foolish King Dhṛtarāṣṭra the root.
>
> (1.1.65)

In the Sanskrit epic the *Mahābhārata*, the blind king Dhṛtarāṣṭra is at the centre of the catastrophe that befalls the Bhāratas.[1] His journey from passed-over primogeniture, to ruler, to destitution and the loss of his one hundred sons in the Bhārata war has the pure arc of a tragic life.[2] While the source of his downfall is 'overdetermined',[3] Dhṛtarāṣṭra usually blames his bad decisions on his affection for his eldest and favourite son, Duryodhana.[4] Indeed, Dhṛtarāṣṭra's self-identity as a father both informs his disastrous decisions and actions before the war, and fuels his moving expressions of grief during and after it. What role do Dhṛtarāṣṭra's numerous expressions of sorrow play in the overall moral and aesthetic tone(s) of the epic?

In this chapter, I explore the issue of gender through the category of fatherhood. More specifically, I examine the relationship between time, grief, and fatherhood in the laments of Dhṛtarāṣṭra.[5] In addition to investigating what these laments tell us about Dhṛtarāṣṭra as a father, I argue that a careful consideration of their interaction with certain structural features that manipulate time reveals that Dhṛtarāṣṭra's despair, that is, the anguish of a father who has lost his sons in battle, is one of the dominant leitmotifs of the epic.

With these goals in mind, I will examine two of Dhṛtarāṣṭra's laments: Dhṛtarāṣṭra's lament at the news of his son Duryodhana's death in the epic's outer frame in the *Ādiparvan* (1.1.95–190) and Dhṛtarāṣṭra's lament at the news of Bhīṣma's (Dhṛtarāṣṭra's own father's)[6] defeat in the frame of the battle books in the *Bhīṣmaparvan* (6.14.1–6.16.6).[7] In both cases Dhṛtarāṣṭra and his grief are located in a framing story,[8] and in both instances Dhṛtarāṣṭra expresses his sorrow in the context of a dialogue with Saṃjaya, his *sūta* and advisor. Two central themes emerge in their discussions that bring to light important dimensions of Dhṛtarāṣṭra's paternal despair. The first is time. In this chapter, I will be referring to three kinds of time: cosmological time (time as the creator and destroyer of all beings in the world); sequential time (past, present, and future time relative to the sequence of the events in the narrative); and consequential time (the inextricable link between past, present, and future and between act and consequence).[9] The second theme is causality, particularly the issue of who or what is responsible for the Bhārata war and the death of Dhṛtarāṣṭra's sons. While Dhṛtarāṣṭra often blames Duryodhana for what has come to pass, Saṃjaya argues that it is Dhṛtarāṣṭra himself who is to blame. How does Dhṛtarāṣṭra's self-identity as a father contribute to his grief? How does his ignorance, particularly about the nature of time, lead to the war and his loss? What does Dhṛtarāṣṭra's 'blindness' teach us about the forces that promote human despair?

Dhṛtarāṣṭra laments the news of Duryodhana's death: the lament as summary in the *Ādiparvan*

The *Mahābhārata* begins when Ugraśravas, a *sūta* and a *paurāṇika*, that is, an expert in telling stories about kings and gods, encounters a group of brahmins performing a ritual and agrees to narrate the story of the *Mahābhārata* to them. However, Ugraśravas does not begin by telling the story of the lineage of the Bhāratas. Instead, he first makes introductory comments about the glories of the story, its origin, its author, and its contents. In the context of these introductory comments, Ugraśravas provides a brief summary of the *Mahābhārata* (1.1.67–95). This summary begins with Pāṇḍu's decision to renounce his kingdom and ends with the decimation of the *kṣatriya*s in the war. Directly after Ugraśravas's summary, Dhṛtarāṣṭra, a character whom Ugraśravas has not yet introduced into the narrative, suddenly speaks for the first time, providing a second summary of the central events of the epic. Dhṛtarāṣṭra's summary is presented in the form of a lament articulated by an aged father who has learned that the last of his sons to survive the battle, Duryodhana, is dead and his army vanquished.[10] Dhṛtarāṣṭra responds to this devastating news by reflecting on the past events that portended in his mind the Kaurava defeat and the deaths of his sons.

In what follows I examine three aspects of Dhṛtarāṣṭra's lament in the *Ādiparvan*: (1) the lament itself and the way that Dhṛtarāṣṭra is characterized by it, particularly in terms of his self-understanding as a father; (2) Saṃjaya's response to the lament; and (3) the location of the lament in the epic's introductory passages.

The lament

Dhṛtarāṣṭra opens his lament by meditating on his own role in the events that led to the war. He attempts to absolve himself of all blame, assuring Saṃjaya that he did not intend the death of the Kauravas,[11] his sons, and adding that he did not favour them over his nephews, the sons of Pāṇḍu.[12] Poignantly, Dhṛtarāṣṭra speaks of his sons killed in the war in the present tense, as though he has not been able yet to accept their deaths cognitively. He tells Saṃjaya:

> My sons who are overcome by anger resent me who am old. But I, who am blind, endure it because of my affection for my sons, which is a weakness.
>
> (1.1.98a–d)[13]

Dhṛtarāṣṭra blames Duryodhana for the war, arguing that a 'bewildered' (√*muh*) Duryodhana motivated him to 'become bewildered' (√*muh*) and therefore to make the bad decisions that led to the conflict. It was because he 'lost his mind' (*acetana*) that he suggested the crooked dice game which caused the war.

Attempting to distance himself further from culpability, Dhṛtarāṣṭra claims to be wise, to have the 'eyesight of insight' (*prajñācakṣus*).[14] All along he has foreseen the approaching war and the Pāṇḍava victory. He says:

> Saṃjaya, hear from me whatever I know about it, so that when you have heard my words which are truly informed with wisdom, then, son of a *sūta*, you will know that I possess the eyesight of insight.
>
> (1.1.101)[15]

Here Dhṛtarāṣṭra defines wisdom in a particular manner, as 'seeing' the outcome of an event from the event's inception.

To prove his point, Dhṛtarāṣṭra lists some fifty-five events which, according to him, presaged the inevitable war and the defeat of the Kurus. Because Dhṛtarāṣṭra foresaw a Kaurava defeat when each event occurred, his point is that in spite of being blind, he has the special ability to see with his insight.

Dhṛtarāṣṭra's list begins with Draupadī's *svayaṃvara* and ends with Aśvatthāman's curse of Parikṣit in the womb,[16] suggesting that Dhṛtarāṣṭra sees these two events as the 'book-ends' of the Kaurava–Pāṇḍava conflict and the defeat of his sons. His list focuses predominantly on the Pāṇḍavas' feats of strength and virtue and the losses suffered by the Kauravas. Examples are: Yudhiṣṭhira's defeat by Śakuni in the game of dice (1.1.105 – and yet still his brothers remained united in their support for him); Draupadī's forced entry into the assembly hall (1.1.106); Arjuna's acquisition of the Pāśupata missile and his sojourn in heaven with Indra (1.1.109–10); the

Pāṇḍavas' alliance with Virāṭa (1.1.115); and the various slayings of Kaurava generals at the hands of the Pāṇḍavas during the battle (e.g. 1.1.126, 144, 147).

Dhṛtarāṣṭra packages each event in the formula 'When I heard *x*, I lost hope of victory'.[17] His repetition of this formula some fifty-five times fashions the lament into a despairing, mournful meditation on the seeds of the Bhārata conflict and the defeat and demise of his sons.[18] Thus, Dhṛtarāṣṭra's speech encourages us to see each of the major epic events from his point of view. However, it also encourages us to ask certain questions of him. One obvious question is: if he 'saw' that each event portended a Kaurava defeat, why didn't he do something to stop the building animosity between his sons and the Pāṇḍavas? What is the use of insight if it is not united with action?

In the last part of his lament Dhṛtarāṣṭra succumbs to utter despair. After reflecting upon the grief of his queen, Gāndhārī, and the other women who lost their husbands and sons in the battle, Dhṛtarāṣṭra tells Saṃjaya:

> Woe! I hear ten have survived the war, three of ours and seven of the Pāṇḍavas'. Eighteen armies were destroyed in the battle, that war of *kṣatriya*s. Now dark confusion seems to overpower me. I have no clarity. Sūta, my mind is unsteady.
>
> (1.1.158–9)[19]

Tormented, he falls to the ground in a faint, and upon regaining consciousness he tells Saṃjaya that he sees no profit in continuing to live (1.1.161).

What are we to make of the shift from the almost prideful arrogance that Dhṛtarāṣṭra exhibited in his prefatory remarks (he does claim, after all, to have special wisdom) to the despair that he succumbs to here? Remember, Saṃjaya has told Dhṛtarāṣṭra that Duryodhana, the head of the Kaurava army, is dead. Any lingering hopes that the Kauravas would prevail have been utterly dashed, and Dhṛtarāṣṭra struggles to come to terms with this devastating news.

The response

Saṃjaya responds to Dhṛtarāṣṭra's words of despair by urging him not to grieve. Saṃjaya makes his 'argument-against-grief' by also discussing the war's cause.[20] However, while Dhṛtarāṣṭra blamed Duryodhana, Saṃjaya considers several other candidates, on which he focuses with varying intensity. First, he points a finger at the destructive power of time,[21] particularly as it affects even the most mighty:

> You have heard about many kings, kings of great energy and strength. You have heard talk of them from Dvaipāyana [Vyāsa] and wise Nārada. They who were born in great lineages, who were

> endowed with virtues, skilled in weapons, possessed splendour that resembled Indra's. They who conquered the earth with *dharma*, offered up sacrifices with many gifts, and acquired fame in this world, all succumbed to the decree of time.
>
> (1.1.163–5)[22]

Saṃjaya recites the names of twenty-four kings, and a second list of sixty-five more kings, making the point that despite their strength, wisdom, and a host of other virtues, they all succumbed to death.[23] Second, Saṃjaya targets Dhṛtarāṣṭra's sons whom he calls 'wicked' and 'consumed by anger': and therefore, he concludes, they should not be mourned.[24] Third, Saṃjaya more quietly and indirectly implicates Dhṛtarāṣṭra himself in the events since Dhṛtarāṣṭra 'knows [how to implement] both restraint and favour',[25] implying that he went too far in protecting his son Duryodhana.[26] Fourth, Saṃjaya turns to the topic of fate: 'It was to be thus, and therefore you must not grieve. With [even] superior wisdom, who can divert fate?'[27] Finally, Saṃjaya returns to the theme of time with one of the epic's signature statements:

> Time ripens creatures and time rots them. Time again extinguishes the time that burns creatures. Time alters all beings in the world, virtuous or not virtuous. Time destroys them and creates them again. Time moves in all creatures, unchecked and impartial. Those beings who were in the past will come again and those that exist now, they are all fashioned by time. Know this and do not abandon your intelligence.
>
> (1.1.188–90)[28]

Saṃjaya devotes the most attention and art to his first and last points, both of which have to do with the destructive power of time. He also targets fate (which he seems to assume is closely related to time), Dhṛtarāṣṭra's sons, and Dhṛtarāṣṭra himself. While Saṃjaya's statements about Dhṛtarāṣṭra are indirect, they do implicate him, particularly in terms of his failings as a father. Specifically, Saṃjaya implies that Dhṛtarāṣṭra did not do enough to prevent the conflict. In spite of the fact that he 'knew better', he did not restrain his wicked sons.

In locating the cause of the war predominantly in the destructive power of time, Saṃjaya is attempting to dispel Dhṛtarāṣṭra's grief by helping him to see that he should not mourn over the death of his sons and the destruction of the Bhārata line because time does not just bring death and destruction selectively. Dhṛtarāṣṭra is not special in terms of his situation. In making this point, Saṃjaya is attempting to shift Dhṛtarāṣṭra's focus from the narrow lens of his own particular situation to the level of the experience of all living creatures. From this vantage point, Dhṛtarāṣṭra's view of things would look radically different. He would see that the sorrow he feels now has been experienced by every creature on earth since all creatures are, after all, creatures of time; he would see that his grief is just a tiny drop in the ocean of sorrow caused by the ravages of all-destroying time. Such a shift would, presumably, snap Dhṛtarāṣṭra out of his despair. It would encourage a transformation in his emotional responses from grief and self-pity to emotions like stoic acceptance and fortitude.

To state clearly the key points of my analysis so far and to consider their implications for Dhṛtarāṣṭra's depiction as a grieving father: Dhṛtarāṣṭra makes three basic points in his lament. First, he blames Duryodhana for the war; second, he claims to be wise, i.e. to have the eyesight of insight (the only time he makes this claim, to my knowledge); and third, he says that he is 'blinded' by sorrow and no longer wants to live. To think about what motivates Dhṛtarāṣṭra to articulate his grief in this way, we should consider what these statements reveal about the psychology of sorrow. A close look at Dhṛtarāṣṭra's lament brings to light a complicated web of emotions that lie at the heart of the loss he feels as a father: grief, fear, guilt, regret, and pride. His grief over the loss of his sons is inextricably linked to his fears of being responsible for the conflict, as well as to his regret for not having taken actions to prevent the war, and to his pride, which prevents him from facing his mistakes and their enormous consequences. This nexus of emotions explains in part why Dhṛtarāṣṭra blames, even censures, Duryodhana at the same time as lamenting his death. It also explains why Dhṛtarāṣṭra claims to be wise at the moment that he deceives himself about the role he played in causing the war (i.e. by telling himself that he was not responsible).

The location of the lament and the response

Let us now consider the significance of the location of this lament and response in the *Ādiparvan*. I argue that the placement of Dhṛtarāṣṭra's lament in the introductory portions of the epic, in the text's outer frame, signals to the audience that Dhṛtarāṣṭra's grief concerning the death of his sons is a dominant motif. It introduces an emotional tone or 'flavour' (grief due to loss) that colours our reception of the central events in the text to come.[29]

To explain how the lament's location does this, it is helpful to make a distinction between where the lament and response take place in the text and where they take place in the story. The lament is located at the beginning of the text, but in the story it takes place some time after the death of Duryodhana, which occurs in the tenth *parvan* at the conclusion of the war in the latter half of the story. Therefore, an event that takes place well into the story is placed in the very opening passages of the text.[30] To determine what kind of 'work' this placement is doing and how it is doing it, it is necessary to turn briefly to the issue of the function of the text's framing technique.

As I mentioned earlier, the *Mahābhārata* does not begin with the central story of the great Bhāratas. Instead it begins with two outer frames that introduce the circumstances of the epic's two earlier tellings – who told it to whom, where, and under what circumstances. Further, these frames provide the opportunity for the epic's two main storytellers Ugraśravas and Vaiśaṃpāyana to reflect on the *Mahābhārata*'s genre, its central messages, its contents, etc. They provide the text with the ability to present itself in specific ways and thus to gain control, to some extent, of the way the audience views it. They also grant the text the capacity to manipulate time by moving backwards and forwards in time (i.e. sequential time).[31] In the case of the location of Dhṛtarāṣṭra's lament, these devices manipulate time by altering the sequence of events in the story. To put it differently, an event that is yet to come (the lament), and that is a response to other events that have yet to come (e.g. Duryodhana's death), is placed at the beginning of the text. Thus it affects the way that the audience understands the text as a whole, as well as events as they come.[32] It does so in several ways.

First, the location of Dhṛtarāṣṭra's lament at the opening of the epic encourages us to see each of the major events that the blind king mentions through the lens of his grief, i.e. through the sorrow of a father broken by the defeat and deaths of his sons in the war. The form of the lament, as a summary of the epic, serves a similar function since Dhṛtarāṣṭra's expression of paternal despair encapsulates the epic in miniature.

Second, Dhṛtarāṣṭra's lament reveals the outcome of the conflict: war and devastation on a massive scale. This structural feature suggests that each of the major events listed in the lament are, in some sense, foreordained stepping stones that inevitably lead to the inescapable outcome of the conflict, namely, the catastrophic end of the great Bhāratas. In this way, cosmological time, the time that drives all creatures towards a foreordained doom, and that is thus a perpetrator of suffering, is woven into the narrative fabric of the text.

Third, Saṃjaya's speech on the destructive nature of time also provides a critical interpretive lens, since his argument for why Dhṛtarāṣṭra should not grieve for the loss of his sons prepares the epic's audiences to deal properly with *their* grief.[33] This preparation is intimately linked with Saṃjaya's meditation on the destructive aspect of time, a major theme of the epic. Just as Saṃjaya tells Dhṛtarāṣṭra that he should not grieve because death comes even to the most mighty, so too the text is telling its audiences that they should not despair at the deaths of the mighty warriors they encounter in this tale, because death is inevitable for all living beings. Indeed, the *Mahābhārata* could be viewed as containing an extended argument for why one should not grieve for the losses that are inevitably brought about by time.[34]

Finally, Dhṛtarāṣṭra's lament and Saṃjaya's response both focus on the cause of the disaster, but they do not supply a consistent account.[35] The text raises at the outset the question 'Who or what caused the deaths of Dhṛtarāṣṭra's sons and the destruction of the great Bhāratas?' – no final answer is given, but several possibilities are suggested. This remains an open-ended question in the text; one possibility is of course Dhṛtarāṣṭra himself, which renders his expressions of despair multi-dimensional, even ironical, and which complicates his characterization as a father. Because the *Mahābhārata* war not only brings death to Dhṛtarāṣṭra's sons, but wreaks devastation on a universal scale (universal in terms of the world of the text, because no one is untouched by it), the broader question here is 'Who or what is responsible for death?'; or, even more to the point, 'Who or what is responsible for grief and sorrow?'[36]

Listen but do not grieve: Dhṛtarāṣṭra laments Bhīṣma's fall in the frame of the *Bhīṣmaparvan*

Now let us turn to Dhṛtarāṣṭra's second lament, which appears in the frame of the battle books.[37] I am interested in the significance of the fact that we 'hear' the events of the war as if we are sitting next to Dhṛtarāṣṭra as he listens to Saṃjaya's narration. As Dhṛtarāṣṭra's fellow listeners, we are privy to his reactions.[38] Since most of the events that Saṃjaya narrates concern the deaths of Dhṛtarāṣṭra's sons, friends, family members, and allies, Dhṛtarāṣṭra's responses are responses of despair. What do we learn from Dhṛtarāṣṭra about his grief by sitting next to him as we listen to Saṃjaya narrate the events of the war?

To answer this question, I first briefly examine Dhṛtarāṣṭra's lament at the news of Bhīṣma's fall in the frame of the *Bhīṣmaparvan*, as well as Saṃjaya's response.[39] I will be particularly interested in Dhṛtarāṣṭra's self-understanding as a father in these articulations of despair. Next, I turn to a consideration of two structural features of the battle books, backshadowing and frame-switching, both of which are used to manipulate the narrative construction of time.

At the end of the *Udyogaparvan*, when it is clear that the peace negotiations have failed and that war is inevitable, Dhṛtarāṣṭra asks Saṃjaya to tell him everything that happened to the armies of the Kauravas and the Pāṇḍavas.[40] In the course of posing this request, Dhṛtarāṣṭra also makes several revealing comments. He tells Saṃjaya that he thinks 'fate is supreme and human effort is useless',[41] because despite the fact that he knows the evils of war, he cannot restrain his deceitful son (i.e. Duryodhana).[42] Upon further reflection he offers, 'I do have the wisdom to perceive evil, but when I am with my son, it is concealed from me.'[43]

Saṃjaya chastises Dhṛtarāṣṭra, telling him that he should not put all the blame (*doṣa*) on his son. Further, 'the person who obtains that which is inauspicious because of his own misdeeds'[44] should not blame time or fate. After reprimanding the king, Saṃjaya agrees to report the details of the war. Significantly, he tells Dhṛtarāṣṭra how he should listen: he should remain calm and not despair.[45] Saṃjaya says,

> So, then, hear from me in full the news of the slaughter in the war of horses, elephants, and boundlessly august kings. And while you are hearing, great king, what happened in the great war that gave rise to the destruction of all the world, remain calm and do not despair.
>
> (5.156.12–13)[46]

Saṃjaya's narration of the war events commences in the *Bhīṣmaparvan* when he, 'griefstricken' (*duḥkhita*, 6.14.2), rushing from the battlefield to Hāstinapura, approaches the 'brooding' (*dhyāyat*, 6.14.2) Dhṛtarāṣṭra and tells him that Bhīṣma has fallen:

> I am Saṃjaya, great king. My homage, bull of the Bhāratas! Bhīṣma, son of Śaṃtanu, the grandfather of the Bhāratas, has been killed! The chief of all warriors, the light of all archers, the grandfather of the Kurus now lies on a bed of arrows.
>
> (6.14.3–4)[47]

To drive the magnitude of this point home, Saṃjaya juxtaposes many of Bhīṣma's great feats of strength with the fact that he now lies helpless:

> He who conquered all the assembled kings in a great battle in the city of the Kāśis, the great warrior, the offspring of the Vasus, who fought Rāma Jāmadagnya and was not killed by him, now has been felled by Śikhaṇḍin.
>
> (6.14.6–7)[48]

Significantly, he concludes his speech by blaming Dhṛtarāṣṭra for what has happened:

> He who, unshakable like Śakra, rained arrows by the thousands and killed a hundred million warriors in battle, lies on the ground, moaning, like a tree broken by the wind, undeserving of his death, because of your ill-conceived plan, Bhārata!
>
> (6.14.12–13)[49]

Dhṛtarāṣṭra responds to this disastrous news by voicing his grief. First he expresses his despair by asking a string of questions (6.15.1–5). How did his father fall from the chariot? Who was protecting him? Next, he reflects on how his sons must feel now that Bhīṣma lies felled, and worries about the implications of the loss of the great warrior for the safety and security of his sons and their army: 'The army of my son is now like a woman whose hero has been killed.'[50] Dhṛtarāṣṭra also expresses how he feels. He says 'Profound grief overwhelms me',[51] and 'I know no peace',[52] only grief. Finally, he questions how this could possibly have happened to someone as mighty and powerful as Bhīṣma. First he blames himself,[53] but later he places the blame on time, coming to the conclusion that 'time certainly is very powerful, inevitable for the whole world',[54] since mighty Bhīṣma has been defeated. At the end of his lament, he exhorts Saṃjaya to tell him everything that happened, pinning the blame on Duryodhana once again:

> Saṃjaya, tell me what befell the kings of the earth in battle, whether it was well-conducted or misguided as a result of the ignorance of that fool [i.e. Duryodhana].
>
> (6.15.73)[55]

Saṃjaya agrees to report the details of Bhīṣma's fall, but before he does so he berates Dhṛtarāṣṭra for not accepting responsibility for his role in the war. Dhṛtarāṣṭra, Saṃjaya says, should not place all the blame on Duryodhana, for 'a man who is faced with misfortune because of his own evil actions must not blame someone else'.[56] Exhorting Dhṛtarāṣṭra to listen to what he, Saṃjaya, has seen with his own eyes or through the power of *yoga*, he instructs him 'not to indulge his mind in sorrow', because 'surely all this was destined long ago'.[57]

In this lament Dhṛtarāṣṭra distances himself from responsibility for the war, just as he did in his 'When I heard . . .' dirge in the *Ādiparvan*. Although in the middle of this lament he does point a finger at himself, he quickly drops this line of thought and turns to causal forces such as time and Duryodhana to locate responsibility for the conflict. Saṃjaya's comments also focus on the issue of the war's cause. Although here he explicitly blames Dhṛtarāṣṭra (as well as fate), Saṃjaya is often inconsistent when he talks to Dhṛtarāṣṭra about the causal forces of the war. When he chastises Dhṛtarāṣṭra for blaming Duryodhana, he always points out that Dhṛtarāṣṭra is to blame. However, when he provides instructions for how Dhṛtarāṣṭra should listen to his narration of the battle events, he often tells him to remain calm, because, he says, all this was destined and thus there was nothing Dhṛtarāṣṭra could have done about it (see, for example, 6.16.6). However, as Lawrence McCrea points out, there is a rationale behind Saṃjaya's ambiguity: Saṃjaya employs two different rhetorical strategies for two different purposes. When Dhṛtarāṣṭra attempts to play 'the blame game', Saṃjaya stops him short by pointing to his own culpability; but when Dhṛtarāṣṭra begins to wallow in despair, Saṃjaya points to the inexorability of fate and the universality of death and loss. In both cases, as McCrea puts it, 'his aim is essentially therapeutic – to lead him away from self destructive emotions and towards stoic acceptance and fortitude' (personal communication, March 2006).[58]

The exchanges between Dhṛtarāṣṭra and Saṃjaya in the frames of the other three battle books follow the format of the *Bhīṣmaparvan* exchange closely: Saṃjaya reports the details of the war to Dhṛtarāṣṭra; Dhṛtarāṣṭra responds with a lament in which he mourns the loss of the particular character who has died, reflects on the implications of the event for the security of his sons, Duryodhana in particular, and then turns to the broader issue of the cause of the war and blames variously himself, fate, time, and, most frequently, Duryodhana. Saṃjaya chastises Dhṛtarāṣṭra for not accepting his responsibility, and tells him that he is reaping the results of his bad acts, since he allowed the Pāṇḍavas to be treated cruelly by Duryodhana. Saṃjaya then exhorts Dhṛtarāṣṭra to listen to what he has to tell him, and to remain calm and not to grieve.

* * *

Moving now to an examination of the battle books' structure, I want to explore how certain structural features related to the text's framing technique – backshadowing and frame-switching – make a specific argument about Dhṛtarāṣṭra's role in the production of the war as well as his weaknesses as a father.

Each battle book begins with a flashforward in which Saṃjaya rushes back from the battlefield to announce to Dhṛtarāṣṭra the death of the Kaurava general after whom the book is named. The rest of the book contains Saṃjaya's narration of the days of the battle that conclude with the general's killing.[59] What is notable about this structure is that each book begins with a declaration of its own outcome (i.e. the news of the death of the Kaurava general), and the rest of the book involves the narrative's effort to 'catch up' with this outcome. I will refer to this device as backshadowing, since Saṃjaya's reports are after-accounts, not running commentaries.[60] While this narrative technique is similar to the placement of Dhṛtarāṣṭra's lament in the *Ādiparvan* discussed above, it does not function in quite the same manner. The difference has to do with the fact that Duryodhana's fall – the source of Dhṛtarāṣṭra's grief in the *Ādiparvan* – is not the outcome of the epic story (the events that the lament frames), but only a later event. Bhīṣma's fall – the source of Dhṛtarāṣṭra's grief in the *Bhīṣmaparvan* – on the other hand, is the outcome of the book. Thus, while the technique is similar in both instances, it is saying something fundamentally different about time in each case – it is making a point about cosmological time in the first instance, and about consequential time in the second.

The second aspect of the battle books' structure that I want to focus on is the device of frame-switching. While frame-switching is used throughout the *Mahābhārata*, it is particularly effective in the battle books because Saṃjaya and Dhṛtarāṣṭra's conversations provide a framing meta-commentary on the events of the war. Significantly, this conversation is between the character who is, ostensibly, an agent of the war (Dhṛtarāṣṭra), and the character who forces him to see himself as such (Saṃjaya).

Backshadowing and frame-switching are narrative devices that manipulate time, and therefore make specific points about it. These points have to do with the implicit connection in the text between causation (seed and fruit) – a theme that has been surfacing throughout this chapter – and consequential time (i.e. the inextricable link between past, present, and future, and between act and consequence).

Backshadowing is a convention that encourages us to view the events of a particular battle book as informed by the outcome of the book (i.e. the death of the Kaurava general). Accordingly, it 'treats the past as though it inevitably led to the present'; it suggests that 'the present, as the future of the past, was already immanent in the past in a more or less straight line' (Morson 1994: 3, 234).

The use of backshadowing in the battle books makes a past catastrophe visible in temporal advance. By treating the present as already immanent in the past, backshadowing makes the point that the fruit of an act is contained in its act, as seed. This device, then, provides us with a clue concerning Dhṛtarāṣṭra's role in the war, a recurring topic of Saṃjaya and Dhṛtarāṣṭra's framing conversations. Following this structural logic, Dhṛtarāṣṭra's fatal error was that he did not have a proper understanding of time, and therefore of causation. When he made his decisions to give in to his sons (particularly Duryodhana whose jealousy of the Pāṇḍavas is evident throughout the epic) and allow the Pāṇḍavas to be treated unfairly, Dhṛtarāṣṭra did not properly understand this intimate connection between past and present (as the future of the past), and therefore between seed and fruit.[61] Or, if he did understand it, he failed to act on this knowledge. Either way, his failure contributed significantly to the great tragedy, for the decision to cheat the Pāṇḍavas contained the fruit of the war and the death of his sons. It was not a question of whether or not the war would come to pass (and Dhṛtarāṣṭra held out hope against hope that it would not, as we know from his 'When I heard . . .' dirge), it was just a matter of time.

The second structural feature, the strategy of frame-switching, plays with time by placing two different narrative moments, the time of the war and the time of the war's telling (and Dhṛtarāṣṭra's grieving), in close proximity to one another. What this device provides, then, is the juxtaposition of the moment when a character (Dhṛtarāṣṭra) is forced to see that he is the agent of an event (the war), and the moment of the event itself. This switching back and forth between agent and event, or seed-sower and fruit, suggests that the present (as the future of the past) and the future are inextricably linked, that the effect and its cause are inseparable. As in the case above, the point is that Dhṛtarāṣṭra did not have a proper understanding of this intimate connection; because of this fundamental misunderstanding, he now finds himself facing inconceivable consequences for his misguided actions and his over-indulgent affection for his sons.

As noted above, Dhṛtarāṣṭra claims to have the eyesight of insight, which he defines as the ability to see the consequences of an action at an event's inception. However, if this is the case, then we encounter the paradox of the blind king: that he sees with insight but does not act with it. The reason why he fails to make the connection between insight and action, following the logic of the structure of the battle books, is because he is blind to the intimate link between act and consequence. He fundamentally misjudged this connection by clinging to the small hopes he harboured that he would not reap the bad consequences of the seeds that he sowed, even though he was able to 'see' these consequences in temporal advance.

The extent to which Dhṛtarāṣṭra acted as a loving father motivated by his affection for his sons, indeed 'blinded' by such affection, makes the consequences of his misguided actions all the more tragic, if not ironic, since these actions led to the deaths of those very sons in whose name he claimed to act. Further, the tension between his grief over the loss of his sons, and his tendency to blame them (particularly Duryodhana) for the disaster, distorts his understanding of his past actions and the function of time more generally. It is these issues precisely (time and confronting his past actions) that Saṃjaya argues Dhṛtarāṣṭra must come to terms with in order to move beyond his grief. Dhṛtarāṣṭra's inability to face and accept his hand in the war prevents him from being able to move beyond his sorrow; ultimately it prevents his moral awakening in the epic. Sadly, at the end of his life Dhṛtarāṣṭra still speaks of being tormented by the memory of the destruction of the Bhāratas, and still blames Duryodhana for the catastrophe (15.36.26–33).

Conclusion

I have explored two laments of Dhṛtarāṣṭra and argued that they reveal a complicated group of emotions at the heart of his identity as a father. I have also argued that the interactions between Dhṛtarāṣṭra's laments and several structural features related to the epic's framing device render Dhṛtarāṣṭra's despair as a grieving father one of the central leitmotifs of the epic. Further, they make a specific argument about Dhṛtarāṣṭra's moral blindness and his consequent role in the production of the war and the deaths of his sons.

To conclude, I turn briefly to the thoughts of B.K. Matilal, who characterizes Dhṛtarāṣṭra's moral failure in terms of moral weakness. This is typified by the following apt quotation:

> I know what *dharma* is, but I cannot persuade myself to act accordingly; I know what *adharma* is, but I am unable to refrain from it.
>
> (Matilal 2002: 61)[62]

All along, according to Matilal, Dhṛtarāṣṭra knew that Duryodhana's behaviour was immoral, but he did nothing to stop it. His blind affection for his son led him to ignore the advice of well-meaning persons, and it was not until the end of the war – when everyone was dead – that Dhṛtarāṣṭra admitted his weakness and regretted it (ibid.: 62).

While there is much merit in these insights, I believe that our analysis of Dhṛtarāṣṭra's laments leads us to characterize his moral failure somewhat differently. What we have discovered in these articulations of despair, beyond moral weakness, is active self-deception. Ironically, while Dhṛtarāṣṭra claims to have the eyesight of insight, the sad truth is that he consistently and actively refuses to acknowledge the power of karmic retribution in the name of his affection for his sons. The effect of Dhṛtarāṣṭra's self-deception is that he lays the seeds for the enmity of his sons and nephews, and then he reaps the horrors that these seeds bear. After the war, when the consequences of his actions are irreversible, he persists in deceiving himself by 'seeing and not seeing' his role in the conflict. Blind in this way to the very end, Dhṛtarāṣṭra and his downfall in the epic serve not only as a cautionary tale for over-indulgent fathers, but also as a warning for those who are tempted foolishly to dismiss the power of consequential time. As Vidura warns Dhṛtarāṣṭra in the *Udyogaparvan* when there is still hope for peace, so too does the epic warn us:

> One should not do at the outset what will cause one to climb in bed and suffer, for life is unstable.
>
> (5.39.27)[63]

Notes

1 I would like to thank Lawrence McCrea, Anne Monius, Parimal Patil, and Laurie Patton for reading drafts of this chapter and making many helpful comments and suggestions. Surprisingly, very few scholars have focused on Dhṛtarāṣṭra and his significance in the epic. One notable exception is Chaitanya 1985: 45–64.

2 Dhṛtarāṣṭra does have one son who survives the war: Yuyutsu, a bastard son.

3 'Overdetermined' is a term that Wendy Doniger takes from Freud; it means that too many reasons are given for any one of them to explain why a particular event occurred. See O'Flaherty 1984: 42–53.

4 While Dhṛtarāṣṭra often blames his bad decisions on his affection for his sons, Duryodhana in particular, he also blames fate (*daiva*) and time (*kāla*). For example, see 2.45.57; 5.56.27 and 5.156.2–7.

5 Because the *Mahābhārata* contains a series of catastrophic events that affect characters in a variety of adverse ways (e.g. the abuse of Draupadī in the dicing scene, the Pāṇḍavas' unjust exile, the failed peace negotiations, the war, the decimation of the Bhāratas, etc.), the text also contains many accompanying passages where characters express their grief. I use the word 'lament' to refer to such expressions of grief.

6 Because of the complex circumstances of Dhṛtarāṣṭra's birth, he has three fathers: Vicitravīrya (his genealogical father), Vyāsa (his biological father), and Bhīṣma (the father who raised him).

7 In addition to these two laments, there are several other places in the epic where Dhṛtarāṣṭra expresses his grief at length. See 8.5; 9.2.3–47; 11.1.10–20.

8 The *Mahābhārata* has two outer frames which contextualize the epic's telling:

the Ugraśravas frame and the Vaiśaṃpāyana frame. Furthermore, framing devices are used throughout the *Mahābhārata*, most significantly during the battle books (Books 6–9) where Saṃjaya narrates the events of the war to Dhṛtarāṣṭra. The first lament that I will examine is located in the Ugraśravas (outer) frame, and the second is located in the dialogue between Dhṛtarāṣṭra and Saṃjaya that frames the battle books. For scholarship on the framing device in the *Mahābhārata*, see Minkowski 1989; Reich 1998: 4–6, 56–64; Hiltebeitel 2001a: 92–130.

9 For scholarship on the subject of time in the *Mahābhārata*, see González-Reimann 2002; Vassilkov 1999; Hiltebeitel 2001a: 38–9, 89, 95–7, 166.

10 The exact timing of this lament in the epic story is not made explicit by the text.

11 *na vigrahe mama matir*, 1.1.97.

12 *na me viśeṣaḥ putreṣu sveṣu pāṇḍusuteṣu ca //* 1.1.97. This statement, we will come to discover, is false. Is Dhṛtarāṣṭra self-delusional or consciously lying here? We do not know.

13 *vṛddhaṃ mām abhyasūyanti putrā manyuparāyaṇāḥ / ahaṃ tv acakṣuḥ kārpaṇyāt putraprītyā sahāmi tat /* The grammar and style in this passage is entirely different from other *Mahābhārata* laments, which are characterized for the most part by a string of questions concerning the circumstances of the loved one's death, the tendency to juxtapose the condition of the deceased with how they appeared in life, and a meditation on the causes of the victim's misfortune (which Dhṛtarāṣṭra does do here). No other lament in the epic, to my knowledge, employs this strange use of the present tense that refers to the loved one as though he or she is still living. For some 'characteristic' *Mahābhārata* laments, see Yudhiṣṭhira's at 7.49; Aśvatthāman's at 9.64.12–38; and Gāndhārī's at 11.16–25.

14 This term is a polite epithet for a blind person. However, it takes on a broader (even ironic) meaning in the *Mahābhārata*, particularly with respect to its application to Dhṛtarāṣṭra. The narrative voice applies this term to Dhṛtarāṣṭra frequently (e.g. 2.45.2; 3.5.1; 3.8.23; 9.1.21; 11.10.2). The term is also linked to knowledge of *karma* at 3.181.26 (in Mārkaṇḍeya's discourse to Yudhiṣṭhira), and to knowledge of impermanence at 3.200.48 (in the hunter's discourse to the brahmin).

15 *tatra yad yad yathā jñātaṃ mayā saṃjaya tac chṛṇu / śrutvā hi mama vākyāni buddhyā yuktāni tattvataḥ / tato jñāsyasi māṃ saute prajñācakṣuṣam ity uta //*

16 In the story, Aśvatthāman hurls his weapon not just at Uttarā's womb, but at the wombs of all the Pāṇḍava women. Kṛṣṇa assures everyone that Parikṣit will be revived in Uttarā's womb. See 10.15.28–31 and 10.16.1–15.

17 *yadāśrauṣaṃ . . . / . . . tadā nāśaṃse vijayāya saṃjaya //* See, for example, 1.1.102.

18 I should stress that Dhṛtarāṣṭra's main preoccupation here is with whether or not the Kauravas' final defeat could have been avoided, not with whether or not the war could have been avoided.

19 *kaṣṭaṃ yuddhe daśa śeṣāḥ śrutā me trayo 'smākaṃ pāṇḍavānāṃ ca sapta / dvyūnā viṃśatir āhatākṣauhiṇīnāṃ tasmin saṃgrāme vigrahe kṣatriyāṇām // tamasā tv abhyavastīrṇo moha āviśatīva mām / saṃjñāṃ nopalabhe sūta mano vihvalatīva me //*

20 For more on the 'genre' of the argument-against-grief in the *Mahābhārata*, see Hudson 2006, chapter 4.

21 There are four other major arguments-against-grief that espouse a view of time consistent with Saṃjaya's view here. Three are delivered by Vyāsa (6.2–4; 12.26; 16.9) and one by Vidura (11.2). Kṛṣṇa's statements to Arjuna in the *Bhagavadgītā* could be considered an argument-against-grief as well, since Kṛṣṇa says that Arjuna should not grieve for those 'he' is going to kill because Kṛṣṇa, as Time, has already killed them (*Bhagavadgītā* 11.32–4). In this way, the *Gītā* can be seen as both an argument-against-grief and an argument for war.

22 *śrutavān asi vai rājño mahotsāhān mahābalān / dvaipāyanasya vadato nāradasya ca dhīmataḥ // mahatsu rājavaṃśeṣu guṇaiḥ samuditeṣu ca / jātān divyāstraviduṣaḥ śakrapratimatejasaḥ // dharmeṇa pṛthivīṃ jitvā yajñair iṣṭvāptadakṣiṇaiḥ / asmiṃl loke yaśaḥ prāpya tataḥ kālavaśaṃ gatāḥ //*
23 Literally 'went to their destruction' (*nidhanaṃ gatāḥ*, 1.1.182).
24 *tava putrā durātmānaḥ prataptāś caiva manyunā / . . . na tāñ śocitum arhasi //* 1.1.183.
25 *nigrahānugrahau cāpi viditau te narādhipa /* 1.1.185.
26 *nātyantam evānuvṛttiḥ śrūyate putrarakṣaṇe //* 1.1.185.
27 *bhavitavyaṃ tathā tac ca nātaḥ śocitum arhasi / daivaṃ prajñāviśeṣeṇa ko nivartitum arhati //* 1.1.186.
28 *kālaḥ pacati bhūtāni kālaḥ saṃharati prajāḥ / nirdahantaṃ prajāḥ kālaṃ kālaḥ śamayate punaḥ // kālo vikurute bhāvān sarvāṃl loke śubhāśubhān / kālaḥ saṃkṣipate sarvāḥ prajā visṛjate punaḥ / kālaḥ sarveṣu bhūteṣu caraty avidhṛtaḥ samaḥ // atītānāgatā bhāvā ye ca vartanti sāṃpratam / tān kālanirmitān buddhvā na saṃjñāṃ hātum arhasi //*
29 In Indian aesthetics, *rasa* (juice, taste, flavour) is a term for emotional experience in drama or poetry.
30 This particular lament is not repeated in the battle books. However, Dhṛtarāṣṭra does lament Duryodhana's death and the defeat of his army at the beginning of the *Śalyaparvan* (9.2.3–47, when he first hears the news of it from Saṃjaya) and at the beginning of the *Strīparvan* (11.1.10–20, when the news has sunk in).
31 For more on frames in the *Mahābhārata* and their relation to time, see Hiltebeitel 2001a: 38.
32 For a good discussion of the significance of the introduction and its impact on interpretation in works of literature, see Swanson 1999: 107–16. On this point she writes, 'Because the literary narrative is an aesthetic medium of communication, the manner in which the narrative opens is furthermore significant in determining the reader's reception of the narrative's entirety. The passage that is presented first thus possesses not only a discursive primacy, but also a primacy in the reader's understanding and interpretation of all that follows . . . It also follows that the central function of a narrative's beginning is to serve as a point of entrance into the fictional world of the story and the character's situations' (ibid.: 110).
33 For more on the role of the audience in the *Mahābhārata*, see Hudson 2006, chapter 1; see also Chapter 3 below.
34 For discussions in the epic on the perils of grief, see 3.206.20–5 and 5.36.42–3.
35 The source of the *Mahābhārata* war is undoubtedly overdetermined. The possible candidates in the text are almost endless. Various characters are blamed (e.g. Duryodhana, Dhṛtarāṣṭra, and less frequently Kṛṣṇa – see 18.1.7–9; 6.62.38–54; 1.1.92; 2.33.19; 15.5.7). Impersonal forces like time, fate, and *karma* are also blamed. For a good discussion of fate, time, and *karma* as causal forces of the war, see Hill 2001: 193–230. There is even a cosmic explanation for why the war had to take place. According to this explanation, the battle is really a conflict between the *asura*s and the *deva*s, whose mission is to relieve the earth of her burden (1.58.25; 11.8.20–6). See Brodbeck in press a. However, I would caution those who want to see this cosmic explanation as all-encompassing, for it may overshadow the human dimension of the conflict, which the epic narrative undoubtably emphasizes. Ramanujan cautions us on this point as well (1991: 434 n. 4).
36 Upon the death of Abhimanyu, Yudhiṣṭhira, heartbroken, asks Vyāsa, 'What is the cause of death?' Vyāsa responds by making reference to a famous dirge, 'The Passing of the Sixteen Kings', recited by the seer Nārada to King Sṛñjaya, who mourned the death of his young son (7.app8). This speech, similar to Saṃjaya's in the *Ādiparvan* in many ways, appears at 12.29 in the Critical Edition.

37 The four battle books are, in order: the *Bhīṣmaparvan*, the *Droṇaparvan*, the *Karṇaparvan*, and the *Śalyaparvan*.
38 Dhṛtarāṣṭra's immediate fellow listeners are, of course, the women of the court. We know this because at the beginning of the *Śalyaparvan* Dhṛtarāṣṭra dismisses them when he hears the news of Duryodhana's death, and then he asks Saṃjaya to narrate the story in detail once they are alone (9.2.1). Also, the text notes their response to Karṇa's death at 8.3.1–8.
39 While Bhīṣma is felled by Arjuna in the first of the four battle books, he does not die until the end of the *Anuśāsanaparvan* (Book 13), after he has delivered his lengthy sermon to Yudhiṣṭhira on the duties of kings.
40 Even though Saṃjaya does not receive his divine eyesight until the beginning of the *Bhīṣmaparvan* (6.2.4–6), he begins his narration here.
41 *diṣṭam eva paraṃ . . . pauruṣaṃ cāpy anarthakam* / 5.156.4.
42 . . . *ahaṃ jānamāno 'pi yuddhadoṣān . . . // . . . nikṛtiprajñaṃ putraṃ . . . / na śaknomi niyantuṃ . . .* // 5.156.4–5.
43 *bhavaty eva hi me sūta buddhir doṣānudarśinī / duryodhanaṃ samāsādya punaḥ sā parivartate* // 5.156.6.
44 . . . *ātmano duścaritād aśubhaṃ prāpnuyān naraḥ* / 5.156.9.
45 To my knowledge, Saṃjaya is the only narrator in the epic who instructs his audience in such a manner, with the exception of Nārada at 15.45.9. Interestingly, Nārada in this context is reporting to Yudhiṣṭhira the news of Dhṛtarāṣṭra's – Yudhiṣṭhira's 'father's' – death in a forest fire.
46 *hayānāṃ ca gajānāṃ ca rājñāṃ cāmitatejasām / vaiśasaṃ samare vṛttaṃ yat tan me śṛṇu sarvaśaḥ // sthiro bhūtvā mahārāja sarvalokakṣayodayam / yathābhūtaṃ mahāyuddhe śrutvā mā vimanā bhava* // Saṃjaya provides the same kind of instructions to Dhṛtarāṣṭra at 6.16.5 and 6.73.1–5.
47 *saṃjayo 'haṃ mahārāja namas te bharatarṣabha / hato bhīṣmaḥ śāṃtanavo bharatānāṃ pitāmahaḥ // kakudaṃ sarvayodhānāṃ dhāma sarvadhanuṣmatām / śaratalpagataḥ so 'dya śete kurupitāmahaḥ* //
48 *yaḥ sarvān pṛthivīpālān samavetān mahāmṛdhe / jigāyaikarathenaiva kāśipuryāṃ mahārathaḥ // jāmadagnyaṃ raṇe rāmam āyodhya vasusaṃbhavaḥ / na hato jāmadagnyena sa hato 'dya śikhaṇḍinā* //
49 *yaḥ sa śakra ivākṣobhyo varṣan bāṇān sahasraśaḥ / jaghāna yudhi yodhānām arbudaṃ daśabhir dinaiḥ // sa śete niṣṭanan bhūmau vātarugṇa iva drumaḥ / tava durmantrite rājan yathā nārhaḥ sa bhārata* //
50 *yoṣeva hatavīrā me senā putrasya saṃjaya* / 6.15.49.
51 *ārtiḥ parā māviśati . . .* / 6.15.4.
52 *na hi me śāntir astīha . . .* / 6.15.69.
53 *sa śete niṣṭanan bhūmau vātarugṇa iva drumaḥ / mama durmantritenāsau yathā nārhaḥ sa bhārataḥ* // 6.15.15.
54 *kālo nūnaṃ mahāvīryaḥ sarvalokaduratyayaḥ* / 6.15.56.
55 *saṃgrāme pṛthivīśānāṃ mandasyābuddhisaṃbhavam / apanītaṃ sunītaṃ vā tan mamācakṣva saṃjaya* // Note that *saṃbhavam* goes with *apanītam*, making what was caused by Duryodhana a bit ambiguous.
56 *ya ātmano duścaritād aśubhaṃ prāpnuyān naraḥ / enasā tena nānyaṃ sa upāśaṅkitum arhati* // 6.16.2.
57 . . . *mā ca śoke manaḥ kṛthāḥ / diṣṭam etat purā nūnam . . . narādhipa* // 6.16.6.
58 For more on Saṃjaya's 'inconsistencies', see Hill 2001: 299.
59 For a slightly different interpretation of the chronological arrangements of Saṃjaya's reports, see Belvalkar 1946: 323–6.
60 See Mehendale 1995a: 3. On my use of the term 'backshadowing', see Hiltebeitel and Kloetzli 2004: 582.
61 Vidura and Saṃjaya make this very same point to Dhṛtarāṣṭra at 5.34.1–25

and 11.1.30–5 respectively; see also 3.225.22–7 (where, interestingly, Dhṛtarāṣṭra himself is speaking about the likelihood that the Pāṇḍavas will defeat the Kurus in battle).

62 *jānāmi dharmaṃ na ca me pravṛttiḥ jānāmy adharmaṃ na ca me nivṛttiḥ //* Matilal gives no reference for this line, which is not to be found in the Sanskrit *Mahābhārata*.

63 *yena khaṭvāṃ samārūḍhaḥ paritapyeta karmaṇā / ādāv eva na tat kuryād adhruve jīvite sati //*

3

EAVESDROPPING ON THE EPIC

Female listeners in the *Mahābhārata*

Brian Black

Introduction

This chapter will explore the theme of female listeners in the *Mahābhārata*, both in terms of how the text represents its projected audience and in terms of how the female characters claim authority to speak on matters of *dharma* and *mokṣa*.[1] Despite the text's orientation towards men, its focus on war, and the way it characterizes the ideals of heroism, honour and courage as specifically masculine traits, subsequent Sanskrit texts have accepted the *Mahābhārata* as the Veda for women and *śūdra*s, a re-packaging of Vedic teachings in a format made accessible to a universal audience. This chapter asks the questions: to what degree is the *Mahābhārata*, a text whose 'main business is the legend of men who were heroes' (van Buitenen 1978: 168), a text for women? Is there any indication within the *Mahābhārata* that the text does in fact aim to reach the ears of women? If so, which women, and in what circumstances? This chapter will explore these questions by looking at how the dialogical presentation of the text gives us an indication of its projected audience, paying particular attention to the frame stories. As we will see, the *Mahābhārata* does explicitly include a female listenership, both by addressing unnamed women in *phalaśruti*s, and by depicting particular female characters as audience members. The female characters who are most often portrayed as auditors are Gāndhārī and Draupadī, both of whom hear large portions of the text while – at the sides of their husband kings – fulfilling their function as queens. Yet, despite the symbolic significance of their presence, for Gāndhārī and Draupadī listening is far from passive, as both of them have consequential speaking parts and are major contributors to a number of pivotal episodes in the story. Indeed, for both Gāndhārī and Draupadī their role as listeners, although sometimes relegated to the background, is intrinsically related to what they do and what they say. Despite the fact that the *Mahābhārata* does not explicitly state that it is a text for women, through the characters of Gāndhārī and Draupadī it includes some women as a crucial part of its audience within the very structure of the text.

Mahābhārata as the universal Veda

Let us begin with the *Mahābhārata*'s status as a fifth Veda. According to the *Bhāgavata Purāṇa*, Vyāsa composed his story out of compassion for women, *śūdras* and uneducated twice-borns (*Bhāgavata Purāṇa* 1.4.25).[2] The text goes on to tell us that Vyāsa's story contains the same message as the Vedas and that its presentation was specifically designed for the purpose of transmitting Vedic knowledge to women and *śūdras* (*Bhāgavata Purāṇa* 1.4.29).[3]

There are some passages within the *Mahābhārata* that seem to agree that the epic is for a wide-reaching audience, but the formulaic description of a text 'for women and *śūdras*' is not to be found anywhere in the Critical Edition. In the *Śāntiparvan*, for example, Vyāsa instructs his disciples to teach his story to members of all four *varṇas*, but he does not specify that women should be part of the audience (12.314.45). Similarly, Ugraśravas equates his story with the Vedas, but he does not mention anything about a female audience (1.1.200–10).[4] Yet clearly this characterization of the text as composed 'for women and *śūdras*' has been accepted by some *Mahābhārata* traditions, as reflected in the legend that Gaṇeśa put the entire text in writing as Vyāsa recounted it to him. James Fitzgerald suggests that the Gaṇeśa episode – which is not found in the Critical Edition – was introduced in order to incorporate 'into the imagination of the text' a new audience: 'the majority of Indian people' (1991: 169). Before the inclusion of the Gaṇeśa episode, the *Mahābhārata* was simply the fifth Veda. Now it 'came to be the Veda of women and śūdras' (ibid.: 170).

If these claims about a universal version of the Veda only come after the final redaction, then what are the claims within the Critical Edition of the Sanskrit *Mahābhārata* regarding its intended reception? And, for the purposes of this chapter, are there any indications within the epic that the text addresses a female audience? A number of scholars have offered their speculations. Madeleine Biardeau imagines a woman 'just beyond voice range' during the composition of the text.[5] Following Biardeau, Alf Hiltebeitel suggests that the *Mahābhārata* authors 'listened to their mothers, wives, sisters and daughters, and probably listened well' (2001: 166). In the Introduction to his translation of the *Āraṇyakaparvan*, J.A.B. van Buitenen considers the question of a female audience in relation to the Nala story: 'It is profitless to speculate whether the story was written by a woman, but it is fair to assume that it was written for a woman' (1975: 184). Building on these comments, I would like to explore ways in which the text portrays female listeners. I will argue that women are integrated into the imagined audience of the *Mahābhārata* and that their presence as listeners impacts on the text in a number of ways. However, rather than speculate about the participation of women in relation to the original composition of the text, I will look at ways in which female characters are depicted as audience members in the story itself.

Phalaśrutis

First let us look at the numerous passages that address an audience directly. At the end of the *Mahābhārata*, as well as at the end of a number of sections within the text, there are passages that explicitly state the benefits of hearing it (or the immediately preceding section). These passages, known as *phalaśrutis*, promise rewards and transformative powers, and often designate benefits specific to class and gender. Most *phalaśrutis* particularly address male *kṣatriyas* and brahmins, promising the likes of wealth and fame, while some *phalaśrutis* suggest a less specific audience.[6] Additionally, a number of *phalaśrutis* are addressed to the primary listener of a particular section of the text. In the *Śāntiparvan*, for example, several of the fruits of hearing are explicitly stated for the benefit of Yudhiṣṭhira.[7]

Despite the *Mahābhārata*'s orientation towards a male audience, there are several *phalaśrutis* that are specifically addressed to female listeners. In the final *parvan*, after the frame dialogue featuring Vaiśaṃpāyana and Janamejaya is closed, Ugraśravas lists a number of wonderful things that happen if one reads, hears or recites the *Mahābhārata*, at the same time indicating that brahmins, kings and women are part of his projected audience (18.5.39–43). There are similar *phalaśrutis* at the end of particular stories or sections of the text. For example, after Bhīṣma recounts to Yudhiṣṭhira the story about a pigeon and his devoted wife, he tells the king that a woman who follows after her husband, as the wife of the pigeon did, will shine in heaven (12.145.15). Strictly speaking, this is not a *phalaśruti*, as it addresses the benefits of behaving rather than of listening. Nevertheless, Bhīṣma's comments – which link being a devoted wife with reaching heaven – seem to imply a female audience.

Yet, while Bhīṣma's story clearly has lessons meant for the ears of women, seemingly there are no female characters present when he recounts this tale. Why would Bhīṣma mention the benefits for female listeners when he is addressing Yudhiṣṭhira? Are there any women to be found listening in the background? This story is told in the context of Bhīṣma's long post-war instructions to Yudhiṣṭhira, at the beginning of which we learn that Kṛṣṇa, Sātyaki, Arjuna, Bhīma, the twins, Kṛpa, Yuyutsu and Saṃjaya all accompany the king to the battlefield where Bhīṣma is lying on a bed of arrows (12.47.69–70). As with other sections of the story, Vaiśaṃpāyana is specific about who is present, and by not mentioning any female characters when Bhīṣma's teachings begin, he implies that there are no women in attendance for most of the *Śāntiparvan* and the entirety of the *Anuśāsanaparvan*.[8] However, despite not being mentioned at the beginning, Draupadī is named as a listener towards the end of Bhīṣma's teaching, when she, in unison with the other Pāṇḍavas, applauds Yudhiṣṭhira's decision to lead the life of a householder (13.57.42–4). Hiltebeitel has commented that Vaiśaṃpāyana's mentioning Draupadī here – midway through the *Anuśāsanaparvan* – represents

> a lovely piece of pacing, leaving Draupadī to chime in just when she has a very good reason to do so, and answering for attentive readers a question they might have had in the back of their minds all along: who are the listeners there around Bhīṣma in this twilight scene?
>
> (personal communication, October 2005)

Another *phalaśruti* that explicitly addresses a female audience is promised by Kuntī, after recounting the dialogue (*saṃvāda*) between Vidurā and her son:[9]

> [A] pregnant woman who hears it again and again is sure to bear a hero, a champion in learning, austerity, self-control, an ascetic, blazing with the luster of brahman, honored with applause, fiery, strong, lordly, a great warrior, daring, unassailable, an invincible conqueror.[10]
>
> (5.134.18–20)[11]

As this list demonstrates, often when women are addressed as audience members, the fruits of their listening are not for themselves, but for their unborn children. Yet why would Kuntī's *phalaśruti* address a female audience when Kṛṣṇa is the only character in her presence when she tells this story? Evidently, as her instructions for Kṛṣṇa to relay her words to the Pāṇḍavas suggest, Kuntī anticipates the female auditors in future narrations of this dialogue.[12]

Although there are not many of them, I would suggest that the *phalaśruti*s that explicitly address female listeners indicate that women, at least to some degree, were part of the text's projected reception. Indeed, it seems unlikely that the text as a whole, or particular sections within the text, would promise rewards for female listeners if women were not an anticipated audience. However, nowhere among the *phalaśruti*s does the text claim that Vyāsa's motivation for composing the *Mahābhārata* was an attempt to convey Vedic knowledge to a universal audience including women. In other words, despite addressing some women on a few specific occasions, there are no claims that the *Mahābhārata* as a whole is for the benefit of women. In fact, in contrast to male listeners who are promised rewards such as wealth, power and the attainment of heaven, female auditors are addressed almost exclusively in their roles as wives and child-bearers, and the rewards available to them usually benefit their children and husbands as much as – if not more than – themselves.

Characterizing the audience: the king as primary listener

In addition to *phalaśruti*s, the *Mahābhārata* draws attention to its auditors by its portrayal of audience members throughout the frame dialogues that introduce both the main narrative and the various sub-stories and didactic sections. Before we direct our attention towards the female audience in particular, let us first look at the more general interest in audience that is displayed by the frame dialogues, especially the way in which the king is constituted as the primary listener.

One of the unique features of the *Mahābhārata* is its complexly interwoven dialogical structure. In addition to the two dialogues that frame the text as a whole, there are several embedded stories within the main narrative, some of which contain further nested stories within them. This technique of multiple embedding is used to great effect in a number of different ways. Sometimes embedded stories provide past information about a central character (e.g. Karṇa at 3.287–93); sometimes they provide important information about a particular place (e.g. the *tīrthayātrā* section at 3.79–153); or sometimes they put a particular event from the main story into a cosmological context (e.g. Draupadī's marriage at 1.189). Another – and I would argue equally important – function of this framing technique is to highlight the social context of telling tales and offering teachings. In other words, the *Mahābhārata* is not merely a collection of stories within stories, but its framing structure brings attention to how stories are told, in what contexts they are told, who does the telling, and who listens. As Christopher Minkowski has remarked: 'An epic frame story is more than embedded; it is a story about the telling of another story' (1989: 402). In this way, the frame dialogues give us a social context for the transmission of knowledge.[13] This does not necessarily mean that the social contexts depicted in the text represent real social contexts in ancient India, but the technique of multiple framing suggests that the composers and compilers were concerned with the question of the text's reception. Moreover, I would submit that the audiences represented in the text give us an indication of the ideal receivers that were in the imaginations of the composers and the compilers.

James Hegarty has made similar comments, suggesting that the *Mahābhārata* presents us with a reflexive model of how the text should be read or heard and that this model invokes 'idealized participants' (2006: 57). More generally, Philip Lutgendorf has proposed that framing is a metacommunicative strategy employed to give listeners or readers clues for interpreting the message of a text (1994: 18). I would only add that in the case of the *Mahābhārata* the multivocality of the narrative, as well as the multiple contexts within which narratives are framed, provide us with a number of different audiences within which such idealized participants might be found. Yet, despite providing us with many possible audiences, clearly the central one depicted in the text is the king. Within the main story Dhṛtarāṣṭra and Yudhiṣṭhira are the paradigmatic receivers, as they are the characters who are most often presented as listeners. Much of the *Āraṇyakaparvan*, for example, consists of eminent seers recounting stories and teachings to

Yudhiṣṭhira; while much of the *Udyogaparvan* features Dhṛtarāṣṭra hosting meetings and hearing reports in his *sabhā*.[14]

Additionally, the prominence of the king as listener is reflected in the framing dialogues that organize the text as a whole: two outer frames that give a context for the telling of the main story, and two inner frames that are long dialogical sections whose participants are characters from the main story. These four frames[15] depict different social contexts, as well as different dynamics between speaker and listener. Significantly, a king features as the primary listener in three of these frames, all of which connect the content of what the king hears to his role as king, thus making the stories and teachings part of his ability to rule and part of his claim to regal power. In other words, what a king hears and his role as a listener are integral aspects of what constitutes him as king. In order to explore this point, let us briefly look at the four major frame dialogues:[16]

(1) Ugraśravas recites the *Mahābhārata* to Śaunaka at a twelve-year *satra* in the Naimiṣa Forest.[17] This is the only one of the four frame dialogues that does not include a king. Minkowski has remarked on the fact that the outer frame addresses a brahmin audience, whereas the inner frames address kings; he points out that both the *Mahābhārata* and the *Rāmāyaṇa* have the pattern of a royal audience embedded within a priestly audience (2001: 178).

(2) Vaiśaṃpāyana recites the *Mahābhārata* to King Janamejaya during the intervals of his *sarpasatra*. Janamejaya, whom Minkowski calls the 'paradigmatic listener' (1989: 419), is a consecrated *yajamāna* at the time he is listening to Vaiśaṃpāyana; and the particular *sarpasatra* taking place is conducted in order to take revenge on Takṣaka, the leader of the snakes, who killed Janamejaya's father, Parikṣit. As Minkowski has pointed out, Janamejaya's sacrifice is the latest link in a vendetta between the snakes and the Bhārata clan (1991: 390, 397). Thus, what Vaiśaṃpāyana narrates to Janamejaya is specifically related to his kingship, both because his royal status is based on his being a direct descendant of the Pāṇḍavas, and because – by assuming the role of a *yajamāna* while he is listening to Vaiśaṃpāyana's story – he is ritually carrying out one of his primary functions as king.

(3) Saṃjaya reports the battlefield events to King Dhṛtarāṣṭra. According to Minkowski (1989: 406), this is the most highly elaborated of the frame stories, as it is the dialogue that is most integrated into the main narrative. On several occasions during his narration, Saṃjaya points out Dhṛtarāṣṭra's complicity in bringing about the terrible events that he is describing. In this way, Dhṛtarāṣṭra's roles as king and as primary listener are interlinked – not only because it is his army that is fighting the war, but also because the war is inextricably related to his own responsibilities and failures as king (see Chapter 2).

(4) Bhīṣma recounts many stories and teachings to King Yudhiṣṭhira after the war. Bhīṣma's instruction, which comprises most of the *Śāntiparvan* and the entirety of the *Anuśāsanaparvan*, is addressed to Yudhiṣṭhira in an attempt to alleviate his suffering and prepare him for the kingship. As such, Bhīṣma's teaching is explicitly directed towards Yudhiṣṭhira in his role as *dharmarāja*.

There are a number of aspects of these frame dialogues that we do not have time to go into here. However, what I would like to point out is that all four dialogues are characterized by their own unique circumstances, that in all four cases the meaning of what is said is inextricably linked to the dynamics between speaker and listener.[18] In the three conversational frames that feature kings, the dialogues are addressed to the specific situations that face their auditors as kings. For Janamejaya, he learns about his ancestors; for Dhṛtarāṣṭra, he hears accounts of his army on the battlefield; and for Yudhiṣṭhira, his role as a listener is in preparation for his duties as a *dharma* king. In these cases, neither Janamejaya, Dhṛtarāṣṭra nor Yudhiṣṭhira are listening to stories or receiving instructions merely for their amusement. All of them have something very personal at stake in their role as listeners, and for all of them what they hear is indelibly connected to their position as king.

Another way that the text makes the connection between kingship and receiving knowledge is through the sequence of the two major frame dialogues within the main story, with Yudhiṣṭhira replacing Dhṛtarāṣṭra as the main audience member only after Yudhiṣṭhira's army defeats the Kauravas. This transfer of the role of primary listener is reflected in the structure of the *Sauptikaparvan*.[19] The *parvan* opens with the familiar frame dialogue between Saṃjaya and Dhṛtarāṣṭra; however, exactly halfway through the *parvan* (10.9.58) Saṃjaya loses his divine sight, precisely at the moment when Dhṛtarāṣṭra's son goes to heaven. Of course, Saṃjaya was only given divine sight for the sake of reporting the war to Dhṛtarāṣṭra, so it is not surprising that Duryodhana's death, signifying the end of the war, is where Saṃjaya's narration ends.[20] Yet this is not only the moment when Saṃjaya's report comes to a close, it is also the symbolic ending of Dhṛtarāṣṭra's kingship.[21]

As if to highlight this transition in power, the tenth *adhyāya* of the *Sauptikaparvan* begins with Yudhiṣṭhira listening to Dhṛṣṭadyumna's charioteer report the details of the night massacre (10.10.1). It should be pointed out that the dialogue between Dhṛṣṭadyumna's charioteer and Yudhiṣṭhira does not continue throughout the *parvan*, and thus Yudhiṣṭhira's role as a listener is not a formal feature of the second part of this *parvan* in the way that Dhṛtarāṣṭra's role as listener frames the first part. Nevertheless, the shift in perspective is clear, indicating that the transition from Dhṛtarāṣṭra to Yudhiṣṭhira as the primary listener reinforces the transition of regal power. There are some actions that take place 'offstage', such as Nakula breaking the news to Draupadī about the deaths of her five children (implied at

10.10.27); some past events are recounted to Yudhiṣṭhira, including the episode when Aśvatthāman had asked Kṛṣṇa for his discus (10.12.11–40); and for much of the *parvan* Yudhiṣṭhira merely watches passively while other characters take centre stage. But throughout, Yudhiṣṭhira is present for all the speeches and actions, and the *parvan* ends the same way as the second half of it begins, with Yudhiṣṭhira in a conversation, this time with Kṛṣṇa hearing about the deeds of Śiva (10.17–18). In this way, the second half of the *Sauptikaparvan* presents Yudhiṣṭhira as the gravitational centre of the narrative: sometimes he is barely noticed or mentioned, but throughout all the events he is present, listening.

Yudhiṣṭhira's role as a listener is also highlighted by the manner of his response to what he hears, with his responses often mirroring the emotional displays of Dhṛtarāṣṭra throughout the battle books. This is demonstrated when Yudhiṣṭhira falls to the ground overcome with grief after hearing about the night massacre and the deaths of his son and four nephews (10.10.7–9). Dhṛtarāṣṭra's suffering has been a recurring theme throughout the battle books (see Chapter 2), but the tenth *adhyāya* of the *Sauptikaparvan* marks the beginning of Yudhiṣṭhira's suffering. From the moment he hears about the death of his own son until the end of the *Mahābhārata*, the narrative primarily focuses on Yudhiṣṭhira's despondency – all the instructions and teachings that he hears in the *Śāntiparvan* and *Anuśāsanaparvan* are prompted by his grief.

In this section we have seen that one of the many effects of frame dialogues in the *Mahābhārata* is to bring attention to the listeners, with the audience often creating the context in which stories are recounted and knowledge disseminated.[22] The primary audience for much of the text is the king, with Janamejaya, Dhṛtarāṣṭra and Yudhiṣṭhira all depicted as paradigmatic receivers: in their capacity as king, they are the ones to whom news is reported, stories are recounted and discourses are presented. This portrayal of the king as the ideal audience member suggests that being a listener can be a way of assuming a position of power. However, if the *Mahābhārata* presents listening as an empowering activity for kings, what does it offer to others who are also within earshot? Who, besides the king, is listening in on the epic?

From the *yajamāna*'s wife to the *dharmarāja*'s wife

Despite the fact that the king features as the primary auditor for much of the story, the multivocality of the narrative indicates that there are several target audiences for the *Mahābhārata* as a whole, as well as for particular sections within it. The remainder of this chapter will focus on Gāndhārī and Draupadī, examining how the frame dialogues incorporate and characterize them as listeners. These two female characters between them listen in on some of the principal teachings and tales that are recounted in the text. Yet it is important to point out that neither Draupadī nor Gāndhārī represents 'woman' as a universally constructed category, as both of them – in addition to other women from the court – are systematically differentiated from other women on the basis of their *varṇa* status.[23] As such, the presence of Gāndhārī and Draupadī as prominent auditors does not point to a universal female audience, but rather to a very specific group of female listeners, namely the *kṣatriya* women of the court and most particularly the queen. Moreover, neither one of them features as the primary receiver of the vast corpus of information she hears, as both do most of their listening at their husband's side, when the king is the main audience.

Before going into more detail about Gāndhārī and Draupadī, let us briefly return to the two outer frame dialogues and their implications regarding a female audience in attendance. Although neither conversation contains explicit references to any female characters, both take place during the intervals of Vedic rituals. As Stephanie Jamison has explored in detail, the ritual texts make it clear that the *yajamāna*'s wife is required to be present for all Vedic rites: 'One of the main technical requirements for being a Sacrificer is that he must be a householder (gṛhastha); he must be *married*. Not only that but the presence and participation of his wife is required at all the solemn rituals' (1996: 30).[24] Furthermore, the particular ritual taking place in the two outer frame stories is a special kind of rite called a *satra*, for which theoretically there is no *yajamāna*, thereby requiring that all the priests function as *yajamāna*s. Consequently, as Jamison observes:

> As they are all yajamānas, they all need wives. The śrauta sūtras in their meticulous (and argumentative) way treat the order and manner in which the wives are consecrated in this type of ritual, whether separately along with their respective husbands or as a group.
>
> (1996: 31–2)

Hiltebeitel points out that during the *satra* the wives were known to make a lot of noise and that there are parts of the rite that include 'lewd exchanges and ritual copulation' (2001: 166). Taking all of this into consideration, he suggests that 'the epic poets cannot have forgotten the women they omit to mention at the Naimiṣa Forest sattra' (ibid.). If we assume that the brahmins in the *Mahābhārata* are following the ritual texts, then this would imply that for Vaiśaṃpāyana's telling of the *Mahābhārata*, Janamejaya's wife, as well as the wives of all the *satrin*s, would be present; and during Ugraśravas's recitation, Śaunaka's wife would be on hand, as well as the wives of all the other brahmin ritualists (see Chapter 6).

To be sure, the text does not mention the presence of any female character during these scenes and we should not overstate the mere possibility of their presence. Nevertheless, the role of the *yajamāna*'s wife during the Vedic rituals may help us to understand why the *Mahābhārata* would bring attention to the presence of Gāndhārī and Draupadī on the occasions that it does:

perhaps the attendance of the *dharmarāja*'s wife during the transmission of certain teachings and stories mirrors the required presence of the *yajamāna*'s wife during the ritual. Similarly, perhaps the depiction of Gāndhārī and Draupadī as listeners is linked to their role as queen in the same way that Dhṛtarāṣṭra's and Yudhiṣṭhira's role as listeners is connected with their status as king. That the queen's attendance is part of the representational dimension of the king is particularly true in the case of Draupadī, who is a manifestation of the goddess Śrī.[25] As both Hara (1996–7) and Hiltebeitel (1976: 143–91) have explored, Śrī is connected with royalty and her presence bestows royal power upon her consort. As an incarnation of Śrī, the presence of Draupadī is necessary for the Pāṇḍavas, and Yudhiṣṭhira in particular, to claim the kingdom.

Yet, despite the representational aspect of the queen, there is more to the significance of Gāndhārī and Draupadī as two of the text's most frequent listeners than merely that they ornamentally symbolize their husbands' royal power. As Jamison demonstrates in great detail, the wife of the *yajamāna* 'acts independently of her husband; she is not merely his double or shadow in ritual performance' (1996: 38). Similarly, despite the fact that they are present because of their husbands (or – as we will see – fathers), the way in which Gāndhārī and Draupadī speak and act upon what they hear is often independent from, and at odds with, their husbands. In other words, their presence as listeners not only represents their husband's power, but also their own. For both of them listening is connected with their particular responsibilities as queen, as well as their unique contributions to the main events of the story.

Gāndhārī: listening in the court

As a strong critic of the war, as a witness to Saṃjaya's account of events on the battlefield, and as the one who issues a curse against Kṛṣṇa contributing to his death and the destruction of the Vṛṣṇi clan (see Chapter 11), Gāndhārī is one of the most prominent female characters in the *Mahābhārata*. During her years as queen in the Kaurava court she is present for many of the pivotal events that lead to the fateful encounter at Kurukṣetra. In particular, she attends the weapons display (1.124–7), the first public contest between her sons and the Pāṇḍavas; she witnesses the dicing match and the disrobing of Draupadī (2.53–70); and she monitors a number of the attempts to negotiate a peaceful settlement described in the *Udyogaparvan* (5.66–9; 5.127–9; 5.136–48). Although she remains silent during most of these scenes – with her presence only occasionally mentioned – she does speak up on a number of occasions, trying to persuade her son Duryodhana not to go to war (5.67.9–10; 5.127.19–53; 5.146.28–35), and criticizing her husband for not standing up to their son (5.127.10–15). Her attempts to avert the war are of no avail, yet her ability to intervene effectively is illustrated just after the disrobing of Draupadī, when she and Vidura, after hearing the cry of a jackal, tell Dhṛtarāṣṭra about this bad omen, convincing him to step in and put an end to the abuse inflicted upon Draupadī (2.63.22–4). Although Gāndhārī's involvement here is subtle, it prompts the king to grant Draupadī a boon, which in turn leads to setting the Pāṇḍavas free from the conditions of the first dicing match.

In addition to her attendance at events leading up to the war, Gāndhārī is present throughout most of Saṃjaya's account of the war, as indicated by several explicit references to her and the other ladies of the Kuru court in *parvan*s 6 to 9. The preamble to the conversation between Saṃjaya and Dhṛtarāṣṭra – the dialogue that frames the battle books – describes Vyāsa offering to grant the divine eye (*divya cakṣus*) to Dhṛtarāṣṭra, so that he can witness the impending events on the battlefield (6.2.4–6). Dhṛtarāṣṭra, however, declines this offer, preferring to hear an account: a preference that leads to Vyāsa offering divine eyesight to Saṃjaya. Dhṛtarāṣṭra's decision to hear rather than see the war has pertinent consequences in terms of how knowledge about the conflict is disseminated. Rather than choosing to have unmediated access to the events on the battlefield – which might imply that the king would witness the war on his own – his preference to have Saṃjaya see for him, and thus put this epic confrontation into a communicable narrative, creates the conditions for a multi-subjective audience that includes Gāndhārī and the ladies of the Kuru court.

Attention is thus focused on those who listen to Saṃjaya's narration and on the manner in which his reports are received. At the beginning of the *Droṇaparvan*, for example, Dhṛtarāṣṭra is 'severely tormented with heartache' (*hṛcchokenārdito bhṛśam*, 7.9.1) and falls on the ground when he hears that Droṇa has been slain. At this point Vaiśaṃpāyana tells Janamejaya that the Bhārata ladies surrounded the king when he fell and rubbed him with their hands (7.9.3). Similarly, at the beginning of the *Karṇaparvan*, Dhṛtarāṣṭra faints after hearing Saṃjaya report the death of Karṇa (8.3.4), and the ladies of the household wail and weep aloud. Then Gāndhārī and all the ladies fall down and lose their senses. Again, at the beginning of the *Śalyaparvan* when the death of Duryodhana is announced, Dhṛtarāṣṭra collapses, as do Vidura, Gāndhārī and all the Kuru ladies (9.1.38–9).

These references to the audience in Dhṛtarāṣṭra's court not only establish Gāndhārī and other women as listeners to Saṃjaya's report of the war,[26] but also bring attention to how the news of events on the battlefield is received, with the scenes of intense mourning by Dhṛtarāṣṭra, Gāndhārī and the Kuru ladies adding further drama and tragedy to the epic struggle between the Pāṇḍava and Kaurava warriors. The Pāṇḍavas are the protagonists throughout most of the *Mahābhārata*, but these scenes highlight the sense of loss experienced by the mothers and wives of their enemies, making an emotional response to the main events of the story part of the story itself, and thereby connecting the audience in the text to the audience outside of the text.[27]

Despite the importance of Gāndhārī's presence when she is mentioned, on several occasions it is unclear whether or not she is hearing everything that Saṃjaya is reporting. She is mentioned at the beginning of all the battle books and sometimes at the end,[28] yet both the *Śalyaparvan* and the *Strīparvan* suggest that she was not within earshot of Saṃjaya's report of the later stages of the battle. After the death of Duryodhana is announced, and Dhṛtarāṣṭra, Vidura, Gāndhārī and all the Kuru ladies collapse from grief, the ladies are dismissed (9.1.49–50), implying that they are not there to hear the remainder of the *Śalyaparvan*. The *Strīparvan* also opens with Dhṛtarāṣṭra fainting. Here he is revived by Vyāsa, Vidura and Saṃjaya, and in the next scene he sends for Gāndhārī (11.9.3), indicating that she had not been present at the beginning of the *parvan*. Although it thus seems that she was not present to hear the entirety of the war narration, her role as a listener and her reaction to hearing the events on the battlefield are integral aspects of the battle books.

Gāndhārī's presence in the Kaurava court before and during the war has particular relevance in connection with her descriptions of the grieving on the war-torn battlefield after the war, when Vyāsa grants her the divine eye, allowing her to see – despite her blindfold – and hear the mourning of the Kuru women.[29] Her narration of what she witnesses is presented in a dialogue with Kṛṣṇa (11.16–25), during which she describes in vivid detail the dismembered bodies that are strewn across the blood-soaked battlefield, mourns the deaths of her sons, speaks of the losses suffered by the Kuru women, and makes several statements denouncing the war. Although their conversation is not a frame dialogue – there are no embedded scenes within their exchange – Gāndhārī's having the divine eye marks her out as the primary speaker of this section and gives her narration a similar status to that of Saṃjaya's account of the war. Yet her ability to communicate everything to Kṛṣṇa is not entirely explained by her temporary acquisition of the divine eye, as her role as speaker is also informed by the tremendous loss that she has suffered, and by her experience as one who has heard an account of the battle as well as other narrations and instructions in her husband's court. In her dialogue with Kṛṣṇa she makes a number of remarks that indicate her awareness of how events are reported, pointing out the irony that warriors who were 'regularly celebrated by bards singing their praises' are now surrounded by the cries of jackals (11.16.32),[30] and referring to how 'clever bards would celebrate [the warriors] in the wee hours of every night' (11.16.41).[31] Subsequently, Gāndhārī suggests that part of the suffering of the many widows is due to the fact that they do not know each other's stories: 'Hearing only incomplete snatches of others' lamentations, these women do not understand each other's wailings' (11.16.46).[32]

In contrast to these wailing women, Gāndhārī is able to verbalize her sorrow, with her remarks suggesting that there is a direct connection between her role as a listener, and her role as speaker and chief articulator of the grieving and suffering of the Kuru women. Because she has been present for a number of pivotal episodes leading up to the war, she understands its complexities and is able to look back and reflect on what she has seen and heard. Even when she grieves for her firstborn son, Duryodhana, she remembers that she had resigned herself to his defeat (11.17.6–7). She then tells Kṛṣṇa that she does not mourn for her son, but for her husband Dhṛtarāṣṭra and the suffering he endures. Despite her own losses, Gāndhārī primarily reports to Kṛṣṇa about the grief of others, and it is in the context of the many mourning widows – who only hear bits and pieces of each others' wailings – that Gāndhārī's narration is so poignant and so unique. Her divine sight gives her access to all of the women's stories, yet her role as listener informs her ability to articulate these disparate accounts in a transmittable narrative that gives a voice to the otherwise silent Kuru women.

Furthermore, her narration takes on a cosmic importance, as the primary audience of her lamentations is Kṛṣṇa, who, according to several sections of the *Mahābhārata*, is God. Not all of the characters in the main story know about Kṛṣṇa's divine status, but the text makes it clear that Gāndhārī does, as she was in attendance when Saṃjaya first disclosed this information to Dhṛtarāṣṭra (5.66–8). Subsequently, she was present in the Kaurava court when Kṛṣṇa revealed his divine form (5.129.4–11); yet she did not see his divine form herself because only Droṇa, Bhīṣma, Vidura, Saṃjaya, *ṛṣi*s and ascetics had been given the divine eyesight on this occasion. We also know that, because of her attendance for Saṃjaya's account of the *Bhīṣmaparvan*, she has heard the *Bhagavadgītā*, which contains Kṛṣṇa's most famous teaching, as well as Saṃjaya's description of Arjuna's vision of Kṛṣṇa's divine form. That Gāndhārī is aware of the full extent of Kṛṣṇa's divine status is significant because much of her narration in the *Strīparvan* is delivered as a diatribe against Kṛṣṇa, whom she holds responsible for the war's tragic outcome. She ends her narration by using her ascetic powers – which she has acquired through obedience to her husband – to make a curse against Kṛṣṇa: he will slay his own family and suffer a shameful death (11.25.36–42). Kṛṣṇa responds that only he can bring about his own and his family's destruction, and then he criticizes Gāndhārī for blaming him, saying that she should hold herself accountable instead. Yet, despite these accusations against her, we are left to wonder if perhaps Kṛṣṇa has taken Gāndhārī's criticisms to heart. As God, he must already be aware that Gāndhārī had been one of the strongest critics of the war; and, despite taking agency away from her, the events proclaimed in her curse describe exactly what happens to Kṛṣṇa and his family, as reported subsequently in the *Mausalaparvan*. Perhaps he is persuaded by her narration, but takes credit for bringing about his own destruction to spare Gāndhārī the karmic consequences of bringing about the death of God.

Draupadī as listener: the education of the *dharma* queen

Draupadī is the other female character whose role as a listener is highlighted on a number of occasions. Like Gāndhārī, Draupadī is a queen who is present when her husband is told a number of important stories, teachings and reports. Her role as an auditor is most fully developed in the *Āraṇyakaparvan* where she accompanies her husbands for twelve years of wandering, during which they encounter a number of eminent brahmins, *ṛṣi*s and storytellers. We should remember that throughout the *Āraṇyakaparvan*, Yudhiṣṭhira is the primary audience for all the tales and lessons; he is the only one addressed in the vocative by the various dispensers of knowledge and he is the one most often asked about by Janamejaya. Indeed, it is often unclear if Draupadī is on hand for every story and lesson that is delivered to the king – but for that matter it is often ambiguous to what extent her other husbands are there as well.[33] Yet, whether or not Draupadī is there all the time, hearing everything that is communicated to Yudhiṣṭhira, the text brings attention to her presence on several occasions.

Draupadī's attendance by her husbands' side is highlighted at the very beginning of the *Āraṇyakaparvan* when Janamejaya asks specifically about her, suggesting that her exploits remain significant throughout the Pāṇḍavas' period of exile (3.1.6). Additionally, there are several references to Draupadī throughout the *parvan*, reminding us that she is hearing the same tales and lessons as Yudhiṣṭhira and her other husbands. For example, when Mārkaṇḍeya arrives to teach the Pāṇḍavas he notices Draupadī first (3.26.5). On another occasion Yudhiṣṭhira brings attention to the fact that Draupadī had been with him for the teachings of a number of the text's most eminent sages. When arguing with Draupadī, Yudhiṣṭhira says:

> You yourself have seen with your own eyes the great ascetic and seer Mārkaṇḍeya when he came here, a man of boundless soul and long-lived in the Law; Vyāsa, Vasiṣṭha, Maitreya, Nārada, Lomaśa, Śuka, and other seers of good thoughts have found perfection through Law alone. With your own eyes you have seen them, possessed of divine Yoga, equally capable of curse and grace, greater even than the Gods.
>
> (3.32.10–12)[34]

It is notable that in this passage Yudhiṣṭhira comments on Draupadī's presence, but as an eyewitness rather than as a listener.[35] Nevertheless, this remark establishes Draupadī's physical proximity on these particular occasions of receiving instruction.

Additionally, Draupadī is mentioned on a number of occasions in the *tīrthayātrā* section. The first part of this section begins when Nārada tells the Pāṇḍavas a dialogue in which Pulastya describes to Bhīṣma the rewards that one receives from visiting the ancient *tīrthas*. Draupadī's attendance as a listener to this dialogue is established by Vaiśaṃpāyana who, as he recounts Nārada's entrance, describes Draupadī as not leaving the side of her husbands: 'As the Sāvitrī [*mantra*] does not desert the Vedas, nor the light of the sun Mount Meru, so the good Yājñasenī did not according to Law relinquish the Pārthas' (3.80.4).[36] Draupadī's presence is made explicit again at the beginning of the subsequent conversational frame in this *tīrtha* section, when Lomaśa specifically names Draupadī as part of his audience before he begins speaking (3.89.9).[37]

These references to Draupadī clearly establish her presence for most of the stories and instructions conveyed to Yudhiṣṭhira in the *Āraṇyakaparvan*. Yet Draupadī's role as a listener is far more substantial than these seemingly offhand remarks – reminding us that she is there – would suggest. The relevance of her proximity is established by means of the content of a number of stories, as well as the context in which these particular tales are told. As we shall see, there are several tales and instructions where Draupadī is not only present, but also implied as a primary listener. Indeed, a number of sections of the *Āraṇyakaparvan* seem to be as much about preparing Draupadī to be a dharmic queen as they are about preparing Yudhiṣṭhira to be *dharmarāja*.

Perhaps the story that is the most relevant to Draupadī in particular, and has the most parallels with the main *Mahābhārata* story in general, is the tale of Nala.[38] Despite the fact that the preamble to this story does not specifically mention Draupadī, its narrator Bṛhadaśva mentions her at the end (3.78.8), and the circumstances under which it is told imply that she is as much the primary audience for this tale as Yudhiṣṭhira is.[39] As Hiltebeitel points out, Draupadī can recognize herself emotionally in Damayantī when she hears Nala's wife 'wondering whether it is her "impoverished share" or "ill fortune" (*mandabhāgya*) that makes her suffer' (2001: 219). Not only is Draupadī's individual character further developed by similarities with Damayantī, but so is her relationship with Yudhiṣṭhira. Hiltebeitel is right to point out that Arjuna is absent during the telling of Nala and that the 'tale is primarily for the ears of Draupadī and Yudhiṣṭhira' (ibid.). This is a keen observation because throughout the *Āraṇyakaparvan*, it is not just Draupadī's presence as a listener that is established, but also her particular role as a listening queen. Whereas at other moments in the story Draupadī's relationship with Arjuna or Bhīma tends to be highlighted, the *Āraṇyakaparvan* is one of the few sections of the epic where her connection to Yudhiṣṭhira is distinctly developed, and listening together to stories, many of whose characters parallel their relationship as king and queen, is one of the main ways the text explores their relationship. Hiltebeitel remarks: 'if Yudhiṣṭhira and Draupadī have a love story, it must take a long time to work out' (2001: 220) – perhaps through listening to the stories of Nala and Damayantī, Rāma and Sītā, and Satyavat and Sāvitrī. As with the Nala story, Draupadī is not specifically named as a listener to either the Rāma or the Sāvitrī tales, yet both imply her presence because they are introduced with particular connection to her: both are told after Draupadī has been retrieved by the Pāṇḍavas following her abduction by Jayadratha.

The Rāma story is prompted by Yudhiṣṭhira's comments about the difficulties of life in exile and his inquiry as to whether anyone has suffered as much as he has (3.257.9–10). This question would seem to reflect a man obsessed with his own misfortune. However, it is clear from the context that he is not merely thinking about his own suffering, but also about the despair of his companions in exile, in particular that of Draupadī. He asks, 'how could such a happening befall our Law-wise and Law-abiding wife . . .? Not a sin had Draupadī committed, not a blameworthy deed anywhere; indeed, among the brahmins themselves she had perfectly carried out the great Law' (3.257.5–6).[40] These remarks bring attention to the particular relevance of this story to Draupadī, because, like Sītā, she both accompanies her husband to the forest and is abducted.[41] We should remember that the Rāma story heard by Draupadī does not end in the same manner as Vālmīki's poem: Mārkaṇḍeya's version has husband and wife reunited at the end, serving as a message to Yudhiṣṭhira and Draupadī not to be despondent.

The Sāvitrī story is also told in response to a statement of Yudhiṣṭhira's about Draupadī:

> When we were brought to grief by evil men at the dicing, we were saved by Kṛṣṇā, and now again she was abducted forcibly from the forest [by] Jayadratha. Has there ever been a woman, or has one been heard of, who was so devoted to her husband and great as Drupada's daughter?
>
> (3.277.2–3)[42]

Here Yudhiṣṭhira's question seems to anticipate a connection between Draupadī saving him and his brothers at the dicing match, and Sāvitrī saving her husband from Yama in the tale he is about to hear. At the end of the story Mārkaṇḍeya indirectly addresses Draupadī as a listener by predicting that, like the heroine of his story, she will save her husbands in the future: 'Thus Sāvitrī by her toils saved them all – herself, her father and mother, her mother-in-law and father-in-law, and her husband's entire dynasty. Likewise the well-augured Draupadī, esteemed for her character, shall rescue you all, just as the nobly-descended Sāvitrī!' (3.283.14–15).[43] Exactly to which episode Mārkaṇḍeya is referring is unclear, especially because the occasion for which Draupadī is most known for saving her husbands is the dicing match, which has already happened when Draupadī hears the story of Sāvitrī. Perhaps Mārkaṇḍeya is referring to another episode where Draupadī listens, this time not only silently, but without the knowledge of the speaker. In the *Virāṭaparvan* Draupadī overhears the arrogant Uttara boast about his martial skills, yet make the excuse that there is no charioteer fit to drive him to the battlefield (4.34.1–9). Draupadī suggests that Uttara send for Arjuna, disguised as Bṛhannaḍā. In this scene, Draupadī not only listens, but overhears – in the sense that her identity is not known to the speaker. Her intervention saves her husbands because Arjuna is called to the battlefield and is able to stave off the Kauravas until the Pāṇḍavas' year in hiding ends.

Returning to the *Āraṇyakaparvan*, although Yudhiṣṭhira is the primary listener in ways that Draupadī is not, the fact that he includes her when he asks to hear these stories suggests that he may be asking questions on behalf of Draupadī or perhaps because these are the kinds of stories that he thinks she should hear. This certainly seems to be the case a bit earlier in the *parvan* when Yudhiṣṭhira asks Mārkaṇḍeya about 'the unsurpassed beneficence of women' (*strīṇāṃ māhātmyam uttamam*) and the subtleties of *strīdharma* (3.196.2–10). Significantly, these questions are specifically related to faithful wives:

> The obedience of women who are devoted to their husbands seems to me very difficult. Pray, my lord, tell of the greatness of devoted wives who continuously think of their husbands as Gods, while restraining their senses and controlling their minds . . . I do not see anything harder than the terrible Law of the women.
>
> (3.196.5–8)[44]

Mārkaṇḍeya responds to this request by reciting the story of the devoted wife (3.197). In this tale a wife neglects a brahmin who is begging at her door because she is dutifully waiting on her husband. When the brahmin becomes angry because he has been left waiting outside, the wife responds that, despite her reverence for brahmins, the *dharma* most pleasing to her is obedience to her husband. In fact, she demonstrates the power of this *dharma* by telling the brahmin that she knows he burned a female egret (*balākā*)[45] before coming to her door and that her ability to know this comes from her devotion to her husband. The wife then goes on to describe the virtues of a true brahmin and sends her brahmin guest to visit a hunter who will explain more about *dharma*.

One of Mārkaṇḍeya's lessons is that women attain heaven by means of their obedience to their husbands and that this obedience is more important than sacrifice, *śrāddha* or fasting (3.196.20). When we look at the story of the devoted wife alongside the tales of Nala, Rāma and Sāvitrī we see that many stories in the *Āraṇyakaparvan* address the themes of the devoted wife and are directed towards Draupadī as a primary listener. When we consider the scenes at the beginning of the *parvan* that depict Draupadī questioning the authority of her husband (3.28–33),[46] these particular stories seem to offer relevant lessons for Draupadī as she prepares to assume the role of a *dharmarāja*'s wife.

From listening to speaking

That Draupadī is educated by listening to the stories and instructions in the *Āraṇyakaparvan* is indicated further by the teaching that she delivers to her cousin-in-law Satyabhāmā (3.222–3). This scene, which appears towards the end of the *Āraṇyakaparvan*, is one of the few dialogues between two female characters in the *Mahābhārata* (see Chapter 5).[47] Apart from Yudhiṣṭhira and her other husbands, Draupadī must be one of the most schooled characters at this point in the story. Yet this is one of the few occasions where she has an opportunity to articulate what she has learned. When she tells Satyabhāmā how she selflessly serves her husbands (3.222.18–31), this is reminiscent of the devoted wife in Mārkaṇḍeya's story (3.197.10–15). And at one point in her instruction to Satyabhāmā, Draupadī explicitly refers to one of her sources for her knowledge, explaining that she has heard about the '*dharma*s of the household' (*dharmāḥ kuṭumbeṣu*) from Kuntī, her mother-in-law (3.222.32). This reference to what she has learned from Kuntī could refer to one of several occasions where Draupadī was instructed by her mother-in-law: when she returns with the Pāṇḍavas just after her *svayaṃvara* (1.184.4–12); before her marriage to the Pāṇḍavas (1.191.1–12); and before setting out for thirteen years of exile (2.70.1–10).[48]

The connection between what Draupadī hears and what she says is highlighted on a number of other occasions, with the text often referring to her role as a listener to explain how she has acquired the knowledge that she has. Indeed, throughout the *Mahābhārata* the way in which listeners are constituted as particular subjects has significant implications for who can speak, and how characters present themselves and their arguments when they are speaking. In other words, seemingly casual references to a listener in the background are interwoven back into the narrative at different points when the one-time barely mentioned audience member is the primary speaker.

There are several occasions when Draupadī refers to her role as a listener in order to claim authority for her speech. At the beginning of the *Āraṇyakaparvan* (3.13.43–108), for instance, Draupadī questions Kṛṣṇa about why he was not present when she was humiliated after the dicing match in King Dhṛtarāṣṭra's court. During this exchange, Draupadī displays her knowledge of Kṛṣṇa's divine status and is able to address him as the sacrifice (*yajña*), Viṣṇu and the Supreme Person (*puruṣottama*). By addressing him in this way, Draupadī not only reveals that she is conversant with one of the most important secrets of the text, but she also makes a point of explaining how she knows what she knows, recounting that she has heard about Kṛṣṇa's divine status when 'Nārada told us' (*nārado 'bravīt*) – suggesting another occasion when Nārada addressed the Pāṇḍavas[49] – and mentioning also the authority of Asita Devala, Jāmadagnya, the *ṛṣi*s and Kaśyapa to support her statements.

Similarly, Satyabhāmā makes reference to what she heard when she claims to know Draupadī's fate after the war. When she says goodbye to Draupadī in the forest, she tells her not to worry: 'Inevitably, so I have heard, you will enjoy the earth with your husbands, their rivals destroyed, and set free from discord' (3.224.6).[50] This comment hints at the possibility that her husband shares with her some of his cosmic knowledge, which in this case would make her one of the few human characters to know the divine plan that guides the events in the narrative.[51]

Returning to Draupadī, another occasion where she invokes what she has heard is when she is arguing with Yudhiṣṭhira in the forest. We have already seen that on this occasion Yudhiṣṭhira refers to the fact that Draupadī was present for the instructions of some of the *Mahābhārata*'s most renowned storytellers and teachers (3.32.11). When Draupadī delivers her counter argument, maintaining the need for action, she cites Manu, indicating that she is literate in the discourse of *dharma*. At the end of her argument, she once again brings attention to how she has acquired her knowledge:

> My father once lodged a learned brahmin in our house; and he told my father of this matter, bull of the Bhāratas. He taught this same policy, which was first propounded by Bṛhaspati, to my brothers at the time; and I listened to their conversations at home. He talked to me comfortingly, when I came in with an errand, or was sitting on my father's lap, listening eagerly, King Yudhiṣṭhira.
>
> (3.33.56–8)[52]

This remark illustrates that female listeners can learn important teachings through eavesdropping. In this instance Draupadī is allowed to be present because she is the king's daughter. We do not know the degree to which the brahmin and her father are aware of her presence as they carry on with their discussion, but whether she is noticed by them or not, there she is 'listening eagerly' (*śuśrūṣamāṇām*) and remembering the brahmin's teaching for a future occasion. Despite the fact that she was not the intended audience, she uses this episode to give her words authority and to explain how she knows what she knows.[53] One of the main issues at stake for Draupadī is establishing authority to speak by making claims to be part of a chain of knowledge. Draupadī does not have a proper *paramparā*; she is not part of a traditional educational lineage passed from teacher to student. In this speech, however, she claims for herself a succession that, like a traditional *paramparā*, traces her knowledge all the way back to an original source, in this case Bṛhaspati.[54]

Sulabhā is another female character who creates a makeshift lineage in order to establish her claims to knowledge. In the *Śāntiparvan*, at the end of her debate with Janaka – during which she challenges the king's claim to have achieved *mokṣa* – Sulabhā explains how she has come to know the path to *mokṣa*:

> I am of the same Order as you, king, a woman of clean birth, and chaste. There was a seer who was a king called Pradhāna. Obviously you have heard of him. Understand that I came to be in his family and am named Sulabhā. Droṇa, Śataśṛṅga, Vakradvāra, and Parvata used to gather, along with Maghavan at the Soma sacrifices of my forebears. In that clan was I born. Since there was no husband suitable to me, I was trained in the rules for gaining Absolute Freedom, so, all alone, I live according to the hermit way of life.
>
> (12.308.181–4)[55]

These words indicate that Sulabhā, like Draupadī, was privy to the teachings of eminent brahmins because she was brought up in her father's court. The childhood memories of both women suggest that overhearing and eavesdropping function as a kind of *pramāṇa* for female characters, that listening in when their fathers and husbands receive important teachings is one of the main ways for female characters to justify their authority to speak.

These episodes featuring Draupadī, Satyabhāmā and Sulabhā demonstrate that the *Mahābhārata* takes into account how female characters know what they know: the text explains the knowledge and eloquence of its female characters – who would have been barred from a formal education – by showing them informally listening in on the education of men. As such, the *Mahābhārata*, although sometimes indirectly, deals with the complex logic of how female characters can follow the *dharma* of women, yet at the same time speak articulately about *dharma* in the company of men. Draupadī, for example, not only has to authorize her knowledge in the same way that a male character would rely on his *paramparā*, but she also has to explain how she knows how to be a wife. When she argues with Yudhiṣṭhira about *dharma* she invokes the authority of Bṛhaspati, but when she discusses the duties of a wife with Satyabhāmā she refers to the instructions of Kuntī. Both cases illustrate that there is a textual logic linking what Draupadī is saying on one occasion to what she has heard on another.

Conclusion

The *Mahābhārata* gives us glimpses of its potential audience in a number of different ways: *phalaśruti*s address listeners both inside and outside of the text; frame dialogues describe a number of different social contexts for telling tales and delivering teachings; and characters in the text often comment about how their words and actions will be received. These instances, where the text anticipates its own reception, not only indicate an awareness of audience, but also reflect ways in which the anticipated audience has an impact on the narrative.

When we recognize the importance of audience in the *Mahābhārata*, then the female listeners, although sometimes silently in the background, emerge as primary characters in shaping the story and giving it direction. This is particularly true for Gāndhārī and Draupadī, both of whom are in attendance for some of the text's most significant speeches, instructions and stories. Despite the fact that their status as listeners is often ambiguous, and that for most of the time they are present they are barely mentioned, these scenes are crucial episodes in the character development of both heroines.

Thus, for both Gāndhārī and Draupadī there is more to being a listener than merely their symbolic presence. The way in which both of them are constituted as subjects shows that they are not merely defined and portrayed in relation to male characters, that what they hear and say is linked up with their specific duties and circumstances as queens: Gāndhārī's role as a listener is part of her characterization as matriarch of the Kuru women, who guides the widows of the court through mourning, who articulates their emotions into a communicable narrative, and who curses Kṛṣṇa for allowing the horrible events at Kurukṣetra to take place; similarly, Draupadī's role as a listener informs her debate with Yudhiṣṭhira, gives her the authority to speak about the duties of a good wife to Satyabhāmā, and educates her for her role as *dharma* queen. In the cases of Gāndhārī and Draupadī – as well as Satyabhāmā, Sulabhā and others – listening is an essential aspect of the depiction of female characters that is well integrated into their other activities throughout the text.

Notes

1 I would like to thank: Alf Hiltebeitel for reading an earlier draft and offering insightful comments; all the people who offered comments and criticisms to an earlier version of this paper presented in London, July 2005, in particular Laurie Patton, Jim Fitzgerald and Emily Hudson; and Julia Leslie to whose memory this paper is dedicated.

2 'As the three Vedas cannot be learnt by women, *śūdras* and brāhmaṇas [or any twice born] (who are so only by birth), the sage (Vyāsa) composed the story of the Bhārata out of compassion for them' (*Bhāgavata Purāṇa* 1.4.25, quoted from Sharma 2000: 235). In his translation of this passage, Arvind Sharma takes the term *dvijabandhu* to mean something similar to *brahmabandhu*, or 'pseudo-brahmin' (see ibid.: 267 n. 90).

3 Sharma describes these passages from the *Bhāgavata Purāṇa*: 'In a nutshell, then, the *Mahābhārata* was composed by Kṛṣṇa Dvaipāyana Vyāsa to convey the message of the Vedas to those who were formally debarred from studying it' (2000: 235). According to Sharma (ibid.: 268 n. 93), Vyāsa's positive attitude towards *śūdra*s and women is also apparent in the *Viṣṇu Purāṇa* (6.2). However, the *Viṣṇu Purāṇa* does not assign a motive to Vyāsa for his composition of the *Mahābhārata*.

4 However, he does seem to imply a female audience in this passage by claiming that even the crime of wilful abortion will be expiated by hearing a recitation of the *Mahābhārata*.

5 'If it were necessary, I would imagine a father, a son, and a maternal uncle of the father or son working together, and in a corner out of the way, just beyond voice range, a woman, wife of the father, mother of the son, and sister of the uncle. This

schema is drawn from the *Mahābhārata* itself' (Biardeau and Péterfalvi 1985: 27; Hiltebeitel's translation 2001a: 165).

6 For example, the *phalaśrutis* at the end of the *Mahābhārata* promise a number of quite general rewards, seemingly anticipating an audience outside the text: by reciting the *Mahābhārata* one can be cleansed of every sin and conquer heaven (18.5.35); by hearing the *Mahābhārata* one can attain heaven or victory (18.5.40).

7 See, for example, 12.111.29, 122.54, 124.69.

8 This is in contrast to earlier sections of the *Śāntiparvan*. For example, when Yudhiṣṭhira first approaches Bhīṣma he is accompanied by Draupadī, Kuntī, Gāndhārī and all the Kuru women (12.38.40).

9 This dialogue is one of the few scenes in the *Mahābhārata* that is narrated by a female character. Kuntī is also the only female character in the text to narrate an *upākhyāna* (see 1.112). For more on *upākhyānas*, *saṃvādas* and other genres within the *Mahābhārata*, see Hiltebeitel 2005a; Gombach 2005; and Chapter 6.

10 Unless otherwise stated, translations – sometimes slightly amended – are from the Chicago edition.

11 *abhīkṣṇaṃ garbhiṇī śrutvā dhruvaṃ vīraṃ prajāyate // vidyāśūraṃ tapaḥśūraṃ damaśūraṃ tapasvinam / brāhmyā śriyā dīpyamānaṃ sādhuvādena saṃmatam // arciṣmantaṃ balopetaṃ mahābhāgaṃ mahāratham / dhṛṣṭavantam anādhṛṣyaṃ jetāram aparājitam //*

12 The dialogue also somehow reaches the Kaurava court (5.136.1–3), where Gāndhārī is present.

13 Elsewhere I discuss similar issues in relation to the dialogues in the Upaniṣads (Black 2007).

14 During the course of the *Āraṇyakaparvan*, Yudhiṣṭhira hears teachings and instructions from a number of the text's most eminent sages and storytellers, including Mārkaṇḍeya, Vyāsa, Śaunaka, Nārada, Lomaśa, Dhaumya, Baka Dālbhya and Bṛhadaśva; similarly, while remaining in his court in the *Udyogaparvan*, Dhṛtaraṣṭra hears reports from Saṃjaya, Vidura, Sanatsujāta, Bhīṣma and Duryodhana.

15 Hiltebeitel adds the comings and goings of Vyāsa as a fifth frame – which he calls the 'outermost' or 'authorial' frame (2001a: 92). I agree with Hiltebeitel that the *Mahābhārata*'s depiction of its own author, particularly concerning his transmission of the text to his disciples, is an important lens through which to view 'the poetics of the *Mahābhārata* "at large" ' (ibid.: 279). However, I have not treated these scenes here, because formally – i.e. in terms of the structure of the text – they do not constitute a frame.

16 For more on frame dialogues in the *Mahābhārata* see Minkowski 1989; Hiltebeitel 2001a; and Hegarty 2004.

17 Minkowski suggests that because of its length and many breaks, the *satra* provided a believable context for the narration of the *Mahābhārata* (1989: 403). It is also significant that Ugraśravas's brahmin audience is in the Naimiṣa Forest, which Minkowski describes as 'the utopian setting of Sanskrit literature' (2001: 176; see also Hiltebeitel 2001a: 92–130).

18 For example, despite the fact that the content of what Ugraśravas and Vaiśaṃpāyana narrate is almost exactly the same, the meaning and significance of what Śaunaka hears and what Janamejaya hears are quite different. Whereas the king wants to know what happens in the story, the interest of the Naimiṣa brahmins, Minkowski remarks, 'is based on the ontological status of the epic, and not on the content of the main story' (1989: 404). See also M. Mehta 1973.

19 The shift depicted here is more symbolic than actual, because after the *Sauptika-*

parvan – at the beginning of the *Strīparvan* – the text briefly returns to the Saṃjaya/Dhṛtarāṣṭra dialogue, and then presents Gāndhārī's dialogue with Kṛṣṇa (see pp. 64–5), before the frame dialogue featuring Yudhiṣṭhira as primary listener begins.

20 As Belvalkar notes, Saṃjaya loses his divine sight 'as soon as [its] purpose is served' (1946: 321).

21 The actual end of Dhṛtarāṣṭra's kingship does not come until the *Āśramavāsikaparvan*.

22 As Minkowski has pointed out, the audience is often established first and the storyteller 'wanders in' later (1989: 408).

23 For example, one of the ways in which the tragedy of the mourning widows is represented in the *Strīparvan* is the contrast between the luxuries they once enjoyed and the hardships that they suffer now: they now walk on 'the blood-soaked earth with their ornamented feet' (11.18.3); they can be seen by ordinary men (11.18.16); they have to lie on the ground when they are used to their well-spread beds (11.25.9). See also Fitzgerald 2004a: 9–10.

24 Jamison also briefly refers to the presence of female listeners during Vedic rituals: 'Women were barred, at least theoretically, from studying the Veda, though their presence at and participation in Vedic solemn ritual attests to the fact that they were not prevented from hearing it or indeed from speaking Vedic mantras' (1996: 14).

25 On the representational dimension of kingship, see Chapter 4.

26 The presence of female listeners back in Dhṛtarāṣṭra's court is alluded to by some of the participants in the battle as well. For example, when only two of the king's sons are still alive on the battlefield, Arjuna imagines how the news will be received back in the capital: 'Hearing of the slaughter of their husbands and sons at the hands of the Pāṇḍavas in battle, all the ladies in Hāstinapura will utter loud wails' (*adya tā api vetsyanti sarvā nāgapurastriyaḥ / śrutvā patīṃś ca putrāṃś ca pāṇḍavair nihatān yudhi //* 9.26.22, tr. Ganguli 9.27, p. 72).

27 This interest in the role of the audience that is displayed in the battle books is illustrative of an attention to how knowledge and information is received that is explored throughout the *Mahābhārata*. Similarly, there are a number of references to the 'people of Hāstinapura' and to the soldiers' wives who are on the side of the battlefield during the war.

28 At the end of the *Karṇaparvan*, after Dhṛtarāṣṭra collapses again, Gāndhārī falls down as well. When Vidura and Saṃjaya revive the king, the Kuru ladies pick up the queen (8.69.41–3).

29 Gāndhārī's divine sight consists of much more than being able to see the battlefield. It also lets her listen in on all of the conversations and know the thoughts of those on the battlefield. Similarly, Saṃjaya's divine eye gives him a universal perspective that allows him to know the thoughts, and even the dreams, of the warriors of Kurukṣetra. As Belvalkar comments: 'There are minor miracles without end that Saṁjaya is able to perform as a consequence of Vyāsa's boon' (1946: 317). For more discussion about Saṃjaya and the powers of the divine eye, see Belvalkar 1946 and Hiltebeitel 2001a: 32–91.

30 *bandibhiḥ satataṃ kāle stuvadbhir abhinanditāḥ /*

31 *sarveṣv apararātreṣu yān anandanta bandinaḥ /*

32 *āsām aparipūrṇārthaṃ niśamya paridevitam / itaretarasaṃkrandān na vijānanti yoṣitaḥ //*

33 We know that Arjuna is absent for a good portion of the instructions and stories that Yudhiṣṭhira hears, including the entire *tīrthayātrā* section. Whether Bhīma, Nakula and Sahadeva hear everything that is told to Yudhiṣṭhira is far from clear. However, given the emphasis on their unity and togetherness, I would assume that

they, along with Draupadī, are present except for on the occasions where the text is explicit that they are not.

34 *pratyakṣaṃ hi tvayā dṛṣṭa gacchan mahātapāḥ / mārkaṇḍeyo 'prameyātmā dharmeṇa cirajīvitām // vyāso vasiṣṭho maitreyo nārado lomaśaḥ śukaḥ / anye ca ṛṣayaḥ siddhā dharmeṇaiva sucetasaḥ // pratyakṣaṃ paśyasi hy etān divyayogasamanvitān / śāpānugrahaṇe śaktān devair api garīyasaḥ //* Among Yudhiṣṭhira's list of seers, we have only seen Vyāsa and Mārkaṇḍeya teach in the presence of Draupadī at this point in the story. Nārada and Lomaśa give instruction to the Pāṇḍavas later in the *Āraṇyakaparvan*; Vasiṣṭha appears several times in the *Āraṇyakaparvan*, but not in the main narrative; Maitreya, who only appears once in the *Mahābhārata*, teaches Duryodhana in the Kaurava court (3.11) shortly after Draupadī and the Pāṇḍavas have ventured into the forest. Perhaps Yudhiṣṭhira is referring to some episodes that occur 'offstage'.

35 This comment about seeing these eminent teachers is perhaps an allusion to the idea of *darśana*, suggesting that part of the authority of these *ṛṣi*s is in their appearance, and not just in their teachings.

36 *yathā ca vedān sāvitrī yājñasenī tathā satī / na jahau dharmataḥ pārthān merum arkaprabhā yathā //*

37 In addition to hearing tales and philosophical discourses, the text makes it clear that Draupadī participates in the religious practices associated with *tīrtha*s. She, along with her husbands, bathes in the Vaitaraṇī River and makes offerings to the ancestors (3.114.13). In the verse summary of this section Vaiśaṃpāyana says that Yudhiṣṭhira 'laved his limbs in all these fords, always followed by Kṛṣṇā, in his brothers' van' (*sa teṣu tīrtheṣv abhiṣiktagātraḥ kṛṣṇāsahāyaḥ sahito 'nujaiś ca* / 3.118.6). Draupadī's presence as a receiver of traditional lore at the various *tīrtha* sites brings up the question of the degree to which women were regular visitors to pilgrimage sites. Pulastya seems to imagine a female audience when he lists a number of *phalaśruti*s during his dialogue with Bhīṣma: 'Whatever evil a woman or a man has done since birth is all destroyed by just a bath at Puṣkara' (*janmaprabhṛti yat pāpaṃ striyo vā puruṣasya vā / puṣkare snātamātrasya sarvam eva praṇaśyati //* 3.80.54). It is important to remember that Draupadī is not in the vicinity when Pulastya is speaking to Bhīṣma, but rather hears this dialogue secondhand through Nārada. This suggests that Pulastya has in mind a more general female audience. The inclusion of women is consistent with other claims of Pulastya, who suggests that visiting *tīrtha*s is a practice accessible to a wide spectrum of people: 'But hear to what injunction even the poor can rise, equaling the holy rewards of sacrifices' (*yo daridrair api vidhiḥ śakyaḥ prāptuṃ nareśvara / tulyo yajñaphalaiḥ puṇyais taṃ nibodha yudhāṃ vara //* 3.80.37).

38 Both Biardeau (1984; 2002) and Hiltebeitel have pointed out how this *upākhyāna* 'mirrors' the *Mahābhārata*, with Hiltebeitel suggesting that Nala is 'perhaps the exemplary subtale . . . "encapsulating" the epic narratively as the *Gītā* does theologically' (2001a: 216). Whether or not the Nala story encapsulates or mirrors the entire *Mahābhārata*, undoubtedly this story has a particular relevance to Draupadī. Van Buitenen has commented that this story features Damayantī as its protagonist: 'In spite of its traditional name it is much more the story of Damayantī than of Nala' (1975: 183).

39 Keeping her in mind as a listener we would also assume that she is addressed by the *phalaśruti* (3.78.13).

40 *patnīm . . . dharmajñāṃ dharmacāriṇīm / . . . // na hi pāpaṃ kṛtaṃ kiṃ cit karma vā ninditaṃ kva cit / draupadyā brāhmaṇeṣv eva dharmaḥ sucarito mahān //*

41 At this point in the story the Rāma tale is not unfamiliar to Draupadī, as Mārkaṇḍeya has already spoken about Rāma in front of her when he first

approached her and the Pāṇḍavas in the forest (3.26.7). It is not clear, however, whether this episode represents a different occasion when Mārkaṇḍeya visits the Pāṇḍavas, or if the earlier section, which is presented in *triṣṭubh*, represents an introductory summary of events that will later be described in *śloka*. Either way, Mārkaṇḍeya's remarks link Draupadī with the Rāma story.

42 *dyūte durātmabhiḥ kliṣṭāḥ kṛṣṇayā tāritā vayam / jayadrathena ca punar vanād apahṛtā balāt // asti sīmantinī kā cid dṛṣṭapūrvātha vā śrutā / pativratā mahābhāgā yatheyaṃ drupadātmajā //*

43 *evam ātmā pitā mātā śvaśrūḥ śvaśura eva ca / bhartuḥ kulaṃ ca sāvitryā sarvaṃ kṛcchrāt samuddhṛtam // tathaivaiṣāpi kalyāṇī draupadī śīlasaṃmatā / tārayiṣyati vaḥ sarvān sāvitrīva kulāṅganā //*

44 *pativratānāṃ śuśrūṣā duṣkarā pratibhāti me // pativratānāṃ māhātmyaṃ vaktum arhasi naḥ prabho / nirudhya cendriyagrāmaṃ manaḥ saṃrudhya cānagha / patiṃ daivatavac cāpi cintayantyaḥ sthitā hi yāḥ // . . . / . . . // strīṇāṃ dharmāt sughorād dhi nānyaṃ paśyāmi duṣkaram /*

45 Van Buitenen translates *balākā* as heron or crane, but here I am following Leslie's rendering (1998: 464, 475).

46 See Chapter 4; Bailey 1983a; 2005.

47 Also, this scene implies that Draupadī and Satyabhāmā do not, in fact, hear all of Mārkaṇḍeya's teaching. The dialogue begins when they leave Mārkaṇḍeya and go inside together. However, when Mārkaṇḍeya first arrives it is clear that both Draupadī and Satyabhāmā are present because Yudhiṣṭhira names them when he addresses the sage (3.180.42–3).

48 In these scenes we glimpse a genealogy of *strīdharma*: Satyabhāmā hears from Draupadī, who has learned from Kuntī. Perhaps Kuntī was taught by Ambālikā or Satyavatī. Does this female '*paramparā*', like the Bhārata clan itself, go all the way back to Śakuntalā?

49 The only occasion recounted in the story before this incident where Nārada proclaims the divine status of Kṛṣṇa is in the *Sabhāparvan*, when he reflects these things to himself. Draupadī may be referring to some incident 'offstage'. However, it is also possible that the text, in this case, does not distinguish between what is said aloud and what is said to oneself (see Brodbeck in press a). We would expect Draupadī to have been present at the time of Nārada's musings, because this was at Yudhiṣṭhira's *rājasūya*, where Draupadī's attendance as wife of the *yajamāna* would have been required.

50 *avaśyaṃ ca tvayā bhūmir iyaṃ nihatakaṇṭakā / bhartṛbhiḥ saha bhoktavyā nirdvaṃdveti śrutaṃ mayā //*

51 Simon Brodbeck further suggests: 'Perhaps Satyabhāmā was there as Śrī-Lakṣmī on the occasion when Kṛṣṇa-Viṣṇu received his mission after Earth complained to Brahmā (1.58.35–51) – in which case maybe her "so I have heard" refers not to something Kṛṣṇa has told her, but to her act of eavesdropping in the celestial court' (personal communication, September 2005).

52 *brāhmaṇaṃ me pitā pūrvaṃ vāsayām āsa paṇḍitam / so 'smā artham imaṃ prāha pitre me bharatarṣabha // nītiṃ bṛhaspatiproktāṃ bhrātṝn me 'grāhayat purā / teṣāṃ sāṃkathyam aśrauṣam aham etat tadā gṛhe // sa māṃ rājan karmavatīm āgatām āha sāntvayan / śuśrūṣamāṇām āsīnāṃ pitur aṅke yudhiṣṭhira //*

53 Another occasion where Draupadī claims to have heard a teaching from brahmins appears in the *Virāṭaparvan* (4.20.28).

54 Bṛhaspati's name goes back to the *Ṛgveda*, where he was known as the priest of the gods. In the *Mahābhārata* he is often quoted as an authority on *dharma* (e.g. 12.23.14; 12.56.38; 12.58.13), and his instructions to Indra are often cited as prototypical wisdom (e.g. 2.46.9; 2.66.7; 5.33.60; 12.21.1).

55 *tava rājan savarṇāsmi śuddhayonir aviplutā // pradhāno nāma rājarṣir vyaktaṃ te*

śrotram āgataḥ / kule tasya samutpannāṃ sulabhāṃ nāma viddhi mām // droṇaś ca śataśṛṅgaś ca vakradvāraś ca parvataḥ / mama satreṣu pūrveṣāṃ citā maghavatā saha // sāhaṃ tasmin kule jātā bhartary asati madvidhe / vinītā mokṣadharmeṣu carāmy ekā munivratam //

4

ARGUMENTS OF A QUEEN

Draupadī's views on kingship

Angelika Malinar

The dialogue between Draupadī and Yudhiṣṭhira in the *Āraṇyakaparvan* is one of many debates in the *Mahābhārata* to feature a female character accusing a male character of not doing his duty, and demanding him to act properly.[1] The depiction of women as self-confident, critical of their male relatives and rhetorically skilled, stands in contrast to the role usually accorded them in the law books and elsewhere in the epic. As is well known, women are regarded as being subordinate, weak and dependent, and it is commonly held that they should be kept in this position. Stephanie Jamison has put this contradiction as follows: 'These fearsomely able women and the women who "don't deserve independence" do not seem to inhabit the same conceptual planet. What is the source of the narrative pattern that contradicts the explicit doctrine of female weakness?' For her this pattern is an 'almost accidental byproduct of . . . conflicting (male) religious goals' (Jamison 1996: 15–16).[2] While such conflicts are certainly influential, I propose to understand what seems to be an ambiguity, or even a contradiction, as the interplay – and sometimes also clash – of different levels of a gender relationship that is construed as one of mutual dependence. In analysing this interdependence one needs to employ a relational notion of gender, since men and women are defined in relation to each other and in relation to the social role they must fulfil. Thus, we are dealing here not with a binary opposition based on fixed attributes or intrinsic, essential properties ascribed to each sex, but with a hierarchical structure in which attributes depend on the relationships between the different actors, and this means that they can change according to context and situation.

In the following, the arguments that are exchanged between a man and a woman – here Yudhiṣṭhira and Draupadī – will be analysed against the background of the mutual dependence implied in their social relationship. It will be shown that the debate serves to negotiate a relationship that has become problematic because the partners have been deprived of the chance to perform their inherited social roles. This seems to be especially critical when the husband and wife are a king and a queen. The reason for the special quality of this relationship lies in the fact that, in the social structure depicted in the *Mahābhārata*, gender relationships are defined by marriage or other kinship ties, which in turn reflect the status of the partners in the social hierarchy. Moreover, this status has to be represented and performed, since it is observed and commented upon by others, be they those who appear in the epic as characters, bards or 'the people' (*jana*), or the audience of epic text when it is recited, read or otherwise published.[3] The task of 'representation' was a particular challenge for the aristocracy, as they were charged with representing society not only as an ordered whole, but also as legitimate, beneficial and – not to be neglected – aesthetically satisfying. When I use the term 'representation', I do not understand it primarily in the more modern sense of 'political representation' as it is the case, for instance, in the *pars pro toto* structure of democratic systems. Rather, I refer to a pre-modern sense in which the upper strata of a hierarchically organized society represent the values and powers that guarantee the functioning of society.[4] In this case representation is located on two interrelated levels: firstly – and this is well studied – the king must be able to exercise his power and maintain social order; secondly – and less studied – he should represent the orderliness, appropriateness and legitimacy of this social order by living up to its values, in brief by incorporating them as the king. However, this incorporation is only complete with a queen at his side. It is the very corporeal dimension of representation, its visibility and material character, that constitutes its attraction in the eyes of the others, be they family members, other kings, gods and goddesses or – not to be forgotten – the other social strata. I am going to argue that this 'representational' quality of kingship is an important feature of the discourse between exiled Draupadī and Yudhiṣṭhira in the *Āraṇyaka-parvan*.[5] It is a feature closely connected to the implications of the socially accorded roles of husband and wife. The discourse is a negotiation of a crisis in their relationship, because Yudhiṣṭhira is no longer the royal husband Draupadī once married. In losing everything during the dice game, he has lost their status; therefore she demands him to take action. Seen from the perspective of the aforementioned construction of gender relationships, the crisis emerges because their customary roles as each other's husband and wife are no longer in harmony with their royal status. This causes grief, complaints and controversies. The question then is: how does one represent one's status when one has lost it? Or, to address the issue of the debate in the *Āraṇyakaparvan*, how can one be Yudhiṣṭhira's wife without being a queen, and, conversely, how can one be Draupadī's husband and not be a king?

These questions indicate that the situation both partners find themselves in does not at all facilitate the ideal relationship between a king and his queen (representing his *śrī*) because royal status has been lost and its representation has become a problem.[6] Let's see how this problem unfolds in the exchange of arguments in 3.28–33. For the sake of orientation, I will first provide an overview of the main points of the debate.

The discussion between Draupadī and Yudhiṣṭhira is transmitted as a part of the *Āraṇyakaparvan*, and is said to have occurred after one year of exile. It is a debate on the pros and cons of putting up with the miserable situation of exile and refraining from immediate retaliation for Duryodhana's transgressions which made him king.[7] Before going into some of the arguments more closely, a survey of chapters 3.28–37 will be given. Chapters 28–33 contain the dialogue between Draupadī and Yudhiṣṭhira, while in 3.34 Bhīma puts forward his point of view and Yudhiṣṭhira continues arguing with him.

Chapter 3.28 starts with a very brief description of the dialogue situation. One evening the five brothers and Draupadī are sitting together in their forest abode, absorbed by pain and grief. Then Draupadī turns to Yudhiṣṭhira and begins to complain about Duryodhana's lack of pity and remorse. She vividly reminds Yudhiṣṭhira of what he and his brothers have lost, and wonders where his enthusiasm for self-assertion (*manyu*) has gone. The chapter ends with the unexpected statement that forgiveness (*kṣamā*) is sometimes called for. The word *kṣamā*, mentioned in the last verse of 3.28, gives Draupadī the opportunity to report a conversation between the former kings Prahlāda and Bali Vairocana. Bali asks Prahlāda whether forgiveness (*kṣamā*) or the demonstration of power (*tejas*) is better. The diplomatic answer is that there is a time and a place for both. Draupadī concludes that the time has come for taking action against Duryodhana. In 3.30 Yudhiṣṭhira replies that uncontrolled demonstrations of power will result in nothing but destruction. In 3.31 Draupadī accuses Yudhiṣṭhira of delusion (*moha*). Instead of following the heroic path of his ancestors, he subjects himself to some dubious 'distributor' (*vidhātṛ*) of the fruits of action. She points out that this 'distributor' does not care for appropriate retribution.

Yudhiṣṭhira, in turn, accuses Draupadī of being an 'unbeliever' (*nāstika*) and asks her to stop (3.32). Although Draupadī complies, she continues arguing her cause, and ends with a final demand for action (3.33). There is no reply from Yudhiṣṭhira at this point; rather, at the beginning of 3.34 Bhīma is made to speak up against his brother, fighting for Draupadī's cause – as always – but with a different set of arguments. The dialogue between Bhīma and Yudhiṣṭhira gets stuck in 3.37 and ends in mutual embarrassment when Bhīma finds no answer to Yudhiṣṭhira's confession of weakness. This situation is only solved by the appearance of Kṛṣṇa Dvaipāyana Vyāsa, the epic's composer, who announces the Pāṇḍavas' future victory and teaches Yudhiṣṭhira a *vidyā*, a magic means for consecrating weapons. A remarkable feature of this sequence of arguments is that there is no clear solution to the conflict addressed in the debate between king and queen. Rather, if one takes Vyāsa's word as final, both of their positions are partially accepted: one should put up with the situation, but meanwhile get ready to fight.

This outline shows that chapters 3.28–37 form a unity in the sense that Vyāsa's appearance is necessary to bring the awkward situation to an end. This does not mean that all these chapters have been incorporated into the *Mahābhārata* at the same time (3.29 especially raises questions). However, my analysis will consider the extant text, and concentrate on the dialogue between Draupadī and Yudhiṣṭhira, since this part of the passage invites an analysis of gender relationships. In the present context this cannot include all the twists and turns of the argument. Rather, I will deal with the main topics of the debate, and closely analyse some of the themes related to the problem of representation and the crisis in the relationship between king and queen.

Duryodhana the winner versus Yudhiṣṭhira the loser

Draupadī, described by the four attributes *priyā, darśanīyā, paṇḍitā* and *pativratā*,[8] begins her speech by complaining about Duryodhana. She does not, as in other speeches, refer to Duryodhana's misbehaviour against herself, but rather blames him for his lack of sympathy for Yudhiṣṭhira's misery. Having a heart made of iron (*āyasa hṛdaya*), a typical epithet for a merciless person (see also 5.133.1), he did not show any sympathy when Yudhiṣṭhira was sent into exile clad in antelope skin (3.28.3–7). Draupadī bitterly contrasts the past and the present by recalling the visible requisites of royalty and their former conjugal happiness. Thus, she starts by recalling the matrimonial bed: 'I see your bed before my eyes, the one of old, and I pity you, who deserve to be happy, not to suffer' (3.28.10).[9] She then conjures up the throne: 'When I see your throne before my eyes, made of ivory, in the middle of the audience hall, adorned with jewels, covered with a cushion made of *kuśa* grass, grief tears me apart' (3.28.11).[10] By putting the bed first, she reminds Yudhiṣṭhira that their marriage has been the precondition for his accession to the throne and, *vice versa*, that losing the throne has deprived them of this 'old' (*purātana*) bed and thereby of their appropriate conjugal life. She continues the list of losses with the *sabhā* and the assembly of allied kings. Then she contrasts his being anointed with sandal paste with his now being covered with mud, his silk dress with the rags he is now wearing,[11] and his feeding of brahmins and renouncers with their present forest diet. In the last seventeen verses of the chapter she describes the poor condition of his brothers, who are condemned to brooding in inactivity. Her lament turns into a complaint, which is orchestrated by the following question repeated eight times: 'Why doesn't your anger (*manyu*) grow?'[12]

The key word of this refrain is *manyu* (anger, wrath). As Malamoud has shown in his study of Vedic texts, *manyu* is not just another word for *krodha* or *kopa*, that is, anger as a passion or transient emotion. Rather, *manyu* is regarded as an essential quality and capacity of (royal) gods like Indra or Varuṇa, which allows them to maintain their status and enact their power. According to Malamoud the '*manyu* of a god is that vigour which brings him to accomplish those deeds through which his divinity is affirmed' (1989: 186, my translation).[13] In this sense it can also be applied to warriors. Draupadī's demand for Yudhiṣṭhira's *manyu* seems to draw on this dimension, because she regards the lack of this capacity in her husband to be the cause of their situation. She states in 3.28.34: 'There is no *kṣatriya* without *manyu* – this saying is well known in the world. In you, however, I now see a *kṣatriya* who is (acts) like the opposite.'[14] For Draupadī, *manyu* is positive because it is a necessary quality of a warrior and thus a quality which she, as the daughter of a king (*rājaputrī*, 3.32.2), must expect from her husband. This positive evaluation of *manyu* is not only in accordance with the Vedic meaning of *manyu*, but also with other passages in the epic, in which it is attributed to or demanded from a hero (e.g. 5.131.2, 5).

In her speech Draupadī places their misery[15] in its visible context and thereby touches upon the very problem of representation pointed out above. She does not draw on the symbolism certainly implied in the paraphernalia listed, but uses them to confront Yudhiṣṭhira with the obvious, that is, with those things whose absence could be noticed by anyone. It is the visibility of the loss which makes the situation so painful and intolerable; and this pain increases when this loss is contrasted with Duryodhana's happiness. For Draupadī's status as the wife and queen of Yudhiṣṭhira, it is this referential framework which counts. She does not hesitate to have a closer look[16] and point out that a king who no longer represents (that is, enacts and incorporates) kingship is no longer a king, even if he claims to be the virtual, rightful or appropriate king. For Draupadī, this is a situation a warrior and king should not tolerate, if he still claims the title 'king' and wants to be regarded as one.[17] Yudhiṣṭhira has turned into a husband who no longer lives up to his social position; he is, as we have heard, a husband who does not even own a proper bed. All this threatens the desirable symmetry of the relationship, as Draupadī has to deal with a weakness she has not learned to tolerate – although she has certainly been brought up to be a wife, that is, simply to put up with her husband's decisions.[18] Her argument points to a conflict of role models and social values that has been caused by the situation of exile. However, at the very end of the chapter, in the last *śloka* (3.28.37), Draupadī's complaint is suspended by the authors, or later redactors,[19] by her statement that sometimes forgiveness (*kṣamā*) is called for.

Self-assertion versus forgiveness in 3.29–30

With this we turn to the next main theme of the debate, the question of which norm should be followed in this situation: striving for retaliation, thus displaying *tejas* and *manyu*, or *kṣamā*, putting up with it? This is the topic of Draupadī's speech in 3.29 and Yudhiṣṭhira's reply in 3.30. I will only give the gist of the argument that is put forward in 3.29 by means of a report of a conversation between Bali Vairocana and Prahlāda. According to Prahlāda there is a time for both, and thus one has to decide according to the situation. The referential framework of this interpretation is not symbolic or philosophical, but consists of a discussion of various concrete situations in which a king or a superior might find himself. We are thus given a casuistic, situational interpretation of the criteria for displaying one faculty or the other. In consequence, Draupadī draws the conclusion that their present situation meets the criteria for displaying *tejas* and not *kṣamā*.

In his reply in 3.30 Yudhiṣṭhira disagrees and, in doing so, shifts the level of argument. First of all, he does not address the issue of *manyu* as a capacity, but the problem of *krodha*.[20] 'Wrath' is thereby no longer regarded as an essential quality, but as a passion that must be controlled. This is a favourite strategy for turning down demands, whereby capacities or powers regarded by the other as desirable for asserting one's social position are re-interpreted as problematic emotions or undesirable passions that need to be controlled (see for example 1.37; 5.133–4). It is denied that *krodha* is a capacity, rather it is condemned as a lower, destructive passion that has to be controlled and erased; at best it can be used as an opportunity for developing forgiveness, *kṣamā*. Rather than viewing both *kṣamā* and *manyu* (or *tejas*) as capacities to be used according to the situation, as suggested by Draupadī on the authority of Prahlāda,[21] Yudhiṣṭhira builds up a binary opposition between them, and asserts that *kṣamā* is always better.[22] He employs a strategy that favours and enforces binary oppositions, instead of situational, casuistic considerations which take the ambiguity of values and attitudes into account. Such ambiguity leaves one with the difficult task of making decisions in various situations and not with a general principle that can be applied at all times.

Thus Yudhiṣṭhira's line of argument changes not only the vocabulary, but also the referential framework. Although concrete situations were adduced in the discourse of Prahlāda in order to explain the different contexts that demand from the king a display of either anger or endurance, Yudhiṣṭhira interprets both as matters of principle, and assesses their metaphysical or even ontological value without applying it to any of those concrete situations. Only twice does he address aspects of the issue put forward by Draupadī. In the first instance, he states that a weaker person, who lacks strength and power, should not show his anger against a stronger one (3.30.10–11). He thereby indicates, again on a rather abstract level, that he may not be strong enough to face Duryodhana in battle. (As mentioned above, the open concession of the Pāṇḍavas' actual weakness in front of Bhīma will close the whole debate and invite Vyāsa's entrance.) In the second instance, he compares himself to Duryodhana by taking *kṣamā* as the point of comparison (3.30.49). Yudhiṣṭhira praises himself as superior to merciless, intransigent Duryodhana by declaring: '*Kṣamā* has found me because I am worthy of it' (3.30.49).[23] What is remarkable about this expression is the active role ascribed to *kṣamā*. This is reminiscent of the goddess Śrī, who finds and chooses as king that man who has the right qualities and is therefore worthy of her. If one pursues this association one might say that, instead of the royal virtues symbolized by Śrī and incorporated by Draupadī as the queen, *kṣamā* seems now to have become Yudhiṣṭhira's essential quality and thus the functional equivalent of Śrī. *Kṣamā* is the virtue that now, in times of crisis, guarantees his future well-being and prosperity. In saying this, he claims that a virtue which later in the text is identified as belonging to the earth is the basis and object of kingship. Yudhiṣṭhira seems to hint at an inversion of his role as king, the protector of the earth, when he compares those who possess *kṣamā* – that is, people like him – with the earth (3.30.25b, 31b: *kṣamiṇaḥ pṛthivīsamāḥ*). In shifting the level of the argument, Yudhiṣṭhira avoids facing the misery by refusing to mirror his situation in Draupadī's arguments. He identifies himself with the earth by claiming one of the goddess's characteristics, endurance. It seems that the ideal symmetry of king and queen with regard to royal virtues has been broken off, and other values prevail.

However, as this is a position taken by her husband, Draupadī, in her role as *pativratā*, the dedicated wife, should now give in and be silent. To put it pointedly, she should practise wifely *kṣamā* with regard to her suffering from her husband's inactivity. However, should she? Not necessarily. According to the very logic of her position in the gender relationship, as a *pativratā* it is not only her duty to support and propel her husband,[24] but she also has to take care that her man does not go astray or fail to live up to social standards. Ideally, as part of her role as queen, she 'guarantees the social construction of a man in accordance with the aristocratic standards' (Wenzel 2003: 24, my translation).[25] Once already Draupadī has cleared up the mess created by her husband's dicing and rescued them all from enslavement. Seen from Draupadī's perspective, her husband is now endangered by another cherished idea turned into an obsession. His clinging to *kṣamā* seems to drive him away from her again, without his thinking about the consequences for his wife and queen. He claims the metaphysical superiority of *kṣamā*, but disregards the contexts in which it is recommended by the 'learned'. These contexts are royal power, as we have seen in the teaching of Prahlāda, and asceticism and female suffering, as Hara has shown.[26] At present, Yudhiṣṭhira cannot claim any of these contexts for himself. As if it were not enough that he cannot use *kṣamā* from a position of strength, he also mixes up the two other contexts, asceticism and female suffering. Yudhiṣṭhira wants to have it both ways: while he is currently comparable to a *tapasvinī*, a woman who suffers from an intolerable situation but cannot do anything against it, he claims to behave like an ascetic, whose strength lies in his capacity to control anger through *kṣamā* and who therefore does not lose his *tapas*, ascetic power. It comes as no surprise that this invites critique because Yudhiṣṭhira is neither a woman, a *tapasvinī* for whom *kṣamā* would be a respectable thing, nor really an ascetic, because he has not renounced his social life, but lost it unintentionally. However, Yudhiṣṭhira interprets what Draupadī regards as weakness as a test case for his strength as a *siddha*, a successful ascetic, and this allows him to ignore her arguments about their royal status. According to Draupadī, this is only *moha*, delusion.

Yudhiṣṭhira makes it clear that restoring *śrī* and freeing Draupadī from her grief are currently not on his agenda. In consequence, he never actually faces Draupadī's words, appearance and emotions. He deflects and escapes her arguments by shifting to a different context. This does not necessarily point to his weakness, but rather confirms what I propose to regard as the structure of mutual dependence which determines the representation of status and gender roles in the epic. Social relationships are in general construed as mirror situations of looking and looking back, that is, as being based on the capacity to face each other. This becomes increasingly difficult during a conflict or in a situation where the image that usually attracts its reflection is distorted (Malinar 2005; Tschannerl 1992: 101–26). Thus, to accept Draupadī's point of view Yudhiṣṭhira would need to take a look at himself, but this is not desirable when the gaze of the queen, which serves to define him according to the norms of their social position, is unfavourable. Yudhiṣṭhira is not only intensively looked at by Draupadī, but also looked up and down, as we have seen in her vivid depiction of his appearance.[27] He, in turn, does not deal directly with her line of thought. Instead, he re-frames her whole argument.

What about retribution?

It seems that Draupadī has very well understood the message whereby their miserable situation is reinterpreted as a test case for a superior value. At the beginning of 3.31 Draupadī again goes on the offensive and in her own way re-establishes a symmetry between the two of them, by also stepping out of *her* roles of obedient, enduring wife and respectable queen. Without hesitation she rejects her husband's praise of himself as better than Duryodhana because *kṣamā* has become his *dharma*. For her this is just a delusion (*moha*): 'Praise to both the "arranger" and the "distributor" who have deluded you! Although you should carry on in the way of your fathers and grandfathers, you have a different outlook (*mati*)' (3.31.1).[28] Now it is her turn to re-frame Yudhiṣṭhira's argument by declaring that regaining *śrī* should be the primary aim of all his activities and that *dharma* defined as *kṣamā* does not serve this purpose.[29] Draupadī points out that their suffering seems to leave Yudhiṣṭhira comparatively cold, because his heart beats more for *dharma* than for his life (and thus for her or his brothers).[30]

In contrast with the rather abstract level of Yudhiṣṭhira's argument, Draupadī comes back to the actual situation and again takes a look at her husband. This time the emphasis is not on his physical appearance and the requisites of kingship. Rather, the outcome of his pious observance of dharmic duties comes under scrutiny. Draupadī's evaluation is guided by the following definition of the working of *dharma*: 'The Law, when well protected, protects the king who guards the Law, so I hear from the noble ones, but I find it does not protect *you*' (3.31.7, tr. van Buitenen).[31] Here she defines *dharma* as a principle of just retribution and almost equates it with *karma*. She takes her husband as the test case for the truth of this definition, and she shows that there is something wrong with it since the observance of *dharma* is not only inefficient and fruitless, but even counter-productive in that it yields the wrong fruits and thus produces injustice (*viṣama*). Although Yudhiṣṭhira has meticulously followed all the prescriptions, he has met misery. Again she vividly describes his former dharmic activities such as sponsoring sacrifices and feeding brahmins, guests and ascetics (3.31.9–16). In spite of this, she observes, everything went wrong during the dice game. This seems to suggest that this was a situation in which *dharma* should have protected Yudhiṣṭhira, because he had protected *dharma* before, but it did not. What does this tell about the efficacy of human efforts and the justice of dharmic retribution? At this point in her argument Draupadī goes into matters of principle too, and inquires who or what is in charge of the business of retribution. This brings her to the *dhātṛ* (arranger) and the *vidhātṛ* (distributor), the *īśvara*s, the lords who rule over the fruits of one's efforts.

Once again she cites ancient lore (*itihāsa purātana*, 3.31.20) on the unpredictable decisions of the lord (*īśvara*), who distributes happiness and suffering amongst the creatures according to his will. Living beings are not free in what they do, and what they achieve is not in their own hands, but in those of this hidden 'arranger', whom Draupadī compares to a puppet-player. He moves his dolls in this or that direction according to a script as secret as he himself:

> This blessed God, the self-existent great-grandfather, hurts creatures with creatures, hiding behind a guise, Yudhiṣṭhira. Joining and unjoining them, the capricious blessed Lord plays with the creatures like a child with its toys. The arranger does not act towards his creatures like a father or mother, he seems to act out of fury, like every other person.
>
> (3.31.35–7, tr. van Buitenen, slightly changed)[32]

In order to demonstrate the fundamental injustice implied in the distribution of fruits, Draupadī again contrasts the pleasures Duryodhana enjoys, because 'the arranger has given him *śrī*, royal prosperity' (3.31.40),[33] with the misery of noble Yudhiṣṭhira. Far from putting up with this by drawing on 'superior values', she draws her own conclusions about the nature of power. She complains about this injustice (*viṣama*) and in the end condemns this 'arranger' who does nothing against it (*dhātāraṃ garhaye*, 3.31.39). Diagnosing that the law of *karma*, the law of just rewards, does not work and seems to be suspended in their case, she ends her speech as follows: 'If the evil that has been done does not pursue its doer, then mere power is the cause of everything, and I bemoan powerless folk!' (3.31.42, tr. van Buitenen).[34] With this statement Draupadī has reached the very end of her argument, which brings her back to the *abala*, the powerless, that is, folk like Yudhiṣṭhira and herself. She has now made explicit what has remained only hinted at throughout this discourse, that is, that the Pāṇḍavas lack the strength to fight, a situation warriors had better not find themselves in. Her argument is double edged. On the one hand, it establishes a symmetry between Yudhiṣṭhira and Draupadī, in that they are now equally in a situation of weakness. On the other hand, in order to keep the ideal symmetry necessary for representing their status as the royal couple, Yudhiṣṭhira should not be weak, as he then would not deserve his wife and queen as the representative of *śrī*. Draupadī has touched a sore point: her metaphysical interpretation of their fate cannot easily be rejected, but nonetheless Yudhiṣṭhira cannot concede. It is only at the end of the whole exchange of arguments, and after Bhīma has entered the discussion, that Yudhiṣṭhira concedes this central point and indirectly (that is, not addressing Draupadī) agrees with his wife that *kṣamā* may not be enough. This is why he so readily accepts Vyāsa's special *vidyā* (3.37.25ff.). In his exchange with Draupadī, however, he rejects this reasoning.

Draupadī the heretic

This rejection essentially consists in an attempt to call Draupadī to order. After having politely praised Draupadī's rhetoric (3.32.1ab), Yudhiṣṭhira puts the brakes on her and accuses her of propagating *nāstikya*, 'heresy' and 'unbelief' (3.32.1cd). In his view she is guilty of a serious transgression, because she doubts the inner or ultimate orderliness of the created world and that things are, in general, right and good as they are. His reply is basically an argument *ex negativo* (a *prasaṅga*), because he points to the undesirable consequences of her thought. However, if one considers the dialogue as a re-negotiation of the relationship between the king and the queen in a situation of crisis, Yudhiṣṭhira's reply succeeds in re-establishing a symmetry between the two. Draupadī has suggested that Yudhiṣṭhira's view (*mati*) has proved unsuccessful and brought him into a situation whereby he no longer represents and embodies kingship and thus has stepped out of his role. This is balanced by Draupadī, the queen, expressing her deepest suspicions about that very order, the very *dharma* she otherwise (that is, officially and *per officium*) represents and enacts. A *nāstika* queen on the throne is as scandalous as a king turned into a deplorable weakling. By depicting her crossing the line and falling out of her role too, the authors re-establish the symmetry of the relationship between the dialogue partners. As Wenzel notes with regard to the construction of gender in the medieval epic *Erec et Enide*:

'When the man steps out of his socially codified role, then the woman also steps out of her social role; in this way, the symmetry of the relationship . . . is still kept' (Wenzel 2003: 265, my translation).

Draupadī's view is therefore denounced as a transgression throughout Yudhiṣṭhira's reply. This can be seen by the many occurrences of the prefix '*ati-*', signifying an excessive or deviant performance of the activity denoted by the verb. Thus, Draupadī is said to 'doubt too much' (*ati+śaṅk*, 32.6 – twice; 32.7, 9, 15, 17, 21), to 'argue too much' (*ati+vad*, 32.6), to 'transgress' (*ati+gam*, 32.9, 20) and to 'violate' (*ati+vṛt*, 32.18) norms. The checking of Draupadī's deviant reasoning is substantiated by the depiction of a Yudhiṣṭhira who does not sway under Draupadī's attack but is a husband in control. Being absolutely determined, he tells the 'king's daughter' (*rājaputrī*, 3.32.2) that he does not pine for the fruits of *dharma* (*nāhaṃ dharmaphal-ānveṣī*, 3.32.2). Reminding her of teachings about 'disinterested action' (*niṣkāma karman*) and the fulfilment of one's social obligations as *l'art pour l'art*, Yudhiṣṭhira claims that his belief in *dharma* is not based on retribution. However, this is not the whole truth, since Yudhiṣṭhira does not exactly relinquish the fruits, but rather employs a different time-perspective so that he can tolerate a postponement of retribution. In contrast to Draupadī's insistence on immediate justice and retribution, he opts for the long-term growth of his dharmic capital. Being a true believer in '*āstikya*', he trusts in the proper functioning of the economy of *dharma*. He is therefore convinced that in the end the fruit will come, even if this might only happen in some after-world or through the attainment of salvation. *Dharma* never fails to produce fruit, and this is confirmed by the fact that all the wise and respected persons fulfil their dharmic duties (3.32.29, 31, 37). They never doubt the orderliness of order, of *dharma*, whatever its outer appearance may be. Thus *āstikya*, belief and confidence, is in any case better than *nāstikya*, unbelief, as this will certainly lead nowhere, or to degradation. In consequence, Yudhiṣṭhira reminds Draupadī that she might easily find herself reborn as an animal (3.32.6) if she does not control her passion for logical reasoning – a passion which only results in establishing herself as the means of proof (*pramāṇa*) instead of the elderly, male experts (3.32.15).

However, it is not only wrong to cast doubt on the integrity of *dharma* and the divine administrative forces behind it, but also inappropriate and embarrassing. Yudhiṣṭhira suggests that Draupadī is inquisitive and seems to have lost her sense of modesty, because she speculates about what the gods are doing behind the scenes (3.32.33–6). It is not only that Draupadī speaks as if she might know better than the gods what should be done, but also that she has missed the crucial point about lords of all kinds: they are not only hidden, they also hide. Gods live by their secrets and it is up to them alone to keep or disclose them. The distribution of the fruits of one's deeds is a 'secret of the gods' (*devaguhya*, 3.32.33). Thus, to be a believer means to accept that the miraculous power of the gods is hidden (*gūḍhamāyā hi devatāḥ*, 3.32.34).

This secrecy cannot be overcome by human beings, and this indicates the fundamental divide between the human and the divine: while human beings can be stripped of everything, the curtain between gods and men can never be torn down, but only lifted up. Yudhiṣṭhira is sure that the ultimate outcome will be a happy one and that, by the grace of the hidden lords, they will reach immortality. Consequently, at the end of his reply he warns Draupadī about doubting and arguing too much.

While this does not leave Draupadī unimpressed, she does not withdraw completely. Her final reply in 3.33 moves on two levels. On the one hand, she obeys Yudhiṣṭhira's admonition and stops expressing her suspicions. She moves back to her accorded role in which she represents an order, the *dharma* she actually believes in. On the other hand, her retreat is turned into another discourse about the different causes of success.[35] Thereby she not only proves her qualification as a *paṇḍitā*, a learned woman, but also manages to substantiate her primary argument, and can in the end demand again that something be done.

Conclusion

What does this tell us about the gendered presentation and articulation of values and ideas in the *Mahābhārata*? Throughout the epic speech and argument are based on the relationship between the speakers, that is, first of all, on their position in the social hierarchy. Arguments serve not only to put forward philosophical doctrines, but also to define and negotiate social relationships. This seems to be especially true of arguments that are exchanged between husbands and wives, which in the epic usually means between kings and queens. Their relationship is characterized by a complementary structure. However, this structure operates in two directions: on the one hand, it is construed vertically according to the normative gender hierarchy, and thus implies an asymmetry in the sense that the wife depends on the husband and is not free in her decisions; on the other hand, there is the horizontal dimension in which both partners move on the same level in order to represent their social status. Here we find a symmetry in that a husband has to maintain the status of his wife in order to keep his own, and the wife has to ensure that her husband lives up to the standards of their class. The specific characteristic of the gender relationships in the epic is that they combine the symmetry of representation with the asymmetry of female subordination.

Therefore the question of the appropriate 'representation' of social status, especially royal status, is an important referential framework which determines the structure not only of gender relationships, but also of gender-related discourses about kingship. Draupadī's verbal attacks on Yudhiṣṭhira are directed at his being displaced from the social context of 'status representation'. Through this displacement a certain asymmetry has set in between the two, as he has lost his position. The dialogue can be regarded as compensating for this asymmetry, as Draupadī is shown to cross the line too. For a moment she stops being the obedient wife and respectable queen, as she doubts the very order she must otherwise represent. In this way the symmetry between king and queen is re-established: Yudhiṣṭhira asserts his position and depicts himself as the one who, as a stout believer in the ultimate efficacy of *dharma*, continues to represent social order even in the moment of crisis and exile. Different arguments can be put forward in order to sustain or re-establish this complementarity, and no typical 'female' argument can easily be identified. Thus, although the idea of fate can also be expressed by a male voice, its use, and thus its quality, is determined by the social identity (which includes gender) of those who are communicating in debate. This does not imply that the relationship between the dialogue partners is negotiated in every debate. In situations where a king is counselled (as for instance King Dhṛtarāṣṭra by Vidura), or where we have a didactic discourse, the very basis of the whole relationship is not necessarily at stake. But in many of the verbal encounters between men and women in the epic, the foundation of their interdependence is the central topic. This is true for the dialogue between Draupadī and Yudhiṣṭhira, as it is, for instance, for that between Śakuntalā and Duḥṣanta (1.68–9). However, given the structure of the relationship that combines the symmetry of representation with the asymmetry of female subordination, the relationship is never broken up by the woman.[36]

These gendered verbal encounters thus have to be distinguished from the construction and usage of gender in normative and even philosophical texts, where gender relationships are used to exemplify the principles of existence (as is the case in Sāṃkhya philosophy),[37] or the duties of men and women are defined on the basis of a certain cultural construction of their 'way of being' (*svabhāva*).[38] However, what seems to be a current topic in those speeches in which women (usually Draupadī) demand their men to act, is that they are not willing to put up with a man who puts up with whatever happens to him, who suffers degradation and defeat without fighting back and who, on top of everything, finds reasons to feel good about it. Faced with passive, suffering men, women, especially aristocratic ones, seem to lose their belief in the sense and value of putting up with the very passivity and suffering they are destined to tolerate in order to gain their merits (cf. Mallison 1979). Their status can only be kept when their husband acts as a *kṣatriya*. As Draupadī states, if it is only power and strength that count, then one should pity those who are powerless. Thus, better to have power. It comes as no surprise that this line of thought has to be dismissed vehemently when proposed by a woman, especially if this woman is one's wife. To doubt that things are fine and right as they are is dangerous, and transgresses the very order that the royal couple has to sustain and to represent, that is, to embody. Doubt is harmful and, as we have seen, Draupadī yields to her husband's admonition. However, at the very end of her speech she nevertheless manages to argue for self-assertion in the realm of politics and sovereignty. As she ends her speech she resorts to yet another method by recalling her experiences in the house of her father, King Drupada (3.33.56–8). When a visiting teacher gave learned discourses, she stresses, she was sitting next to her father. This is the final image and the final message that her husband has to deal with. Yudhiṣṭhira has to legitimize his view not only against his wife, but also against his father-in-law. However, by returning to the court of her father, she signals that she has come back from what Yudhiṣṭhira regards as a verbal, intellectual and emotional excess.

It is significant that the authors refrain from putting a reply in Yudhiṣṭhira's mouth, so neither Draupadī nor Yudhiṣṭhira is made to lose face. Rather, Bhīma takes over and argues Draupadī's case from his own understanding of the situation. The whole debate gets stuck when Bhīma cannot offer a reply to Yudhiṣṭhira's analysis of their weakness, that is, their lack of weapons. This cannot be compensated for by any dharmic behaviour or merely by strong belief, but only by acquiring them. It very well suits the inner logic of the discourse that in this moment of silence the epic's composer Vyāsa appears in order to announce that Yudhiṣṭhira, and with him faith in victory, will prevail. His message is as much a narrative link motivating the further course of events during the exile, as it is a comment on the previous debate. Vyāsa supports Yudhiṣṭhira's position when he indirectly confirms that *kṣamā* is the choice of the moment since there is no other left; however, he also sides with Draupadī by emphasizing that one must actively secure final victory (and thus dharmic retribution), and he therefore offers Yudhiṣṭhira a (magic) means, a *vidyā* that allows the Pāṇḍavas to acquire superior weapons.[39] Yudhiṣṭhira is in no way disinclined to accept this offer. Thus, after the often rather twisted and sophisticated exchange of arguments, the epic authors manage to establish the symmetry of the relationship between the two protagonists: Yudhiṣṭhira and Draupadī not only keep face, but both get their due.

Notes

1 Other instances are 4.16–20; 5.80; 5.131–4; 12.14; 12.18.

2 See also Falk (1977: 91–2), who discusses the view that the strong portrayals of female characters belong to older parts of the epic, and that the contradictions in the depiction of female characters result from the coexistence of different textual layers in the extant epic. She points out that later redactors could not have recast Draupadī 'without destroying their work. Her words are too important to the epic, too crucial to the delineation of its central problem' (ibid.: 92). While this certainly goes too far and does not pay enough attention to the absence of Draupadī's voice during much of the epic, I would also not completely subscribe to Mary Brockington's view that 'Draupadī . . . in fact has hardly any influence on the plot, and is not a person in her own right' (2001: 257). According to Brockington, her role as a minor character in the epic can be equated with that of the younger brothers in that their function is to stress the accuracy of Yudhiṣṭhira's view and therefore they have to be 'automatically wrong' (ibid.: 256). While I follow Brockington

when she points out that the narrative techniques implied in the presentation of minor characters must be taken into consideration, I would allow for the possibility that they are not always totally wrong. In the dialogue under discussion in this chapter, the crucial point is not primarily to teach the audience about right and wrong, but to negotiate the relationship between the characters.

3 On the 'implied audience', see Mangels 1995; on the importance of 'seeing' and 'observing' as a form of social communication, see Malinar 1996: 97–114; 2005; Tschannerl 1992.

4 This has been labelled the '*caput*' or head-form of representation typical, for instance, for monarchic organizations. On the concept of 'representation' with regard to pre-modern societies, see Wenzel 1990, Hofmann 1974, Kantorowicz 1957 and, in contrast with the functional differentiation in sub-systems in modern societies, Luhmann 1998.

5 The importance of this dimension has also been stressed in my study of the epic context of the *Bhagavadgītā* and the 'political' aspects of the manifestation of Kṛṣṇa as God; see Malinar 1996.

6 Important studies on the symbolic aspects of the construction of sovereignty in the *Mahābhārata* have been made by Hiltebeitel (1976). He especially focuses on Draupadī's connection with the goddess Śrī and thus with the symbolic and mythological background of epic stories. He has shown that as a queen Draupadī represents the goddess whose presence is necessary for making a king prosper. Accordingly, in many epic and Puranic texts we meet a king either united with Śrī, or separated from her – and therefore from his kingdom. These are the two possible relationships between the goddess Śrī and a king, and thus between the divine and the human realm. They demonstrate the two opposite ends of ideal kingship: to be or not to be with Śrī. In the symbolic realm there is no other way. This topic is discussed in some passages in the epic, such as the dialogue between Bali and Indra in the *Śāntiparvan* (12.216–18, 220), and has also led to the depiction of Śrī as 'fickle' and 'unreliable', as she leaves the king who loses his power. As far as I know, Śrī is not met in any situation of crisis where she is attacked, appears helpless or is sent into exile. If such things happen, she seems to have already left the king beforehand (a fact which can then serve as an explanation for the crisis). In contrast, epic literature is full of princesses and queens who are in exactly such a situation of being separated from their royal husband, but are still wives and queens. My emphasis here is less on divine, dharmic or mythological symbolization, and more on the human or social level and thus on how the relationship between Draupadī and Yudhiṣṭhira is embedded in a framework of social relations.

7 Seen in the larger context of the pre-war books of the *Mahābhārata*, this dialogue of a royal couple is one of several that are to be found in these books. We come across other narratives of royal couples in crisis, for instance Duḥṣanta and Śakuntalā (1.62–9), Nala and Damayantī (3.50–78) and Rāma and Sītā (3.258–75). The situation of Draupadī and the Pāṇḍavas is refracted and recast in these adjacent stories. A different case is the dialogue between a mother and her son in the *Udyogaparvan* (5.131–4), called 'fierce speech of encouragement' (*uddharṣaṇaṃ bhīmam*), in which the son is blamed for his unmanliness. See Malinar 1996: 175ff.

8 This list confirms the representative dimension of Draupadī's status as wife and queen. Four attributes are given that characterize the queen: she is *priyā*, beloved, *darśanīyā*, beautiful, *paṇḍitā*, learned, and *pativratā*, dedicated to her husband. While the last attribute refers to the essential duty of every wife, her subordination to her husband and her responsibility for his well-being, learnedness seems to be a result of her aristocratic upbringing, which is also confirmed at the end of her

discourse when she recalls wisdom she imbibed at her father's court (3.33.56–8). This learnedness also extends to her rhetorical knowledge, which Yudhiṣṭhira cannot but praise (3.32.1ab), as she is depicted as a skilful rhetorician. She knows how to raise emotions through vivid images of the past, supports her arguments by citing acknowledged authorities under the heading of ancient lore (*itihāsa purātana*) and what she herself has learned by listening to learned conversations, and, last but not least, she demonstrates her reasoning skills by drawing her own conclusions about *dharma*, however dangerous. Of course she is beautiful; otherwise she could not incorporate Śrī and be the queen. As a consequence, this beauty has to be kept or at least reinstalled at all costs, and this is only possible by being dressed and adorned according to status. See also Hiltelbeitel 1980a; 1980–1.

9 *idaṃ ca śayanaṃ dṛṣṭvā yac cāsīt te purātanam / śocāmi tvāṃ mahārāja duḥkhānarhaṃ sukhocitam //* This contrast of actual suffering and deserved happiness is pointed out by means of the repeated expressions *sukhocita aduḥkhārha* and *duḥkhānarha*, 'for whom happiness is appropriate' and 'who does not deserve unhappiness' (see 3.28.6; 28.10; 28.18; 28.20; 28.26). For a study of the topic of suffering, see Bailey 1983a.

10 *dāntaṃ yac ca sabhāmadhye āsanaṃ ratnabhūṣitam / dṛṣṭvā kuśabṛsīṃ cemāṃ śoko māṃ rundhayaty ayam //* For an analysis of the symbolism of the throne, see Auboyer 1949.

11 3.28.14. Dress also signifies status in the case of Draupadī, as Hiltebeitel has shown (1980a; 1980–1).

12 *kasmān manyur na vardhate* (3.28.20, 21, 25, 27, 29–32); cf. the variation in 3.28.33 (*tava naivāsti manyur*).

13 'le manyu d'un dieu est l'élan qui le porte à accomplir des actes par quoi sa divinité s'affirme' (see also p. 182: 'manyu est une qualité permanente, mieux, une faculté essentielle').

14 *na nirmanyuḥ kṣatriyo 'sti loke nirvacanaṃ smṛtam / tad adya tvayi paśyāmi kṣatriye viparītavat //*

15 According to Greg Bailey the cause of Draupadī's suffering is that she finds herself in a situation in which *adharma* overrules *dharma* (1983a: 113–15). This summarizes the whole situation precisely. However, in the dialogue under discussion Draupadī is struggling not only with Duryodhana's adharmic prosperity, but also with Yudhiṣṭhira's interpretation of *dharma*, which seems to make him abandon his dharmic duties as a warrior and king. Hence it is argued that fulfilling dharmic duties does not necessarily yield dharmic results (see p. 87).

16 This passage confirms the importance of 'seeing' as a way of acquiring and expressing knowledge in the epic (see Malinar 1996; 2005), which is corroborated by the numerous occurrences of verbal forms of *paś* and *dṛś*: twenty-three times in 3.28.3–35.

17 To put it pointedly and to give the compound *dharmarāja* a different, rather ironic connotation certainly not in accordance with the dominant interpretation of Yudhiṣṭhira, one could say that he is only a *dharmarāja*, that is, a king only with regard to or according to the law, or morally, but not *de facto*.

18 This education is eloquently displayed in her conversation with Satyabhāmā in *Mahābhārata* 3.222–4.

19 From a text-historical perspective chapter 3.29 could be regarded as an interpolation, because the last verse of the previous chapter (3.28.37) is anti-climactic: it contradicts Draupadī's emphasis in the previous verse, in which *kṣamā* is definitely ruled out. A change in terminology also points in this direction since throughout chapter 3.29 *tejas*, not *manyu*, is regarded as the opposite of *kṣamā*.

20 Consequently, the word *krodha* is primarily used throughout the chapter. There are twenty-one occurrences of the noun and thirteen verbal forms; in addition, the participle of the verbal root '*kup*' (to be angry) appears three times. In contrast, there are only five occurrences of *manyu*, which is used on each occasion directly to reject Draupadī's diagnosis. Firstly, Yudhiṣṭhira explains that perfected men (*siddhas*) are free from anger and this is why his wrath does not grow (*etad draupadi saṃdhāya na me manyuḥ pravardhate* // 3.30.8); secondly, he argues that a weak and powerless person should suppress *manyu* (*tasmād draupady aśaktasya manyor niyamanaṃ smṛtam* // 3.30.11); thirdly, the wise praise victory over *manyu* (*manyor hi vijayaṃ kṛṣṇe praśaṃsantīha sādhavaḥ* / 3.30.14); fourthly, *manyu* is said to lead to destruction (*tasmān manyur vināśāya prajānām abhavāya ca* // 3.30.30); fifthly, it is claimed that the yonder worlds belong to those who have eliminated *manyu* through *kṣamā* (*yeṣāṃ manyur manuṣyāṇāṃ kṣamayā nihataḥ sadā* / *teṣāṃ paratare lokās* . . . // 3.30.43).

21 This view, that a king has to know how and when to use both, is also presented by Draupadī at 12.14.17.

22 While *krodha* leads to destruction and non-existence, forgiveness is better, because it secures a pleasant sojourn in the yonder worlds. By also citing an external authority, the '*gāthā*' of Kāśyapa (3.30.36–9), Yudhiṣṭhira praises *kṣamā* as the source of everything.

23 *arhas tasyāham ity eva tasmān māṃ vindate kṣamā* //

24 Jamison calls this 'the Barbara Bush syndrome' (1996: 262 n. 37); cf. Falk 1977: 98.

25 Wenzel is writing on Chrétien de Troyes's medieval epic novel *Erec et Enide*.

26 Hara (1977–8) has dealt with the importance of *kṣamā* for the definition of *tapas* and the *tapasvinī* by arguing that the two rather different meanings of *tapas*, suffering and ascetic heat, are connected in that they both require *kṣamā*: the ascetic practises *kṣamā* in order to prevent his *tapas* being reduced by his giving in to anger; the suffering woman (*tapasvinī*) practises *kṣamā* because she is caught in a hopeless situation, and her *kṣamā* is thus a consequence of weakness and dependence.

27 See n. 16 above.

28 *namo dhātre vidhātre ca yau mohaṃ cakratus tava* / *pitṛpaitāmahe vṛtte voḍhavye te 'nyathā matiḥ* // It should be noted that the manuscripts of the Southern Recension read *rājye* instead of *vṛtte*.

29 *neha dharmānṛśaṃsyābhyāṃ na kṣāntyā nārjavena ca* / *puruṣaḥ śriyam āpnoti na ghṛṇitvena karhi cit* // 3.31.2.

30 *nādya bhārata* / *dharmāt priyataraṃ kiṃ cid api cej jīvitād iha* // 3.31.4 ('There is nothing here on earth which is dearer to you than *dharma*, not even your life'). This also corresponds to Hiltebeitel's observation that the depiction of Draupadī's departure into exile bears 'the connotation of widowhood' (1980–1: 195).

31 *rājānaṃ dharmagoptāraṃ dharmo rakṣati rakṣitaḥ* / *iti me śrutam āryāṇāṃ tvāṃ tu manye na rakṣati* //

32 *evaṃ sa bhagavān devaḥ svayambhūḥ prapitāmahaḥ* / *hinasti bhūtair bhūtāni chadma kṛtvā yudhiṣṭhira* // *saṃprayojya viyojyāyaṃ kāmakārakaraḥ prabhuḥ* / *krīḍate bhagavān bhūtair bālaḥ krīḍanakair iva* // *na mātṛpitṛvad rājan dhātā bhūteṣu vartate* / *roṣād iva pravṛtto 'yaṃ yathāyam itaro janaḥ* //

33 *dhārtarāṣṭre śriyaṃ dattvā dhātā* . . . //

34 *atha karma kṛtaṃ pāpaṃ na cet kartāram ṛcchati* / *kāraṇaṃ balam eveha janāñ śocāmi durbalān* //

35 This is a discourse about the different factors that influence the success of one's work, and belongs to the topics of '*daiva*' and '*puruṣakāra*', which are discussed time and again in the epic. A detailed discussion is not possible within the scope

of this chapter. For general discussion of these topics, see Scheftelowitz 1929; Woods 2001.

36 Usually the men turn away, as for instance Nala, who flees from Damayantī (3.59); Duḥṣanta, who leaves Śakuntalā in the hermitage (1.67); Rāma, who rejects Sītā (3.275); and Yudhiṣṭhira, who does not look back when Draupadī falls into the snow during the '*mahāprasthāna*', but blames her affection for Arjuna (17.2). All this underscores women's dharmic dependence and subordination.

37 See for example *Bhagavadgītā* 7.4–10 where Kṛṣṇa describes his relationship to *prakṛti* in terms of procreational activities. Cf. Malinar 1996: 228ff.

38 For later traditions, see Leslie 1986.

39 Vyāsa confers the so-called '*vidyā pratismṛti*' on Yudhiṣṭhira, which allows the magical consecration of weapons; see J.L. Mehta 1990.

5

HOW DO YOU CONDUCT YOURSELF?

Gender and the construction of a dialogical self in the *Mahābhārata*

Laurie L. Patton

When Satyabhāmā, the wife of Kṛṣṇa, and Draupadī, wife of the Pāṇḍavas, retire to catch up in the forest, they have a confidential conversation (*saṃvāda*). Satyabhāmā asks Draupadī,

> How do you conduct yourself towards the Pāṇḍavas, Draupadī? How are they obedient to you, and how are they never angry with you, lovely one? (*kena draupadi vṛttena pāṇḍavān upatiṣṭhasi / . . . / kathaṃ ca vaśagās tubhyaṃ na kupyanti ca te śubhe //*)
>
> (3.222.4)

Satyabhāmā is convinced that Draupadī must be using a spell. Draupadī's answer is a long, varied, and quite rich description of what she does as a wife, throughout which she is adamant that none of her wifely duties involves a spell or any form of deceit. As we will see, her wifely duties engage a surprising variety of roles.

The larger issues

We spend a large amount of time thinking about the topic of *dharma* in the *Mahābhārata*, occasionally forgetting that the issue of multiple *dharma*s is at the heart of the tragic nature of the story. While some might argue that this view is a truism almost not worth repeating, it does not translate into our interpretive frameworks in a very sophisticated way. While we are perfectly willing to admit Yudhiṣṭhira's multiple *dharma*s as a king and a husband, or Arjuna's as a warrior and a beloved cousin, we frequently still choose the singular theme, rather than the plural, when we conduct our studies ('kingship in the epic', 'fate in the *Mahābhārata*', and so on).[1]

Elsewhere I have argued against the singular hermeneutic of 'gender' in ancient India.[2] Until recently we have tended to view 'woman' as a singular category, replete with queens, goddesses, maids, farmers, and courtesans, all joyfully lumped into a single hermeneutical pile. The last decade has seen a change in this approach, but it remains a challenge for us in terms of the study of the epic. The idea of 'gender' in the *Mahābhārata* tempts us to come up with a single ideology of gender in the epic, but it has become quite clear to me in my recent explorations that such a conclusion is impossible.

The clarity comes not only from the ideological commitment that all feminist hermeneutics must be plural. It also comes from the dialogical structure of the *Mahābhārata* itself. Many recent and not-so-recent studies[3] have given us great insight into the nature of the frame tale – particularly how a switch in narrative voice gives us multiple perspectives from which to think about the unfolding scene. These frame switches involve temporal, narratological, and dramatic juggling of a mind-boggling complexity. And yet we very rarely think about the ways in which the actual characters – *Mahābhārata* 'selves' – are built through this narrative technique. We struggle with the idea of 'character development' in the epics, but we may have turned a blind eye to the ways in which selves might be constructed through dialogue itself.[4]

Yet we have, happily, a meeting of dialogical textual form and recent hermeneutical theory to help us think about the issue of multiply layered selves and multiple gender ideologies in the *Mahābhārata*. Recent theories of gender have argued that gender is constructed through social relationships – enacted hierarchy, speech acts and other forms of performance, conversation in which multiple selves are instantiated. Philosophers as well as feminist theorists in particular have come up with the term 'the dialogical self' to show the ways in which gender is constructed not only through the binary roles of male and female, but also through a series of multiple roles within both male and female repertoires.[5] To put it succinctly, the dialogical, gendered self is a multiple self, with a variety of momentary roles to choose from.

Let us begin with a more general exploration of gender theory. Recently Judith Butler has argued for the idea that identity is performative and discursive, particularly when it comes to gender (1993: 2). She writes that the very idea of a 'culturally intelligible subject' is a result of rule-bound discourse, iterated throughout a series of performative instances (Butler 1999: 184ff.). And the idea of a *gendered* subject is no different. If Butler is right – and I think she is at least partly correct – then her theory can provide us with important insights into the nature of the epic. The idea of a knowing subject, constructed in this way, could well include any persuasive character in an epic, and Butler does include characters in novels and plays in her analyses. So the characters in the *Mahābhārata* are 'constructed' through performance, through a series of utterances that build our confidence in them as subjects. And thus we might read any given dialogue in the *Mahābhārata* as a building of characters – the creation of persuasive selves, and by implication, the building of gendered selves through performative speech acts (see also Butler 2001). Draupadī, Sudeṣṇā, and Satyabhāmā can be analysed in this light (as we shall see below), as could other characters.

Yet this self is not a simple self. Butler and other theorists are interacting with a recent turn in psychological and literary theory which proposes an idea called 'the dialogical self'. Two of the founding figures in this field are H. Hermans and H. Kempen, who write that characters in a novel resist a singular description: 'Different voices, often of a markedly different character and representing a multiplicity of relatively independent worlds, interact to create a self narrative' (Hermans and Kempen 1993: 208).[6]

Here Hermans and Kempen are drawing upon Bakhtin's notion of the polyphonic novel. Using the literary critic's essay on Dostoyevsky's poetics, they view the self as 'voices in dialogical relation with each other' (ibid.).[7] In other words, the self is internally plural, and dialogical relationships between voices lend the self coherence. It is 'only when an idea or thought is endowed with a voice and expressed as emanating from personal position in relation to others that dialogical relations emerge' (ibid.; see also Hermans 2002: 74). Not surprisingly, a set of important ideas is developing about the South Asian dialogical self in relation to the diaspora, and the multiple worlds that such a self must contain.[8]

But surely these ideas are equally relevant, if not more so, to the characters – or selves – of an ancient text which is composed entirely of dialogue? Indeed, it strikes me that the *Mahābhārata* is the exemplar *par excellence* of Hermans's, Kempen's and Bakhtin's ideas. For each character there are a series of dialogical positions, not all of them consistent, not all of them transparent, but each of them most clearly a voice taken in relationship to other voices within, as well as in relationship to other selves without. In fact, in the *Mahābhārata* one would be hard pressed to find character development *outside* of dialogue.

However, there are also very clearly specified dialogues – intensified exchanges – throughout the *Mahābhārata*. Many of these exchanges are designated as *saṃvāda*, generally translated as dialogue, but they can also be named as *upadeśa*, *pradeśa*, and *anuvāda*. There are also moments in the text when these dialogues are simply indicated by a change in metrical form.[9] In many cases, the characters involved encounter each other in a specific moment of intensity, where some particular issue at stake is discussed and resolved. In the *Mahābhārata* all selves are dialogical selves, but some are even more dialogical than others.[10]

And yet such intense dialogical structure within the *Mahābhārata* has not been viewed against the background of a theory of the dialogical self. And so we might turn to significant exchanges in the *Mahābhārata* with this lens in mind. Although there are many fruitful paths that the hermeneutic approach of the dialogical self in the *Mahābhārata* could follow, I have chosen two particular dialogues in which gender ideology plays a significant role, and I discuss the multiply constructed self in gendered terms. I have preferred dialogues in which two women talk about gender roles, among many other topics: the dialogue of Draupadī and Satyabhāmā in the *Āraṇyakaparvan* (3.222–4, with particular reference to 3.222.1–57), and the dialogue of Draupadī and Sudeṣṇā in the *Virāṭaparvan* (4.8). I choose these same-sex dialogues because of their particular take on gender ideology. In these dialogues, the appropriate conduct and roles *for* women are discussed and emphasized as much as, if not more than, the difference *between* men and women.

The dialogue between Draupadī and Satyabhāmā

This dialogue begins in the forest, during the Pāṇḍavas' exile, right after the sage Mārkaṇḍeya has told them the stories of Skanda's birth and demon-killing adventures. Satyabhāmā and Draupadī take a private seat inside, laughing because they have not seen each other in a long time. Satyabhāmā asks how Draupadī keeps the affection and obedience of her husbands, and suggests a variety of means, such as spells and sacrifices. Draupadī condemns the use of deceitful manipulations in marriage, and describes her own behaviour in relationship to her husbands, their retinue, and her mother-in-law. She describes her duties in their former kingdom, and its vast wealth. She emphasizes that her actions are truthful, and not a 'spell' of any kind. Satyabhāmā apologizes, and suggests that such joking questions, as hers were, are common among friends. Draupadī then gives a versified description of her actions. Satyabhāmā reassures Draupadī that her wounded pride will be avenged, and that her sons are happy and well cared for, and then departs with Kṛṣṇa.

An initial reading of this passage would easily reveal a single gender ideology: Draupadī happily speaks of servitude, of treating one's husband like a god – the classic *pativratā* devotion. As she puts it to Satyabhāmā early and often in their conversation, she serves her husbands without regard for her own likes and dislikes. Draupadī also speaks of her obedience; she never bathes nor eats nor sleeps until her husband has; she renounces what he renounces, eats and drinks what he does, and so on (3.222.23–4, 29–31). Later Draupadī declares that she never, in sleeping, eating, or talking, acts against the wishes of her Lord, and that she is always guided by her husbands (3.222.35–6).

In a sense, the rhetorical force – indeed, some might say sanctimoniousness – of such statements could overwhelm a subtler reading of Draupadī's words. When we look for a single gender ideology in a tradition, we tend to find it. Yet there are some very intriguing ideas in this dialogue which would not be brought to light by such a reading: Draupadī's awareness of the basic power dynamics between men and women, as well as her sense of her own power and agency within a given situation.[11] Indeed, Draupadī is constructing a dialogical self – a loosely connected set of voices in dialogical relation to each other.

Let us first look more closely at what exactly is at stake in this *saṃvāda.* The two women are not just concerned with wifely behaviour *per se*, but the question of control and deceit – indeed, one might say, agency itself. When Satyabhāmā asks her question, she is particularly interested in the Pāṇḍavas' inclination to do Draupadī's bidding. It is not simply that she wants to know how they are never angry (*na kupyanti*) but also why they obey her (*vaśagās tubhyaṃ*, 3.222.4). Satyabhāmā also uses the word 'obedient' again in verse 5 (*tava vaśyā hi satataṃ pāṇḍavāḥ. . .*). Her possible solutions to her own question are not unreasonable, and she gives us a long list of practices which, without the context of the dialogue, we would not be surprised to see in a *yoga* commentary, or even an Āgama or a Purāṇa. Satyabhāmā wonders about the practice of vows, or asceticism, or ablutions, or *mantra*s, or herbs, or some special knowledge of roots, or recitation, or fire-sacrifice, or drugs.[12] All of these are mentioned as efficacious means of action in the Vidhāna literature, and indeed, as auspicious forms of action. They are not spoken of as 'black magic' (*abhicāra*) of any kind. Nor is there any mention of an *ari* or *śatru* (enemy). And the *Mahābhārata* does not hold back from using this kind of terminology when necessary. Even Satyabhāmā calls the knowledge that she seeks *yaśasyam* (auspicious or glorious). So one can't really blame Satyabhāmā for asking a straightforward question about family harmony. However, when Draupadī replies (3.222.9), she says that Satyabhāmā is asking her about conduct that is *asat* – that does not have the quality of truth. And she, Draupadī, must reply in truth (*satye*). She comments that the path of *asat*, non-truthful conduct (*asadācarite*), is a difficult one to praise.

Draupadī goes on to say something which displays her knowledge of the 'balance of power' in any given relationship between a husband and a wife – an element she will refer to again and again in the dialogue. As she puts it, if a man knows that his wife has begun the practice of *mantra* recitation and the application of magical roots, then the husband fears her as if she is a poisonous serpent in the house (3.222.11).[13] And this state will lead to a permanent situation of unhappiness, for where will a man of fear find peace, and where will a man without peace find happiness?[14] Here Draupadī is arguing that in a world where the gender roles of a female involve deceit, that deceit will give power to the woman and incite fear in the man. And she goes on to speak of these acts as a form of injury, using verbs such as *upasṛjanti* (for misfortune or calamity, oppressive action) to describe this behaviour. Draupadī, then, fully acknowledges that a wife can create fear in and oppress her husband. Indeed, at one point (3.222.13–16) she argues that such actions can and do cause disease and death.

Intriguingly, Draupadī then goes on in the next verses to state the kinds of *pativratā* behaviour we are all familiar with: the renunciation of that which her husbands renounce, the daily offerings to the gods, ancestors, and guests, the restraint of anger and jealousy, and the observance of patience and humility. But in the context of her initial strong awareness of the power dynamics within any given relationship, we might read these verses rather differently. Even the 'quintessential statement' of a *pativratā* might be read with some subtlety. At 3.222.35 Draupadī states, 'The husband is a god, he is a path, and nothing else. What woman then would do injury?' (*sa devaḥ sā gatir nānyā tasya kā vipriyaṃ caret //*). Draupadī may not simply be articulating the norm here, as a simpler, univocal reading might suggest. Rather, she could be articulating the actual state of affairs: a woman has no other option in life, so why would she act against her own self-interest in this regard? Again, if we read Draupadī as a sophisticated, thoughtful character, capable of many different approaches and containing many different voices, then this realistic voice – one that is knowledgeable about power dynamics – would indeed be consistent with voices of Draupadī that we have seen earlier.

In addition, Draupadī shows an understanding of the other side of the power equation: just as a manipulative wife is like a snake in the house, so too Draupadī uses a comparable simile in describing her protectiveness towards her husbands. Her statement is quite an elegant *śloka* in its use of contrasting images: 'I serve my truthful, gentle husbands, who have the ethics and the *dharma* of truth, and watch over them as if they were poisonous angry snakes' (*mṛdūn sataḥ satyaśīlān satyadharmānupālinaḥ / āśīviṣān iva kruddhān patīn paricarāmy aham //* 3.222.34). The contrast between the traditional interpretation of the Pāṇḍavas as gentle lords of *dharma* in the first part of the *śloka*, and the second interpretation of them as volatile and toxic reptiles, is striking indeed. The contrast is elegant, and on the surface it serves to illustrate the depth of Draupadī's devotion. And yet we might also wonder about the force of *iva* here: is Draupadī speaking about the ludicrousness of the Pāṇḍavas' behaving in this manner, as a contrastive or ironic simile might suggest? Or is she hinting at the fact that the Pāṇḍavas *do* actually act this way from time to time? Certainly there are enough episodes in the epic to give us reason to believe that the Pāṇḍavas, especially Bhīma, may well be prone to such behaviours. Moreover, there is no reason to think that Draupadī would be using one snake simile in a non-ironic way in verse 3.222.11 (women who use deceitful means of controlling their husbands are like snakes in the house), and later, another snake simile in an ironic way (the Pāṇḍavas can act like poisonous volatile snakes). While it is not entirely clear which way one might read the text, one thing is indeed clear: Draupadī understands the power dynamics involved. She could have chosen a simile of gentle animals such as rabbits or gazelles to describe the gentle Pāṇḍavas who need to be guarded so zealously. Indeed, the compound *mṛduromakaḥ* – using the same word *mṛdu* (soft, gentle) – is a common epithet for a hare. And yet she did not. Instead she chose the opposite, as snakes imply danger and volatility from within a marriage as well as from without.

Draupadī shows another significant awareness of power dynamics in terms of her relations with other women. First we might take note of the fact – often glossed over – that Draupadī must serve the Pāṇḍavas' other wives. At 3.222.18 Draupadī states, 'I always serve the Pāṇḍavas with devotion, along with their wives' (*sadārān pāṇḍavān nityaṃ prayatopacarāmy aham //*). The compound *sadārān* is a common one to denote an entire household retinue that includes many wives.

And yet there is an even more significant dynamic that she is aware of – the forceful presence of Kuntī. Draupadī declares to Satyabhāmā in verse 3.222.38: 'I always wait upon the worthy mother of heroes, truth-telling Kuntī' (*nityam āryām ahaṃ kuntīṃ vīrasūṃ satyavādinīm / . . . paricarāmy. . .*). In addition to serving Kuntī, Draupadī never claims superiority over her in matters of food and dress, nor does she speak ill of that Pṛthā (Kuntī) who is equal to the earth itself.[15] Here Draupadī again shows awareness of the need for acknowledging a power balance between two members of a household. Notice that she doesn't simply speak of serving, or being subservient to, or honouring. She also states the negative possibility – that she could upstage or reprove her mother-in-law, but chooses not to. We see the same pattern of speech a little earlier, at 3.222.36, when she declares that, always guided by her husbands, she never speaks ill of her mother-in-law.[16] Most intriguingly here, Draupadī suggests indirectly that her husbands' gentle speech about their mother inspires her, but once again the subtle implication is also that their guidance is necessary, and she might not necessarily be so inclined if she were left to her own devices. In these subtle ways, then, and particularly by stating the negative possibility that she avoids, Draupadī shows an awareness of a domestic power balance.

Finally, Draupadī shows keen understanding of where her actual power does lie. She describes her former activities in the palace of Yudhiṣṭhira, before the banishment into the forest. Here Draupadī becomes very particular about numbers: she has served eight thousand brahmins, eighty-eight thousand *snātaka*s, and ten thousand *yati*s, all eating their meals on plates of gold and each with a retinue of serving maids. The king himself, Draupadī reminds Satyabhāmā, had one hundred thousand serving maids and one hundred thousand horses and elephants (3.222.40–8). After she has enumerated all of these in Puranic fashion, she sums up the retinue and her responsibility for it in the following manner: 'It was I who watched over the regulation and the number [of chores] among them, and I who listened to them' (*yeṣāṃ saṃkhyāvidhiṃ caiva pradiśāmi śṛṇomi ca //* 3.222.49). Draupadī goes on to note in verse 3.222.50 that she alone knew the activities of the maids and the cowherds. And finally, in verse 51, she makes an ultimate power statement: 'Among the renowned Pāṇḍavas I alone, good lady, knew the incomes and expenses of the king's revenues' (*sarvaṃ rājñaḥ samudayam āyaṃ* *ca vyayam eva ca / ekāhaṃ vedmi kalyāṇi pāṇḍavānāṃ yaśasvinām //*). Moreover, she alone supervised the treasury, which was inexhaustible like the hoards of Varuṇa.[17] Here is the true power of Draupadī: her supervision of household affairs and her singlehanded financial mastery over the treasuries of the palace.

Such language of mastery (phrases such as *ekāhaṃ vedmi*) is not the only language that indicates Draupadī's awareness of her own power. At two points in her reply to Satyabhāmā she actually speaks of her husbands' obedience to her. Right after her use of the snake simile where she speaks of her guardianship of her husbands, Draupadī declares to Satyabhāmā: 'O blessed lady, through constant care, continuous exertion and submission to (my) teachers, my husbands have become obedient' (*avadhānena subhage nityotthānatayaiva ca / bhartāro vaśagā mahyaṃ guruśuśrūṣaṇena ca //* 3.222.37). The same sentiment is echoed at 3.222.56, when Draupadī sums up her long statement of her strength in the palace, their former place of residence, with how she uses this kind of model behaviour as her only charm (*saṃvananam*) to make her husbands obedient to her. In other words, obedient dutifulness begets obedience. In both passages the question of submission is understood as 'two way' in nature.

With this theoretical lens, then – the idea of a polyphonic 'voice' which builds a single character – we can read Draupadī's speech in a new way: these are not simply the monochrome statements of a *pativratā*, but rather, various voices of Draupadī which alternate between fierceness and meekness, savvy and servitude, authority and submission. She is both the one who does not spend too much time in the privy, who does not laugh except at a jest (3.222.25–30), and the one who guards her husbands, oversees crores of personnel, and alone knows the amounts in the treasury. Indeed, in the various roles she assumes, we are tempted to think of Draupadī as the *ādi*-superwoman.

Most important for our analysis, though, is the fact that Draupadī does take on roles of strength and authority with clear knowledge of the particular power dynamics of a palace household. We learn from her something that most feminist analyses might not suggest: being a *pativratā* is a two-way street. And in the eyes of theorists of 'the dialogical self' such as Hermans and Kempen, this is exactly what the construction of a dialogical self might look like. There is a polyphonic voice and a set of multifaceted roles which make it impossible to think of a single woman's voice embracing a single gender ideology. The *Mahābhārata* does not speak with a single voice when it comes to 'women' or even 'gender ideology'. Moreover, it is clear that Draupadī's speech lends support to Butler's idea of gender as performative: when Satyabhāmā asks about instruments to make husbands obedient, Draupadī answers by narrating of a series of acts. By answering in this way, Draupadī emerges as a 'culturally intelligible subject' within a rule-bound discourse – a discourse which is polyphonic in nature.

Draupadī as Sairandhrī

For further ideas on this topic let us turn to another, somewhat smaller example – again a conversation between two women. At the beginning of the *Virāṭaparvan*, the Pāṇḍavas are thinking of how best to enter the kingdom of Virāṭa, and how to design their disguises.[18] Draupadī decides to pose as a *sairandhrī*, a chambermaid, who is willing to do work for whoever will take her. When they have entered the royal court, Draupadī, in her disguise, has a dialogue with Sudeṣṇā, the chief wife and queen of Virāṭa. Again we see multiple voices at play in building a character, but here this takes place at a more intense level than in the earlier dialogue with Satyabhāmā.

Vaiśaṃpāyana begins narrating the story in *anuṣṭubh* verse. After the Pāṇḍavas have chosen their disguises and hidden their weapons in an old, distant tree near the cremation grounds, they enter the kingdom. Here Vaiśaṃpāyana switches into *triṣṭubh* verse. Yudhiṣṭhira puts on his glorious cloak, and when King Virāṭa sees him he asks his court who this could possibly be. There is then a *saṃvāda* between the king and Yudhiṣṭhira, who is asked to explain truthfully who he is and what his purposes are. Yudhiṣṭhira expounds his identity as a great brahmin who has lost all his wealth – a wise counsellor, a formidable gambler, once in the service of Yudhiṣṭhira himself (4.6).

The same occurs for Bhīma: Vaiśaṃpāyana narrates the warrior's arrival, and the dialogue between Bhīma and the king ensues. Only this time, Virāṭa is more incredulous than he was with Yudhiṣṭhira. He says, 'Pride giver, I cannot believe you are a cook, for you mirror the god of a thousand eyes'[19] (*na sūdatāṃ mānada śraddadhāmi te sahasranetrapratimo hi dṛśyase* / 4.7.6). Bhīma informs the king that he is especially good at sauces beloved long ago by Yudhiṣṭhira. We see the same pattern in the cases of Sahadeva, disguised as a cowherd (4.9), Arjuna, as a transvestite and maid versed in all the feminine arts (4.10), and Nakula, disguised as a horse groom (4.11).

Intriguingly, these *saṃvāda*s of persuasion are all presented in *triṣṭubh* verse. The only negotiation that is not in *triṣṭubh* is the one between Sudeṣṇā and Draupadī, which occurs at 4.8, between Bhīma's arrival and Sahadeva's. One wonders at the reason for the change in metre – perhaps it is because Draupadī does not want to engage fully in a dialogue given her circumstances. We see a similar pattern at 4.13.1–21. Here Kīcaka approaches her in *triṣṭubh*, and she responds in *anuṣṭubh*, until the very end of her response, where in her most emotional spurning of his advances, she breaks into *triṣṭubh*. It is on the *anuṣṭubh saṃvāda* between Draupadī and Sudeṣṇā that we will now focus.

Draupadī begins by dressing herself as a maid, concealing her hair, and wearing expensive yet dirty clothes. Townspeople query her, and she tells them that she seeks anyone who will hire her (4.8.1–4). Sudeṣṇā, the chief queen of Virāṭa, sees her from her terrace, and, impressed by her beauty and her forlorn state, asks her who she is. Draupadī replies as she has previously (4.8.6–8). But Sudeṣṇā asserts that she is too beautiful to be a chambermaid and that, if anything, she is the mistress of servants both male and female. Her physical appearance, comments Sudeṣṇā, is what gives her away: among many other physical attributes, Draupadī's heels are not overly large, her palms, soles, bust and hips are well developed, her speech is sweet, her words are solemn, and her intelligence is great. In fact, in all of her attributes, thinks Sudeṣṇā, Draupadī is more like the goddess Śrī. Might she be a *yakṣī*, or a *gandharvī*, or even a goddess herself (4.8.9–14)?

Here we see a compelling way in which status and gender combine to betray any attempt at disguise; the 'signs' of Draupadī's high station in life are simply too numerous for her to fool anyone at first glance. Indeed, Sudeṣṇā speaks to her in part as a lover would to praise a beloved's attributes – but Draupadī seems to be a lover who would exist in the heavens, rather than on earth. She must be divine or at least semi-divine. Thus it is impossible at the very beginning of this dialogue to avoid the polyphonic voices of social status and gender.

Moreover, Sudeṣṇā observes, Draupadī can oversee servants of *both* genders – a theme we have seen earlier in her description of her overseeing Yudhiṣṭhira's palace. The text is very careful to mention both male and female servants in the Draupadī–Satyabhāmā dialogue (3.222.50) as well as in this one in the *Virāṭaparvan* (4.8.9). The earlier dialogue indicates Draupadī's authority over both male and female genders; this one indicates her attractiveness to both genders.

Draupadī tries to reassure Sudeṣṇā that she is neither divine nor royal, and then provides an assertion of her appropriate class as a *sairandhrī*. She then goes on to describe the various labours of a chambermaid – the dressing of hair, the pounding of cosmetics, the making of garlands. In a delightful play of identities, Draupadī asserts that she has served both Draupadī and Satyabhāmā.[20] She earned good food from Draupadī, and was given the name Mālinī, 'garland girl'. But she also wanders about alone, looking for work – hence her presence in the Virāṭa kingdom.[21]

Sudeṣṇā replies that Draupadī, as Sairandhrī, will make her husband swoon over her. To justify this assertion, she points out that women are looking at her, attracted by her beauty. No male person will be able to resist her attractiveness either.[22] So too the king will surely leave Sudeṣṇā once he sees Draupadī, and turn to her with his whole heart.[23] Here Sudeṣṇā utilizes a lovely metaphor for her own predicament in taking Draupadī in: 'Just as a crab conceives an embryo which is her own death, so I think the same of giving you shelter, O Sweet-Smiling One' (*yathā karkaṭakī garbham ādhatte mṛtyum ātmanaḥ / tathāvidham ahaṃ manye vāsaṃ tava śucismite //* 4.8.26).[24]

Here there is a multiplicity of roles. Sudeṣṇā herself is clearly attracted to Draupadī, and wants to take her in for her own sake. But at the same time, she is aware of Draupadī's potential attractions for the king, and states them outright. Sudeṣṇā is patron, friend, and rival, all in one single relationship. Notice here that for Sudeṣṇā it is not simply a matter of rivalry – frequently classed as 'co-wifery' (*sapatnī*) in epic and other early texts – or of blind friendship, but something much subtler and more multi-layered.

Draupadī replies to Sudeṣṇā very clearly and stridently that no man will touch her, and that her five husbands are *gandharva*s, sons of a powerful *gandharva* king, who will always protect her.[25] Most importantly, and perhaps most reassuringly for Sudeṣṇā, Draupadī explains that anyone who attempts to take her as one might a common woman will meet with their death that very night.[26] Draupadī's *gandharva*s are always engaged in a form of secret protection.

Draupadī's use of the image of the *gandharva*s is doubly meaningful here. First, we might note that in the earlier dialogue Draupadī mentions marriage to a *gandharva* in the context of those *asat* (deceitful) marriages which she decries to Satyabhāmā. As she puts it there, Draupadī's heart belongs to her husbands, not to any other god, mortal, or *gandharva* (3.222.22). Thus it is both fitting and somewhat ironic that, from within her disguise, she refers now to her five husbands as *gandharvas*.[27] Even though Draupadī's own sense of loyalty to her husbands would prohibit such extra marriages to *gandharva*s, deceit is the name of the game in the Virāṭa kingdom. Thus, in that context, her choosing to have *gandharva* husbands is appropriate. And, while marriage to a *gandharva* is explicitly understood as a *lack* of protection and safety between husband and wife in the earlier dialogue,[28] here it is indeed the best protection possible to guard against the (albeit friendly) jealousy of Sudeṣṇā and the potential sexual advances of Virāṭa.

Both Draupadī and Sudeṣṇā prove to be right in their forebodings. Draupadī's discomfort after Kīcaka's lewd advances is, of course, part of the motivation for the killing of Kīcaka (4.13–23), an episode which both oddly echoes the previous gambling scene and foreshadows the war to come.[29] Yet the important point for us here is that both women express these forebodings in multiple voices, exploring multiple roles. Draupadī is at once temptress and chaste woman, chambermaid and goddess. Sudeṣṇā is at once protectress of the forlorn itinerant, sexual rival, and friend. And all of these very gendered roles are explicitly explored and discussed within the dialogue itself, through the use of imagery and clever repartee that allows the subtleties of the situation to emerge.

* * *

We have seen, then, two powerful instances of the multiplicity of gender roles within a single conversation (*saṃvāda*). I can only gesture here towards the possibility of exploring multiple gender roles, and the development of a dialogical self, in other famous *saṃvāda*s in the epic. We might think of Agastya and Lopāmudrā, who alternately switch back and forth between the appropriateness of asceticism and householder life for both men and women, and who are in a multi-layered battle for the well-being of Agastya's ancestors (3.94–7). We might also explore the dialogue of Sulabhā and Janaka (12.308), where the appropriateness of gender behaviour is explored in a wide variety of contexts: the roles of *yogin*s; the conduct of kings, queens, and their courts; the influence of *gotra*s; the teachings of various philosophical schools; the possibility of meditative union; the relationship between meditative union and sexual union.

This brief study suggests, then, that gender ideology is a multi-layered issue, even in the epic's poetics of *dharma*. In their understandings of male and female roles these dialogues about gender are as complexly constructed as anything that Judith Butler might propose for our consideration. And this complexity comes about precisely through dialogue – not narrative summary, not paraphrase. If dialogical selves are the new models for thinking about gendered selfhood in the Euro-American academic tradition, we might do well to turn back to that master of dialogues, the *Mahābhārata*, for some sophisticated tutelage on the subject.

Notes

1 The issue of multiple voices has been aptly raised by James Fitzgerald (2003); see also A.K. Ramanujan (1989) on the subtlety and multiplicity of *dharma*.

2 For a longer discussion of this idea, and related references on the treatment of the 'women's issue' in the singular, see Patton 2002a. For a discussion of this issue particularly in relation to the epic, I look forward to Arti Dhand's *Woman as Fire, Woman as Sage: sexual ideology in the Mahābhārata* (in press); see also Dhand 2002; 2004.

3 See, among many others, Ramanujan 1991; Minkowski 1989; Reich 1998; and Hiltebeitel 2001a, esp. pp. 93–129. Emily Hudson's dissertation (2006) also argues for the ontological and aesthetic as well as the literary value of the 'frame' structure of the epic; see also Chapter 2.

4 When I teach the *Mahābhārata*, I have often noted that Irawati Karve's *Yuganta* (1969) is a favourite reference work amongst students. I believe this is because Karve very clearly begins from a perspective of the personal experience of each of the characters treated. Moreover, she assumes that such experience is multifaceted.

5 See in particular Hermans, Kempen and van Loon 1992; Scott 2001.

6 See also Hermans, Kempen and van Loon 1992; Hermans, Rijks and Kempen 1993; Barresi 2002.

7 See also Bakhtin 1973; 1990; Todorov 1988.

8 See for example Moya 1996; Bhatt 2002.

9 We have several examples of such a switch in metre in the passages describing each of the Pāṇḍavas' entry into the Virāṭa kingdom (see, for example, the dialogue between Virāṭa and Yudhiṣṭhira at 4.6.1–16; and the dialogue between Virāṭa and Bhīma at 4.7.1–11). It should be noted that the narrator, Vaiśaṃpāyana, also briefly switches metre in introducing his narration, in addition to representing the voices of the interlocutors.

10 I am grateful to Jim Fitzgerald and Angelika Malinar for their comments on the idea of *saṃvāda* here (*Epic Constructions* conference, SOAS, London, 8 July

2005). Although it is tempting to see 'identity' at stake for each of the dialogues, it may be better described as a salient but not universal characteristic.

11 For recent discussions of women's agency in early India, see, among many others, H.-P. Schmidt 1987; Leslie 1991; Porter and Teich 1994; Jamison 1996; Leslie and McGee 2000; McGee 2002; Findly 2002; Patton 2002b; Jamison 2002; Patton 2004.

12 *vratacaryā tapo vāpi snānamantrauṣadhāni vā / vidyāvīryaṃ mūlavīryaṃ japahomas tathāgadāḥ //* 3.222.6.

13 *udvijeta tadaivāsyāḥ sarpād veśmagatād iva //*

14 *udvignasya kutaḥ śāntir aśāntasya kutaḥ sukham /* 3.222.12.

15 *naitām atiśaye jātu vastrabhūṣaṇabhojanaiḥ / nāpi parivade cāhaṃ tāṃ pṛthāṃ pṛthivīsamām //* 3.222.39.

16 *nāpi parivade śvaśrūṃ sarvadā pariyantritā //*

17 *adhṛṣyaṃ varuṇasyeva nidhipūrṇam ivodadhim / ekāhaṃ vedmi kośaṃ vai patīnāṃ dharmacāriṇām //* 3.222.54.

18 According to the terms agreed at the dice match, the Pāṇḍavas and Draupadī must spend the final year of their exile in society but in disguise.

19 Here I am following van Buitenen's translation.

20 *ārādhayaṃ satyabhāmāṃ kṛṣṇasya mahiṣīṃ priyām / kṛṣṇāṃ ca bhāryāṃ pāṇḍūnāṃ kurūṇām ekasundarīm //* 4.8.17.

21 *tatra tatra carāmy evaṃ labhamānā suśobhanam / vāsāṃsi yāvac ca labhe tāvat tāvad rame tathā // mālinīty eva me nāma svayaṃ devī cakāra sā /* 4.8.18–19.

22 *striyo rājakule paśya yāś cemā mama veśmani / prasaktās tvāṃ nirīkṣante pumāṃsaṃ kaṃ na mohayeḥ //* 4.8.21.

23 *rājā virāṭaḥ suśroṇi dṛṣṭvā vapur amānuṣam / vihāya māṃ varārohe tvāṃ gacchet sarvacetasā //* 4.8.23.

24 On this simile van Buitenen has commented: 'I find no folklore on the belief that the crab dies in giving birth' (1978: 534).

25 *nāsmi labhyā virāṭena na cānyena kathaṃ cana / gandharvāḥ patayo mahyaṃ yuvānaḥ pañca bhāmini // putrā gandharvarājasya mahāsattvasya kasya cit / rakṣanti te ca māṃ nityaṃ duḥkhācārā tathā nv aham //* 4.8.27–8.

26 *yo hi māṃ puruṣo gṛdhyed yathānyāḥ prākṛtastriyaḥ / tām eva sa tato rātriṃ praviśed aparāṃ tanum //* 4.8.30.

27 Marriage to a *gandharva* should not be confused with the so-called '*gandharva* marriage', in which two (human) lovers choose and marry each other independent of parental involvement or permission (see Chapter 8). However, in light of the facts here – that Draupadī seems to be personally attracted to the Pāṇḍavas, and Sairandhrī to her *gandharva* husbands – some kind of *double entendre* is no doubt intended.

28 Draupadī there compares the Pāṇḍavas to the sun, fire, and the moon, emphasizing that they are great, fierce, and fiery chariot-warriors who can kill just by looking (3.222.21). It is in light of the Pāṇḍavas' consequent ability to protect her that she says in the next verse that no other husband would do, not even a god or *gandharva*.

29 In fact, after Kīcaka falls the Kauravas, seeing an opportunity for engagement, propose a raid. In the ensuing mock battle we have the occasion for another *saṃvāda*, introduced by Vaiśaṃpāyana and involving Arjuna and Uttara.

6

AMONG FRIENDS

Marriage, women, and some little birds

Alf Hiltebeitel

> Draupadi, the heroic princess of the Hindu epic of Mahabharata is the epitome of feminism and feminity [*sic*]. Through out history Draupadi has remained an enigmatic woman of substance. Fragile, with a granite will, compassionate yet volcanic enough to reduce her enemies to ashes. Draupadi alone enjoyed the unique relationship of *sakhi* (female-friend) with her *sakha* (male-friend) Krishna. Krishna's divine presence was constant in her life, whenever life's obstacles seemed insurmountable, there was Krishna gently guiding her.

These words, 'compiled by: Anu Simlote' for a rendition of 'Draupadi' by Hema Malini in Washington DC on 25 September 2004, comprise the opening paragraph of a two-page account of the themes and episodes to be developed in a 'fusion stage' performance in which the famous danseuse plays the part of Draupadī supported by a well-choreographed troupe, with intervals for cinematic soliloquies in which Draupadī meditates on the quandaries she faces. I found Anu Simlote's description interesting for its opening insistence that Draupadī, as 'the epitome' of feminism and femininity, has 'remained an enigmatic woman of substance', for it reminded me of a passage I highlighted in my book, *Rethinking the Mahābhārata*: '*bṛhatī śyāmā buddhisattvaguṇānvitā* / *draupadī*' (17.3.36) – a description whose philosophical import I will return to in closing, but which we might, given this opening, retranslate for the moment (and with an eye to further consideration) as 'Draupadī, the great enigma endowed with intellectual substance'.[1] I also found it interesting that before this playbill goes into anything specific about her story, it invokes the 'unique' *sakhī–sakhā* friendship of Draupadī and Kṛṣṇa.[2] The 'uniqueness' of Draupadī and Kṛṣṇa's *sakhī–sakhā* relationship is well noted, and has important moments in the Sanskrit epic that I will also come to. But first, some differences between this performance and the classical text are also noteworthy.

Subtales and soliloquies

On the fusion stage, Draupadī turns to Kṛṣṇa far more frequently than she does in the Sanskrit epic – and notably in her soliloquies. For instance, as regards the ticklish subject of her polyandry, Draupadī gets marital advice from Kṛṣṇa in soliloquized dialogues, whereas in the Sanskrit epic the only marital counsel on this matter is given not to her by Kṛṣṇa but to her father by Vyāsa and to her husbands by Nārada. First, Vyāsa tells Drupada the divine secret that makes his daughter's polyandry legal – that Draupadī is Śrī incarnate and the Pāṇḍavas five former Indras to whom she had already been serially wed (in the *Pañcendra-Upākhyāna* or 'Subtale of the Five Indras', 1.189); second, Nārada tells the Pāṇḍavas how and why they must regulate this marriage – by taking yearly turns with Draupadī to avoid such rivalries over a woman as led to the mutual destruction of the demon brothers Sunda and Upasunda (in the *Sunda-Upasunda-Upākhyāna*, 1.201–4). Instructively, this information is conveyed not through soliloquies but through two *upākhyānas* or 'subtales' – in these two early cases, ones that Draupadī does not herself hear.

I would like to build on my recent research on the *Mahābhārata*'s subtales or *upākhyānas* (Hiltebeitel 2005a) to explore further how subtales are worked into the epic's textual weave, particularly in the ways they set off differences in the portrayal of male and female characters.[3] The *Mahābhārata* has sixty-seven *upākhyānas*, or sixty-eight if one adds the story of Śvetadvīpa ('White Island'), which the *Nārāyaṇīya* seems to call the essence of them all:

> Of those hundreds of other virtuous subtales (*anyāni . . . upākhyānaśatāni . . . dharmyāṇi*) that are heard from me, king, this is raised up as their essence (*sāro*); just as nectar was raised up by the gods and demons, having churned (the ocean), even so this nectar of story (*kathāmṛtam*) was formerly raised up by the sages.
>
> (12.326.114–15)

The full sixty-seven includes sixty called *upākhyānas* in the colophons and/or running heads for units in the Critical Edition; six more (including the aforementioned *Pañcendra-* and *Sunda-Upasunda-Upākhyānas*) are named in the epic's table of contents – the *Parvasaṃgraha*,[4] and one (the *Indra-Namuci-Upākhyāna*, 9.42) is mentioned additionally only in passing in the text (at 9.42.28a).[5] In treating this sample, it should be clear, as the *Nārāyaṇīya* passage suggests by mentioning *upākhyānas* in the hundreds, that it would not be a boundaried group without overlap with other 'ancillary story' material (see Gombach 2000).

Most notably, some narratively well-developed 'tales' (*ākhyānas*), 'dialogues' (*saṃvādas*), 'adventures' (*caritas*), and 'birth/origin stories' (*utpattis*) such as the 'Birth of Skanda' (*Skanda-Utpatti*), the 'Birth of Śuka' (*Śuka-Utpatti*), and the 'Origins of the Sword' (*Khaḍga-Utpatti*, 12.160) and 'Origins of the Daṇḍa' (*Daṇḍa-Utpatti*, 12.122) could and should be grouped with the *upākhyāna*s. Indeed, the colophons often reveal overlap in titling these narratives, as with the *Kapota-Upākhyāna* or 'Pigeon Subtale' (12.141–5), discussed briefly below, which Stephanie Jamison refers to as the *Kapota-Lubdhaka-Saṃvāda* or 'The Dialogue of the Pigeon and the Fowler' (1996: 163).[6]

In probing the main story through the subtales, let us note that the *upākhyāna*s in their 'hundreds' are said to be *dharmyāṇi* – 'virtuous', that is, 'concerned with *dharma*'. In thinking through the relation between the main story and the *upākhyāna*s and the way they construct gender together as it has to do with *dharma*, I believe it is fruitful to invoke Masaji Chiba's 'three-level structure of law' (Chiba 1986: 5–7), and Werner Menski's opening of Chiba's approach to a treatment of 'Hindu Law' (Menski 2005: 71 and *passim*), as involving official law, unofficial law, and basic legal postulates. Although the *Mahābhārata* skirts posing as a vehicle of official law like the Dharmasūtras and Dharmaśāstras, it often invokes such official law in the main story, as, for example, when Bhīṣma enumerates the eight modes of marriage before abducting the Kāśi princesses (1.96.8–11),[7] when Kṛṣṇa (5.138.1–9) and Kuntī (5.142.25)[8] tell Karṇa he is 'legally' a son of Pāṇḍu, and fairly regularly during the *Rājadharmaparvan*. In contrast, I would suggest that the *upākhyāna*s are more often vehicles of unofficial or informal law, posed for the heroes and heroines of the main story to ponder grey areas as they set *dharma* as their lodestar. Meanwhile, basic postulates,[9] like, for instance, the indissolubility of marriage, are often unstated and implicit values by which we can read back and forth between these two types of interwoven narrative. Here I will take the sixty-seven *upākhyāna*s and the reverberations between them only as an extendable base set from which to probe gender construction in the epic's main story, principally as it concerns (or might concern) Draupadī.

First, there are differences – at least in degree – in the ways male and female characters are drawn into the story from prior existences. Generally, this can occur in two ways: prior divine and demonic identities and the *karma* of previous human lives. While there are many males with prior divine/demonic identities in the *Mahābhārata*, there are few females with them, and Draupadī as the incarnation of Śrī is the only one of any significance.[10] As far as I am aware, incarnations tend to occur mainly in the main story as part of the *aṃśāvatāraṇa* or 'partial descent' of gods, demons, and other supernaturals, and do not figure among characters developed in the *upākhyāna*s. The revelation that Draupadī is an incarnation of Śrī, amplified in the *Pañcendra-Upākhyāna*, is thus doubly exceptional.

On the other hand, main characters in the Sanskrit epics have little karmic depth from previous human lives, such as there is, for instance, in several *upākhyānas*,[11] in the Buddhist Jātakas and many other Buddhist stories, and in the Tamil epics influenced by Buddhism and Jainism. Nonetheless, it is a trait especially of women characters[12] to exclaim that the sins they committed in previous lives must have been considerable to have brought them to their present impasse, as if their present life must have emerged out of some personal karmic morass that they are now unaccountably accounting for. I have so far found five such instances, two of which are spoken by Gāndhārī. Blindfolded yet seeing the corpse-strewn battlefield with the divine eye given her by Vyāsa, she says to Kṛṣṇa:

> Obviously I did evil in earlier births, Keśava, since I behold my sons, grandsons, and brothers killed.
>
> (11.16.59, tr. Fitzgerald)[13]

And again, speaking not only of herself but also of her daughters-in-law:

> O you who are blameless, I guess the evil these women beyond criticism did in past lives – and I as well, so dim-witted am I – must not have been small. The King of Law [Yama] now repays us, Janārdana, O Vṛṣṇi, there is no erasing either good or bad deeds.
>
> (11.18.11–12, tr. Fitzgerald)[14]

But the other three occur in *upākhyāna*s. In the *Śakuntalā-Upākhyāna* (1.62–9) – the very first *upākhyāna* in the Northern Recension and the second in the Southern Recension (where it swaps first and second positions with the *Yayāti-Upākhyāna*) – Śakuntalā presses her case that King Duḥṣanta has sired the son she has brought before him to his royal court, and asks him just before he tells her all women are liars:

> What evil deeds have I done before in another life that in my childhood I was abandoned by my kin, and now by you?
>
> (1.68.70, tr. van Buitenen)[15]

In the *Vyuṣitāśva-Upākhyāna* (1.112), the only *upākhyāna* spoken by a woman, Kuntī tells Pāṇḍu how Bhadrā Kākṣīvatī addressed the corpse of her husband King Vyuṣitāśva, who had just died of 'consumption' from their sexual overindulgence:

> Surely, in previous bodies, my prince, I must have sundered faithful companions or separated those that were united! The misery that I have piled up with evil deeds in previous bodies has now come upon me in my separation from you.
>
> (1.112.25–26, tr. van Buitenen)[16]

– all this said before Vyuṣitāśva's voice announces that he can still impregnate her on certain days that lie ahead, from which she will have seven sons (all as quoted by Kuntī, preparing the impotent Pāṇḍu for her revelation that she could still bear him sons, which results in Pāṇḍu's choosing Dharma to sire his first son, Yudhiṣṭhira, and so on).

And finally in the *Ambā-Upākhyāna* (5.170–93), the estranged and embittered Ambā, preparing to seek a male reincarnation whereby she can avenge herself against Bhīṣma, tells the sympathetic hermit-sage Śaikhāvatya:

> I want to wander forth. I shall practice severe asceticism. Surely there must have been evil deeds that I foolishly committed in previous bodies, and this as surely is their fruit.
>
> (5.173.14–15, tr. van Buitenen)[17]

These passages express this anguished sentiment in varied and non-formulaic terms,[18] which suggests that it is more than a trope or a convention. I believe it finds its deepest analogue in the utterances of women about to become *satī*s who hold themselves at fault for their husbands' predeceasing them.[19]

I do not find a place in the Sanskrit *Mahābhārata* where Draupadī invokes her own or others' unknown past *karma* like this, although I recall her making such exclamations in Tamil Draupadī cult *terukkūttu* (street theatre) dramas.[20] But she is perhaps unique in the epic's main story in being not only the incarnation of a deity, but in having at least one known prior human life with antecedent *karma* that affects her in this one:[21] she was an overanxious maiden who pressed Śiva too insistently – five times – to grant her a husband, with the result that the god destined her to have five husbands. Vyāsa first tells this story to the Pāṇḍavas (1.157.6–13) to set them *en route* to Pāñcāla to attend Draupadī's *svayaṃvara* (the 'self-choice' ceremony where she will obtain a husband), and he repeats it to Drupada in the *Pañcendra-Upākhyāna*.[22] Thus even though the early *upākhyāna*s in Book 1 – and also the *Ambā-Upākhyāna* which Bhīṣma tells Duryodhana in Book 5 – are told out of Draupadī's earshot, they circumscribe what we know about her as the rare if not only woman whose *karma* from a previous life *is revealed* – again, in an *upākhyāna* whose importance is underscored by its being a double revelation from Vyāsa, the author.

What then of the *upākhyāna*s that Draupadī does hear? Let me interject a suggestive comment of Madeleine Biardeau's as to the primal scene of the epic's composition (see Hiltebeitel 2001a: 165).

> If it were necessary, I would imagine a father, a son, and a maternal uncle of the father or son working together, and, in a corner out of the way, just beyond voice range, a woman, wife of the father, mother of the son, and sister of the uncle.
>
> (Biardeau and Péterfalvi 1985: 27, my translation)

At first sight this silently listening woman would hardly remind us of Draupadī, who is certainly the most active woman in the epic not only in deeds but also in words. On the reputation of her being a lady *paṇḍitā* (learned scholar),[23] she makes long speeches when debating with Yudhiṣṭhira early in their time in the forest, demanding Kṛṣṇa's reassurances of revenge against the Kauravas, revealing wifely duties to Kṛṣṇa's wife Satyabhāmā, and deriding Yudhiṣṭhira's wish to renounce the kingdom after the war. But she is also certainly the epic's most frequently present silent listener (see Chapter 3). This speaking/listening contrast is illuminating with regard to the modern stage's use of cutaway soliloquies and the epic's use of cutaway subtales. In the Sanskrit epic, women characters, at least,[24] do not have soliloquies. But they do listen to subtales. Kuntī, for instance, must have listened to *upākhyāna*s to be able to tell one.[25] Indeed, all of the *upākhyāna*s would have been heard by such missing characters from Sörensen's *Index* (1963) as Mrs Janamejaya and Mrs Śaunaka and the other wives of the *ṛṣi*s of the Naimiṣa Forest (performers of *satra* sacrifices – at which both of the epic's frame story recitals occur – cannot come without their wives; Jamison 1996: 31; Hiltebeitel 2001a: 166). But clearly Draupadī is the main female auditor of subtales within the main story. Once the fine points of her polyandry are sanctioned by Vyāsa's and Nārada's subtales that are meant privately for male ears only in Book 1, and after she has been abused in the public 'men's hall' of Book 2, from the time she is with her husbands in the forest to the epic's last subtale at the end of the *Āśvamedhikaparvan*, Draupadī hears all forty-four *upākhyāna*s that her husbands hear, including three told by Kṛṣṇa early in Book 12. Indeed, as mentioned in previous chapters, Draupadī offers a vignette on a female's listening position to tell Yudhiṣṭhira an 'old story' (*itihāsaṃ purātanam*, 3.31.20b), first propounded by the god Bṛhaspati, that she heard as a child when a learned brahmin came to her father's house and spoke to her brothers while she listened in, doing errands and sitting on her father's lap (3.33.56–8). The story is featured in Draupadī's 'puppet speech' (Hiltebeitel 2001a: 214 n. 106, 269), in which she tells Yudhiṣṭhira that God (Īśvara) as the Placer (Dhātṛ) assembles and manipulates beings like a grand puppeteer. She thereby suggests something of her state of mind at the beginning of her years in exile, shortly after the trauma of her disrobing.

Most prominently, and, I would argue, setting the tone for all the *upākhyāna*s that the adult Draupadī hears, are three *upākhyāna*s in Book 3 that Biardeau calls 'mirror stories' (2002, vol. 1: 412–13): tales that mirror the listeners' – the Pāṇḍavas' and Draupadī's – current tribulations. These are the *Nala-Upākhyāna* (3.50–78), the love story about Nala and Damayantī told by the seer Bṛhadaśva while Arjuna is visiting Śiva and Indra and Draupadī misses her favourite husband; the *Rāma-Upākhyāna* (3.257–76), a '*Mahābhārata*-sensitive' version of the Rāma story (see Hiltebeitel in press) focused on Sītā's abduction and told to all five Pāṇḍavas and Draupadī by

Mārkaṇḍeya just after Draupadī's abduction by Jayadratha Saindhava; and the *Sāvitrī-Upākhyāna* (3.277–83), the story of a heroine who saved her husband from Yama, told also by Mārkaṇḍeya just after the *Rāma-Upākhyāna* when Yudhiṣṭhira asks, having already heard about Sītā, if there ever was a woman as devoted to her husband(s) as Draupadī. As the frames of these three mirror stories show, Yudhiṣṭhira is very much aware of Draupadī as listener.[26] So this implicit slighting of Sītā is rather curious, and could be Yudhiṣṭhira's way of affirming that, unlike the Sītā of the *Rāma-Upākhyāna*, to whom Rāma says, 'Whether you are innocent or guilty, Maithilī, I can no more enjoy you than an oblation that has been licked by a dog' (3.275.13), Draupadī's fidelity after her handling by Jayadratha goes without question, and need not be affirmed by the gods, as Sītā's has just been by a heavenly host including Brahmā, Vāyu, Agni, Varuṇa, and Bhagavat, whoever that is (3.275.17–34).[27] Indeed, when Jamison writes, 'The Brāhmaṇas and the Mahābhārata present a series of female types, both positive and negative, but the Adulterous Wife is not in this gallery of archetypes' (1996: 92), she would seem to have momentarily overlooked not only the innuendos of this scene but also the *Cirakāri-Upākhyāna* (12.258) and its tale of how Cirakārin took so long reflecting on his father Gautama's command to kill his mother Ahalyā for her adultery with Indra that finally Gautama changed his mind.[28] Moreover, this story, which Draupadī hears with her husbands in the *Mokṣadharmaparvan* of Book 12, The Book of the Peace, seems to offer a peaceful resolution to a case of *real adultery* as an advance beyond the violent response to a woman's mere *thought of adultery* in the *Kārtavīrya-* (or *Jāmadagnya-*) *Upākhyāna* (3.115–17) in the pre-war Book 3, in which Rāma Jāmadagnya beheads his mother Reṇukā at the command of his father Jamadagni.

This brings me to a point I would now like to open up on a bit: while Draupadī endures virtually every imaginable strain on her marriage to five men in the *Mahābhārata*'s main story, and yet remains unquestionably faithful to them, she hears *upākhyāna*s that probe 'fringe' matters bearing on female sexuality – mainly in response to questions asked by Yudhiṣṭhira. Indeed, she is there to hear Yudhiṣṭhira ask Bhīṣma, seemingly quite out of the blue, 'In the act of coition, who derives the greater pleasure – man or woman?' (13.12.1; Dandekar 1966: lix), whereby Yudhiṣṭhira gives his grandfather, the lifelong celibate, the opportunity to make his case that the luckier ones are women by telling the *Bhaṅgāśvana-Upākhyāna* (13.12). Or is Yudhiṣṭhira's question so out of the blue? With the turn from the *Mokṣadharmaparvan* of Book 12 to the *Dānadharmaparvan* of Book 13, he has just turned his mind from matters of ultimate liberation, which cannot be his if he is to rule as all require of him, to the householder life that he – and Draupadī, and his brothers – must accept for what lies ahead in the rest of their lives together. One could take this as a 'jolt of sexuality' like those centred on the wife that Jamison finds energizing the structures of brahmanic rituals[29] – and as a timely reminder to Draupadī of the pleasures Yudhiṣṭhira would like to think she once enjoyed and, who knows, could enjoy again.[30] Indeed, it is just a short time later, when Bhīṣma has completed his main run of Book 13 *upākhyāna*s, that Draupadī jolts us with the one confirmation (13.57.42–4) that she has been silently listening all along to Bhīṣma's battle-field oration by voicing her approval when – as Vaiśaṃpāyana reports – Yudhiṣṭhira finally says he 'no longer longed to dwell in a hermitage'.

Birds and friendship

Birds play in and out of numerous epic stories, as no one saw better than Julia Leslie, to whose memory I would like to dedicate this chapter.[31] Since I cannot detail all the *upākhyāna*s that bring birds to bear upon marital 'fringe matters', let me focus on little birds, and let it suffice to note two themes that run through a few *upākhyāna*s, and explore a few such matters from this double angle. The two themes are birds and friendship, and let us bear in mind that this combination has a well-known precedent in the relation of the two birds who nestle in the same tree (*dvā́ suparṇā́ sayújā sákhāyā samānáṃ vṛkṣáṃ pári ṣasvajāte*) in *Ṛgveda* 1.164.20 – a line that gets reinterpreted in a *bhakti* parable about the soul and the Lord in the *Muṇḍaka* and *Śvetāśvatara Upaniṣad*s, to which I will return. As Biardeau has emphasized, birds are *dvija*s, 'twice-borns', especially as implying brahmins, and thus *upākhyāna*s featuring birds can work out norms and implications of *dharma* especially as they bear on brahmins – although clearly some birds are more brahmin than others. Now there are a number of stories that treat the themes of birds and/or friendship while bringing into focus deeper 'fringe matters' of marriage and sexuality. One that weaves in these themes is the aforementioned *Kapota-Upākhyāna* (12.141–5), which, in Book 12, entertains the theme of implied *satī* when the female pigeon joins her overly hospitable husband on his funeral pyre.[32] Also interesting, though without a couple, is the *Śuka-Vāsava-Saṃvāda* (13.5), where the friendship is not between birds or humans, but a bird and a tree. Here a parrot, out of 'devotion (*bhakti*) to the tree' (*tasya bhaktyā vanaspateḥ*, 13.5.6), refuses to leave it withering from a poisoned arrow, and explains to Indra (in brahmin guise), who cannot believe that a bird could demonstrate such 'non-cruelty' (*ānṛśaṃsya*), that because it received the tree's protection, it stays out of devotion to non-cruelty, and because compassion (*anukrośa*) is the great *dharma* and perennial happiness of the respectable (*sadhūnām*) and 'always extends kindness' (*sadā prītiṃ prayacchati*, 13.5.23d) – with *prīti* implying 'in a friendly way'. Indra then revives the tree (Hiltebeitel 2001a: 213). Though not an *upākhyāna*, it comes in the series of them that runs from the end of Book 12 through the beginning of Book 13. But here I would like to give fuller attention to two *upākhyāna*s which, taken together, allow us to explore what *Mahābhārata* subtales have to say about *dharma* or Law as it bears upon a tension between implied marital indissolubility and 'irretrievable marital breakdown' – terms I use advisedly, since in India the latter is not, even today, considered a legal ground for divorce.[33]

First of these is the *Śārṅgaka-Upākhyāna* (1.220–5), a tale about seven Śārṅgaka birds told to the Pāṇḍavas' great-grandson Janamejaya by Vaiśaṃpāyana at the end of Book 1, where it is notched into the episode of the Burning of the Khāṇḍava Forest. It thus occurs in the epic well before one gathers, in Book 3, that Draupadī is a frequent listener to subtales; and since it is told three generations after her life, she would not be alive to hear it anyway. But there are still things that Mrs Janamejaya and Mrs Śaunaka might connect at this juncture with Draupadī, whose favourite husband Arjuna has just returned with a second wife, and who will lose her sons in a great conflagration.

The *ṛṣi* Mandapāla, 'Slow-to-protect',[34] having learned from the gods who sit around Dharmarāja (i.e. Yama)[35] that he cannot enjoy the fruits of his acts in heaven without fulfilling his obligation to beget sons (1.220.8–12), has the inspiration to fulfil this debt to his ancestors quickly by becoming a bird.

> So he became a Śārṅgaka bird and coupled with a female (*śārṅgikā*) named Jaritā. On her he begot four sons who were wise in the Veda (*brahmavādinaḥ*), deserted them on the spot (*tān apāsya sa tatraiva*), and ran after Lapitā.
>
> (1.220.16c–17)[36]

Now just as Agni is about to burn the Khāṇḍava Forest, the distraught Jaritā lovingly oversees the four's hatching. Mandapāla knows Agni's intention and lauds him with a Vedic-sounding hymn full of pralayic overtones by which he obtains the god's promise to spare the children, whose survival of this conflagration will in some manner – as Biardeau saw (1971–2: 141) – be reminiscent of the four Vedas.[37] But of course Jaritā and the children do not know of Mandapāla's intervention, since he is still flitting about the woods with Lapitā (1.220.20). Jaritā, now described for the first of three times as a *tapasvinī*,[38] a 'suffering woman' (used now and then for Draupadī, especially beginning with three usages describing her mistreatment in the gambling hall[39]), bewails her plight:

> Here this dreadful Fire is coming, burning the underbrush, setting the universe aglow (*jagat saṃdīpayan*),[40] and terrifyingly he increases my miseries. And these children of little wit (*śiśavo mandacetasaḥ*) pull at me – still without feathers or feet, yet the final recourse of our ancestors (*pūrveṣāṃ naḥ parāyaṇam*). Here is the Fire coming, terrifying, licking the trees.
>
> (1.221.3–4)

Two things to note here: Jaritā underestimates the wit of these precocious sons, and she is raising them for 'our ancestors'. Despite the haste with which she and the kids have been abandoned, the indissoluble union conferred by her marriage has bought her surprisingly quickly into her husband's ancestral program. Indeed, we now learn that his abrupt departure was not without words on this point. As Jaritā begins to ponder her options, and first among them is covering her children with her limbs and 'dying with' (*maraṇaṃ saha*) them,[41] she tells them that Mandapāla's parting words included the prediction that their second son Sārisṛkva would 'beget offspring, increasing the lineage of the ancestors' (*prajāyeta pitṝṇāṃ kulavardhanaḥ*, 1.221.8). Immediately the children also buy into the ancestral program, telling her:

> Cast off your love (*sneham utsṛjya*), and fly away to where there is no Fire (*havyavāṭ*). For when we have perished, you shall have other sons. But when you have died, the continuance of our line will be cut (*naḥ syāt kulasaṃtatiḥ*). Reflect on these two outcomes and do what is best for our family (*kṣamaṃ syād yat kulasya naḥ*) – the ultimate moment has arrived for you to do so, mother. Don't be misled by your love for us your sons (*snehaṃ kārṣīḥ suteṣu naḥ*) into destroying the family (*kulavināśāya*); for this deed of our father, who wishes for his worlds (*lokakāmasya naḥ pituḥ*), must not be in vain.
>
> (1.221.12–14)

To follow the children's use of the first person plural pronoun *naḥ* is to realize that their concern for their mother is not her love (*sneha*) for them, which she should disregard,[42] but the 'desire for worlds (*lokakāma*) of our father', which – they are already shrewd enough to know – provides 'what is *best* for our family' as well as ultimate 'safety' (*kṣema*, 1.222.16) for their mother through her status as a joint sacrificer in the ancestral rites. For as the little ones soon clarify further, Jaritā is beautiful and can win her husband back and have other 'beautiful sons' (1.222.4).[43] As for themselves, the four fledglings tell Jaritā they prefer a purifying death by fire to the uncertainties of being hidden in a rat hole, which is the best idea she has to offer; 'or, perchance, Fire will not burn us, and you shall come back to us again' (1.222.15). When she has flown off to a 'safe country (*deśaṃ*[44] *kṣemam*) devoid of fire' (1.222.16), the fledglings ask Agni to 'protect us young *ṛṣi*s' (*ṛṣīn asmān bālakān pālayasva*, 1.223.11c) by lauding him one by one themselves (1.223.7–19). Agni is gratified by their *stotra*, but has of course already promised their safety to Mandapāla, as he tells them (1.223.22ab); but since their laud is also weighty to him, he asks what else he can do for them, to which the little darlings' reply is, 'Burn these cats!' – which Agni does while continuing on his eating binge (1.223.20–5).

Whereupon the scene shifts to Mandapāla and Lapitā. Vaiśaṃpāyana leads off by telling that Mandapāla was anxious about his sons even though he had spoken to Agni. But this is just indirection by which we find direction:

> In his anxiety over his sons, he said to Lapitā, 'Why, my little sons are incapable of flying,[45] Lapitā! When the Fire spreads and the wind begins to blow hard, my sons will be unable to make their escape (*asamarthā vimokṣāya*). Why, their poor mother (*mātā teṣāṃ tapasvinī*) is unable to save them; she must be anguished when she sees no way of saving her sons. Why, suffering (*saṃtapyamānā*) for my sons, who are still incapable of either running or flying, she must be screeching and fluttering about! How is my son Jaritāri, how my Sārisṛkva, how Stambamitra, how Droṇa, and how that poor woman (*kathaṃ sā ca tapasvinī*)?'
>
> (1.224.2–6)

As we have noted, the *tapasvinī* theme is set in motion when Jaritā starts bewailing the onset of Agni. Now, suddenly, it occurs twice from the beak of Mandapāla, which is too much for Lapitā, who sees correctly that Mandapāla cannot really be worried about his sons, whom he knows Agni has agreed to protect, and zeroes in, 'as if jealously' (*sāsūyam iva*, 1.224.7d):

> You do not care at all for your sons! You yourself said they were *ṛṣi*s of splendour and power, and had nothing to fear from Fire. Also, before my very eyes[46] you commended them to the Fire, and the great-spirited god gave you his promise. The World Guardian won't ever tell a lie! And they are eloquent speakers. Your mind (*mānasam*)[47] is not on them. You are suffering (*paritapyase*) because you are thinking about only her, my rival (*mamāmitrīm*)! Your love for me is not firm as it once was for her. Surely, it is not right for a bird (*pakṣavatā*) [to be] loveless to a friend, [and] able to overlook [her] when he himself is somehow pained. Go to your Jaritā, for whose sake you suffer (*paritapyase*) so! I shall wander alone, as [befits having attached myself] to a bad man.[48]
>
> (1.224.8–13)

Here the theme of friendship among birds takes on a double meaning, since when Lapitā says it is 'not right for a *bird* to be loveless to a friend', *pakṣavat*, 'one possessing wings', can also be translated 'one who has two causes' (van Buitenen) or '[one] that hath two parties dividing his attention' (Ganguli 1.235, p. 453). Moreover, Lapitā's word for 'rival' is *amitrī*, 'enemy, adversary' – literally 'non-friend'. Mandapāla has brought a very human mess into his life as a bird, which he thought would be such a quick fix. But the point seems to be that he now realizes this and is deciding to do something about it: indeed, he is deciding to do 'the right thing'. When Lapitā twice tells him 'you suffer' (*paritapyase*) for Jaritā, she is matching his double reference to 'my poor wife' (*tapasvinī*). And that is where he is headed (1.224.14–16). Chagrined at the trouble his children are in, and realizing that the world despises a 'slow-witted' (*mandadhīḥ*) man who 'abandons the present (or past) for the sake of the future' (*bhūtaṃ hitvā bhaviṣye 'rthe*), he tells Lapitā, 'Do as you wish. For this blazing fire is licking the trees and brings a hateful malign sorrow to my heart (*dveṣyaṃ hi hṛdi saṃtāpaṃ janayaty aśivaṃ mama*)'.

Vaiśaṃpāyana now shifts to the site just left by Agni, to which Jaritā now dashes, 'screeching pitifully' (*rorūyamāṇā kṛpaṇā*), where she sees 'the most incredible sight' (*aśraddheyatamam . . . darśanam*) of her sons; she embraces them again and again and weeps (1.224.17–19).

> Then suddenly Mandapāla himself arrived there, Bhārata, and none of his sons welcomed him. Though he chattered at each of them time and again, and at Jaritā, they spoke not a word to the *ṛṣi*, good or bad.
>
> (1.224.20–1)

Not a word until he tells his sons, 'I made [you] over to the Oblation Eater, but from this I found no peace' (*kṛtavān asmi havyāśe naiva śāntim ito labhe* // 1.224.23). Mandapāla's hesitation and ambiguity are important here.[49] He is not quite making it explicit that he obtained Agni's promise to protect them, which he does not know that they now already know from Agni. But more importantly, he would not be willing to make it explicit because Jaritā, who does *not* yet know that he got Agni's protection for the children, would realize that he did not get Agni's protection *for her*. In any case, Mandapāla's 'From this I found no peace' finally gets the parents talking:

> Jaritā said, 'What does your eldest son matter to you, or the second one? What does the middlemost matter, or this poor youngest? You left me completely destitute and went your way. Go back to your tender sweet-smiling Lapitā!'
>
> (1.224.24–5)

This sour reception is enough for Mandapāla to put a bad twist on her response and a good twist on his own actions:

> Mandapāla said, 'Apart from another man, nothing in the world is so fatal (*bhavitavyam*) to women as rivalry with another wife (*sāpatnakam*)! For even the faithful and good Arundhatī, famous in all the worlds, distrusted Vasiṣṭha, the eminent *ṛṣi*. He was always completely pure-hearted and devoted to her happiness and well-being, yet she despised that hermit among the Seven Ṛṣis. Because of this

contempt she is now a tiny star like a red ember overlaid by smoke, not very lovely, sometimes visible sometimes not, which appears like a bad omen. You yourself obtained me to get offspring, and giving up what you wanted,[50] now that it has come to this pass, you become like her. A man should never put trust (*viśvāsaḥ*) [in the word] 'wife' (*bhāryeti*), for a wife who has sons does not look to her duty.'

(1.224.26–31)

Mandapāla thus passes off his relationship with Lapitā with a maxim about what is 'fatal' to women: another man, above all, but then rivalry among co-wives – even as it is *he* who, not 'fatally' at all, has had another woman, and one with whom it is not so clear that he was actually married. For as would be typical of brahmanical marriages, at least as they are viewed in post-Independence Indian courts, a public marriage to a first wife would be considered sacramentally 'irrevocable' through the 'seven-step' rite of *saptapadī*, which makes a wife a 'friend' (*sakhā*), whereas marriage to a second wife or concubine would not.[51] Moreover, more outrageously, Mandapāla's comparison of Jaritā to Arundhatī lets him get away with his implicit comparison of himself with the ever-faithful Vasiṣṭha. Indeed, he seems to have made up this story about Arundhatī and Vasiṣṭha, the two stars that newlyweds look to as emblems of fidelity (see Hiltebeitel 1977: 345), just for the occasion.[52] And most outrageously, he tries to pass off a maxim that a wife cannot be trusted once she has sons when it is he, the husband, who was not to be trusted! But his poppycock is enough to have won over the children, who now 'waited on him properly (*saṃyag upāsire*)' as he began 'to reassure' (*āśvāsayitum*) them, telling them, with a few choice words also tucked in for their mother, what they already know but she up till now does not:

I had commended you [boys] to the Fire, so that he might spare you; and he promised to me he would do so. Thus, knowing the Fire's promise, and your mother's piety in the Law (*dharmajñatām*), and your own great power, I did not come sooner. You had no need to worry about your death, sons. Even the Bearer of Oblations knew you were *ṛṣi*s, and the *brahman* is known to you.

(1.225.1–3)

Somehow Mandapāla leaves out that another reason he did not come sooner is that he was having a good time with Lapitā. Jaritā too is now silent on this point and others as well, and Lapitā is still flying around somewhere. But the good news is that despite male infidelity and wife- and child-desertion this marital reconciliation is complete, without anyone having had to go to counselling or to court – like, say, Śakuntalā, or Draupadī. For so Vaiśaṃpāyana now ends the tale: 'Having thus reassured (*āśvāsya*) his sons, Mandapāla took them and his wife, O Bhārata, and went from that country to another country (*deśād anyaṃ deśaṃ jagāma ha*)' (1.225.4).

Now somewhere along the line, I think probably when Mandapāla had his change of heart and left Lapitā, but certainly by now, attentive readers and listeners like Mrs Janamejaya and Mrs Śaunaka, who, as noted, might be alert to the pertinence to Draupadī of a wayward yet returning husband and the nearly slaughtered children, would realize that Mandapāla's name 'Slow-to-protect' would refer not to his children, whom he protects from the very beginning, but to his 'poor wife' to whom he returns. And who would not wish the avian couple and their children well as they depart for another country? But as they fly off, leaving us poised to enter the *Sabhāparvan*, such listeners might also reflect that they are coming to the scene in the main story in which a husband will be all too horribly 'slow-to-protect' his 'poor wife' – as Draupadī is called for the first time, and then repeatedly, when she is dragged into the *sabhā* (see n. 39).

* * *

This bring us to our second story, not an *upākhyāna* but a *saṃvāda*, the *Brahmadatta-Pūjanī-Saṃvāda* (12.137),[53] which occurs amid several animal tales in the *Āpaddharmaparvan* of Book 12 that precede the *Kapota-Upākhyāna*, which, as mentioned, ends in a female bird's implied *satī*. The bird Pūjanī – nicely translated as 'Adorable' by James Fitzgerald – would seem to experience a surprising number of the *Śārṅgaka-Upākhyāna*'s main issues, but with contrary results. When Adorable tells King Brahmadatta that she rejects his offer to restore their friendship because her 'trust' (*viśvāsa*) is broken, she says, 'A fool is trapped by trust (*viśvāsād badhyate bālas*) . . . Some who cannot be captured easily, not even with well-sharpened weapons, get captured with conciliation, the way elephants are trapped by other elephants' (12.137.34c–35). Adorable thus says that she would be a fool to restore a friendship on the basis of coinciding interests, for, as with forest elephants, such interests lead into traps.[54]

Adorable had lived for a long time in the women's quarters (*antaḥpura*) of Brahmadatta's capital of Kāmpilya (12.137.5). Each had a son, but one day at the beach the king's son killed the bird's. Reflecting upon this turn of events, Adorable says,

> There is no association (*saṃgatam*) in a *kṣatriya* – neither affection (*prītir*) nor goodheartedness (*sauhṛdam*). They participate with others to get something done and then, when their interests have been accomplished, they abandon them. There is no trust (*viśvāsaḥ*) among *kṣatriya*s. They harm everyone. And after wronging someone they are always conciliatory, but uselessly. I will now wreak fitting vengeance upon this horribly cruel ingrate who has slain my trust

> (*viśvāsaghātinaḥ*). Triple is his sin, because he killed someone born and raised with him, one who ate with him, and who depended upon him for protection.
>
> (12.137.13–16)

Adorable then puts out the little prince's eyes. This case of Adorable and King Brahmadatta is interesting for having been a *sakhya* friendship before their falling out. When Brahmadatta tries to coax Adorable back, she says to him:

> Friendship (*sakhyam*) can *not* be forged again between one who does injury and the victim. The perpetrator knows that in his heart (*hṛdayaṃ tatra jānāti*), and so does the victim.
>
> (12.137.32)

Brahmadatta disagrees:

> Friendship (*sakhyam*) *can* be forged again between one who does injury and the victim. Cessations of hostilities have been seen to happen (*vairasyopaśamo dṛṣṭaḥ*); neither meets with evil again.
>
> (12.137.33)

But, recalling the elephants, Adorable says, in effect, forget it. It is suggestive that while *sakhya* describes the baseline of their friendship, Adorable reviews her impasse in other friendship terms as well. She gears up for her revenge against the little prince with the thought that *kṣatriya*s lack affection (*prīti*) and goodheartedness (*sauhṛdam*), and says to Brahmadatta that both perpetrator and victim know how injuries linger in the heart (*hṛdayam*). And with regard to *mitra* ('alliance') friendship, she tells Brahmadatta that the only friends one can truly trust are one's innate friends (*mitrāṇi sahajāni*), the friends one is born with – that is, one's own good qualities:

> Knowledge, bravery, initiative, strength, and fortitude the fifth – these they say are one's innate friends by which the wise make things happen here (*vidyā śauryaṃ ca dākṣyaṃ ca balaṃ dhairyaṃ ca pañcakam / mitrāṇi sahajāny āhur vartayantīha yair budhāḥ //*).
>
> (12.137.81)

K.M. Ganguli, in his translation of the *Mahābhārata*, once takes *mitra* and *suhṛd* to imply a juxtaposition between 'interested' (*mitra*) friendship and 'disinterested' (*suhṛd*) friendship.[55] This nice contrast presents *suhṛd* in what could be taken as its ideal form, while, as regards *mitra*, Adorable says the only truly dependable 'allies' would be one's innate good qualities. Perhaps she echoes a Buddhist emphasis: that one must begin by being a friend to oneself as the opening to the beneficial practice of 'unlimited' mindfulness on 'friendship' (*maitrī* or *mettā*).[56] In any case, contradicting the axiomatic 'non-independence' (*asvatantratva*) one is supposed to expect from a real woman in the epic and in the *Mānava Dharmaśāstra*,[57] Adorable is gearing up to be an 'independent woman'.

Ultimately, and with further unpacking of these and further friendship and kinship terms, Adorable concludes with an intriguing commentary on marriage, kinship, and the state:

> One should keep away from a bad wife (*kubhāryām*), a bad son (*kuputram*), a bad kingdom (*kurājānam*), a bad friend (*kusauhṛdam*), a bad relative (*kusaṃbandham*), a bad country (*kudeśam*). There is no trust in a bad friend (*kumitre nāsti viśvāsaḥ*). How could there be pleasure in a bad wife? There is no satisfaction in a bad kingdom. No one can make a living in a bad country. There is never any association (*saṃgatam*) with a bad friend (*kumitre*), whose friendship (*sauhṛde*) is always inconstant. A bad relative becomes contemptuous when one loses one's wealth. She is a real wife who says what is dear (*sā bhāryā yā priyaṃ brūte*);[58] he is a real son in whom one takes satisfaction. He is a friend (*mitram*) where there is trust; a real country is a place where one can survive. When there is no oppression with violence, then the king rules with properly strict governance. When he seeks to support the poor, it is not just some personal tie of his own. Wife, country, friends (*mitrāṇi*), sons, kinsmen (*saṃbandhi*), relatives (*bāndhavāḥ*) – all of these are excellent when the king looks with the eye of Law (*etat sarvaṃ guṇavati dharmanetre mahīpatau*).
>
> (12.137.89–94)

Adorable actually concludes the first verse of this passage, 'One should keep *far* away (*dūrataḥ*) from a bad country.' Presumably, unlike Lapitā who is left where she is, or Jaritā who flies off to another country with her husband and children, Adorable flies off to a distant country alone. Nor does she even have to say, like Lapitā, that she will be better off without a 'bad man' (*kupuruṣa*). Gender is constructed to show that these three *pajaritas* – or as Jamison puts it, 'little (female) birdikins' (1996: 70) – hold the stories together, and that each in her own way is more virtuous than her male partner. Unlike female characters in general, who, as we have seen, are prone to fault themselves with unknown sins even from previous lives, Mandapāla has the tenuous no-fault clause that comes with being a man – a clause, no doubt 'soteriologically'[59] nuanced, that finds elegant and precise expression in the *Pativratā-Upākhyāna* (3.196–206) when the virtuous hunter of Mithilā proclaims, 'Having committed a sin, a man (*pūruṣa*) should think, "Not I!"'.[60] No doubt alert to such dodges, Jaritā knows how to weigh what she hears from her husband and the boys to keep her family together. Meanwhile,

Lapitā reads things truly when she sends Mandapāla home to her. And Adorable knows the bottom-line basic legal postulate that, deeper than her own revenge against the king's son, for which she is ostensibly exonerated, a king is responsible for protection that does not occur.

But what are we to make of this baseline *sakhya* friendship between a male king and this 'adorable' female bird, one based on a trust (*viśvāsa*) that both admit has been broken, one that, with the breach, calls so many friendship terms and ties under such thorough review and ultimate forsaking? As we have noted, *sakhya* friendship can imply marriage, and marriage itself can forge such friendship in the seventh step. Indeed, in so far as Adorable calls her relation to the king a *sakhya* friendship, one *could* take her to be implying that she is King Brahmadatta's *first* wife, the one with whom his bond would be made truly indissoluble by the sacramental seven steps. Here a number of species-crossing unimaginables could reflect deeper logics of the text, which I thank Simon Brodbeck for suggesting that I consider. Were Adorable to regard her own slain son to be Brahmadatta's true heir, she would now have put a blind half-brother in his place, which could remind listeners of the blind Dhṛtarāṣṭra whose rule, like Brahmadatta's, was untrustworthy; and of Dhṛtarāṣṭra and Gāndhārī's sons, who by the time this story is told have been both disinherited and killed. But a bird's story must keep to certain bounds.

This little bird from the king's 'women's quarters' makes an analogy between good friendship, good marriage, and a peaceable kingdom and country. It seems that with Adorable and Brahmadatta's parallel relationship as parents with sons but with no mention of their spouses, Adorable's story involves an implicit reflection on the unthinkable grounds of 'irretrievable marital breakdown' that would, after all, even if only in theory, justify a wife who leaves her husband – as must have happened more often than we are told. For given the prior presumption of marital indissolubility, irretrievable marital breakdown cannot actually be admitted for creatures of the same species – or at least, should a rare exception be found, it is easier to say it about creatures of different ones. And where would trust or its breach finally have to lie? In both cases, in the treatment of sons, for, in contrast to the story of the Śārṅgaka birds where reconciliation can begin from the mother's and father's mutual if uncoordinated care for the children, here we have the opposite outcome of one son killed and the other maimed in revenge – by Adorable herself. Indeed, what she seems to be really saying, as so often by displacement, is that she can no longer be 'a real wife who says what is dear'. Don't forget who is listening directly to all this: not just Draupadī and her husbands, but also Kṛṣṇa.

Friends among friends

Coming now to Draupadī's 'unique' *sakhā–sakhī* relationship with Kṛṣṇa, I will discuss the few occurrences that play out this relationship explicitly in the text, and some of those that do so implicitly, and conclude with some speculation on Yudhiṣṭhira's closing description of Draupadī mentioned at the beginning of this chapter.

In relationships with individual males, a woman's husband could consider her to be an exemplary 'intimate friend', as Yudhiṣṭhira does in answering the *yakṣa*'s questions in the *Āraṇeyam Upākhyānam* or 'Firesticks Subtale' (so called at 1.2.127c).

> . . . What is the friend made by fate (*kiṃ svid daivakṛtaḥ sakhā*)?
> . . . The wife is the friend made by fate (*bhāryā daivakṛtaḥ sakhā*).
> (3.297.50b, 51b)

Note that *sakhā*, for the wife, is in the masculine. But for a woman to have a *sakhā* outside of marriage is something rare. The *Gautama Dharmasūtra*, one of the earliest texts on *dharma*, introduces such a relationship probably before the *Mahābhārata*,[61] but fleetingly, with the following rules:

> Sex with a female friend (*sakhī*) or uterine sister,[62] a woman belonging to one's lineage, the wife of one's pupil, one's daughter-in-law, and a cow is equal to sex with the wife of an elder. According to some, it is equal to a student's breaking the vow of chastity.[63]
> (*Gautama Dharmasūtra* 23.12–13, tr. Olivelle)

But Gautama does not develop the idea of the *sakhī* in any other rule, and when one gets to the *Mānava Dharmaśāstra*, the rule is sanitized so that it no longer concerns the delicate matter of sex with a female friend (or a cow) but only with the wives of male friends or their sons: 'Sexual intercourse with uterine sisters, unmarried girls, lowest-born women, and the wives of a friend or son, they say, is equal to sex with an elder's wife' (*Mānava Dharmaśāstra* 11.59, tr. Olivelle).[64] In the epics, as far as I know, the only case of such a relationship is that of Kṛṣṇa and Draupadī, which confirms not only its uniqueness but also the singularity with which the *Mahābhārata* brings it to life. I find it mentioned explicitly in only two contexts: first, three times with reference to Draupadī's disrobing; and then, much later, in an ostensibly lighter scene.

Its first mention is thus in a scene of evident great intensity. Dragged into the men's gambling hall by her hair, dashed to the ground in a single blood-stained garment, wretched with misery, hearing her question about *dharma* only ducked and bandied about by the men, Draupadī calls for the last time for it to be answered, mentioning for the first time in the epic that she is the *sakhī*-friend of Kṛṣṇa:

> From of old, we have heard, they do not bring virtuous women into the hall (*dharmyāḥ striyaḥ sabhāṃ pūrvaṃ na nayantīti naḥ śrutam* /).

> This ancient eternal law (*pūrvo dharmaḥ sanātanaḥ*) is lost (*naṣṭaḥ*) among the Kauravas. How can I, wife of the Pāṇḍus, sister of Pārṣata, a good woman (*satī*), and friend of Vāsudeva (*vāsudevasya ca sakhī*), enter the hall of kings? Is the wife of Dharmarāja, whose birth matches his, a slave or not a slave (*dāsīm adāsīṃ vā*)?
>
> (2.62.9–11)

It is shortly after this that she prays to Kṛṣṇa, who, in conjunction with Dharma (her *dharma*?), multiplies her sarees to prevent her disrobing – at least so it is in all Sanskrit texts prior to the Critical Edition. As I see it, the Critical Edition, in taking stock of a kind of Genghis Khan effect in which a rampant breeding of variants has made it impossible to trace earlier 'generations' (Stokes 2004), has taken Kṛṣṇa's part in this intervention to suggest that there would once have been an original in which he did not intervene and it was Draupadī's own *dharma* that saved her.[65] Indeed, as the war approaches in Book 5, Draupadī specifically connects her being Kṛṣṇa's *sakhī* with her having called upon him to 'save' her in the *sabhā*:

> It has been said often enough, but I repeat it confidently, Janārdana: has there been a woman like me on earth . . . risen from the middle of the altar . . . your dear friend (*tava . . . priyā sakhī*), Kṛṣṇa? . . . Yet I . . . was molested in the men's hall . . . The Pāṇḍavas watched it without showing anger or doing anything, so it was you I desired in my heart, Govinda, crying 'Save me!' (*trāhi mām iti govinda manasā kāṅkṣito 'si me //*).
>
> (5.80.21–6)

There is the suggestion here that only an 'intimate friend' (*sakhā*) could touch her sarees in her husbands' presence. But the main thing about the intimacy of their *sakhā–sakhī* relationship in this episode is that it is steeped in *bhakti*, as Draupadī herself also makes evident earlier in the Forest Book when she questions how, as Kṛṣṇa's *sakhī*, she could have suffered such insults. Seeking Kṛṣṇa's refuge (*śaraṇyaṃ śaraṇaiṣiṇī*) and acknowledging at length that he is the supreme deity (3.13.42–50), she asks:

> And here am I, about to tell you of my grief, out of love (*praṇayāt*), Madhusūdana – for are you not the lord of all beings, both divine and human? Then how was it that a woman like me, wife to the Pārthas, sister of Dhṛṣṭadyumna, your friend (*tava . . . sakhī*), Kṛṣṇa, came to be dragged into the hall, Lord?
>
> (3.13.52–3)

If, as I have argued elsewhere, Draupadī's question about *dharma* questions the 'ownership' of women,[66] it would seem that being Kṛṣṇa's *sakhī* simply nullifies such ownership at a higher plane. But on a more down-to-earth plane, Draupadī's *sakhī* relation with Kṛṣṇa is, at least in these scenes, one of the main things that keeps her marriage to five men going, and with it the *dharma* that they are all born to protect and restore.

* * *

And now, much later into the epic, that seemingly lighter moment. Kṛṣṇa has just told Yudhiṣṭhira what he has learned from spies: Arjuna is returning, quite emaciated after many fights, from his mission of guarding the horse for Yudhiṣṭhira's postwar *aśvamedha*; preparations for the rite should begin. Yudhiṣṭhira is very glad to hear of Arjuna's imminent return, but he is troubled by the report of his brother's gaunt look and asks Kṛṣṇa whether Arjuna bears some 'unfavourable[67] mark by which he experiences such miseries' (*aniṣṭaṃ lakṣaṇaṃ kṛṣṇa yena duḥkhāny upāśnute* // 14.89.4). 'Reflecting for a very long interlude' (*dhyātvā sumahad antaram*, 14.89.6b) – and let me mention that Vaiśaṃpāyana sometimes likes to cue us that Kṛṣṇa is an entertainer[68] – Kṛṣṇa replies:[69]

> O king, I surely do not detect this one's having anything unfavourable except that this lion among men's cheekbones[70] are overly developed (*na hy asya nṛpate kiṃ cid aniṣṭam*[71] *upalakṣaye / ṛte puruṣasiṃhasya piṇḍike 'syātikāyataḥ //*). On account of these two, this tiger among men is always hitched to the roads (*nityam adhvasu yujyate*). I do not see anything else by which this Jaya has a share of misery.
>
> (14.89.7–8)

His curiosity satisfied, Yudhiṣṭhira says, 'So it is, Lord' (*evam etad iti prabho*, 14.89.9d).

> But Kṛṣṇā Draupadī indignantly[72] glanced askance at Kṛṣṇa (*kṛṣṇā tu draupadī kṛṣṇaṃ tiryak sāsūyam aikṣata /*). The Slayer of Keśin, Hṛṣīkeśa, approved that showing of her affection (*pratijagrāha tasyās taṃ praṇayam*)[73] as if he were Dhanaṃjaya in person (*sākṣād iva*),[74] a friend of a friend (*sakhyuḥ sakhā*). Having heard, Bhīma and the other Kurus and Yādavas[75] there took pleasure in this story about Dhanaṃjaya whose manner was amusing,[76] O lord (*remuḥ śrutvā vicitrārthā dhanaṃjayakathā vibho //*).
>
> (14.89.10–11)

Now if Kṛṣṇa's remark and his approval of Draupadī's show of affection were all we had to go on, we might begin by noting that he seems to be teasing his friend Draupadī. Vaiśaṃpāyana's initial cues would reinforce this: Kṛṣṇa took a very long time to come up with this *vicitrārthā . . . kathā* – this 'amusing', 'entertaining', or 'colourful' *tale* about Arjuna.

But what do we have here in this *sakhyuḥ sakhā*, 'friend of a friend'? Who is whose friend? Let us return to the last line of the three-line verse where this phrase occurs: 'Hṛṣīkeśa [approved that showing of her affection], as if he were Dhanaṃjaya in person, a friend of a friend (*sakhyuḥ sakhā*)' (14.89.10ef). The commentator Nīlakaṇṭha is silent. Georges Dumézil, while trying to make a comparative point about the facial distortions of Indo-European warriors, seems to take *sakhyuḥ sakhā* as referring to Kṛṣṇa as the friend of Arjuna: 'Draupadī, . . . who has a preference for Arjuna, . . . takes strong exception to a challenge of this kind to the hero's perfect beauty; she throws an angry glance at Kṛṣṇa, who, in his own affection for Arjuna, enjoys her feminine reaction' (1970: 164 n. 9).[77] This is certainly grammatically plausible, since the genitive *sakhyuḥ*, 'of the friend', is in the masculine. But Ganguli takes *sakhyuḥ sakhā* as referring to Kṛṣṇa and Draupadī, translating, 'The slayer of Kesi, *viz.*, Hrishikesa, approved of that indication of love (for his friend) which the princess of Panchala, who also was his friend, displayed' – to which he adds in a note: 'It is worthy of note that Draupadi was always styled by Krishna as his *sakhi* or "friend". Krishna was highly chivalrous to the other sex at an age when women were universally regarded as the inferiors of men' (Ganguli 14.87, p. 149).[78] That is, Ganguli takes 'friend of a friend' to refer to Kṛṣṇa (the *sakhā*) as the friend of Draupadī (*sakhyuḥ*, even though it is in the masculine), while reminding us in parentheses that Arjuna, for whom Draupadī makes her show of affection, is also Kṛṣṇa's friend. Somewhat in favour of this reading, the genitive *tasyās*, 'of her', in 'that showing *of her* affection' which precedes *sakhyuḥ sakhā*, could be taken as pointing to Draupadī in the genitive masculine 'of the friend', and it is instructive that three Malayalam manuscripts[79] replace *sakhyuḥ* with the feminine genitive *sakhyāḥ* to make this explicit: that 'friend of a friend' means 'friend of a female friend'. Actually, it is perfectly ambiguous. The masculine genitive *sakhyuḥ* could refer to either Draupadī or Arjuna as 'friend' of Kṛṣṇa, for as William Dwight Whitney observes, 'forms of [the masculine] *sakhi* are sometimes found used with feminine value' (1960: 342) – we have noticed such a usage when Yudhiṣṭhira describes the wife as the 'friend (*sakhā*) made by fate'. Moreover, since Kṛṣṇa sees Draupadī 'as if he were Dhanaṃjaya in person (*sākṣād iva*)', it could even be saying that *he* is sympathetically seeing what Arjuna would be seeing as the friend in the nominative, leaving the genitive – the friend whose friend is Arjuna – to be either Draupadī or Kṛṣṇa.

But there are other clues in Vaiśaṃpāyana's narration, for we are actually in the midst of another highly charged ritual situation involving not only Draupadī and Arjuna but also the returning horse. In this regard, Draupadī could have more on her mind to be indignant about than just this slight of Arjuna, whose return with the horse after its year of wandering signals that

Draupadī must now ramp herself up for a ritual highlight of the *aśvamedha*. For if one were following the old ritual texts, as the queen or chief wife (*mahiṣī*) of the king, she would soon be lying down and exposing herself sexually to the horse after it has been suffocated. Even though it is certainly selective in describing other details of the *aśvamedha*, the *Mahābhārata* does not omit this 'sexually jolting' ritual scene, which it soon describes with manifest restraint:

> When the bulls among priests (*yājakarṣabhāḥ*) had made the horse agree [i.e., when they had killed it] according to rule, they caused the wise (*manasvinīm*) daughter of Drupada to lie down beside it for three minutes (*kalābhis tisṛbhī*) according to rule, O king.
>
> (14.91.2)[80]

Let us note that Vyāsa plays a supervisory priestly role at both Yudhiṣṭhira's *rājasūya* and his *aśvamedha*, and would thus be one of the chief 'bulls among priests (*yājaka*s)' mentioned here.[81] But what is most noteworthy is that Kṛṣṇa's friendship with Draupadī comes explicitly into play around these two ritually defined scenes: one in a development from the dice match as an extended narrative sequel to the *rājasūya*,[82] and the other in an underplayed portrayal of the role of the *mahiṣī* in exposing herself sexually to the sacrificed horse in the *aśvamedha*. I suspect that in each case Kṛṣṇa intervenes to lighten Draupadī's sexual humiliation. As the epic wife takes her role as victim[83] within the arena of the great Vedic royal sacrifices, she has a new friend to turn to in the text's *bhakti* theology: God. But really, he is not a new friend but an old one, for as the earlier Vedic Brāhmaṇa texts are fond of repeating, *yajño vai viṣṇus*, 'Viṣṇu is the sacrifice'.[84]

Further, I believe that Vaiśaṃpāyana offers hints that the Yādavas, among others, or, even more interestingly, the *yājaka*s or 'sacrificial priests' (see n. 75), among others, would have found even more to be amused about in Kṛṣṇa's 'colourful' tale about Arjuna. This would be that Kṛṣṇa seems to be referring not only to Arjuna but to the horse; or, more exactly, that if Kṛṣṇa were reading, or perhaps better, reading *into*, his 'intimate friend' Draupadī's mind, he would be hinting that Arjuna and the horse would have a somewhat fused or interchangeable profile as they approach together. While *piṇḍikā* can indeed designate 'a globular swelling or protuberance' on a man's cheeks, it could also describe the same on a horse.[85] Kṛṣṇa's *bon mot* would thus be a *śleṣa* or *double entendre*: one that would be especially amusing to the *yājaka*s, who are thinking not only of Arjuna but also – or perhaps more so – of the horse he is bringing for them to sacrifice. Indeed, the *yājaka*s, as we have seen, are headed by Kṛṣṇa Dvaipāyana Vyāsa, the author, who would be the first to understand double meanings. Or alternatively, the Yādavas know their kinsman Kṛṣṇa better than most.

The narration and Kṛṣṇa's own words offer further clues in this direction.

That Kṛṣṇa approves Draupadī's show of affection under his name Slayer of Keśin is more than curious, since Keśin is a horse Kṛṣṇa slew in his childhood.[86] Even the name Hṛṣīkeśa is worth noting here, since it can mean 'Master of the Senses' (Biardeau 2002, vol. 1: 595) and, with that, convey the familiar Upanishadic image of 'yoking' the senses, with the senses evoking horses.[87] But most tellingly, these meanings apply when Kṛṣṇa says in his own words that Arjuna's facial protuberances come from his being 'always hitched to the roads' (*nityam adhvasu yujyate*), like a family workhorse. If so, no wonder Draupadī looks at him askance. She would understand this play on words just as well as the *yājaka*s or Yādavas do.

In short, when Vaiśampāyana tells us that Kṛṣṇa responded to Draupadī's indignation as a friend of a friend (*sakhyuḥ sakhā*), the *sakhā* could be either Kṛṣṇa or Arjuna, and the *sakhyuḥ* could be either Arjuna, Draupadī, or Kṛṣṇa. If Vaiśampāyana is cuing us to take Kṛṣṇa's 'story' about Arjuna's cheekbones to be 'amusing', he is probably also leaving us with at least some of these ambiguities as to the triple intimacies of the *sakhā–sakhī* friendship of Draupadī, Kṛṣṇa, and Arjuna. One could probably say that it is the relation of these principal characters – the leading man, leading woman, and their friend God – as they act, wink, and listen, that provides the epic's armature of gender throughout. I have in mind principally Draupadī's colloquy with Kṛṣṇa's wife Satyabhāmā in The Book of the Forest (3.222–4), Arjuna's disguise in The Book of Virāṭa (see Hiltebeitel 1980b), and above all the persona of Kṛṣṇa, a devious divinity (Matilal 1991) of whom it can be said that part of his charm is that you don't have to believe a word he says.

The *Mahābhārata* does not really tell us where these friendships start. Perhaps Arjuna's with Kṛṣṇa is among the friendships and rivalries the Pāṇḍavas form with others – notably Aśvatthāman and Karṇa – who receive Droṇa's martial training, since the Vṛṣṇis and Andhakas are mentioned among that lot (1.122.46), but without Kṛṣṇa being personally identified there. But by the time of Draupadī's *svayaṃvara*, Kṛṣṇa is there with Balarāma to recognize Arjuna, restrain the vying suitors, and seal the deal as 'lawful' (*dharmeṇa*, 1.181.32) – before it becomes a matter of polyandry (which calls for the additional interventions, mentioned above, of Kṛṣṇa's congeners Vyāsa and Nārada). Draupadī does not much appreciate Kṛṣṇa's next entanglement: encouraging Arjuna to marry Subhadrā, his (Kṛṣṇa's) sister (1.211–12). Indeed, when Kṛṣṇa uses the phrase 'always hitched to the roads' to explain Arjuna's high cheekbones, Draupadī could also be reminded of this tour (provoked by Nārada's intervention) that brought Arjuna home with this new bride. In any case, the Burning of the Khāṇḍava Forest is framed by these now developed friendships. Before the fire starts, Arjuna and Kṛṣṇa decide to go, as each puts it, 'surrounded by [our] friends' (*suhṛj-janavṛta*) – including Draupadī and Subhadrā[88] – for water sports and a picnic with liquor and music on a bank of the Yamunā (1.214.14–25). And when the conflagration is over, Agni grants Kṛṣṇa the boon of 'eternal friendship with Arjuna' (*prītiṃ pārthena śāśvatīm*, 1.225.13)[89] – like marital friendship, friendship between males can be sanctioned by circling around fire.[90] Moreover, in the grisly scene between these two bookmarks of confirmed amity, the Burning of the Khāṇḍava Forest reveals Arjuna and Kṛṣṇa for the first time as 'the two Kṛṣṇas' (1.214.27, 32; 1.219.3) riding together on one chariot, as they will do in the war (see Hiltebeitel 1984). By that point one also knows that Kṛṣṇa, Arjuna, and Draupadī are three enigmatic 'Kṛṣṇas' along with a fourth, the author Kṛṣṇa Dvaipāyana Vyāsa. As we have now seen, all this has been further developed when Draupadī and Kṛṣṇa are mentioned as two Kṛṣṇas at the beginning of the passage about Arjuna's return with the horse, where Vyāsa not only stands behind everything Vaiśaṃpāyana says, but also is the chief of the priests overseeing the whole *aśvamedha* when Draupadī and the dead horse take their three minutes to cohabit.

* * *

Now with regard to *sakhi*[91] as 'intimate friend', we have seen that there is an Upanishadic usage of that term in describing two birds who as 'companions and friends' nestle in the same tree:[92]

> Two birds, who are companions and friends (*sayujā sakhāyā*), nestle on the very same tree. One of them eats a tasty fig; the other, not eating, looks on. Stuck on the very same tree, one person grieves, deluded by her who is not the Lord (*anīśayā*). But when he sees the other, the contented Lord (*īśam*) – and the Lord's majesty – his grief disappears.
>
> (*Śvetāśvatara Upaniṣad* 4.6–7, tr. Olivelle 1996; also *Muṇḍaka Upaniṣad* 3.1.1–2)

It would seem that the *Muṇḍaka* and *Śvetāśvatara*[93] *Upaniṣad*s put a *bhakti* twist on the first of these two verses – which is originally the first in a sequence of three Rigvedic riddle verses[94] about two male birds without a female birdikins to complement them – by introducing the feminine as 'her who is not the Lord',[95] the 'tasty fig' that deludes the one friend who eats while 'the other, the contented Lord', 'not eating, looks on'. Indeed, given the preceding verse that contextualizes this parable at *Śvetāśvatara Upaniṣad* 4.5, 'she', as one of the three 'unborns' or *ajalajā*s, is none other than tricolored primal matter whom the one unborn male 'burning with passion, covers' while the other 'unborn male leaves her after he has finished enjoying her pleasures' (tr. Olivelle 1996).[96] To put it briefly, the exemplary *sakhi* friendship of the two male birds passes entirely over 'her' head.

I have been suggesting in this chapter that the *Mahābhārata* has done something to correct this in Kṛṣṇa's *sakhi* friendship with Draupadī. But we must finally see this not from within this 'dark' circle of *sakhi* friends named Kṛṣṇa/ā ('black'), but from the dying consciousness of the almost infinitely educable Yudhiṣṭhira, who is always slightly outside that circle (that is, one barely finds him mentioned as Kṛṣṇa's *sakhi* friend – see for example 5.70.91ab; Arjuna is after all his brother, and although Yudhiṣṭhira does speak of the wife as *sakhā*, he knows that among his brothers this relation to Draupadī would belong above all to Arjuna).

Yudhiṣṭhira knows that Draupadī has died on the path up into the Himālaya that he and his brothers take on their final great setting forth (*mahāprasthāna*) accompanied by a dog who is Dharma in disguise. Draupadī is the first to fall, leaving Yudhiṣṭhira to explain to Bhīma that she fell as the result of her one fault in life: that she had a partiality for Arjuna (17.2.6). Without looking back he climbs ahead. But he continues to think about her, and once the dog has revealed himself to be Dharma, Yudhiṣṭhira is taken in a chariot to heaven in his own body, with all his human feelings still intact; and once there, desiring to be wherever his brothers and Draupadī are, he brings Book 17 to a resounding close by asking where *bṛhatī śyāmā buddhisattvaguṇānvitā / draupadī* is (17.3.36). Then, as Book 18 begins, finding Duryodhana rather than his loved ones there, he soon finds Draupadī (and the rest) at the end of her post-mortem but still 'human' path in Hell (18.2.11–41). There he dramatically curses the gods, *dharma*, and Dharma as his father (*devāṃś ca garhayām āsa dharmaṃ caiva yudhiṣṭhiraḥ //* 18.2.50) for all the awful tests they have made him and his loved ones endure. And having reentered heaven himself, just as he has his last longing to question Draupadī (18.4.8), Indra breaks in to tell him he cannot do so because she has already returned to her divine identity:

> O Yudhiṣṭhira, she is Śrī, who took the form of Draupadī for your sake, becoming human though not born of a womb, beloved of the world, she who smells good (*śrīr eṣā draupadīrūpā tvadarthe mānuṣaṃ gatā / ayonijā lokakāntā puṇyagandhā yudhiṣṭhira //*).
> (18.4.9)

In questioning where Draupadī is in this interval between death and what is next for her, I would speculate that Yudhiṣṭhira may be evoking an even deeper identity of Draupadī than Śrī,[97] whose 'good smell' is surely but also merely that of the earth, which Yudhiṣṭhira must now leave behind. If so, this would call for us to think that the epic's concatenation of friends named Kṛṣṇa/ā would be co-configured (by the epic's author, another Kṛṣṇa, no less) against the full background of what Madeleine Biardeau nearly forty years ago[98] introduced as the epico-puranic 'universe of *bhakti*', a cosmology in which on the grandest scale – on top, that is, of the 'occasional dissolutions' in which the earth is periodically dissolved into the single ocean – there are the 'great dissolutions' in which all the elements are dissolved into primal matter, the third *ajā*. If so, Kṛṣṇa and Arjuna, 'the two Kṛṣṇas on one chariot'[99] as images of the soul and the Lord, would be *sakhi*s with a 'great enigmatic dark Lady' (*bṛhatī śyāmā*) indeed. The *sakhi* relation that connects the three of them would apply not only to the two males as Lord and soul, but also to the three as Lord, soul, and primal matter – that is, primal matter in her highest sattvic aspect as *pradhāna*, which reveals itself / who reveals herself, or is revealed, at eschatological moments of both individual and cosmic illumination. If so, Yudhiṣṭhira would be not only asking after the woman of substance and intellect, the lady *paṇḍitā* (or learned scholar) he knew in life, but also giving homage to the deepest nature she could possibly have in this more than occasionally philosophical text: the great enigmatic dark one (*bṛhatī śyāmā*) who is *buddhisattvaguṇānvitā*, primal substance as intellect. The 'great enigmatic dark one' who is *buddhisattvaguṇānvitā* would then be that tasty fig come to life in parity, the mysterious third friend who is, precisely for Yudhiṣṭhira, the friend of the friend of the friend.

Notes

1 See Hiltebeitel 2001a: 272–3, where I discuss some possible translations, beginning with 'the great dark one rich in spirit, character, and virtue'.

2 This chapter owes deep debts to Derrida 1997 regarding – amongst other things – his discussions of friendship with and among women (pp. 101, 155–7, 164–86, 191 n. 6, 201, 239, 273–4, 281–3, 291, 293); friendship and love (pp. 20–1); self-friendship and self-enmity (pp. 177 and 190 n. 5); how many friends may be too many, and two the ideal (pp. 21–2, 101); the third friend as odd one out or mysterious presence (pp. 260, 276–7, 293); and the question of whether friendship is possible with God and/or animals (pp. 17, 19, 198, 206–7, 211, 222–4, 294). Derrida's book also opens many other paths into the *Mahābhārata* that I hope to explore in additional essays.

3 See Adarkar 2001: 86 and n. 24 on different 'options' open to male and female characters, noting that, for the latter, 'exploring such options would be another study'. For some especially rich discussions of character in this work, see pp. 49–62, 145–8, 234–40.

4 *Pañcendra-* and *Sunda-Upasunda-* are mentioned in the *Parvasaṃgraha* at 1.2.87c and 90cd respectively. Four others mentioned there are narrated in Book 3: the *Śyena-Kapotīya-Upākhyāna* (1.2.115ab, referring to 3.130–1), *Aṣṭāvakrīya-Upākhyāna* (1.2.126a = *Auddālakīya*, referring to 3.132–4), *Vainya-Upākhyāna* (1.2.126b, referring to 3.183), and ' "The Fire-Sticks Subtale" in which Dharma instructs his son' (*āraṇeyam upākhyānaṃ yatra dharmo 'nvaśāt sutam* / 1.2.127, referring to 3.295–9). The *Ambā-Upākhyāna* (5.170–93) is mentioned both in the *Parvasaṃgraha* (1.2.54a and 150f) and the colophons.

5 Two others are mentioned both in passing in the text and in the colophons: the *Dhundhumāra-Upākhyāna* (3.192–5; see 3.195.37c) and the *Indravijaya-Upākhyāna* (5.9–18; see 5.18.16a).

6 Jamison may follow Sörensen 1963: 383, who gives this title. The colophons for the tale's opening *adhyāya* 12.141 mentioned in the Critical Edition favour the *saṃvāda* title by 11 manuscripts to 9, but with representation only in the Northern Recension, whereas '*Kapota-Upākhyāna*' occurs in the three Malayalam manuscripts, M1–3.

7 See Jamison's rich treatment of this passage amid discussion of the eight forms of marriage and the *rākṣasa* mode among them (1996: 210–35, 296 n. 9).

8 Kuntī says, 'Why should this *kānīna* (son of an unmarried girl), who has returned to me as a son, not do my word that is so salutary for his brothers?' Kuntī is right that Karṇa would be covered by the law's retrospective intent regarding unwed mothers. But *Mānava Dharmaśāstra* 9.160 would not allow Karṇa to inherit the kingdom: a *kānīna* is one of six types of sons 'who are *relatives but not heirs*'! But of course Yudhiṣṭhira would 'give' the kingdom to him, as Karṇa has just said to Kṛṣṇa, and Karṇa would give it to Duryodhana. Yet Kuntī is also drawing on a 'basic legal postulate' that worked so well with her other sons when they followed the unintended outcome of her telling them to 'share it all equally' (1.182.2) and jointly married Draupadī: sons should listen to their mothers.

9 'A *legal postulate* is a value principle or value system specifically connected with a particular official or unofficial law, which acts to found, justify, or orient the latter' (Chiba 1986: 6).

10 After three verses on Draupadī-Śrī (1.61.95–7), the epic's fullest list of partial incarnations concludes by accounting for the other three leading females as uneventful incarnations of post-Vedic abstractions: 'The Goddesses Success (Siddhi) and Endurance (Dhṛti) were the two mothers of the five, born as Kuntī and Mādrī; and Wisdom (Mati) became the daughter of Subala [Gāndhārī]' (tr. van Buitenen). See Dumézil 1968: 251 on prominent early Vedic goddesses *not* incarnated: 'Aditi, Uṣas, Pṛthivī, Sarasvatī, the Waters, etc.' Like Sörensen (1963: 599), Dumézil (1968: 252–3) mentions a verse identifying Rukmiṇī as an incarnation of Śrī and Draupadī as an incarnation of Śacī, but it is interpolated (1.*566) and the reference to Śrī is not recorded in the Critical Edition's apparatus.

11 As especially informative on the karmic mechanisms of reincarnation as they have affected a worm and a virtuous *śūdra* hunter, see respectively the *Kīṭa-Upākhyāna* (13.118–20, discussed in Hiltebeitel 2001a: 198–9) and the *Pativratā-Upākhyāna* (3.196–206; Hiltebeitel 2001a: 204–5). Interestingly enough, where we do learn how karmic outcomes – overridden by curses or vows – have affected characters of the main story, it is still in *upākhyānas*: Śaṃtanu in the *Mahābhiṣa-Upākhyāna* (1.91); Vidura in the *Aṇīmāṇḍavya-Upākhyāna* (1.101); the Pāṇḍavas etc. in the *Pañcendra-Upākhyāna*; and Śikhaṇḍin in the *Ambā-Upākhyāna*.

12 One exception was pointed out to me by Emily Hudson at the London *Epic Constructions* conference: a passage where Dhṛtarāṣṭra, like his wife Gāndhārī (see p. 113), wonders whether it is his past deeds from previous births that occasion his postwar grief: 'Saṃjaya, I do not recall doing anything wrong in the past that might have yielded as its fruit what I suffer here and now as a dazed fool. But obviously I did something wrong in earlier births, since the Disposer has joined me to such wretched deeds' (*na smarāmy ātmanaḥ kiṃ cit purā saṃjaya duṣkṛtam / yasyedaṃ phalam adyeha mayā mūḍhena bhujyate // nūnaṃ hy apakṛtaṃ kiṃ cin mayā pūrveṣu janmasu / yena māṃ duḥkhabhāgeṣu dhātā karmasu yuktavān //* 11.1.17–18; see Fitzgerald 2004a: 31; Hill 2001: 33). Hill 2001: 30–4 discusses this utterance as well as two of the other passages now cited, and likewise observes how few the instances are 'where any character, beset by misfortune, contemplates or expresses remorse at how the actions and desires of previous lives may have brought about their current lot' (ibid.: 31).

13 *nūnam ācaritaṃ pāpaṃ mayā pūrveṣu janmasu / yā paśyāmi hatān putrān pautrān bhrātṝṃś ca keśava /* Fitzgerald has 'brother' rather than 'brothers'.

14 *pūrvajātikṛtaṃ pāpaṃ manye nālpam ivānagha / etābhir anavadyābhir mayā caivālpamedhayā // tad idaṃ dharmarājena yātitaṃ no janārdana / na hi nāśo 'sti vārṣṇeya karmaṇoḥ śubhapāpayoḥ //* Brodbeck in press a interprets Gāndhārī's words here as 'subversive, ironic, even sarcastic', which may be so, given her

distrust of Kṛṣṇa; but I do not think the characterization applies to these usages generally.

15 *kiṃ nu karmāśubhaṃ pūrvaṃ kṛtavaty asmi janmani / yad ahaṃ bāndhavais tyaktā bālye saṃprati ca tvayā //*

16 *abhāgyayā mayā nūnaṃ viyuktāḥ sahacāriṇaḥ / saṃyogā viprayuktā vā pūrvadeheṣu pārthiva // tad idaṃ karmabhiḥ pāpaiḥ pūrvadeheṣu saṃcitam / duḥkhaṃ māṃ anusaṃprāptaṃ rājaṃs tvadviprayogajam //*

17 *pravrājitum ihecchāmi tapas tapsyāmi duścaram // mayaivaitāni karmāṇi pūrvadeheṣu mūḍhayā / kṛtāni nūnaṃ pāpāni teṣām etat phalaṃ dhruvam //*

18 That is, there are no repeated lines, half-lines, or even phrases in these utterances; each is an 'original'. One line in the stanza following the two cited in n. 12 'feels' formulaic, where Dhṛtarāṣṭra goes on to say, 'Is there a man in the world more miserable than I?' (*ko 'nyo 'sti duḥkhatitaro mayā loke pumān iha //* 11.1.19). This is reminiscent of three lines that introduce the *Nala-Upākhyāna* – the first one uttered by Yudhiṣṭhira describing himself (3.49.34ef) and the other two (36cd; 38cd) describing Nala. But in 11.1.19 Dhṛtarāṣṭra has stopped attributing his troubles to *karma* from previous lives and has turned to fate (*daiva*) as an explanation (Hill 2001: 33).

19 See Weinberger-Thomas 1999: 26 (on *karmadoṣa*, 'the 'fault of *karma*'), 45, 86, 102, 106–8, 132, 143–51, 163–7; Hiltebeitel 1999c.

20 I checked the likely Tamil chapbook dramas where I thought I recalled a line where Draupadī laments that she must be suffering on account of *karma* or sins from a past life, but could not find what I was looking for. Perundevi Srinivasan then kindly read several of them also at my request, and likewise found nothing so explicit. But she did find in 'Eighteenth-Day War' (*Patiṉettāmpōr Nāṭakam*) that after Aśvatthāman kills the Pāṇḍavas' and Draupadī's five children, Draupadī laments, 'Is it a lesson, or a curse, a curse, a curse expanded from the past?' (*pāṭamō, paṇṭai virittiṭṭa cāpamō, cāpamo, cāpamo*; Kiruṣṇappiḷḷai 1980: 79) – which no doubt contains something of the idea, again overridden by a presumed curse (see n. 11). Both Srinivasan and I recall a more explicit statement at least from oral performances.

21 Her uniqueness would seem to be paralleled by that of Sītā in the *Rāmāyaṇa*, with her former life as Vedavatī (*Rāmāyaṇa* 7.17). In fact, considering the short list (see n. 11) of main characters having prior existences affected by vows or curses, the only other person in the main story to have had her or his life affected by known or unknown *karma* from a previous *human* life would be Śikhaṇḍin: likewise a woman reborn as a girl, but with the difference that she turns into a man. Of the others mentioned in n. 11, only Śaṃtanu had a prior human life as the former King Mahābhiṣa, but the act that led Mahābhiṣa to be reincarnated as Śaṃtanu occurred in heaven. The situation contrasts with that in numerous vernacular oral epics, where the Pāṇḍavas, Draupadī, and other epic figures are reincarnated due to the 'unfinished business' of their *Mahābhārata karma* (see Hiltebeitel 1999a).

22 Indeed, the Southern Recension of the Sanskrit epic and Tamil (including Draupadī cult) variations on it identify this overanxious maiden to have been Nāḷāyaṉi, wife of the *ṛṣi* Mudgala. See Hiltebeitel 2001a: 237. Mudgala's own story is told as the *Mudgala-Upākhyāna* (3.246–7), which Draupadī does hear, along with her husbands.

23 3.28.2; see Hiltebeitel 2001a: 261 n. 58, 268.

24 At 12.17, Yudhiṣṭhira responds to his family's urging to abandon his aspiration to renounce the just-won kingship with what James Fitzgerald takes as 'a kind of soliloquy' (2004a: 694) in which '[t]he inner battle that Bhīma predicted now takes place within Yudhiṣṭhira' (ibid.: 179). But I think this is unlikely; see Hiltebeitel

2005c: 252. In that one could soliloquize in others' company, Dhṛtarāṣṭra could be the epic's main soliloquizer – and as Emily Hudson shows (Chapter 2), from right near the start.

25 See also Kuntī's narrative of the *Vidurā-Putra-Anuśāsana* (or *Vidurā-Putra-Saṃvāda*, 5.131–4). Cf. Dumézil 1968: 55: Kuntī 'sait sa théologie' when Pāṇḍu instructs her to invoke three gods for her impregnations.

26 See Hiltebeitel in press for a discussion of the frame of the *Rāma-Upākhyāna*, and Hiltebeitel 2001a: 216, 239 for the frame of the *Nala-Upākhyāna*.

27 Bhagavat is mentioned at 3.275.18d, and is clearly a coy allusion to Viṣṇu, for which there is a parallel in the *Nala-Upākhyāna*'s deployment of the charioteer Vārṣṇeya. For discussion, see Hiltebeitel in press.

28 Jamison does discuss the *Cirakāri-Upākhyāna* as a tale of 'adultery' slightly later (1996: 291 n. 2), but she focuses mainly on the *Rāmāyaṇa*'s version of Ahalyā's seduction for its emphasis on the theme of hospitality (ibid.: 156–7).

29 Jamison 1996: 96, 283 n. 221; cf. 95 ('sexual "kick" '), 98 ('frisson of forbidden sex'), and *passim*. If so, it would not be the only one in the sequence, as it is preceded by the *Sudarśana-Upākhyāna* (13.2) in which Sudarśana's wife Oghavatī performs hospitality by sleeping with a guest.

30 At least in popular traditions, with some possibility that the Sanskrit epic is the basis for their depiction, Draupadī has been celibate since her violation at the dice match; see Hiltebeitel 1981.

31 See Leslie 1998, and my discussion of her findings in relation to the *Śuka-Utpatti* in Hiltebeitel 2001a: 318–22.

32 For discussion, see Leslie 1989: 306–7; Bowles 2004: 227–35.

33 See Menski 2005: 449–80. The closest the *Mānava Dharmaśāstra* comes to even imagining divorce comes right after the famous verse denying women independence: 'As a child, she must remain under her father's control; as a young woman, under her husband's; and when her husband is dead, under her sons'. She must never seek to live independently. She must never want to separate herself from her father, husband, or sons; for by separating herself from them, a woman brings disgrace on both families' (5.148–9, tr. Olivelle).

34 Cf. van Buitenen 1973: 467: 'the slow protector'.

35 Who has the habit of appearing frequently in *upākhyāna*s; see Hiltebeitel 2005a: 480–4, 492.

36 Here and below I generally follow van Buitenen's translation (and later Fitzgerald's) except for small changes, unless otherwise indicated.

37 'Jaritāri', one of the names of the four sons, recalls the Rigvedic *jaritṛ* as a term for Agni as a singer (Macdonell 1974: 97; Lubotsky 1997, vol. 1: 559–60). Another of the sons, Sārisṛkva, addresses Agni with the Vedic name Jātavedas. In Söhnen-Thieme's comparison (2005) of the *Śārṅgaka-Upākhyāna* with the *Vaṭṭaka Jātaka* (Jātaka 35; for translation, see Cowell 2005, vol. 1: 88–90), this name is noted as central to an 'act of truth' in a *gāthā* verse uttered by the Buddha in one of his previous lives as a baby quail, by which he called upon Agni to cease his approach in the form of a great forest fire. Söhnen-Thieme regards the *gāthā* and three other verses as the nucleus of a Buddhist 'transformation' of a presumably non-Buddhist story, but not of this *Mahābhārata* story, which she sees as an indirect amplification – all of which seems cautious, plausible, and curious in that both traditions build their stories around pseudo-Vedic idioms. But note that the Jātaka story also includes a pralayic theme: the baby quail's words create the 'aeon miracle' of protecting the spot from fire for an entire aeon (*kalpa*), and thus protect the Buddha and his monks who have found themselves there. In effect, the Buddha, by his former truth-act as a quail, now protects his disciple-sons as Mandapāla does.

38 At 1.221.2. Cf. 1.224.4 and 6 (discussed on p. 120), where Mandapāla settles his thoughts on her as the one he is really worried about, and breaks with Lapitā.
39 At 2.62.3; 2.71.2; 2.72.12; cf. also 4.12.10; 4.34.11; 14.68.12. See Hara 1977–8: 58: the word 'makes frequent appearance . . . when a pitiable heroine in distress is described by her lamenting friends, both male and female, showing their sympathy with her'. He cites Nala's description of Damayantī at *Mahābhārata* 3.64.10 as an example.
40 See 1.220.24c, 28b; 1.223.12b, 15b (Agni as *jagat-pati*) on Agni and the entire *jagat*, and 1.221.11ab and 224.3 on release from the cosmic blaze as *mokṣa* (on which see the discussion of *pralaya* themes below).
41 The term is evocative of *satī* as *sahagamanam*. As Söhnen-Thieme nicely points out (2005), Jaritā is 'naturally not able to stop the fire with a hymn or a prayer'.
42 Indeed, they offer her some typical *mokṣadharma* wisdom on this point: 'We have done you no favours, you do not know us at all. Who are you, so virtuous (*satī*) that you support us under much anxiety, and who are we to you?' (1.222.13).
43 I thank Simon Brodbeck (personal communication, February 2006) for the following astute comment: 'In general, in this whole Śārṅgaka story the ones who face the fire are males (Mandapāla and the sons, because they must ensure the patriline survives), whereas the females can just fly off "around somewhere" and have other children: it is only the chicks who are so keen when Jaritā leaves them that her future sons might be their father's sons too. But the gendering of this "ancestral-heavenly" salvation and the gendering of the "freedom from future rebirth" *mokṣa* are slightly different' – the former requiring 'cooperation with the female'; the latter, 'rejection of the female'.
44 I translate *deśa* mainly as 'country' in this story and the next, as van Buitenen does only at the end of this story.
45 Van Buitenen has 'escape' for *plavane*.
46 1.224.9b: *mama saṃnidhau*. Van Buitenen somewhat overtranslates this phrase, which literally means no more than 'in my presence', but I have translated it as 'before my very eyes' to evoke the sense of being a witness since it might remind one of the story's bearing as 'unofficial law', and also since it might, with Lapitā as the *female* witness, be *slightly* suggestive in relation to the parable of the two birds in the one tree, discussed below.
47 From here through to the end of this passage, I do not follow van Buitenen's translation.
48 Cf. Ganguli 1.235, p. 453.
49 Van Buitenen trims this to, 'I left you to the Fire, but I found no peace' (not translating the '*itas*' – 'thence', 'from this'), which makes Mandapāla sound more as if he is simply exhibiting a regret.
50 Van Buitenen has 'the man you wanted' for *iṣṭam* (1.224.30c), which seems gratuitous.
51 See Menski 2005: 276–301, 317, 396–403, 433, 526–7 on *saptapadī* in Hindu marriage law; Nicholas 1995 on the invisibilization of divorce through emphasis on the marriage *saṃskāra* as a rite that leaves no mental room for marital dissolution; Jamison 1996: 121, citing *Śāṅkhāyana Gṛhyasūtra* 1.14.6 etc. (*sakhā saptapadī bhava*, 'Become a companion [friend] of the seventh step') and *Āpastamba Śrautasūtra* 10.23 (*sakhāyaḥ saptapadā abhūma*, 'We have become companions [friends] at the seventh step').
52 Hopkins 1969: 182 cites no corroborating passage when he briefly mentions, 'Arundhatī, though a model of faithfulness, yet suspected Vasiṣṭha and became "smoky-red" '. One cannot, of course, prove that a story is intentionally mis-told for effect, and that alert audiences would raise their eyebrows, but that is what I suspect here. The *Mānava Dharmaśāstra* seems to rely on this *Mahābhārata*

mis-telling when it relates both stories through the supposed low birth of Arundhatī to make the point that the cases of 'Śārṅgī' (= Jaritā) with Mandapāla and 'Akaṣmālā' (= Arundhatī) with Vasiṣṭha prove that 'women of low birth attained high status in this world by reason of the eminent qualities (*guṇas*) of their respective husbands' (*Mānava Dharmaśāstra* 9.23–4, tr. Olivelle)! But whether or not the *Mānava Dharmaśāstra* has the *Mahābhārata* story as precedent, its totally different emphasis and conclusion show the originality of the authors of both texts – as may also be said of the comparison between this story and the *Vaṭṭaka Jātaka* (see n. 37 above).

53 Belvalkar (1954: 737) calls attention to parallels in the *Harivaṃśa* (now appendix 5 in its Critical Edition) and the *Kuntanī Jātaka* (Jātaka 343), as Gombach notes (2000, vol. 1: 274). For further discussion, see Bowles 2004: 199–202.

54 This explains a statement in the previous story, the *Mārjāra-Mūṣaka-Saṃvāda*, in which a mouse tells a cat, 'no one is really anyone's friend – interests just coincide with other interests like elephants in the forests' (12.136.104).

55 Ganguli 13.10, p. 25, translating Critical Edition 13.10.1: 'Yudhisthira said, "I wish to know, O royal sage, whether any fault is incurred by one who from interested or disinterested friendship [*mitrasauhṛdabhāvena*] imparts instructions unto a person belonging to a low order of birth . . ." '.

56 The practice is the first of the four 'unlimited mental states' (*apramāṇacittas*), also known as the four *brahmavihāras* or 'stations of Brahmā': friendliness, compassion, sympathetic joy, and impartiality (see Conze 1967: 80–91). Buddhaghoṣa says the purpose of developing 'friendliness is . . . to seclude the mind from hate' (*Visuddhimagga* 9.3; see Ñāṇamoli 1975); first and foremost, friendliness 'should be developed . . . towards oneself' (9.8), on which the Buddha said, 'I visited all quarters with my mind / Nor found I any dearer than myself / Self is likewise to every other dear / Who loves himself will never harm another' (9.10). Some statements that the self (*Bhagavadgītā* 6.5–6) or one's *dharma* (merits, virtue, *Mānava Dharmaśāstra* 4.239) is one's true friend occur elsewhere in classical brahmanical sources, and are also, I think, varied ripostes to such Buddhist teachings. The *Gītā* citation, for instance, refers to *anātman* as an inimical outlook (6.6c) and occurs amid references to (*brahma-*)*nirvāṇa* (5.24–5; 6.15) and the friendship of Arjuna and Kṛṣṇa as two aspects of the self. See Sukthankar 1957: 94–102 on these verses and matters.

57 See *Mānava Dharmaśāstra* 5.147–8 (as partially cited in n. 33 above); 9.3. For the epic, see Jamison 1996: 236–7 and 305 n. 98, citing also the *Tapatī-Upākhyāna* (1.161.14), and noting contradictions of Manu's dictum. The issue and the key terms *svatantrā*/*asvatantrā* return in other substory material: the *Vyuṣitāśva-Upākhyāna* (1.113.4, 26); the *Sulabhā-Janaka-Saṃvāda* (with five references between 12.308.64 and 140); and the *Aṣṭāvakra-Dik-Saṃvāda* ('The Dialogue Between Aṣṭāvakra and Lady North', with seven references between 13.21.11 and 18). Meanwhile, the main story brings the terms to the fore when Sūrya is seducing Kuntī and telling her she is free to follow her desires (3.291.13), and at Karṇa's lowest moment when he tells Draupadī, now wagered, that she is not only *asvatantrā* but also the wife of a slave (2.63.1). See also the *Vivāha-Dharmāḥ* or 'The Laws Governing Marriage' at 13.46.13.

58 12.137.92a; for the translation 'dear', cf. the *Yājñavalkya-Maitreyī-Saṃvāda* at *Bṛhadāraṇyaka Upaniṣad* 2.4.1–13; 4.5.1–15.

59 Neither *puruṣa* nor *ātman* can commit *karma*, whether good or bad, so a 'man' (both terms are of masculine gender) is really saved no matter what he has done; see pp. 133–5.

60 *pāpaṃ kṛtvā hi manyeta nāham asmīti pūruṣaḥ* / 3.198.51. See similarly Nala's disclaimer about abandoning Damayantī: 'It was not my own fault' (*nāhaṃ*

tat kṛtavān svayam, 3.74.16b, tr. van Buitenen). On both passages, see Hiltebeitel 2001a: 235.

61 Olivelle 1999: xxviii–xxxiv places *Āpastamba Dharmasūtra* in the early third century BCE and *Gautama Dharmasūtra* in the mid-third century BCE as the two earliest Dharmasūtras.

62 I have added 'uterine', as Olivelle himself does when translating the parallel at *Mānava Dharmaśāstra* 11.59.

63 *Gautama Dharmasūtra* 23.17–20 lists penances for this and comparable sins, as do *Baudhāyana Dharmasūtra* 2.2.12–14 and *Vāsiṣṭha Dharmasūtra* 20.16 for comparable sins.

64 The expiation is provided at *Mānava Dharmaśāstra* 11.171.

65 James Hegarty (2004: 202 n. 298), speaking of 'the shifting identification of the being responsible for the replenishing of Draupadī's skirts', cites 2.*544.1–4 as yielding 'alternately, Dharma's intervention'. But he omits to mention that in the first two lines of this passage Draupadī invoked Kṛṣṇa, Viṣṇu, Hari, and Nara to make this happen. Nearly all manuscripts have Draupadī make some prayer to Kṛṣṇa, while the four that do not are in agreement with the rest that Duḥśāsana taunted her that she would do so (2.60.26). Given that Kṛṣṇa (5.58.21) and Draupadī (5.80.23–6) both agree later that he did so, it would seem that she made some private prayer even in the manuscripts where it is not so stated and where it is left, rather delicately (and perhaps originally), for one to piece things together from these other attestations. The epic has many ways of saying, 'Where Kṛṣṇa is, there is *dharma*.' For discussion of these matters, which continue to cause a lot of wishful readings, see Hiltebeitel 2001a: 250–7.

66 And it is most notably, and ironically, Karṇa – the *sakhā* of Duryodhana – who rises to defend the husband's ownership of the wife after the attempted disrobing (2.63.1); see Hiltebeitel 2001a: 259 and n. 57 above.

67 For *an-iṣṭa*: 'unwished, undesirable, disadvantageous, unfavourable; bad, wrong, evil, ominous' (Monier-Williams).

68 See 12.29.6, where Kṛṣṇa, speaking to Yudhiṣṭhira 'disarmingly' (*abhivinodayan*, Fitzgerald 2004a: 228) or 'entertainingly', launches into amusing stories, among them that of Svarṇaṣṭhīvin, 'Excretor of Gold', in the *Nārada-Pārvata-Upākhyāna* (12.30), to begin to dissolve some of Yudhiṣṭhira's postwar grief. See Hiltebeitel 2005c: 254–5 on this passage; on the generally gloomy and depressed character of Yudhiṣṭhira during the *aśvamedha*, see Jamison 1996: 76, to which p. 277 n. 151 adds, with only slight but, as I am trying to suggest, significant exaggeration, 'This, of course, is true for all of the postwar Mahābhārata. The Pāṇḍavas seem to live in a state of clinical depression for parvan after parvan.'

69 Note that at 14.89.6 he is called Hṛṣīkeśa, Viṣṇu, and 'increaser of the Bhoja princes'.

70 Dumézil 1970: 164 n. 9: '*Piṇḍikā*, which designates "a globular swelling or protuberance," here certainly has the meaning "cheekbone." '

71 Instead of *aniṣṭam*, the Vulgate (14.87.8b; see Kinjawadekar 1929–36) reads *saṃśliṣṭam*, on which Nīlakaṇṭha suggests something confounded, bristling, fleshy, and extending broadly and from behind.

72 I translate *sāsūyam* here as 'indignantly', noting that I have followed van Buitenen's 'jealously' in the response of Lapitā to Mandapāla's newfound concern for his 'poor wife' (1.224.7d; see p. 120 above). In fact, 'indignantly' would do for both usages, whereas 'jealously' would not fit the present one. For the adjectival *sāsūya*, Monier-Williams gives 'having envy, envious; disdainful, scornful, angry at or with'. Ganguli 14.87, p. 149, has 'angrily', which I would regard as the next best thing in this context.

73 Again, *praṇayam*; cf. the early Forest Book passage just cited.

74 'Visibly, really, actually' (Monier-Williams); with his own eyes.
75 The Vulgate reads *yājakās*, 'sacrificers' (14.87.12d) rather than *yādavās*.
76 Whose goal was varied; whose concern, manner, or meaning was charming, entertaining, amusing, colourful.
77 Dumézil would probably have in mind behind this the Vedic precedent of Viṣṇu's being the 'intimate friend of Indra' (*índrasya yújyaḥ sákhā*, *Ṛgveda* 1.22.19).
78 Note, however, that Ganguli turns matters around to make this point for Kṛṣṇa who, as far as I can see, leaves it entirely to Draupadī to affirm their friendship in *sakhā–sakhī* terms.
79 Those called M1–3 in the apparatus of the Critical Edition.
80 With little change from Jamison, who comments, 'Three minutes sounds about right. For whatever reason, at the Aśvamedha depicted in the Rāmāyana a whole night is required' (1996: 66), and describes in detail what the traditional ritual would expect of Draupadī (ibid.: 68–9).
81 See Sullivan 1990: 31–4; Hiltebeitel 2001a: 50–1, 77–9.
82 As van Buitenen demonstrated (1972), the *Mahābhārata*'s second book transposes the dice match that should end a *rājasūya* from Yudhiṣṭhira's ceremony at the Pāṇḍava capital, which ends without a dice match, to the ostensibly independent sequel that occurs when Yudhiṣṭhira is invited to play dice at the Kaurava capital.
83 See Jamison 1996: 256 on the 'sacrificed' sacrificer's wife playing the role of mediator between men and gods. I would suggest that this is the Vedic ground from which this aspect of Draupadī's relation to Kṛṣṇa is developed by the epic poets.
84 See Hiltebeitel 1976: 105, 293–4, 333, 356.
85 Cf. Monier-Williams: '*Piṇḍika*, n. the penis, *LiṅgaP.*; (*ā*), f., see *piṇḍaka*'; *piṇḍaka*, '. . . a round protuberance (esp. on an elephant's temples) . . . (*ikā*), f. a globular fleshy swelling (in the shoulders, arms, legs, &c., esp. the calf of the leg)'. Similar meanings also apply to *piṇḍa*. I will not press the late attestation of 'penis'.
86 On the principle that names of multiply named characters are often used selectively for their contextual fit, see Biardeau 2002: *passim*.
87 See *Kaṭha Upaniṣad* 3.3–9 and other *Mahābhārata* ramifications in Hiltebeitel 1984. See also n. 128 of Chapter 7.
88 Friendships between women in classical sources deserve further study, for which Pintchman's ethnography (2007) of women's friendships in Benares has important pointers.
89 Curiously, these are the same terms Drupada uses when he disingenuously asks Droṇa for 'eternal friendship' (1.128.13d) after the latter has returned to him half of the kingdom he conquered from him with the help of his just mentioned martial trainees.
90 As with the friendship forged between Rāma and Sugrīva (*Rāmāyaṇa* 3.68.13; 4.5.16).
91 Henceforth I use the stem form *sakhi* of the masculine noun generically rather than the nominative singulars *sakhā* and *sakhī*. I will not treat in this chapter the alternate meaning of *sakhi* as 'pact friend' or *socius*, on which see Hiltebeitel 1976: 254–66; Dumézil 1970: 20, 30.
92 Biardeau sees the parable of the two birds standing behind Kṛṣṇa's story (*Mahābhārata* 2.13.36–42) of the two allies of Jarāsaṃdha: Haṃsa (whose name 'Gander' evokes the supreme self or *ātman*) and Ḍimbhaka ('Sot', 'Fool'); see Biardeau 2002, vol. 2: 756.
93 I would not go as far as Oberlies, who argues that the *Śvetāśvatara* is from around 0–200 CE (1997: 86; 1988: 57–9), though he may be right (even if I doubt it) that it is younger than the *Gītā*. Cf. Olivelle 1996: 252: 'Its thought and vocabulary are close to those of the other famous theistic document, the Bhagavad Gītā.'

94 *Ṛgveda* 1.164.20–2; see most recently Houben 2000: 520–2.

95 *Anīśayā* is the instrumental of the feminine *anīśā*, 'not-lord', which Olivelle translates by this whole phrase.

96 See also Olivelle 1996: 399: the 'expression' *anīśā* 'probably refers to the female cosmic power, that is, *prakṛti*, which is distinct from the Lord and which is the cause of human ignorance. The opposition between the two principles is more pronounced in the SU [*Śvetāśvatara Upaniṣad*] [than it is in the *Muṇḍaka Upaniṣad*].'

97 This paragraph, and indeed this whole chapter, carries along a meditation on this description of Draupadī in Hiltebeitel 2001a: 271–7, especially 272–3 and nn. 88–90, the latter on the ' "darkly illuminating" sattvic quality' that the 'three Kṛṣṇas' Draupadī, Kṛṣṇa, and Vyāsa share. I would suggest that the identity of the Goddess as Yoganidrā in the *Devī Māhātmya* (1.54–71) and elsewhere would emerge from this range of ideas. As Viṣṇu's 'yogic sleep', it is she who, at Brahmā's behest, awakens Viṣṇu to defeat the demons Madhu and Kaiṭabha, thereby securing the continuance of creation.

98 Principally in the 1967, 1968, and 1971 articles reprinted in Biardeau 1981a.

99 Whose friendship also recalls their identity as Nara and Nārāyaṇa: '. . . the two dear friends who were the seers Nara and Nārāyaṇa' (*āstāṃ priyasakhāyau tau naranārāyaṇāv ṛṣī* // 1.210.5).

7

GENDERED SOTERIOLOGY

Marriage and the *karmayoga*

Simon Brodbeck

This chapter explores the interface of gender, analogy, and narrative.[1] The Sanskrit tradition up to and including the *Mahābhārata* contains certain gendered discourses which, when applied as background to our reading, yield a new perspective on one reiterated *Mahābhārata* motif: that of the man who, for individual interpersonal circumstantial reasons, wants to leave his wife. I will consider this motif as an allegory of a soteriological situation in which the soul 'wants to leave' *saṃsāra*,[2] and, *vice versa*, I will consider that soteriological situation as an allegory of this motif.

By 'soteriology' I mean the post-Vedic (or, at the very least, late Vedic, and also non-Vedic) *mokṣa*/*nirvāṇa*/*kaivalya* soteriology, which inverts and debases the parallel conventional *telos* of long life, family success, fame, wealth, heaven, excellent rebirth, etc. From this soteriological perspective, as *Mahābhārata* 12.190–1 has it, any rebirth is 'hell' (*niraya*), including this one. Textual traditions variously labelled 'Vedic', 'Hindu', 'Buddhist', 'Jain' etc. all admit a soteriological step in which an individual karmic career comes to an end. Varying perspectives are immediately possible. Is one thing, the 'subject' of the soteriological process, separating from and discarding another? In what sense does the 'subject' become transformed? Is there really a 'subject' both before and after the step?

If unsaved (and this is the soteriological situation – it is aspirational), we look at this step 'through a glass, darkly';[3] and so although we may think in terms of the departure of a soul (as in Hindu and Jain philosophy and in the *Mahābhārata*), we may also think of the situation as psychological and existential, and as invoking secondary and derivative metaphysical postulations – emergent properties, as it were, of a human social predicament. For the possibility of radical change to appeal, one must be persuaded that things are currently awful; but the turn to the psychological and the existential suggests that the idea of possibly effecting change may be a key component of any current awfulness. Hence determinism may be a meta-soteriological discourse;[4] hence also the traditional idea that marriage is indissoluble; and the *lokāyata* idea that there is no soul separable from the material world.

Early Indian soteriological discourse is androcentric, and soteriological achievement is narratively associated with men leaving their possessions, family, and social obligations, and going forth to wander.[5] Fellowship with other seekers may initially be useful (and apparently is the basis of many early Indian texts), but ultimately, as the *Suttanipāta* has it, 'One should wander solitary as a rhinoceros horn' (1.3.35, tr. Norman).[6] The wife is left behind along with everything else, even if she is relinquished last.

Initially, my proposal is threefold: firstly that there is considerable narrative cross-fertilization between the motif on the human level (a man wanting to depart on a private quest) and the soteriological situation on the metaphysical level (a soul or spiritual entity could depart or emerge from a gross material process); secondly that, either as a result of or as a contributing factor to that cross-fertilization, the motif and the soteriology are at least implicitly gendered, perhaps even in contexts where the gendered aspect is not stressed; and thirdly that the *Mahābhārata*, at least in part, resists and/or modifies the motif and the soteriology. In the *Mahābhārata*'s narrative, Yudhiṣṭhira and many others lose or relinquish or attempt to relinquish or nearly relinquish or nearly lose their wives, but do not actually do so, or at the very least only do so temporarily; and the text's more didactic sections – most famously the *Bhagavadgītā* – contain the message that soteriological success is attained not through physical renunciation, but through an inner renunciation which neutralizes *karmabandha* (the bondage generated by good and bad action) at source, allowing continued performance of social *dharma*s in a spirit of *karmayoga* (see also Chapter 12).

The chapter will pan out into an examination of Yudhiṣṭhira's masculinity – so-called because this character turns on his negotiation of the duty of *rakṣaṇa* (protection; Fitzgerald 2004a: 10–13), which, in the presumably male-authored *Mahābhārata*'s patrilineal world, is an almost entirely male prerogative. (Maternal child-protection is a rather neglected theme in the text[7] – usually *rakṣaṇa* does not figure as a duty for mothers, and *kṣatriya* ladies willingly send their sons to possible death in battle.[8]) The discussion of Dharmarāja's masculinity will proceed, as it does in the *Mahābhārata*, in counterpoint with another idea of how to be a man, that is, the renunciative ethos of what might very loosely be termed the '*śramaṇa* traditions', which the text presents in terms of defective masculinity, with *nāstika* and *klība* (impotent)[9] being partially interchangeable. In the *Mahābhārata*'s *kṣatriya* discourse, the king's duty to wield the *daṇḍa* and satisfy Śrī and Earth (see below) is presented in quasi-sexual terms, and soldiers who die heroically in battle are fit for sexual pleasures with the *apsarā*s in heaven. Insofar as it implies a rejection of these duties, renunciation is by implication the rejection of a certain normative masculinity.[10] Such a normative masculinity is of course not unknown outside ancient India; indeed, recent European and North American narrative traditions (such as the 'cop show', the 'western', and the normative presentation and discussion of 'news' in the national media) regularly evoke something like *rakṣaṇa* as a baseline of moral masculinity, particularly in the justification of violent action.

Gendered genesis and its soteriologico-narrative ramifications

Our project is complicated because the terms in which the *Mahābhārata* presents the dualism of 'spirit' and 'matter' (often *puruṣa* and *prakṛti*, though many other words are also used) are often not explicitly gendered within the text, and there is debate over the extent to which we may understand them as such. The general scholarly presumption has been that these are gendered categories (and such an interpretation is encouraged by the feminine grammatical gender of '*prakṛti*' and the basic meaning of '*puruṣa*' as 'male person', as well as by several textual suggestions[11]), but Knut A. Jacobsen has recently suggested – mentioning also the work of Mackenzie Brown (1986) in this regard – that *prakṛti* was 'feminized' only latterly, in a period post-dating the *Mahābhārata* and the basic philosophical *sāṃkhya* texts, through the influence of tantric ideas of *śakti* and the goddess (Jacobsen 1996).[12]

Jacobsen is an expert on *prakṛti* (Jacobsen 1999), but in the present context it is important that we sidestep certain implications of his work, in two ways.[13] Firstly, there are suggestions of *prakṛti*'s femininity in the philosophical literature even preceding *prakṛti*'s 'feminization': gendered metaphors are used to explain what *prakṛti* is. Jacobsen mentions some of these, principally the 'dancing girl' image of *Sāṃkhyakārikā* 59, and interprets them as mere metaphors. From this perspective *prakṛti*, as an impersonal unconscious principle, must be non-gendered;[14] but this is an analytical philosophical edge of a wider discourse in which two basic principles, variously labelled, feature in narratives many of which emphasize the gendered aspects omitted or at least downplayed by Jacobsen and the *Sāṃkhyakārikā*. Our concern is narrative interpretation, and hence much of the more philosophical literature is peripheral. Secondly, and relatedly, Jacobsen's argument that *prakṛti* was originally non-gendered is in many ways an argument *ex silentio*, and as such is overdependent on the choice of what exactly to listen for. If we listen for basic conceptual patterns, we find evidence in the late Vedic texts, Dharmaśāstras, and *Mahābhārata* that a polarity similar to that expressed in *sāṃkhya* texts by the terms *prakṛti* and *puruṣa* was narratively portrayed in explicitly gendered terms.

From the *Ṛgveda* onwards cosmogony is often presented, by analogy with human son-production, as dependent on a union of gendered entities. This analogy is pervasive, and it is often impossible to tell whether the main subject of discussion is the cosmos, or the individual person within it.[15] The gendered entities combining to create the cosmos are also indispensable personal constituents: every person has two parents, and also two metaphysical aspects. Selected quotations will demonstrate the gendered idea of the cosmic parents at some length (although examples could easily be multiplied), as this idea forms an essential backdrop for the remainder of the chapter. Procreation is not the only evident old Indian cosmogonic theory;[16] but nonetheless the identifiable gendered cosmo-parental mythology formed an implicit symbolic background for the *Mahābhārata*'s gendered narratives and metaphysical speculations.

The *Mānava Dharmaśāstra* says that 'the Lord who is Self-existent, himself unmanifest, caused this (universe) to become manifest . . . he of whom all creatures are made – he is the one who actually appeared' (1.6ab, 7cd, tr. Doniger with Smith).[17] Then we are told how:

> first he emitted the waters, and then he emitted his semen in them. That (semen) became a golden egg,[18] as bright as the sun with his thousand rays; Brahmā himself, the grandfather of all people, was born in that (egg) . . . The one who is the first cause, unmanifest, eternal, the essence of what is real and unreal, emitted the Puruṣa, who is known in the world as Brahmā.
>
> (*Mānava Dharmaśāstra* 1.8c–9, 11, tr. Doniger with Smith)[19]

The Lord is male, the waters female,[20] and the son (cosmos-as-person) differs from the father only in name, age, and level of manifestation. This cosmogony draws on a tradition of thinking apparent in the Veda in many variations. Sometimes the waters (*āpaḥ*, *salila*) appear to produce the incipient cosmos by themselves, without fertilization.[21] Sometimes both Lord and waters apparently preexist, neither being marked out as primary.[22] Sometimes, as here, the preexisting male produces the waters.[23] Often, as here, the incipient cosmos is a male person, and the two males are identified.[24] The role of the waters as the means for a non-manifest male to become manifest has unilineal implications matching the patrilineal emphasis on the obtaining of a son.[25] The unilineal tendency may render the gendered aspect less visible:

> . . . Such is his greatness, and Puruṣa is yet more than this. All creatures are a quarter of him; three quarters are what is immortal in heaven. With three quarters Puruṣa rose upwards, and one quarter of him still remains here. From this [quarter] he spread out in all directions, into that which eats and that which does not eat. From him Virāj was born, and from Virāj came Puruṣa. When he was born, he ranged beyond the earth behind and before.
>
> (*Ṛgveda* 10.90.3–5, tr. O'Flaherty)[26]

Here Virāj appears to be the mother through whom the father manifests one-quarter of himself as the son.[27]

In cosmogony, unity is perhaps instinctively more original than duality. Although one might suppose that the pre-cosmic Lord should initially be non-gendered, only latterly polarizing into male and female sexually productive aspects,[28] his gender is pronominally marked in advance, and carries over into the cosmic person. Clearly one must be (or become) two before one can be (or become) another one or many; and the prioritization of the pre-cosmic male, requiring as it does his ability independently to create a mate for himself, explains how, if the Lord and the waters only have one cosmic son (per universe), that son might himself manage to procreate:[29]

> In the beginning this was self (*ātman*), in the likeness of a person (*puruṣa*). Looking round he saw nothing but himself (*ātman*) . . . He was afraid . . . He had no pleasure either . . . He desired a companion. He became as large as a woman and a man embracing. He made that self split (*pat-*) into two: from that husband (*pati*) and wife (*patnī*) came to be. Therefore Yājñavalkya used to say, 'In this respect we two are each like a half portion'. So this space is filled up by a wife. He coupled with her, and from that human beings were born.
> (*Bṛhadāraṇyaka Upaniṣad* 1.4.1–3, tr. Roebuck)[30]

Puruṣa's way of creating human beings[31] mirrors the way the Lord created him. Only when offspring are multiple and of both genders (as implied here by their being human) can the line continue in the normal manner.

In the *Mahābhārata* Kṛṣṇa combines the extra-cosmic and intra-cosmic scenarios: 'Great Brahman is my womb; I put the embryo in it. Thence arises the production of all beings. Brahman is the great womb; I am the seed-giving father of the forms which arise in all wombs' (*Bhagavadgītā* 14.3–4).[32] Here '*brahman*', despite its grammatically neuter gender, plays an explicitly female role often played by (*mūla* or *avyakta*) *prakṛti* or the waters. But Kṛṣṇa claims his fertile companion as a possession or a part of himself.[33]

In the *Mānava Dharmaśāstra*, after Puruṣa-Brahmā hatches, he bifurcates and reproduces sexually, and the son is called Virāj; but the text then presents another reproductive method: 'By heating himself up with ascetic toil, that man, Virāj, brought forth a being by himself – know, you best of the twice-born, that I [Manu] am that being, the creator of this whole world' (1.33, tr. Olivelle).[34] Here *tapas* replaces the 'other half', and the female is unnecessary in all but name ('Virāj'). Manu then uses the same method to produce the ten 'mind-born' *ṛṣi*s. To be productive the male must polarize into himself plus another (*tapas*, mind, waters), so some mate/mother may always be identified, however disguised: 'the general principle of necessary gender complementarity is symbolically maintained' (Pintchman 1998: 271; see also Zwilling and Sweet 2000: 101). In the *Mahābhārata*, in microcosmic versions of the cosmogonic scenario where the Lord is paired with his *māyā* or *vidyā*,[35] Droṇa, Kṛpa, Śuka *et al.* are produced when a sage sees an *apsarā* and his consequent seminal emission is incubated in some impersonal or makeshift *yoni*.

The gendered cosmogonic principles necessarily pre-exist the infant cosmos, but are also integral aspects within it: thus sexual production is iterated at different levels in the ongoing analogical process. The analogy between microcosm and macrocosm is persistent and extensive;[36] and so, like the cosmos (male Puruṣa is male-plus-female), a human person has two essential constituents (*prakṛti* and *puruṣa* in *sāṃkhya* theory), internal representations of the parents.[37]

This analogical approach,[38] when applied iteratively, throws up a specific type of problem. Although each individual human is physically and nominally of unipolar gender, he/she has two gendered parents, and two gendered aspects (Goldberg 2002: 77). So if male and female characters are narratively to 'stand for' the Lord and the waters, or heaven and earth, or *puruṣa* and the material principle, it appears that there is sleight of hand. But we cannot allow this interesting problem[39] to stop us reading in this way, for that would be to scruple where some authors do not, and would impoverish our textual understanding.

If the cosmic parents are ranked (the male creates the waters), so are the two constituents of humans: the microcosmic Lord ('soul', *dehin*, *ātman*, *jīva*, *puruṣa*, *prāṇa*) is presented as essential; the body-stuff is not. The *mokṣa* soteriology attempts to re-claim the essence entirely: traditionally, according to the *nivṛtti* impulse, to be saved is to abandon materiality, the cosmic and microcosmic representation of the female principle[40] – by analogy, the wife of the soteriological subject. We see this in the *Śvetāśvatara Upaniṣad*, where the three colours of the female goat remind us of *prakṛti*'s *guṇa*s: 'With the nanny-goat, red, white and black, who brings forth many offspring like herself, lies one billy-goat, taking pleasure. The other billy-goat abandons her, who has had her enjoyment' (4.5, tr. Roebuck).[41] Old Indian narrative traditions prominently juxtapose soteriological attainment and wife-abandonment: Yājñavalkya, Mahāvīra and the Buddha abandoned their wives.[42] The *Buddhacarita* makes this into a general rule: 'All the *bodhisattva*s of matchless character, knowing sensual enjoyments, pleasures and delights, went to the forest once a son was born to them' (2.56).[43] This allows a man's wholehearted pursuit of *mokṣa/nirvāṇa* to follow the fulfilment of patrilineal duties within one lifetime,[44] and resembles the classical Hindu scheme of four successive *āśrama*s, which however values social duties more highly, prohibiting renunciation until much later (when the man's sons are independent, *Mahābhārata* 12.277.8; when he has grandchildren, *Mānava Dharmaśāstra* 6.2).[45] In all these cases a wife is necessary because sons are necessary.[46]

When, in the *Mahābhārata*, we see men ambivalent towards their wives, we can read this, on one level,[47] as discussion of the *mokṣa* soteriology (which resembles the gendered cosmogony in reverse). However, in the *Bhagavadgītā* Kṛṣṇa proposes a soteriological variant whereby one need not abandon one's wife to attain *mokṣa*.[48] In allowing both procreation and *mokṣa*-attainment, the *karmayoga* – or the *rājavidyā*[49] – parallels the mature *āśrama* system and the *bodhisattva* rule; but it is more thoroughgoing, obviating in principle the need ever to renounce the wife.[50] Hence many *Mahābhārata* stories dramatize the possibility of the man abandoning the wife: she is sometimes temporarily abandoned, but never for long. Our heroes must learn to live with her. The next two sections of the chapter will explore several such stories in terms of the soteriological dynamic between *puruṣa* and the material principle; but this is only possible now that we have established that there is already a long narrative tradition of presenting this dynamic in hierarchically gendered terms.

In emphasizing the wife, we single out one of several female symbolic units in the *Mahābhārata* which may stand for that which must be physically abandoned, according to the traditional soteriology, for salvation to occur. Others are Śrī (the goddess of fortune) and Earth (Pṛthivī, Bhūmi, Mahī). The king husbands Earth (his realm),[51] and Śrī is his consort; the queen represents his being Lord of Earth (*mahīpati*) and Śrī's favourite.[52] Because the *Mahābhārata*'s main characters are royal *kṣatriya*s, it exemplifies the renuciative impulse in terms of abandonment of the duties and trappings of kingship (including the citizens), and/or the wife. Wife-abandonment is sometimes partial or implicit, since she may still be there with the husband in emaciated form, suffering, without her finery.

The matter is complicated because in the *Mahābhārata* the wife is not just a cipher, an object in connection with male subjects; she is also a subject herself. As Olivelle has made clear (1997: 437–42), the traditional *mokṣa* soteriology implies every person's soteriological independence. The *Mahābhārata* is probably the earliest Sanskrit text explicitly to anticipate (Sanskrit-knowing subsets of) women and the 'lower' classes amongst its audience, and Kṛṣṇa's new soteriology is universally available.[53] The brief for women and *śūdra*s is one of unstinting service; but the *pativratā* wife, who cleaves to her husband for better, for worse (even if and as he rejects her), and who refuses to be abandoned because her destiny depends on him, could be a soteriological exemplar herself, regardless of her symbolic role in *his* story.

The case of Yudhiṣṭhira

Our primary example is the story of Yudhiṣṭhira, who becomes Dharmarāja.[54] As mentioned earlier, we are particularly interested in aspects of his masculinity bearing on the duty of *rakṣaṇa*, which in his case – his being a king – is theorized in specific symbolic and gendered terms, whereby his relations with his queen are glossed with his relations with the seven *prakṛti*s that constitute kingship ('The king, the minister, the country, the fortified city, the treasury, the army and the ally', *Arthaśāstra* 6.1.1, tr. Kangle).[55] In light of the dialogue with the renunciative traditions, particular attention will be paid to the ideas of loss or abandonment of one's wife, and loss or abandonment of one's (i.e. the king's, the good protector's) proper self, the primary ordinal of the *prakṛti*s, the *prakṛti*-that-is-*puruṣa*-too.

We will survey Yudhiṣṭhira's biography selectively, highlighting events particularly indicative of his character and his attitude to wife and kingdom, and comparing the stories of Pāṇḍu, the Buddha, Nala, and Rāma along the way. We will see that in Yudhiṣṭhira's case, focused as it is through these allied stories, brief wife-abandonment, despite and through being a failure of *rakṣaṇa* in the face of *śramaṇa* ideology, marks the way to self-knowledge and eventual dutiful success. But the dilemma arises for Yudhiṣṭhira repeatedly, and in different forms, and in my view the cumulative effect cannot properly be dealt with unless the dramatic situations are seen in Yudhiṣṭhira's biographical context. Hence this section is organized chronologically, like Norbert Klaes's book of 1975, with details of the story sketched in when required. The section is further broken down into subsections dealing with Yudhiṣṭhira's father; Yudhiṣṭhira's acquisition of a spouse and the Khāṇḍava kingdom; his loss of the same; his rehabilitation while in exile; his acquisition of the united kingdom; and his last days.

Yudhiṣṭhira's father Pāṇḍu (1.105–16)

Yudhiṣṭhira hardly knows his father Pāṇḍu; since he has problems coming to terms with his masculinity, this omission seems significant. It would then also be significant that Pāṇḍu doesn't know *his* father (Vicitravīrya) either.[56] Pāṇḍu's story may be viewed in light of the absence of a paternal example; and, since apparently he doesn't hear this story, so may Yudhiṣṭhira's.

Pāṇḍu, tired of kingship, retired childless, with his wives, to a forest life of hunting. Dhṛtarāṣṭra, regent in his absence, obtains many sons, and the narrators explain Pāṇḍu's childlessness: after a hunting accident, he is cursed to celibacy or death, and decides on a solitary ascetic life, striving for *mokṣa*. His wives are 'intent on the world/s of our husband' (1.110.27)[57] and insist on joining him in the ascetic life, and he agrees with apparent indifference; but when eventually 'he set out together with his wives from the hundred-peaked (mountains) facing north, wanting to cross to the other side of heaven' (1.111.5),[58] the *ṛṣi*s prevent him, saying the path is too hard for women. But Pāṇḍu blames his childlessness, which now obsesses him, and eventually sons are produced *via* celestial sperm-donation, Yudhiṣṭhira's 'biological' father being the god Dharma. 'Then Pāṇḍu, seeing those five beautiful sons guarded by the strength of his own arms in the great mountain forest, became happy' (1.116.1);[59] but his death by sexual misadventure follows immediately.

Pāṇḍu shows no desire for children until the *ṛṣis* check his progress, even though one might have expected the king's childlessness to have caused concern much earlier. The text describes three separate renunciations: of the kingdom, of sex (enforced, with one fatal exception), and of hunting (in favour of *mokṣa*). We might superimpose these renunciations, imagining that Pāṇḍu's accident and curse led to his renouncing the kingdom, sex, and hunting all together. The narrators are particularly concerned with the question of royal heirs (Pāṇḍu's premature renunciation of the kingdom helps set up the conflict between the cousins), but Pāṇḍu's triple renunciation is due to *duḥkha*, the down-side of knowledge about mortality: you may enjoy yourself, but it can't last (Piatigorsky 1993: 111–25). Pāṇḍu 'misunderstands' the *ṛṣis*, whose reason for intervening fits the traditional renunciative soteriology: perhaps they would expect Pāṇḍu to dismiss his wives and continue alone, but instead he comes to terms with his ancestors, his wives, and his sexuality. His career has three phases: comparatively carefree early days; asceticism; and dharmic compromise. His death in Mādrī's arms, though ostensibly the result of desire, is also a paradigm of desirelessness: we know from the *Bṛhadāraṇyaka Upaniṣad* that 'As a man embraced by a woman he loves is oblivious to everything within or without, so this person embraced by the *ātman* consisting of knowledge is oblivious to everything within or without' (4.3.21, tr. Olivelle);[60] and in a karmayogic light this may be seen as more than a simile.

Yudhiṣṭhira before the dicing

Kuntī brings the children to the Hāstinapura court, but they soon find themselves in exile for their own safety (1.137ff.). Disguised as brahmins, the Pāṇḍavas attend Draupadī's *svayaṃvara*, where all five fall in love with her and Arjuna wins her hand. They already know that Draupadī was not born from a womb, but was summoned from the fire for *kṣatriya* doom in a rite of black magic (1.154–5). Yudhiṣṭhira, perhaps fearful of trouble, perhaps green with envy, hastens from the *svayaṃvara* scene even before Draupadī has given Arjuna the garland. Kuntī proposes they share Draupadī; Yudhiṣṭhira tells Arjuna to have her; Arjuna, speaking also for the others, tells Yudhiṣṭhira to have her; and Yudhiṣṭhira, realizing they all love her, and mindful of Vyāsa's earlier advice, acquiesces to Kuntī's proposal. Drupada is persuaded that this is dharmic, the marriage is held (1.190–1), and the Pāṇḍava juggernaut has begun to roll, with Yudhiṣṭhira, bewitched by Draupadī and bound by his priority, inadvertently in the van.

Yudhiṣṭhira's other wife is Devikā, mentioned only once (1.90.83):[61] daughter of Govāsana Śaibya, she chose him at her *svayaṃvara*, and they have a son Yaudheya.[62] Draupadī, princess of Pāñcāla, Yudhiṣṭhira's royal wife, is first his brother's wife; when he later tries to leave her and the kingdom, Yudhiṣṭhira might regret how things have turned out.

Dhṛtarāṣṭra partitions the kingdom between his own sons and Pāṇḍu's, who found Indraprastha. Arjuna, sensitive to Yudhiṣṭhira over their wife,[63] spends some time away, contracting various other marriages; when he seeks Yudhiṣṭhira's blessing for his abduction of Kṛṣṇa's sister Subhadrā, it is immediately provided. Subhadrā produces Abhimanyu, and Draupadī (only later?) five sons, one per husband (1.213.58–82).

The juggernaut rolls: Arjuna and Kṛṣṇa burn Khāṇḍava Forest; *asura* Maya builds the Pāṇḍavas a *sabhā* (at Kṛṣṇa's suggestion – the deal is done before Yudhiṣṭhira knows of it); Indraprastha hosts celebrities (2.1–4). Nārada reports Pāṇḍu's post-mortem wish for Yudhiṣṭhira to perform the *rājasūya*, and Yudhiṣṭhira considers the idea. He is urged by brothers, friends, and ministers; Kṛṣṇa proposes to canvass support by killing Jarāsaṃdha in his name. Yudhiṣṭhira is uneasy ('I think that if it is begun, the principal object will not be obtainable', 2.14.5),[64] but Kṛṣṇa uses emotional blackmail for his assent,[65] his brothers perform the *digvijaya* for him, and, overtaken by the momentum of events, Yudhiṣṭhira orders the *rājasūya*.

At the ceremony, the host is unsure which *kṣatriya* guest should receive his primary honour: his choice of Kṛṣṇa, proposed by Bhīṣma, is opposed by Śiśupāla, and a rumpus ensues, during which Kṛṣṇa kills Śiśupāla (2.33–42). Welcome to the hot seat, *samrāj* (universal monarch)!

Yudhiṣṭhira the gambler

Dhṛtarāṣṭra invites Yudhiṣṭhira to Hāstinapura to dice with Duryodhana (2.44–67).[66] Yudhiṣṭhira accepts the invitation,[67] despite Vidura's warnings and his own uneasiness. Finding that Śakuni, a dice expert,[68] will be playing for Duryodhana, he still goes ahead. He stakes and loses his wealth and land, his brothers, himself, and finally, at Śakuni's suggestion, Draupadī. But she will not be lost, and protests that her staking was unlawful, Yudhiṣṭhira having already lost himself and thus any claim over her; and Dhṛtarāṣṭra is convinced (by her protest, by Karṇa, Duryodhana, and Duḥśāsana's insults to her during the ensuing debate, and by other omens) to grant her boons and annul the match. Duryodhana persuades his father to recall the Pāṇḍavas for a shorter game: the stake this time is exile for thirteen years, with Draupadī, and when Yudhiṣṭhira loses she accepts the result. During their exile Bṛhadaśva tells them the story of Nala and Damayantī (3.50–78, after Yudhiṣṭhira calls himself the unluckiest man), and Mārkaṇḍeya tells them the story of Rāma and Sītā (3.258–75, after Yudhiṣṭhira repeats the claim), amongst others.

Yudhiṣṭhira gives Vidura several explanations for his initial acceptance of Dhṛtarāṣṭra's invitation (2.52.14–18): the *kṣatriyadharma* of accepting challenges, the *kuladharma* of obeying one's uncle, and the inexorability of Dhātṛ (the 'Placer') and *daiva* (the business of the gods). Such dharmic-explanatory details are a *Mahābhārata* speciality, but may obscure a more direct narrative sense. That dicing was an integral part of the *rājasūya* ritual[69] the *Mahābhārata* nowhere mentions: although this is suggested by Vedic ritual manuals, and may help explain why the authors put the dice match here, such a proposal can only take us so far – it would be one more dharmic explanation to add to Yudhiṣṭhira's list. Behind his excuses and fondness for dice, where Yudhiṣṭhira's real motivations should be, questions remain. Why did Yudhiṣṭhira agree to play this game, and then, why did he stake Draupadī?

In terms of our interest in the soteriological overtones of wife-abandonment, we can observe immediately that Yudhiṣṭhira did not play in order to lose his wife. But that is not the whole story. Yudhiṣṭhira knows nothing of his destiny in terms of the destruction of the demonic *kṣatriya*s (1.58–61), and his comments about *daiva*, though correct, are out of range. In the wider picture, the puppet-masters play out their drama with Yudhiṣṭhira in a leading role, and at his expense (amongst many others; see Brodbeck in press a) – but we are presently interested in his business, not theirs. Perhaps, spurred by his recent success, he was trying to play politics – in those terms there was something to be gained. Shulman says that 'Latent desire appears to motivate a gesture rationalized as *noblesse oblige*' (1992: 362). Mehendale highlights Balarāma's speech at 5.2.9–11: 'According to Balarāma's version, the compulsion for playing the game was Yudhiṣṭhira's own urge to play; he lost, because his confidence was misplaced' (1995b: 37). Mehendale also highlights Yudhiṣṭhira's account to Bhīma (3.35.1–5): he wanted Duryodhana's half of the kingdom;[70] when Śakuni's superiority became clear, instead of cutting his losses, he became angry.

Perhaps Yudhiṣṭhira, if allowed, would have led a quiet dharmic life; but he is led into power by circumstances (his being 'first-born'; his brothers' extraordinariness, including Arjuna's winning Draupadī; Kuntī's sealing the polyandrous marriage; Dhṛtarāṣṭra's partitioning the kingdom; Maya's *sabhā*; his various advisors' machinations). In this position, he tries to make more of himself. He agrees to dice; going it alone, he overreaches himself – and second-hand ambition is precarious. Having willingly contrived a situation of maximum embarrassment, his self-confidence misplaced, he responds by throwing it all away.[71] He loses control, effectively tries to burn his bridges.

The renunciative urge is presented, in soteriological texts, as *duḥkha*'s consequence, and for our purposes this existential prompt outweighs the hypothetical goal. The Buddha-to-be sees an old man, a diseased man, and a dead man (*Buddhacarita* 3.26–62); learning the facts of life, in *duḥkha* he rejects his harem (4.1–103); meeting a *śramaṇa*, he decides to renounce (5.16–21; cf. Pāṇḍu). Yudhiṣṭhira, recently in splendour, discovers his success is ill-founded, unsustainable by his own merits; he is *samrāj par hazard*, and the coin's dark side looms. What now? Remain in the *pravṛtti* game, and strive in pain, embarrassment, and uncertainty to restore what's lost, however ephemeral and (now) hollow the prize? This is not his first-choice option.

Yudhiṣṭhira stakes himself, and loses. Śakuni says, 'This is the worst you could have done, losing yourself! Self-loss is wicked, king, when a stake remains' (2.58.29).[72] Draupadī is 'something left', and now becomes Yudhiṣṭhira's final stake at Śakuni's suggestion. Śakuni's critique fits the *Mahābhārata*'s quarrel with the *śramaṇa* paradigm: accepted responsibilities must be taken seriously, or others suffer – the renouncer leaves someone behind.[73] Yudhiṣṭhira cannot choose the quiet life now; he is already rolling on other tracks. From Draupadī's perspective, if Yudhiṣṭhira lost himself while another stake remained, then he forfeited rights over that remainder: she had better now seek protection (*rakṣaṇa*) elsewhere, or even take charge of herself, rather than remaining 'his'.[74]

Yudhiṣṭhira errs in ordering his stakes, but perhaps only having lost himself is he able to stake his wife. To illuminate this suggestion, which implies a severe critique of renunciation, we will compare Nala's story, where loss of self precedes loss (i.e. renunciation) of wife.[75] King Nala is possessed by the demon Kali, and falls prey to gambling; challenged by his brother, he loses his kingdom (the dice are possessed by another demon, Dvāpara); retaining only himself and his wife Damayantī (whom he would not stake), the two of them go to the forest. Nala, ashamed, cannot persuade Damayantī to abandon him, and dithers over abandoning her. 'But he was dragged away by Kali; Nala, deluded, fled, moaning pitifully again and again, leaving that wife sleeping' (3.59.24).[76]

Kali makes Nala abandon Damayantī: he is not himself (hence, perhaps, the question of staking himself never arises). Yudhiṣṭhira, *sans* demon, must lose himself to get to this point. The renunciative urge, marked by wife-abandonment, requires loss of self.[77] Thus the text can reverse events by having the character regain himself.

Dhṛtarāṣṭra intervenes and restores to Yudhiṣṭhira whatever was lost; then, when called back for the re-match (his stated reasons for accepting are the same as for the first match), Yudhiṣṭhira stakes neither himself nor his family members. The Pāṇḍavas and Draupadī are exiled in rags, but though down they are not out.[78]

Dhṛtarāṣṭra's role is played in Nala's story by the snake Karkoṭaka,[79] who, rescued by Nala from a forest fire, bites him, turning him temporarily into a hunchback but also poisoning Kali within him, thus initiating his gradual restoration. By returning for the second dice match Yudhiṣṭhira rescues Dhṛtarāṣṭra from the Duryodhana-fire; by losing it he is bitten, and temporarily transformed, distorted, and diminished. Yudhiṣṭhira's Kali to conquer is Duryodhana (who incarnates him),[80] and the urge to abandon self and wife.

Nala is apart from Damayantī for some time before she engineers their reconciliation, but Draupadī wins back Yudhiṣṭhira on the spot, through

Dhṛtarāṣṭra's boon. After this they are somewhat estranged: Draupadī, without regal apparel, says that until her humiliation is redressed she will have no husbands at all.[81] While Draupadī fears that Yudhiṣṭhira has no intention of activating his patrilineal *kṣatriya* self and demanding that redress,[82] this seems appropriate; but 'he thought about it for almost an hour and worked out the proper thing to do' (3.37.2).[83] She accepts that he is just biding time, and after the exile they are a public couple again, and scores are settled. As Paul Bowlby observes, 'the war between the Pāṇḍavas and their cousins . . . is the completion of the . . . dice match for Yudhiṣṭhira and his brothers' (1991: 4). Structurally, the Kurukṣetra war matches Nala's second, triumphant dice game, at which, after reuniting with his wife, he wins back his kingdom. On that occasion Nala stakes Damayantī and himself, both at once; but by that stage he is self-possessed and has learned to play expertly.

Comparing Yudhiṣṭhira and Nala's wife-abandonment with the Buddha's, we note that in the former, dicing frames the motif, and no soteriological goal is explicitly mentioned. But because of this second difference, the stories converge: each man succeeds, in rajadharmic or in soteriological terms. In the *Mahābhārata*'s terms, wife-abandonment is a failure of *rakṣaṇa*, but for all three characters it marks the way to self-knowledge and eventual success. The *Mahābhārata*'s dharmic *kṣatriya*s may lose self, wife, and kingdom through death in battle; but if they lose these through folly or mistaken attraction to the *śramaṇa* life, they must survive and come back the stronger for it. According to Kṛṣṇa's soteriological variant, discarding proper self, wife, and kingdom in hope of avoiding further embodiment just leads to further, probably degraded, embodiment; but a dharmic *kṣatriya* death leads to glorious heavens, and, for *karmayogin*s, perhaps *mokṣa* too. And in Yudhiṣṭhira's case, though he leaves the kingdom, he keeps his self and wife,[84] a preferable option should one's career involve *duḥkha*, leading as it does to his subsequent restoration.

Whatever potlatch-esque or men's-club scenarios may lie behind an inferred tradition of high-stakes gambling,[85] *Mahābhārata* dicing stories comment on the *śramaṇa* option in the context of kingship as well as exploring the marital responsibilities of both genders in terms of the twin ideologies of *rakṣaṇa* and *pativratā*. The interrelationship of these two is shown when a failure of the former is answered by a demonstration of the latter, and the former's resumption. (Presumably a similar story can be told with the boot on the other foot – i.e. a negligent wife won back through her husband's faith in his duty – but we do not see that here.) Whilst wife and kingdom fall out of the Buddha's story before the main event occurs, the *Mahābhārata*, using the same pieces, focuses elsewhere.

Compare Rāma's career. Like Yudhiṣṭhira, he seems initially uninterested in kingship: he goes into exile with his wife and brother ostensibly in fidelity to his father's word, but this may be a dharmic mask concealing distaste for the throne the squabbles for which have killed his father. Due to a political error of Rāma's, Sītā is abducted; eventually he locates her and kills her captor Rāvaṇa. At the reunion, Rāma takes a good look, and rejects Sītā.

> Rāma suspected her of having been touched, and he said to Vaidehī, 'Go, Vaidehī, you are free. I have done what I had to do. Once you found me as a husband, good woman, you were not to grow old in a Rākṣasa's house – that is why I killed the night-stalker. For how would a man like me, who knows the decision of the *dharma*, maintain even for an instant a woman who had been in another man's hands? Whether you are innocent or guilty, Maithilī, I can no more enjoy you, no more than an oblation that has been licked by a dog.'
>
> (*Mahābhārata* 3.275.10–13, tr. van Buitenen)[86]

Here again is the dharmic mask. Perhaps Rāma wants no longer to do what he had/has to do. After kingdom troubles, he left the kingdom; after wife troubles, he would leave the wife. Perhaps Lakṣmaṇa would have been next – but Sītā, like Draupadī, will not be abandoned: at her call, Wind, Fire *et al.* confirm her purity, and Rāma's deceased father bids him take back the kingdom too. He cannot refuse.

If Rāma is to be seen in allegorical terms, like Yudhiṣṭhira and Nala, as a *mokṣa* seeker, a would-be renouncer, then Sītā and the kingdom are his *prakṛti*, his body – Sītā is replete with telluric symbolism. Like Yudhiṣṭhira, Rāma shies away from the burden of kingship (of patrilineal householdership writ large, and/or of embodiment writ sideways – the burden of *rakṣaṇa*). Like Yudhiṣṭhira and Nala, after suffering he tries unsuccessfully to throw it all away. But while Rāma's scene with Sītā ends his exile, and he takes up his kingdom forthwith, Yudhiṣṭhira must wait, and fight.[87]

With regard to the stories of Yudhiṣṭhira, Nala, and Rāma, one might wonder whether the *Mahābhārata* sets up renunciation/exile/attempted wife-abandonment as a necessary and prescribed stage in the archetypal king's career, in the manner of the *āśrama* system with its successive stages. On the whole I think not. Although at some level there is a symbolic need for the king to experience and subdue the wilderness (Falk 1973; Parkhill 1995), this can happen in a variety of ways. The drama of the wife-abandonment stories adds to their didactic effect, but surely they are told at least partly in hope that audience members and future kings may learn from these characters' mistakes, and not repeat them. We see such a possibility when the Pāṇḍavas hear the story of how Sunda and Upasunda fought over a woman, and so take measures not to fight over Draupadī (1.200–4). On the other hand, the situation in which Yudhiṣṭhira hears Nala's story and Rāma's shows that these stories may also reassure kings who *have* made grave mistakes, demonstrating that it is not all over yet.

Draupadī's other indignities

While exiled Yudhiṣṭhira recovers composure and resolve for kingship, partly due to Draupadī's promptings. But the focus of his shame drifts easily from Draupadī's plight to his own self-image: when she faints at high altitude on their *tīrthayātrā*, he comforts himself with self-pity, and Dhaumya and other brahmins minister to him, Draupadī's recovery being secondary (3.144). This example may show Yudhiṣṭhira's love for Draupadī (Mary Brockington 2001: 257), but also reveals his self-absorption – rare now is the crisis in which he does not make himself the centre of attention. It seems that the authors are trying to keep Yudhiṣṭhira at the centre of audience attention, and to emphasize, in his case, the existential negotiations attendant upon being a dharmic actor.

Draupadī is abducted by Jayadratha (3.248–56),[88] and molested at Virāṭa's court (by the *sūta* Kīcaka and family, 4.13–23) as she was at the dicing (2.60–3). During Draupadī's dice-match molestation Yudhiṣṭhira remained silent; Bhīma came to her defence, thirsting for vengeance; and Arjuna steered a middle course, sympathetic to Bhīma's instincts but mindful of Yudhiṣṭhira's authority. But when Jayadratha abducts Draupadī, Yudhiṣṭhira, sensing trouble, brings the Pāṇḍavas home from their hunting trip. He scolds the maid for reminding them to rescue their wife, and all the brothers fight against Jayadratha. Once Draupadī is safe, Yudhiṣṭhira makes Bhīma spare Jayadratha.[89] So here Yudhiṣṭhira demonstrates *rakṣaṇa* towards Draupadī.

When Kīcaka molests Draupadī,[90] their need to remain unrecognized during the last year of exile – Draupadī blames Yudhiṣṭhira[91] – compromises the Pāṇḍavas' ability to protect her. However, through virtue and piety Draupadī has obtained an invisible *rākṣasa* bodyguard from the sun,[92] so her 'husbands' need not intervene: Yudhiṣṭhira restrains Bhīma, and Draupadī's public outrage targets Virāṭa, the host. Yudhiṣṭhira's frustration is clear, but when Bhīma privately kills Kīcaka, this is impolitic: Kīcaka's kin now seek Draupadī's death, so Bhīma kills them too, making Virāṭa wary of continuing to host Draupadī.

King Yudhiṣṭhira

After the exile, Yudhiṣṭhira's old *kṣatriya* advisors and allies reappear. Unprompted, Yudhiṣṭhira asks Śalya, who will fight on Duryodhana's side, to turn this to the Pāṇḍavas' advantage by weakening Karṇa somehow (5.8). To Saṃjaya, the Hāstinapura emissary, Yudhiṣṭhira proposes to regain his kingdom whatever it takes; but just as Saṃjaya is leaving, Yudhiṣṭhira offers to settle for five villages (5.31), and then he sends Kṛṣṇa on a similarly futile peace mission. These gestures suggest ambivalence towards needless slaughter rather than towards *rakṣaṇa* – and the strength of Duryodhana's armies is well known. Overall, in Books 5–11, Yudhiṣṭhira follows Kṛṣṇa's advice (Klaes 1975: 88–107).

Yudhiṣṭhira fights valiantly but loses relatives, allies, and his son Prativindhya. Afterwards, discovering Karṇa to have been his elder brother, he is overcome by *duḥkha*, curses all women (for Kuntī's secret), and wants to retire.[93] His brothers reason with him. Draupadī takes it personally, calls him mad (i.e. not himself), and groups him with the *nāstika*s:

> My mother-in-law, who knows all and sees all, lied to me. 'Yudhiṣṭhira will bring you the highest happiness, O princess of Pāñcāla, after he who is so quickly aggressive kills many thousands of kings.' I see that that was wrong, because your mind is muddled, O lord of people. When the eldest in a group is insane, all the others follow after him; so all the Pāṇḍavas are insane, O Indra among kings, because you are insane. If they were not insane, O lord of people, your brothers would imprison you along with the unbelieving *nāstika*s, and govern the earth.
>
> (*Mahābhārata* 12.14.30–3, tr. Fitzgerald)[94]

She then recommends pharmaceutical treatment. *Nāstika*s recur in these rajadharmic arguments against Yudhiṣṭhira:[95] this brahmanical objection to *kṣatriya* renunciation highlights the failure to protect and please females (kingdom and citizens being symbolically female).

Arjuna tells Yudhiṣṭhira about Janaka (12.18), who exchanged wife and kingdom for asceticism as Yudhiṣṭhira threatens to, but did so with clear soteriological intent – his story can help us understand Yudhiṣṭhira's otherwise vague intentions.[96] Janaka's wife seeks out Janaka and scolds him for irresponsibility, using – as do the other Pāṇḍavas[97] – karmayogic arguments already heard by Arjuna in the *Bhagavadgītā* in a similar situation. Allegedly Janaka, presumably after his wife's speech, became a *karmayogin*,[98] although Arjuna does not say so here.

Earlier, Yudhiṣṭhira has heard hints of the *karmayoga* and mentioned it to Draupadī (3.2.30; 3.32.2–5, 24). Yudhiṣṭhira and Arjuna trust Kṛṣṇa; but do they become *karmayogin*s? The text, describing deeds and words only, will not tell us, for *karmayogin*s are externally unmarked. Kṛṣṇa says, 'As the unknowing ones act, attached to action, Bhārata, just so should the knowing, non-attached one act, desiring to effect the holding-together of the world/s' (*Bhagavadgītā* 3.25).[99] Arjuna says (for Janaka's wife), 'Behaving as if attached, though non-attached, aloof, free of bonds, impartial towards enemy and friend: that one indeed is released, O lord of the earth' (*Mahābhārata* 12.18.30).[100]

Yudhiṣṭhira is persuaded to rule the reunited kingdom from the Hāstinapura throne.[101] After his coronation he receives the local trade secrets from Bhīṣma at length. The *mokṣadharma* section of these teachings, despite occasional karmayogic moments, has a *nivṛtti* tone contrasting with the *rājadharma*, *āpaddharma* and *dānadharma* sections and the *Bhagavadgītā*. The two teaching sessions – Kṛṣṇa's to Arjuna in the *Bhagavadgītā*, and Bhīṣma's to Yudhiṣṭhira in the *Śāntiparvan* and *Anuśāsanaparvan* – fit their characters. Arjuna's *Bhagavadgītā* paralysis and *nivṛtti* impulse[102] are uncharacteristic of him (except when deferring to Yudhiṣṭhira), and Kṛṣṇa is a *pravṛtti* paradigm (Great Brahman's impregnator, his incarnation corrects the local dharmic balance in protection of Earth). Bhīṣma, however, who rejected kingship and swore celibacy years earlier,[103] is an imperfect sovereign representing a *kṣatriya* problem, so his *mokṣadharma* is hardly surprising.[104] That he also teaches the family *rājadharma* he has personally refused matches his geriatric conversion to Kṛṣṇa-*bhakti*: before Bhīṣma teaches, Kṛṣṇa puts his *buddhi* into him (12.54.27–30). Yudhiṣṭhira represents the same *kṣatriya* problem (von Simson 2000a: 311, 316), but is also on the turn, having rallied after his latest lapse.[105] However, after Bhīṣma's *mokṣadharma* and death, Yudhiṣṭhira again wants to renounce (14.2.11–13). Kṛṣṇa repeats the gist of the *Bhagavadgītā* (minus the *bhakti*, which has served its purpose), recommending that Yudhiṣṭhira conquer his inner enemy (14.11–13); but although Yudhiṣṭhira performs the *aśvamedha* and rules, he is unhappy, burdened by his grisly past and denied his preferred tonic.

Yudhiṣṭhira's rule is something of a biographical gap. He did not like being king, but we hardly see him being king; his reign's salient feature is his distaste for it. Practically, he acquiesces, and his idealistic instincts have been immaterial, except (there's the rub) as a tale for others: he is paternally commanded from beyond the grave, pushed around by teachers, spooked by his indominable devoted wife. His self-assertions are fancies – the identity he proposes is not his. He joins the ancient dharmic kings who were beloved of Śrī, sponsored rituals, overcame difficulties, made donations, fought glorious battles, and went to heaven. But reading Yudhiṣṭhira's story we suspect they might not have liked it; after the dicing, Yudhiṣṭhira never believes the hype. Those kings are in stories, we now suspect, to encourage others – otherwise (the story goes) the world degenerates, women are molested, and brahmins go hungry. Perhaps this message is subversive. Yudhiṣṭhira, like the war-widows, is royally ruined; resistance is futile, but also *right* somehow – and so Yudhiṣṭhira can be a hero (Mary Brockington 2001: 256–7). His integrity as Dharmarāja requires him to distrust his *rājadharma*.

Yudhiṣṭhira's retirement and death

When Dhṛtarāṣṭra asks permission to retire, finally leaving him in sole charge (Dhṛtarāṣṭra has been King Yudhiṣṭhira's close consultant), Yudhiṣṭhira says the kingdom is a disease, and if Dhṛtarāṣṭra is retiring, he will too – Yuyutsu, for example, should be king (15.6.5–8). Yudhiṣṭhira allows Dhṛtarāṣṭra's retirement because Vyāsa insists. Later, while visiting the elders in the forest,

Yudhiṣṭhira is weirdly entered by Vidura, whose body is left lifeless. At the end of the visit Yudhiṣṭhira, loath to return to Hāstinapura, tells Gāndhārī: 'O queen, my heart [*buddhi*] no longer turns as of old towards kingdom. My mind [*manas*] is wholly set upon penances now' (15.44.30, tr. Ganguli 15.36, p. 57)[106] – he must again be ordered to rule, this time by Kuntī. But eventually he does retire, with his brothers, Draupadī, and a dog, to circumambulate the subcontinent (17.1).

Beyond the Himavat, Yudhiṣṭhira's human companions severally fall and die.[107] Draupadī falls first, and Bhīma asks why; Yudhiṣṭhira identifies her partiality for Arjuna. Is he jealous? Does his ambivalence suggest he thinks Draupadī is ambivalent towards him? Do his explanations for his brothers' deaths suggest jealousy of their qualities and skills? Yudhiṣṭhira continues without looking back, finally alone with the beasts; but while becoming alone he demonstrates desire and aversion.

Yudhiṣṭhira, citing particulars of *dharma*, will not let Indra take him to heaven without the dog (he must protect it – or he is clinging to life). He says he did not abandon his brothers and Draupadī while they were alive, which we suspect for a lie; but the dog reveals itself as Dharma, whose test he has just passed.[108] He ascends to heaven in his own body, apparently a rare honour[109] (but a prakritic connection nonetheless), and he is immediately desperate to find Draupadī and his brothers. He wanted to do without them, but now cannot do without them; the renunciative impulse is presented as symptomatic of attachment. Indra and Nārada rib Yudhiṣṭhira for retaining human affections and enmities, but he is furious that Duryodhana *et al.* are in heaven, and when he finds Draupadī and his brothers in hell he resolves to stay with them, censuring Dharma and the gods (he cannot remain non-attached to the fruits of their deeds).[110] This is a key double response; now hell becomes heaven, Indra says Yudhiṣṭhira may cease fretting, Dharma says he has passed another test by choosing hell for love,[111] and Yudhiṣṭhira bathes in the celestial Gaṅgā, obtains a celestial body, and sheds all grief and enmity.

Kṛṣṇa emphasizes the moment of death:

> The ancient governor-sage, more minute than the minute, *dhātṛ* of all, of unthinkable form, the colour of the sun beyond the darkness: the one who, at the time of death, thinks about this one with unwavering, devoted mind, yoked with the forces of *yoga*, delivering the entire breath between the eyebrows, attains to that divine highest *puruṣa*.
>
> (*Bhagavadgītā* 8.9–10)[112]

Yudhiṣṭhira may have died when he went to heaven after the dog test; but he still has his body. His death comes after he passes the next test by censuring Dharma and accepting *duḥkha*. It is unclear whether we should view this as the death of a human, or the end of a karmic life-chain; if the latter, then this implies a framing *mokṣa* validation, a definitive level outside what is said to be dharmic. But the end is as fluid and various as the beginning. Yudhiṣṭhira has passed Dharma's third test; but having rebuked Dharma, what can this mean? Is Yudhiṣṭhira pleased to be para-dharmically dharmic? Is there any interval in which to react? No indication is given: he is told, and he bathes. Perhaps the key double response, and bathing in the celestial Gaṅgā, are somehow the same, not successive events. And are the two prongs of the response successive? Does he accept hell before or after censuring Dharma, or neither?

After his celestial bath 'Yudhiṣṭhira' is shown his old earthly acquaintances in their celestial bodies, and is told who incarnated whom. He has a question for Draupadī, but, out of time, he dissolves into Dharma. This final episode, expanding out of logical nowhere, hardly provides Yudhiṣṭhira (it is no longer him) with closure over *daiva*'s mysteries, and leaves the first two 'levels of death' – respectively, a *pravṛtti* frame, and a *nivṛtti* frame with two prongs (traditional *mokṣa* soteriology and the *karmayoga* variant) – undercut and contextualized by an axiomatically unformulable question from the male to the female.

Listening to the wife

When a king is inclined to abandon his wife, *Mahābhārata* stories often trace his failure to do so (his success not to do so) to that wife.[113] We see this with Pāṇḍu, Yudhiṣṭhira, Rāma, Janaka, and also Duḥṣanta. Duḥṣanta promises the kingdom to the son of his brief liaison with Śakuntalā, but when mother and child come to court he refuses them both (1.62–9). His stated doubts resemble Rāma's – tongues will wag if he accepts Bharata as his on her authority – but Śakuntalā unleashes a detailed *pravṛtti* defence, invoking the need for sons, the benefits of conjugality, and the evils of deception, particularly self-deception. As with Draupadī and Sītā (who wastes few words of her own), her perspective is accredited through a hypernatural intervention. Śakuntalā is justified by a voice from the sky (the celestials speaking through a messenger, Vaiśampāyana suggests); Draupadī is protected from Duḥśāsana by an unseen hand, and from Kīcaka by the sun's *rākṣasa*; Sītā calls upon the five elements.[114]

In other stories too a man's failure of *rakṣaṇa* is remedied by instigation of the neglected female: Kaśyapa and Earth (12.49.56–79); Indra and Śacī (5.10–18); Satyavat and Sāvitrī (3.277–83).[115]

Rāma Jāmadagnya, who has massacred the *kṣatriya*s, gives Earth to Kaśyapa, who banishes Jāmadagnya, gives Earth to 'the brahmins', and retires. (Kaśyapa's initial negligence is qualified – he is no *kṣatriya*.) Suffering unprotected, Earth finds Kaśyapa and says: 'Brahmin, there are some *kṣatriya* bulls who were born in the clan of the Haihayas whom I have preserved in the midst of other men; let them guard me, sage' (12.49.66, tr. Fitzgerald).[116] Kaśyapa installs these and other survivors as kings.

Indra, mortified at having killed Viśvarūpa and Vṛtra,[117] retires. 'He lived hidden in the water, moving like a snake' (5.10.43).[118] We recall Yudhiṣṭhira and Nala's ophidian encounters; living hidden in the water suggests the disguised state of the defected *kṣatriya*, as well as the gestation of the true-*kṣatriya*-to-be. New king Nahuṣa covets Indra's abandoned wife Śacī; after stalling him at Bṛhaspati's suggestion, she invokes her wifely dharmicness and truthfulness, and with the aid of Night and Whisper (*upaśruti*) visits Indra beyond the Himavat. After giving him her news, Śacī agrees to facilitate Indra's plan for overcoming Nahuṣa; but on returning she also, through Bṛhaspati, sends Agni in the form of a woman[119] to find Indra so that he might come and fight Nahuṣa. By the time Indra is ready Nahuṣa has already fallen thanks to Indra's plan.[120] These parallel plans for Nahuṣa's defeat have different gendered emphases, but each requires both genders; in any case, Śacī starts the ball rolling.

Sāvitrī marries Satyavat, knowing that he has one year to live and that his blind father has lost his kingdom. She performs an ascetic *vrata* and insists on accompanying Satyavat into the forest on what should be his last day alive; when Yama comes for Satyavat, Sāvitrī's punditry makes him grant her boons, eventually including the restoration of Satyavat's family's kingdom and his life.[121] Satyavat's loss of kingdom and impending loss of life and wife are involuntary – the renunciation is impersonal, not his – but Sāvitrī reverses them.

We return now to the analogy between a person's origin (mother plus father) and composition (*prakṛti* plus *puruṣa*), and to the *karmayoga* soteriology. By viewing narrative through philosophy and philosophy through narrative, that is, by seeing how the *Mahābhārata* discursively superimposes (as well as juxtaposes) these categories, we can move towards a description of the text's gendered soteriology.

Kṛṣṇa locates the salvation process (leading to the isolation of *ātman* or *puruṣa*) within the person's *buddhi*, that is, within the female, material pole.

> Action is far less important than being yoked with *buddhi*. Seek refuge in *buddhi*! The miserable ones are those whose motive is the fruit. The one yoked with *buddhi* leaves both good and bad actions here. So be yoked for *yoga*! *Yoga* is skilfulness in actions. The wise, yoked with *buddhi*, having renounced the fruit born of action, free from the bond of [re]birth, go to the undiseased station.
>
> (*Bhagavadgītā* 2.49–51)[122]

This fits our stories. If the person is composed as a polarized couple, the husband cannot be saved except through his wife. If he attempts solitary salvation, abandoning her physically while still prey to *kāma* and *krodha*, he will be joined to another body, another parcel of materiality, the wife. Similarly, suicide (body-abandonment) results in rebirth whenever *kāma* and *krodha* are operating (Sullivan 2006).

In fact *ātman* cannot act, nor try, however futilely, to save himself.[123] So whence is the attempt at renunciation, the urge to separate from *prakṛti*? It comes from *prakṛti*, not *ātman*. As Kṛṣṇa points out (*Bhagavadgītā* 3.6), renouncers can be as self-centred as anyone. So counter-productive renunciation and salvific *karmayoga* may be correlated with, respectively, mental ascendancies of *ahaṃkāra* and of *buddhi*.[124] Within the person-couple, one of two competing females gets her way. Sulabhā, descendant of Pradhāna, appearing as a belle, says that, to be saved, Janaka must renounce (12.308); his wife says he must come home (12.18). These separate events are not explicitly linked – we cannot say which comes first[125] – and this seems to emphasize (as Yudhiṣṭhira's story does) the recurring nature of the internal battle.[126]

In the *Mahābhārata*'s principal statement of the *karmayoga* soteriology, Arjuna's renunciatory impulse is refuted and *varṇadharma* enforced by Kṛṣṇa, a man.[127] Kṛṣṇā Draupadī, Kṛṣṇa Vāsudeva, and Kṛṣṇa Dvaipāyana Vyāsa are united in name and, at least partly, in effect (Hiltebeitel 1976: 60–76; 1984; 1991b). Kṛṣṇa Vāsudeva is Arjuna's charioteer at Kurukṣetra; this role, following the chariot metaphor of *Kaṭha Upaniṣad* 3.3–9, would make him *buddhi* to Arjuna's *ātman*.[128] 'Kṛṣṇa', as mentioned earlier, spans both genders: 'Kṛṣṇa' plants the world-seed; 'Kṛṣṇā' is the womb; 'Kṛṣṇa'/Kāla sustains then devours the product.[129] When he revives the stillborn Parikṣit, Yudhiṣṭhira's non-biological heir (14.65–8), Kṛṣṇa Vāsudeva appears to be the only man in the delivery room. Using a truth-act (a technique elsewhere in the text used largely by women), he invokes his own dharmic record to miraculous effect.

Collins writes that 'enlightenment for a man connotes a sex-change' (2000: 61): it is the realization that *ahaṃkāra*, part of *prakṛti*, has been mistaken for *ātman*, together with the realization that this very realization (and so on) is *buddhi*'s. If this marked-male body-and-mind is to be the last in an *ātman*'s career, it must feature, in *buddhi*, correct discrimination between *ātman* and non-*ātman*, and the knowledge that *ātman*, the subject of potential *mokṣa*, is soteriologically helpless; thus it must feature coexistence with the consort, without contrary ideals. Perhaps *ātman* will become henceforth non-embodied, but making this happen is none of his business. We see that the *karmayoga* soteriology is a logical concomitant of *ātman*'s non-agency, and an analogical concomitant of the almost infinitely attenuated role of the father in reproduction. But it is no longer clear that a separative soteriological ideal can be sustained.

Conclusion

In the Vedic and epic traditions traced here, cosmos and person have gendered parents. Cosmic *pravṛtti* implies cosmo-parental superimposition; cosmic *nivṛtti* follows cosmo-parental disjunction (the 'night of *brahman*'). People have personal parents (father and mother) and metaphysical 'parents' (*ātman/puruṣa*, and prakritic karmic stains from before); together these compose a person as *ātman/puruṣa* plus mind-and-body. Personal *nivṛtti* is the physical death of a mind-and-body; the *nivṛtti* of a karmic life-chain is the wiping-off of karmic stains and the removal of *ātman/puruṣa* from *prakṛti*.

In disjunction, the perspective of either gender is unbalanced. But in Vedic and epic cosmogonies, the duality is usually not original: first there was an incipiently male *tád ékam*. Or, what was *ātman* before it met (or made and mated with) the material principle, making a karmic life-chain (or cosmos)? If *ātman* can attain *mokṣa*, this must be a return, not just a departure. The initial solitary male features at the (pre-)cosmic level, but, because *duḥkha* is existential, the final solitary male[130] features on the (post-)personal level (the days and nights of *brahman* continue indefinitely). In any case the subject is male, so, irrespective of the *karmayoga* variant, female *mokṣa*-seekers are symbolically anomalous,[131] and we see longstanding debates elsewhere over whether or not a karmic life-chain can end in a female body. In the *Mahābhārata*'s royal patrilines, too, the paradigmatic person – the protective *kṣatriya* king – is male, as are his origins and ends: he may have female relatives, but his cultural 'who's who' is largely male,[132] and his main task is to obtain an heir.

What would it be to say that the text's patrilineal, androcentric concerns are self-selected by its authorial culture? Ostensibly it would be to say nothing about *my* gender or culture! Elsewhere in Indian tradition there are gynocentric cosmologies and soteriologies (this is labelled, '*śakti*-ism'). Some might suggest that their stellar role in the procreative process makes the production of such discourses less pressing for women as a whole than for men. Though it has no special connection with female seekers, philosophical *sāṃkhya-yoga* texts mention the salvation-state of *prakṛtilaya* (dissolution into *prakṛti*; Jacobsen 1999: 273–320), attainable without knowledge of *puruṣa*; but this is trumped as merely penultimate.

We can imagine a tradition of seeking *mokṣa/nirvāṇa*, and by analogy a tradition, which threatens the brahmanical economy/ideology, of (thinking of) abandoning wives, kingdoms, bodies, or other *prakṛti*s. The *karmayoga* response, stressing *ātman*'s non-agency, makes the female the leading partner in the male's salvation, combines *pravṛtti* and *nivṛtti* impulses in one lifestyle, and elevates the gendered ideologies of *rakṣaṇa* and *pativratā* to soteriological as well as practical importance. But there is now a means/ends paradox dogging Yudhiṣṭhira and his *alter ego*s, who doubt whether being dutiful is really worth it. And if the mutually supportive ideologies of *rakṣaṇa* and *pativratā* are especially orientable to *mokṣa* through *karmayoga*, might they not become false external markers just like physical renunciation? Perhaps Yudhiṣṭhira and Draupadī, slightly ambivalent towards *rakṣaṇa* and *pativratā*,[133] fear their becoming ideal pathologies.

Kṛṣṇa states that women also are soteriological subjects (*Bhagavadgītā* 9.32). This remains fully to be explored: might the hypothetical unitary gendered extremities (beginning and end) somehow lose rhetorical power, even while we are gendered bodies, extrapolating wildly from the fact of sexual reproduction in past, present, and future generations, prey to possibilities, anxieties, holy *duḥkha*, and its standard emollients? A Godhead or a soteriological subject, to have an existential analogical counterpart, cannot be non-unitary or neuter,[134] since from birth we are unitary and non-neuter. In theory certain Buddhist philosophies tackle this problem most thoroughly (by dismantling the soteriological subject, dismissing cosmogony as speculation, and/or setting up the *bodhisattva* paradigm of remaining in *saṃsāra* voluntarily even after enlightenment), but with mixed results.

In closing, we visit the scene where Arjuna and Śikhaṇḍin fell Bhīṣma.[135] Bhīṣma cannot consider union with a woman, and is non-committal with regard to *pravṛtti*, but Arjuna, Kṛṣṇa's friend and disciple and Kṛṣṇā Draupadī's favourite husband, represents – whether or not he actualizes it – the new *karmayoga* soteriology, a spiritualized *pravṛtti* outlook requiring union with the female. Having spent a year in female guise, he moves the Bhāratas beyond Bhīṣma (and dharmic neglect) by standing behind Draupadī's brother-sister Śikhaṇḍin, whom Bhīṣma regards as female and will not face. Bhīṣma is defeated through Arjuna's partnership with the female Bhīṣma has rejected (Śikhaṇḍin was previously Śikhaṇḍinī, the reincarnation of Bhīṣma's would-be wife Ambā), a partnership that involves each sharing the other's gender. Arjuna receives Śikhaṇḍin's *rakṣaṇa*, and Ambā, having given up looking for a *pati*, finds one in Arjuna. But this is Ambā's revenge against Bhīṣma, and if instead of pursuing it she had settled for the forest, then Arjuna would not have had the power to fell Bhīṣma alone.

Notes

1 The chapter contains what to scholars will be some shocking generalizations; but it does so on the supposition that the *Mahābhārata*'s formative cultural context did so too. Some of these ideas have been aired in papers given at the 213th Annual Meeting of the American Oriental Society, Nashville, April 2003, and at the Annual Spalding Symposium on Indian Religions, Harris Manchester College, Oxford, April 2005. I am grateful to those who responded to those papers; and also to Sîan Hawthorne, Adam Bowles, and Knut Jacobsen.

2 On this perspective, see also Bailey 1983a: 119–26; Biardeau 1984–5; Collins 2000; Hiltebeitel 1980a: 107; 2000: 117–20; 2001a: 272–3; see also the final pages of Chapter 6.

3 1 Corinthians (King James version) 13.12.

4 See Brodbeck 2003: xvi–xxi; 2003/4: 98; 2004: 88–101.
5 See also Brodbeck in press a.
6 The Indian rhinoceros has one horn.
7 With one prominent exception: Karṇa's basic complaint against Kuntī at 5.139 and 144 is her failure of *rakṣaṇa* towards him. Like Draupadī, in trying to provide for himself what others who should have known better did not, Karṇa acts more assertively than his station would normally allow; the text problematizes this, but also contextualizes it, making it understandable.
8 The *Strīparvan*'s female mourners do not blame themselves for the deaths of their menfolk in terms of their own failures of *rakṣaṇa*.
9 See Zwilling and Sweet 2000: 101–2 (on 'the virility obsession or complex of the late vedic period'), 105–9, 120 (on *klība* as defective male).
10 See *Bhagavadgītā* 2.1–38; *Mahābhārata* 12.7–34 (discussed below); Fitzgerald 2004a: 692–3. '*Klība*' is usually an insult – sometimes translated 'coward' (van Buitenen) or 'sissy' (Fitzgerald); see also Hejib and Young 1981 – and is applied to Yudhiṣṭhira on many occasions (at 8.49.104 by himself). At 12.281.23 it refers to the wise, humble, friendly, dharmic *ārya* – quite possibly a *śramaṇa*; but at 3.198.35 the proliferation of *klība*s is a symptom of negligent kingship.
11 See *Mahābhārata* 12.206.8; 12.292.27; 12.293.12–19; 12.295.
12 For the presumption of *prakṛti*'s femininity, see Jacobsen 1996: 61–3; Indradeva 1966; Falk 1977: 106–8; Collins 2000; Natarajan 2001; Kelkar 2003. Jacobsen has elaborated his thesis with specific reference to the *Mahābhārata* (2005); it fits in part with Ruth Vanita's claim that *ātman* is not male (2003: 81).
13 Others are possible: perhaps *prakṛti*'s gender was downplayed in order that the *sāṃkhya* be philosophically relevant, without narrative symbolic interference, to a wide audience including women and *karmayogins*.
14 In *sāṃkhya* texts the terms *avyakta* and *pradhāna*, both of neuter gender, are often used as synonyms of *prakṛti*.
15 On this problem in the classical texts of the *sāṃkhya* system, see Parrott 1986; Bronkhorst 1999; Burley 2007: 108–32.
16 On Vedic cosmogony, see Kuiper 1983; Roy 1996. Other scenarios include the creator as craftsman; the Indra–Vṛtra fight (on which see Thomas 2006a); and the churning of the ocean (featured at *Mahābhārata* 1.15–17 and perhaps symbolically continuous with the 'gendered parents' scenario). See also Penner 1965–6; Bailey 1983b: 85–121 (featuring *Mahābhārata* cosmogonies); Pintchman 1998; N.N. Bhattacharyya 1971; and, for gendered Norse cosmogonies, Linke 1989.
17 *tataḥ svayaṃbhūr bhagavān avyakto vyañjayann idam / sarvabhūtamayo . . . sa eva svayam udbabhau //* For a study of this text's cosmogony, see Laine 1981.
18 The egg is an apt image, being dually composed – and it is the yolk which grows and hatches. An egg is externalized as a womb is not: unlike mammalian birth, the mother is not necessarily present when it hatches (and the albumen has all but gone). In a variant (see *Mahābhārata* 12.200.8–13), the Lord lies on the waters face-up, and the egg is replaced by the flower of a lotus plant.
19 *apa eva sasarjādau tāsu bījam avāsṛjat // tad aṇḍam abhavad dhaimaṃ sahasrāṃśusam aprabham / tasmiñ jajñe svayaṃ brahmā sarvalokapitāmahaḥ // yat tatkāraṇam avyaktaṃ nityaṃ sadasadātmakam / tad visṛṣṭaḥ sa puruṣo loko brahmeti kīrtyate //*
20 Rivers also are female, and often personified: 'all of them are the mothers of everything, and indeed all of them are very powerful' (*viśvasya mātaraḥ sarvāḥ sarvāś caiva mahābalāḥ // Mahābhārata* 6.10.35). For the waters as mothers, see also *Taittirīya Saṃhitā* 1.2.1; *Śatapatha Brāhmaṇa* 6.8.2.2–6.
21 *Śatapatha Brāhmaṇa* 11.1.6.1–2; *Ṛgveda* 10.82. Kuiper stresses the fatherless picture, seeing it as primary, both logically (1970; 1975; 1983: 10, 98–103) and

chronologically ('The mystery of Agni's birth is unquestionably the central motif of the Indo-Iranian mythology', 1983: 29). Neither judgment is material to our purpose.

22 *Taittirīya Saṃhitā* 5.6.4 (Prajāpati and the waters); *Śatapatha Brāhmaṇa* 2.1.1.3–5 (Agni and the waters); *Ṛgveda* 9.74.5 (Agni and Aditi). This matches the *sāṃkhya* tradition (*prakṛti* and *puruṣa* as twin ultimates).

23 *Ṛgveda* 10.121.7–9; *Śatapatha Brāhmaṇa* 6.1.3.1; *Mahābhārata* 12.321.28–9; 12.327.24–5; 12.339.17. At *Śatapatha Brāhmaṇa* 6.1.1.8–10 and *Bṛhadāraṇyaka Upaniṣad* 1.2.1 the waters are created through Vāc (speech), an intermediate fertile female offshoot (on whose creative role see Norman Brown 1968; Sutherland Goldman 2000: 71–2). *Ṛgveda* 10.129.1–3 presents several scenarios (Brereton 1999).

24 *Ṛgveda* 10.121 ('he' is the son in v. 7, the father in vv. 8–9); 10.129 ('that one' is the father in v. 2, the son in v. 3). See Varenne 1977–8: 383–4 – Agni is father, husband, and son of the waters – and 386: 'fire is at the very centre of . . . nature and its relation to it resembles the relation of *ātman* to an individual (or *puruṣa* to *prakṛti* in the Sāṃkhya)'. For the equation of father and son, see also *Śatapatha Brāhmaṇa* 6.1.2.26; *Aitareya Brāhmaṇa* 7.13; *Mahābhārata* 1.68.36, 47–8, 62–5; Olivelle 1997: 431–3.

25 Patrilineal males must offer regular *śrāddha*, feeding the heaven-dwelling ancestors, and have sons (who have sons, etc.) that this may continue (Kane 1968–77, vol. 4: 334–515; *Bhagavadgītā* 1.38–44). Several *Mahābhārata* characters (e.g. Droṇa, Jaratkāru, Pāṇḍu) produce a son only to satisfy the ancestors.

26 *etā́vān asya mahimā́to jyā́ yāṃś ca pū́ruṣaḥ / pā́do 'sya víśvā bhūtā́ni tripā́d asyāmṛ́taṃ diví // tripā́d ūrdhvá úd ait púruṣaḥ pā́do 'syehā́bhavat púnaḥ / táto víṣvaṅ ví akrāmat sāśanānaśané abhí // tásmād virā́ḷ ajāyata virā́jo ádhi pū́ruṣaḥ / sá jātó áty aricyata paścā́d bhū́mim átho puráḥ //* The suggestion that the father is the son risen upwards (rather than or in addition to the son being the father descended) has interesting implications concerning the phenomenologically situated order of enquiry.

27 I take manifesting one-quarter of oneself and reproducing *via* a self-created female as the same process. On Virāj, see *Mahābhārata* 12.254.*704 (she is Earth); *Atharvavedasaṃhitā* 8.9–10 (she is also Svadhā, Māyā, and Tirodhā); Penner 1965–6: 288, 292, 294.

28 Goldberg insists that the Godhead which is a juxtaposition of polarized opposites is not the ultimate Godhead (2002).

29 This stage may also involve the intermediate or superimposed duality of heaven and earth. When the egg hatched, the shell's two halves became the sky and earth (*Chāndogya Upaniṣad* 3.19; see also *Śatapatha Brāhmaṇa* 6.1.1.11–2.4; *Mānava Dharmaśāstra* 1.12–13; *Mahābhārata* 12.299.4); these two may then parent all creatures in between, the father fertilizing the mother through rain (Gonda 1974: 93–117; Macdonell 1974: 126–7; *Atharvavedasaṃhitā* 12.1.12, 42; *Aitareya Brāhmaṇa* 4.27; Das 2000: 244–5). This fertilizing function is evident in the *Mahābhārata* character Bhīṣma, incarnation of the sky god, whose celibacy infuriates Ambā ('mother', who consequently changes her name and gender) and causes problems for the Bhārata dynasty. See also *Bṛhadāraṇyaka Upaniṣad* 6.4.20 ('I am sky, you are earth: let us two join together, mix our seed together, to get a male child', *dyaur aham pṛthivī tvaṃ tāv ehi saṃrabhāvahai saha reto dadhāvahai puṃse putrāya vittaye iti //* tr. Roebuck); *Mahābhārata* 12.183.15. The vertical dualism (sky/earth, Lord/waters) fits the 'missionary position'.

30 *ātmaivedam agra āsīt puruṣavidhaḥ so 'nuvīkṣya nānyad ātmano 'paśyat . . .// so 'bibhet . . .// sa vai naiva reme . . . sa dvitīyam aicchat sa haitāvān āsa yathā strīpumāṃsau sampariṣvaktau sa imam evātmānaṃ dvedhāpātayat tataḥ patiś ca*

patnī cābhavatām tasmāt idam ardhabṛgalam iva svaḥ iti ha smāha yājñavalkyaḥ tasmād ayam ākāśaḥ striyā pūryata eva tāṃ samabhavat tato manuṣyā ajāyanta //

31 Elsewhere Puruṣa divides into the components of the cosmos, including the four *varṇas*: see *Ṛgveda* 10.90.6–14; *Mānava Dharmaśāstra* 1.31; John Brockington 1998: 13 (for *Mahābhārata* examples).

32 *mama yonir mahad brahma tasmin garbhaṃ dadhāmy aham / saṃbhavaḥ sarvabhūtānāṃ tato bhavati bhārata // sarvayoniṣu kaunteya mūrtayaḥ saṃbhavanti yāḥ / tāsāṃ brahma mahad yonir ahaṃ bījapradaḥ pitā* //

33 See also *Bhagavadgītā* 7.4; 9.8, 17. *Sat* and *asat* at *Bhagavadgītā* 11.37 (also *Chāndogya Upaniṣad* 6.2; *Ṛgveda* 10.129) could denote male and female principles.

34 *tapastaptav āsṛjad yaṃ tu sa svayaṃ puruṣo virāṭ / taṃ māṃ vittāsya sarvasya sraṣṭāraṃ dvijasattamaḥ* //

35 For Lord plus *māyā*, see 12.206.2–3; Roy 1996: 13–14; for Lord plus *vidyā*, see 12.224.33 (where Ganguli 12.232, p. 157 reads *avidyā*); 12.326.66–7; 12.332.12; 12.335.17.

36 On this analogy, see Schreiner 1999b: 132–7; Brodbeck 2003: xxii–xxiv; 2003/4: 91–103; 2004: 90–2. The end and re-beginning of the cyclic cosmos (on which see *Śvetāśvatara Upaniṣad* 4.1, with *śakti* as the female; *Bhagavadgītā* 8.17–19) matches the death of one body and *ātman*'s taking another. The 'evolutionary' cosmic model, whereby the material principle is gradually 'unpacked', fits the sexual model: the fertilized egg/foetus develops and grows. The four sets of five in the *sāṃkhya tattva*-lists are like fingers and toes. For other embryological connections see *Ṛgveda* 10.162.3; *Śatapatha Brāhmaṇa* 6.1.3; *Mahābhārata* 12.308.116–20; Kuiper 1970; 1983: 134 n. 90, 135–6. Knowledge of the emanation-process 'is a condition or a help for turning away and for advancing towards the goal of isolated worldlessness, unworldly isolation' (Schreiner 1999a: 775). Ascetics may burn off their limbs: see 3.135.28; 9.47.20–4.

37 *Mahābhārata* 12.293.12–19 presents *prakṛti* and *puruṣa* as female and male, and indicates which physical aspects of the person come from which human parent. The female constituent is often multifarious: consider the proliferation of the material principle into the various *tattvas*; see *Kauṣītaki Upaniṣad* 4.3–18; *Bṛhadāraṇyaka Upaniṣad* 2.1.1–13; *Chāndogya Upaniṣad* 5.2.1–2. 'Plurality is mentioned as one of the characteristics of the perishable, unity of the imperishable' (Schreiner 1999a: 768). On 'She-of-a-hundred-forms', see Pintchman 1998: 272–4.

38 It rests on the *bandhu* principle: see Gonda 1965; B.K. Smith 1989; 1994:11–12; Hegarty 2006; Kuznetsova 2006: 118–22.

39 For example, consider *Bhagavadgītā* 8.23–6. Rebirth and *mokṣa* are correlated with time of death: death during the daytime, the waxing fortnight, or the year's first half (after the winter solstice, before the summer) means no rebirth; death during the night, the waning fortnight, or the year's second half means rebirth. Added up, the auspicious times comprise seven-eighths of the year, as do the inauspicious times; six-eighths are ambiguous. Yet each ending life must either have or not have a karmic sequel. Similar iterative analogical interference could indefinitely retroject the pre-cosmic male's solitude: to make Puruṣa he needs the waters, to make them he needs Vāc, to make Vāc . . . But although this collects cosmogonies in strings, the concept 'beginning' is nonetheless retained (*Mahābhārata* 12.175.35). Semantically parallel items appear in series; a poet describes a scene of simultaneous birds and bees by using words *in sequence*.

40 See 12.237.13. On *pravṛtti* and *nivṛtti*, see Bailey 1985.

41 *ajām ekāṃ lohitaśuklakṛṣṇām bahvīḥ prajāḥ sṛjamānāṃ sarūpāḥ / ajo hy eko juṣamāṇo 'nuśete jahāty enām bhuktabhogām ajo 'nyaḥ* // *Aja* also means 'unborn' (see above, p. 133); married goats/unborns are unknown.

42 For Yājñavalkya see *Bṛhadāraṇyaka Upaniṣad* 2.4 and 4.5; for Mahāvīra

(Śvetāmbara tradition; the Digambara Mahāvīra never marries), Hemacandra's *Triṣaṣṭiśalākāpuruṣacaritra*, *Mahāvīracaritra* 2.125–55; for Buddha, Aśvaghoṣa's *Buddhacarita* 2–6. Polygyny means that the wife is rarely left for another woman – but see the Śārṅgaka story discussed in Chapter 6.

43 *vanam anupamasattvā bodhisattvās tu sarve viṣayasukharasajñā jagmur utpannaputrāḥ* / For an in-depth study of the *Buddhacarita* as a response to the Sanskrit epics, see now Hiltebeitel 2006, esp. pp. 247–53, 268, 271–5 on the narrative contrast between the Buddha's and various epic kings' attitudes to *dharma* and the necessity of householdership.

44 These duties comprise one of the three (or more) debts, usually to the *pitṛ*s, *deva*s, and *ṛṣi*s (and to people) (Olivelle 1993: 47–53). Son-production is sometimes presented as unnecessary: Medhāvin tells his father that salvation does not depend on sons (*Mahābhārata* 12.169; Olivelle 1993: 150–1), and the father is convinced. The sonless Bhīṣma tells this story to Yudhiṣṭhira (who has lost his) by way of example. A *paramparā* may replace a *vaṃśa*, the sonless man (Bhīṣma, Yudhiṣṭhira, Vyāsa) leaving a text instead: 'Scholarship, in establishing and indulging a nexus of authority, serves a reproductive function' (Hawthorne 2004: 42).

45 On the *āśrama* scheme, see Olivelle 1993: 136–60. Apparently following a *Buddhacarita*-type model, Jaratkāru considers marriage only at his endangered ancestors' request, and then insists that his wife have the same name as him, and that he not have to support her or the child. He as it were tests the universe, which confirms the ancestors' request as valid, but he then makes the additional condition that his wife never displease him (*Mahābhārata* 1.43.7–8; cf. Gaṅgā's demand that Śaṃtanu never criticize her, 1.92.34–5), enabling him to abandon her while she is yet pregnant (1.34.10–36.7; 1.41–3).

46 Yājñavalkya's sons are not mentioned, but nor is their non-existence; he seems to have the best of both worlds successively. Nonetheless, as Brian Black points out, 'he is the one philosopher in the Upaniṣads who challenges the soteriology that is based on having sons' (personal communication, May 2006; see Black 2007: 94–8, 146). At *Mahābhārata* 4.20.27 Draupadī says that self-protection depends on child-protection and hence on wife-protection.

47 This is not to dispute or replace other interpretations. Note von Simson's qualification of his calendrical interpretation of the Nala story: 'An open disclosure would have made the text a dull, pedantic allegory' (2005: 133). Using a musical analogy, we may think of overtones, resonances, and/or simultaneous accompaniments in different registers.

48 The karmically deleterious effect of activities (*karmabandha*) can allegedly be neutralized by knowledge (*Śatapatha Brāhmaṇa* 1.6.1.21; *Bṛhadāraṇyaka Upaniṣad* 4.4.23; 5.14.8; *Kauṣītaki Upaniṣad* 1.4; 3.1).

49 See *Bhagavadgītā* 9.2–3; Biardeau 1981b; Malinar 1996; Slaje 2000a.

50 Just as the Mahāyāna *bodhisattva* model obviates in principle the need ever to stop being reborn: see Kuznetsova 2006: 123.

51 His failures of husbandry may cause drought, i.e. depletion of the waters.

52 On royal representation, see Chapter 4; on the king, Earth, and Śrī, see Hara 1973; 1996–7; Gonda 1969: 176–231; on Draupadī, Śrī, and Earth, see Bailey 1983a: 118–19; Brodbeck in press a.

53 See *Bhagavadgītā* 9.30–2; *Mahābhārata* 14.19.56. For discussion of the *Mahābhārata*'s anticipated female audience, see Chapter 3 and Chapter 6.

54 On Yudhiṣṭhira, see also Klaes 1975 (following him step by step); Zaehner 1962: 114–24 and *passim*; Fitzgerald 2004a: 81–142. In terms of the *Mahābhārata* as a whole Janamejaya might be considered the 'primary example', but his context is more complicated and will not be treated here.

55 See also *Arthaśāstra* 8.1.5; *Mānava Dharmaśāstra* 9.294; *Mahābhārata* 12.69.63.

56 Moreover, after Bhīṣma's abdication, Śaṃtanu died while his new heirs Citrāṅgada and Vicitravīrya were yet young (1.95.4). Pāṇḍu and Yudhiṣṭhira are both produced through *niyoga*; there are specified biological fathers and adoptive fathers in both cases, but one aspect of the net result is the marking of a contrast with the (narratively) normative paternal situation in which the son is raised to adulthood by the biological father, in his patriline. I am grateful to Paul de Villiers for stimulating discussions of Pāṇḍu's story.

57 *bhartṛlokaparāyaṇe*; see Olivelle 1997: 436–7.

58 *svargapāraṃ titīrṣan sa śataśṛṅgād udaṅmukhaḥ / pratasthe saha patnībhyām. . . /*

59 *darśanīyāṃs tataḥ putrān pāṇḍuḥ pañca mahāvane / tān paśyan parvate reme svabāhubalapālitān //*

60 *tad yathā priyayā striyā sampariṣvakto na bāhyaṃ kiṃ cana veda nāntaram evam evāyam puruṣaḥ prājñenātmanā sampariṣvakto na bāhyaṃ kiṃ cana veda nāntaram*; see also *Bṛhadāraṇyaka Upaniṣad* 2.1.19.

61 Though also a river (6.10.15; 13.26.9; 13.134.16; 13.151.14; *Mānava Dharmaśāstra* 3.9), 'Devikā' has brahmin connections (2.47.5; 3.80.110–15; 3.212.20–4).

62 Yaudheya is not mentioned again, although 'the Yaudheyas' attend Yudhiṣṭhira's *rājasūya* (2.48.13) and fight at Kurukṣetra (7.18.16; 7.132.25 – against Yudhiṣṭhira himself; 7.136.5; 8.4.46).

63 On this triangle, see Hiltebeitel 2001a: 264ff. Later, during the thirteen-year exile, while the family visit *tīrtha*s, Arjuna visits Indra.

64 *ārambhe pārameṣṭhyaṃ tu na prāpyam iti me matiḥ //* See also 2.15.1–5.

65 'If your heart knows, if you have confidence in me . . .' (*yadi te hṛdayaṃ vetti yadi te pratyayo mayi* / 2.18.7, tr. van Buitenen). Gönc Moačanin says 'Yudhiṣṭhira did nothing on his own. He acquired the title of *samrāj* with the help of Kṛṣṇa who obviously had his own plans'; as she points out, these are implicit in Kṛṣṇa's speech at 2.30.23 (2005: 153).

66 For bibliographical references on the dicing episode, see Gönc Moačanin 2005: 149. On Yudhiṣṭhira in the dicing scene, see Mary Brockington 2001; 2003.

67 At 2.44.18 and 2.45.38 Śakuni says Yudhiṣṭhira loves gambling; at 2.60.43 Draupadī says he is inexperienced.

68 Commentators have pointed out that Śakuni does not seem to cheat (Gönc Moačanin 2005: 156), but nonetheless there is a common misperception that he did.

69 See van Buitenen 1972. The main weakness of this position is that in the *Mahābhārata* dicing is not part of the *rājasūya*, and not a formality. Claiming dicing as a cultural necessity for kings (Gönc Moačanin 2005: 158–9) is susceptible to similar criticism: the text does not show us that culture. (Hence also I discuss Yudhiṣṭhira without reference to the *vrātya*s.)

70 Discrepancies between the two accounts of Yudhiṣṭhira's motives may or may not indicate that different versions (or texts) of the dicing have been combined. Such is Mehendale's conclusion from these and other data, but he does not factor in Yudhiṣṭhira's addressees.

71 This is to traduce the gambler's role. Howsoever infinitesimal the chances of victory, the universe could provide it; definitive agency falls beyond the gambler. Cf. Jaratkāru, n. 45 above.

72 *etat pāpiṣṭham akaror yad ātmānaṃ parājitaḥ / śiṣṭe sati dhane rājan pāpa ātmaparājayaḥ //* I follow van Buitenen for the first half of the *śloka*.

73 Youthful renouncers leave parents bereft (e.g. Vyāsa: see Hiltebeitel 2001a: 278–322, esp. the final page). For proud *kṣatriya* parents, any son refusing family expectations is effectively renouncing – (although) the *Mahābhārata*'s main parental losses are military.

74 Draupadī calling on Kṛṣṇa for help (2.60.26; also 5.58.21; 5.80.26) compares with Earth calling on Brahmā when *asura* kings oppress her (1.58.25–51), and with

Ambā calling on Rāma Jāmadagnya and Śiva after Bhīṣma rejects her (5.176, 188). The substitute *pati*'s identity is often ambiguous or multiple. On Draupadī in the dicing scene, see Hiltebeitel 1980a: 103, 108 (contrasting and comparing Earth); 2000: 114–15; and Chapter 6. See *Aitareya Brāhmaṇa* 7.16 for a similar scene.

75 On Nala (with further references), see Hiltebeitel 2001a: 215–39 (also comparing Nala and Yudhiṣṭhira); von Simson 2005.

76 *so 'pakṛṣṭas tu kalinā mohitaḥ prādravan nalaḥ / suptām utsṛjya tāṃ bhāryāṃ vilapya karuṇaṃ bahu //*

77 We are reminded of Buddha's *anātman* theory, and of the possibility of faulty discrimination of *prakṛti* and *puruṣa*, *ahaṃkāra* and *ātman* (see further below).

78 In exile Yudhiṣṭhira hears Nala's story, of a lost kingdom regained through acquisition and use of the *akṣahṛdaya*, the heart (or secret) of the dice; Yudhiṣṭhira receives the *akṣahṛdaya*, and uses it for his disguise in the *Virāṭaparvan*. As Adam Bowles says, '*akṣahṛdaya* may reflect the adage that "the king makes the age" ' (personal communication, February 2006): see González-Reimann 2002: 118–37. Paul Bowlby, following Heesterman, sees *akṣahṛdaya* as the knowledge and ability to rule dharmically, passions conquered, and mediate through ritual with unseen powers to prosper the *loka* (Bowlby 1991). This looks like the *rājavidyā*, but lacks the soteriological context. Bowlby suggests that a king really needs various specific skills (the *akṣahṛdaya*, knowledge of weapons, etc.) *and* the *karmayoga* (pp. 16–17). On *akṣahṛdaya* as text-receptive competence, see Hegarty 2001; Brodbeck 2006: 16 n. 46.

79 'Dhṛtarāṣṭra' is also a snake: see 1.3.142; 1.31.13; 1.52.13; 2.9.9; 5.101.15; Minkowski 1991: 388–9, 396.

80 And Śakuni incarnates Dvāpara: see 1.61.72, 80. On *kali* and kings, see 12.12.27 (Nakula defines Kali as any non-protective king); González-Reimann 2002: 53–62.

81 See 3.13.112; 10.16.28. Draupadī is labelled *anāthavat* (as though unprotected /husbandless) at 1.1.106; 2.60.24; 2.61.52; 4.17.29; 5.88.86.

82 3.31.1; see again Chapter 4.

83 *sa muhūrtam iva dhyātvā viniścityetikṛtyatām* / The interpretation of *muhūrtam* is uncertain (it may mean just a moment, or a 48-minute measure); see also n. 86 below. Some manuscripts add a speech-to-self just before this line.

84 In exile, Yudhiṣṭhira builds some self-knowledge. See 3.2.66.

85 For the potlatch theory, see Mauss 1990; Held 1935; Tieken 2004; Gönc Moačanin 2005.

86 *uvāca rāmo vaidehīṃ parāmarśaviśaṅkitaḥ / gaccha vaidehi muktā tvaṃ yat kāryaṃ tan mayā kṛtam // mām āsādya patiṃ bhadre na tvaṃ rākṣasaveśmani / jarāṃ vrajethā iti me nihato 'sau niśācaraḥ // kathaṃ hy asmadvidho jātu jānan dharmaviniścayam / parahastagatāṃ nārīṃ muhūrtam api dhārayet // suvṛttām asuvṛttāṃ vāpy ahaṃ tvām adya maithili / notsahe paribhogāya śvāvalīḍhaṃ havir yathā //*

87 Compare Scharf 2003: 24–5: 'Rāma represents pure consciousness (*puruṣa*) . . . Sītā represents the individual body, senses, mind, and intellect which are the manifest evolutes of original nature (*prakṛti*) . . . In the stage of enlightenment known as cosmic consciousness (*kaivalya*), the self, identified with pure consciousness, recognizing its own purity, views the body and other evolutes of nature as belonging to the field of change from which it dissociates itself. However, in the ultimate stage of development of consciousness (*brahman*), the self recognizes the transcendent original pure state of nature in all the active states of nature and embraces all levels of nature as one with itself.'

88 This event provides the opportunity for the *Rāma-Upākhyāna* to be told.

89 Although Jayadratha's grudge later contributes to Abhimanyu's death (3.256.24–9; 7.41–2), we must factor in Bhīma's humiliating him as well as Yudhiṣṭhira's leniency.

90 For discussion of this episode, see Bailey 1983a: 118.
91 She also blames *daiva*, and herself (for unknown past sins come to fruition).
92 Damayantī too engineers her own safety from a menacing hunter after Nala's flight; both women use a *satyakriyā* ('truth-act').
93 As promised at 3.173.19. Yudhiṣṭhira tells Arjuna to rule instead (12.7.40), and seems to anticipate solitary renunciation (12.9.3, 10, 15; see also Bronkhorst 1998: 33–4; Fitzgerald 2004a: 685).
94 *anṛtaṃ mābravīc chvaśrūḥ sarvajñā sarvadarśinī / yudhiṣṭhiras tvāṃ pāñcāli sukhe dhāsyaty anuttame // hatvā rājasahasrāṇi bahūny āśuparākramaḥ / tad vyarthaṃ saṃprapaśyāmi mohāt tava janādhipa // yeṣām unmattako jyeṣṭhaḥ sarve tasyopacāriṇaḥ / tavonmādena rājendra sonmādāḥ sarvapāṇḍavāḥ // yadi hi syur anunmattā bhrātaras te janādhipa / baddhvā tvāṃ nāstikaiḥ sārdhaṃ praśāseyur vasuṃdharām //* Yudhiṣṭhira married Draupadī in order that Kuntī not be a liar. See also *Bhagavadgītā* 3.21.
95 See also 12.10.20; 11.27; 12.4; 12.25; 15.33; 19.23; 36.43.
96 Janaka is bald, with water pot, triple staff, and robe (adopted by *śaiva* ascetics pursuing *mokṣa*). His interest in *mokṣa* is proverbial; see also 12.18.26, 30. At 12.9 Yudhiṣṭhira implies that he wants *mokṣa*, but this is rarely explicit. At 12.161.40–6 he insists on *mokṣa* as a transcendent other to *dharma*, *artha*, and *kāma*; as Bowles suggests (2005), that scene continues the family's discussion here (which continues those in Books 3 and 5).
97 See 12.11.14–25; 12.19–23, 33–5; 13.1–11; 16.21–4; 18.29–33; Hiltebeitel 2005c: 250–8.
98 See *Bhagavadgītā* 3.20; *Mahābhārata* 3.2.30–2; 12.297; 12.308; 14.32.
99 *saktāḥ karmaṇy avidvāṃso yathā kurvanti bhārata / kuryād vidvāṃs tathāsaktaś cikīrṣur lokasaṃgraham //*
100 *asaktaḥ saktavad gacchan niḥsaṅgo muktabandhanaḥ / samaḥ śatrau ca mitre ca sa vai mukto mahīpate //* See also Slaje 2000b: 176–7, 183.
101 Vyāsa, who suggests ritual expiation of the war-guilt (12.34–6), probably tips the balance by addressing Yudhiṣṭhira's problem at face value.
102 Arjuna voices *pravṛtti* concerns (for his family, not *mokṣa*), but proposes *śramaṇa*-type behaviour.
103 Ostensibly that his father might enjoy Satyavatī, a *dāśī* half his age (1.94). Bhīṣma repeatedly refuses responsibilities (kingship; marriage; impregnating widows) from behind a dharmic mask, invoking his old filial vow. Like Rāma, having seen his father brought to irresponsibility through passion and manipulation, he himself doesn't feel inclined towards or fit for responsibility. Both characters renounce kingdom then wife (Ambā, Sītā), but Bhīṣma is the more stubborn – Śaṃtanu doesn't re-instruct him after dying.
104 It fits also that he champions Sulabhā when narrating her debate with Janaka (12.308; see Chapter 12), and fails to support Draupadī in the dice-match debate.
105 Yudhiṣṭhira is heirless *pro tem.* (see above, n. 44), Parikṣit unborn.
106 *mamāpi na tathā rājñi rājye buddhir yathā purā / tapasy evānuraktaṃ me manaḥ sarvātmanā tathā //*
107 On this and the subsequent scenes, see Hiltebeitel 2001a: 271–7.
108 On the dog episode, see Bailey 1983a: 126. Yudhiṣṭhira earlier encountered Dharma as a heron/*yakṣa* (3.295–8; Leslie 1998: 475, 481). On Dharma's tests, see also Adarkar 2005b.
109 Von Simson links this with Yudhiṣṭhira's connections, *via* Dharma and his *alter ego* Kaṅka, to Yama: 'It might have occurred to the authors . . . that Death himself cannot die' (2000a: 318). On dogs, dice, and death, see White 1989.
110 On this scene, see Shulman 1996: 158, 160–4; Emily Hudson 2005. At 12.192.119–21 Bhīṣma says that delighting in heaven indicates attachment, 'But

if on the other hand he goes there freed from passion, and hesitantly, wishing for the highest immutable, he enters exactly that' (*atha tatra virāgī sa gacchati tv atha saṃśayam / param avyayam icchan sa tam evāviśate punaḥ //* 12.192.121). But Yudhiṣṭhira reacts to others' deserts, not his own. He reminds us of *Bhagavadgītā* 18.66: 'Abandon all *dharmas* and go to me [Kṛṣṇa], the only refuge. I will free you from all misfortunes: grieve not' (*sarvadharmān parityajya mām ekaṃ śaraṇaṃ vraja / ahaṃ tvā sarvapāpebhyo mokṣayiṣyāmi mā śucaḥ //*). Dharma was cursed, for being unfair, to be born as Vidura (1.101), who is now Yudhiṣṭhira – so perhaps Yudhiṣṭhira's curse of Dharma is pre-discharged.

111 He has been doing this all along, in his way, but for the odd lapse – and these become increasingly theatrical. For Yudhiṣṭhira voicing renunciative intent, see Klaes 1975: 99, 109–13.

112 *kaviṃ purāṇam anuśāsitāram aṇor aṇīyāṃsam anusmared yaḥ / sarvasya dhātāram acintyarūpam ādityavarṇaṃ tamasaḥ parastāt // prayāṇakāle manasācalena bhaktyā yukto yogabalena caiva / bhruvor madhye prāṇam āveśya samyak sa taṃ paraṃ puruṣam upaiti divyam //* See also *Bhagavadgītā* 2.72; 7.30; 8.5; *Mahābhārata* 5.44.16; 5.61.2; 12.207.25; 12.210.13, 20; 13.17.18; 14.46.54; *Chāndogya Upaniṣad* 3.17.6; Edgerton 1926.

113 On the wife as essential partner-in-*dharma*, see 12.142; 12.340–353; Jamison 1996: 29–149.

114 Damayantī's predator (see n. 92) dies 'like a tree burned by fire'; she later calls upon wind, sun, and moon that Nala may be assured of her purity. For discussion of the authorizing effect of the 'outside intervention' in the stories of Draupadī, Śakuntalā and Gārgī, see Black 2007: 154–5.

115 See also 12.215–21. Prahlāda says *svabhāva*, not Indra, has caused Indra's success (and also causes knowledge of *ātman*, 12.215.23); other defeated *asuras* identify the agent as Kāla or, usually, Śrī.

116 *santi brahman mayā guptā nṛṣu kṣatriyapuṃgavāḥ / haihayānāṃ kule jātās te saṃrakṣantu māṃ mune //*

117 'New to the Pāṇḍava narrative's symbolic version of this ancient battle is the assistance given to Indra by Śrī (i.e. in the Pāṇḍava narrative, the energizing of the Pāṇḍavas by Draupadī)' (Fitzgerald 2004b: 62). On this story see also Hiltebeitel 1977; Thomas 2006b. Indra's withdrawal links with the Pāṇḍavas' exile and with Yudhiṣṭhira's plans after the war.

118 *praticchanno vasaty apsu ceṣṭamāna ivoragaḥ //*

119 *hutāśanaḥ / strīveṣam adbhutaṃ kṛtvā*, 5.15.27.

120 This corresponds to what Śalya, the story's narrator, is hoping may happen with Karṇa. Nahuṣa, having angered the *ṛṣis*, goes down the snake: see 3.175–8.

121 On this story, see also Aklujkar 1991; Chapple 2006: 107–9.

122 *dūreṇa hy avaraṃ karma buddhiyogād dhanañjaya / buddhau śaraṇam anviccha kṛpaṇāḥ phalahetavaḥ // buddhiyukto jahātīha ubhe sukṛtaduṣkṛte / tasmād yogāya yujyasva yogaḥ karmasu kauśalam // karmajaṃ buddhiyuktā hi phalaṃ tyaktvā manīṣiṇaḥ / janmabandhavinirmuktāḥ padaṃ gacchanty anāmayam //* See also 2.41–3, 52–3, 63–6.

123 See 12.337.16–27 (creator Brahmā is impotent until Nārāyaṇa sends Buddhi); *Bhagavadgītā* 3.27–8; 5.8–9; Collins 2000; Parrott 1990; Burley 2007: 141–7.

124 For the *tattvas* in classical *sāṃkhya*, see Parrott 1986: 56–9. The non-renouncing Vedic hedonist of *Bhagavadgītā* 2.42–4 is also *ahaṃkāra*-ascendant.

125 Janaka expounds the *karmayoga* to Sulabhā, but says he learned it from Pañcaśikha.

126 Analogical re-application may introduce polarization within either or both poles (e.g. *Bhagavadgītā* 7.4–5). *Ātman* being inactive, the choice between *ahaṃkāra* and *buddhi* may fall to a masculinized aspect of *prakṛti*. At *Mahābhārata*

14.20–50 *manas* is *buddhi*'s husband, but *kṣetrajña* (i.e. *ātman*) is *manas*'s teacher. Such finesse allows the male to retain a soteriological role.

127 Male friends (e.g. Yudhiṣṭhira's brothers) also share this role elsewhere. At 1.57.1–31 Indra persuades Vasu, who has renounced kingship, to take it up again. Indra's gender is not unambiguous in the *Mahābhārata* (see 12.329.14; 13.34.25–6; 13.41.21); at *Kauṣītaki Upaniṣad* 3.1 he plays Kṛṣṇa's *Bhagavadgītā* role as supreme object of knowledge and paradigmatic *karmayogin*.

128 Arjuna must seek refuge in *buddhi* (*Bhagavadgītā* 2.49c) and in Kṛṣṇa (18.66). See Hiltebeitel 1984: 12–15; 2001a: 273 n. 90; Brassard 1999; Sutton 2000: 344–7; Dasti 2005. For *buddhi* as charioteer, see *Mahābhārata* 5.127.25–6. The charioteer is *manas* at 14.50.1–6 (with *buddhi* as reins); *sattva* at 11.7.13–15; *jñāna* at 12.228.8–12; *νόος* at Plato's *Phaedrus* 247. Elsewhere *ātman* (variously construed) or *kṣetrajña* plays the charioteer (3.2.62; 3.202.21–3; 5.34.57–8; 12.238.2; 12.280.1; Goudriaan 1990). The discrepancy may track the difference between a chariot of war or state (featuring a dedicated driver) and a single-occupant chariot (cart). Nala's charioteer is initially 'Vārṣṇeya'; later, in hunchback form, Nala himself is the driver (3.57, 69). The chariot analogy is applied also to the cosmos: see 8.24, where Śiva and Brahmā are warrior and charioteer. Jāmadagnya says his chariot is Earth, his horses the Vedas, his charioteer the wind (*mātariśvan*, from *mātṛ*, mother), his armour the Vedas' mothers (5.180.3–4). At 5.183.15–27 Gaṅgā drives Bhīṣma's chariot. At 12.246.9–15 the body is a city, with Buddhi its queen (*svāminī*).

129 See also 1.16.39–40 for Viṣṇu's female form. On Viṣṇu's three steps as covering one pole, the other, and the totality, see Kuiper 1962; 1975; 1983: 20, 41–55.

130 At *mokṣa* the *ātman* joins its analogical counterpart, Kṛṣṇa-*puruṣottama*, the pre-cosmic Lord (*Bhagavadgītā* 7.5; 8.20–2; 15.7).

131 According to an androcentric symbology. Despite the textual support for this symbology, there always were female renouncers: see e.g. Khandelwal 2004: 36–9 for Hinduism; Horner 1999 for Buddhism; Dundas 1992: 48–52 for Jainism.

132 There are many important women in the generations the *Mahābhārata* spotlights, but in some ways we are led to suppose that this should be anomalous, a symptom of dharmic crisis. In the frame story of Earth's oppression (1.58–61), for example, Earth features as a character only because the kings are bad.

133 On the contrast between Draupadī and Sītā in terms of the *pativratā* model, see Sutherland 1989.

134 '[S]ince this formless Brahman is also understood to be the ultimate identity of an essentially male god . . . how androgynous can Brahman really be?' (Pintchman 1998: 275).

135 On the gendered dynamics here, see also Dennis Hudson 1996: 72–8.

8

BHĪṢMA AS MATCHMAKER

Nick Allen

It is well known that Dyu (or Dyaus or Dyaùṣ pítar), the god incarnate in Bhīṣma, is etymologically cognate with Zeus, Jupiter, Tyr, and other gods, but the Indo-European dimension of the hero himself is not so widely appreciated. Georges Dumézil's work is fundamental. Deemphasizing the etymology, he compared Bhīṣma to the gods Janus, Heimdall, and Lug (Roman, Norse, and Irish respectively), and also, briefly, to Rome's founder-hero Romulus (2000: 151–88; 1979: 73–6). In a similar vein, I have compared Bhīṣma with the Trojan hero Sarpedon (son of Zeus) in the *Iliad*, with Zeus and Ouranos in Hesiod's *Theogony*, and (more fully than Dumézil did) with Romulus (Allen 2004; 2005a; 2005b).

Both Romulus and Bhīṣma have careers that fall into a small number of contrasting phases, and in each tradition one such phase is devoted to matchmaking – to arranging marriages for other people with a view to their reproducing: Romulus's 'Rape of the Sabine Women' parallels Bhīṣma's 'Abduction of the Kāśi Princesses'. But this abduction is only one episode within Bhīṣma's career as matchmaker, and we need to study this career as a whole. Apart from some remarks on Heimdall at the end of the chapter, I shall concentrate on the Sanskrit narrative.

Bhīṣma organizes in succession the marriages of five of his male relatives, namely those of his father Śaṃtanu, his younger half-brother Vicitravīrya, and his three nephews – Dhṛtarāṣṭra, Pāṇḍu, and Vidura. The matchmaking is covered at 1.94–106, but is interspersed with other material and does not constitute a single block of text.[1] Moreover, although Bhīṣma marries off five relatives, he arranges six matches, since Pāṇḍu gets two wives. Bhīṣma also organizes Vyāsa's impregnation of the two widows who are left childless at Vicitravīrya's death, but the resulting offspring are attributed to the dead man; thus the arrangement completes the latter's marriage, rather than constituting a separate union. My central question is whether Bhīṣma's matchmaking presents any patterning or structure.

This question was clearly formulated by Dumézil, who observed that the matchmaking extends over three adjacent generations (1979: 66–71; 2000: 166). Relative to the epic's central heroes, Bhīṣma belongs to the grandparental generation, and he is indeed often referred to simply as 'The Grandfather' (*pitāmaha*). So if Bhīṣma is located in the second ascending generation (henceforth G+2), his matchmaking extends from the third ascending generation (henceforth G+3) to the first (henceforth G+1), as is shown in the following table. For a reason that will emerge later, the table includes Śaṃtanu's first wife, Gaṅgā (the Ganges), the union from which Bhīṣma was born.

Generation	*Groom*	*Bride(s)*
G+3	Śaṃtanu I	Gaṅgā
"	Śaṃtanu II	Satyavatī
G+2	Vicitravīrya	Ambikā, Ambālikā, (slave)
G+1	Dhṛtarāṣṭra	Gāndhārī
"	Pāṇḍu I	Kuntī
"	Pāṇḍu II	Mādrī
"	Vidura	unnamed *pāraśavī*

One notices that within each generation the last female listed is of very low social status. In G+3, Satyavatī has the menial job of operating a ferry and is the adopted daughter of the king of the *dāśa*s or fisher people – an impure occupation. In G+2, the king marries only the two princesses, but when Vyāsa is called upon to impregnate them, his third and last partner is Ambikā's unnamed servant or slave (*dāsī*, 1.100.23, 24; cf. *śūdrayonau*, 1.57.81), who gives birth to Vidura (see Dhand 2004). In G+1, Vidura's bride is, like himself, of mixed and inferior birth, a *pāraśavī*, the daughter of a king and a *śūdrā*. This patterning, whereby fisher-girl, servant, and bastard enter the final union in successive generations, already suggests that the unions are more than a random juxtaposition of disparate tales.

However, the obvious question for a comparativist is whether the table relates in any way to the Indo-European classificatory ideology – that is, to the three or four functions into which speakers of the Indo-European languages so often organized their cultural heritage, including their narratives. This remark may require a gloss. Anthropologically speaking (Allen 2000: 39–60), it is common for world-views (i.e. ideologies) to partition or compartmentalize continuous contexts: for instance, the time span of a year may be thought of as classified into four seasons, the human life span into a certain number of stages, the chromatic spectrum into a few basic colours, three-dimensional space into six or seven cardinal points,[2] the indefinite number of roles performed by members of society into a handful of occupations or social functions. A modern world-view presents at most only sporadic and unsystematic links between these different contexts (year, life span, colours, cardinal points, social structure), but many societies link them systematically, so that (to use the examples yet again) a particular season corresponds to a particular stage, colour, direction, and role. These correspondences may be rendered non-arbitrary and motivated (in the linguists' sense) by the belief that entities which correspond to each other all have something in common: they share in or relate to some definable essence, which itself need not be named or put into words by the culture.

Thus a classificatory ideology is one which combines two features or dimensions. First, horizontally as it were, or in rows, it compartmentalizes contexts, and secondly, vertically or in columns, it interlinks the compartments. The effect of the interlinking is that the classification of different contexts follows the same abstract pattern. This pattern is the key to the ideology, and although the simplest expository strategy is to start from the contexts and view the pattern as deriving from their vertical alignment, one can equally well reverse the direction of thought and start from the pattern. A classificatory ideology is one patterned by a (smallish) number of well-defined compartments which are projected onto and manifested in the conceptualization of multiple contexts.

What Dumézil thought he had discovered (in 1938) was that the proto-Indo-European speakers possessed a classificatory ideology consisting of three compartments, which he labelled 'functions'; he was referring to social structures, real or theoretical, for example the schema of the three 'twice-born' *varṇas*, in which each unit has its own social function. People who live out an ideology are not obliged to analyse it, and it is not clear that the proto-culture possessed definitions or labels for the functions. However, from 1938 onwards, by comparing many contexts, Dumézil was able to work out the implicit definitions, and since the functions were often manifested in a particular order, which also expressed their ranking or valuation, he gave them the numerical labels 'first', 'second', and 'third' (conveniently abbreviated as F1, F2, and F3). He and others demonstrated, over many decades, that trifunctional patterns are to be found in all sorts of contexts, often culturally important ones, for example ritual and legal procedures, pantheons, mythologies, and other forms of traditional narrative. Such patterns can be found in all the major branches of the language family, and in some cases are densely interlinked. Although occasional instances of the pattern can be found outside the Indo-European world, they tend to be not only less frequent and important but also less interlinked.

The wide distribution of trifunctional patterns suggests that the three functions were an important feature of the proto-Indo-European world-view, but Dumézil never claimed that they exhausted it. That a fuller account would require recognition of a fourth function was first proposed by Rees and Rees (1961), and the published arguments in favour of the proposal have been accumulating. I believe, however, that one needs to posit a split fourth function, in other words a pentadic schema, of which the two extremes are sometimes at maximum distance from each other but sometimes very close – as close as the Old Year and the New Year (Allen 2005c). I thus look for a pattern that can be expressed abstractly and cursorily as:

> valued otherness or transcendence (F4+);
> sacredness or wisdom (F1);
> physical force or strength (F2);
> wealth or fecundity (F3); and
> devalued or excluded otherness (F4–).[3]

Expressed in terms of social roles, the pattern becomes king, priest, warrior, producer/merchant, slave: from the viewpoint of the middle three (representatives of the 'core' or 'classical' functions), the slave is a devalued outsider (denied the ordinary rights of a member of society), while the king is a valued outsider (transcendent, enjoying a station above and beyond ordinary members of society).

Dumézil's analyses of Sanskritic tradition are scattered across his oeuvre, but his major analysis of the *Mahābhārata* comes in Part 1 of *Mythe et Épopée* (1968). Following up an insight of the Swedish scholar Stig Wikander, he argues (among much else) that the Pāṇḍava brothers are to be analysed as follows:

> the pious Yudhiṣṭhira . . . F1;
> the brutal warrior Bhīma . . . F2;
> the chivalrous warrior Arjuna . . . F2;
> the helpful and subordinate twins . . . F3.

However, a four-functional point of view (Allen 1999) extends the analysis to cover the remaining half-brother, the eldest – the 'baddy' Karṇa (F4–), and reinterprets Arjuna as the 'virtual king' (F4+). Such analyses are based on many details in the texts and must be assessed in the light of them, but for mnemonic purposes the results can be summed up in tables such as the following.

Compartments:	*F4+* *Transcendence*	*F1* *The sacred*	*F2* *Force*	*F3* *Fertility etc.*	*F4–* *Exclusion*
1. *varṇas*	king	brahmin	*kṣatriya*	*vaiśya*	*śūdra*
2. Pāṇḍavas	Arjuna	Yudhiṣṭhira	Bhīma	twins	Karṇa

One of the rows that could be added concerns marital law or, more precisely, modes of marital union. The fundamental text is Dumézil's *Mariages Indo-Européens*, chapters 2 and 3 (1979: 31–45), which I have examined from a four-functional perspective in the light of Arjuna's marital history (Allen

1996). Although Dumézil brings to bear material from elsewhere, particularly from Rome, the concern here is with the Sanskritic modes of union as they are presented both in the legal texts (Rocher 1979) and in the epic: they are mentioned or discussed by Bhīṣma himself at 1.96.8–11 and 13.44.2–9 and by Kṛṣṇa at 1.213.3–5, and they are listed by Duḥṣanta with explicit reference to Manu Svāyaṃbhuva at 1.67.8–9 (cf. *Mānava Dharmaśāstra* 3.20–34). From a trifunctional viewpoint, Manu's first four modes (*brāhma*, *daiva*, *ārṣa*, and *prājāpatya*), variants on the 'gift of a maiden' (*kanyādāna*), are the most dharmic and represent F1 (cf. also Renou 1978: 179). The *rākṣasa* and *āsura* modes, based on force and purchase respectively, represent F2 and F3. The despised *paiśāca* mode is excluded from the trifunctional analysis. The remaining *gāndharva* mode, based on the free choice of both partners, is linked with the characteristic autonomy of *kṣatriya*s (Dumézil 1979: 41–5) and hence with F2. One further mode, the *svayaṃvara,* found in the epics but not in the legal texts, is interpreted as a courtly elaboration of the *gāndharva.*

A four-function approach accepts much of this analysis, but incorporates the devalued *paiśāca* mode under F4–, and relocates the *svayaṃvara* (typical of kings) under F4+. The *gāndharva* mode would now be a privatized version of the *svayaṃvara*. On this basis we can add a further row to the table.

Compartments:	*F4+* *Transcendence*	*F1* *The sacred*	*F2* *Force*	*F3* *Fertility etc.*	*F4–* *Exclusion*
3. modes of union	*svayaṃvara, gāndharva*	*brāhma, daiva, ārṣa, prājāpatya*	*rākṣasa*	*āsura*	*paiśāca*

With this in mind, we can turn to Dumézil's chapter on 'Bhīṣma marieur' (1979: 66–71). After considering all the marriages organized by Bhīṣma, Dumézil narrows down his analysis by excluding the first and last in the sequence. Vidura's marriage is omitted since he is of mixed caste and therefore excluded from the royal line, and Śaṃtanu II is excluded on the grounds that although Bhīṣma makes it possible, he is not 'responsible' for it. The remaining four unions are then argued to relate to the functions as follows.

Generation	*Groom*	*Bride*	*Mode*	*Function*
G+2	Vicitravīrya	Ambikā, Ambālikā	*rākṣasa*	F2
G+1	Dhṛtarāṣṭra	Gāndhārī	*brāhma* or similar	F1
G+1	Pāṇḍu I	Kuntī	*svayaṃvara*	F2
G+1	Pāṇḍu II	Mādrī	*āsura*	F3

For the G+2 union Bhīṣma attends a *svayaṃvara* at Kāśi, but he ends up using force to abduct the princesses – so the result is a mixture of what for the trifunctionalist are two F2 modes. Dumézil suggests (1979: 70) that since Vicitravīrya's mode is barbarous and bloody, it has been projected or rejected into the prehistory of the poem, but whether or not that view is accepted, the G+1 *kṣatriyas* do, on this analysis, present a neat trifunctional set. The different modes enter the story in the standard ('canonical') order, and this order conforms to the ranking implied by the birth order of the two older nephews and by the relative seniority of Pāṇḍu's co-wives.

However, Pāṇḍu's first marriage raises an analytical problem since, as presented above, four-function theory locates the *svayaṃvara* mode not under F2 but under F4+. So is the neatness of the trifunctional argument illusory? Not necessarily, for a given entity need not fall under the same function *in different contexts*. Thus in the context of the Pāṇḍava brothers Karṇa represents F4–, while in the context of the five Kaurava marshals he falls under F2 (Allen 2005b). A similar ambiguity has been noted for several entities that waver between F4+ and F2 (Allen 1999; 2007). Thus Arjuna – so closely linked to the king of the gods, and so often transcendent relative to his brothers – must in general represent F4+; but in the context of the birth order and the fraternal seniority it represents, he appears to represent F2. In the context of the pantheon something similar applies to Arjuna's divine father, Indra, king of the gods; and earthly kings, who in cross-cultural perspective 'ought' to transcend their subjects, are often subsumed, as by Manu, among the F2 *kṣatriyas*.[4] In such cases one might postulate that the F4+ interpretation is the older, but my main point is that marital law in general, where *svayaṃvara* represents F4+, is a different context from this particular stretch of epic text, where Pāṇḍu's *svayaṃvara* – situated in a bounded triad between modes that clearly represent F1 and F3 – seems to represent F2.

For the sake of clarity I should emphasize that this chapter is primarily about the functions attached to marital unions, and not about the functions (if any) attached to the grooms, brides, or offspring of unions. The latter raise issues too complicated for systematic treatment here. Nevertheless, to strengthen the argument for treating the triad of G+1 *kṣatriya* unions as a meaningful analytic unit, two points are worth noting. First, a single *śloka* (1.61.98) brings together the three queens: Kuntī and Mādrī incarnate Siddhi and Dhṛti, and Gāndhārī incarnates Mati. Secondly, taken together, their offspring cover the whole range of functions: Gāndhārī's sons, the incarnate demons, represent F4–; Kuntī's, by birth order, represent F1, F2, F4+/F2; and Mādrī's represent F3.[5]

If the G+1 marriages form a reasonably clear pattern, what of the other generations? Vicitravīrya's marriage in G+2 has already been linked with F2. As for Śaṃtanu II in G+3, it is the bride's father who makes demands, who drives a hard bargain: he parts with his daughter only in exchange for a guarantee that his grandson shall inherit the throne at Hāstinapura. This negotiation resembles what happens when Arjuna falls in love with Citrāṅgadā, only child of King Citravāhana of Maṇalūra, and asks for her hand. The king demands as his brideprice (*śulka*, 1.207.22) that the son born of the marriage shall succeed him (as indeed happens).[6] Among Arjuna's marriages, this one represents F3 (Allen 1996: 16), and the similarities suggest that Śaṃtanu II is of the same type, even if the king of the fishers does not use the term *śulka*. It accords with the low status of the bride that the *āsura* mode is sometimes recommended for a *vaiśya* marrying a *śūdra* female, or is even dismissed as *adharmya* (*Mānava Dharmaśāstra* 3.24–5).

Thus in addition to the horizontal or intragenerational trifunctional set of unions in the canonical or descending hierarchical order (Dhṛtarāṣṭra, Pāṇḍu I, Pāṇḍu II), we have a vertical trifunctional set in the ascending order (Śaṃtanu II, Vicitravīrya, Dhṛtarāṣṭra), spanning the three generations. In other words the dynastic unions follow the sequence F3, 2, 1, 2, 3 – rising, then falling, with Dhṛtarāṣṭra's union as the climax or turning point. If the highest-valued union in the set leads to the birth of the epic's arch-villain, probably this paradox is one among the many symptoms of the cosmic crisis narrated by the epic.[7]

In any case, the results so far can be summed up as follows.

G+3	Śaṃtanu II (*āsura*, F3)
G+2	Vicitravīrya (*rākṣasa*, F2)
G+1	Dhṛtarāṣṭra (*brahmā* . . ., F1); Pāṇḍu I (*svayaṃvara*, F2); Pāṇḍu II (*āsura*, F3)

I now attempt to reinforce this double trifunctional analysis of the unions by three additional arguments.

Perfect polity

After the birth of the nephews and shortly before their marriages, one finds a fourteen-*śloka* account of the prosperity of the Kurus: for crops, animals, and citizens this is a golden age, a *kṛta yuga* (1.102.5). Similarly, after Gaṅgā's departure and shortly before the king's first meeting with Satyavatī, there comes a seventeen-*śloka* account of Śaṃtanu's rule (1.94.1–17). It describes a perfect polity where the ruler is virtuous, the *kṣatriya*s are happy, people fulfil their *varṇa* duties, rituals are properly performed, etc. Thus both of our sets are preceded by an account of a perfect polity. Despite the interruption of the vertical set by the golden age that introduces the horizontal set, the repetition of the motif provides a measure of support for distinguishing two sets.

Framing of the whole sequence of matchmaking

Vidura's non-royal marriage stands apart from the royal ones, but it marks the end of Bhīṣma's matchmaking career and cannot be ignored. The mode of union is not specified. Bhīṣma simply approaches the bride's father, transports the girl, and establishes the marriage;[8] so analysis must fall back on the partners. Vidura is excluded from the throne because of his mixed blood (*karaṇatvāt*, 1.102.23), and like his bride, the *pāraśavī*, he has a *śūdrā* mother. One might therefore speculate that in earlier versions their union was explicitly of the lowest type (corresponding to Manu's *paiśāca*), in which case the unions in G+1 would form the sequence F1, 2, 3, 4–.[9] However, all we can say for certain is that Bhīṣma's final matchmaking involves partners of very low social rank.

This prompts a closer look at the start of the sequence of marriages in Bhīṣma's family. Bhīṣma seemingly cannot arrange Śaṃtanu I, the marriage from which he himself is born, but appearances can be deceptive (1.91–3). Śaṃtanu himself is the reincarnation of Mahābhiṣa, an earthly king whose virtues secure him a place in heaven. However, when he shamelessly exhibits his feelings for Gaṅgā, he is condemned by Brahmā to a further life as a mortal, and chooses to become Śaṃtanu. Gaṅgā, who reciprocates Mahābhiṣa's feelings, now meets a set of eight gods called Vasus, who have offended the sage Vasiṣṭha and have been cursed by him to an earthly incarnation. They urge her to become their mother, and when they choose Śaṃtanu as their father, Gaṅgā welcomes the opportunity to take human form and pursue on earth the love affair that began in heaven. Now although the Vasus address Gaṅgā collectively, their ringleader is Dyu, who thus helps to bring about Śaṃtanu's first marriage. But Dyu is incarnated as Bhīṣma. Thus Bhīṣma's matchmaking on earth has a prelude in heaven: his divine precursor Dyu participates in arranging the marriage of Gaṅgā and the soon-to-be-reincarnated Mahābhiṣa. In that sense Bhīṣma begins his matchmaking before he is born.

In other words the matchmaking sequence that ends with the union of two outcastes starts with the project for the union of two celestials. Moreover, Śaṃtanu I can only be a *svayaṃvara* or *gāndharva* union (depending on whether one emphasizes its start in the divine assembly or its development on earth). Both represent F4+, and we were tempted to view Vidura's union as F4–. However, the contrast between the start and finish is better illustrated by the females: while the river goddess is emphatically pure, Vidura's bride, young and beautiful though she is, is born impure. So even if the modes of union cannot be contrasted with confidence, the two female partners can be, and they form a neat frame around the other unions, reinforcing our attempt to treat them as a meaningful whole.

As for the male partners in the 'framing' unions, although they contrast as king of a perfect polity versus a bastard, they have similar prehistories. It is not only that Śaṃtanu incarnates Mahābhiṣa – at least in the context of his first marriage – while Vidura incarnates the god Dharma; more importantly, both incarnations are punishments. Mahābhiṣa's shameless behaviour angered Brahmā, while Dharma's excessive punishment of a childish peccadillo provoked the curse of the sage Aṇīmāṇḍavya (1.57.77–81). This gives the coming to earth of Śaṃtanu and Vidura a special quality that sets them apart from the warriors participating in the great war; the latter incarnate supernaturals, but not ones who are being punished.[10] When so much incarnation is taking place, it is striking that not one of the three male partners *within* the frame is to be found in the main list of incarnations (1.61). Later, at 15.39.8–15, Vyāsa tells Gāndhārī that Dhṛtarāṣṭra and Pāṇḍu incarnate respectively the king of the *gandharva*s, and the Maruts (*marudgaṇa*), but his is a curious list, in which Bhīma too is from the Maruts and Bhīṣma (coming at the end) is merely a Vasu, no reference being made to Dyu. In any case, even if the half-brothers are taken as incarnations, the passage contains no reference to punishment, so the distinctiveness of Śaṃtanu and Vidura receives some further support.

The *Rígsþula* ('Ríg's list')

Dumézil's rapprochement between Bhīṣma and Heimdall (noted at the start of the chapter) draws on many lines of argument, but I focus here only on the matchmaking. According to an Eddic poem, the *Rígsþula* (tenth–eleventh century),[11] Heimdall the King (Ríg) goes on a journey. His first visit is to the humble home of Great-grandfather and Great-grandmother. He stays three nights, and when he leaves, the woman is pregnant with Thrall, the black and ugly progenitor of slaves. His second visit is to the prosperous home of Grandfather and Grandmother, and here the child is the ruddy Karl, ancestor of peasant farmers. His third visit is to the refined house of Father and Mother, where the child is the fair-haired Jarl, ancestor of the earls or nobility. The obvious repeating pattern is more elaborate than this summary suggests, but it tails off after the third visit when Heimdall comes to teach runes to Jarl, giving him the title *ríg* (a Celtic word) and encouraging him to conquer territory. The rest of the poem deals with Jarl's youngest son, Konr Ungr, 'Young Noblekin' in Dronke's translation, whose name is a pun on Norse *konungr* 'king'. Strong, but also possessing a range of useful and unwarlike skills, he outdoes his father in knowledge of runes, and is pretty clearly the founder of the Norse institution of kingship. The poem breaks off when a crow instructs the (as yet unmarried) king to undertake a military expedition, apparently against Denmark.

Heimdall lies between each married couple on their bed, but (*pace* many analysts) it is not clear that he impregnates the females. What is clear is that his visits promote procreation and lead to the birth of the social classes – slaves, peasants, and nobility; that the couples who originate the three classes are associated respectively with G+3, +2, and +1; and that full Scandinavian royalty emerges from and after the nobility.

The story actually uses generations in two ways, or at two levels. In the larger and encompassing pattern the generations of the three couples visited by Heimdall are related only by their names and sequence, from great-grandparents onwards to G+1; but internally, within each of the parallel episodes, three generations are again presented – the founding couples, their sons (Thrall, Karl, Jarl) with their respective brides, and the latters' children, many of whose names are listed. Konr Ungr is the grandson of Father and Mother, but since his story begins after the larger three-generation pattern finishes, one is tempted to interpret him not as part of the G+1 episode but as representing a fourth generation in the encompassing pattern (G zero).

In any case, this is a story about the origin of four social statuses. The first three must represent F4–, F3, and F2, but the problem lies in the interpretation of Konr Ungr. For Dumézil (2000) Konr Ungr contrasts with Jarl as F1 contrasts with F2, and the king's knowledge and magical skills support this view. On the other hand, viewed four-functionally, the founder of the kingship must represent F4+.[12] Part of the explanation may lie in the fact that the ancient Germans lacked a hereditary priesthood corresponding to brahmins, but comparison with the *Mahābhārata* suggests a further line of thought. Heimdall says that Jarl (G+1 in the larger pattern) is his son (*son kveðz eiga*, 37.6), and since he says nothing similar of Thrall or Karl, he thus implicitly locates himself in G+2. This is precisely the location of 'Grandfather' Bhīṣma, and two generations down from Bhīṣma and Heimdall brings one to Yudhiṣṭhira and Konr Ungr. After the great war, albeit reluctantly, Yudhiṣṭhira becomes king, but at the same time he represents the first function among the Pāṇḍava brothers. So perhaps, despite the many complexities, Yudhiṣṭhira and Konr Ungr are cognate figures. In any case, both the Sanskrit epic and the Eddic poem share the motif of a three-generation rising hierarchy, starting in G+3.

One complication is that the rising hierarchy starts with the F4– slaves in the Norse, but with the F3 mode of union in the Sanskrit. But it seems to me that the bards were capable of interweaving more than one functional pattern in a single stretch of text, and that if we shift analytic attention from the modes of union to the epic brides, the discrepancy resolves. In G+3 Satyavatī, of *dāśa* status, represents F4–. In G+2 the princesses not only marry a husband who represents F3 (Allen 2005b: 35–8), but within seven years they wear him out so that he dies of excessive love-making; thus the princesses could well represent F3 (their pairing resembles the twinning so characteristic of that function).[13] But in G+1 – to pursue the central line of succession – Kuntī can hardly be taken to represent anything but F2. If this is on the right tracks, both rising hierarchies start in G+3 with representatives of the devalued fourth function.

The aim of this Scandinavian excursion has not only been to publicize and reinforce Dumézil's argument that Bhīṣma and Heimdall are cognate figures from cognate Indo-European traditions, but to go a little further. Despite performing different roles in the various marriages (Bhīṣma initiates the unions, Heimdall ensures offspring for couples who already exist), both figures spread their activity over three successive generations, starting in G+3, and this activity expresses a rising hierarchy linked to the functions; and both are in some sense located in G+2.

Does the rapprochement suggest that the vertical set of unions in the *Mahābhārata* has been part of the tradition for longer than the horizontal one? Possibly, but such speculation seems premature. The Indo-European tradition, mythic and/or epic – the 'proto-narrative', as I call it – can, I believe, be reconstructed, up to a point, by drawing together the various rapprochements involving Bhīṣma that were mentioned at the start, plus any new ones that are discovered; but it will be a lengthy and very intricate undertaking, and it remains to be seen whether an acceptable degree of scholarly consensus is attainable, comparable to that of linguists when they reconstruct the Indo-European proto-language.

Meanwhile, I have tried to exemplify the sorts of insight offered by Indo-European cultural comparativism. Some of them are aesthetic: to recognize the play of the functions in the unrolling of a complicated narrative is like recognizing the variations of a melody that recurs in a symphony. Others bear on the history of the story, enabling us not only to distinguish what is definitely old from what may be new, but also to recognize patterns that were presumably incorporated as wholes, not piecemeal. For instance, if the unions of Śaṃtanu I and Vidura form a frame around the other unions arranged by Bhīṣma, both probably entered the tradition at the same time.

For those who prefer a synchronic reading of the epic, and are less interested in aesthetics than analysis, an approach *via* the functions brings to light unexpected patterns, but it is often unclear exactly how to interpret them. For instance, one might wonder to what extent bards and their audience or compilers were consciously aware of the functional ideology; but the question seems not only unanswerable (what evidence could be used, apart from the existence of the patterns?), but also ill formulated (to what extent are we consciously aware of our grammar?). Quite possibly any narrator who devised a new functional pattern was guided by what 'felt natural' or 'seemed right', not by an ideology that the narrator could have expounded.

One wonders also about the identity of these innovatory narrators. For how long did the old ideology continue to inspire the composition of new functional patterns? Again we are stymied, not only by lack of evidence but also by a conceptual problem – how to define novelty and distinguish it from adaptation of the old. Nevertheless, the general thrust of the comparative approach is towards identifying what is old, and at least some of the three- or four-functional innovators must have lived outside India and long before the Vedas reached their current form.

However, the situation varies for different functional patterns. Like the *varṇa* schema, to which it is explicitly related, the functional classification of marital unions must have entered the oral epic tradition in early Indo-European times, as is shown by the comparison between the marital histories of Arjuna and Odysseus (Allen 1996). Thereafter, within the epic tradition, it was of course adapted to the realities of Indian geography, anthroponymy, material culture, etc., and expressed in new language as Sanskrit developed. But in this case the classification cannot have been solely a survival from the distant past: it must have related in some way to current social life, or it would hardly have appeared so regularly in the legal texts. Even here, one must be cautious in drawing conclusions about the realities of social life around the turn of the eras, since the legal texts themselves surely contain some very old ideas, and may sometimes represent brahmanical aspirations or ideals rather than practices. Nevertheless, we can be sure that there existed doctrines concerning the modes of union, and anthropological work on topics like dowry and bride-price in India (cf. Allen 2007) suggests that the doctrines cannot have been wholly theoretical.

The broader question of how gender articulates with the old functional ideology needs further work. Provisionally, it seems to me that if many more comparativist analyses concern males than females, this merely reflects the male bias in our sources (a bias that varies over space and time, being for instance less marked in the Roman pantheon than the Vedic one). Functional analysis sometimes applies to females in themselves, as well as to the unions into which they enter, as has been suggested above for several of the female partners considered; but my main point here has been that these unions themselves draw on an ancient classificatory tradition.

Notes

1 For Śaṃtanu see 1.94.41ff., for Vicitravīrya 1.96, and for the nephews respectively 1.103; 1.105.1–5; 1.106.12–14.

2 The conventional four cardinal points, plus zenith, nadir, and often 'centre' (location of speaker – as it were the default direction or zero direction).

3 For Dumézil's full definitions of F1–3 see Dumézil 1958: 19. His definition of F1 includes 'sovereignty', which makes it excessively broad. As I have argued in previous papers, a fourth function with two 'aspects' fits the facts better than would a fifth function (which in addition would have to be awkwardly expressed as F0).

4 Though the brahmins might well welcome the demotion of representatives of F4+ into F2 (their 'secularisation'), I doubt if this massive trend within the ideology can be explained solely by conscious machinations of brahmins who control the texts.

5 It is interesting too that dynastic continuity, to Parikṣit and beyond, is maintained *via* the middle marriage (Kuntī's), *via* Pāṇḍu's middle son (Arjuna), and *via* the wife (Subhadrā) whom Arjuna acquires by the mode associated with the middle function (the F2 *rākṣasa* mode).

6 Compare also Śakuntalā's demand (1.67.17), where however no reference is made

to *śulka* and the marriage is presented as *gāndharva* mode. The epic explicitly recognizes the mixing of modes (*miśrau*, *miśrāḥ*, 1.67.13; 13.44.9).

7 But it is debatable exactly how the two trifunctional sets are related and whether Dhṛtarāṣṭra's union belongs more to one than to the other. One hypothesis would be that this unusual structure resulted from combining two trifunctional sets of different origin.

8 *tatas tu varayitvā tām ānāyya puruṣarṣabhaḥ / vivāhaṃ kārayām āsa vidurasya mahāmateḥ //* 1.106.13. The information is sufficient to eliminate the F4+ and probably the F2 types.

9 As we noted near the start, Vidura's marriage can be compared with Vyāsa's third union. If the female partner in a *paiśāca* union is not her real self because she is asleep, drunk, or mad (*Mānava Dharmaśāstra* 3.34), can one say that Vidura's mother is not her real self because she is disguised as her mistress? I leave such questions for future work.

10 The Vasus too, including Dyu/Bhīṣma, come to earth as a punishment, but we are concerned here only with the frame figures.

11 The *Rígsþula* is in Old Icelandic, a Norse dialect. See Dronke 1997: 161–238; Larrington 1996: 246–52; for a trifunctional interpretation, Dumézil 2000: 151–65. The identification of the protagonist, Ríg, with the somewhat obscure Norse deity Heimdall depends on a medieval commentator, but has been widely accepted by Germanists.

12 Allen (2005b) argues that Rome's first king, Romulus, represents F4+, as does his cognate Bhīṣma. This interpretation of Bhīṣma accords with the fact that, though he arranges other people's marriages, he himself stands *outside* the institution.

13 1.110.3–4; 5.145.23. One is reminded of Mādrī, F3 from several points of view, including the explicit twinning of her sons and of her divine partners: Mādrī's sexual charms cause the death of Pāṇḍu.

9

BHĪṢMA BEYOND FREUD

Bhīṣma in the *Mahābhārata*

James L. Fitzgerald

Introduction

The vast *Mahābhārata* epic teems with interesting characters, and one of the most stunning and consistently intriguing is the centrally important figure of Bhīṣma, the ironic patriarch of the Bhārata clan, known to all as 'grandfather', though in fact a lifelong celibate. Not only was Bhīṣma the most dominating figure of the epic and one of its most thematically 'male' warriors, the very core of Bhīṣma's persona was constituted by a tangle of issues that centre upon the sexual dimorphism of human beings, human sexual experience, and intrafamilial and intergenerational conflict. And there is more to him than all this! A reincarnation of the god Sky, he was, at an age of about one hundred years (Allen 2005b: 23 n. 4), the most learned *kṣatriya* sage of the passing age, the man who taught the victorious new king Yudhiṣṭhira after the war that the rule of a kingdom could be understood as truly righteous (truly constituting deeds of *dharma*) in spite of all appearances to the contrary (Sinha 1991; Fitzgerald 2006: 280–2). And in the Sanskrit *Mahābhārata* Bhīṣma is one of the principal and most open advocates of Kṛṣṇa as a divinity.

Bhīṣma has not been neglected by twentieth-century historical scholarship on the epic. He is noted in due course by J.J. Meyer in his *Sexual Life in Ancient India* (1930). We have Georges Dumézil's very general and comparative discussion of Bhīṣma in volume 1 of *Mythe et Épopée* (1968), Alf Hiltebeitel's treatment of him in *The Ritual of Battle* (1976), Robert Goldman's extensive psychoanalytic discussions of him in 'Fathers, sons and gurus: oedipal conflict in the Sanskrit epics' (1978) and fifteen years later in 'Transsexualism, gender, and anxiety in traditional India' (1993), Hiltebeitel's 'Bhīṣma's sources' (2001b), and Nick Allen's interesting and important 'Romulus et Bhîshma: structures entrecroisées' (2005b) (and now his chapter in this volume, 'Bhīṣma as matchmaker'). All of these treatments of Bhīṣma focus upon crucial elements of him, but none of them attempts to comprehend the whole of this curious figure in a considered, analytic way. Only Irawati Karve treats him comprehensively, in the second chapter of her moralizing reflections[1] on the epic and many of its characters, *Yuganta* (1969). Karve brings the helpful touch of a modern Indian woman to the reading of Bhīṣma,[2] but as valuable and important as the essays in her book are, she is engaged in an essentially different enterprise from ours. So it is time to look at Bhīṣma again, and he is a most apt subject for the themes of this volume. However, a complete study in depth of this ironic old epic 'patriarch' would require a very large effort, far beyond what is possible at the moment. So my contribution here will be limited to the first instalment of what I hope will be a series of investigations of Bhīṣma filling out the whole of the sweeping paper I presented at the memorable *Epic Constructions* conference at SOAS in July 2005,[3] and I begin at Bhīṣma's end.[4]

The end of Bhīṣma

Bhīṣma's three mothers

As all readers of the *Mahābhārata* know, Bhīṣma died at the time of the winter solstice, many weeks after the great Bhārata war ended.[5] His death was as grand and majestic as his life had been. Employing *yoga* in a process very similar to that used by Droṇa just before Dhṛṣṭadyumna lopped off his head on the fifteenth day of the war,[6]

> Bhīṣma stabilized his mind (or soul – *ātman*) in the 'holding-meditations' (*dhāraṇā*s), and his life breaths, which were now completely bottled up within his body (*saṃniruddha*), rose upwards within him. Then a miracle occurred in the midst of those exalted men: as Bhīṣma engaged in *yoga* and successively released different limbs of his body, each released limb healed – it became free of the arrows and arrow-wounds that had caused him great suffering since his fall on the tenth day of the war. His whole body healed in a moment as Kṛṣṇa Vāsudeva and Vyāsa and other sages looked on and were amazed. Then Bhīṣma's soul (*ātman*), completely obstructed in all the stations of its normal operation (the senses and the *manas*), split through his head and left his body, rose up into the sky, and, like a giant meteor, disappeared in a moment. Thus did the son of Śaṃtanu, that family-supporting scion of the Bharatas,[7] rejoin his proper realm.
>
> (13.154.2–7)[8]

The Pāṇḍavas and Vidura then prepared Bhīṣma's body and a pyre for his cremation, performed the Vedic offering for a departed ancestor (*pitṛmedha*), had oblations made and *sāman*s sung over the body, and then burned it. The whole party then proceeded to the river Gaṅgā for the pouring of the funeral libation in the river. When the party reached the Gaṅgā[9] and was joined by some of the inhabitants of Hāstinapura, Bhīṣma's mother, the river herself, rose up from her waters and lamented her son:

> A perfect master of the ways kings act, and richly endowed with wisdom and noble birth; dutiful caretaker of his Kuru elders; devoted to his father; scrupulously true to his vow – that mighty man whom Rāma Jāmadagnya once failed to conquer with his marvelous weapons has now been killed by Śikhaṇḍin! Kings! My heart must now be hard as a rock since it does not split, even though I no longer see my dear son.
>
> (13.154.20–2)

Gaṅgā recounted Bhīṣma's seizing the Kāśi princesses (told at 1.96), and then returned again, dirge-like, to his having been killed by Śikhaṇḍin. And yet again she recurred to his battle with Rāma – she was amazed that Śikhaṇḍin killed Bhīṣma, who had pressed Rāma so easily. Kṛṣṇa then offered her solace by assuring her that her son – 'an illustrious Vasu become human only because of a curse' – had reached the highest level of attainment through *yoga* (*paramā siddhi*) and now has gone to heaven and rejoined the Vasus at a time of his own choosing. Otherwise no one could have put him down in battle, not even Indra, not even all the Gods attacking in concert.[10] But most importantly, he informed her that it was Arjuna, doing his duty as a *kṣatriya*, and not Śikhaṇḍin, who had cut Bhīṣma down in the battle. The River Goddess then sank back into her own waters and, given leave by her, everyone left (13.154.23–34).

There is jealousy as well as confusion in these words of Bhīṣma's mother, as she repeatedly recurs to Śikhaṇḍin's role in Bhīṣma's fall.[11] For whether Gaṅgā knows it well or not, the authors of the epic have made the audience fully aware that Śikhaṇḍin is a male embodiment of the reincarnation of 'Mother', Ambā,[12] who was the eldest of the three Kāśi princesses seized by Bhīṣma as brides for his brother, and who became Bhīṣma's fatal nemesis. Through an interesting and important series of narrative complications this 'mother' had become a possible wife for Bhīṣma, but he refused even to think of her as such.[13] Bhīṣma had earlier pledged lifelong celibacy as he procured Satyavatī as a second wife for his father, his 'Yamunā wife' to complement his earlier Gaṅgā wife. In the case of Satyavatī Bhīṣma transformed a woman who might well have been his bride into a mother (stepmother); with Ambā he turned a woman named 'mother' into a bride he should have taken but instead scorned. All three of Bhīṣma's 'mothers' hover here over Bhīṣma's last rites.[14] His relations with each of these 'mothers' is qualitatively quite distinct, though each relationship records significant 'mother'–son antagonism,[15] and in the case of Ambā, as we shall see, the antagonism becomes something of an abstract theme centred upon the idea of 'womanhood ruined'. I shall return to Bhīṣma's mothers in a future instalment; but first to the 'son' who helped 'Mother' kill him.

Father, son, and 'Mother'

Although Kṛṣṇa's assurance that it was really Arjuna who felled Bhīṣma might have been comforting to Gaṅgā's sense of the dignity of her son, Kṛṣṇa's correction of her points to even more disquieting ironies at the heart of Bhīṣma's story. As Goldman has pointed out (1978: 333), Bhīṣma was Arjuna's beloved 'grandfather' psychologically even if not biologically. In attacking Bhīṣma Arjuna assaulted, felled, and fatally wounded the dominant man of his patriline. As Goldman emphasized, he effectively committed parricide, even if he did not kill his actual father. And there is another short chapter to the parricidal violence that has not been discussed previously.[16]

The epic records a little-known act of aggression by Arjuna against Bhīṣma, an act presented as a kindness on the surface, but a re-enactment of father-murder nonetheless. At the end of that tenth day of the war, everyone gathered around the fallen Bhīṣma as he lay upon a 'hero's bed of arrows' (*vīraśayana*, *śaratalpa*): he was so thoroughly pin-cushioned, with arrows protruding from his body in every direction, that no part of his body touched the ground. Bhīṣma saluted them all and asked for a pillow because his head hung back unsupported (6.115.27ff.). Many of the kings present produced finely made pillows which Bhīṣma refused as unsuitable for a hero's bed. He asked Arjuna to produce a fitting pillow. His eyes full of tears, Arjuna strung his bow, took up three arrows, consecrated them with *mantra*s, and used them to form a pillow supporting Bhīṣma's head. That is to say – though the text does not say it explicitly – Arjuna shot the arrows into the ground just past Bhīṣma's head, from point-blank range, re-enacting the parricide face to face. Similarly, on the following morning Bhīṣma asked the assembled kings and warriors for a drink of water to allay his suffering. As before, various kings fetched water (and food) in various pots which they placed around Bhīṣma. But lying upon a bed of arrows as he was, Bhīṣma was not able to make use of normal human implements. Bhīṣma turned to Arjuna for proper satisfaction and Arjuna mounted his chariot, strung his bow again, drove round the prostrate grandfather in a circle, consecrated an arrow as the 'rain-water missile' (*parjanyāstra*), and shot it into the ground to Bhīṣma's right. From the point where it entered the earth there came a fountain of pure, cool, fragrant water with which Bhīṣma could satisfy himself at will. All present were amazed at Arjuna's power and Bhīṣma praised Arjuna extravagantly, saying that such a feat was entirely normal for him. This second exercise of Arjuna's virtuosity with a bow (6.116.9–31) makes two important points: first, it describes, more elaborately and explicitly than the first instance did, Arjuna's use of the bow to fulfil Bhīṣma's request; second, it underscores the unique relationship between Bhīṣma and Arjuna. It also represents a profound ambivalence – after representing the terrifying aggression of Arjuna's fashioning a pillow with arrows, it portrays an unalloyed act of kindness.

Another unsettling element of Arjuna's felling of Bhīṣma is that Bhīṣma himself designed the basic plan of his death, encouraged its happening, and became completely passive in the face of the attack. Only Arjuna could be the cause of Bhīṣma's fatal wounds, and Arjuna could succeed only because he would be screened by Śikhaṇḍin. Bhīṣma's father Śaṃtanu had conferred upon his son the wonderful power of not dying until he chose to do so (1.94.94), as a reward for Bhīṣma's swearing perpetual celibacy to enable Śaṃtanu's marriage to Satyavatī of the Yamunā.[17] This power (*svacchandamaraṇa*) amounted to Bhīṣma's being invincible in battle (6.114.33), as Kṛṣṇa said to Gaṅgā at the water rites for Bhīṣma (13.154.30–1). And it was Bhīṣma's will that only Kṛṣṇa or Arjuna slay him. He told the Pāṇḍavas and Kṛṣṇa on the eve of the tenth day of battle, 'I do not see anyone in the world who might kill me if I am resisting, except for the illustrious Kṛṣṇa or the Pāṇḍava Dhanaṃjaya' (6.103.80). Though this statement looks as if Bhīṣma is simply making a declaration of his relative might, that cannot be the case here, for the basic premise of the entire episode is that not even Kṛṣṇa or Arjuna could kill him if he did not wish it (see 6.41.41). As Kṛṣṇa had pledged to help the Pāṇḍavas in the war only as a non-combatant, Arjuna alone had the responsibility to kill Bhīṣma. Arjuna had sworn before the war began that he would attack and kill Bhīṣma first of all in the battle,[18] but he was less than wholehearted about doing so during the battle's first nine days. Twice (once on the third day and again on the ninth[19]) Kṛṣṇa got impatient with what he perceived as Arjuna's reluctance to attack the grandfather (*mṛduyuddhatā*, 'fighting softly'), and he jumped from their chariot and rushed at Bhīṣma to slay him. Both times Bhīṣma laid his weapons down and happily welcomed Kṛṣṇa as his killer. Both times Arjuna followed Kṛṣṇa and grabbed him from behind, digging his heels in and bringing the charging Kṛṣṇa to a halt on his tenth step. Arjuna swore both times that he would perform the deed as promised, so Kṛṣṇa relented. In the wake of Kṛṣṇa's second loss of patience, in the evening after the ninth day of battle, Yudhiṣṭhira recollected that Bhīṣma had promised to advise the Pāṇḍavas how he could be defeated in battle when the time for him to die arrived (6.41.4–44). The Pāṇḍavas and Kṛṣṇa went to Bhīṣma's tent that night and, in an emotionally wrought conversation, Bhīṣma instructed the Pāṇḍavas to have Arjuna attack him from behind Śikhaṇḍin, as Bhīṣma would not fight against Śikhaṇḍin, the incarnation of Ambā, because of that man's earlier existence as a woman.[20] And thus, on the tenth day of battle, Arjuna led a general attack against Bhīṣma from behind Śikhaṇḍin, and shot the grandfather full of arrows as Bhīṣma put up no resistance to the missiles coming from Arjuna's chariot. Eventually, Bhīṣma toppled headfirst from his chariot to the ground.[21]

Bhīṣma's fall and (eventual) death at the hands of Arjuna screened by a variable 'peacock'-man[22] who was formerly a girl called 'Peahen' (Śikhaṇḍinī) and before that a woman called 'Mother' forces us to pause and consider why the epic poets dreamt up such a strange way to bring down the hoary old patriarch of the Bhāratas. Robert Goldman developed one answer to that question, and we must now consider his Oedipal interpretation of this passage and the more general interpretation of Bhīṣma that he draws from it.

Does Bhīṣma (or Arjuna) need Freud?

Goldman interprets this attack as a representation of the Oedipal triangle:

> Clearly Śikhaṇḍin who, despite his change of sex, remains a woman for Bhīṣma, can only represent the missing mother in this curious displacement of the oedipal triangle. Like a mother, he/she intercedes for the son to ward off the destructive rage of the father.
>
> (Goldman 1978: 334)

With explicit support from the *Mahābhārata* itself,[23] Goldman connects Arjuna's fatal assault upon Bhīṣma to two other apparently Oedipal struggles: Bhīṣma's own prior, determined, but ultimately non-fatal assault upon a father-figure, his *guru* Rāma Jāmadagnya (5.179–86; this fight was occasioned by Rāma's commanding Bhīṣma to take Ambā back); and, after the war, the fatal assault upon Arjuna by one of his own sons, Babhruvāhana (told at 14.78–82). Babhruvāhana's (only temporary) killing of Arjuna was, according to Ulūpī, Babhruvāhana's 'mother', the means for Arjuna to put to rest (*śānti*) his killing of Bhīṣma. To quote Goldman's account:

> [Ulūpī] tells Arjuna that his 'death' at the hands of his son is in fact his penance or expiation for his immoral killing of Bhīṣma during the great Bhārata war. She reminds him that since he wrongfully killed the great Kaurava patriarch while he was engaged with Śikhaṇḍin, he would, by virtue of this crime, have gone to hell forever had he died without having expiated it. The expiation fixed is death at his own son's hands. The rationale given for this sequence is that the Vasus, divine figures reckoned to be the older brothers of Bhīṣma, learning of the unchivalrous murder of that hero, resolved – with the concurrence of their mother, the sacred river Ganges – to curse Arjuna.
>
> (Goldman 1978: 331–2)

At the same time, according to Goldman, being killed by Arjuna was Bhīṣma's punishment for disobeying a command of his *guru* Rāma (to take Ambā back) and then trying to kill him in battle.

> [The *Ambā-Upākhyāna*'s] detailed account of the highly charged encounter of Bhīṣma and his guru provides the psychological as well

> as narrative explanation for the former's subsequent death at the hands of . . . his son.
>
> (ibid.: 336)

Goldman continues, pointing out that Bhīṣma and Arjuna are the central links in a chain of parricides stretching across much of the *Mahābhārata*.

> Thus the battle over the Kāśi princess is but another link in the chain of oedipal struggles that links and indeed identifies the defeat of the great Bhārgava sage [Rāma] with the deaths of first Bhīṣma and finally Arjuna.
>
> (ibid.)

It is clear that Goldman has called our attention to a striking and disturbing thematic continuum within the *Mahābhārata*. But Goldman's 1978 paper was more concerned to make the case that Oedipal themes were present and important in the epics than to explain how any particular such theme contributed to the larger literary context in which it was found. In my judgment, Goldman's principal achievements in that paper were to collate many episodes of the Sanskrit epics that involve Oedipal representations and to argue persuasively that we must not confine ourselves to a literal reading of the surface of the text. And I agree with him in accepting the Freudian principle that the authors of these texts would have been behaving in perfectly normal and understandable ways if and when they filled the roles of fathers, sons, and mothers in their stories with figures who only *resembled* the actual father, son, or mother of the protagonist of a given episode, and if they expressed ambivalence about such deeds in a variety of temporizing ways.

A serious and thoughtful objection to seeing the presence of Oedipal themes in these stories has been sounded by William Sax in an important essay in his recent book *Dancing the Self: personhood and performance in the pāṇḍav līlā of Garhwal* (2002).[24] Sax analyses a series of ritual performances (which form part of the occasional mounting of a *pāṇḍav līlā*[25]) surrounding the enactment of elements of local Garhwali *Mahābhārata* traditions, particularly the 'Rhinoceros Tale', which represents a transformed version of the Sanskrit text's story of Babhruvāhana's fatal attack upon Arjuna. After discussing Goldman's Freudian interpretations of the relevant Sanskrit stories, Sax argues, 'If I can propose an explanation that makes sense to local participants as well as to outside observers, then why invoke the hidden messages and secret codes of psychoanalysis?' (2002: 80).

After expressing sympathy with the attempts of Gananath Obeyesekere (1990) and Stanley Kurtz (1992) (see p. 199 below) to 'modify psychoanalytic theory so as to take account of culturally variant socialization patterns and family relationships', Sax characterizes his own method as follows:

> . . . in the main, my analysis is ethnographic, not psychoanalytic . . . I rely upon empirical entities such as public ritual performances, ideas about masculinity and father–son relationships, child-rearing patterns, and the complex institutions of family and caste – what a psychoanalytically oriented analyst might call 'surface features' – to explain why the battle between father and son is central to *pāṇḍav līlā*, and why its dramatic representation evokes such a powerful response from the audience.
>
> (Sax 2002: 79–80)

The primary ideas he sees at the centre of the Rhinoceros Tale – and the re-enactment in dance of the fatal fight between Arjuna and his son (here called Nagarjuna) that concludes each of many recitations of it during the multiple days of *pāṇḍav līlā* – are the affiliation of fathers and sons, and a man's acting with the courage and resolve required of a genuine *kṣatriya* warrior.

The fight between Arjuna and his son Nagarjuna (represented in story and re-enacted in dance)

> . . . is all about solidarity and continuity between fathers and sons. It is a way of resisting death by ensuring the continued life of the patriline.
>
> (ibid.: 87)

Furthermore:

> The duty of a Kshatriya king or warrior is to fight bravely, against his own relatives, against his father himself if need be. Is this not implicit in the *Mahābhārata* and explicit in the *Bhagavad Gītā* at its core? Textual and dramatic representations of fratricide or parricide are terrible not because they enact suppressed wishes but because they violate the values of filial piety and fraternal solidarity that are so deeply embedded in Indian culture. The tension between filial piety and the dharma of the warrior king is precisely what provides the dramatic interest of the *Mahābhārata*, which is after all about a devastating fratricidal war.
>
> (ibid.: 90)

And in concluding the chapter:

> The battle between Arjuna and Nagarjuna can thus be seen as a didactic episode stressing the ambivalent tension between the principle of filial piety and the principle of Kshatriya valor, and thus consistent with the enduring themes of the *Mahābhārata* story.
>
> (ibid.: 92)

While I appreciate very much Sax's detailed explication of one community's appropriation and use of a remarkable *Mahābhārata* tradition, and while I am more than sympathetic to his insistence upon examining the details of the story in terms of the understanding of this community and the 'surface features' of its social and cultural life, I must dissent from his turning his back on the prospect of a new and improved, non-ethnocentric psychoanalysis. I find his explanations of the importance of patrilineal solidarity, father–son bonds, and the active sense of *kṣatriya* duty very helpful as far as they go, but he has not, in fact, accounted for all the major features of the story and its performance in terms of these themes, and I doubt he could. I think that the ambivalence in the danced re-enactments of the battle of Arjuna and Nagarjuna is more than an ambivalence 'between the principle of filial piety and the principle of Kshatriya valor'.

In Sax's explanation, the value of this story's representation of intergenerational violence lies in its being an affirmation of his sense of *kṣatriya* duty and personal courage for every man who positively identifies with either warrior in the fight. Sax accounts for the intrafamilial aspect of this test of a warrior's resolve by his reference (cited above, p. 196) to the need for a *kṣatriya* to fight even against members of his family, and even his father, if necessary. But what is the reason for imagining the test of courage in parricidal and filicidal terms? Any number of other terrifying and difficult struggles would serve the same purpose.[26] Of course Sax is right when he goes on immediately to say 'Textual and dramatic representations of fratricide or parricide are terrible not because they enact suppressed wishes but because they violate the values of filial piety and fraternal solidarity that are so deeply embedded in Indian culture.' But the question is not why such narrative themes are 'terrible', but why they exist in the first place and replicate themselves so successfully. Such grotesque narrative themes – and the fascination they seem to hold for participants in traditions of the *Mahābhārata* – are not adequately explained by the need to affirm or demonstrate one's courage or sense of duty.[27]

Sax notes the fact that – but does not explain why –

> [t]he actual moment of Arjuna's death [in the dance performances] is ambiguously represented: as the drums reach their climax, the two dancers merely 'hop' once or twice, and this is quickly followed by an embrace that, as informants are quick to point out, signifies reconciliation.
>
> (ibid.: 75–6)

There seems to be genuine discomfort with the concept of Arjuna's death, while the representation of the father and son fighting is the occasion for enthusiastic displays of dancing skills with a partner before an appreciative audience. Sax's explanation accounts for the dancing, but not for the

Garhwalis' simultaneously retaining the traditional narrative of Arjuna's being killed but shrinking from the portrayal of its narrative and logical outcome. If the actual death of Arjuna makes these men uncomfortable, why have they retained it? The tradition has altered many aspects of the story, and if Nagarjuna's killing his father did not mean something important to them (evidently below the surface of their primary awareness), why would they not have eliminated it long ago?

Sax leaves unexplained the closely related fact that Arjuna's killing the rhinoceros also seems to be some form of intrafamilial slaughter. Arjuna has been commanded to acquire the hide of a rhinoceros so his nominal father Pāṇḍu's funereal rites might be completed. Arjuna's son Nagarjuna had acquired the rhinoceros from Arjuna's physical father, Indra (thus Nagarjuna's grandfather), and when Arjuna finds the rhinoceros it is in Nagarjuna's care. Further in the background, the rhinoceros is an expiatory 'penalty-form' of a son who is in the final stage of expiating an act of disobedience to his father. It is difficult to judge whether the rhinoceros should be seen as a surrogate for Arjuna's father (it has associations with Pāṇḍu and Indra and even Bhīṣma, who was a disobedient 'son',[28] and whom Arjuna actually did kill prior to being killed by his own son[29]) or for his son, but it clearly seems to represent one or the other or some fusion of both. Sax's explanation does not deal with the valorization of the rhinoceros. Nor does he explain the strange fact that the story focuses upon the rhinoceros with its single horn so prominently positioned in the middle of its face. The son expiating his disobedience in the form of a rhinoceros – and dealt with so brutally – is overtly marked with what would seem to be unambiguously phallic imagery. Given his election to forgo Freudian mechanisms of explanation, Sax has no obligation to see the rhinoceros's horn as a phallic metonym of whomever it is the rhinoceros represents; but some explanation of this strange animal's appearance in the story, and some rebuttal to the predictable Freudian interpretation of it, were in order.

The entire Rhinoceros Tale revolves around issues of fathers and sons, as Sax tells us, but the tale portrays brutal intergenerational violence that appears to be disproportionate to the social functions Sax ascribes to it. I think we do in fact need to make some kind of use of 'the hidden messages and secret codes of psychoanalysis'. But what kind of use? And how best do we interpret traces of the Freudian unconscious in myths?

Towards a 'langue' of narratives of Indian family relations

As significant as Goldman's achievement was – and it truly was a groundbreaking contribution[30] – it was only a beginning. Just what does it mean for a text to put such terrifying representations in the foreground? What might it have meant for the author(s)? What meanings might it have had for those who have assimilated and used the text over the centuries? Is the Freudian analysis of these themes as universal as Goldman seemed to believe thirty years ago?[31] And whatever such representations of desire and antagonism across the sexes and generations within the family might mean in people's actual lives, how do these representations fit into the broader picture the *Mahābhārata* narrative develops?[32] Why are they there? What contribution do they make? In the case of Bhīṣma, Goldman's presentation leaves unresolved the apparent inconsistency that Bhīṣma at different times represents strongly both the passive and aggressive types of Oedipal relation to the father (he did desexualize himself to become a self-sacrificing instrument of his father's will, and he fought ferociously with his *guru* Rāma Jāmadagnya). Furthermore, there are major Oedipal representations of Bhīṣma as both a son and a father (on the one hand his acquiescence to Śaṃtanu and his disobedience of, and going to war with, Rāma, and on the other his fatal struggle with Arjuna on the tenth day of the war), and his struggle with the surrogate son has no history of conflict or obvious interpersonal antagonism.[33] Equally puzzling is the fact that even in his fatal encounter with his 'son', shielded by the reincarnated 'Mother', Bhīṣma assumed the same kind of passivity he had shown earlier towards his father Śaṃtanu. Consequently, even while agreeing with Goldman on the presence and importance of these themes, I think it necessary to push past the bounds of the classical Oedipal triangle.

Towards a truly universal psychology of family relations

I more than agree with Sax's nod of approval toward Obeyesekere and Kurtz (Sax 2002: 79), who have both written at length to argue for the need to enrich psychoanalysis – and the Oedipal theory in particular – by incorporating into it understandings of the social and psychological phenomena of other groups of human beings (specifically, in their writings, South Asian peoples). Freud's Oedipal theory has been aptly characterized as 'an extraordinary analytic invention, a framework for conceptualizing family dynamics and their residue in the psychic life of the child' (Greenberg 1991: 5), but it was not formulated at one point in time in a single dogmatic promulgation (Mitchell and Black 1995: 15ff.; Obeyesekere 1990: 87), and it has long been one source of great controversy among psychoanalysts (see Mitchell and Black 1995, esp. pp. 85–111). Gananath Obeyesekere's essay, 'Oedipus: the paradigm and its Hindu rebirth' (1990: 71–139), is a particularly thoughtful set of reflections upon it and a contribution towards its development into a genuinely universal theory of the psychodynamics of family relations (my term).

Obeyesekere's essay sketches out a regrounding of psychoanalytic theory against a much more heterogeneous background of social and cultural experience than that to which Freud had access. Regarding an earlier debate over the psychodynamics of human development within the family in the

Trobriand Islands (sparked by Bronislaw Malinowski's objections to the claimed universality of Freud's theories), Obeyesekere remarks:

> There is no nuclear Oedipus complex of which the Trobriand is a variation; there are several, possibly finite, forms of the complex showing family resemblances to one another. One might even want to recognize the likelihood of different forms of the Oedipus complex within a single group, especially in complex societies . . .
>
> (Obeyesekere 1990: 75)

Later he adds: 'The Oedipus complex is much more complex than the simple triangular relationship where the son hates the father and loves the mother!' (ibid.: 86).

Obeyesekere emphasizes Freud's own uncertainties across time in formulating the Oedipal theory (ibid.: 88) and Freud's statements admitting that the fundamental human drives 'cannot be neatly disaggregated' (ibid.: 72). Arguing *contra* Wittgenstein and others, and broadly parallel to Freud, Obeyesekere sketches out the ontological foundation of a universal human nature underlying the variety of social and familial forms, and he postulates a fundamental psychodynamic matrix in which wide spectra of infantile experiences – of gratification, love, frustration, and hate – might fix themselves on 'objects' of the child's environment (cathexis).

> The ontological ground of the Oedipus complex then is the existence of the powerful bond between mother and infant, and the family, nuclear or extended, in which a male (or males) care for the helpless infant, not just a caretaking role required for the survival of the human infant, but a *sense* of caring that is specifically human. *Yet, one must emphasize, it is impossible to infer a universal (and uniform) Oedipus complex on the basis of a universal form of a human family life, as it is to infer a universal family model from a common human nature* [my italics]. Diverse grafts, exhibiting at best family resemblances, can be implanted on a universal human nature . . . [G]iven the existence of human family living, there is no way one can escape from ambivalence and the desirability of *all* intimate familial persons. The power of the mother–son bond, for example, is undisputed; but, insofar as the sibling is also a member of the family, why is it that it also cannot be an intrinsic object of erotic attachment? If the father is loved and feared, why not other intimate members in the circle of familial relations, like the mother's brother? And . . . how is it possible to divorce one affect or drive or motive from the other in this context of intense, yet diffuse, emotional relationships, especially of power or domination and nurture? Freud rightly noted that in this kind of situation the individual has developed automatic techniques

> for coping with his complex emotions – the most significant being repression, followed by displacement and projection and the other mechanisms of defense.
>
> (Obeyesekere 1990: 95–6)

What I think is important here is that Obeyesekere preserves the Freudian commitment to a common human world (including the structure of the human body and mind) and at the same time has the twentieth-century anthropologist's respect for social and cultural variability. The 'Oedipal' theory Obeyesekere posits is no longer an *Oedipal* theory, but rather a theory of the development of the psyche that posits much greater variability in the objects a subject may cathect.

> In the context of Hindu familial relationships, can one reasonably speak of a universal Oedipus complex – the Greek model – that then, through various symbolic mechanisms (especially displacements), is expressed in the kind of mythic representations presented earlier [by Goldman]? Goldman follows the classic Freudian argument that there is everywhere a positive Oedipus complex and that the Hindu is but a transformation of it. But the Hindu son is in fact born into a family system where these relationships are pregiven. If so it is meaningless to speak of a set of infantile relationships paralleling the Western model, since no such relationships exist (except in unusual and individual cases). Thus the Oedipus complex in the Indian family must be structured in terms of these pregiven relationships, rather than in terms of a nonexistent Western model. The Greek Oedipus can hardly exist in the Hindu joint family; even if he does exist in an individual example he rarely survives as a mythic representation.
>
> (Obeyesekere 1990: 82)

What I draw from Obeyesekere (and Kurtz as well, though I have not discussed his work) are two things: (1) a deeper confidence that Freud's basic theoretical commitments and ideas do form one potentially valuable interpretive template for the examination of Indian narrative materials alongside others; and (2) the conviction that while some themes of an Indian 'Oedipal' theory are already in place, in fact there is still a great deal to learn from reading the myths again while looking out for indications of the more 'variable' version of the theory which Obeyesekere imagines.

Integrating representations of intrafamilial love and hate into a mythic 'langue' of Indian narratives

Even if we agree that all representations bearing a 'family resemblance' (I employ Wittgenstein's term *via* Obeyesekere's discussion) to those of the

Oedipal complex do express repressed wishes – hidden infantile motives of one sort or another – we still need to understand how such representations of family love and aggression function in the creation and use of cultural artifacts such as the Indian epics. And we need to have a way that helps alert us to the possibility that other cathected objects besides those of the classical Oedipal triangle are represented.

For the identification and interpretation of such representations in their original symbolic settings, I propose simply that we use the highly serviceable method for analysing mythic narratives first outlined by Claude Lévi-Strauss (1955). That is, we should identify representations that are clearly, or possibly, cathected objects just as we do all the other repeated 'subject-function'[34] relations which that analytic technique culls from the *parole* of the diachronic linear narrative and discovers as its synchronic *langue*. The myth as a whole functions as a timeless logical statement of some kind of relation (e.g. opposition, coincidence, reduction, exclusion, ranking) between or among the terms of its *langue*. Whatever their sources in conscious or unconscious psychic processes, all the representations found in poetic[35] narratives have been fashioned and presented by poets who were engaged in some (implicitly or explicitly intersubjective) cultural process that transcended their own ego psychology. The representations of cathected objects of family relations (a menacing father, an erotically desirable mother) occur in connection with the other elements of symbolic art which make up the poet's creation, and they play some role in that creation. Representations of cathexes must be evaluated through those connections (in a structuralist way) in addition to being interpreted in terms of any intrinsic expressive power it may be argued they have of their own.[36] Such representations may intrinsically have some of the same kind of emotional power as the representation of particular symbols which are experienced by poets or some of their audiences as sacred. And like sacred symbols, cathected representations may lose some of their autonomy and power in a larger narrative (or they may not), but they acquire the fullness of their meaning in such a narrative only through their parallels with and oppositions to other meaningful elements of the narrative, thereby contributing to whatever timeless, implicitly normative rehearsal the myth as a whole makes.

At least as regards the interpretation of complex and extended verbal artifacts like the *Mahābhārata*, it is not sufficient simply to focus on recurrent patterns of cathected objects in isolation from the rest of the narrative. We may find, for example, that it was not the connection of Arjuna's parricide of Bhīṣma with Bhīṣma's attempted parricide of Rāma that mattered most to the epic poets as they conceived the death of Bhīṣma and its manner of occurrence; but rather the contrast between Bhīṣma's monovalent asexuality and might, and the polyvalent mixture of sexualities and strength in his dyadic killer (Arjuna and Śikhaṇḍin are both transsexual, but Arjuna is a prolifically sexual male, while Śikhaṇḍin, though male now, embodies a woman whose life was asexual because of Bhīṣma's actions). That is only one way we might untangle the 'triangle' resulting in Bhīṣma's death. Or we may find that a *kṣatriya* who is an uncompromisingly celibate 'father' (Bhīṣma) succumbs to a *kṣatriya* 'son' who is prolifically sexual and fertile (Arjuna), while a naturally adult celibate brahmin father who compromises his celibacy (Vyāsa) is outshone by his brahmin son who is uncompromisingly celibate (Śuka, our 'parrot'). For *kṣatriyas* uncompromising asexuality is a serious wrong, while for brahmins uncompromising asexuality is ideal. At the same time, Vyāsa's mere humiliation by Śuka may show that Vyāsa's willingness to see the propriety of an *āpaddharma* is superior to Bhīṣma's failure to do so, which may be a failing that did, in fact, put the stamp of fate on Bhīṣma's death warrant.[37] That warrant was executed by the two prime representatives of the groups whom Bhīṣma's celibacy injured.

So the reading of the story of Bhīṣma that will come in the next instalment of this series will be based on such a structuralist reading and the *langue* it discloses. One of the advantages of this method is that it forces our attention to all the overdetermined elements of the story, whether these correspond to our initial sensibilities or not, whether these fit the Freudian Oedipal theory or not, and whether a mother or father is the object of cathexis or not. This mechanism will prove salubrious. As readers of the *Mahābhārata*, we often succumb too easily to the 'known' trajectory of the epic story and the grand rhetorics of fatalism and heroism that define it for us. The story is so immense and sprawling that, it seems, we unconsciously seek for ways to reduce it to manageable size and conceptuality. Some may find it surprising, perhaps, but apart from its speeches and side-stories the *Mahābhārata* narrative moves along quite quickly. And it is all too easy for us to assimilate into the 'known' general narrative a host of truly stunning points introduced by the text with little comment.[38] A structuralist analysis of the text slows the rushing narrative down and will give us a chance to tarry over the array of colourful wild flowers with which it constructs its ironically celibate patriarch.

We shall see that elements that definitely resemble the classic 'Oedipal' triangle occur and recur in this story, but we shall also see that these contribute only a part to some larger tableau of meaning that can be ethically construed in pragmatic, social settings such as those William Sax presents to us. And we may learn things that will help those who care to further the agenda of Obeyesekere and Kurtz to extend and complicate the Freudian theory of human development. We have already noted that Bhīṣma does not conform to the Oedipal type of the menacing father when he does fatal battle with Arjuna. When his father Śaṃtanu first encounters the post-infantile Bhīṣma, the boy is shooting arrows that have stopped the flow of the Gaṅgā towards Śaṃtanu's capital (1.94.21–5). Is this 'subject-function' an act of aggression by Bhīṣma towards his mother for having tried to drown him at birth (1.92.46ff.)? Or is it an act of aggression towards his mother for having abandoned the father with whom the boy thoroughly identifies (as will be shown in the narrative shortly after this episode)? Or is the boy merely 'playing' in a way that signifies that Śaṃtanu's having finally acquired a son from his super-charged sexual relationship with Gaṅgā spelled the end of the relationship?[39] We will address such matters when we take up 'The origins of Bhīṣma' in future.

Notes

1 I use the word 'moralizing' in the sense that Karve intentionally offers the evaluative comments of a person who stands within the direct tradition of the text. I do not imply that her drawing moral judgments is illegitimate or tedious, for it is neither.

2 For example, regarding his treatment of the Kāśi princess Ambā, she writes, 'Because of his oath of celibacy Bhishma refused [Ambā's demand he marry her], and finally the slighted, dishonoured, shelterless Amba committed suicide by burning herself. Up to this time Bhishma's life had been blameless, no one had to die cursing him. Amba was the first person he had ever injured. Later there were to be many others.' Regarding Bhīṣma's procuring other brides for his kin, she writes: 'How all these women must have suffered! How they must have cursed Bhishma! He alone was responsible for their humiliation . . . In his zeal to perpetuate his house he had humiliated and disgraced these royal women. There is no mention of what people felt about Kunti, Madri, or Gandhari, but for his treatment of the princesses of Kashi Bhishma was strongly denounced by Shishupala . . .'. And, 'Fortunately Bhishma did not have to find brides for Duryodhana and Dharma. In that generation no woman suffered because of his doing' (Karve 1969: 36–8).

3 I would like here to express my appreciation to William Sax for his challenges and helpful suggestions in response to my presentation at that conference.

4 I wish to dedicate this series of articles to the memory of Julia Leslie who did so much to further the study of gender and women's issues in South Asian civilization and whose leadership and inspiration engendered the 2005 conference. Furthermore, she always watched the birds in the text, and two birds will appear sooner or later in the complete tracing of the arc of Bhīṣma's figure, one the peacock (*śikhaṇḍin*), the other the parrot (*śuka*). Additionally, I would like to subdedicate the first instalment of this series to A.K. Ramanujan, one of my great *gurus*, who first conjured for me Arjuna and Uttara (a real *śikhaṇḍin*, if ever there was one) together on the chariot in a memorable lecture on the *Bhagavadgītā* in 1975.

5 For an account of Bhīṣma's long instructional pacification of the new king Yudhiṣṭhira during these weeks, see Fitzgerald 2004a: 79–164; Fitzgerald 2006.

6 Peter Schreiner has described and discussed the death of Droṇa from the point of view of its presentation of *yoga* (Schreiner 1988). Being focused upon Bhīṣma's persona in the *Mahābhārata*, I do not here take up any of the interesting issues of *yoga* these episodes present.

7 This not uncommon phrase, *bharatānāṃ kulodvahaḥ*, has special connotations when applied to Bhīṣma. The verb *ud-√vah* has, in addition to its general meanings of 'bear up, lift up, elevate', and so on, the special sense 'to take or lead away (a bride from her parents' house)'. As we shall see, Bhīṣma's bringing three brides back for his stepbrother Vicitravīrya is one of the defining acts of his life and career in the *Mahābhārata*.

8 My text here translates, paraphrases, expands, and adapts the Sanskrit.

9 There is a fact of some importance here, namely that when moving between the capital city Hāstinapura, which is on the Gaṅgā, and the important old site of 'the Field of Kuru' (Kurukṣetra; see Fitzgerald 2004a: 623–4), one must cross the Yamunā. (The *Mahābhārata* explicitly notes this fact only occasionally, as, for example, at 15.30.16, when the Pāṇḍavas went out from the capital to visit their mother and elders who had retired to the forest. On the way, 'Yudhiṣṭhira went down to Kurukṣetra, crossing the River Yamunā . . .'. Madeleine Biardeau has also noted the defining importance of the two rivers in this account; Biardeau 2002, vol. 1: 218.) The land between the capital and the battlefield (the doab) was defined by these two rivers, each of which provided a bride to Bhīṣma's father Śaṃtanu – Gaṅgā, Bhīṣma's actual mother, and Yamunā, his fateful stepmother. (Satyavatī was a woman of the Yamunā, the daughter of a celestial *apsarā* who was temporarily embodied as a fish in the river and accidentally impregnated by King Vasu Uparicara's semen. Satyavatī's origins and her giving birth to Kṛṣṇa Dvaipāyana Vyāsa are told at 1.57.32ff.) There is at least a small note of poetic justice in the funeral party's having to cross the Yamunā as they make their way across the doab to the Gaṅgā for the penultimate act of Bhīṣma's story. (Bhīṣma's final appearance in the epic is when he descended with the other war-dead brought down from heaven in the Gaṅgā by Vyāsa to visit Dhṛtarāṣṭra, Gāndhārī, Kuntī, and the Pāṇḍavas and others at 15.40.)

10 For not only was Bhīṣma a mighty warrior, his father Śaṃtanu had given him the privilege of choosing for himself the time of his death (as compensation for swearing perpetual celibacy so Śaṃtanu could marry Satyavatī); see 1.94.

11 This is one of at least two instances where the epic's authors deliberately constructed a mother's ignorance regarding a son's death in the war as a narrative device. At 11.14.12–19 Bhīma seized upon Gāndhārī's mistaken knowledge of events on the battlefield to attenuate the horror of his having drunk Duḥśāsana's blood. I discussed that instance in two notes to that exchange in my translation of The Book of the Women (Fitzgerald 2004a: 670). The purpose of portraying Gaṅgā as mistaken is that it underscores the ambiguities surrounding Śikhaṇḍin. See Chapter 10.

12 As Robert Goldman once wrote, Ambā 'is one of the commonest words for "mother" in the Sanskrit language' (1978: 336).

13 The whole story of Ambā and Śikhaṇḍin is told in detail in the epic's *Ambā-Upākhyāna*, 5.170–97, which picks up from Bhīṣma's sending her to Śālva at 1.96.47–51. When Rāma commanded Bhīṣma take Ambā back, Bhīṣma said he would not give her to his brother (5.178.5–9). It is never explicitly suggested that Bhīṣma marry Ambā or that he might do so. There is awareness throughout the episode of his famous vow of celibacy and his strictness to his word.

14 Satyavatī is present here only implicitly and metonymically, by the implied allusion to her mother the Yamunā. See n. 9 above.

15 Bhīṣma shot arrows against Gaṅgā, stopping her flow (1.94.21–5). He adamantly refused his stepmother Satyavatī's request that he inseminate his stepbrother Vicitravīrya's widows (1.97.1–99.2). And having kidnapped Ambā in the first place, he refused to remedy the wrong after Śālva rejected her (5.178.1–22).

16 I report this incident more fully than some others since it is very striking and many readers may be unfamiliar with the narrative details.

17 According to Goldman, this vow on Bhīṣma's part represents the 'prevailing type of the oedipal myth in traditional India', in which a son adopts an attitude of 'total passivity and perfect, unhesitating obedience' toward his father (1978: 337). '[F]orceful examples of filial subservience in the Indian epics frequently involve either the formal abdication of sexuality on the part of the son, often explicitly in

the favor of the father, and/or an illustration of the wrath of the angry father unleashed upon elder brothers who are insufficiently subservient' (ibid.: 338). An example of this latter type of story occurs in the story of Yayāti and his youngest son Pūru. It is told in the *Saṃbhavaparvan*, at 1.70.33–46 and at 1.78–80.

18 *hantāsmi prathamaṃ bhīṣmaṃ miṣatāṃ sarvadhanvinām* // 5.160.8.

19 6.55.80–102; 6.102.50–70. These passages are very similar in their narrative details. The former, which forms part of a nearly classical *upajāti* passage, seems to have been developed from the latter.

20 The name Śikhaṇḍin means 'peacock', and this identification is appropriate to the Pāñcāla prince who was born as a female incarnation of Ambā named Śikhaṇḍinī ('Peahen'). One of the principal attributes of the peacock, according to 12.120.4–7, is its mutability and variability. At 12.120.4–16 the king is advised to pattern his behaviour after the peacock in a number of interesting ways. See Fitzgerald 2004a: 465–6.

21 *evaṃ vibho tava pitā* [Saṃjaya is addressing Dhṛtarāṣṭra] *śarair viśakalīkṛtaḥ / śitāgraiḥ phalgunenājau prākśirāḥ prāpatad rathāt* / 6.114.81.

22 The most telling statement in Bhīṣma's 'peacock exhortation' (see n. 20 above) is: 'He should take whatever coloration would be good for some particular affair' (*yasminn arthe hitaṃ yat syāt tad varṇaṃ rūpam āviśet* / 12.120.6). The *śloka* continues nicely, 'Even his very delicate affairs succeed when a king can take on many different forms' (*bahurūpasya rājño hi sūkṣmo 'py artho na sīdati* //, transforming the negative statement into a positive one).

23 The statement made to Arjuna by Babhruvāhana's 'mother' Ulūpī after she had revived him following his death at Babhruvāhana's hands (14.82.5ff.).

24 This essay was originally published as Sax 1997.

25 Popular festivals centred upon recitations from the *Mahābhārata*, re-enactments, sometimes in dance, of selected episodes, and various rituals. The primary referent of the word *līlā* (game, play, actions done without any compulsion, for one's own purposes) is the activity of a deity, which is what is usually portrayed at such festivals in one medium or another. The *pāṇḍav līlā* centres upon the activities of the semi-divine Pāṇḍava heroes of the *Mahābhārata*.

26 For example, Nagarjuna's entering the rhino's cage and mastering it, or Arjuna's killing the rhino with bow and arrow.

27 Nor can the enduring fascination with them in European history be explained by the dialectic of fate and resignation, as Freud noted in *The Interpretation of Dreams* (1938: 306–7).

28 When he defied his *guru* Rāma's command to take Ambā back. It is worth noting too that one of the principal characteristics of the single-horned South Asian rhinoceroses noted in Indian literature is their solitariness (they are *ekacara*, 'solitary-grazers'), a trait which, along with their being exceptionally aggressive and tough, fits Bhīṣma rather well. For a wide-ranging discussion of the treatment of the rhinoceros in ancient India, see Jamison 1998.

29 And we have seen that the *Mahābhārata* explicitly links Babhruvāhana's killing Arjuna to Arjuna's killing Bhīṣma.

30 It is important to mention, however, that while Goldman's work definitely represented a 'minority report' among Sanskrit literary scholars in the late 1970s, he was not entirely alone. Besides the work of social scientists Morris Carstairs, Georges Devereux, and Phillip Spratt, upon which his work was based to some extent, Indologists A.K. Ramanujan and Jeffrey Moussaieff Masson had also recently broken the ground of psychoanalytic studies of Indian narrative themes.

31 Goldman did address several of these points in subsequent papers published across the 1980s and culminating in 1993 with his dazzling 'Transsexualism, gender, and anxiety in traditional India'. The reliance of the 'Transsexualism' paper

on 'Fathers, sons and gurus' shows that Goldman was as confident in 1993 as he was in 1978 of the universality of the classic Freudian Oedipal theory. And where the 1978 paper left implicit how Goldman saw Oedipal representations actually working (either as expressions of their authors or as images operating upon or within their audiences), the 1993 paper is quite explicit in ascribing didactic functions to these representations and fantasies as 'cautionary tales', 'punitive representations of the father', etc. He gives a nice summation of how he sees the unconscious being connected to the public world: 'This theme [the male fantasy of becoming a woman] represents, I believe, an effort to master a powerful complex of anxieties that is generated by specific features of traditional South Asian family and social life and is heavily reinforced through the use of literary and religious texts whose contents, in the form of myths and legends structured as cautionary or exemplary tales, deeply inform the consciousness of the cultures of the region' (1993: 394).

32 Though he describes and explicates the linkages of the chain of three father–son struggles centring upon Bhīṣma and Arjuna in the *Mahābhārata*, Goldman has nothing to say about how these function in the structure of the *Mahābhārata*. Analysis of the *Mahābhārata* as a literary or cultural artifact as such was not the task he had undertaken in 'Fathers, sons and gurus'. His 'Rāma sahalakṣmaṇaḥ' (1980) addresses the overall poetic effort of Vālmīki to a much greater extent.

33 Regarding such complexities and the *Rāmāyaṇa*, Goldman says: '. . . if one is to search for testimony of oedipal conflict in the *Rāmāyaṇa*, one is confronted with an *embarras de richesses*. Indeed, the epic presents a most complicated oedipal situation. To put it briefly, there are too many fathers, too many mothers and too many sons. What is more, *several of the characters play more than one of these roles at the same time or different roles with respect to different characters while a single role is frequently split between two figures*' (1980: 155, my italics).

34 Lévi-Strauss's technical term for the smallest meaningful narrative statement within a myth. See Lévi-Strauss 1968: 207.

35 I use this term as an adjective referring to the inspired creative activity (*poiesis*) of artists. It does not refer directly to those objects we call 'poems' and their attributes except insofar as they are the products of such *poiesis*.

36 Cathected objects lying repressed in the unconscious are not arbitrary symbols whose meaning is established only by their mutual delimitation with other arbitrary symbols. But representations of such objects are symbols and may be qualified by the other symbols with which they co-operate. Judging by their abundance and variety, however, they are never completely effaced by their structural relations, and thus they never lose their power for the unconscious. Perhaps the overdetermination of such symbols is protection against such effacement.

37 Satyavatī tried to persuade Bhīṣma that circumstances warranted a temporary lapse of his celibacy. She specifically invoked the concept of *āpaddharma* at 1.97.21. For a discussion of the *Mahābhārata*'s frequent latitudinarianism, see my discussions of *āpaddharma* in Fitzgerald 2004a: 152ff.; 2006.

38 In this regard it does not help when our sense of 'exotic otherness' or 'mythology' – or worse, both – are at high levels.

39 Gaṅgā had agreed to marriage with Śaṃtanu only on the condition that he never question her or interfere with anything she did; see 1.92.34 *inter alia*.

10

'SHOW YOU ARE A MAN!'

Transsexuality and gender bending in the characters of Arjuna/Bṛhannaḍā and Ambā/Śikhaṇḍin(ī)

Andrea Custodi

In the introduction to his translation of the fifth book of the *Mahābhārata*, van Buitenen writes: 'Epic myth [as opposed to Puranic myth] has a different character: it is frankly more manly . . . Duryodhana's final taunt to Yudhiṣṭhira, "Show you are a man!" is the essence of the *Mahābhārata* as epic' (1978: 168). On the one hand, one might respond that van Buitenen is simply seeing the epic through masculinist lenses, and that a feminist analysis of the epic might reveal many rich currents of femininity animating and propelling the epic. This is partly what I am doing. Yet on the other hand, one might, also from a feminist perspective, agree with him, as I also do. Masculinity and its symbolic correlates are highly charged and contested themes in the epic, permeating the *dharma* that undergirds the *Mahābhārata* and constituting some of its most poignant preoccupations in a way that femininity does not.

The lengths to which male characters will go to prove or defend their manhood simply have no equivalent for the female characters, whose femininity is rarely if ever contested. Even in contemporary culture femininity must rarely be proven in the way masculinity must be – one is rarely challenged to 'be a woman' or 'show your womanhood' in the way men are regularly exhorted to prove themselves as such. Masculinity is charged with a symbolic investment that is qualitatively different from that of femininity, and is constructed in a way that makes it more vulnerable to challenge and subversion. But why, and how? In exploring transsexuality and gender bending in the characters of Arjuna/Bṛhannaḍā and Ambā/Śikhaṇḍin(ī), I hope to shed some light on constructions of gender and sexual difference in the epic and bring Lacanian theory to bear as a reflecting surface that both illuminates these examples and is in turn illuminated by them.

Wendy Doniger (O'Flaherty), in her comprehensive study of androgyny in

Indian mythology, notes the vast range and variety of forms that can be grouped together under that heading:

> . . . liminal figures [that] include the eunuch, the transvestite (or sexual masquerader), the figure who undergoes a sex change or exchanges his sex with that of a person of the opposite sex, the pregnant male, the alternating androgyne (male for a period of time, female for a period of time), and twins.
>
> (O'Flaherty 1980: 284)

Beyond the 'true' androgynes who are equally male and female, there are also numerous cases of androgynes who are either primarily male or primarily female, though 'male androgynes by far outnumber female androgynes and are generally regarded as positive, while female androgynes . . . are generally negative' (ibid.: 284). The Sanskrit word that is commonly used in many of these cases is *napuṃsaka*, which can 'designate non-men of such different natures as eunuch, impotent man, and androgyne' (ibid.: 308). *Klība* is another, with a wide, pejorative range of meanings:

> A *klība* is not merely an androgyne . . . [it] is a defective male, a male suffering from failure, distortion, and lack. This word has traditionally been translated as 'eunuch,' but . . . it includes a wide range of meanings under the general homophobic rubric of 'a man who does not act the way a man should act,' a man who fails to be a man. It is a catchall term that a traditional Hindu culture coined to indicate a man who is in their terms sexually dysfunctional . . . including someone who was sterile, impotent, castrated, a transvestite, a man who committed fellatio, who had anal sex, a man with mutilated or defective sexual organs, a man who produces only female children, or finally a hermaphrodite.
>
> (Doniger 1999: 279–80)

Indeed, the *Mahābhārata* is not always explicit about the exact status of an ambiguous character's sexual organs, and deities especially might manifest a fluidity of gender that would be a stretch for even the most sexually malleable of epic hero(in)es. Śiva, of course, is the quintessential androgynous god, widely worshipped in his *ardhanārīśvara* (god-who-is-half-woman) form, but we also see female or androgynous characteristics in Agni, the Vedic fire god (5.15.26–7), out of whom both Draupadī and her brother are born (1.155), and Kṛṣṇa, known as 'Vāsudeva . . . because he is the womb of the Gods' (5.68.3).[1] As fluid as sexual characteristics and gender may be among deities and in mythological escapades, however, *dharma* as it structures and orders this-worldly affairs revolves around a firm conception of the two genders, and is very much based upon their clear distinction and eternal

binary gendering of dharma

stability. In the *Mahābhārata* a lack of clear distinction between the sexes has inauspicious resonances – for example, 'women seemed to look like men, and men like women, when . . . Duryodhana fell' (9.57.56, tr. Dutt [9.58.57][2]) – and gender ambiguity or reversal is used broadly throughout the epic as a sign of dharmic decline.

Not only is having no clear marker of gender inauspicious and ignominious, having (as one would say in Lacanian terms) no phallus[3] is one of the worst things a man can impute to himself or another, for it is the possession of the phallus upon which masculinity is predicated. In these instances we see manhood contested in a way for which there is no feminine equivalent, and disparaging references to oneself or another as impotent or a eunuch are among the most common forms of insult in the epic. Śiśupāla accuses Bhīṣma of living 'like a eunuch'[4] (2.38.2) and suggests that his 'celibacy is a lie that you maintain either from stupidity or impotence [*klībatvād*]' (2.38.24). Duryodhana remarks that he 'would be neither a woman nor not a woman, neither a man nor not a man' if he tolerated the Pāṇḍavas' good fortune (2.43.29), and Bhīma attempts to incite his brother Yudhiṣṭhira to action by wondering out loud if 'despair has prompted [him] to the life of a eunuch' (3.34.13). Though Damayantī, in fondly recollecting her lost husband, muses 'my [Nala] has no vices, he has been like a eunuch to me' (3.71.14) – an exceptional instance in the *Mahābhārata* when this is a positive quality – Draupadī, less kindly, wonders how her powerful husbands can 'like castrates suffer that their beloved and faithful wife is kicked by a *sūta*'s son' in Virāṭa's hall (4.15.21). Vidurā, in a parable recited by Kuntī, incites her son to battle by calling him 'a man with the tools of a eunuch' (5.131.5) and a castrate (5.131.17). She admonishes him that 'the forgiving man, the meek man is neither woman nor man' (5.131.30) and that 'standing tall means manhood' (5.132.38), instructing him to 'harden yourself and rise to victory' (5.134.7)!

As Lacan suggests, being a man – and fulfilling the manly roles of king, warrior, and husband – is intimately wound up with possessing the phallus, which paradoxically, however, is a function of the castration involved in becoming a subject.[5] Whereas Freud places the discovery of sexual difference at the moment when young children see and recognize the genitals of their parents or each other, Lacan speaks of sexual difference symbolically in terms of either *being* or *having* the phallus. As Dylan Evans notes,

> For Lacan, masculinity and femininity are not biological essences but symbolic positions, and the assumption of one of these two positions is fundamental to the construction of subjectivity; the subject is essentially a sexed subject. 'Man' and 'woman' are signifiers that stand for these two subjective positions.
>
> (1996: 178)

Though Man assumes the status of full subject whereas Woman occupies a more nebulous subjective position, Man's possession of the phallus is always tenuous, premised as it is on the condition of castration, and encounters with the Other[6] continually serve as reminders of this instability inherent in phallic subjectivity. Thus his ostensible phallic plenitude remains simultaneously a site of lack, failure, and frustration.

If gender is one of the foundational pillars upon which the elaborate edifice of *dharma* rests in the *Mahābhārata*, interesting possibilities emerge when we see these seemingly stable categories subverted, challenged, and transgressed. It is in liminal states such as transsexuality that the boundaries of the symbolic binaries of gender are thrown most starkly into relief, and it is here also where Law and the Symbolic Order[7] must weigh in on what is acceptable, what must be modified, and what must be denied. Though there are multiple examples of transsexuality and other forms of gender bending in the *Mahābhārata*, I focus here on what I find to be two particularly striking cases: Arjuna/Bṛhannaḍā and Ambā/Śikhaṇḍin(ī). It is in these two examples that I find traditional categories of gender and sexuality most poignantly challenged and transgressed in ways that provide suggestive insights into contemporary theorizing on selfhood and subjectivity. If we examine these cases closely, we can see themes of gender and subjectivity intricately interwoven in ways that might offer feminists, Lacanians, and South Asianists food for thought.

Arjuna/Bṛhannaḍā

The exact nature of Arjuna's gender as Bṛhannaḍā during the Pāṇḍavas' year of disguise is not exactly clear – that is, the text never states explicitly whether Arjuna is simply cross-dressing or has undergone some physiological transformation as well. The one potential moment of truth – in which Virāṭa orders that Arjuna be inspected to ensure that he is safe to put in the princess's quarters – is dealt with ambiguously and even playfully, for the answer comes back that Arjuna's 'non-masculinity was firm (*apuṃstvam . . . sthiram*)' (4.10.11, tr. Hiltebeitel 1980b: 155). Even his name Bṛhannaḍā is playfully ambiguous, meaning 'great man' but in the feminine gender (Hiltebeitel 1980b: 157), or as van Buitenen translates it, 'large reed' or 'having a large reed' – likely 'a joke that he who condemns himself to an effeminate life is endowed with a large reed' (1978: 9). Indeed the text seems almost intentionally titillating, weaving in and out of these ambiguous references as if to insist that the reader remain piqued by these paradoxes but unable to resolve them definitively. As Alf Hiltebeitel puts it, 'the epic descriptions leave it amusingly imprecise and ambiguous whether Arjuna is physiologically a eunuch, a hermaphrodite, or simply a transvestite' (1980b: 154). Arjuna himself is no help, announcing his disguise as they begin their year in hiding as matter-of-factly as his brothers announce theirs:

> Sire, I am a transvestite [*ṣaṇḍhaka*], I'll vow, for these big string-scarred arms are hard to hide! I'll hang rings from my ears that sparkle like fire, and my head shall sport a braid, king! I shall be Bṛhannaḍā. Listen, I'll be a woman, and tell sweet little tales and tell them again and amuse the king and the other folk in the seraglio. I myself shall teach the women in the palace of King Virāṭa to sing, king, and to dance in many ways, and to make music in still others! . . . 'I was at Yudhiṣṭhira's palace, a maid of Draupadī's; I lived in!' so I'll tell the king if he asks me, Bhārata.
>
> (4.2.21–6)

Indeed, the text alternates between affirming the undeniable masculinity underneath Arjuna's effeminate exterior and revelling in his disguise's convincingness. The moment of recognition, in which Arjuna comes to the rescue of the young prince of Matsya, is both a humorous vignette and an appreciation of the man behind the disguise:

> [Arjuna] leaped from that fine chariot and pursued the running prince; his long braid was trailing and his red skirts fluttering. Not knowing that it was Arjuna running there with the fluttering braid some of the soldiers burst out laughing at the spectacle. But on seeing him run nimbly the Kurus said: 'Who is that behind his disguise, as fire below its ashes? He has something of a man and something of a woman. He is built like Arjuna and wears the form of a eunuch [*klībarūpa*]. That is his head, his neck, his bludgeonlike arms, that is his stride, he is no one but [Arjuna]!'
>
> (4.36.27–31)

But as playfully and matter-of-factly as the text ostensibly treats the ambiguous gender of one of its central heroes, there are also deep symbolic dynamics at work, or as Hiltebeitel puts it, 'it is in their disguises that the Pāṇḍavas and Draupadī reveal their "deepest" symbolism' (1980b: 153). Yudhiṣṭhira chooses to be a dicemaster and brahmin, Bhīma a cook and part-time wrestler, Nakula and Sahadeva horse- and cow-tenders respectively, all occupations easily in keeping with their already established proclivities as characters. Arjuna's, then, is striking – how can this most virile of heroes' latent self, deepest self, be a eunuch, a transvestite, a transsexual? Is his hypermasculinity – his famous martial prowess and well-known philandering – overcompensation for this latent effeminacy? Is this a weakness in a staunchly patriarchal culture, a subtle subversion of it, or a testament to its subtlety and elasticity? What can this crossing of genders in the hero of the story mean?

Hiltebeitel argues that Arjuna's transsexual disguise is a 'clear evocation' of the androgynous Śiva (1980b: 153), which, if this link bears out, might support the idea that in the *Mahābhārata* genders may cross as much as the realms of human and divine. If Arjuna's human body can be transformed into a divine one through wrestling with Śiva (ibid.: 149), his masculine body may also be transformed into a feminine or androgynous one through identification with this god-who-is-half-woman. Here also Arjuna's moniker as the left-handed archer is relevant, since the left side of the body is considered the feminine half, and is the half of Śiva's body that Umā occupies. Furthermore, if Arjuna and Draupadī can be understood as evoking Śiva and the Goddess (ibid.: 153), not only does his gender bending become relevant, but hers does too.

As much as Draupadī is extolled as the perfect wife – chaste, demure, and devoted to her husbands – she also repeatedly shows herself to be intellectual, assertive, and sometimes downright dangerous. Not only is Draupadī a manifestation of Śrī-Lakṣmī, the auspicious goddess of good fortune, she also represents the destructive forms of the Goddess in her totality (ibid.), driving her husbands to the bloody revenge that will empty the earth of kings. This is signalled at the moment of her birth: as Draupadī rises from the altar, a 'disembodied voice spoke: "Superb among women, the Dark Woman [*kṛṣṇā*][8] shall lead the baronage to its doom" ' (1.155.44). During the year in disguise, while Arjuna is singing and dancing with the girls, Draupadī vents her anger and frustration to Bhīma, who, in clear contrast to Arjuna, fulfils his duty as husband and protector, vindicating Draupadī against the lustful Kīcaka (4.13–23). We should note here, too, that Bhīma himself poses as a woman (as Draupadī, in fact) to accomplish this. Sally Sutherland uses this episode to refer to 'the transsexual roles of both Bhīma and Arjuna' (1989: 70)[9] in the *Virāṭaparvan*, though Bhīma's is employed for a specific purpose whereas Arjuna's seems to be more gratuitous. Indeed, Arjuna, whose philandering and martial prowess might on the one hand suggest hypermasculinity, could in another sense be read as a failed husband, as it is Bhīma who, here and elsewhere, finally comes through in this pivotal marital duty.

Though the sexual behaviour of Arjuna and Draupadī does not become the stuff of classical myth as has that of Śiva and Pārvatī,[10] the alternating complementarity of their behaviour has a suggestive salience to gender bending in the *Mahābhārata*. As Sutherland writes, this and other episodes such as the dicing match 'all depict Draupadī as an aggressive and dynamic character. In these episodes she is effectively contrasted with her cautious and ineffectual husband Yudhiṣṭhira and his subservient, although less passive, younger brothers Bhīmasena and Arjuna' (1989: 71). Furthermore, Sutherland astutely notes that 'the repeated attacks on Draupadī [are] enhanced by the fact that the insults are overtly sexual and thus raise questions about their masculinity' (ibid.: 72). Especially during the year in disguise, not only are physical sexual characteristics put into question, but on a psychological and behavioural level as well, Draupadī wears the proverbial pants while Arjuna wears the skirt.

Returning to the divine implications of Arjuna's transsexual episode, Robert Goldman, approaching the question of transsexuality in the epics from a Freudian perspective, emphasizes the eroticized nature of *bhakti* and the god/devotee relationship: if the god is male, the devotees must become female to intensify the experience of his love; if the god is female, the devotees must also become female in order to disavow any sexual desire for her (1993: 389). As Doniger notes, too,

> The devotee visualizes himself as a woman not merely because god is male but because in the Hindu view the stance of the ideal devotee is identical with the stance of the ideal woman: '. . . Women yield; proud men don't. Men must renounce their masculinity if they would be devotees'.
>
> (O'Flaherty 1980: 88, citing Yocum 1977: 19)

The significance of Arjuna's transsexuality thus becomes dual, as he is intimately linked with both Kṛṣṇa and Śiva. As Kṛṣṇa's primary friend and devotee in the epic and recipient of the *bhakti* message of the *Bhagavadgītā*, his feminine tendencies could be read within a register of devotion. Furthermore, if Arjuna is identified with Śiva in relation to the Goddess, not only could his feminization be erotic,[11] but it could also be a renunciation of sexuality towards her. Hiltebeitel, citing Biardeau, notes the theme of sexual abstinence or renunciation (*brahmacarya*) in Arjuna's role as a eunuch (1980b: 150), and Draupadī herself is symbolically abstinent throughout the period of exile (Hiltebeitel 1981).

The picture becomes even more complex when we realize that Kṛṣṇa himself is by no means univocally masculine! We see him throughout the Purāṇas (though not in the *Mahābhārata*) as Viṣṇu in the persona of Mohinī the enchantress, and, in folk traditions, on the eve of the great epic battle as Aravān's soon-to-be-widowed bride. In the former case, Doniger recounts an episode in the *Brahmāṇḍa Purāṇa* where Viṣṇu as Mohinī first seduces demons and then is raped by Śiva – though in both cases he 'retains his male memory and his male essence, and so he can be regarded as having male homosexual relations,[12] playing first the active role with the demons . . . and then the passive role with Śiva' (1997: 137). In the latter case, the warrior Aravān, a son of Arjuna, agrees to be sacrificed for the victory of the Pāṇḍavas before the great battle, on the one condition that he be married before he dies:

> The only one willing to be widowed in this way was Kṛṣṇa, who became a woman, married Aravān, made love to him all night on the wedding night, saw him beheaded at dawn, and, after a brief period of mourning, became a man again.
>
> (Doniger 1997: 138)[13]

In a variant of that story, Aravān is actually a *son* of Kṛṣṇa – which would mean, as Doniger provocatively suggests, 'Aravān thus one-ups Oedipus, by sleeping with (a transformation of) not his mother, but his father' (ibid.)!

To return again to Arjuna's disguise as Bṛhannaḍā, the obvious question is *why* – or as put by the young Matsya prince, 'By what quirk of fate could a man of such virile appearance and with all the marks of manhood become a eunuch [*klība*]?' (4.40.10). Arjuna responds: 'It is at the behest of my eldest brother that I observe for this year a vow of chastity; I swear this is the truth. I am not a eunuch . . . but under another's orders and compliant with [*dharma*]' (4.40.12–13). Here we see not only a continuing ambiguity about the exact nature of Arjuna's role as Bṛhannaḍā – is he or is he not, then, a eunuch? – but also the question of how he could become a eunuch sidestepped with the response that he is observing a vow of chastity at the behest of his elder brother. For Goldman, this resonates with Oedipal themes in which a son's sexuality is deferred in favour of his father's, since in ancient Indian society an elder brother is in the position of father to his younger brother (1978: 328, 359). But whatever the exact nature of Arjuna's disguise, and however much he might insist on his masculinity, Arjuna's non-masculinity is nonetheless firm enough for him to be allowed into the princess's quarters. Were he 'truly' a man underneath his disguise, it is doubtful that his charade could have passed the vigilant eyes of the king to whose daughter he was given access.

Another episode in the *Mahābhārata* provides a seemingly explicit explanation for Arjuna's transsexuality, which Goldman employs to make an Oedipal analysis of his predicament:

> [T]he virile hero Arjuna, visiting the heavenly court of his father Indra, rejects the sexual advances of the *apsaras* Urvaśī, precisely because her well-known liaison with his ancestor Purūravas places her in the position of a 'mother' to him. The nymph is furious at being thus spurned and curses Arjuna to lose his manhood and become a *napuṃsaka*, a feminized transvestite of ambiguous sex and feminized gender. But, like the curse of his forefather Ila,[14] this one too is modified so as to have its effect restricted to only a limited period. Indra intervenes on his son's behalf and sets the term of the curse at one year. It is Urvaśī's curse, thus modified by Indra, that provides the underlying explanation for the necessity of Arjuna's having to adopt the humiliating guise of the feminized transvestite Bṛhannaḍā during the Pāṇḍavas' year of enforced concealment at the court of Virāṭa.
>
> (1993: 380)

Grundlage der TV-Version

According to Goldman, Arjuna thus having refused the sexually voracious mother and having been cursed to sexual impotence (read castration) for it, is rewarded for this gesture by his father who restores him his phallus, with only a traumatic trace of the original punishment to live out. Doniger, too, frames this episode in a Freudian light:

> [Urvaśī] plays the roles of the spurned, vengeful goddess and the incestuous mother who punishes her unwilling son. Arjuna's response to these threats is to disguise his manhood twice over: he pretends to be a eunuch pretending to be a woman; that is, he castrates himself symbolically in order to avoid being actually castrated by the mother . . . This myth has been interpreted as a 'collective male fantasy of the child's encounter with the sexual mother (and of) anxiety about his inadequacy to fill her sexual needs. The conflict is resolved through a self-castration which appeases the mother' (Kakar 1978, pp. 96–98). Here, as in other instances that we will encounter, androgyny is a denial of sexuality, an antierotic state.
>
> (O'Flaherty 1980: 298)

These Freudian analyses are useful and interesting, but I would suggest that there is more to Arjuna's transsexuality than that. Towards the conclusion of this chapter I will revisit Goldman's analysis as a springboard to showing how a Lacanian approach might expand our set of interpretive tools and enrich our understanding of these stories, but for now I will simply suggest that we broaden our psychoanalytic interpretation from a strict Oedipal focus to a more fluid and appropriately open-ended exploration of the question of sexual difference. What makes a man? What makes a woman? And what makes a 'man child who is a woman'? As we shall see, the plot only thickens when we turn to Ambā.

Ambā/Śikhaṇḍin(ī)

Ambā's story is one that spans two lifetimes, in the second of which she is Śikhaṇḍin(ī), the 'man child who is a woman'[15] (5.189.5). Although it is in this second life that Śikhaṇḍin(ī)'s transsexuality is made an explicit focus, the state in which she ended her first life is already evocative of what is to come: 'deprived of the world of a husband, neither a woman nor a man!' (5.188.4). Both Goldman and Doniger note that female-to-male transsexuality is a much rarer occurrence in the epics and Purāṇas than male-to-female; it is also more difficult, less stable, and with often lethal connotations (Goldman 1993: 380; Doniger 1997: 140). Accordingly, even though Ambā pursues a life of austerities, receives a guarantee from a god, and finally immolates herself in the fire to be reborn a man – *and* her future father Drupada performs rites for a son – Ambā is actually reborn as a female, and only effects the sexual transformation with the help of a sympathetic *yakṣa*[16] after her guise as a male has been revealed by her bride. Even then, there is some cosmic gender balance that must be maintained, for Śikhaṇḍin(ī) only receives her masculinity at the cost of the *yakṣa*'s, who becomes female, and the swap can only be temporary, for their genders will revert back upon Śikhaṇḍin's death.[17]

Whereas the status of Arjuna's penis remains ambiguous, Śikhaṇḍin(ī)'s is made explicit: her dialogue with the *yakṣa* leaves no doubt that she will wear his male organ, and he her female organ, and 'The women [who were] sent found out the truth and fondly reported . . . that Śikhaṇḍin was male . . . of potency puissant'[18] (5.193.26). But even once the swap has been effected, and the status of Śikhaṇḍin's genitalia has been confirmed in a test reminiscent of Arjuna's, the authenticity of his/her masculinity remains in question. Bhīṣma, for example, acquiesces in his own death at Śikhaṇḍin's hands by refusing to fight 'a woman, a former woman, one with the name of a woman, and an apparent woman' (5.193.62); as Doniger puts it, for Bhīṣma it is imperative that 'Śikhaṇḍin is in essence a woman, despite her outer male form' (1997: 141). As striking as this incongruence is, it makes sense. It is easier to go down than up, in gender as it is in caste. If a man wants to become a woman, for devotional or other reasons – or, as the story of Bhaṅgāśvana (13.12) suggests, because women derive greater pleasure from sex – he can forsake the privileges of manhood and do so, for it is he who, at least in the scheme of the social hierarchy, loses. For example, it is doubtful that a woman could be cursed to manhood the same way that both Arjuna and the *yakṣa* are cursed to femininity.[19] A woman who wants to become a man, on the other hand, constitutes a direct challenge to the social and political *status quo*, and her sexual transformation thus must be allayed, undermined, inauthenticated, made only temporary, or outright denied.

So though the epic permits the transsexuality of Ambā/Śikhaṇḍin(ī) – indeed it must, perhaps as valuable catharsis, for Ambā is spurred to her transformation in order to take revenge for injustices that could only be perpetrated upon a woman – it must subvert it, undermine it, and ultimately deny it. After Ambā's arduous austerities and self-immolation for the sake of becoming a man, she is re-born as a woman, re-dies as a woman,[20] and doesn't even really ever accomplish what she set out to do. As Doniger notes:

> There is therefore something anticlimactic about the killing of Bhīṣma by Śikhaṇḍin . . . Śikhaṇḍin does not kill Bhīṣma outright, but merely functions as a human bulwark for Arjuna (or, in Robert P. Goldman's nice phrasing, Bhīṣma is slain by 'Arjuna hiding, as it were, behind the skirts of his "mother" Ambā in her sexually ambiguous form of Śikhaṇḍin'). And Bhīṣma does not die

> immediately of his wounds but withdraws and dies long, long afterwards (after declaiming thousands of verses of renunciant philosophy . . .).
>
> (1997: 141)

Furthermore, I would add, Ambā's vow to become a man in order to kill Bhīṣma was in a sense nullified from its inception, since Bhīṣma had the boon of being able to choose the moment of his own death – she, therefore, could only ever really accomplish what Bhīṣma would be willing to allow anyway. This ambiguity is further overdetermined by the fact that, though both Arjuna and Śikhaṇḍin discharge multitudes of arrows towards Bhīṣma, Arjuna's are in certain places given greater credit, yet on the other hand, there are also numerous references throughout the epic to Bhīṣma being killed by Śikhaṇḍin (5.47.35; 6.14.5; 6.15.45–7; 6.115.*482; 14.59.11)! The epic is thus ambivalent on whether or not to allow Ambā as Śikhaṇḍin to be credited as the cause of Bhīṣma's death, weaving in and out of the question, circling around it, repeatedly contradicting and undermining itself. The question of who ultimately is responsible for Bhīṣma's death – Śikhaṇḍin, Arjuna, or Bhīṣma himself – seems destined to remain as ambiguous as Śikhaṇḍin's ultimate gender.

Several feminist and psychoanalytic themes emerge in Ambā's story, one of which Doniger calls 'lethal transsexuality' – frustrated by love, denied fulfilment in marriage, 'Ambā thus epitomizes the no-win situation of a woman, tossed like a shuttlecock between two men, each of whom ricochets between inflicting upon her sexual excess or sexual rejection' (1997: 141) – and her sexual and social frustration turns male to effect revenge. Second, as the passage of Goldman's quoted by Doniger above indicates, Oedipal dynamics can be found at work in Ambā's association as the mother goddess earth, Bhīṣma as the father sky,[21] and Arjuna as occupying the position of (grand)son to both.[22] Indeed, it is a veritable Oedipal soap opera: Bhīṣma symbolically and socially rapes Ambā, not for himself but for his brother, whom she rejects for her former lover who in turn rejects her as second-hand goods (5.170–2). Ambā then turns to Bhīṣma's father-figure *guru* Rāma Jāmadagnya, who fights Bhīṣma to make him take her back, but he will not because he has already symbolically castrated himself in deference to his father's sexuality (5.177–8). When Bhīṣma defeats Rāma Jāmadagnya, Ambā is left desolate, 'neither man nor woman', and she takes up a life of austerities before finally immolating herself in the fire, vowing Bhīṣma's destruction (5.188), which she finally accomplishes with the help of Arjuna, who on the one hand is as a son to her, and on the other (in her reincarnation as Śikhaṇḍin) is the husband of her sister Draupadī, and thus brother-in-law! So, Oedipally speaking, the alliance we have against Bhīṣma the father is either brother–brother or (grand)mother–(grand)son, and it is this transformability that makes it all the more psychoanalytically compelling. Even more provocatively, we have an alliance of two transsexuals against a father figure whose symbolic castration makes his own sexuality dubious.

Van Buitenen makes some interesting observations about Ambā/Śikhaṇḍin(ī). First of all, he notes that the names of the three sisters Ambā, Ambikā, and Ambālikā are 'variations on the vocative *ambe*, *amba*, a hypocorism for "mother, mommy" ', and suggests that these three Ambās might well have 'given rise to an old epithet of Rudra,[23] *tryambaka*: "he of the three mothers," which was later reinterpreted as "three-eyed" ' (1978: 173–4). He also notes that after Bhīṣma's initial telling of the story of Ambā/Śikhaṇḍin(ī), it is pretty much forgotten, only recurring in connection to Bhīṣma's imminent death. Van Buitenen's theory is that the story of Ambā and the references to the invincibility of the warrior Śikhaṇḍin in relation to Bhīṣma's death were unrelated, until some internal logic in the development of the epic linked the two in the story of Ambā's vow and Śikhaṇḍin's sex change (ibid.: 176–8). Why? Because 'it is so utterly appropriate: the great Bhīṣma, fearfully famed for his abjuration of all women, in the end finds his undoing at the hand of one of them, whom he had cheated out of her rightful marriage' (ibid.: 178). For van Buitenen, this logic requires a diachronic view of the text: two chronologically disparate elements in the original epic material that would have been later linked as the *Mahābhārata* grew into the vast opus that it is, becoming a fantastic, funny, instructive story that made absolute moral sense and tied loose strands up into a tidy little knot of transsexual reincarnation.

> If we were to take this story seriously as simultaneous to the epic portions of the *Mahābhārata*, we would ultimately have to lay the death of Bhīṣma at the fragrant door of the yakṣa Sthūṇākarṇa's mansion in a wood off Kāmpilya. I, among my trees of different ages, find this view of the enchanted forest absurd.
>
> (van Buitenen 1978: 178)

For the purposes of my analysis, however, it does not matter so much *how* the epic's stories were forged as that they exist as such. Can it not be just as meaningful that as concentrated and intentional a design as Ambā's – so overdetermined – should only finally be realized by a seemingly fortuitous encounter in a forest? Is that not ironic, and might not the epic's seeming avoidance till the last minute of something it is obliged to do tell us something? I would lay Bhīṣma's death 'by' Śikhaṇḍin (in inverted commas because its attribution as such remains equivocal) at the door of whatever constitutes the node of gender and sexual dynamics in the epic – whatever it is that makes female-to-male transsexuality so much harder to accomplish and maintain than the reverse, whatever continually undermines the staunchest affirmations and exemplars of masculinity, whatever effects the dizzying transformations that complexify and question the *dharma* that ostensibly stabilizes and grounds sexuality and gender relations in the epic. In fact, let us return to the statement of van Buitenen's that I cited at the outset of this chapter: ' "Show you are a man!" is the essence of the *Mahābhārata* as epic'. If we understand Ambā/Śikhaṇḍin's mini-epic in this context, we see the elements of her/his story come together in a delightfully intriguing interweaving of themes surrounding masculinity, its construction *and* deconstruction as such, its juxtaposition to femininity, and the transformations, disavowals, and masquerades that are implicated in their relationship.

First of all, as both Doniger and Goldman note, there is a dark, destructive, lethal undercurrent to Śikhaṇḍin's female-to-male transsexuality that simply does not exist even in the deepest symbolic currents underlying Arjuna's male-to-female transsexual episode. As Goldman puts it, not only is female-to-male transsexuality 'far more complicated, gradual, and overdetermined', but it also 'has as its purpose neither the avoidance nor the facilitation of an erotic relationship. Instead, its goal is vengeance' (1993: 391). We have noted the destructive undertones in the character of Draupadī, who never switches genders but does challenge the epic's explicit dharmic formulations of what a woman and wife should be.[24] Both of these characters' trajectories away from 'traditional' femininity are towards vengeance, and I would suggest that this current of feminine vengeance – which I might also argue drives the major events of the epic – is an important strand of femininity in the *Mahābhārata* not articulated in the *strīdharma* that constitutes the dominant conscious discourse on femininity in the epic.

For example, though motherhood is spoken of dharmically in terms of maternal love, breasts flowing with milk, self-sacrifice, and tearful loyalty, we see mothers such as Vidurā and Kuntī sharply inciting their sons to battle; in Vidurā's case, insulting his manhood to rouse his valour. Draupadī speaks of herself as a submissive, docile wife (3.222–3) but prods her husbands on to revenge when they might have settled for peace – dharmic discourse leaves out the reality of feminine vengeance that is an indispensable element to female figures in the epic and Hinduism more broadly. The vengeance that hovers around the edge of Draupadī's character and the undertones of destruction that are rumbled at her birth, as well as the femininity that, though wearing a male organ for revenge, nonetheless continues to hover around Śikhaṇḍin's masculinity 'of potency puissant', come out of the gap, the blind spot, the absence that is Woman constructed according to the phallic signifier. Behind the masquerade of *strīdharma*, behind the idealized constructions of feminine sexuality embodied by the *apsarā*s (though, as we have seen with Urvaśī, *apsarā*s can be vengeful too!), behind the passivity and 'meek hearts' consistently avowed in speech by the epic's female protagonists, there is agency, there is insistence on recognition of rights, wrongs, and some balance to be enforced, and there is an undeniable presence as a shaping force to their own lives, the course of history, and the destiny of male characters. But this is oblique; it can be seen only out of the corner of the epic eye. The lacuna of what is disavowed in Woman may exist as a gap or absence in the Symbolic Order, but I would suggest that it literally returns with a vengeance in the transsexual figure of Śikhaṇḍin, and, refracted differently, in the provocative figure of Draupadī.

Second of all, the phallus recurs throughout the epic as an unstable construct, at least inasmuch as it is supposed to be the bedrock of masculinity and the *dharma* that is predicated upon it. On the level of signification and subjectivity, and in the context of Lacanian theory, the phallus represents a unity that is as symbolically suggestive as it is impossible – for subjects inhabiting a Symbolic world of law and language, the phallus stands as an example of coherence where there exists fragmentation, of full presence where there is lack, of meaning where there is dissonance, of law where there is chaos. For Woman who is constructed and projected beyond the borders of this Symbolic world, who occupies the role of the phallus in relation to male subjectivity in the sense that – like God – unity, meaning, truth, and full presence are attributed to her, the possession of the phallus is not a requirement for her status as subject, though she may desire it for its symbolic value and cultural capital. For Man, however, subjectivity is predicated upon the possession of the phallus, which can only ever be an ideal, a master signifier that defines and bounds the realm of male subjectivity by necessarily being located apart from and outside of it. There is a constant striving towards it, coupled with inevitable confrontation of the fact that it escapes out of reach.

Susan Bordo draws a compelling contrast between the phallus as cultural ideal and the penis as the reality of embodied masculinity. The phallus as it represents Man is a 'timeless symbolic construct . . . singular, constant, transcendent', whereas the penis, representing actual men as 'biologically, historically, and experientially embodied beings, . . . evokes the temporal not the eternal. And far from maintaining steady will and purpose, it is mercurial, temperamental, unpredictable' (Bordo 1994: 265–6). Indeed, we see a sense of failure read as impotence in heroes' references to themselves and each other as eunuchs – if masculinity is constructed upon possession of the phallus, the inevitable failure to possess the phallus fully is poignantly and tellingly described in the image of a castrate.

Third, returning more specifically to the case of Śikhaṇḍin, the fact that Bhīṣma as patriarch of the epic is involved should draw our attention to the role of *dharma* in this story, and the story's dharmic implications. I would be tempted to put a bar through 'patriarch' as Lacan puts a bar through the S that stands for subject.[25] Bhīṣma occupies the role of patriarch in the epic without actually being so, an absence holding a place around which the royal genealogy is arranged, a lack – or more strongly, a failure – at the origin that both sets in motion and continually spurs the intergenerational dysfunctionalities and fratricidal neuroses that culminate in the final devastating breakdown. Yet as primary exponent of *dharma* in the epic, Bhīṣma is a very real presence, though his actions much like his words seem to be continually contradicting and undermining themselves. He expounds upon the *dharma* of kingship as the kingdom that he watched over lies shattered, the *dharma* of fraternal relations as his family ruthlessly kill one another, the *dharma* of relations between the sexes as he lies dying at the hands of a 'woman' upon whom he had effected a travesty. Indeed, beyond the weak excuse that he is 'bound by wealth' (6.41.36, tr. Dutt [6.43.41]) to the Kurus, it is never really clear why, as patriarch and ostensible embodiment of *dharma*, he ends up fighting on the side that (he admits) is clearly in the wrong.

I note above the strange ambiguousness of his death 'at the hands of' Śikhaṇḍin. On the one hand it must be so, for it was a vow taken by Ambā, and a boon granted twice by Śiva; on the other hand, it cannot be so – a warrior and patriarch of Bhīṣma's stature being felled by an otherwise undistinguished prince, and even more so a 'former woman', an inauspicious transsexual who wears the penis she received from a *yakṣa*. It both must be and cannot be, and it exists in the epic in precisely this ambiguous, tenuous, unresolved balance. This is suggestive of *dharma* in the epic – a seemingly staunch patriarchal order, firm laws, all the answers, eternal and unchanging; yet also a tension of contradictions, a dynamic flux of rationalizations and inverted mirror images, continually folding back upon itself and coming out the other end upside down, a circle of discourse that continually seems to be on the verge of lapsing into either tautology or radical contingency. Much like Bhīṣma's death at the hands of Śikhaṇḍin, *dharma* in the *Mahābhārata* is simultaneously overdetermined and continually receding; it must be so, it must be so, yet in the final analysis it is not necessarily so.

Concluding reflections

To move from the dharmic and sexual ambiguities surrounding the character of Bhīṣma towards concluding theoretical reflections, let us dwell for a moment on Goldman's analysis of transsexuality in the epic as an illustration of how a Freudian approach may sometimes take one down paths that are better avoided with Lacan. In his reading of several transsexual episodes in the epic, Goldman suggests that, along the lines of the 'Indian Oedipal' pattern he identifies elsewhere, the pervasive male fantasy of becoming a woman is really more about and between men than anything actually having to do with women: it is either a 'demeaning punishment for some kind of Oedipal transgression against a powerful and dreaded male figure', or 'a deeply longed for metamorphosis that makes possible an erotic liaison with a powerful and desired male' (1993: 392). So any fear of Woman is really 'a more deeply rooted but far less explicitly stated anxiety derived from the coercive and potentially castrative power of dominant males such as fathers, older brothers, gods, gurus, and sages' (ibid.: 395), and any identification with Woman is a 'fantasy of sexual possession by the very father the fear of whom lies at the root of the focal anxiety centering on one's own maleness' (ibid.: 394). According to Goldman's Oedipal analysis, therefore, no matter how recurrent certain themes of femininity, motherhood, or female sexuality may be in the epic, and throughout all these episodes of transsexuality and the *Mahābhārata* in general, it really is all about men and male relationships – or as he puts it, women are simply 'a screen for a power struggle between males' (ibid.: 397 n. 115).

The feminist objections to this line of reasoning and the conclusions he draws are probably rather obvious. First of all, if it were indeed as Goldman describes, what a drab *Mahābhārata* it would be! Why rob the rich and dynamic female characters of their agency, their motivations, their own feelings and actions in the epic? Furthermore, is there really no other reason why men might want to become women? There seems to be nothing in Goldman's analysis that women characters can show us or tell us that actually has to do with them as women, and he seems content simply to see the female characters, in all their depth and complexity, as but a 'screen for a power struggle between males'. The epic's challenge to 'show you are a man!', however, is not just about or between men, for, as Lacan reminds us, an essential component in the performance of masculinity is Woman – as spectator and as Other. Thus, not only would I want to call out the masculinist bias in Goldman's analysis that threatens to undermine an otherwise rich and ground-breaking study of transsexuality in the epics, I would also want to highlight the limitations of Freudian analysis and the unfruitful paths down which it may sometimes lead us. Though I would not want to dispense with Freudian analyses altogether, and though I too find provocative Oedipal material in the *Mahābhārata*, there is simply more going on in these epic explorations of sexual difference than Goldman's analysis admits. Especially in a contemporary theoretical climate that widely credits Lacan for taking psychoanalysis into the twenty-first century, psychoanalytic studies of Indic material should begin to engage with the sorts of interpretive innovations and contributions that Lacan offers.

There are fertile openings already. Margaret Trawick, in a passage on transvestism in contemporary south India cited by Doniger, moves the discourse rightly, I think, into broader questions of desire and *jouissance*:[26] 'We might consider the proliferation of androgyny there to be one aspect of a pleasure in sexuality in its original polymorphous nature that we ourselves miss, together with an intellectual enjoyment of paradox, which, also, we fail to share' (Doniger 1997: 145, citing Trawick 1990: 253). Desire drives all humans, though it may be channelled differently according to sexual and subjective formation, and these transsexual episodes explore transformations of gender and desire through provocative yet innocuous narrative means. What attracts us as readers and scholars, men and women, two thousand years later is precisely the plural philosophical possibilities in these stories, their resonances with contemporary questions, and the fact that Woman is also intrinsically, though perhaps obliquely, implicated in showing that one is a Man.

Taking a different yet similarly fertile tack, Doniger returns the problem of the mythical androgyne or transsexual to an attractively pithy (and classically Hindu) solution: 'To the question posed by these myths – How deep is gender? Is it skin deep, superficial, or truly deep, essential? – Hinduism answers Yes' (1999: 301). It is this kind of a response – one that does not require airtight formulations, tidy knots, or erudite explanations, one that in fact resists and avoids such reductionist or essentialist approaches to matters so big, complex, and ultimately unanswerable – that makes Lacanian theory well suited to address these questions. If on some level we can agree that these myths of transsexual transformation revolve around the compelling question of sexual difference, then Lacan can offer a way of thinking about this question that moves us beyond the Freudian focus on the nuclear family and phylogenetic, biologistic explanations and toward cultural, unconscious, and linguistic explanations that provide much greater theoretical flexibility and feminist possibilities (Grosz 1990: 70).

Whereas for Freud women really are in a sense castrated, in that they lack the biological penis, the sense in which women are castrated within the Lacanian framework has more to do with their perceived powerlessness in relation to phallic structures of signification and authority, and in fact *all* subjects must experience symbolic or psychic castration in order to successfully negotiate the Oedipal complex and accede to full sexed subjectivity. This 'relation of the subject to the phallus . . . is established without regard to the anatomical difference of the sexes' (Lacan 1977: 282), and indeed, 'woman has to undergo no more or less castration than the man' (Lacan 1982: 168). Castration, as the advent of the Symbolic, interrupts the child's specular illusion of wholeness and narcissistic mirroring with the mother and introduces the lack that will continue to dog all subjects no matter how they are gendered. The child must renounce the attempt to be the object of the mother's desire and give up 'a certain *jouissance* which is never regained despite all attempts to do so' (Evans 1996: 22) – or as Lacan says, 'castration means that *jouissance* must be refused, so that it can be reached on the inverted ladder (*l'échelle renversée*) of the Law of desire' (1977: 324). The way one negotiates this Oedipal gauntlet will determine which position one takes as desiring subject, and who or what one will desire. It could be argued that in these Hindu narratives of transsexuality, as in Lacan's treatment of sexual difference, the presence or absence of the phallus – *being* or *having* it – is the crucial determinant of gender and the subject's position in the Symbolic, though, as opposed to Western notions of gender that demand clear designation, the exact status of the phallus with regard to these subjects is often playfully and intentionally obscured, confused, or questioned.

For feminists, it may seem counterintuitive to accept the notion that the phallus is the sole determinant and signifier of sexual difference – why can't we determine sexual difference by saying that men don't have a uterus or vulva? Luce Irigaray (1985) has done groundbreaking work in shifting philosophical and psychoanalytic dialogue toward a feminine paradigm of duality and contact, and Julia Kristeva (1984) has articulated a feminine Semiotic to contrast and complement Lacan's masculine Symbolic. Without taking either of those fertile directions here, however (though I do elsewhere), we may also remind ourselves of Lacan's crucial emphasis on the *symbolic* nature of the phallus and its position as a master signifier in the Symbolic Order. Of course female and male sexual organs have equal ontological status and functional value, but, for Lacan, 'the question of sexual difference revolves around the symbolic phallus' (Evans 1996: 142–3), and 'the phallus is a symbol to which there is no correspondent, no equivalent. It's a matter of a dissymmetry in the signifier' (Lacan 1993: 176). In other words, there simply is no feminine signifier on the level of the Symbolic that corresponds to the phallus, because the phallus itself bounds and structures Symbolic functions of law and language. And because of this Symbolic inability to signify the feminine position, Woman is always constructed as the mysterious 'other sex', the 'dark continent' both for herself and for Man. *Women* may exist within the symbolic world of law and language bounded and ordered by the phallic signifier, but *Woman* is located outside it, in the position of Other, a place functionally similar to that of God. Jacqueline Rose writes:

> As negative to the man, woman becomes a total object of fantasy (or an object of total fantasy), elevated into the place of the Other and made to stand for its truth. Since the place of the Other is also the place of God, this is the ultimate form of mystification . . . In so far as God 'has not made his exit' . . . so the woman becomes the support of his symbolic place.
>
> (1982: 50)

Whereas God is in the Western context constructed as a male with whom men would form a positive father-figure sort of identification, however, not only can God be female in the Hindu context, but even when he remains masculine, the male devotee may assume a feminine position towards him.[27] This is, I would argue, not simply a homosexual desire for and fear of the father, as Goldman's Freudian analysis suggests. Coming from a feminist Lacanian direction we might also see the act of feminization, and other examples of the desire to be female, as a fascination with and desire to occupy this position of Other that has such a profound and powerful role in the forming and sustaining of male subjectivity. Just as women may want the phallus for the authority, agency, and mastery it confers – in Ambā's case the ability to take up arms, go into battle, and effect vengeance, or in Draupadī's, the active shaping of the fate of her husbands, family, and kingdom – men desire to occupy the role of Other to which the phallic structure of signification has relegated Woman. The mysterious 'dark continent' holds great attraction as such. If Woman *is* the phallus, and if Man *possesses* the phallus, but this possession of the phallus always risks being undermined by lack and failure, then it makes sense that Woman would be a position that Man, at some level, would want to occupy.

Furthermore, along those lines, and as I suggested earlier, *jouissance* is another element of Lacanian theory that might figure into the fascination with transsexuality that we see in these epic sub-plots. Though on the one hand Lacan describes *jouissance* as phallic, 'in keeping with Freud's assertion that there is only one libido, which is masculine' (Evans 1996: 92), he later writes that, in being '*not all* [*pas tout*] . . . excluded by the nature of things', Woman has 'in relation to what the phallic function designates of *jouissance*, a supplementary *jouissance*' (Lacan 1982: 144). This is

> a *jouissance* of the body which is . . . *beyond the phallus* . . . a *jouissance* proper to her, to this 'her' which does not exist and which signifies nothing. There is a *jouissance* proper to her and of which she herself may know nothing, except that she experiences it.
>
> (Lacan 1982: 145)

Men are not wholly excluded from this *jouissance*, though it is not the 'normal' man who will experience it: 'Despite, I won't say their phallus, despite what encumbers them on that score, they get the idea, they sense that there must be a *jouissance* which goes beyond. That is what we call a mystic' (ibid.: 147).

Here we return to the spiritual/mystic implications of androgyny and transsexuality in the Hindu context. Putting aside her Freudian hermeneutic of suspicion for a moment and allowing herself a more typically Hindu interpretation, Doniger writes:

> [T]he image of the androgyne expresses with stark simplicity the problem of how one may be *separated* from god when one is united with god . . . As a theological image, therefore, the androgyne may represent either the bliss of union with god or the ironic agony of eternal longing for a deity with whom one is in fact consubstantial.
>
> (O'Flaherty 1980: 333)

The god may be androgynous (in Śiva's case) or transsexual (in the case of Viṣṇu as Mohinī), and the devotee may either feminize himself in an ecstatic merging with a male god (as in the *bhakti* tradition) or seek to combine both male and female elements simultaneously in his body in order to experience the ecstatic sensation of the merging of God and Goddess (as in the Tantric tradition). None of these examples really conflicts with Lacanian thinking on mysticism, indeed they may even surprisingly corroborate it.

These spiritual or mystic images of androgyny or sexual transformation all have feminine erotic resonances, and draw their ecstasy (*ex-stasis*) and enlightenment from a symbolic position that may be God, Woman, or the Other. As Lacan asks – and it seems these images might even offer answers – 'why not interpret one face of the Other, the God face, as supported by feminine *jouissance*?' (1982: 147).

We saw above that Arjuna's transsexual episode has resonances both of identification with the androgynous Śiva and of *bhakti* devotion to Kṛṣṇa. Though Śiva presides over Ambā/Śikhaṇḍin's female-to-male transformation, however, the symbolic themes are more secular, probably because Ambā is more concerned with pursuing this-worldly privileges of the phallus rather than other-worldly *jouissance*. Yet beyond the quest for vengeance driving Ambā/Śikhaṇḍin's story that seems to differentiate it from other examples of transsexuality in the epic, there remains a male fascination with the mystery of feminine *jouissance* that is at least hinted at in her case when s/he is referred to as 'Śikhaṇḍin, tiger among men . . . who has realized in himself the pleasures of manhood and femininity'[28] (7.9.41, tr. Dutt [7.10.46]). In the transsexual story of Bhaṅgāśvana elsewhere in the epic, male curiosity about feminine *jouissance* (and the sneaking suspicion that women actually have it better) is made explicit; and Ila, too, embodies in his/her alternating genders the excessive erotic pleasure that is attributed to women as opposed to the dharmic rectitude of men. So, to respond once more to Goldman, there are many good reasons in and of themselves why a man might want to become a woman, and why the feminine in the epic is so much more than a screen for power struggles between men. There is, as Lacan suggests, the prospect of *jouissance* beyond the phallus that must be attractive to 'normal' men and mystics alike; there is the feminine gaze that constitutes and affirms frail subjectivity; and beyond that, the Otherness of Woman's place in the Symbolic Order holds the promise of knowledge, full presence, and most compellingly, absence of the lack that dogs the ostensible possessor of the phallus. The transsexual episodes in the *Mahābhārata*, I would suggest, are ways of playfully and poignantly exploring these possibilities, ways that continue to capture our imagination and challenge our intellects. Though with both Arjuna and Śikhaṇḍin the text offers no definite answers, it does offer more than enough material to hold our philosophical attention two thousand years later.

Notes

1 All translations in this chapter are those of van Buitenen, except where otherwise stated.

2 References to M.N. Dutt's translation of the *Mahābhārata* are given in square brackets.

3 My use of the term 'phallus' throughout this chapter will be in its particular Lacanian sense. For Lacan, what concerns psychoanalytic theory is not the actual

penis as much as its imaginary and symbolic functions, so his use of the term 'phallus' distinguishes it from its biological counterpart and emphasizes its role on the level of fantasy, language, sexual difference, and symbolic production. Elsewhere, I use capital letters to designate specifically Lacanian usages of otherwise common terms.

4 Literally, 'living in the third nature' – *tṛtīyā*, meaning 'third gender' in the feminine.

5 For Lacan, castration is a symbolic and linguistic process that is integral to both masculine and feminine subjectivity, but is negotiated differently for each. Man is constructed as possessing the symbolic phallus, whereas Woman does not, but Man 'can only lay claim to the symbolic phallus on condition that he has assumed his own castration' (Evans 1996: 141).

6 The Other designates that 'radical alterity' which cannot be assimilated through identification, both another subject and also the Symbolic Order – language and the law – that 'mediates the relationship with that other subject' (Evans 1996: 133).

7 The Symbolic Order is, for Lacan, the all-pervasive structure of law and language that governs our entry into culture, our position as sexed subjects, and our perceptions of reality. Elsewhere I make the argument that the Symbolic functions for Lacan as *dharma* functions in the *Mahābhārata*, as they both act in a normative, representational, and ordering capacity, especially in the regulation of desire and the construction of sexual difference.

8 Kṛṣṇā, meaning 'dark in complexion', is another name for Draupadī.

9 Hiltebeitel notes the transsexual implications of this scene as well (1980b: 163).

10 Though it does take on a fascinating vitality in vernacular folk traditions – see Hiltebeitel 1988.

11 Doniger cites a passage in the *Rāmāyaṇa* in which Śiva is making love to Pārvatī, having 'taken the form of a woman to please her' (1997: 130), and another in the *Mahābhāgavata Purāṇa* in which Pārvatī takes the form of Kṛṣṇa, and Śiva that of Rādhā, Kṛṣṇa's lover, 'in order to make love in reverse' (ibid.: 137).

12 In a Telugu variant, Mohinī turns back into Viṣṇu as Śiva is making love to her, and Śiva continues – 'a very rare instance of a consummated, explicit, male homosexual act in Hindu mythology' (Doniger 1997: 137).

13 For a fascinating study of the folk cult that surrounds the mythology of Aravān, see Hiltebeitel 1998.

14 Ila/Ilā is cursed to alternate genders, spending one month as a man, then one as a woman. Though this story is only referred to briefly in the *Mahābhārata*, it is recounted more elaborately in the *Rāmāyaṇa* (7.78–81), and no doubt forms part of the broader historical and mythological context in which the *Mahābhārata* is set.

15 Literally, a female-male – *strīpumāṃs*.

16 Goldman notes that *yakṣa*s are 'often represented in Indian legend and literature as having the power to exchange their sex with people' (1993: 381 n. 40).

17 Originally, the deal was intended to make Śikhaṇḍin a man only long enough to pacify his father-in-law. But when Kubera, lord of the *yakṣa*s, passed by and found Sthūṇākarṇa with female genitals, he became so enraged that he cursed the *yakṣa* to continue to wear Śikhaṇḍin's female organ for life, a curse that he then mitigated to expire upon Śikhaṇḍin's death.

18 This is a case of van Buitenen waxing poetic, and perhaps slightly Gallic, in his translation – but overall he has such a good sense of the language and feel for the epic's 'mood' that it seems right to retain this charming phrase.

19 Goldman cites a passage from the story of Thera Soreyya in which the Buddha explains that 'men who indulge in adultery must, after suffering in hell for hundreds of thousands of years, suffer the further indignity of a hundred successive

rebirths as women. Women, on the other hand, who perform meritorious acts with the desire of escaping their feminine condition or who are utterly devoted to their husbands can, he asserts, thereby be reborn as men' (1993: 377).

20 We never receive an explicit confirmation that Śikhaṇḍin reverts back to a woman after his death, but this was the agreement that was struck.

21 Bhīṣma is a reincarnation of Dyaus, one of the divine Vasus and sky god.

22 Though Bhīṣma is technically Arjuna's great-uncle, and Ambā would have been his great-aunt had she married either Vicitravīrya or Bhīṣma, the titles of (grand)-father and (grand)mother are widely used to address any relative of a preceding generation.

23 Another name for Śiva.

24 Though Doniger sees Draupadī's 'hypersexuality' as standing in 'dramatic contrast with the reborn Ambā's ambiguous sexuality' (1999: 283).

25 Lacan does this primarily to illustrate that the subject is essentially divided, but it also points toward the failure, lack, and castration at the origin of the subject.

26 Generally translated as enjoyment or pleasure of a sexual nature, in its Lacanian sense this term also has undertones of pain or suffering.

27 It bears noting here, however, that assuming a sexualized relationship toward the deity is not the only form of *bhakti* – another form developed throughout the epic is that of *sākhya bhāva*, the *bhakti* of friendship, that we see most poignantly in the relationship between Arjuna and Kṛṣṇa but also, interestingly, between Kṛṣṇa and Draupadī, one of the few if only instances of true male–female friendship in the epic (see Chapter 6).

28 *strīpūrvo yo naravyāghro yaḥ sa veda guṇāguṇān / śikhaṇḍinaṃ*. The text here is nuanced – it could be more conservatively translated as 'he who knows both the merits and defects of masculinity and femininity', but the Dutt translation sexualizes it, casting it in the language of pleasure. As in earlier choices, I find this telling and interesting, and thus choose to retain this language.

11

KṚṢṆA'S SON SĀMBA

Faked gender and other ambiguities on the background of lunar and solar myth

Georg von Simson

Introduction

Among the issues of gender in the *Mahābhārata*, those concerning some form or other of border-crossing deserve our special interest. Besides the better-known case of transsexualism, the case of Śikhaṇḍinī/Śikhaṇḍin, which is a story of major importance within the main plot of the *Mahābhārata*, we meet a case of cross-dressing which seems to be of less weight: the story of Sāmba, a young man who on one occasion is presented in the outfit of a woman, a pregnant woman at that. In the end, the pregnant woman is found to be a man, but the pregnancy nevertheless becomes real, with disastrous effect. Is this bizarre episode[1] just a whimsical idea of the epic's author(s), defying any attempt at further explanation? Probably not. The more one gets acquainted with the *Mahābhārata*, the more one becomes aware of the fact that details like this are used to create a tight net of meaning by which the whole epic structure is held together. In the case of Sāmba we shall see that it is hardly sufficient to study his character as it is depicted in the *Mahābhārata*: the scarce information given there has to be supplemented by information from the *Harivaṃśa* and the Purāṇas. But to understand the cross-dressing incident attributed to Sāmba in more detail, we will have to refer to levels of meaning that are hidden under the surface of the texts and belong to the large realm of basic conditions for the epic's coming into being. More specifically, we shall see that gender opposition may also reflect certain phenomena of nature, particularly the sun and moon, which during their monthly and annual cycles undergo states that can be interpreted as sexually ambiguous.

The assumption of hidden meanings is, of course, burdened with the risk of misinterpretation and overinterpretation. To reduce this risk to a minimum, it is necessary to keep the interpretation within the limits of basic human interest – in our case the problematics of gender – and/or within the sphere of ancient Indian speculation – here speculation about the course of sun and moon, the seasons of the year, and time in general, so characteristic for both the Vedic and the classical culture of India. In addition, we have to stipulate that the results be consistent with each other and, as far as possible, in agreement with the results of accepted scholarship within our field.

The story of Sāmba

According to the *Mahābhārata*, the *Harivaṃśa*, and other Purāṇas,[2] Sāmba is a son of Kṛṣṇa and one of his wives, Jāmbavatī, daughter of Jāmbavat, king of the bears.[3] Throughout the *Mahābhārata* he is often mentioned together with other Vṛṣṇis, particularly his half-brother Pradyumna,[4] or Kṛṣṇa's younger half-brother Gada,[5] or both of them.[6] Though depicted as a brave fighter during the siege of Dvārakā by Śālva,[7] he does not take part in the great battle between the Pāṇḍavas and the Kauravas, instead joining his uncle Balarāma on his pilgrimage (5.154.16).[8] If we had no more information about him than this, we would take him as one of those minor members of the Vṛṣṇi-Andhaka clan whose names are mentioned frequently, but who otherwise remain rather colourless characters.

There is only one scene in the *Mahābhārata* where Sāmba plays a role that seems so special that it deserves our attention, and that is when he becomes a decisive factor in the causal chain that leads to the destruction of his clan. To understand this episode fully, we have to place it in the greater context of the main plot of the epic. The disaster which Sāmba is involved in does not happen out of the blue, but is the result of events occurring many years earlier. After the great war between the Pāṇḍavas and Kauravas which ended with the death of almost all participants, the women gather on the battlefield to lament their dead husbands and sons. Gāndhārī, the mother of the one hundred Kaurava brothers who are all slain by the Pāṇḍava Bhīma, meets Kṛṣṇa, the friend and cousin of the five sons of Pāṇḍu and the charioteer of Arjuna. Considering him the main person responsible for the disaster of the war, which he in her opinion could have prevented, she hurls a terrible curse against him: thirty-six years from now he will be the cause of the annihilation of his whole clan and will himself meet with a humiliating death (11.25.36–42).

The curse is one of the epic poets' favourite means of providing the story with a moral background and giving meaning to events that otherwise would be inexplicable. It assumes personal guilt for anything negative that happens to a person, but unlike the classical *karma* doctrine that prefers the idea of retribution in a future existence, the curse establishes a direct connection between offender and offended and normally produces its effect within a shorter period. As P.V. Ramankutty shows in his monograph on curses in the *Mahābhārata* (Ramankutty 1999),[9] the person who curses tends to be one who disposes of the magic potency of the spoken word, that is a priest or sage (*ṛṣi*), and the typical reason for the curse is that he feels offended by disrespect on the part of the offender. Gāndhārī's curse of Kṛṣṇa is exceptional in several respects: it is a woman who curses, the offence is of an unusually vague nature (the responsibility for the war in general – not the committing of an offence, but the omitting of morally required action), and, finally, there is a large temporal distance between the curse and its effect. Also peculiar is Kṛṣṇa's reaction: instead of being shocked, he accepts Gāndhārī's prophecy with a smile, as something inevitable. He himself will be the cause of his people's annihilation and they will kill each other because nobody else would be able to do this (11.25.24–5). Though not depicted as God in this scene, it is clear that the poet wants us to understand that Kṛṣṇa himself – as a time-controlling deity – is destiny.

But destiny needs tools to come into effect. The sixteenth book of the epic, *Mausalaparvan*, relates how, thirty-six years after the great battle, Gāndhārī's curse is – with the active help of Kṛṣṇa[10] – fulfilled. The story runs as follows.[11]

Replying to a question of Janamejaya, Vaiśaṃpāyana relates that once when the *ṛṣi*s Viśvāmitra, Kaṇva, and Nārada were visiting Dvārakā, some young men of the Vṛṣṇi clan tried to make fun of them: disguising Sāmba as a woman, they presented him to the *ṛṣi*s as the wife of a certain Babhru and asked them about the nature of the child to be born from her. The *ṛṣi*s answer with a curse: Kṛṣṇa's son Sāmba will give birth to a terrible iron club which will lead to the destruction of the Vṛṣṇis and Andhakas (16.2.4–9). On the following day Sāmba delivers a club, which by order of the king is pulverized and thrown into the sea (16.2.15–17). From now on, any production of alcoholic drinks is forbidden (16.2.18–20). The god of time and death (Kāla) is seen sneaking around the houses and other bad omens appear (16.3.1–20). Kṛṣṇa, noticing these inauspicious signs, orders his people to undertake a pilgrimage to the sea coast (16.3.21–2). The whole population of Dvārakā (i.e. the clans of the Yādavas, Vṛṣṇis, Andhakas, and Bhojas) settles at a place on the shore called Prabhāsa (16.4.9–10). A great drinking bout takes place there, resulting in a brawl in which all the heroes gradually get involved (16.4.14–33). On seeing his friend Sātyaki and his own son Pradyumna killed, Kṛṣṇa angrily grasps a handful of *erakā* grass, which is immediately converted into an iron club. He kills those who stand next to him (16.4.34–5). Then all the warriors kill each other with terrible clubs which come into being as soon as they take up *erakā* blades (16.4.36–41). Kṛṣṇa's wrath is enhanced when he sees his son Sāmba, Pradyumna's son Aniruddha, and other members of his family killed. He takes active part in the massacre (16.4.42–4). The end of Kṛṣṇa and his brother Balarāma, the only adult male survivors, is told at 16.5: Balarāma enters into a state of *yoga* and leaves his body through the mouth in the form of a large white snake. He enters the sea where he is received by the great divine snakes and god Varuṇa himself (16.5.12–15). Kṛṣṇa, too, knowing that his time has come, enters into a state of *yoga*. He is killed by a hunter named Jarā ('Old Age') and ascends to heaven where he is received by the gods (16.5.16–25).

Psychology versus theology

What makes the *Mahābhārata* difficult to interpret and appreciate is the peculiar blend of psychological motivation on the human level and theological interpretation on the divine level. Gāndhārī behaves as a normal human mother, cursing the man whom she regards responsible for the death of her children. Kṛṣṇa, on the other hand, has to play two parts simultaneously: he is human, allying himself with the Pāṇḍavas in the great war, but he is also the highest god, knowing everything that is going to happen beforehand and making sure that destiny takes its infallible course. He thus receives Gāndhārī's curse with utter calmness, accepting its content as inevitable destiny. In the same way, when the brawl starts, 'he did not give way to anger, knowing (the effect of) the revolution of time' (*na cukrodha . . . jānan kālasya paryayam* // 16.4.30). But only a few verses later, he gets into a rage when he sees his friend and son killed, and triggers the disaster by converting the blades of grass into a deadly weapon.

Reasons for the *ṛṣis*' wrath

In contradistinction to the curse of Gāndhārī, which in more than one respect goes beyond the normal, the curse that the wise men direct against Sāmba represents the standard type of relation between offender and offended: young men, Sāmba and his fellows, have grossly neglected their duty of showing respect to the elders, in this case holy men belonging to the priestly order. What remain to be explained are the specific circumstances: Sāmba's transvestism, the extraordinary violent reaction of the *ṛṣi*s, the iron club (or rather 'pestle', see below), and the *erakā* grass.

Before we have a closer look at Sāmba, let us try to define the specific nature of the offence more precisely. Of course, it was highly inappropriate behaviour of the young men of the Vṛṣṇi clan to test the divinatory talent of their holy guests in the first place, but what apparently was felt to be particularly offensive was the masquerade, the man acting as a pregnant woman, and the frivolous attempt to fool the wise men by this masquerade. To mention one possibility, the *ṛṣi*s could have understood the seemingly pregnant Sāmba as an ironic attack on (their own?) yogic asceticism: even today there is a current belief in India that 'the yogi becomes "pregnant" as his stomach swells with the retained seed' (O'Flaherty 1980: 44).

But one gets the impression that more than one border has been crossed here. The confusion of sexes might have been felt repulsive in itself, but even more so in this case because Sāmba – as a man changing into a woman and presenting himself as the pregnant wife of another man – was degrading himself by voluntarily losing his manhood.[12] There might also have been the suspicion of homosexuality playing a role here, although there is nothing in the information about Sāmba we get elsewhere that seems to point in that direction.

It is perhaps not out of place to compare the situation and the reaction of the *ṛṣi*s with concepts we meet in the North Germanic culture of pre-Christian Scandinavia. Here the term *ergi* denotes lack of manhood/manliness and is used with regard to men who play the female part in a homosexual relationship. There was no greater insult to a man than to accuse him of *ergi*. Strangely enough, Odin, the highest god, was denounced for committing this sinful behaviour. Odin was also associated with *seid*, a kind of shamanic magic and divination that normally belonged to the domain of women.[13] There is enough evidence to show that Odin can be considered as a counterpart of Viṣṇu,[14] so it is not surprising that change of sex is attributed to both of them. As far as Viṣṇu is concerned, best known is his transformation into a woman in the *amṛtamanthana* ('Churning of the Ocean') myth, where in the shape of Mohinī he seduces the *asura*s to win back the *amṛta* which they have stolen.[15] Even more interesting is the fact that in the iconography of later Hindu art, Viṣṇu and Śiva can be combined in the half-male, half-female figure of Hari-Hara, and that Viṣṇu here regularly appears on the left, female side, which is regarded as mild and friendly (*saumya*)[16] in contrast to the 'terrible' (*raudra*) side of the male Śiva.[17] The *Brahmāṇḍa Purāṇa* even tells a story where Śiva rapes Viṣṇu in his form as enchantress (*mohinī*) (Doniger 1999: 263–5). In other words, Viṣṇu was attributed the same gender ambiguity as his Scandinavian counterpart Odin, and this ambiguity could apparently be transferred to Sāmba, the son and replica of Kṛṣṇa, Viṣṇu's *avatāra* on earth.

A European parallel: the legend of emperor Nero

In western tradition we find a quite different parallel to the Sāmba story in the case of the legend of the Roman emperor Nero, which never ceased to stimulate people's imagination from Roman antiquity to the Christian Middle Ages. Roberto Zapperi has followed the development from history to legend in detail (see Zapperi 1991: 112–21). It started with the reports of the Roman historians Tacitus and Suetonius on Nero's sexual extravagances and transgressions. Relevant in our context are his homosexual marriages, in which he played the part of the bride, and his acting on stage, where, among other parts, he played the part of a woman who gives birth. According to Plutarch, Nero was reincarnated as a frog (Zapperi 1991: 113). The Christians developed these historical records into a legend suited further to denigrate their persecutor, who was stylized as the Antichrist and identified with the Beast of the Revelation of St John. Here again we meet the frog as a devilish animal, whose form is taken by the unclean spirits vomited by the Dragon, the Beast, and the False Prophet (Revelation 16.13–14; Zapperi 1991: 116). This may have triggered the idea of the emperor getting pregnant and giving birth to a frog (ibid.: 115), which we may compare with the more complicated story of Sāmba, who first gives birth to a pestle, which is then pulverized and thrown into the water from where it reappears as *erakā* grass (rushes?) until, in the end, the grass is reconverted into pestles or clubs. In one of the early medieval versions of the Nero legend, contained in the Chronicle of John, Bishop of Nikiou (*c.* 700 CE), 'even the priests of the idols hurled maledictions against' the emperor – compare Sāmba being cursed by the *ṛṣi*s – who then gets pregnant and, unlike Sāmba, dies of his pregnancy (Zapperi 1991: 112).

By pointing to these parallels we do not want to suggest any historical connection between the Indian story of Sāmba and the European story of Nero: our intention is to show how popular imagination in both cultures reacts to sexual misbehaviour, forming tales of a certain similarity.

The prehistory of Sāmba's birth

The audience of the *Mahābhārata*, puzzling over Sāmba in a woman's outfit, could be referred to a passage of Book 13 of the epic, *Anuśāsanaparvan*, where an account of the circumstances of Sāmba's birth is given (13.14–16). The context is a lengthy and probably late Śaiva text (13.14–18) culminating in a *sahasranāmastotra* of the Great God (*adhyāya* 17). This Śaiva passage is embedded in Bhīṣma's teaching on morality, which is, after all, the main purpose of the *parvan*. It follows almost immediately after the story of Bhaṅgāśvana (13.12), the king whom the offended god Indra converts into a woman and who in the end, to the god's great surprise, prefers to remain a woman. The reason for his decision, to be sure, is not the social position of women, but their greater potential for sexual enjoyment.[18] It thus seems as if the issue of changing sex which is addressed in the Bhaṅgāśvana story[19] has reminded the epic author of Kṛṣṇa's son Sāmba, even if the story of Sāmba's transvestism is told much later, in Book 16, whereas here, in Book 13, we only learn about the prehistory of Sāmba's birth. The story runs as follows.

Kṛṣṇa Vāsudeva relates how, by exercising *tapas* in the hermitage of Upamanyu in the Himālaya, he won Śiva's favour. He was acting on behalf of his wife Jāmbavatī who, seeing all the sons of her co-wife Rukmiṇī, wants to have a son herself. The god finally appears before his worshipper Kṛṣṇa, but – and this point seems to be of primary importance – he shows himself not alone, but in the company of his consort:

tejaḥ sūryasahasrasya apaśyaṃ divi . . . //
tasya madhyagataṃ cāpi tejasaḥ . . . /
indrāyudhapinaddhāṅgaṃ vidyunmālāgavākṣakam /
nīlaśailacayaprakhyaṃ balākābhūṣitaṃ ghanam //
tam āsthitaś ca bhagavān devyā saha mahādyutiḥ /

tapasā tejasā kāntyā dīptayā saha bhāryayā //
rarāja bhagavāṃs tatra devyā saha maheśvaraḥ /
somena sahitaḥ sūryo yathā meghasthitas tathā //

I (i.e. Kṛṣṇa) saw a brilliance of one thousand suns in the sky . . . and in the centre of this brilliance . . . a compact mass (or cloud)[20] whose body was covered by rainbows and which had loopholes consisting of garlands of lightning. It was like a heap of black stones and adorned by cranes. On it stood the Lord in his full glory of heat, energy and beauty together with the Goddess, his blazing wife. There the Holy One, the Great Lord, shone together with the Goddess like the sun united with the moon in the midst of a cloud.

(*Mahābhārata* 13.15.6–9)

In what follows, the divine couple acts together: both Śiva and Umā are pleased by Kṛṣṇa's devotion and grant him wishes (13.16). This happens in a peculiar way which seems to underline the cooperation of Śiva and his consort: whereas the god rather taciturnly accepts Kṛṣṇa's wishes – which include hundreds or thousands of sons[21] – with the words 'So be it' (*evam astu*, 13.16.3), it is Umā who explains to him that her husband has granted him a son who shall be named 'Sāmba' (13.16.5). The whole arrangement is apparently meant to give a hint as to the name's meaning: 'Sāmba' can be understood as a *bahuvrīhi* compound derived from *sa* + *ambā*, meaning '(Lord Śiva) accompanied by the Mother (i.e. his consort Umā)'. In fact, in the version of the story of Sāmba's birth which is given in the *Śiva Purāṇa*,[22] the connection between the name Sāmba and Śiva as *sa-amba* is made quite explicit:[23] first Kṛṣṇa[24] exercises *tapas* with regard to 'Śiva Sāmba' in order to get a son,[25] and then, at the end of the rainy season, 'Śiva Sāmba' appears before him[26] and grants him a son who is thus called Sāmba.[27] It bears witness to the greater subtlety of the *Mahābhārata* poet that he avoids being overly explicit, leaving it to his audience to draw the necessary conclusions.

Soma, the *musala*, the *erakā* grass, and lunar mythology

Instead of Ambā, Śiva's consort in the epic story is called by her ordinary name Umā (13.15.29, 49; 13.16.4), which means that, by analogy with the explanation of the name Sāmba, the god, being united with Umā, could be understood as *sa* + *umā* = *soma*.[28] But what could such a hint of *soma* mean? In the *Mahābhārata*, the word *soma* is used to mean 'moon', but if we take into account the possibility of a ritualistic interpretation,[29] the older meaning of the term, still prevalent in the *Ṛgveda*, should be taken into consideration. The word *soma* originally signified a plant and its juice, a drug that was used for ritualistic purposes. The annihilating battle of the *Mausalaparvan* could hint at the ritual of *soma*-pressing. The *musala*[30] to which Sāmba gives birth may then be interpreted as a development of the upper, pestle-shaped press-stone (*grāvan*) in the so-called *ulūkhala* type of *soma*-pressing device.[31] It is now no longer conceived as a stone, but as consisting of iron. In our epic story, the *musala* is first pulverized and thrown into the ocean. But from the ocean it apparently reappears in the form of a certain rush or reed (*erakā*), and when the Vṛṣṇi-Andhakas get into that fatal row that will destroy them, the blades of reed are miraculously reconverted in Kṛṣṇa's hands into an iron club, and then into many clubs when the other warriors follow Kṛṣṇa in taking up the reeds. It is thus Kṛṣṇa himself who becomes instrumental for the disaster. Kṛṣṇa is Viṣṇu incarnate, the god who from the late Vedic period is identified with the sacrifice (*yajña*), an idea that is still very much present in later texts like the *Harivaṃśa*. It must also be noted that according to the *Āpastamba Śrautasūtra* (16.26.3–4), mortar (*ulūkhala*) and pestle (*musala*) symbolize the space that is traversed by Viṣṇu (as Trivikrama).

It is Sāmba who brings forth the *musala* in the first place. Here we have to note the – at least partial – identity of Sāmba and his father Kṛṣṇa. The author of the story of Sāmba's birth in the *Anuśāsanaparvan* emphasizes that the son to be born will be like his father: this is what Sāmba's mother Jāmbavatī asks her husband for – 'grant me a son who is like yourself' (*ātmatulyaṃ mama sutaṃ prayaccha*, 13.14.14) – and this is what the sage Upamanyu prophesies to Kṛṣṇa – 'you will get a son who is like yourself' (*lapsyase tanayaṃ kṛṣṇa ātmatulyam*, 13.14.48). Thus on the ritual level Sāmba and his father Kṛṣṇa cooperate: the son gives birth to the *soma*-grinding pestle, and the father puts into operation the ritual process, which he symbolically represents.

The question remains why the *erakā* grass had to be inserted between the first 'birth' of the pestle and its reappearance during the fight of the Vṛṣṇis. This issue seems to be connected with the second scene of action, which is no longer the capital town Dvārakā, but Prabhāsa on the sea shore. Readers of the *Mahābhārata* are familiar with this place through the description of the pilgrimage (*tīrthayātrā*) which was undertaken by Kṛṣṇa's elder brother Balarāma during the great battle.[32] Prabhāsa is the first and most prominent of the holy places on the banks of the Sarasvatī,[33] situated at the point where the holy and mythical river discharges into the sea. The story connected with this place – and this is of utmost importance in the context of the *Mausalaparvan* club-fight – is the aetiological myth of the waning and waxing moon. According to this tale, the moon was cursed by his father-in-law, Dakṣa, because he regarded only Rohiṇī, neglecting the other 26 sisters (= the *nakṣatra*s, forming the lunar circle of constellations) who were his wives as well. As the moon was dwindling away and about to disappear altogether, the curse was finally moderated by the intervention of the gods, with the effect that the moon from now on should regularly wax and wane. For his regeneration he had to take a bath at Prabhāsa[34] on the new-moon night (*amāvāsyā*). We may therefore assume that the fight with the clubs had to take place at the holy place at the sea shore because this was associated with the curse of the moon.[35] The *erakā* grass, which we have to imagine as a kind of reed or rush growing near the water, is to remind us of the ritual grasses (like *darbha* or *kuśa*) that are closely connected with Viṣṇu, the personal representative of the sacrifice (*yajña*).

The next place which the author of the description of Balarāma's pilgrimage dwells upon, Udapāna, is also intimately connected with *soma* sacrifice and, in my opinion, lunar mythology focusing on the new-moon period (9.35). Here the story is told of Trita[36] who, after being deserted by his two elder brothers, falls into a well. He saves himself by performing a *soma* sacrifice in his imagination, defining a plant that happens to grow in that well as a *soma* plant.[37] There can be little doubt that Trita represents the moon on the third day of the new-moon period[38] when the moon, caught as it were in a well (*kūpa*), is about to reappear. The new-moon symbolism in this story is palpable; in our context it seems significant that the well is described as being covered by (juicy) herbs (*vīrudh*) and (dry) grasses (*tṛṇa*) (9.35.29), because if the herbs represent the *soma* plant to be pressed, the grasses are the counterpart of the *erakā* grass of the *Mausalaparvan* club-fight episode. Considering that the new-moon genius Sāmba is the descendant of Jāmbavat, king of monkeys or bears, it also seems to be significant that Trita's brothers, the representatives of the first two days of the new-moon period, are punished by being converted into wolves[39] (9.35.49) while their children or descendants shall be different kinds of monkeys and bears.[40] This reflects the original inauspiciousness of the new-moon period, a time when the world is out of order as it were, and Kṛṣṇa has to interfere to reestablish *dharma*.

Sāmba disguised as a pregnant woman is said to be the wife of Babhru. This is the name of a well-known Yādava warrior, but as *babhru* 'the brown one' in Vedic texts is also used as a designation of the *soma* juice, a hidden hint to the *soma* ritual may be intended as well. But, at the same time, the name could also contain an allusion to the god Śiva since Yudhiṣṭhira refers to Śiva as 'Babhru' in the very first verse of the large Śaiva passage which contains Sāmba's birth story (13.14.1). And, as we have seen, *soma* could indeed be interpreted as *sa* + *umā* and thus also be a designation of the Great God!

On the other hand, Sāmba's disguise invites us to detect yet another symbolic value of the *musala*. Sāmba pretends to be a pregnant woman. The *ṛṣi*s, seeing through the masquerade, expose him as a man, making at the same time bitter earnest of the feigned pregnancy. Expecting that the punishment would correspond to the crime, we feel entitled to a symbolic interpretation according to which the pestle brought forth by Sāmba represents his penis,[41] which is hidden in the faked woman's womb and now, when detected by the angry *ṛṣi*s, is converted into a deadly weapon.[42] It should be noted in this connection that Sāmba's sexual potency is emphasized in some Purāṇas, where Kṛṣṇa curses his son for having sexual relations with his, Kṛṣṇa's, 16,000 wives (Mani 1979: 677, item 5).

The drinking bout as a kind of perverted *soma*-pressing and *soma*-drinking ritual of the Vṛṣṇis, in which the *musala* becomes multiplied to destroy the whole clan, may also be interpreted as a warning against the excesses of the warrior class, where drinking of alcohol combined with sexual transgressions was probably experienced as a constant threat. That this phenomenon was symbolically associated with the waning moon can be shown if one analyses certain myths concerning Indra, Kutsa, and Gaṇeśa (von Simson 1992; 2000b). In this connection it should be noted that the *musala* (pestle) is also one of the attributes of Balarāma, also known as Saṃkarṣaṇa – who in my opinion is the representative of the waning moon in, respectively, the group of five Vṛṣṇi heroes and the group of four *vyūha*s (see below) – and that the characteristic feature of this hero is his being addicted to spiritual drinks![43]

Sāmba and the lunar circle; the five heroes of the Vṛṣṇi-Andhakas

The circumstances of Sāmba's birth, which are initiated by Kṛṣṇa's worship of Śiva and the theophany of the divine couple, invite us to see additional levels of meaning referring to Sāmba's lunar character.

When the Great God, accompanied by his wife Umā, appears before Kṛṣṇa, he is compared with the sun being in conjunction with the moon[44] (*somena sahitaḥ sūryo*, 13.15.9, quoted above, p. 236), in other words, at the time of the new-moon period; and we may thus expect also that the child whose birth is announced on this occasion will bear features of the new moon, particularly because his father Kṛṣṇa, 'the Black One', whose likeness he shall be, can be interpreted in this way as well.[45] The comparison of Śiva accompanied by Umā with the conjunction of sun and moon implies that Śiva here is compared with the sun and Umā with the moon. This means that the moon, though normally conceived as male (*candramas*, *candra*, *soma*, and other designations of the moon are grammatically masculine), appears as a female in this situation,[46] a circumstance that helps to explain the gender ambiguity of both Kṛṣṇa and his son Sāmba.

The full- and new-moon days are so-called *parvan* days, *parvan* meaning 'knot' or 'joint', referring both to plants like bamboo and to the course of the moon. In a line occurring twice in the *Mahābhārata* in contexts where people with blameworthy ways of life are listed, we meet the rare word *parvakāra*, '*parvan*-maker'. This is explained at the second occurrence of the verse (13.90.9 in the Vulgate and the Critical Edition) by the seventeenth-century commentator Nīlakaṇṭha as *veṣāntaradhārī*,[47] 'he that puts on disguises' (thus Ganguli). Nīlakaṇṭha here quotes the dictionary *Medinikośa*, where one of the meanings of *parvan* is given as '*lakṣaṇāntara*', '(having) a different mark/sign'. The origin of this meaning is probably the lunar meaning of *parvan* as the point where the moon changes (its appearance or character). As the word for mark or sign (*lakṣaṇa*) may also have the pregnant meaning 'sexual organ', we may assume that Sāmba's association with the new-moon period invited him to be seen as a cross-dressing man, a *parvakāra* in the sense of one who disguises himself as a woman. The occurrence of this term among others that express contemptible behaviour is quite significant.

We have seen not only that Sāmba is disguised as a woman, but also that after being cursed by the *ṛṣis* he actually gives birth, not to a child, it is true, but to an iron pestle. This seems again to be an association with the idea of the new-moon period, a period of pregnancy as it were, when the birth of the young moon's crescent was expected. That Sāmba is indeed associated with the new-moon period can also be deduced from his position among the group of 'Five Heroes' (*pañca vīrāḥ*) of the Vṛṣṇi-Andhaka clan. The group consists of Kṛṣṇa Vāsudeva's elder brother Saṃkarṣaṇa (= Balarāma), Kṛṣṇa himself, Kṛṣṇa's sons Pradyumna and Sāmba, and Pradyumna's son Aniruddha. Whereas the worship of the two divine brothers Saṃkarṣaṇa and Vāsudeva is attested at least from the second century BCE (Joshi 1979: 22), there is hardly any evidence for an early cult of exactly those five Vṛṣṇi heroes.[48] Their names appear in the common tradition of the *Brahmāṇḍa Purāṇa* and the *Vāyu Purāṇa* for which Kirfel would give a *terminus a quo* of 335 CE (Bock-Raming 2002: 313–20). There is thus no good reason to defend the opinion (e.g. Härtel 1987) that this group is older than that of the four *vyūha*s of the Pāñcarātra philosophy[49] which includes the same names with the exception of Sāmba. Both groups seem to have originated in speculations around the phases of the moon and then to have developed in different directions.

On the basis of this assumption, the names can easily be explained. 'Saṃkarṣaṇa' can be derived from the verbal root *kṛṣ*, 'to draw/drag/pull', with the preverb *sam*, 'together', *saṃkarṣaṇa* thus being understood as 'drawing/pulling together', 'contracting' (cf. Bigger 1998: 66 and n. 203) – this would be a precise designation of the phase of the waning moon. The name Rāma, which the epic normally uses for Kṛṣṇa's elder brother instead of Saṃkarṣaṇa,[50] may be derived from the verbal root *ram*, the middle voice of which means 'to stand still, rest'. This name, too, may thus refer to the waning moon approaching the new-moon phase. Kṛṣṇa, 'Black', would designate the dark moon during the new-moon phase, and Sāmba, explained as *sa* + *ambā*, would, as we have seen, point in the same direction, meaning sun and moon in conjunction, Sāmba's identity with his father Kṛṣṇa being especially emphasized in the *Mahābhārata*. The two remaining names could then be understood as originally referring to phases of the moon as well: Pradyumna as 'Shining Forth' for the first appearing of the young moon[51] after the new-moon period, and Aniruddha, 'the Unobstructed One', as a designation for the full moon, Indra who has overcome Vṛtra, the demon of obstruction.[52] We thereby get the following scheme:

	FULL MOON Aniruddha	
WAXING MOON Pradyumna		WANING MOON Balarāma/Saṃkarṣaṇa
	Kṛṣṇa Vāsudeva NEW MOON Sāmba	

This does not mean that we have to think either of a division of the month into four sections of equal duration, or of four strictly defined points within the month; the figures should rather be understood as representations of characteristic manifestations of the moon. Kṛṣṇa Vāsudeva is the dominant figure in the scheme, developing gradually into the highest god of a branch of Hinduism that focused on Viṣṇu. In order to take care of minor functions – perhaps connected with certain seasonal aspects – he was provided with a double, his son Sāmba. In the *vyūha* speculation of the Pāñcarātrins this was apparently not felt necessary; here the original lunar mythology was replaced by cosmological speculations and Kṛṣṇa, in conformity with his significance, ranked first. Aniruddha plays a prominent part in these speculations, which in my opinion reflects an original main dichotomy between two opposites only, full and new moon. This pair can also be seen in the pair Nara-Nārāyaṇa upon which the late layers of the epic focus and which they equate with Arjuna, 'the White One', and Kṛṣṇa, 'the Black One'. The black moon seems to have been regarded as the real self (*ātman*) of the white moon, and this explains why Aniruddha (corresponding to Indra, Arjuna, and the white moon) by the end of these philosophical speculations is more or less absorbed by Kṛṣṇa Vāsudeva/Nārāyaṇa. He is now identified with 'agent, cause and effect', the origin of everything mobile and immobile (*Mahābhārata* 12.326.37), or with the 'ego-maker, I-consciousness' (*ahaṃkāra*, 12.326.39).[53] But he still preserves traces of his original white-moon nature, for instance when the demons Madhu and Kaiṭabha see the god Hari (Viṣṇu) with a white moon-like appearance when he takes the Aniruddha form,[54] though he is also depicted here as being under the influence of *yoga*-sleep and lying on the coils of the serpent Śeṣa (Saṃkarṣaṇa). This gradually increasing blending of symbolic images may be the reason why the origin of the *vyūha*s in lunar mythology has not been seen by previous scholars who have dealt with this topic.

The moon as measurer

One of the main functions of the moon was measuring time, hence its name *candramas*, 'the shining measurer'. The monthly cycle was either measured from full moon to full moon or from new moon to new moon, and if we are right in suspecting that both Kṛṣṇa and his son Sāmba had some connection with the new-moon period, then we might be able to find hints in the texts pointing in that direction. The *Mahābhārata* seems to be silent about this topic, but its appendix the *Harivaṃśa* contains a passage that might be interpreted as pointing to measuring in connection with Sāmba. Right after mentioning that Jāmbavatī's son was born in the same month that Pradyumna, his half-brother, was abducted by the demon Śambara,[55] the text adds a *śloka* which is apparently meant to express something fundamental about the newborn child:

> *bālyāt prabhṛti rāmeṇa māneṣu viniyojitaḥ* /
> *rāmād anantaraṃ caiva mānitaḥ sarvavṛṣṇibhiḥ* //
>
> From the days when he was a child, he was commissioned by Rāma [= Balarāma] with the '*māna*s', and next after Rāma he was honoured by all the Vṛṣṇis.
>
> (*Harivaṃśa* 100.2)

What does the term *māna* mean in this verse? The word *mānitaḥ* ('honoured') in the next line seems to suggest that the author wants us to take *māna* as also meaning 'honour'. But are we really supposed to understand that Rāma commissioned the child with 'honours', in the sense of 'tributing honours (to others)'? Considering Sāmba's misbehaviour before the *ṛṣi*s in the episode at the beginning of the *Mausalaparvan* – and we have hardly any reason to doubt that Sāmba's disguise as a pregnant woman belongs to an ancient tradition – this would sound like a highly ironic statement implying that his uncle's attempt to educate the boy had proved to be an utter failure. I would therefore suggest that we have to take the second meaning of *māna*, 'measure', so that the line would mean: 'From the days of his childhood he was commissioned by Rāma with the measures (or measurements).' I have to admit that there is nothing in the information we get about Sāmba's life that would give support to this interpretation, but nor is there anything to support the other meaning. In my opinion, this *Harivaṃśa* verse represents a trace of an ancient tradition about Sāmba that was inserted at this decisive place, right after mentioning the approximate date of his birth: 'in the same month when Pradyumna was abducted by Śambara' (*Harivaṃśa* 100.1). We might even suspect that the words *tam eva māsam* ('in the same month') have something to do with Sāmba's concern with measuring that is expressed in the next line, as both *māsa* ('month') and *māna* ('measure') are derived from the root *mā*, 'to measure'.

Sāmba as *vidūṣaka* (*Harivaṃśa*)

In the *Harivaṃśa* Sāmba accompanies his brother Pradyumna in their enterprise against the demon Vajranābha. The whole story does not seem to belong to the older parts of the text,[56] and even here Pradyumna is more important than Sāmba. It is worthwhile though to have a closer look at these late passages as well. There is at least one incident where Sāmba plays a role that seems to be more characteristic of him than the superficial reader might notice. Again we meet Sāmba in disguise: Pradyumna has fallen in love with Vajranābha's daughter Prabhāvatī, and in order to get access to her the Vṛṣṇi heroes sneak into the enemy's palace under cover, disguised as actors. To the delight of the *asuras*, they put on a play for them about Rambhā and Nalakūbara, in which Nalakūbara, the main hero (*nāyaka*), is played by Pradyumna, whereas Sāmba plays the *vidūṣaka*. This casting of the parts seems well weighed. Pradyumna in these late parts of the *Harivaṃśa* is seen as the reincarnate Kāma, the god of love. In terms of lunar mythology he seems to represent the crescent of the young moon in the evening. Derived from *pra*, 'forth', a particle which often expresses beginning, and *dyumna* which is to be connected with the verbal root *dyu*, 'to shine', Pradyumna's name already seems to indicate the meaning 'shining forth', the start of the monthly cycle after the new-moon period. Sāmba, on the other hand, reflects the centre of the new-moon period: he is an *alter ego* of Kṛṣṇa, and the pair Pradyumna-Sāmba can be regarded as replicating the gods Indra and Viṣṇu. In classical Sanskrit drama the *vidūṣaka* is the friend and companion of the hero (*nāyaka*), but at the same time in several ways he is his opposite, a kind of anti-hero. In spite of Kuiper's arguments which would suggest that the *vidūṣaka* reflects the god Varuṇa (Kuiper 1979), I consider it much more natural to see in the pair *nāyaka-vidūṣaka* a continuation of the divine pair Indra-Viṣṇu, which is also present in the *Mahābhārata* pair Arjuna-Kṛṣṇa.

Sāmba's *virūpatva*

As *vidūṣaka*, Sāmba would have to be ugly, *virūpa*, which again reminds us of his character as new moon, the moon which has lost his splendour, which has become black or ugly or invisible. In this connection, attention should be paid to the fact that his mother Jāmbavatī is the daughter of Jāmbavat, king of the bears.[57] The story in the *Anuśāsanaparvan* which contains the prehistory of Sāmba's birth calls Jāmbavatī 'daughter of the king of the apes' (*kapīndraputrī*, *Mahābhārata* 13.14.24) and, in the following verse, 'daughter of the king of the Vidyādharas' (*vidyādharendrasya sutā*).[58] This shows that there might have been different traditions about the nature of this Jāmbavat. As we know from the *Rāmāyaṇa*, where Jāmbavat figures as king of the *ṛkṣa*s (bears), there does not seem to have been any strict borderline between *ṛkṣa*s (bears) and *kapi*s (apes or monkeys). By choosing the expression *kapīndra*, 'king of the apes', for Jāmbavat, who is going to be Kṛṣṇa's father-in-law, the author of our *Anuśāsanaparvan* passage places him a step nearer his son-in-law: in the *Viṣṇu-Sahasranāma* which is included in the same *parvan*, both *kapi* (13.135.109) and *kapīndra* (13.135.66) are mentioned among the thousand names of Viṣṇu. And the *kapi* who figures on Arjuna's banner (*dhvaja*) may be a multiform of Viṣṇu, standing on the Pāṇḍava's chariot as he does with his human form as Kṛṣṇa Vāsudeva. We may also think of the Rigvedic Vṛṣākapi ('the Virile Ape') who, as Indra's companion and rival in sexual matters, can be understood as a parody of Viṣṇu and an anticipation of the *vidūṣaka* of the later drama.[59] It is certainly more than a coincidence that the highest god of the *Nārāyaṇīya* introduces the ritual for the ancestors (*pitaraḥ*, 'fathers') under the name Vṛṣākapi (12.333.16, variant reading; 12.333.21, 23). The episode is connected with Viṣṇu's *avatāra* as a boar (*varāha*, 12.333.11), and the fact that the god in this chapter is also called Govinda (12.333.25),[60] Viṣṇu (12.333.24), and Nārāyaṇa (12.333.25) shows that for the poet all these names refer to one and the same god. It is also highly significant that the *Mahābhārata* elsewhere recommends the waning-moon period and especially the new-moon night (*amāvāsyā*) as the most suitable time for the ritual dedicated to the ancestors (*śrāddha*).[61]

The *vidūṣaka* in the *Nāgānanda*: new-moon imagery

That there may be a connection between the *vidūṣaka* and Sāmba, on the one hand, and the new-moon period, on the other, can be shown by an example from Harṣa's play *Nāgānanda* (seventh century CE). Here we meet in the third act a *vidūṣaka* who, in order to avoid bees who are molesting him, wraps himself up in red garments like a woman(!)[62] with the effect that the drunk *viṭa* (*bon vivant*) mistakes him for his love Navamālikā, who also appears on the scene. The *viṭa* and the girl make fun of the *vidūṣaka*, calling him a 'tawny little monkey' (*kapilamarkaṭaka*),[63] and Navamālikā, who remembers having seen the *vidūṣaka* sleeping with his eyes closed and looking handsome[64] while she was keeping watch during the marriage ceremony,[65] wants – in imitation of that situation – to paint his face black. Cumulatively, the imagery – a man dressing as a woman (hinting at the sexual ambiguity of the moon), the red garments (= *uṣas*, 'dawn'[66]), the bees (bees and honey from the Vedic period being associated with the sun), the *vidūṣaka* sleeping and closing his eyes and the colouring black of his face (= the moon going to sleep, closing his eyes and becoming black) – points towards the new-moon period, and it fits when at the end of the act (verse 49) Jimūtavāhana, the hero of the play, praises the sun as the benefactor of all people. At the same time this *vidūṣaka* resembles Sāmba in at least two respects: he is compared with a monkey – Sāmba is the grandson of Jāmbavat, king of the monkeys (*kapīndra*) – and he dresses himself like a woman, thus like Sāmba concealing his male identity. We see how the phenomena of nature lead the imagination of the poets to produce similar results, even if Harṣa was not necessarily inspired by the Sāmba story of the *Mahābhārata*.[67]

Purāṇic sources: Sāmba introduces the sun cult from Śākadvīpa

That Sāmba always retained some importance within the history of Indian religion[68] is evident from the fact that there exists an Upapurāṇa under his name, the *Sāmba Purāṇa* (von Stietencron 1966; Rocher 1986: 217–19), in which Sāmba is credited for having introduced the sun cult from Śākadvīpa by fetching Maga priests from there. The aetiological legend for this enterprise is interesting for us insofar as it focuses on a feature that was brought forward in our analysis of Sāmba more by implication than by direct evidence of the texts, i.e. his ugliness (*virūpatva*). It tells how Sāmba was cursed by his own father Kṛṣṇa Vāsudeva because he had offended Nārada when the latter together with other *ṛṣi*s paid a visit to Dvārakā.[69] Kṛṣṇa also had another reason to be angry with his son because Nārada had asserted that the attractive young boy had seduced his father's 16,000 wives. Thus Kṛṣṇa curses his son to be struck by leprosy (*kuṣṭharoga*) and so to lose his beauty.[70] In order to get rid of the disease and regain his lost beauty,[71] Sāmba has to win the favour of the sun god (Bhāskara). He shows his gratitude by erecting an image of the god on the bank of the river Candrabhāgā (Chenab).[72]

A version of the Sāmba story which is close to the *Mahābhārata* version (*Mausalaparvan*, see above, p. 232) is given in the *Bhaviṣya Purāṇa*: here it is told how Sāmba offends the *ṛṣi* Durvāsas by caricaturing him and deriding him for his ugliness. The *ṛṣi* curses him both to be struck by leprosy and to give birth, at a later point in time, to the pestle (*musala*).[73] It is interesting to note that in this version of the story Sāmba imitates Durvāsas, because this *ṛṣi* is considered to be a partial incarnation of Śiva/Rudra, the god who, accompanied by his consort Umā, according to the *Anuśāsanaparvan* granted the birth of Sāmba. Sāmba could thus be understood both as a replica of Śiva – as such he would represent the Great God under his destructive aspect as Kāla, bringing forth the iron pestle – and as the son and replica of Kṛṣṇa/Viṣṇu, whom he resembles by having sexual relations with the 16,000 women. All this confirms our hypothesis that Sāmba represents the conjunction of sun and moon at the new-moon period. This is the point when the sun has withdrawn its splendour (light) from the moon, or, in terms of the myth, Sāmba is struck by leprosy. Correspondingly, the sun is about to start casting its splendour upon the moon again, meaning that Sāmba has to win the sun god's favour to get rid of the disease.

Sāmba and Guṇavatī (*Harivaṃśa*)

Returning to the Vajranābha story of the *Harivaṃśa*, there is one more detail concerning Sāmba that might be of interest: the main purpose of the Vṛṣṇi enterprise is the marriage of Pradyumna to Vajranābha's daughter Prabhāvatī. But the demon has two more daughters, Candravatī and Guṇavatī, who marry Pradyumna's companions, his uncle Gada[74] and his half-brother Sāmba respectively. These girls probably do not represent characters of their own, they are just invented to provide the young heroes with appropriate wives and to make the expedition a full success. We may therefore expect that their names are chosen to indicate characters who match their husbands. It is obvious that Pradyumna and Prabhāvatī are a perfect match: 'the Shining Forth (of the young moon)' and 'she who is Provided with Splendour'. The name Gada is apparently just the masculine variant of *gadā*, 'club, mace', and if this Gada is to marry a girl named Candravatī, 'the one who Owns the Moon', we may presume that Gada could be understood as a phase of the moon when it resembles a mace.

But why does Sāmba acquire a consort called Guṇavatī? One could, of course, be satisfied with the trivial meaning of the name: Guṇavatī, 'the Virtuous One'. But I think we should credit the *Harivaṃśa* poet (or whoever invented that name) with more ingenuity. If we are right in taking Sāmba as a representative of the moon during the new-moon period, we must be aware that the moon while passing the sun is invisible – he is, in a way, *nirguṇa*, devoid of tangible qualities. There is evidence in late Vedic literature that the new-moon period was imagined to be the place of the moon's *ātman*, personified by the mythical character Kutsa. As I have shown elsewhere (von Simson 2000b), the story of Indra vacillating between Kutsa and Luśa as told in the *Jaiminīya Brāhmaṇa* may be interpreted on the basis of early lunar mythology. Here Kutsa is associated with Indra's *ātman*, his real self. We may find here the origin of philosophical speculations about *ātman* as *puruṣa*, as reflected for instance in the thirteenth chapter of the *Bhagavadgītā*, where the *puruṣa* experiences the *guṇa*s which have their origin in *prakṛti* (*Bhagavadgītā* 13.20ff.). Guṇavatī, the consort of Sāmba, might thus contain a hint in this direction: 'she who is Provided with the *Guṇa*s' is to be married to Sāmba, the ambiguous one who lacks definite qualities – as we saw in the story of his disguise as a pregnant woman, and also in his disguise as a *vidūṣaka*, a character who can be defined by his lack of the specific virtues of a hero. Since in the *Anuśāsanaparvan* passage he is twice called *ātmatulya* with reference to his father Kṛṣṇa, one might even feel tempted to detect another ambiguity concerning Sāmba: perhaps we are invited to understand *ātmatulya* here not only to mean 'like yourself', i.e. like Kṛṣṇa, but at the same time in an absolute way to mean 'one who is like *ātman*'?[75] I shall not try here to explain Sāmba's absence from the *vyūha*s, the cosmological personifications of the four Vṛṣṇi heroes in the philosophy of the Pāñcarātrins. In this group appear, as we have seen, Kṛṣṇa himself, Kṛṣṇa's elder brother Saṃkarṣaṇa (= Balarāma), Kṛṣṇa's son Pradyumna, and Pradyumna's son Aniruddha, but not Sāmba. Whatever the reason for his absence was, it cannot have been the impossibility of associating him with philosophical concepts! The Purāṇas, on the other hand, accept Sāmba as one of the 'five heroes' (*pañca vīrāḥ*) of the Vṛṣṇis and thus underline his importance.

Sāmba and the cycle of the year

When Śiva and Umā appear before Kṛṣṇa to grant his wish to have a son with his wife Jāmbavatī, the divine couple are seen standing upon a cloud which is adorned by rainbows, garlands of lightning, and cranes (*Mahābhārata* 13.15.6–9; see above, pp. 235–6) – imagery that clearly belongs to the rainy season.[76] This would suggest a seasonal interpretation of the Śiva-Pārvatī myth as represented for instance by Kālidāsa in his epic poem *Kumārasaṃbhava*. Here the Great God is first depicted as performing intense asceticism (*tapas*) and burning to death the god of love (Kāma) who is accompanied by his friend Vasanta ('Spring')[77] (meaning: the sun's developing intense heat, *tapas*, spells the end of springtime and impedes sexual activity). After a long period of ascetic exercise (meaning: the hot season, *grīṣma*), Umā/Pārvatī, the daughter of the personified Himavat mountain, overcomes Śiva's resistance. The divine couple are married and indulge in sexual activity (meaning: at the end of the *uttarāyaṇa* the sun reaches the Himālaya, its northernmost position, and then, after the summer solstice, the rainy season starts).

In the *Anuśāsanaparvan* theophany scene the divine couple, Śiva accompanied by Umā, could then in fact symbolize the summer solstice and thereby the start of the summer monsoon; and this would suggest that the *Mausalaparvan* events which are triggered by Sāmba's misbehaviour are symbolically associated with the rainy season.[78] This is also borne out by the fact that the *musala* is first pulverized and thrown into the water, from where it reappears as *erakā* grass/rush/reed. Several times the poet compares the blades of this grass, reconverted into iron clubs, with thunderbolts (*vajra*, Indra's weapon).[79] We thus find a parallelism with the *Nala-Upākhyāna*, where the hero's name, Nala (derived from *naḍa*, 'reed'), is a clear indicator of the rainy season (von Simson 2005: 114).[80] It thus seems that the destruction of the Vṛṣṇi-Andhaka clan by the club/pestle (*musala*) not only reflects the pressing of *soma* (which again is a reflection of the meeting of *agni* and *soma* and of the monthly cycle), but, more specifically, the coming down of *soma* with the rain, this too being a Vedic concept (cf. Oberlies 1999: 40–2). At the same time, the sexual connotation of the *musala* is corroborated by the already Rigvedic identification of *soma* with *retas*, seminal fluid (ibid.: 42).

Sāmba, Śikhaṇḍin, and the solstices

Śiva is not only involved in the story of Sāmba, but also in that of Ambā/Śikhaṇḍin (on which see Chapters 9 and 10), and we have to ask ourselves whether there is any relation between these stories. We remember that Ambā, daughter of the king of Vārāṇasī and engaged to be married to Śālva, the king of Saubha, was abducted by Bhīṣma. Intent on taking revenge, she wins the favour of Śiva and, after committing suicide, is reborn as Śikhaṇḍinī, daughter of the Pāñcāla king Drupada. She finally succeeds in getting her sex converted so that she can confront Bhīṣma in the great battle as a man. Because of Śikhaṇḍin's past as a woman, Bhīṣma refuses to fight against him and can thus be subdued by the Pāṇḍavas on the tenth day of the battle. Here Śikhaṇḍin is placed in front of Arjuna who thus can shoot his deadly arrows against the defenceless Bhīṣma. Considering the multiple connections between Arjuna and Śiva described by Alf Hiltebeitel (1980b: 153–60), one could feel tempted to identify the pair Arjuna-Śikhaṇḍin here as Śiva Ardhanārīśvara, with Arjuna, who is often identified with the mythic figure Nara, representing the male and Śikhaṇḍin(ī) the female part. But Arjuna, according to the epic tradition, represents the god Indra, and as I would take Indra as a representative of the (full) moon, the scene rather means that the moon at the time of the winter solstice is able to conquer the old and declining sun of the *dakṣiṇāyana* at the moment when he allies himself with the young sun of the coming *uttarāyaṇa*. This is represented by Śikhaṇḍin, the sun which is still so weak that one may be in doubt as to whether it is man or woman. Born as a woman, the reborn Ambā, the female part of Śiva, is converted into Śikhaṇḍin, the male part of the god, whom I would consider to be an original sun god. The *Bhīṣmaparvan* scene thus reflects the winter solstice and the beginning of the *uttarāyaṇa* when Bhīṣma according to the unanimous *Mahābhārata* tradition has to die.

We thus recognize a clear distinction between the seasonal associations of Sāmba and Śikhaṇḍin: Śiva's and Umā's theophany in the *Anuśāsanaparvan* seems to refer to the summer solstice, the point of the year when the Great God's asceticism is neutralized by his sexual union with the Goddess and the rainy season is about to start. Kṛṣṇa's ascetic exercise bears fruit at precisely this point. He is granted the fulfilment of his wish to have a son with Jāmbavatī, and we may assume that this son's nature is in some way defined by the special circumstances of the situation, the meeting of Kṛṣṇa with the divine couple. If we compare this with the Śikhaṇḍin story, we notice a clear scheme of correspondences:

Point of year	*Moon*	*Sun*	*Results*
Winter solstice (persons involved:)	Full/white Arjuna	Weak Śikhaṇḍin	Arjuna + Śikhaṇḍin defeat Bhīṣma[81]
Summer solstice (persons involved:)	New/black Kṛṣṇa	Strong Śiva + Umā	Sāmba will be born; catastrophic results[82]

Śikhaṇḍin reflects the sexual ambiguity of the sun at a certain point of the year. The case of Sāmba is a little more complicated. He inherits the ambiguity of his biological father which is due to the ambiguity of the new-moon period; but this ambiguity seems to be enforced by the fact that the spiritual force that ensures his birth is both male and female, Śiva and Umā cooperating. In a way, Sāmba is the product of Viṣṇu-Kṛṣṇa's subordination to Śiva (by imitating the latter's asceticism), and this may be an explanation for his misbehaviour and the catastrophic events that follow from the redefinition of his sexual organ as a deadly weapon.

Sāmba and the North American trickster

The *Mahābhārata* story of Sāmba does not give a complete picture of this minor epic character. It is only when we take into account information given in the *Harivaṃśa* and later Purāṇas, including the *Sāmba Purāṇa*, that we get an idea of what role he might have played in the popular imagination of ancient India. The fact that he plays the part of the *vidūṣaka* in the theatre episode of the *Harivaṃśa* suggests that he represents one of those trickster characters that we encounter in so many cultures of the world, most prominently in the culture of the Indians of North America.[83] Like Sāmba, a bear figures as the grandfather (or at least as the grandmother's husband) of Nabozho, the trickster of the Algonquin-speaking Indians (Stein 1993: 264), and this is not the only point of resemblance. The trickster is a typical border-crossing character who violates the standards of civilized behaviour in many ways.[84] This would correspond to Sāmba's challenging the *ṛṣi*s and provoking their anger. Like Sāmba, who is cursed by the holy men when trying to make fun of them, and who is caught by the Kauravas when abducting Duryodhana's daughter Lakṣmaṇā,[85] Wakdjunkaga, the trickster of the Winnebago Indians, often gets himself into trouble when trying to make trouble for others (Stein 1993: 302–3). The result may be bodily repulsiveness: Sāmba is punished by leprosy, Wakdjunkaga in one episode by being covered by excrement.[86] Common to both characters is their sexual appetite:[87] Sāmba seduces the 16,000 wives of his father, and Wakdjunkaga is involved in a series of erotic adventures.[88] If our conjecture is correct, the pestle or club (*musala*) Sāmba delivers represents his penis, and likewise the motif of the detached penis is a characteristic of the trickster of North America,[89] a characteristic he would share with Śiva in the Pine Forest myth.[90] And like the *musala* of the Indian epic, this detached penis is often used as a weapon in the American trickster stories as well (Róheim 1952: 193). The death-bringing pestle is first converted into *erakā* blades, as we have seen, and these blades unfold their deadly effect during a drinking bout of the Vṛṣṇi-Andhaka clan. Similarly in one episode the American trickster binds lots of reeds on his back (as camouflage?) before persuading a flock of ducks to perform at a dancing party, on which occasion he starts killing the birds.[91]

What interests us particularly here is that, like Sāmba, the North American trickster is characterized by sexual ambiguity: in one episode he converts himself into a woman, marries the son of a chief, and even gives birth to children.[92]

But there are also positive features associated with both figures: Sāmba introduces the sun cult into India, and the American trickster presents features of a culture hero which are sometimes explicitly connected with his sexual character, as for instance when food plants grow from the remains of his penis.[93] At the end of his story cycle Wakdjunkaga is depicted as wandering along the Mississippi;[94] in the *Mahābhārata* Sāmba is said to accompany Balarāma on his riverine pilgrimage (*tīrthayātrā*), and according to some Purāṇas he establishes the first sun temple on the bank of the river Chenab. Does this reflect a very old tradition of the sacredness of water in general and of rivers in particular in both cultures?

It has to be noted that there exist some striking differences between Sāmba and his American counterpart as well. The American trickster is mostly depicted as a lonely wanderer[95] who gets into one adventure after another and seems unable to adapt himself to the social norms of his group,[96] whereas Sāmba is depicted as fully integrated into his family. The trickster's antagonists are often animals,[97] in relation to whom he displays an unusual degree of cruelty. He often kills them, driven by an insatiable hunger[98] – a motif that is missing with Sāmba, as is the American trickster's scatological side (one of the recurrent themes in his stories), which adds to the impression of his infantility and invites a Freudian analysis (Stein 1993: 298–300).

Regarding Sāmba, we must be aware that we are unable to tell whether the puzzle pieces we gathered from different Sanskrit sources yield a roughly complete picture of him. Some of the more repulsive features of his character may have been eroded when he was converted into one of the five heroes of the Vṛṣṇi clan, and we have to remember that the Vedic Rudra also, the predecessor of the later Śiva (with whom Sāmba as we have seen has several features in common), was mainly depicted as a dreaded and harmful god before he too, in later Hinduism, adopted more positive features. On the other hand, Sāmba's father Kṛṣṇa shows clear trickster features, particularly in the Puranic childhood stories of the god-hero, but also as Yogeśvara, 'the Master of Stratagems' in the *Mahābhārata* war (Mehendale 1995a: 29–45). And we must not forget that with reference to Sāmba the epic particularly emphasizes the likeness of father and son.

Conclusion

We return finally to the issue of gender in the *Mahābhārata*. Though the context of the story of Sāmba's prehistory in the *Anuśāsanaparvan* shows that issues of sex and gender indeed contributed to the motivation of the epic authors, the analysis of all available information reveals a subtle net of relations which can best be explained if we take into account the metaphorical use of the phenomena of nature. Only then does the gender issue find its proper place. The experience of nature with its monthly and annual cycles and the experience of sex/gender are both primary human experiences, and it is certainly not a specific feature of Indian culture that the imagination of their priests and poets tried to see parallels between them. What are specific are the climatic conditions prevailing in India and, in addition, the rather unusual circumstance that both sun and moon were normally regarded as male. At the most critical point of the annual cycle, the winter solstice, when the sun is in its weakest phase, an ambiguity of its gender could therefore be expressed by the figure of Śikhaṇḍin, a gender-changing human being who had to assist Arjuna, the representative of the – bright, strong, and at this point of the year doubtless male[99] – moon in overcoming Bhīṣma, the aged sun of the expiring year. Sāmba, on the other hand, seems to symbolize the moon in its most critical phase, the new-moon period; hence his cross-dressing, his disguise as a pregnant woman. But whereas pregnancy is normally regarded as something auspicious, associated with fertility and the expectation of a child, this pregnancy is stamped with inauspiciousness. Sāmba remains male, and the pregnancy results in the birth of a disastrous weapon. If our interpretation is correct, the hidden penis of the disguised male becomes manifest as a weapon multiplied into many weapons (on the metaphorical level: the thunderbolts of the rainy season with their destructive force). The inauspiciousness must in our view be explained by the special conditions of the Indian climate. At the summer solstice, when the sun god Śiva reaches the climax of his power and marries Pārvatī, the daughter of the Himālaya in the north, the birth-giving new-moon period inaugurates the annual monsoon period, a symbol of chaos, when both sun and moon disappear for a time and give way to demonic powers.

There thus exists a close interdependence of gender symbolism and the symbolism of natural phenomena.[100] A detailed study of the *Mahābhārata* can help us to gain a better understanding of both, and thereby of ancient Indian culture in general.

Notes

1 Even if the idea of pregnant or procreating males occurs more than once in the *Mahābhārata* (see Custodi 2005: 100–54) and elsewhere in the ancient Indian tradition (see O'Flaherty 1980: *passim*), the case of Sāmba, where a sexual masquerade unleashes dire effects, seems to be unique.

2 See Mani 1979: 677–8; Dikshitar 1995, vol. 3: 586–7; Dange 1989: 1254–5.

3 There is another Sāmba in the *Mahābhārata* (15.15.11), a brahmin whom the citizens of Hāstinapura entrust with delivering the goodbye address for Dhṛtarāṣṭra when the old king is about to retire into the woods. This brahmin does not bear any resemblance to Kṛṣṇa's son Sāmba, and it is not easy to see why the authors of the epic chose this unusual name for this minor epic figure, who is not mentioned elsewhere. Perhaps the reason is the name's Śaiva connection? In some manuscripts the name Śakalya or Śākalya is given instead of Sāmba/Śāmba, and a Śākalya is mentioned (13.14.68) among the worshippers of Śiva in the Upamanyu story, which also contains the prehistory of the birth of Kṛṣṇa's son Sāmba (see p. 235).

4 Passages where Sāmba and Pradyumna are mentioned together without any intervening names are 1.211.9; 1.213.27; 2.app1.12; 2.4.29; 3.17.9; 3.120.4; 3.223.10; 5.1.5.
5 3.16.9; 5.154.16; 10.12.32; 14.65.3.
6 2.31.15; 3.48.24; 5.3.19; 7.10.27. The close association of Sāmba with Pradyumna and Gada is continued in the *Harivaṃśa*, where Pradyumna is accompanied by these two heroes in his expedition against Vajranābha.
7 He even subdues Śālva's generals Kṣemavṛddhi and Vegavat (3.17). He is also praised by Sātyaki for his former successful fight against the army of the demon Śambara (3.120.12–14).
8 The *Harivaṃśa* shows him in a less flattering light in an episode where he is caught when trying to abduct Duryodhana's daughter, and Balarāma must intervene to get him free (*Harivaṃśa* 90.8–12; cf. *Viṣṇu Purāṇa* 5.35; *Bhāgavata Purāṇa* 10.65).
9 The curse never ceases to be a popular means of explanation in Indian literature; see for example, for the vernacular *Rāmāyaṇa* epics, W.L. Smith 1986.
10 '(Kṛṣṇa) Vāsudeva, who wanted to make it [i.e. the curse] true' (*vāsudevas . . . cikīrṣan satyam eva tat*, 16.3.21).
11 Similar versions of this story are told in *Viṣṇu Purāṇa* 5.37.6–9; *Bhāgavata Purāṇa* 11.1.11–16.
12 On the 'social opprobrium' attributed to eunuchs and men disguised as women in both ancient and modern India, see Hiltebeitel 1980b: 162 (in connection with Arjuna disguised as Bṛhannaḍā in the *Virāṭaparvan* of the *Mahābhārata*).
13 On Odin's gender ambiguity and association with *seid* and *ergi*, see Solli 2002: 128ff. and *passim*. If the authors of the *Mahābhārata* had similar ideas, the request directed to the *ṛṣi*s to foretell the nature of the child could have been considered offensive because this kind of divinatory activity belonged to the domain of women.
14 See particularly the myth of Odin who in the shape of an eagle fetches the divine mead out of the mountain, and the myth of Viṣṇu's bird Garuḍa who fetches the *soma* from Indra's heaven.
15 *Mahābhārata* 1.16.39. On this myth, see Doniger 1999: 261–2; for parallel stories, see pp. 260–302. It is interesting that even today the Indian *hijra*s (transvestite eunuchs), to legitimize themselves, tell a story about Kṛṣṇa turned into a woman (ibid.: 265, referring to Nanda 1990: 20–1).
16 'One unique feature of Indian iconography is that each of the divinities . . . is endowed with two basic forms: the *saumya* (benign) and the *raudra* (wrathful)' (D.C. Bhattacharyya 1980: 7). Note that *saumya* is derived from *soma* 'moon', and *raudra* from *rudra*, which is frequently a name for Śiva Mahādeva and the main name of his Vedic predecessor.
17 O'Flaherty 1980: 328. On Hari-Hara images, their theological meaning, and their expression of differential gender estimation, see Goldberg 2002: 52–5. D.C. Bhattacharyya (1980: 11–12) quotes the iconographic text *Kāśyapaśilpa* (73.1–9) which prescribes a fearful expression (*ugradṛṣṭi*) for the right (= Śiva) half of the face of a Hari-Hara figure, and a serene (*suśītala*) expression for the left (= Viṣṇu) half. Concerning the relation between Umā and Viṣṇu-Kṛṣṇa see *Kūrma Purāṇa* 1.24.89, in the theophany scene which we will discuss later: Umā emphasizes that there is no difference between Kṛṣṇa and herself (*nāvayor vidyate bheda ekaṃ paśyanti sūrayaḥ //*). She is here presented as *śaṃkarārdhaśarīriṇī* ('possessing half of Śiva's body', 1.24.86), an expression that is apparently meant to remind the reader of Śiva Ardhanārīśvara. In the next *adhyāya* (1.25.60) the identity between Kṛṣṇa (Viṣṇu) and Śiva is also stated.
18 The question of the difference in sexual experience is discussed in the erotic literature of ancient India: see for example *Kāmasūtra* 2.1, where the author, after a lengthy discussion, finally arrives at the conclusion that the pleasure

must be similar for man and woman (*tenobhayor api sadṛśī sukhapratipattir iti*, 2.1.62).

19 On the Bhaṅgāśvana story see O'Flaherty 1980: 305–6. If we follow O'Flaherty, the basic idea is that women should not enjoy sex, and that one who does can be regarded as a phallic woman, a woman who deprives the male of his own virility. This would establish an even closer connection between the stories of Bhaṅgāśvana converted into a woman and Sāmba dressed as a woman: in both cases we would meet the idea of the hidden penis (see p. 238).

20 The term *ghana* in the *Ṛgveda* has the meaning of a crushing weapon or club: could this be understood as a foreboding of the *musala* which will be brought forth by Sāmba?

21 *sutānāṃ . . . śataṃ śatāni*, 13.16.2; the expression may also mean '10,000'.

22 *Śiva Purāṇa* (Rāmateja's edition) 7, *Vāyusaṃhitā*, *Uttarabhāga*, *adhyāya* 1 (this *adhyāya* is missing from Bareli's edition of 1966, and from Pañcānana Tarkaratna's Calcutta edition of Śaka Era 1812, i.e. 1890 CE).

23 According to Mani 1979: 677, this is also the case in *Devībhāgavata Purāṇa*, *skandha* 4.

24 Kṛṣṇa is here identified with Viṣṇu (v. 24).

25 *kṛṣṇaḥ . . . / tapaś cakāra putrārthaṃ sāmbam uddiśya śaṃkaram //* v. 21.

26 *tapasā tena varṣānte dṛṣṭo 'sau parameśvaraḥ / śriyā paramayā yuktaḥ sāmbaś ca sagaṇaḥ śivaḥ //* v. 22.

27 *yasmāt sāmbo mahādevaḥ pradadau putram ātmanaḥ / tasmāj jāmbavatīsūnuṃ sāmbaṃ cakre sa nāmataḥ //* v. 25.

28 Instead of *sāmba*, Śiva can in fact be called *soma* (= *sa* + *umā*). See for example *Śiva Purāṇa* (Tarkaratna's edition; see n. 22), *Vāyavīsaṃhitā*, *Uttarabhāga*, 1.1: *namaḥ śivāya somāya sagaṇāya sasūnave /*. In the *Kūrma Purāṇa*, too, we find that in this scene Śiva is described as manifesting himself in the sky '*somaḥ*', in the sense of 'accompanied by Umā': *tato bahutithe kāle somaḥ somārdhabhūṣaṇaḥ / adṛśyata mahādevo vyomni devyā maheśvaraḥ //* 1.24.51; cf. v. 79. See also Bhattacharyya's interpretation of the term *dvā-someśvara* in the Gaya Śītala temple inscription (eleventh century) as 'the form showing the two deities (*dvā*): Īśvara or Śiva with (*sa*) Umā' (D.C. Bhattacharyya 1980: 27).

29 For the Vedic ritual being used as model for the plot of the *Mahābhārata*, see Oberlies 1995 (with references to further literature).

30 The word *musala* normally designates the pestle used to grind grain in the *ulūkhala* (mortar).

31 Cf. Oberlies 1999: 140: 'ein keulenförmiges Pistill'.

32 *Mahābhārata* 9.29–53; cf. Hiltebeitel 2001a: 140–54. On this and other pilgrimages in the *Mahābhārata* see also Oberlies 1995; Bigger 2001.

33 *prabhāsaṃ paramaṃ tīrthaṃ sarasvatyā(ḥ)*, 9.34.69.

34 The name means, in this context quite appropriately, 'splendour'.

35 'The whole story has been related to you of how the moon was cursed and how Prabhāsa became the foremost of the holy places' (*etat te sarvam ākhyātaṃ yathā śapto niśākaraḥ / prabhāsaṃ ca yathā tīrthaṃ tīrthānāṃ pravaraṃ hy abhūt //* 9.34.75).

36 Trita Āptya is already known in the *Ṛgveda* and has his roots in Indo-Iranian tradition.

37 'Imagining that that plant was *soma*' (*tāṃ vīrudhaṃ somaṃ saṃkalpya*, 9.35.33).

38 The name Trita is derived from the numeral three as the names of his brothers, Ekata and Dvita, are from the numerals one and two.

39 The context makes it probable that *daṃṣṭrin* is to be translated by 'wolf' here; the Vulgate reading (*vṛkākṛtī*, 'having the shape of wolves') is more explicit.

40 *prasavaś caiva yuvayor golāṅgūlarkṣavānarāḥ* // 9.35.50.
41 The *Smaradīpikā*, a treatise on erotics, compares the penis with a *musala*; see quotation in R. Schmidt 1922: 256.
42 Cf. the Norse story of the stolen hammer of the god Thor, told in 'The Lay of Thrym' in the Edda: here Thor, in order to get back his weapon that was stolen by the giant Thrym, is disguised as a bride, the goddess Freyja whom the giant wants to marry. When the latter lays the hammer on the bride's lap(!), Thor grabs it and kills Thrym and all the other giants. Doniger (1999: 262–3) underlines the similarity with the Indian myth of Viṣṇu as Mohinī.
43 On Balarāma, see von Simson forthcoming.
44 'Conjunction' as an astronomical term signifies the coincidence of moon and sun at the same celestial longitude, which means new moon, when the moon is invisible. This is not equivalent to an eclipse of the sun, because normally moon and sun pass each other at slightly different celestial latitudes.
45 For Arjuna representing the white and Kṛṣṇa the black or invisible moon, see von Simson 1984: 197.
46 Cf. also *Taittirīya Saṃhitā* 3.5.1.4, where Sarasvatī, the female goddess, is identified with the new moon, and Sarasvat, her male equivalent, with the full moon.
47 At the first occurrence, 5.35.39 (= 5.35.46 in the Vulgate), Nīlakaṇṭha gives the meaning '*śarakṛt*', 'maker of arrows' (thus Ganguli), 'arrow-wright' (thus van Buitenen), which does not seem to fit well in the context. Besides, an arrow-wright would rather remove the knots (on the shaft) than make them.
48 The *pañcavīra* concept does not yet appear in the *Mahābhārata*, where Aniruddha as Kṛṣṇa's grandson – though not unknown to the epic poets – would anyway have been too young to play any major part in the main plot. At 2.13.56 Sāmba belongs to a group of seven Vṛṣṇi heroes, the six others being Cārudeṣṇa, his brother, Cakradeva, Sātyaki, Kṛṣṇa, and Pradyumna.
49 For the problem of the *vyūha*s and the question of the priority of the *pañcavīra*s in relation to them, see Bock-Raming 2002: 313–20. In the *Mahābhārata* the *vyūha*s (sometimes called *mūrti*s, 'shapes') are mentioned at 6.61.64–7 (as *paramaṃ guhyaṃ*, 'highest secret'); 12.326.31–9; 12.336.53; 13.143.37; see Grünendahl 1997: 213–15. All these passages are part of or closely related to the *Nārāyaṇīya* (*Mahābhārata* 12.321–39), which belongs to the youngest layers of the epic (for a thorough analysis see Schreiner 1997). As they do not contain any reference to Sāmba, they will not be further discussed here.
50 The name Balarāma is late and does not appear in the *Mahābhārata*. Bigger, who takes only the evidence of the *Mahābhārata* into consideration, thus denies the identity of Balarāma and Saṃkarṣaṇa (Bigger 1998: 62–4). There is, on the other hand, good evidence for the name Baladeva for Kṛṣṇa's elder brother. His two attributes, the pestle (*musala*) and the plough (*hala*), might refer to shapes of the waning moon, and his capacity to handle them could have resulted in his name 'God of Strength' (*bala-deva*); see von Simson forthcoming.
51 The *vyūha* Pradyumna is identified with the divine Sanatkumāra, 'the Eternal Youth', and with Kāma, the god of love.
52 According to the Vedic ritual literature, the full-moon ritual (*paurṇamāsya*) symbolizes Indra's victory over Vṛtra; see for example *Śatapatha Brāhmaṇa* 1.6.4.2–12; *Kauṣītaki Brāhmaṇa* 3.5.15–16.
53 At 12.326.69 this idea is further developed: Brahmā, the creator of the world, emanates from Aniruddha's navel, and Aniruddha is a shape taken by Kṛṣṇa. Cf. also 12.335.16–18.
54 *śvetaṃ candraviśuddhābham aniruddhatanau sthitam* / 12.335.57.
55 This happened seven days after Pradyumna was born, so both children according

to the *Harivaṃśa* were born within a period of some weeks only. This is probably an older tradition than that of the *Anuśāsanaparvan* which says that at the time when Jāmbavatī announced her wish to have a son, twelve years had already passed since Pradyumna had slain Śambara (13.14.12).

56 In the Critical Edition the episode is relegated to the apparatus (appendix 29F).

57 The story of Kṛṣṇa winning Jāmbavatī as his wife after overpowering the bear in his cave is told in *Harivaṃśa* 28. The real object in dispute in this lengthy story is the Syamantaka jewel. For the Purāṇa version of the Syamantaka story, see Kirfel 1927: 437ff.

58 Both verses are in *triṣṭubh* meter.

59 The *Sūryā-Sūkta* (*Ṛgveda* 10.85), which celebrates the solemn marriage ritual against the background of the marriage (astronomically the conjunction) of sun (here represented by his daughter Sūryā) and moon (*soma*), is followed by the *Vṛṣākapi-Sūkta* (*Ṛgveda* 10.86), a burlesque celebrating sexuality and fertility. Here, in my opinion, the moon is split into its two aspects, the white moon (Indra), and the black moon masquerading as the virile monkey Vṛṣākapi, Indra's companion and best friend (like Viṣṇu elsewhere in the *Ṛgveda*), who in the context of marriage has to perform the sexual act. A linguistic connection with the *vidūṣaka* is given by the verbal form *vy adūduṣat* (*Ṛgveda* 10.86.5), and with Viṣṇu-Kṛṣṇa by Vṛṣākapi's epithet *janayopana* (10.86.22), which corresponds to Kṛṣṇa's common epithet *janārdana* ('exciting or agitating men': people get nervous when the moon changes!).

60 Govinda is a frequent name for Kṛṣṇa in the *Mahābhārata*.

61 13.24.35; 13.87.17–19; 13.92.19; cf. also 13.91.12 (the first *śrāddha* was performed by Nimi at new moon); see also Kane 1968–77, vol. 4: 369 ('Śrāddha originally meant a sacrifice performed for the Fathers on Amāvāsyā').

62 *rattaṃsuajualeṇa itthiāvesaṃ vihia* (i.e. *raktāṃśuyugalena strīveṣaṃ vidhāya*), *Nāgānanda* 3.5. Note that *aṃśu* may mean both 'thread, cloth, garment' and 'sunbeam'.

63 *kabilamaṃkaḍaa*, *Nāgānanda* 3.16 (cf. 3.20 and 3.60).

64 In order to persuade the *vidūṣaka* to allow his face to be painted black, Navamālikā flatters him, calling him 'handsome' when sleeping; this is hardly more than a trick and would probably be understood as irony by the audience.

65 *ajja tumaṃ mae vivāhajāgaraṇe nijjāamāṇanimīliaacho sohaṇo diṭṭho* (i.e. *ārya tvaṃ mayā vivāhajāgaraṇe nidrāyamāṇanimīlitākṣaḥ śobhano dṛṣṭaḥ*) / *Nāgānanda* 3.61.

66 The scene takes place early in the morning (*pabhāde*, i.e. *prabhāte*, 3.3).

67 One may however note that the poet uses Kṛṣṇa's family as points of comparison: the drunk *viṭa* compares himself with Baladeva (= Balarāma) and with Kāmadeva (who is regularly identified with Sāmba's half-brother Pradyumna) (*Nāgānanda* 3.1: verse 32).

68 On Sāmba's gradually falling into disgrace with the Bhāgavatas and the possible reasons for this development (his association with Śiva, his introducing an Iranian sun cult, his being descended from a monkey king, his incestuous conduct with his 16,000 stepmothers, and his being the cause of the annihilation of the Yādavas), see Banerjea 1944: 90–1.

69 *Sāmba Purāṇa* 3.6ff. = *Bhaviṣya Purāṇa* 1.72.10ff.; see von Stietencron 1966: 30–1 (text), 126–7 (German translation). See also *Skanda Purāṇa* 4.48; 6.213.

70 The text relates that he is handsome to begin with, but this seems to be no more than a prerequisite of his later ugliness, the latter probably being the original feature which had to be explained by the aetiological story.

71 See also *Sāmba Purāṇa* 24.28–9; von Stietencron 1966: 41, 136.

72 *Sāmba Purāṇa* 3.48ff.; von Stietencron 1966: 35, 130–1.

73 *Bhaviṣya Purāṇa* 1.72.14–20, 51–2; von Stietencron 1966: 51–3, 145–7. Only the leprosy is an appropriate punishment for Sāmba's misbehaviour, whereas the birth of the pestle seems to be due to tradition and not further motivated.
74 According to *Harivaṃśa* 25.7, Gada is a son of Vasudeva's wife Sunāmā.
75 The *Kūrma Purāṇa* version insists in a peculiar way on the term *ātman* in one of the verses that Umā speaks to Kṛṣṇa: *paśya tvam ātmanātmānam ātmīyam amalaṃ padam* / 1.24.89. In the preceding verse the goddess addresses him as Sarvātman, 'the *Ātman*/Self of the Universe', but cf. '*viśvātmanā*' referring to Śiva at 1.24.85.
76 According to *Śiva Purāṇa* 7 (*Vāyusaṃhitā*), 2 (*Uttarabhāga*), 1.22, the theophany takes place at the end of the rainy season (*varṣānte*).
77 The mention of *vasanta* (spring) is, as far as I can see, the only explicit reference to the seasons of the year; the rest follows by implication.
78 This would be in keeping with my symbolic year-myth scheme for the whole *Mahābhārata*, where I tentatively place the *Mausalaparvan* in the rainy season (von Simson 1994: 237).
79 16.4.35, 37; cf. 16.4.39 (*tad vajrabhūtaṃ musalaṃ vyadṛśyata tadā*, 'then that club, converted into a thunderbolt, became manifest').
80 This *naḍa*/*nala* ('reed') appears also in 'Bṛhannaḍā/Bṛhannalā', the name Arjuna assumes while in disguise at the court of King Virāṭa; see Hiltebeitel 1980b: 160. The *Virāṭaparvan* too in my opinion represents the rainy season (von Simson 1994: 237, 240).
81 Bhīṣma represents the old sun which is to die at the beginning of the *uttarāyaṇa*.
82 The catastrophic results take place in the rainy season (according to the mythical year scheme of the *Mahābhārata*), following immediately after the summer solstice.
83 Babcock-Abrahams 1975; Hynes and Doty 1993. For texts and commentaries, see Radin 1979; Stein 1993.
84 For examples see Stein 1993: 302. Róheim (1952: 193), using Freudian concepts, tries to explain this on a psychoanalytical basis: 'Id as hero is a counterbalance to social pressure.'
85 *Harivaṃśa* 90.8; see also Mani 1979: 677.
86 Episode no. 24; see Radin 1972: 27; Stein 1993: 121.
87 This is one of the basic features of the American trickster (Radin 1972: 167; Stein 1993: 142).
88 For examples see Stein 1993: 301.
89 Episode nos. 15–16; see Radin 1972: 18–20; Stein 1993: 112–14 (Wakdjunkaga), 280 (Nabozho).
90 Mani 1979: 728–9 (item 16.1); O'Flaherty 1973: 180.
91 Episode no. 12; see Radin 1972: 14–16; Stein 1993: 109–11.
92 Episode nos. 19–20; see Radin 1972: 22–3; Stein 1993: 116–17 (Wakdjunkaga), 280 (Nabozho).
93 Episode no. 39; see Radin 1972: 39; Stein 1993: 132.
94 Episode no. 47; see Radin 1972: 52; Stein 1993: 139.
95 Radin (1972: 165) emphasizes his 'uncontrollable urge to wander'; cf. Stein 1993: 309.
96 'Er ist unfähig, sich in eine soziale Gemeinschaft einzufügen' (Stein 1993: 304).
97 The trickster himself sometimes appears as an animal or with the name of an animal, e.g. Hare, Coyote.
98 Radin 1972: 165, 167; Stein 1993: 142 (the trickster's hunger as his basic motive), 302 (his aggressiveness and destructive behaviour).
99 Arjuna's sexual ambiguity as Bṛhannaḍā (in the *Virāṭaparvan*) reflects in my view another season of the year, the rainy season, when the bright moon is under cover as it were.

100 It is beyond the scope of this chapter to attempt a similar analysis for the American trickster. As Wolfgang Stein points out, there have been several attempts to explain him on the basis of lunar mythology (Stein 1993: 38, 48–9), which were *en vogue* in the first part of the last century. As he correctly remarks, astral-mythological explanations are today generally rejected, mainly as a result of the extremely one-sided interpretations produced by this school in the past (ibid.: 126). However, exaggeration and misuse of a certain theoretical approach is hardly a sufficient reason for its complete rejection. The analysis of the *Mahābhārata* as a whole has convinced me that metaphorical references to phenomena of nature indeed pervade the epic on a certain level and that this approach helps us to understand details that would otherwise remain unexplained.

12

PARADIGMS OF THE GOOD IN THE *MAHĀBHĀRATA*

Śuka and Sulabhā in quagmires of ethics

Arti Dhand

Although the *Mahābhārata* is arguably a text devoted to *śānti* (peace, tranquility) and the achievement of *mukti* (i.e. *mokṣa*), actual models of enlightened souls are few.[1] Several enlightened figures are mentioned in the work: Mudgala, Medhāvin, Asita Devala, Jaigīśavya, Sanatkumāra, and Mārkaṇḍeya, among others. Studying references to these characters, however, we learn very little about them beyond what we may infer from the detritus of other tales: that the *mukta* have privileged knowledge of people's thoughts and actions, that they pass freely through portals of space and time; that they have a penchant for being somewhat meddlesome, with a knack for turning up in moments of nail-biting intensity; that they are, of course, beyond death. Other than this, the presence of the *mukta* is shadowy, hazy; they exist like blurred, out-of-focus figures in otherwise sharply vivid family photographs. Two exceptions to this pattern might be Śuka (12.309–18), the son of the author Vyāsa, and to a lesser extent Sulabhā (12.308), the *bhikṣukī* (female mendicant) who matches wits with King Janaka in the *Śāntiparvan*. The narrative of Śuka tells us something about the path to a complete and final acorporeal freedom from the world, for which one shuns all attachment and proceeds on the course of eternity along a solitary path. The story of Sulabhā informs us about the values associated with an enlightened mind, and presents a figure who, although apparently possessing liberating knowledge, nevertheless remains active in the world. Both accounts deal with renunciation and the sacrifices it entails.[2] In the following, I will analyse these narratives with a view to observing both the social aspects of renunciation and the personal ones. My ultimate interest is in the *ethical* import of the *brahmavādin*'s actions as they valorize or contest the persistent categories by which Hinduism orders society. While *brahmanirvāṇam* implies the absolute purge of social values, it would nevertheless appear that the *brahmavādin*'s acts are yet circumscribed by social biases to which s/he pays a muted ideological deference. These matters are of concern to an ethicist. The *Mahābhārata* is a key scriptural text of Hinduism, with tremendous power to shape and form the imagination of modern Hindus. This given, its ethical stances bear scrutiny. What enlightened perspectives do the *mukta* bring to questions of entrenched social hierarchies? Given the text's leanings toward an ethics of non-harm, how do these speak to concerns of social justice? By focusing on two case studies of the *mukta*, I hope to elicit some critical answers to these contemporary questions, bearing in mind that the epics are works that continue to have profound relevance for Hindus.

Śuka

While Hindu texts typically speak enthusiastically about *mokṣa* as a goal, indeed the most worthy of goals, they are more reticent about offering descriptions of the substantive content of *mokṣa*. From this standpoint, the narrative of Śuka is a rarity. In *Śāntiparvan* 309–18 we follow Śuka from the first instructions he receives from his father, to his eventual success in attaining that highly elusive state. The story begins with Vyāsa strongly urging Śuka to shun the lures of the world and to set his goals high. Vyāsa tells him:

> In this existence, the Self lives in a body that is akin to a water bubble. Son! How can you sleep in this transient abode, however pleasant it is? Why don't you realize, child, that the foes internally corrupt the mind and are alert, awake, always ready for action? As the years go by, longevity decreases and life becomes shorter, child! Why don't you get up and flee?
>
> (12.309.6–8)[3]

With the zeal of what in Canada we call a 'hockey dad', an excessively ambitious father, Vyāsa nudges Śuka on, using colourful imagery to impress upon his son that death waits for nobody.

> I try to expound thousands of enlightening examples. However, there is no point in cooking barley if the master does not turn up.
>
> (12.309.61)[4]

> Go! Why do you remain idle?
>
> (12.309.33)[5]

> You have passed sixteen years . . . You are getting old!
>
> (12.309.62)[6]

> What is the use of wealth, kinsmen and sons when you die? Where

> have all our forefathers gone? Seek the *ātman* that is hidden in a cave. What is to be done tomorrow must be done today! What is planned for the afternoon should be completed in the forenoon! The agents of death do not look into things like whether a person is going to do things today or tomorrow.
>
> (12.309.71–2)[7]

> While the barley of noblemen is yet cooking, they will be whisked away by death. So hurry!
>
> (12.309.48)[8]

Vyāsa is unrelenting in his insistence, dwelling with prophetic vehemence on the subject of imminent death:

> Lord Yama (the god of death), who knows no sorrow, will soon take the lives of the entire clan – yours and your relatives'! Nobody will be able to stop him then.
>
> (12.309.35)[9]

> The death-wind will soon blow. On the onset of great fear the quarters of the sky will whirl around in your presence. Your memory, Son, will also soon be blocked in that great confusion . . .
>
> (12.309.37–8)[10]

> Old age will soon weaken your body and take away its strength and the beauty of its limbs . . . Soon the Lord of Death will violently pierce your body with the arrows of diseases . . . Frightening wolves moving in the human body will soon attack on all sides . . .
>
> (12.309.40–2)[11]

So vivid and compelling are Vyāsa's images of imminent apocalyptic doom that Śuka is moved to action. He departs to receive further instruction from the famously sage king of Mithilā, Janaka. Janaka, of course, is the legendary monarch of Upanishadic lore who outclasses the brahmins in knowledge of the Absolute and eventually becomes their teacher.[12] After travelling long but without exhaustion, and after remaining unmoved even when in the company of the most alluring women, Śuka eventually meets Janaka, who confirms him in his knowledge and meditative accomplishments. His confidence thus boosted, Śuka returns to live quietly with his father until once again urged, this time perhaps mischievously by Nārada in Vyāsa's absence, to undertake the radical path of no return. Now Śuka sets himself to the task without equivocation. He is impervious even to his father's plea for a one-night delay, and thus becomes the only figure in the *Mahābhārata* whose trajectory into *mokṣa* is charted in detail.

Sulabhā

The story of Sulabhā directly precedes the Śuka episode in *Śāntiparvan* 308, and is recounted to the ever-earnest Yudhiṣṭhira by the ailing yet loquacious Bhīṣma. Sulabhā is described as a peripatetic *bhikṣukī* (mendicant) who, happening through the town of Mithilā and having heard much about the wisdom once again of its ubiquitous sovereign Janaka, tarries a day to test him. It is quite striking that both *Mahābhārata* stories should have chosen to employ a Janaka. While Śuka's Janaka, however, is comfortable in his traditional role as the dispenser of uncommonly insightful royal advice, the Janaka of Sulabhā is presented as a brash and boastful man, a callow amateur at the game of *mokṣa*. The story goes as follows.

Encountering Sulabhā disguised as a strikingly beautiful young mendicant, Janaka is overcome with curiosity. He invites her into his palace and greets her with the appropriate rites, but is perplexed to find her entering not only his palace but also, through her *yoga* prowess, his body and mind. This disconcerts him, and shortly into their conversation Janaka launches into a *vita* of his accomplishments. Somewhat defensively, Janaka insists that even though he retains his royal sceptre, he is *mukta*, free, and as wise and perfected as any renouncer may be. Indeed, he argues, warming to his subject, his wisdom exceeds hers, because she has committed cardinal sins in violating his body – sexual sins of *varṇasaṃkara* (intermingling of *varṇa*s) and *āśramasaṃkara* (mixing of the stages of life). Viewing her possession of him as some kinky form of sexual union, he berates her for her lack of propriety.

> Through your mental contact with me, you have destroyed me. This is another sin of yours. I see in you clearly signs of a deceitful wicked woman. You want to exert power over others. Your intention is not to defeat me alone. You wish to subjugate my entire court. Again you look askance at me. That is to disparage my followers and glorify yourself. Being jealous of my powers and deluded by a desire for supremacy over me, you released the weapon of *yoga* that mingled the nectar with poison. The sexual enjoyment of man and woman who are in love is equal to the taste of nectar. But if the man does not love the woman then their union is devoid of pleasure. The detrimental effect of this union is venomous. Do not touch me. Understand thoroughly. Follow your scriptures. You did all this apparently out of your desire to learn if I am liberated, but in fact you conceal secret motives.
>
> (12.308.65–70)[13]

Sulabhā hears out his rant, and then gives an apt response. First she tackles the question of who she is. In proto-Sāṃkhya categories, she describes a human being as the composite of various strands of matter (12.308.96–125).[14] Finally, she comes to the point:

> You see the Self within yourself with the knowledge of the Self. But if you have attained impartiality, why can't you see the Self in others by the same knowledge? . . . O king of Mithilā! To one who is freed of duality, what is the use of the questions: Who are you? Whose are you? From where have you come?
>
> (12.308.126–7)[15]

Sulabhā suggests to Janaka that his understanding of reality is as yet worldly and naïve.

> If a person who claims to be free treats his enemy, friend, and neutral in war and peace in the same manner as an ordinary man does, does he have any signs of his liberated state?
>
> (12.308.128)[16]

> Therefore you are unworthy of freedom. Supposing you have a desire for it, it should be nipped by your friends as an insane person is treated with medicine.
>
> (12.308.131)[17]

> I am free. I have no connection with my own body. How could it be that I am in contact with the bodies of others?
>
> (12.308.162)[18]

Janaka has no rejoinder for Sulabhā, and the story ends there.

This is a marvelous story for many reasons. It represents a series of reversals and subversions each of which is worth pondering in its own right. First, it shows the humbling of a man by a woman – an event for which there are *some* precedents in the *Mahābhārata*, but which runs decidedly counter to the sexual ideology of the text. Second, it shows the humbling of a Janaka, a monarch famed in legend and lore – indeed, the one who in the Śuka story directly following is the critical dispenser of liberating wisdom – by one who is by all accounts an ordinary mendicant woman. Finally, as Sutton (1999) and Fitzgerald (2002b) have pointed out, it is a powerful denial of the viability of the *karmayoga* doctrine; indeed, an explicit rebuttal of it. Whereas, arguably, the bulk of the *Mahābhārata* didactus is aimed at contending that the highest religious goals *are* achievable while still conforming to *varṇāśramadharma*, Sulabhā's questioning of Janaka expresses great scepticism about this. She upholds a renouncer's standard that true liberating wisdom is *not* possible when one is immersed in the day-to-day business of living life.

Comparing Śuka and Sulabhā

Śuka and Sulabhā, although both relatively minor figures in the *Mahābhārata*, are intriguing because they belong to that elite class of individuals who have mastered the highest religious teachings of the text. Their narratives are presented back to back, hence clearly they are intended to be read in tandem. One is a tale about a man's successful pursuit of *videhamukti*, a freedom premised upon a complete abandonment of the corporeal state; the other would seem to be a tale about a woman living in a state of *jīvanmukti*. Read together, the texts reveal some intriguing thematic connections. Both narratives play with the subject of renunciation. Renunciation, of course, is both a social and a profoundly personal act; in one move, one abandons the values of society as well as all of one's personal relationships and attachments. In what follows, I reflect on the social aspects by observing the *brahmavādin*'s relationship to the congeries of themes surrounding gender and *varṇa*. Following that, I take account of the personal dimension of renunciation highlighted here to poignant effect. What is the literary value of placing the Śuka and Sulabhā stories adjacent to each other?

Gender

While *mokṣadharma* tracts generally disavow constructs of *varṇa* and gender as transient and labile, hence of no ultimate consequence, we know from experience that these are wily and tenacious hierarchies deeply embedded in the warp and woof of Hindu thought; when barred from the front, they are often admitted through the back door. A typical rhetorical move by commentators, for example, is to insist upon the necessity of scriptural study for the achievement of *mokṣa*. Where study of scripture is not permitted to women and *śūdra*s, this of course has the effect of saying that *mokṣa* is in fact not for the lowly; thus the gender and class prejudices of orthodoxy are reinstated even as they are rhetorically denied. To what extent does the *mukta* state of Śuka or Sulabhā prolong or contest these worldly patterns?

Gender play is a significant motif of both tales. In the case of Śuka, to begin with, his father illustrates the meaninglessness of worldly life specifically by deconstructing the facade of wife and family. Ever a good student, Śuka absorbs this, and eventually his achievement is tested through the time-honoured trope of the Indic traditions: his exposure to gorgeous women in varying states of dishabille. We are told that Śuka does not even *need* to resist their charms in Janaka's palace; he is utterly immune to them. Later, our confidence in his detachment is reinforced by the fact that the nymphs of the forest can sport in complete comfort in his presence, even though they are quite unclad. He has moved beyond sex, as one nymph observes; masculinity and femininity are worldly categories that no longer pertain to him.

The Sulabhā story also plays with gender, albeit more mischievously. To attract Janaka's attention, Sulabhā first transforms herself into an alluring young woman. Then she goes further; she undertakes a bold move and occupies Janaka's body. In direct foil to the stoic and resolute Śuka, and thus starkly illustrating Janaka's *unenlightened* status, Janaka takes the bait in both cases; he becomes curious about Sulabhā because of her youth and beauty, and he is viscerally affected when she possesses him. Moreover, he views her yogic possession of his body in expressly sexual terms:

> You live as an ascetic practising *mokṣadharma*. But I am married. You have caused another evil, that is, the intermixture of different modes of life. I don't know your *gotra*, and you don't know mine. If you happen to be of my *gotra*, then by entering my body you have caused an incestuous union. Suppose your husband is alive and living abroad or somewhere else: so . . . your contact with me has caused a dharmic transgression . . . because one must not have sexual union with another's wife.
>
> (12.308.60–2)[19]

Sulabhā instructs him on these points, declaring that differences between male and female are cognized by the unenlightened alone; the *mukta* know these to be mutable and ephemeral categories, of no real significance from the perspective of the enlightened.

It would seem that the text thus successfully makes the point in both cases that gender is inconsequential in the context of *mokṣa*. The Śuka story, however, is inherently troubling. One should already be unsettled by the number of *Mahābhārata* birth stories in which women are viewed as dispensable to the process of generation and childrearing. In addition, any story in which a child is born from a man's thumb or, as in Śuka's case, from a drilling stick – not that that's too transparent a metaphor! – should make us nervous. But the Śuka story etches these assertions of male self-sufficiency deeper – Śuka is, after all, a man born with only the merest aid of a woman and reared independently by his father, himself a loner and a dubious friend of women. The Śuka story thus is a template of ascetic texts of the Indic traditions; it represents a closed dialogue among men in which a man's self-mastery is signalled by his stony indifference to women. Although there is nothing specifically hateful stated about women (as one finds elsewhere in the text – see Dhand in press), they are still represented either as sexual objects or as nooses and fetters that would bind a man to a world of misery and suffering. One might therefore question whether Śuka's nonchalance toward the naked nymphs represents simply the saintly conquest of sexual temptation, or whether it isn't tainted with other colours – whether subtextually it isn't also perhaps a prolongation of the persistent, if latent, misogyny of the text. Śuka's triumph is represented in precisely gendered terms; he is the paradigm of the male *puruṣa* wholly disinterested in the vivacious snare of *prakṛti*.

Varṇa

Similarly mixed messages are present in the Śuka story's representation of *varṇa*. Ultimately, we are told, Śuka achieves *mokṣa* and his essence is disseminated among all the creatures of the universe – hence presumably as much among *śūdra*s as among brahmins. Yet we see that the category of *varṇa* is repeatedly valorized as a criterion in Śuka's quest for *mokṣa*. His brahmin status is underscored by his father numerous times:

> Falling into the snare of the body, a creature rarely gets the rank of a brahmin. Son, therefore protect the state of brahminhood diligently. The body of the brahmin is not meant for sensual pleasures, but for suffering and penance in this world and for unparalleled happiness after death. Brahminhood is obtained by a great many austerities. Having obtained it, one must not disregard it. Be always engaged in the study of the Veda, in penance and in control of the senses. Be intent on virtue, seek eternal happiness and always strive to attain it.
>
> (12.309.21–3)[20]

Vyāsa repeatedly tells him to observe the duties of his own *varṇa* and not to deviate from them. He says:

> (The road to Yama's abode) is infested with highway robbers and protected by monstrous goblins. Hence observe the duties of your own *varṇa*. Only it can take one to the next world (safely).
>
> (12.309.56)[21]

> The person who generates wealth by the observance of duties of another's *varṇa* is afflicted with hundreds of (evil) qualities stemming from ignorance and delusion.
>
> (12.309.68)[22]

A brahmin is uniquely burdened and privileged, and this point is reiterated by Śuka's father several times in his discourse with Śuka.

One might argue that Vyāsa's pronouncements and opinions represent nothing of significance; as we know from later in the story, his wisdom comes into question. Indeed, Vyāsa seems confused on other vital points. For example, while some of his directions point Śuka to *mokṣa*, others seem to suggest that *mokṣa* is an afterlife very much akin to heaven.

> One who is on the path of action prescribed for his *varṇa* duly enjoys the fruits of his action. The person of mean acts (acts inappropriate for his *varṇa*) goes to hell. The person who follows the path of *dharma* attains heaven. Human birth is hard to get and it is a first step to heaven. Therefore meditate on the Self. Do not swerve from the course once again. One whose mind is intent on the path to heaven, and who is not diverted from it, is said to be a person of meritorious acts and his friends and relations need not lament his death.
>
> (12.309.78–80)[23]

When he also urges Śuka to follow his *varṇadharma*, therefore, it could be argued that this is Vyāsa's lack of higher consciousness at work: on the one hand, Vyāsa urges Śuka to cling to his *varṇa* duties; on the other, he exhorts him to rise above the limitations of the world, to be one who sees 'himself in all creatures and all creatures in himself' (*sarvabhūteṣu cātmānaṃ sarvabhūtāni cātmani* / 12.313.29). These facts notwithstanding, however, it seems that Vyāsa's concerns about *varṇa* do impress themselves upon Śuka. Thus, the very first question Śuka asks Janaka is about *varṇa* duties; he says, what are the duties of a brahmin? (12.313.13). Janaka explains these, and later relativizes the *āśrama* scheme, saying it is not entirely necessary to proceed in consecutive stages; one may renounce early if one is competent to do so. Janaka never, however, questions the validity or significance of *varṇa* to the pursuit of *mokṣa*; indeed, in precisely the backdoor manoeuvre anticipated earlier, he tells Śuka that scriptural study is necessary for *mokṣa*. Scripture is a raft that may be abandoned after its utility is exhausted, but to begin with it is indispensable to the search for enlightenment (12.313.22–3). Nor does Śuka question these things. The Śuka story, therefore, while ultimately describing as thorough a renunciation of corporeal existence as possible, nevertheless seems averse to abandoning the privileges of *varṇa*. Śuka's essence may have been disseminated into the mountains, trees, waters, and the souls of all beings, but *varṇa* proves to be a resistant, indurate category whose centrality the text makes no effort to displace or relativize.

The Sulabhā story also raises the spectre of *varṇa*. Janaka berates Sulabhā for transgressing the norms of sexual union. He says:

> You belong to the brahmin class, foremost of all classes. I am a *kṣatriya*. There should not be union of the two of us. Do not cause intermingling of classes.
>
> (12.308.59)[24]

In the Sulabhā story, however, Janaka's assertions are represented as the view of the *unenlightened*. Indeed, Sulabhā contests them. Though she does clarify that her background before renunciation was *kṣatriya*, hence cognate to his own, she explicitly denies the relevance of all social categories for the *brahmavādin*, saying:

> Only those who identify the Self with the body, and who consider distinctions among classes and among different stages of life to be real, entertain the idea of the intermingling of things.
>
> (12.308.177)[25]

Hers would seem to be the last word on the matter in that episode.

The ambiguities surrounding gender and *varṇa* illustrated here bespeak the profound ambivalence that the *Mahābhārata* has about these issues. Although the text repeatedly and volubly expounds a conservative orthodox position, its moral qualms are apparent in tales such as these. As we will observe below, however, the *varṇāśramadharma* has formidable tenacity and is not easily sloughed off. Even where passages such as these question its value, overall in my view the protest is both timid and tepid, and the quasi-resolutions achieved are morally dubious. We will return to this point shortly.

Renunciation of family

Speaking now to the personal dimension of renunciation, the Sulabhā story, as we have seen, contests the possibility of authentic detachment while still immersed in the world of relationships and acts. This is especially so if one is in a position of high responsibility, as is a king. Whereas Janaka grandiloquently proclaims his aloofness from the world, Sulabhā counters that there are many subtle sources of attachment that arise from being a king (12.308.133ff.). Although a king would seem to have complete freedom to effect anything he wants, in fact his power is illusory:

> He is said to have his freedom in giving orders to others. However, his orders are carried out by respective people independently. Though he wishes to sleep, he cannot get to sleep, because of people who want to get their work done. If, permitted by them, he goes to sleep, he is woken up. 'Have a bath, touch, drink, eat, pour libations on the fire, perform sacrifices, speak, listen' – in this way, others cause the king to act without his control over his action. Men always approach seeking gifts. Being the guardian of the treasury, he, however, does not have the power to distribute his gifts even to the most deserving. If he makes a large donation, the treasury will dwindle. If he disappoints the seekers, there will be hard feelings. Very soon he is overcome with weaknesses that cause dissatisfaction in others. He becomes suspicious if the wise, the heroic and the wealthy stay together. He fears the people who wait upon him even though there is no cause to fear them. When these people I have mentioned

> become corrupt, then he is frightened of them. See how the king's fears may arise even from his subordinates?
>
> (12.308.140–6)[26]

A king is thus subject to many misconceptions generated by his royal privilege. Although he considers himself to be above others and in a position of power, in reality he is just another mortal and as susceptible to desire and suffering as anyone else.

> Janaka, all men are kings in their own houses. All men are masters in their own houses. All men may be likened to kings in rewarding and chastising others. Like kings others too have sons, wives and their own selves, treasures, friends and stores. In these respects the king is no different from others. The country is in ruin. The city is in shambles. The best of elephants is dead. Thus the king grieves from false knowledge like commoners do. The king is rarely free of mental anguish caused by desire, aversion and love, or headaches, diseases and pain. The king is afflicted by the pairs of opposites. He has many foes. He serves the kingdom full of foes. Being fearful and suspicious he passes nights without sleep. Hence kingship is fraught with little happiness and much misery. It is basically useless. Who would accept this kind of kingship? Who will have peace of mind having obtained these? You think that this country, the city, the army, the treasury and the cabinet of ministers belong to you. In reality who do they belong to?
>
> (12.308.147–153)[27]

How is it possible for the king to remain detached when he regularly shares a bed with his wife, has children close by, and indulges in numerous enjoyments? Sulabhā casts strong sceptical doubt over the possibility of personal renunciation while one is still immersed in a world of action.

It would seem then that the Śuka story, which follows directly after, is intended to illustrate, if not to Janaka then at least to the reader, what a complete and focused pursuit of *mokṣa* actually entails. It seems intended to drive the point home in a graphic and even brutal way. The story begins innocuously enough and with a series of paradoxes: Vyāsa, himself a forest dweller, first counsels Śuka on renunciation. Then, for further instruction on this topic, he sends Śuka to Janaka, who is neither a renouncer nor even a forest dweller, but a *gṛhasthin* (householder). This *gṛhasthin* then confirms Śuka's readiness for *mokṣa* and *saṃnyāsa*. Śuka takes no direct issue with these paradoxes; he follows the directions of both men studiously. Yet although in the Sulabhā story Janaka insists that renunciation is *not* necessary – nor, in the Śuka story, has Janaka renounced – *Śuka* finds it necessary. He directs himself squarely toward *mokṣa* and gives up the world. In the process of renouncing the world, he also very strikingly renounces his father.[28]

'Don't be cruel'

Alf Hiltebeitel has eloquently argued (2001: 177ff.) that the major moral lesson imparted in the *Mahābhārata* is one against cruelty. As Hiltebeitel notes, the terms *ahiṃsā* and *ānṛśaṃsya* both connote this. It is hard to avoid the conclusion, however, that Śuka's rejection of his father, from the perspective of those yet immersed in the world, is stunningly cruel. Śuka is the beloved son of Vyāsa, the only one whom he actively sought, and whom he received after many years of penance. Vyāsa rears him tenderly on his own, like a champion breeder tending a rare and exotically gifted animal. He takes no help from wife or family; rather, he personally vests everything of himself into Śuka – all his knowledge of the Vedas, his personal wisdom, his habits of asceticism and of ritual. Vyāsa cherishes big ambitions for Śuka; it is he, after all, who plants the seeds of renunciation in Śuka's mind and provides all the means necessary for him to achieve the goal. For such a father, was one night too big a sacrifice? Apparently so, and this is a fact that is shocking to both the father and the reader. Everything in our reading of the *Mahābhārata*, other Hindu texts, and indeed of the Vyāsa-Śuka story, leads us to expect that Śuka, as a good son, even the ideal son, will seek his father's permission and *with his blessing* go the solitary course. Thanks to Nārada's counsel, however, Vyāsa is emphatically *not* a reference point in his son's decision; Śuka acts independently of and indifferently to his father, and cares nothing for his father's blessing. In the context of a culture that strongly advocates filial loyalty, respect, and obedience, this is an extraordinary and striking anomaly. Nor does the text attempt to soften it; indeed, it takes pains to underscore Śuka's complete impassiveness.

It would seem that the most obvious interpretation of Śuka's action is that the text seeks to demonstrate the degree of absolute aloofness necessary for *mokṣa*. We are perhaps meant to understand that Śuka has fully internalized Vyāsa's teachings:

> One has had a thousand parents in past lives, hundreds of wives and children. So will one in future births. But whose are they? Whose are we?
>
> (12.309.84)[29]

> No father, mother, or relative, no intimate beloved friend will follow one in the perilous journey of death.
>
> (12.309.49)[30]

It would seem that Śuka has fully imbibed the import of this teaching and, in a sad irony, turned it against his father himself. *Mokṣa* is a highly personal event, permitting no loyalties to kith and kin; the degree of indifference required by it is striking and brutal, admitting of no partiality even for one's most loving caregivers. The literary effect of placing the Śuka and Sulabhā stories adjacent to each other thus is to illustrate that Janaka's discourse on *mokṣa* is flowery, romantic, and terribly naïve, whereas the truth is hard, radical, and extreme. It entails a visceral and devastating experience of *viraha* or loss. The renouncer's success is marked by his *conquest* of such emotion – he *doesn't* experience loss – while the renouncer's family feels it painfully and bitterly, and this is what betrays the difference between the two. If Janaka in Sulabhā's story has never experienced such a thing, has never had to give up deeply bonded emotional ties, how can he claim victory over attachment? Janaka's claims are thus represented as fluffy and full of bravado. He can prate comfortably about aloofness and indifference while still ensconced in a world of comfort and social ties, but in the Śuka story we are apparently meant to see the hard reality of what true detachment looks like.

We have then two narratives about renunciation, representing both a disavowal of social values as encoded in the concepts of gender and *varṇa*, and a *tyāga* of personal relationships. It is time now to assess their significance in the context of the larger work. What more may we glean from them?

Hiṃsā and *ahiṃsā* on moral terrain

While the Śuka and Sulabhā stories both deal with themes of renunciation in literary terms, the most compelling questions they raise are questions of ethics. In unpacking the ambiguities depicted in these stories, we get an insider view into the difficult moral terrain that the *Mahābhārata* attempts to traverse – trying to retain renunciation as a high religious value while minimizing its impact upon society. The resolutions it eventually achieves, however, are less than perfect in that they raise serious moral concerns of their own.

Before proceeding further, it may be well to pause here to consider what we mean when we speak of morality and ethics. What does it mean to say that something is moral or immoral? Who is entitled to make such judgments, drawing upon what resources? Is there a universal standard of morality, and if so, what is its source? What is it that authorizes individuals to make pronouncements about morality and ethics? These are metaethical questions that need to be considered before any discussion of the moral quality of *mukti* can be intelligible.

In introductory works on the subject,[31] *ethics* is generally defined as the philosophical foundation of *moral* beliefs and practices; thus, whereas morality has a *practical* application, the discipline of ethics represents the *philosophical* platform upon which moral reasoning is based. Put another way, the primary ethical questions are not so much 'what ought we to do', as 'why ought we to do such and such thing' and 'how do we determine what we ought to do'. The question of 'what we ought to do' is the domain of morality.

To make a moral judgment about the rightness or wrongness of actions, therefore, we need to measure them against a recognized standard of morality. Is there any one standard that is applicable to all human beings, and if so, where does it come from?[32]

In the Western tradition, there is no uniformity of thought about these issues; different schools of thought understand morality differently. We act morally because God commands us in particular ways, or because we recognize certain basic principles consistent with being a rational human being, or because we concern ourselves with the development of character, or because we're concerned about achieving a greater good. Moral reasoning is anchored in different suppositions about the purpose of human existence and the ideal human life, and our evaluation of the moral nature of an action is therefore based on the beliefs and assumptions we hold to be true.

Hinduism most inconveniently has no universal code of ethics, is based on no unequivocal authority; it is a notoriously polyvocal tradition that has historically seen its strength in *retaining* ambiguity, in acting *situationally*, questioning at times every parameter of *dharma*.[33] In the *Mahābhārata*, we find that the tradition *always* speaks at two levels – one directed at those struggling *within* the world; the other geared at those seeking freedom from it.[34] The ethics associated with each level are radically different and even diametrically opposed; what the tradition affirms for the mundane, it turns on its head for the supramundane. Thus, the ethics of *mokṣa* are *intended* to be subversive of worldly norms; indeed, at this level the tradition relishes the deconstruction of social values, a process it provocatively calls 'going beyond good and evil' (being *nirdvaṃdva* / *dvaṃdvātīta* / *śubhāśubhaparityāgī*). At this level, the adept is no longer responsible for walking the well-grooved pathways of social morality; s/he has moved beyond it and is hence responsible for upholding a different standard of conduct. This conduct is a quintessentially moral one, whose primary feature is non-harm.

To recap, there are two broad types of ethical discourse in the *Mahābhārata*. One corresponds to the level of life-in-the-world, and may be summarized as the *varṇāśramadharma*, which is contingent upon the social location of the individual. The other is a more embracing universal standard that gives priority to principles such as non-harm and non-cruelty. While the *varṇāśramadharma* is relative to the individual, the other claims ontic authority in that it is aligned with the ontological state of self-realization. At this level, *ahiṃsā* is the unambiguous ideal of moral action. Even where one may argue (with some merit) that *ahiṃsā* was not an ideal valorized as the goal of all segments of the Hindu tradition (it has too many practical problems in application), it is explicitly the cardinal rule of renunciation as pronounced in the *Mahābhārata*, affirmed in numerous statements throughout the text. Thus, *nivṛtti dharma* (the *dharma* of renouncers) defines *dharma* as 'that which strives for the benefit of creatures; *dharma* is so called because it is wedded to *ahiṃsā*' (12.110.10).[35] One who practises *nivṛtti* is one 'whose life is the practice of *dharma*' (*jīvitaṃ yasya dharmārthaṃ*, 12.237.23), who feels distressed at causing grief to others, and who embraces non-injurious conduct (*yo 'hiṃsāṃ pratipadyate*, 12.237.19). Such a person is 'the refuge of all creatures' (*śaraṇyaḥ sarvabhūtānāṃ*, 12.237.20).[36] His/her cardinal ethic is that of non-harmfulness, of avoiding injury to other beings. As one *nivṛtti* practitioner challenges a *pravṛtti* one: 'If there is any ethic evident that is superior to *ahiṃsā*, that is rooted in righteousness instead of the *āgama*s or *śāstra*s, if you see it, do explain it' (12.260.17).[37]

If one is to assess the moral quality of the *mukta*'s actions, therefore, *ahiṃsā* would seem to be the primary scale of measurement. Renouncers must be held to a more rigorous code of ethics than those engaged in the world; they must uphold, first and foremost, the value of *ahiṃsā*, and this would seem to be the moral standard that pertains to both Śuka and Sulabhā according to the text itself.

Bringing these considerations to bear now upon the ethical resolutions achieved in these narratives, let us look again at the topic of *varṇa*. In the Śuka story, Vyāsa describes the virtues of an enlightened man, emphasizing his quintessentially ethical qualities of love and compassion for all. Then he concludes: 'His attachments and various afflictions eradicated through wisdom, [such a man,] his intellect illuminated, never finds fault with the course of conduct that prevails in the world' (12.316.52c–f).[38] Such a response effectively eliminates the need for a social conscience, negates the obligation of the enlightened to work for social justice, and reinscribes the *status quo* – only this time with more force, because it has the authority of the truly *mukta* behind it.

The Sulabhā story is a bit of an improvement, yet not beyond criticism. Although it engages with the moral problems more directly and deconstructs the relevance of *varṇa* for the *mukta*, it is problematic in two ways. First, Sulabhā, in denying any wrongdoing, identifies herself as a *kṣatriya* and in this way tips her hat to the *varṇāśramadharma* – thereby underscoring its pertinence. Second, even in contesting it, she employs a rhetorical move typical in such debates: she questions the relevance of *varṇa*, but *only in the case of the mukta*. Thus it would seem that the text admits its higher moral conscience, but answers it by displacing moral responsibility through an appeal to epistemology; we are given to understand that, at a higher level of religious accomplishment, the boundaries of gender and *varṇa* are porous – and indeed, anyone who avers otherwise is unenlightened. At the lower level of consciousness, however, they are not only left unquestioned, they are re-affirmed.

From a broadly liberal-humanist perspective, this move seems evasive. Like the Śuka story, the Sulabhā story takes no interest in questioning the values of the world; only in subverting them with an eye to soteriology.

Though apparently identifying the ethical insufficiencies of gender and *varṇa* prejudices, it defers the task of acting in true accordance with one's conscience to some long-distant future time, and thus escapes the responsibility of acting to correct moral wrongs. As soon as one is able to identify the insufficiencies of social prejudice, one is by definition re-located onto a new ethical ground whereby there is no necessity to correct such prejudices in others (see *Bhagavadgītā* 3.29ff.).

The ethics of *karmayoga*

In my view, these ethical irresolutions are the result of the text's overall championing of *karmayoga*, which, ironically enough, is itself a response to a different kind of ethical problem. This one stems from the moral difficulties posed by the renunciation of social and familial commitments. A longstanding trope of the Indic narrative traditions is the existentially troubled individual leaving home to seek higher spiritual truths. Perhaps most evocatively expressed in the hagiography of the Buddha, it depicts the rejection of home, family, and society, in favour of an individualistic search for enlightenment. That Hinduism saw moral problems with this is obvious from its development of the *āśrama* system, expressly formulated to counter the trend toward renunciation at an early age, a trend that was considered detrimental to social and familial duties.[39] This moral reservation is particularly acute in the *Mahābhārata*, which functions as an extended meditation on the topic. As we know, the massive bulk of the *Śāntiparvan* and *Anuśāsanaparvan* is directed toward arguing that it is *wrong* to seek personal individual fulfilment prematurely. Yudhiṣṭhira has obligations, duties, miles to go before he can renounce; the text will not release him to pursue his inner spiritual yearnings until he has completed his lifespan's worth of duties in the world. But the *Mahābhārata* goes much beyond this; in segments such as the *Gītā*, not only does it argue that one must complete one's duties, it also proposes that it is possible to do both simultaneously. No sacrifice of personal spiritual longings is necessary; through *niṣkāma karma* (desireless action), one may be in the world performing one's duties while still mentally renounced and free. *Karmayoga* thus is offered as a morally informed way of dissolving the opposition between personal aspirations and worldly duties.

Karmayoga, however, has niggling moral problems of its own. In insisting upon the performance of duty, the *karmayoga* doctrine in the main treats duty not as a contingent act to be determined situationally through active moral reasoning, but as a self-evident quantity most often aligned with the *varṇāśramadharma*. Debate on what constitutes authentic duty thus rarely takes us into genuinely moral turf. For example, even in the most famously charged dilemma of the epic – Arjuna's indecision about engaging in the war – Arjuna's paralysis is not of a *moral* quality so much as of an emotional and intellectual one: he must choose between two *pre-defined* sets of conflicting duties, *kuladharma* (family duty) and *varṇadharma* (*varṇa* duty). The question is not of the morality of war and *hiṃsā*, but of the propriety of killing intimate members of one's family. It would seem then that the *karmayoga* doctrine as most commonly interpreted contributes little to genuine *moral* debate; indeed, it *obstructs* it by reifying the *varṇāśramadharma* as a set of inalienable duties. It fails to interrogate the moral quality of these categories.

Having said this, an important caveat needs to be entered. This is that this apparent abdication of moral consciousness is not logically required of *karmayoga*. It is possible, for example, for *karmayoga* to be both morally and spiritually exigent. The obstruction is created by the indelible link historically drawn between *svadharma* and the *varṇāśramadharma*. Where *svadharma* is interpreted simply as '*varṇa* duty', it leads to a sterile system of ethics that rationalizes and prolongs a pattern of egregious social injustice. Were *svadharma* to be interpreted instead as moral consciousness or, using classical Dharmaśāstra vocabulary, *ātmatuṣṭi*,[40] *karmayoga* would be a compelling and profound religious exercise, promising the highest soteriological rewards while also holding the individual up to exacting standards for moral behaviour within the world. This was precisely the hermeneutical stance assumed, for example, by Gandhi, who elevated *ātmatuṣṭi* above all other *pramāṇa*s that inform one's *dharma* in the world. Gandhi's approach, however, represents the minority of Hindu exegetes on this topic.

* * *

The *Mahābhārata*'s simultaneous embrace of the worldly and the spiritual thus brings it into impossible moral terrain. For if one views Śuka's renunciation – and hence his cool insouciance toward his father – as soteriologically sound but morally perverse, the text's resolution of this problem through *karmayoga* is equally morally doubtful. Thanks to *karmayoga*, all the text's ideals of kindness, compassion, and *ahiṃsā*, though lofty and profound, need never be taken seriously – this is apparent especially in the social realm, in which the *hiṃsā* (harm, injury) attached to gender and *varṇa* discrimination is never soberly scrutinized. Thus the narratives of Śuka and Sulabhā, while a triumph of the soteriological orientation of the text, ultimately would seem to fail to meet the moral benchmarks established by the text's own ideals of non-cruelty and non-harm. While they are tales of religious perfection, we find that on the whole they are not morally exemplary. There is a core disjunction in the ethics of the *Mahābhārata*, which on the one hand embraces high moral ideals in *ahiṃsā* and *ānṛśaṃsya*, but on the other mitigates the necessity for rigorously applying them by recourse to the *karmayoga* doctrine.

* * *

The Hindu epics are works of ancient history; it could be argued therefore that to hold them up to the moral scrutiny of a later time is to tax them unreasonably with burdens they never undertook. This is not, however, quite the case; both epics explicitly present themselves as moral codes exercising transhistorical authority for the tradition as a whole. Moreover, they are not simply dusty volumes of arcane historical interest, but are perhaps the most vital and influential scriptural texts for Hindus in modern times. It is therefore not only fitting that they be subjected to ethical scrutiny, but arguably absolutely necessary that they be so taxed. In an age vitally coloured by the politics of a resurgent Hinduism, it is imperative for Hindus to quiz and examine their received wisdom before embracing it as the proud emblem of a robust and literate Hindu identity – if only to avoid the errors of the past.

I have belaboured the stories of Śuka and Sulabhā because to me they must be of especial import; after all, they represent the perspective of the allegedly fully enlightened, the most free, the very highest ideal of the tradition. The *mukta* are not shackled by bonds of ignorance; they have knowledge, wisdom, vision beyond our ken, and can see well past our shoulders to a greater, circumambient reality. One might reasonably expect then that these tales of religiously perfected souls would affirm a cognate moral perfection as well, to be paradigmatic of moral stances to be emulated by the unenlightened. It is clear, however, that this is far from the case; indeed, the moral stances assumed in these narratives are on the whole troubling. One might even argue that they are insidious and doubly pernicious in that they reinscribe a morality that is socially inequitable and flawed. It would seem that the composers of the epic had a high regard for the ideals of *mokṣa*, but they were unwilling or unable to let go of their social biases, which ultimately betray their historical and social location in the world.

Notes

1 I owe thanks to my research assistants, Maithili Thayanithy and Patrick McGee.

2 The Śuka and Sulabhā episodes have received some discussion before, from different angles. See C. Mackenzie Brown 1996; Doniger 1993; Hiltebeitel 2001a: 278–322; and Shulman 1993: 108–32 for Śuka; and Fitzgerald 2002b; Piantelli 2002; Vanita 2003; and Sutton 1999 for Sulabhā.

3 *phenapātropame dehe jīve śakunivat sthite / anitye priyasaṃvāse kathaṃ svapiṣi putraka // apramatteṣu jāgratsu nityayukteṣu śatruṣu / antaraṃ lipsamāneṣu bālas tvaṃ nāvabudhyase // gaṇyamāneṣu varṣeṣu kṣīyamāṇe tathāyuṣi / jīvite śiṣyamāṇe ca kim utthāya na dhāvasi //*

4 *sahasraśo 'py anekaśaḥ pravaktum utsahāmahe / abuddhimohanaṃ punaḥ prabhur vinā na yāvakam //*

5 *prayāsyatāṃ kim āsyate . . . /*

6 *gatā dviraṣṭavarṣatā . . . / . . . vayo hi te 'tivartate //*

7 *kiṃ te dhanena kiṃ bandhubhis te kiṃ te putraiḥ putraka yo mariṣyasi / ātmānam anviccha guhāṃ praviṣṭaṃ pitāmahās te kva gatāś ca sarve // śvaḥkāryam adya kurvīta pūrvāhṇe cāparāhṇikam / ko hi tad veda kasyādya mṛtyusenā nivekṣyate //*

8 *na yāvad eva pacyate mahājanasya yāvakam / apakva eva yāvake purā praṇīyase tvara //*

9 *purā samūlabāndhavaṃ prabhur haraty aduḥkhavit / taveha jīvitaṃ yamo na cāsti tasya vārakaḥ //*

10 *purā sahikka eva te pravāti māruto 'ntakaḥ / purā ca vibhramanti te diśo mahābhayāgame // smṛtiś ca saṃnirudhyate purā taveha putraka /*

11 *purā jarā kalevaraṃ vijarjarīkaroti te / balāṅgarūpahāriṇī . . . // purā śarīram antako bhinatti rogasāyakaiḥ / prasahya . . . // purā vṛkā bhayaṃkarā manuṣyadehagocarāḥ / abhidravanti sarvato . . . //*

12 See, for example, numerous passages in the *Bṛhadāraṇyaka Upaniṣad* (2.1.1; 3.1.1–2; 4.1–4; 5.14.8); Janaka is also the wise father of Sītā in the *Rāmāyaṇa*. The sagacity of Janaka is legendary in Sanskrit literature; Mario Piantelli (2002) traces some of these texts in his article.

13 *idam anyat tṛtīyaṃ te bhāvasparśavighātakam / duṣṭāyā lakṣyate liṅgaṃ pravaktavyaṃ prakāśitam // na mayy evābhisaṃdhis te jayaiṣiṇyā jaye kṛtaḥ / yeyaṃ matpariṣat kṛtsnā jetum icchasi tām api // tathā hy evaṃ punaś ca tvaṃ dṛṣṭiṃ svāṃ pratimuñcasi / matpakṣapratighātāya svapakṣodbhāvanāya ca // sā svenāmarṣajena tvam ṛddhimohena mohitā / bhūyaḥ sṛjasi yogāstraṃ viṣāmṛtam ivaikadhā // icchator hi dvayor lābhaḥ strīpuṃsor amṛtopamaḥ / alābhaś cāpy araktasya so 'tra doṣo viṣopamaḥ // mā sprākṣīḥ sādhu jānīṣva svaśāstram anupālaya / kṛteyaṃ hi vijijñāsā mukto neti tvayā mama / etat sarvaṃ praticchannaṃ mayi nārhasi gūhitum //*

14 *tasyāpy evaṃprabhāvasya sadaśvasyeva dhāvataḥ / ajasraṃ sarvalokasya kaḥ kuto vā na vā kutaḥ // kasyedaṃ kasya vā nedaṃ kuto vedaṃ na vā kutaḥ / saṃbandhaḥ ko 'sti bhūtānāṃ svair apy avayavair iha // yathādityān maṇeś caiva vīrudbhyaś caiva pāvakaḥ / bhavaty evaṃ samudayāt kalānām api jantavaḥ //* 12.308.123–5. 'The whole world moves perpetually like a galloping majestic horse of good breed. As such, what connection do these questions – who, whose and from where – have with the bodies of living beings? As fire is generated when the sun's rays touch the *sūryakānta* stone or when two sticks are rubbed together, living creatures are the result of the association of the thirty principles.'

15 *ātmany evātmanātmānaṃ yathā tvam anupaśyasi / evam evātmanātmānam anyasmin kiṃ na paśyasi / yady ātmani parasmiṃś ca samatām adhyavasyasi // . . . / . . . dvaṃdvair muktasya maithila / kāsi kasya kuto veti vacane kiṃ prayojanam //*

16 *ripau mitre 'tha madhyasthe vijaye saṃdhivigrahe / kṛtavān yo mahīpāla kiṃ tasmin muktalakṣaṇam //*

17 *tad amuktasya te mokṣe yo 'bhimāno bhaven nṛpa / suhṛdbhiḥ sa nivāryas te vicittasyeva bheṣajaiḥ //*

18 *svadehe nābhiṣaṅgo me kutaḥ paraparigrahe / na māṃ evaṃvidhāṃ muktāṃ īdṛśaṃ vaktum arhasi //*

19 *vartase mokṣadharmeṣu gārhasthye tv aham āśrame / ayaṃ cāpi sukaṣṭas te dvitīyo 'śramasaṃkaraḥ // sagotrāṃ vāsagotrāṃ vā na veda tvāṃ na vettha māṃ / sagotram āviśantyās te tṛtīyo gotrasaṃkaraḥ // atha jīvati te bhartā proṣito 'py atha vā kva cit / agamyā parabhāryeti caturtho dharmasaṃkaraḥ //*

20 *saṃpatan dehajālāni kadā cid iha mānuṣe / brāhmaṇyaṃ labhate jantus tat putra paripālaya // brāhmaṇasya hi deho 'yaṃ na kāmārthāya jāyate / iha kleśāya tapase pretya tv anupamaṃ sukham // brāhmaṇyaṃ bahubhir avāpyate tapobhis tal labdhvā na paripaṇena heḍitavyam / svādhyāye tapasi dame ca nityayuktaḥ kṣemārthī kuśalaparaḥ sadā yatasva //*

21 *anekapāripanthike virūparaudrarakṣite / svam eva karma rakṣyatāṃ svakarma tatra gacchati //*

22 *dadhāti yaḥ svakarmaṇā dhanāni yasya kasya cit / abuddhimohajair guṇaiḥ śataika eva yujyate //*

23 *prayuktayoḥ karmapathi svakarmaṇoḥ phalaṃ prayoktā labhate yathāvidhi /*

nihīnakarmā nirayaṃ prapadyate triviṣṭapaṃ gacchati dharmapāragaḥ // sopānabhūtaṃ svargasya mānuṣyaṃ prāpya durlabham / tathātmānaṃ samādadhyād bhraśyeta na punar yathā // yasya notkrāmati matiḥ svargamārgānusāriṇī / tam āhuḥ puṇyakarmāṇam aśocyaṃ mitrabāndhavaiḥ //

24 *varṇapravaramukhyāsi brāhmaṇī kṣatriyo hy aham / nāvayor ekayogo 'sti mā kṛthā varṇasaṃkaram //*

25 *varṇāśramapṛthaktve ca dṛṣṭārthasyāpṛthaktvinaḥ / nānyad anyad iti jñātvā nānyad anyat pravartate //*

26 *yadā ty ājñāpayaty anyāṃs tadāsyoktā svatantratā / avaśaḥ kāryate tatra tasmiṃs tasmin guṇe sthitaḥ // svaptukāmo na labhate svaptuṃ kāryārthibhir janaiḥ / śayane cāpy anujñātaḥ supta utthāpyate 'vaśaḥ // snāhy ālabha piba prāśa juhudhy agnīn yajeti ca / vadasva śṛṇu cāpīti vivaśaḥ kāryate paraiḥ // abhigamyābhigamyainaṃ yācante satataṃ narāḥ / na cāpy utsahate dātuṃ vittarakṣī mahājanāt // dāne kośakṣayo hy asya vairaṃ cāpy aprayacchataḥ / kṣaṇenāsyopavartante doṣā vairāgyakārakāḥ // prājñāñ śūrāṃs tathaivāḍhyān ekasthāne 'pi śaṅkate / bhayam apy abhaye rājño yaiś ca nityam upāsyate // yadā caite praduṣyanti rājan ye kīrtitā mayā / tadaivāsya bhayaṃ tebhyo jāyate paśya yādṛśam //*

27 *sarvaḥ sve sve gṛhe rājā sarvaḥ sve sve gṛhe gṛhī / nigrahānugrahau kurvaṃs tulyo janaka rājabhiḥ // putrā dārās tathaivātmā kośo mitrāṇi saṃcayaḥ / paraiḥ sādhāraṇā hy ete tais tair evāsya hetubhiḥ // hato deśaḥ puraṃ dagdhaṃ pradhānaḥ kuñjaro mṛtaḥ / lokasādhāraṇeṣv eṣu mithyājñānena tapyate // amukto mānasair duḥkhair icchādveṣapriyodbhavaiḥ / śirorogādibhī rogais tathaiva vinipātibhiḥ // dvaṃdvais tais tair upahataḥ sarvataḥ pariśaṅkitaḥ / bahupratyarthikaṃ rājyam upāste gaṇayan niśāḥ // tad alpasukham atyarthaṃ bahuduḥkham asāravat / ko rājyam abhipadyeta prāpya copaśamaṃ labhet // mamedam iti yac cedaṃ puraṃ rāṣṭraṃ ca manyase / balaṃ kośam amātyāṃś ca kasyaitāni na vā nṛpa //*

28 David Shulman evocatively considers the rivalry and ambivalence in this father–son relationship (1993).

29 *mātāpitṛsahasrāṇi putradāraśatāni ca / anāgatāny atītāni kasya te kasya vā vayam //*

30 *na mātṛpitṛbāndhavā na saṃstutaḥ priyo janaḥ / anuvrajanti saṃkaṭe vrajantam ekapātinam //*

31 See, for example, any elementary textbooks on the subject, e.g. Jones *et al.* 1977; Luper and Brown 1999; and O.A. Johnson 1978.

32 This of course is a question that has exercised Western philosophers for millennia. While some, like Kant, have argued that there *is* a universal standard of morality anchored in certain *categorical imperatives* based on an assumption of human reason, there are also numerous other schools of thought that identify other sources of moral guidance. (1) *Religious* theories locate their source of authority in God and scripture; according to these, the ideal of moral action is acting in accordance with a pre-divined religious goal, of obedience to God, for example. The moral quality of an action is assessed by the degree to which one conforms to religious injunctions. (2) *Deontological* theories isolate uncompromisable core values deemed eternal and transcendent; according to these, the measure of our moral action is the degree to which we conform to the basic value (of Truth, for example), as against the degree to which we deviate from it. (3) Theories of *self-realization* include *virtue* ethics and *character* ethics; these assess the rightness or wrongness of an action by the extent to which it contributes to the cultivation of the individual. (4) *Consequentialist* theories evaluate the rightness of an action against the consequences likely to accrue from it.

33 For more on these questions, see Dhand 2002.

34 I have explored these contentions in greater detail in Dhand in press.

35 *prabhāvārthāya bhūtānāṃ . . . kṛtam / yat syād ahiṃsāsaṃyuktaṃ sa dharma iti . . . //*

36 The ideal of not causing harm to others is retained as one of the cardinal vows of the renouncer in the Saṃnyāsa Upaniṣads, which inscribe it into ritual. The ritual of renunciation also involves the ceremonial promise of imparting fearlessness to others. See Olivelle 1977: 107; 1978.

37 *yady atra kiṃ cit pratyakṣam ahiṃsāyāḥ paraṃ matam / ṛte tv āgamaśāstrebhyo brūhi tad yadi paśyasi //*

38 *jñānena vividhān kleśān ativṛttasya mohajān / loke buddhiprakāśena lokamārgo na riṣyate //*

39 These points are made by Olivelle 1993.

40 Literally translated as 'what is pleasing to oneself' in Olivelle's translation of *Mānava Dharmaśāstra* 2.6, but rendered 'conscience' by Gandhi. The former translation opens a window to egoism, hence cannot function as a satisfactory source for moral guidance, but 'conscience' is a fertile resource, and presents possibilities that could be fruitfully tapped.

APPENDIX

Concordance of Critical Edition and Ganguli/Roy translation

Since its completion in 1966, the Poona Critical Edition has been the predominant edition of the *Mahābhārata* used by scholars. Usually, as in this book, reference to specific places in the text is made by means of the book (*parvan*), chapter (*adhyāya*), and verse (*śloka*) numbers of the critically reconstituted text. These numbers differ from those of any other edition of the Sanskrit *Mahābhārata* because the reconstituted text is shorter, containing only that material which all (or almost all) known *Mahābhārata* manuscripts have in common. However, since the reconstituted text has yet to be translated fully, the convention of using its numbering system effectively prohibits those who cannot navigate within the Sanskrit text from pursuing many of the references that scholars give. Readers may wish to use the concordance below, which allows one to know, given any reference to the reconstituted text, where to look for the same passage in the Ganguli/Roy translation. In the concordance, the Critical Edition chapter (and, where relevant, verse) numbers are on the left; the Ganguli/Roy chapter numbers are on the right. This concordance is intended for use in one direction of conversion only: the Ganguli/Roy edition translates many passages of varying lengths which are not part of the critically reconstituted text (and which appear instead within the Poona Critical Edition's apparatus as footnoted or appendicized material), and the concordance does not trace these passages to their specific locations in the critical apparatus. When a chapter in the reconstituted text and a chapter in the Ganguli/Roy edition are equated, then, it should be remembered that the latter may well contain material omitted from the former.

P.C.E.	ROY
Book 1, *Ādiparvan*	
1–12	1–12
13.1–28	13
13.29–34	14
13.35–45	15
14–18	16–20
19.1–16	21
19.17	22
20	23
21–46	25–50

47.1–16	51
47.17–25	52
48–52	53–57
53.1–26	58
53.27–36	59
54–67	60–73
68–69	74
70–91	75–96
92.1–31	97
92.32–55	98
93–100	99–106
101.1–15	107
101.16–28	108
102–104	109–111
105.1–3	112
105.4–27	113
106–107	114–115
108–118	117–127
119.1–34	128
119.39–43	129
120–121	130–131
122.1–11	132
122.12–40	133
122.41–47	134
123.1–57	134
123.58–78	135
124–128	136–140
129–136	143–150
137–139	152–154
140–141	155
142–149	156–163
150.1–25	164
150.26–27	165
151–155	165–169
156.1–9	170
156.10–11	171
157	171
158–159	172
160–161	173–174
162–163	175
164–166	176–178
167–168	179
169–181	180–192
182–183	193
184–214	194–224
215.1–11	225
215.12–19	226
216–225	227–236

Book 2, *Sabhāparvan*

1–10	1–10
11.1–42	11
11.43–73	12
12–16	13–17
17.1–7	18
17.8–27	19
18–42	20–44
43–49	46–52
50.1–9	53
50.10–28	54
51.1–21	55
51.22–28	56
52	57
53.1–16	58
53.17–25	59
54–61	60–67
62.1–21	68
62.22–38	69
63–65	70–72
66.1–27	73
66.28–37	74
67–72	75–80

Book 3, *Āraṇyakaparvan*

1–2	1–2
3–4	3
5–44	4–43
45.1–8	44
45.9–38	47
46.1–18	48
46.19–41	49
47–65	50–68
66–67	69
68–73	70–75
74–75	76
76–79	77–80
80.1–21	81
80.22–133	82

81–104	83–106
105–106	107
107–108	108–109
109–110	110
111–134	111–134
135–136	135
137–140	136–139
141–142	140
143–146	142–145
147.1–30	146
147.31–41	147
148–149	148–149
150.1–15	150
150.16–28	151
151–153	152–154
154–160	156–162
161.1–16	163
161.17–29	164
162–163	165–166
164–165	167
166–179	168–181
180–181	182
182–187	183–188
188.1–2	188
188.3–93	189
189–190	190–191
191	198
192–202	200–210
203.1–12	211
203.13–51	212
204–212	213–221
213.1–15	222
213.16–52	223
214–219	224–229
220–221	230
222–237	231–246
238.1–37	247
238.38–49	248
239–240	249–250
241.1–14	251
241.15–37	253
242–247	254–259
248–299	262–313

Book 4, *Virāṭaparvan*

1–5	1–5
6–31	7–32
32.1–34	33
32.35–50	34
33–37	35–39
38.1–8	40
38.9–19	41
38.20–35	42
38.36–58	43
39–57	44–62
58	?
59–63	63–67
64.1–18	68
64.19–37	69
65–67	70–72

Book 5, *Udyogaparvan*

1–44	1–44
45–61	46–62
62.1–5	63
62.6–31	64
63–148	65–150
149.1–46	151
149.47–66	152
149.67–84	153
150–165	154–169
166.1–13	169
166.14–39	170
167–173	171–177
174–175	178
176–177	179–180
178–179	181
180–197	182–199

Book 6, *Bhīṣmaparvan*

1–2	1–2
3–4	3
5–15	4–14
16.1–20	15
16.21–46	16
17–21	17–21
22.1–16	22

22.17–22	24
23–44	25–46
45.1–46	47
45.47–63	49
46.1–40	50
46.41–56	50
47–73	51–77
74.1–17b	78
74.17c–36	79
75–94	80–99
95.1–25	99
95.26–53	100
96–111	101–116
112.1–77	117
112.78–138	118
113–114	119–120
115.1–36	121
115.37–65	122
116–117	123–124

Book 7, *Droṇaparvan*

1–4	1–4
5.1–20	5
5.21–33	6
5.34–40	7
6–22	7–23
23	?
24.1–17	?
24.18–61	23
25–47	24–46
48.1–38	47
48.39–53	48
49	49
50–52	72–74
53.1–30	75
53.31–56	76
54–56	77–79
57.1–59	80
57.60–81	81
58–88	82–112
89–90	113
91–101	114–124
102.1–42	125
102.43–105	126
103–141	127–165
142.1–19	166
142.20–44	167
143–163	168–188
164.1–57	190
164.58–110	191
164.111–159	192
165.1–67	193
165.68–125	194
166.1–15	195
166.16–60	196
167–170	197–200
171–172	201
173	202

Book 8, *Karṇaparvan*

1.1–24	1
1.25–49	2
2–3	3–4
4.1–57	5
4.58–87	6
4.88–108	7
5.1–26	8
5.27–110	9
6–11	10–15
12.1–47	16
12.48–71	17
13–16	18–21
17.1–29	22
17.30–47	23
17.48–120	24
18.1–40	25
18.41–76	26
19.1–35	27
19.36–75	28
20–23	29–32
24.1–52	33
24.53–161	34
25	35
26.1–30	36
26.31–74	37
27.1–17	38
27.18–52	39
27.53–105	40

28–29	41–42
30.1–6	43
30.7–47	44
30.48–88	45
31	46
32.1–22	47
32.23–84	48
33–40	49–56
41–44	58–61
45.1–54	64
45.55–73	65
46–48	66–68
49.1–71	69
49.72–116	70
50.1–34	71
50.35–65	72
51–61	73–83
62.1–31	84
62.32–62	85
63–67	87–91
68.1–13	92
68.14–63	94
69	96

Book 9, *Śalyaparvan*

1–2	1–2
3.1–4	3
3.5–50	4
4–64	5–65

Book 10, *Sauptikaparvan*

1–18	1–18

Book 11, *Strīparvan*

1–8	1–8
9.1–2	9
9.3–21	10
10–13	11–14
14–15	15
16–27	16–27

Book 12, *Śāntiparvan*

1–22	1–22
23–24	23
25–26	24–25
27–32	27–32
33–34	33
35	34/35
36	36
37.1	36
37.2–43	37
38	38
39.1–37	39
39.38–49	40
40–49	41–50
50–51	51
52–68	52–68
69–70	69
71–116	70–115
117.1–21	116
117.22–44	117
118–124	118–124
125.1–19	125
125.20–34	126
126.1–26	127
126.27–52	128
127–141	129–143
142.1–10	144
142.11–20	145
142.21–44	146
143–149	147–153
150.1–18	154
150.19–36	155
151.1–18	156
151.19–34	157
152–170	158–176
171.1–54	177
171.55–61	178
172–223	179–230
224.1–31	231
224.32–73	232
224.74–75	233
225–268	233–276
269–274	278–283
275–292	287–304
293.1–11	305
293.12–50	306
294–309	307–322

310–328	324–342
329–330	343
331–340	344–353
341–342	354
343–351	355–363
352–353	364

Book 13, *Anuśāsanaparvan*

1–13	1–13
14–15	14
16.1–12	15
16.12–75	16
17–18	17–18
19–20	19
21–32	20–31
33–47	33–47
48.1–38	48
48.39–49	49
49–57	49–57
58–83	59–84
84–85	85
86–92	86–92
93–95	93
96–98	94–96
99	58
100–111	97–108
112–125	111–124
126–127	139–140
128–129	141
130–134	142–146
135	149
136–146	151–161
147–148	162
149–154	163–168

Book 14, *Āśvamedhikaparvan*

1–47	1–47
48.1–13	48
48.14–29	49
49–78	50–79
79–81	80
82–85	81–84
86–87	85
88–91	86–89
92–93	90
94	91
95–96	92

Book 15, *Āśramavāsikaparvan*

1	1
2–3	2
4–7	3
8	4
9–10	5
11–14	6–9
15–16	10
17–25	11–19
26–27	20
28–35	21–28
36–37	29
38–47	30–39

Book 16, *Mausalaparvan*

1–2	1
3–9	2–8

Book 17, *Mahāprasthānikaparvan*

1–3	1–3

Book 18, *Svargārohaṇaparvan*

1–5	1–5

GLOSSARY

adharma	injustice; improper conduct
adharmya	improper
adhyāya	a subsection of text; chapter
āgama	a type of text
agni	fire
ahaṃkāra	'the maker of I'; ego; reflexive individuation
ahiṃsā	the practice of not harming; non-violence
amṛta	the nectar of immortality
anātman	'no-self/soul'; the Buddhist theory that there is no abiding soul
anuṣṭubh	a type of Sanskrit metre used in the *Mahābhārata*
ānṛśaṃsya	non-cruelty
āpaddharma	behaviour appropriate in times of extremity
apsarā	a type of semi-divine female being; nymph; celestial courtesan
ārṣa	'of the *ṛṣi*s'; a type of marriage (involving a father giving his daughter away and accepting two oxen)
artha	profit; purpose
ārya	refined in behaviour and speech
asat	non-existent; untrue
āśrama	mode or stage of life; hermitage, often the residence of a *ṛṣi*
asura	a type of semi-divine being, enemies of the gods and hence 'demons' or 'antigods'
āsura	'of the *asura*s'; a type of marriage (involving a father selling his daughter)
aśvamedha	the royal ritual of the horse-sacrifice
asvatantrā	dependent
ātman	self; oneself; soul
avatāra	divine incarnation
avidyā	ignorance; nescience
avyakta	unmanifest
bahuvrīhi	a type of Sanskrit compound noun (an English equivalent would be 'paleface')
bandhu	bond; connection

bhakti	devotion; loyalty; reverential service
bodhisattva	an enlightened being repeatedly embodied through compassion for non-enlightened beings
brāhma	'of *brahman*'; a type of marriage (in which a father gives his daughter to a man of learning and good character)
brahman	the absolute
brahmanirvāṇam	a soteriological goal of not being reborn
brahmavādin	one whose speech is in accord with spiritual truth
buddhi	awareness; wit; intelligence
daiva	'of the gods'; fate; a type of marriage (in which a bride is given to a priest)
dakṣiṇāyana	the second half of the year
dānadharma	regulations concerning the practice of giving
daṇḍa	punishment; the rod of royal rule
darśana	auspicious sight of the divine
darśanīyā	beautiful
dāśa	a fisher
dāśī	a female fisher
dehin	'that which has a body'; the soul
deva	a deity; god
dharma	proper, meritorious behaviour in accord with accepted social norms (see Fitzgerald 2004c)
dharmarāja	righteous king; king who protects *dharma*
dhātṛ	'the arranger'
digvijaya	conquest of (all) the directions
duḥkha	suffering
dvaṃdvātīta	beyond the pairs of opposites
dvija	twice-born; member of one of the first three *varṇa*s
erakā	a rush, reed or grass
gandharva	a type of semi-divine being often associated with music, dance, and amorous activity
gāndharva	'of the *gandharva*s'; a type of marriage (involving mutual consent)
gandharvī	a female *gandharva*
gāthā	a type of verse
gotra	family; lineage
guṇa	a quality; in *sāṃkhya* philosophy, one of three basic aspects of the realm of objects
guru	teacher; master
hiṃsā	harm; violence
īśvara	lord; God
itihāsa	history; legend; name of a textual genre that is sometimes used to describe the *Mahābhārata*
jīva	soul
jīvanmukti	one who is released yet alive
jñāna	knowledge
kaivalya	state of isolation and purity
kāla	time; name of the god of time

kali	strife
kāma	desire; passion; sensual pleasure
karma	action; the residual power of previous actions which results in subsequent events and births
karmabandha	the residual 'bond of actions' which compels further rebirth
karmayoga	the *yoga* of (non-attached) action
karmayogin	a practitioner of *karmayoga*
kāvya	a genre of Sanskrit poetry
klība	eunuch; impotent; defective male
krodha	anger
kṣamā	forgiveness; patience; forbearance
kṣatriya	the second social class, comprising aristocrats and warriors
kṣatriyadharma	the duty and appropriate behaviour of *kṣatriya*s
kṣetrajña	'the knower of the field'; soul
kuladharma	family duty
loka	place; world; heavenly world
lokāyata	atheistic, materialistic philosophy
mahāyāna	the 'great vehicle'; a type of Buddhism
mahiṣī	queen; chief wife
manas	mind
mantra	a verbal formula; spell; sacred verse
manyu	self-assertion; vigour; anger
māyā	magic; power of appearances, hence sometimes 'illusion'
moha	delusion
mokṣa	freedom, especially from future rebirth
mokṣadharma	conduct oriented towards the achievement of *mokṣa*
mukti	release; spiritual freedom
mūla	root
musala	pestle
nakṣatra	constellation; star
napuṃsaka	a non-male; a transvestite of ambiguous sex
nāstika	unbeliever; heretic; a term typically applied to those (such as the Buddhists and Jains) who rejected the validity of the Veda
nirdvaṃdva	unaffected by pairs of opposites
nirvāṇa	'blowing-out' (of repeating embodiment); soteriological goal, esp. in early Buddhism
nivṛtti	'turning back'; ideological stance of indifference to and renunciation of worldly values, often in pursuit of freedom from rebirth
niyoga	the practice whereby a wife or widow is legitimately impregated by someone other than her husband, typically the husband's brother or a brahmin
paiśāca	'of the fiends'; a type of marriage (in which a man approaches a woman who is asleep, intoxicated, or otherwise unaware)
pañcavīra	'the five heroes'
paṇḍitā	learned woman; female scholar
paramparā	educational lineage; uninterrupted tradition

pāraśavī	daughter of a *kṣatriya* man and a *śūdra* woman
parvan	'knot' or 'joint'; a section of e.g. a text (thus 'book')
parvasaṃgraha	summary
pati	lord; husband
pativratā	a woman who is devoted to her husband
phalaśruti	a textual passage promising rewards to the listener
pitṛ	father; ancestor
pradhāna	the essential or most important aspect of something; sometimes synonymous with *prakṛti*
prājāpatya	'of the lord of creatures'; a type of marriage (in which the bride is given away and a *mantra* accompanies the ceremony)
prakṛti	the substrate of all psycho-physical phenomenality; matter (including mental matter); nature; (when plural) constituents
pralaya	dissolution; the reabsorption of the universe at the end of a cycle of time
pramāṇa	means of knowing; epistemological criterion
prāṇa	breath; life-force
pravṛtti	'turning forth'; ideological stance embracing the maintenance and development of society, family, economy and environment
priyā	beloved
puruṣa	'person'; the soul; the principle of subjectivity
puruṣakāra	autonomous human action
puruṣārtha	aim of life (namely *dharma*, *artha*, *kāma*, and *mokṣa*)
puruṣottama	'Supreme Person'; world-soul
rājadharma	royal duty; a subsection of the *Mahābhārata*
rājasūya	royal consecration ritual
rājavidyā	royal knowledge
rakṣaṇa	protection; husbandry
rākṣasa	a type of monster; a type of marriage (in which a bride is abducted by force)
ṛṣi	seer; sage
sabhā	court; assembly; assembly hall
sahagamanam	'going with'; a wife's accompanying her husband in death
sahasranāmastotra	hymn of praise, consisting of a list of the deity's (one thousand) names
sairandhrī	chambermaid
śaiva	focused upon the god Śiva
sakhī/sakhā	friend; companion
śakti	power; capability (often personified as a consort-deity)
sāman	song
sāṃkhya	'enumeration'; a metaphysically dualistic philosophy notable for its enumeration of the constituents (*tattvas*) of the phenomenal realm
saṃnyāsa	renunciation
samrāj	sovereign
saṃsāra	the phenomenal realm of repeated embodiment
saṃskāra	rite of passage

saṃvāda	dialogue; conversation
sarpasatra	snake sacrifice
śāstra	a type of didactic text
sat	existent; true
satī	a faithful wife; a wife who burns herself on her husband's funeral pyre
satra	a type of Vedic sacrifice in which the priests are joint sacrificers (*yajamāna*s) and share the benefits of the performance
satrin	one who participates in a *satra*
sattva	'being-ness'; goodness; in *sāṃkhya* philosophy, one of the three *guṇa*s
siddha	an accomplished ascetic
skandha	a section (e.g. of a text)
śloka	a type of metre used in the *Mahābhārata*
snātaka	a brahmin who has completed his Vedic education
soma	psychotropic ritual drink; moon
śrāddha	the ceremony of making offerings to the deceased, particularly ancestors; those offerings themselves
śramaṇa	'one who takes pains'; a renunciatory, ascetic and often peripatetic type of seeker
śrī	royal prosperity
stotra	praise
strīdharma	the duty and appropriate behaviour of women
śubhāśubhaparityāgī	one who has renounced the agreeable and the disagreeable
śūdra	the fourth social class, comprising servile and menial labourers
śulka	price; fee, especially that given for marriage
sūryakānta	'a kind of crystal supposed to possess fabulous properties as giving out heat when exposed to the sun' (Monier-Williams 1964: 1243)
sūta	a low-class court factotum often associated with recounting narratives or driving chariots
svabhāva	way of being; inherent nature
svadharma	one's own duty or appropriate behaviour
svatantrā	independent
svayaṃvara	a type of marriage (in which a bride ceremonially chooses or is won by her partner)
tád ékam	'that one'
tapas	austerity; heat; self-mortification
tapasvinī	a long-suffering woman (see Hara 1977–8)
tattva	'that-ness'; in *sāṃkhya* philosophy, any one of the basic constituents of the phenomenal realm
tejas	fiery energy
tīrtha	a sacred place (almost always a bathing place)
tīrthayātrā	a tour of *tīrtha*s; a pilgrimage
triṣṭubh	a type of Sanskrit metre
tyāga	renunciation

upajāti	a type of Sanskrit metre
upākhyāna	subtale
uttarāyaṇa	the first half of the year
vaiśya	the third social class, comprising artisans and agriculturists
vaṃśa	genealogy
varṇa	any one of four social classes, namely brahmin, *kṣatriya*, *vaiśya*, *śūdra*
varṇadharma	specific duties in accord with social class
varṇāśramadharma	specific duties in accord with social class and stage of life
vidūṣaka	a stock character in classical Sanskrit drama; a comical, gluttonous, degraded brahmin, he is a good friend of the hero
vidyā	knowledge; spell
virūpatva	ugliness
viṭa	a stock character in classical Sanskrit drama; a *bon vivant*
vrata	vow; regimen
vrātya	itinerant and degraded persons known for adventuring together in quasi-military groups
vyūha	any one of four stages in the cosmogony, and the particular deities (or names of deity) associated with them; battle-array
yājaka	sacrificial priest
yajamāna	'sacrificer'; the sponsor of a Vedic sacrifice and the recipient of its benefits
yajña	Vedic sacrifice
yakṣa	a type of semi-divine chthonic being, often associated with a particular locality
yakṣī	a female *yakṣa*
yati	an ascetic who has renounced the world
yoga	spiritual exercise; stratagem; any disciplined personal effort ('yoking') directed towards a specific goal
yogin	one who performs *yoga*
yoni	womb; female organs; origin

BIBLIOGRAPHY

Adarkar, Aditya (2001) 'Karṇa in the *Mahābhārata*', unpublished thesis, University of Chicago.

—— (2005a) 'Karṇa's choice: courage and character in the face of an ethical dilemma', in T.S. Rukmani (ed.) *The Mahābhārata: what is not here is nowhere else (yannehāsti na tadkvacit)*, Delhi: Munshiram Manoharlal.

—— (2005b) 'The untested *dharma* is not worth living', *International Journal of Hindu Studies* 9: 117–30.

Agrawal, Anuja (1997) 'Gendered bodies: the case of the "third gender" in India', *Contributions to Indian Sociology* (new series) 31.2: 273–97.

Aitareya Brāhmaṇa. See A.B. Keith (tr.) (1920) *Rigveda Brahmanas: the Aitareya and Kauṣītaki Brāhmaṇas of the Rigveda, translated from the original Sanskrit*, Cambridge, MA: Harvard University Press.

Aklujkar, Vidyut (1991) 'Sāvitrī: old and new', in Arvind Sharma (ed.) *Essays on the Mahābhārata*, Leiden: Brill.

—— (2000) 'Anasūyā: a *pativratā* with panache', in Mandakranta Bose (ed.) *Faces of the Feminine in Ancient, Medieval, and Modern India*, New York: Oxford University Press.

Allen, N.J. (1996) 'The hero's five relationships: a Proto-Indo-European story', in Julia Leslie (ed.) *Myth and Mythmaking: continuous evolution in Indian tradition*, Richmond: Curzon.

—— (1999) 'Arjuna and the second function: a Dumézilian crux', *Journal of the Royal Asiatic Society* (3rd series) 9.3: 403–18.

—— (2000) 'Primitive classification: the argument and its validity', in *Categories and Classifications: Maussian reflections on the social*, Oxford: Berghahn.

—— (2002) '*Mahābhārata* and *Iliad*: a common origin?', *Annals of the Bhandarkar Oriental Research Institute* 83: 165–77.

—— (2004) 'Dyaus and Bhīṣma, Zeus and Sarpedon: towards a history of the Indo-European sky god', *Gaia* 8: 29–36.

—— (2005a) 'Bhīṣma and Hesiod's succession myth', *International Journal of Hindu Studies* 8 (2004): 57–79.

—— (2005b) 'Romulus et Bhîshma: structures entrecroisées', *Anthropologie et Sociétés* 29.2: 21–44.

—— (2005c) 'The articulation of time: some Indo-European comparisons', *Cosmos, Journal of the Traditional Cosmology Society* 17.2 (2001): 163–78.

—— (2007) 'The close and the distant: a long-term perspective', in G. Pfeffer (ed.) *Periphery and Centre: studies in Orissan history, religion and anthropology*, Delhi: Manohar.

Altekar, A.S. (1959) *The Position of Women in Hindu Civilization: from prehistoric times to the present day*, Delhi: Motilal Banarsidass. First published 1938.

Āpastamba Śrautasūtra. Richard Garbe (ed.) (1882–1902) *The Śrauta Sūtra of Āpastamba belonging to the Taittirīya Saṃhitā, with the commentary of Rudradatta*, 3 vols, Calcutta (Bibliotheca Indica).

Appelbaum, David (1990) 'Tangible action: non-attached action in the *Bhagavadgītā*', in Bimal K. Matilal and Purusottama Bilimoria (eds) *Sanskrit and Related Studies: contemporary researches and reflections*, Delhi: Sri Satguru.

Arthaśāstra. See Kangle 1986.

Atharvavedasaṃhitā. William Dwight Whitney (tr.) (1993) *Atharva-Veda-Saṁhitā, Translated into English with Critical and Exegetical Commentary*, revised and edited by Charles Rockwell Lanman, 2 vols, Delhi: Motilal Banarsidass (first published Cambridge, MA, 1905).

Auboyer, Jeannine (1949) *Le Trône et son Symbolisme dans l'Inde Ancienne*, Paris: Presses Universitaires de France.

Babcock-Abrahams, Barbara (1975) 'A tolerated margin of mess: the trickster and his tales reconsidered', *Journal of the Folklore Institute* 11: 147–86.

Bailey, Gregory M. (1983a) 'Suffering in the *Mahābhārata*: Draupadī and Yudhiṣṭhira', *Puruṣārtha* 7: 109–29.

—— (1983b) *The Mythology of Brahmā*, Delhi: Oxford University Press.

—— (1985) *Materials for the Study of Ancient Indian Ideologies: pravṛtti and nivṛtti*, Turin: Indologica Taurinensia.

—— (1993) 'Humanistic elements in the *Mahābhārata*', *South Asia* 16.1: 1–23.

—— (2004) 'The *Mahābhārata* as counterpoint to the *Pāli Canon*', *Orientalia Suecana* 53: 37–48.

—— (2005a) 'The *Mahābhārata*'s simultaneous affirmation and critique of the universal validity of *dharma*', in T.S. Rukmani (ed.) *The Mahābhārata: what is not here is nowhere else (yannehāsti na tadkvacit)*, Delhi: Munshiram Manoharlal.

—— (2005b) 'The meaning of the word *bhikṣu* in the *Mahābhārata*', paper presented at the *Epic Constructions* conference, SOAS, London, July 2005.

Bakhtin, M. (1973) *Problems of Dostoyevsky's Poetics*, tr. R.W. Rotsel, Ann Arbor, MI: Ardis Press.

—— (1990) *Art and Answerability: early philosophical essays*, eds Michael Holquist and Vadim Liapunov, Austin: University of Texas Press.

Banerjea, Jitendranath (1944) 'The worship of Sāmba among the early Pāncharātrins', *Proceedings of the Indian History Congress* 7: 82–90.

Barresi, J. (2002) 'From "the thought is the thinker" to "the voice is the speaker": William James and the dialogical self', *Theory and Psychology* 12.2: 237–50.

Baudhāyana Dharmasūtra. See Olivelle 2000.

Bedekar, V.M. (1968) 'The doctrine of the colours of souls in the *Mahābhārata*, its characteristics and implications', *Annals of the Bhandarkar Oriental Research Institute* 48–9: 329–38.

Belvalkar, S.K. (1946) 'Saṃjaya's "eye divine" ', *Annals of the Bhandarkar Oriental Research Institute* 27: 310–31.

—— (ed.) (1954) *The Śāntiparvan: being the twelfth book of the Mahābhārata, the great epic of India*, part 2, Poona: Bhandarkar Oriental Research Institute. Vol. 14 of Vishnu S. Sukthankar *et al.* (eds) 1933–66.

Bhagavadgītā. See van Buitenen 1981.

Bhāgavata Purāṇa. K.K. Shastree (Bambhania) (ed.) (1997, 1998) *The Bhāgavata*, vol. 4, part 1 [*skandha* 10]; part 2A [*skandha* 11], Ahmadabad: B.J. Institute of Learning and Research. See also Ganesh Vasudeo Tagare (tr.) (1976) *The Bhāgavata-Purāna*, 5 vols, Delhi: Motilal Banarsidass.

Bharadwaj, Saroj (1992) *The Concept of 'Daiva' in the Mahābhārata*, Delhi: Nag.

Bhatt, Sunil (2002) 'Acculturation, dialogical voices, and the construction of the diasporic self', *Theory and Psychology* 12.1: 55–77.

Bhattacharya, Pradip (1995) 'Epic women: east and west – some observations', *Journal of the Asiatic Society of Bengal* (4th series) 37.3: 67–83.

Bhattacharyya, Dipak Chandra (1980) *Iconology of Composite Images*, New Delhi: Munshiram Manoharlal.

Bhattacharyya, Narendra Nath (1971) *History of Indian Cosmogonical Ideas*, Delhi: Munshiram Manoharlal.

Bhaviṣya Purāṇa. See von Stietencron 1966.

Biardeau, Madeleine (1968) 'Some more considerations about textual criticism', *Purāṇa* 10.2: 115–23.

—— (1970) 'The story of Arjuna Kārtavīrya without reconstruction', *Purāṇa* 12.2: 286–303.

—— (1971–2) 'Seminars on the *Mahābhārata*', *Annuaire de l'École Pratique des Hautes Études* (5th section) 79: 139–47.

—— (1981a) *Études de Mythologie Hindoue*, vol. 1, *Cosmogonies Purāṇiques*, Paris: Adrien-Maisonneuve.

—— (1981b) 'The salvation of the king in the *Mahābhārata*', *Contributions to Indian Sociology* (new series) 15: 75–97.

—— (1984–5) 'Nala et Damayantī: héros épiques', *Indo-Iranian Journal* 27.4: 247–74 (pt 1); 28.1: 1–34 (pt 2).

—— (1989) *Hinduism: the anthropology of a civilisation*, tr. Richard Nice, Delhi: Oxford University Press.

—— (1997) 'Some remarks on the links between the epics, the Purāṇas and their Vedic sources', in G. Oberhammer (ed.) *Studies in Hinduism: Vedism and Hinduism*, Vienna: Verlag der Österreichischen Akademie der Wissenschaften.

—— (2002) *Le Mahābhārata: un récit fondateur du brahmanisme et son interprétation*, 2 vols, Paris: Seuil.

Biardeau, Madeleine (comm.) and Péterfalvi, Jean-Michel (tr.) (1985) *Le Mahābhārata: livres I à V*, vol. 1 of 2, Paris: Flammarion.

Bigger, Andreas (1998) *Balarāma im Mahābhārata: Seine Darstellung im Rahmen des Textes und seiner Entwicklung*, Wiesbaden: Harrassowitz.

—— (2001) 'Wege und Umwege zum Himmel: Die Pilgerfahrten im Mahābhārata', *Journal Asiatique* 289: 147–66.

—— (2002) 'The normative redaction of the *Mahābhārata*: possibilities and limitations of a working hypothesis', in Mary Brockington (ed.) *Stages and Transitions: temporal and historical frameworks in epic and purāṇic literature*, Zagreb: Croatian Academy of Sciences and Arts.

Black, Brian (2007) *The Character of the Self in Ancient India: priests, kings, and women in the early Upaniṣads*, Albany: State University of New York Press.

Bock-Raming, Andreas (2002) *Untersuchungen zur Gottesvorstellung in der älteren Anonymliteratur des Pāñcarātra*, Wiesbaden: Harrassowitz.

Bordo, Susan (1994) 'Reading the male body', in Laurence Goldstein (ed.) *The Male Body*, Ann Arbor: University of Michigan Press.

Bowlby, Paul (1991) 'Kings without authority: the obligation of the ruler to gamble in the *Mahābhārata*', *Studies in Religion / Sciences Religieuses* 20: 3–17.

Bowles, Adam (2004) '*Dharma*, disorder and the political in ancient India: the *Āpaddharmaparvan* of the *Mahābhārata*', unpublished thesis, La Trobe University.

—— (2005) 'Framing Bhīṣma's royal instructions: the Mahābhārata and the problem of its design', paper presented at the Fourth Dubrovnik International Conference on the Sanskrit Epics and Purāṇas, September 2005.

Brassard, Francis (1999) 'The concept of *buddhi* in the Bhagavadgītā', in Mary Brockington and Peter Schreiner (eds) *Composing a Tradition: concepts, techniques and relationships*, Zagreb: Croatian Academy of Sciences and Arts.

Brereton, Joel P. (1999) 'Edifying puzzlement: *Ṛgveda* 10.129 and the uses of enigma', *Journal of the American Oriental Society* 119.2: 248–60.

Bṛhadāraṇyaka Upaniṣad. See Olivelle 1998.

Brinkhaus, Horst (2000) 'The Mārkaṇḍeya episode in the Sanskrit epics and Purāṇas', in Piotr Balcerowicz and Marek Mejor (eds) *On the Understanding of Other Cultures*, Warsaw: Instytut Orientalistyczny, Uniwersytet Warszawski.

Brockington, John L. (1995) 'Concepts of race in the Mahābhārata and Rāmāyaṇa', in Peter Robb (ed.) *The Concept of Race in South Asia*, Delhi: Oxford University Press.

—— (1997) 'The *Bhagavadgītā*: text and context', in Julius Lipner (ed.) *The Fruits of our Desiring: an enquiry into the ethics of the Bhagavadgītā for our times*, Calgary: Bayeux Arts.

—— (1998) *The Sanskrit Epics*, Leiden: Brill.

—— (1999) 'Epic Sāṃkhya: texts, teachers, terminology', *Asiatische Studien / Études Asiatiques* 53.3: 473–90.

—— (2000) 'The structure of the *Mokṣadharmaparvan* of the *Mahābhārata*', in Piotr Balcerowicz and Marek Mejor (eds) *On the Understanding of Other Cultures*, Warsaw: Instytut Orientalistyczny, Uniwersytet Warszawski.

—— (2001) 'Indra in the epics', *Studia Orientalia* 94: 67–82.

—— (2002) 'Jarāsaṃdha of Magadha (Mbh 2,15–22)', in Mary Brockington (ed.), *Stages and Transitions: temporal and historical frameworks in epic and purāṇic literature*, Zagreb: Croatian Academy of Sciences and Arts.

—— (2003) '*Yoga* in the *Mahābhārata*', in Ian Whicher and David Carpenter (eds) *Yoga: the Indian tradition*, London and New York: RoutledgeCurzon.

Brockington, Mary (2001) 'Husband or king? Yudhiṣṭhira's dilemma in the Mahābhārata', *Indo-Iranian Journal* 44.3: 253–63.

—— (2003) 'Husband or slave? Interpreting the hero of the *Mahābhārata*', paper presented at the Twelfth World Sanskrit Conference, Helsinki, July 2003.

Brodbeck, Simon (2003) 'Introduction', in Juan Mascaró (tr.) *The Bhagavad Gita*, London: Penguin.

—— (2003/4) 'Kṛṣṇa's action as the paradigm of *asakta karman* in the *Bhagavadgītā*', in Renata Czekalska and Halina Marlewicz (eds) *Second International Conference on Indian Studies: proceedings* (= *Cracow Indological Studies* 4–5), Cracow: Institute of Oriental Philology, Jagiellonian University.

—— (2004) 'Calling Kṛṣṇa's bluff: non-attached action in the *Bhagavadgītā*', *Journal of Indian Philosophy* 32.1: 81–103.

—— (2006) 'Ekalavya and *Mahābhārata* 1.121–28', *International Journal of Hindu Studies* 10.1: 1–34.

—— (in press a) 'Husbands of Earth: *kṣatriya*s, females, and female *kṣatriya*s in the *Strīparvan*', in Robert P. Goldman and Muneo Tokunaga (eds) *Proceedings of the Twelfth World Sanskrit Conference, Helsinki, 2003 (epic panels)*, Delhi: Motilal Banarsidass.

—— (in press b) 'Cricket and the *karmayoga*: a comparative study of peak performance', in Jeremy D. McKenna (ed.) *At the Boundaries of Cricket: philosophical reflections on the noble game*, London: Taylor and Francis / International Research Centre for Sport, Socialization, Society, De Montfort University.

Brodbeck, Simon and Black, Brian (2006) 'Introduction', *Journal of Vaishnava Studies* 14.2: 1–8.

Bronkhorst, Johannes (1993) *The Two Traditions of Meditation in Ancient India*, Delhi: Motilal Banarsidass. First published 1986.

—— (1998) *The Two Sources of Indian Asceticism*, Delhi: Motilal Banarsidass. First published Bern: Peter Lang, 1993.

—— (1999) 'The contradiction of Sāṃkhya: on the number and the size of the different *tattvas*', *Asiatische Studien / Études Asiatiques* 53.3: 679–91.

Brown, C. Mackenzie (1986) 'The theology of Rādhā in the Purāṇas', in John Stratton Hawley and Donna Marie Wulff (eds) *The Divine Consort: Rādhā and the goddesses of India*, Boston, MA: Beacon.

—— (1996) 'Modes of perfected living in the *Mahābhārata* and the *Purāṇas*: the different faces of Śuka the renouncer', in Andrew O. Fort and Patricia Y. Mumme (eds) *Living Liberation in Hindu Thought*, Albany: State University of New York Press.

Brown, W. Norman (1968) 'The creative role of the goddess Vāc in the Ṛg Veda', in J.C. Heesterman, G.H. Schokker and V.I. Subramoniam (eds) *Pratidānam: Indian, Iranian, and Indo-European studies presented to F.B.J. Kuiper on his sixtieth birthday*, The Hague: Mouton; reprinted in Rosane Rocher (ed.) (1978) *India and Indology: selected articles* [of W. Norman Brown], Delhi: Motilal Banarsidass / American Institute of Indian Studies.

Buddhacarita of Aśvaghoṣa. E.H. Johnston (ed. and tr.) (1972) *The Buddhacarita; or, Acts of the Buddha*, Delhi: Motilal Banarsidass (first published Calcutta, 2 vols, 1935–6).

van Buitenen, J.A.B. (1972) 'On the structure of the Sabhāparvan of the Mahābhārata', in J. Ensink and P. Gaeffke (eds) *India Maior: congratulatory volume presented to J. Gonda*, Leiden: Brill; reprinted in Ludo Rocher (ed.) (1988) *Studies in Indian Literature and Philosophy: collected articles of J.A.B. van Buitenen*, Delhi: Motilal Banarsidass / American Institute of Indian Studies.

—— (ed. and tr.) (1973) *The Mahābhārata*, vol. 1, *Book 1, The Book of the Beginning*, Chicago, IL, and London: University of Chicago Press.

—— (ed. and tr.) (1975) *The Mahābhārata*, vol. 2, *Book 2, The Book of the Assembly Hall*; *Book 3, The Book of the Forest*, Chicago, IL, and London: University of Chicago Press.

—— (ed. and tr.) (1978) *The Mahābhārata*, vol. 3, *Book 4, The Book of Virāṭa*; *Book 5, The Book of the Effort*, Chicago, IL, and London: University of Chicago Press.

—— (ed. and tr.) (1981) *The Bhagavadgītā in the Mahābhārata: a bilingual edition*, Chicago, IL, and London: University of Chicago Press.

Burley, Mikel (2007) *Classical Sāṃkhya and Yoga: an Indian metaphysics of experience*, London and New York: Routledge.

Butler, Judith (1993) *Bodies that Matter: on the discursiveness of sex*, New York: Routledge.

—— (1999) *Gender Trouble: feminism and the subversion of identity*, 2nd edn, New York: Routledge. First published 1990.

—— (2001) 'Performative acts and gender constitution: an essay in phenomenology and feminist theory', in Sue Ellen Case (ed.) *Performing Feminisms: feminist critical theory and theatre*, Baltimore, MD: Johns Hopkins University Press.

Carstairs, G. Morris (1957) *The Twice Born: a study of a community of high-caste Hindus*, London: The Hogarth Press.

Chaitanya, Krishna (1985) *The Mahābhārata: a literary study*, New Delhi: Clarion Books.

Chakravarti, Uma (1999) 'Beyond the Altekarian paradigm: towards a new understanding of gender relations in early Indian history', in Kumkum Roy (ed.) *Women in Early Indian Societies*, New Delhi: Manohar.

Chakravarty, G.N. (1955) 'The idea of fate and freedom in the *Mahābhārata*', *Poona Orientalist* 20: 7–16.

Chāndogya Upaniṣad. See Olivelle 1998.

Chapple, Christopher Key (2005) 'Karṇa and the *Mahābhārata*: an ethical reflection', in T.S. Rukmani (ed.) *The Mahābhārata: what is not here is nowhere else (yannehāsti na tadkvacit)*, Delhi: Munshiram Manoharlal.

—— (2006) 'Yoga and the *Mahābhārata*: engaged renouncers', *Journal of Vaishnava Studies* 14.2: 103–14.

Chiba, Masaji (1986) *Asian Indigenous Law: in interaction with received law*, London: KPI Limited.

Chopra, Ravi and Chopra, Baldev R. (dir. / prod.) (1988–90) *Mahābhārat*, television version, 94 episodes, India: Doordarshan.

Collins, Alfred (2000) 'Dancing with *prakriti*: the Samkhyan goddess as *pativrata* and *guru*', in Alf Hiltebeitel and Kathleen Erndl (eds) *Is the Goddess a Feminist? The politics of South Asian goddesses*, Sheffield: Sheffield Academic Press.

Conze, Edward (1967) *Buddhist Thought in India*, Ann Arbor: University of Michigan Press.

Cosi, Vita Antonella (2005) 'The importance of conceptual analysis in studies of similes: the case of the Śiśupāla episode in the *Mahābhārata*', paper presented at the Fourth Dubrovnik International Conference on the Sanskrit Epics and Purāṇas, September 2005.

Couture, André (1996) 'The *Harivaṃśa*: a supplement to the *Mahābhārata*', *Journal of Vaishnava Studies* 4.3: 127–38.

Cowell, E.B. (2005) *The Jātaka or Stories of the Buddha's Former Births*, 2 vols, Delhi: Motilal Banarsidass. First published 1895.

Custodi, Andrea (2005) 'Dharma and desire: Lacan and the left half of the *Mahābhārata*', unpublished thesis, George Washington University.

Dandekar, R.N. (ed.) (1966) *The Anuśāsanaparvan: being the thirteenth book of the Mahābhārata, the great epic of India*, 2 parts, Poona: Bhandarkar Oriental Research Institute. Vol. 17 of Vishnu S. Sukthankar *et al.* (eds) 1933–66.

—— (gen. ed.) (1971–6) *The Mahābhārata Text as Constituted in its Critical Edition*, 5 vols incl. *Harivaṃśa*, Poona: Bhandarkar Oriental Research Institute.

—— (ed.) (1990) *The Mahābhārata Revisited*, New Delhi: Sahitya Akademi.

Dange, Sadashiv Ambadas (1989) *Enyclopaedia of Puranic Beliefs and Practices*, vol. 4, New Delhi: Navrang.

—— (1997) *Myths from the Mahābhārata*, vol. 1, *Quest for Immortality*, New Delhi: Aryan Books International.

—— (2001) *Myths from the Mahābhārata*, vol. 2, *Study in Patterns and Symbols*, New Delhi: Aryan Books International.

—— (2002) *Myths from the Mahābhārata*, vol. 3, *Probe in Early Dim History and Folklore*, New Delhi: Aryan Books International.

Das, Sadananda (2000) '*Pṛthivī sūkta* of the *Atharvaveda*: a study', *Journal of the Ganganatha Jha Kendriya Sanskrit Vidyapeetha* 56: 235–43.

Dasgupta, Madhusraba (2000) 'Usable women: the tales of Ambā and Mādhavī', in Mandakranta Bose (ed.) *Faces of the Feminine in Ancient, Medieval, and Modern India*, New York: Oxford University Press.

Dasti, Matthew (2005) 'Buddhi-yoga in the *Bhagavad-gītā*: an interpretive analysis', *Journal of Vaishnava Studies* 14.1: 139–54.

Davis, Donald R. (2005) 'Being Hindu or being human: a reappraisal of the *puruṣārthas*', *International Journal of Hindu Studies* 8 (2004): 1–27.

Derrida, Jacques (1997) *Politics of Friendship*, tr. George Collins, London: Verso.

Devereux, Georges (1951) 'The Oedipal situation and its consequences in the epics of ancient India', *Samīkṣā, Journal of the Indian Psychoanalytical Society* 5: 5–13.

Devī Māhātmya. Swāmi Jagadīśvarānanda (1972) *The Devī-Māhātmyam or Śrī-Durgā-Saptaśatī*, Madras: Sri Ramakrishna Math.

Dhand, Arti (2002) 'The *dharma* of ethics, the ethics of *dharma*: quizzing the ideals of Hinduism', *Journal of Religious Ethics* 30.3: 347–72.

—— (2004) 'The subversive nature of virtue in the *Mahābhārata*: a tale about women, smelly ascetics, and God', *Journal of the American Academy of Religion* 72.1: 33–58.

—— (in press) *Woman as Fire, Woman as Sage: sexual ideology in the Mahābhārata*, Albany: State University of New York Press.

Dikshitar, V.R. Ramachandra (1995) *The Purāṇa Index*, 3 vols, Delhi: Motilal Banarsidass. First published Madras, 1951–5.

Doniger, Wendy (1993) 'Why is a parrot the narrator of the *Bhagavata Purāṇa*?', in Wendy Doniger (ed.) *Purāṇa Perennis: reciprocity and transformation in Hindu and Jain texts*, Albany: State University of New York Press.

—— (1997) 'Myths of transsexual masquerades in ancient India', in Dick van der Meij (ed.) *India and Beyond: aspects of literature, meaning, ritual and thought*, London and New York: Kegan Paul International.

—— (1999) *Splitting the Difference: gender and myth in ancient Greece and India*, Chicago, IL, and London: University of Chicago Press.

Doniger, Wendy and Kakar, Sudhir (trs) (2003) *Kamasutra: a new translation*, Oxford: Oxford University Press.

Doniger, Wendy with Smith, Brian K. (trs) (1991) *The Laws of Manu*, London: Penguin.

Doniger, Wendy: see also O'Flaherty, Wendy Doniger.

Dronke, Ursula (ed. and tr.) (1997) *The Poetic Edda: vol. II, mythological poems*, Oxford: Clarendon.

Dumézil, Georges (1968) *Mythe et Épopée: l'idéologie des trois fonctions dans les épopées des peuples Indo-Européens*, vol. 1 of 3, Paris: Gallimard.
—— (1970) *The Destiny of the Warrior*, tr. Alf Hiltebeitel, Chicago, IL: University of Chicago Press.
—— (1973) *Gods of the Ancient Northmen*, ed. Einar Haugen, Berkeley: University of California Press.
—— (1979) *Mariages Indo-Européens*, Paris: Payot.
—— (2000) *Mythes et Dieux de la Scandinavie Ancienne*, Paris: Gallimard. (For relevant English translations, see Dumézil 1973: 118–40.)
Dundas, Paul (1992) *The Jains*, London: Routledge.
Dunham, John (1991) 'Manuscripts used in the critical edition of the *Mahābhārata*: a survey and discussion', in Arvind Sharma (ed.) *Essays on the Mahābhārata*, Leiden: Brill.
Dutt, M.N. (tr.) (2001) *Mahabharata: Sanskrit Text and English Translation*, 9 vols, edited and revised with introduction by Ishwar Chandra Sharma and O.N. Bimali, Delhi: Parimal Publications. Translation first published 1895–1905.
Edgerton, Franklin (1926) 'The hour of death: its importance for man's future fate in Hindu and western religions', *Annals of the Bhandarkar Oriental Research Institute* 8: 219–49.
Eliade, Mircea (1962) *Méphistophélès et l'Androgyne*, Paris: Gallimard.
Eller, Cynthia (2000) *The Myth of Matriarchal Prehistory: why an invented past won't give women a future*, Boston, MA: Beacon.
Evans, Dylan (1996) *Introductory Dictionary of Lacanian Psychoanalysis*, New York: Routledge.
Falk, Nancy (1973) 'Wilderness and kingship in ancient South Asia', *History of Religions* 13: 1–15.
—— (1977) 'Draupadī and the *dharma*', in Rita M. Gross (ed.) *Beyond Androcentrism: new essays on women and religion*, Missoula, MT: Scholars Press.
Feller Jatavallabhula, Danielle (1999) '*Raṇayajña*: the *Mahābhārata* war as a sacrifice', in Jan E.M. Houben and Karel R. van Kooij (eds) *Violence Denied: violence, non-violence and the rationalization of violence in South Asian cultural history*, Leiden: Brill.
Feller, Danielle (2004) *The Sanskrit Epics' Representation of Vedic Myths*, Delhi: Motilal Banarsidass.
Findly, Ellison Banks (2002) 'The housemistress at the door: Vedic and Buddhist perspectives on the mendicant encounter', in Laurie L. Patton (ed.) *Jewels of Authority: women and textual tradition in Hindu India*, New York: Oxford University Press.
Fitzgerald, James L. (1991) 'India's fifth Veda: the *Mahābhārata*'s presentation of itself', in Arvind Sharma (ed.) *Essays on the Mahābhārata*, Leiden: Brill. First published in *Journal of South Asian Literature* 22.1: 1985.
—— (2002a) 'The Rāma Jāmadagnya "Thread" of the *Mahābhārata*: a new survey of Rāma Jāmadagnya in the Pune Text', in Mary Brockington (ed.) *Stages and Transitions: temporal and historical frameworks in epic and purāṇic literature*, Zagreb: Croatian Academy of Sciences and Arts.
—— (tr.) (2002b) 'Nun befuddles king, shows *karmayoga* does not work: Sulabhā's refutation of King Janaka at MBh 12.308', *Journal of Indian Philosophy* 30.6: 641–77.

—— (2003) 'The many voices of the *Mahābhārata*', *Journal of the American Oriental Society* 123.4: 803–18.

—— (ed. and tr.) (2004a) *The Mahābhārata*, vol. 7, *Book 11, The Book of the Women; Book 12, The Book of Peace, part one*, Chicago, IL, and London: University of Chicago Press.

—— (2004b) '*Mahābhārata*', in Sushil Mittal and Gene R. Thursby (eds) *The Hindu World*, London and New York: Routledge.

—— (2004c) '*Dharma* and its translation in the *Mahābhārata*', *Journal of Indian Philosophy* 32.5–6: 671–85.

—— (2005) 'Towards a database of the non-*anuṣṭubh* verses of the *Mahābhārata*', in Petteri Koskikallio (ed.) *Epics, Khilas, and Purāṇas: continuities and ruptures*, Zagreb: Croatian Academy of Sciences and Arts.

—— (2006) 'Negotiating the shape of "scripture": new perspectives on the development and growth of the *Mahābhārata* between the empires', in Patrick Olivelle (ed.) *Between the Empires: society in India 300 BCE to 400 CE*, New York: Oxford University Press.

Flood, Gavin (1997) 'The meaning and context of the *Puruṣārthas*', in Julius Lipner (ed.) *The Fruits of our Desiring: an enquiry into the ethics of the Bhagavadgītā for our times*, Calgary: Bayeux Arts.

Foucault, Michel (1979) *The History of Sexuality: vol. 1, an introduction*, tr. Robert Hurley, Harmondsworth: Penguin.

Freud, Sigmund (1938) 'The interpretation of dreams', in A.A. Brill (ed. and tr.) *The Basic Writings of Sigmund Freud*, New York: Random House.

Ganguli, Kisari Mohan (tr.) (1970) *The Mahabharata of Krishna-Dwaipayana Vyasa Translated into English Prose from the Original Sanskrit Text*, 12 vols, New Delhi: Munshiram Manoharlal. Paperback edition in 4 volumes, 1993. First published in 100 fascicules by Pratap Chandra Roy and Sundari Bala Roy, Calcutta, 1883–96; now also online (http://www.sacred-texts.com/hin/maha/).

Gautama Dharmasūtra. See Olivelle 2000.

Ghosh, Jayatri (2000) 'Satyavatī: the matriarch of the *Mahābhārata*', in Mandakranta Bose (ed.) *Faces of the Feminine in Ancient, Medieval, and Modern India*, New York: Oxford University Press.

Gitomer, David (1991) 'Rākṣasa Bhīma: wolfbelly among ogres and brahmans in the Sanskrit *Mahābhārata* and the *Veṇīsaṃhāra*', in Arvind Sharma (ed.) *Essays on the Mahābhārata*, Leiden: Brill.

—— (1992) 'King Duryodhana: the *Mahābhārata* discourse of sinning and virtue in epic and drama', *Journal of the American Oriental Society* 112.2: 222–32.

Glover, David and Kaplan, Cora (2000) *Genders*, London: Routledge.

Goldberg, Ellen (2002) *The Lord who is Half Woman: ardhanārīśvara in Indian and feminist perspective*, Albany: State University of New York Press.

Goldman, Robert P. (1978) 'Fathers, sons and gurus: oedipal conflict in the Sanskrit epics', *Journal of Indian Philosophy* 6.4: 325–92.

—— (1980) 'Rāmaḥ sahalakṣmaṇaḥ: psychological and literary aspects of the composite hero of Vālmīki's *Rāmāyaṇa*', *Journal of Indian Philosophy* 8.2: 149–89.

—— (1993) 'Transsexualism, gender, and anxiety in traditional India', *Journal of the American Oriental Society* 113.3: 374–401.

—— (1995) 'Gods in hiding: the *Mahābhārata*'s *Virāṭaparvan* and the divinity

of the Indian epic heroes', in Satya Pal Narang (ed.) *Modern Evaluation of the Mahābhārata: Prof. R.K. Sharma felicitation volume*, Delhi: Nag.
—— (1996) 'Vālmīki and Vyāsa: their contribution to India's discourse on ethnicity', *Journal of the Oriental Institute, Baroda* 46.1–2: 1–14.
Gombach, Barbara (2000) 'Ancillary stories in the Sanskrit *Mahābhārata*', 2 vols, unpublished thesis, Columbia University.
—— (2005) 'Born old: story, smṛti and the composition of the Sanskrit *Mahābhārata*', in T.S. Rukmani (ed.) *The Mahābhārata: what is not here is nowhere else (yannehāsti na tadkvacit)*, New Delhi: Munshiram Manoharlal.
Gönc Moačanin, Klara (2005) '*Dyūta* in the Sabhāparvan of the *Mahābhārata*: part of *rājasūya* sacrifice and/or potlatch and/or *daiva* and/or . . .?', in Petteri Koskikallio (ed.) *Epics, Khilas, and Purāṇas: continuities and ruptures*, Zagreb: Croatian Academy of Sciences and Arts.
Gonda, Jan (1965) '*Bandhu* in the Brāhmaṇas', *Adyar Library Bulletin* 29: 1–29.
—— (1969) *Aspects of Early Viṣṇuism*, Delhi: Motilal Banarsidass. First published Leiden, 1954.
—— (1974) *The Dual Divinities in the Religion of the Veda*, Amsterdam: North Holland Publishing Co.
González-Reimann, Luis (2002) *The Mahābhārata and the Yugas: India's great epic poem and the Hindu system of world ages*, New York: Peter Lang.
Goudriaan, T. (1990) 'The Ātman as charioteer: treatment of a Vedic allegory in the Kulālikāmnāya', in T. Goudriaan (ed.) *The Sanskrit Tradition and Tantrism* (Panels of the Seventh World Sanskrit Conference, Leiden, 1987, vol. 1), Leiden: Brill.
Greenberg, J. (1991) *Oedipus and Beyond: a clinical theory*, Cambridge, MA: Harvard University Press.
Greer, Patricia M. (2005) 'Ethical discourse in Udyogaparvan', in T.S. Rukmani (ed.) *The Mahābhārata: what is not here is nowhere else (yannehāsti na tadkvacit)*, Delhi: Munshiram Manoharlal.
Grosz, Elizabeth (1990) *Jacques Lacan: a feminist introduction*, London: Routledge.
Grünendahl, Reinhold (1997) 'Zur Stellung des Nārāyaṇīya im Mahābhārata', in Peter Schreiner (ed.) *Nārāyaṇīya-Studien*, Wiesbaden: Harrassowitz.
Halbfass, Wilhelm (2000) 'Goals of life: observations on the concept of puruṣārtha', in Ryutaro Tsuchida and Albrecht Wezler (eds) *Harānandalaharī: volume in honour of Professor Minoru Hara on his seventieth birthday*, Reinbek: Dr Inge Wezler / Verlag für Orientalistische Fachpublikationen.
Hara, Minoru (1973) 'The king as a husband of the earth (*mahī-pati*)', *Asiatische Studien / Études Asiatiques* 27.2: 97–114.
—— (1974) 'A note on the rākṣasa form of marriage', *Journal of the American Oriental Society* 94.3: 296–306.
—— (1977–8) 'Tapasvinī', *Annals of the Bhandarkar Oriental Research Institute* 58–9: 151–9.
—— (1996–7) 'Śrī: mistress of a king', *Orientalia Suecana* 45–6: 33–61.
—— (1999) 'A note on the phrase *dharma-kṣetre kuru-kṣetre*', *Journal of Indian Philosophy* 27.1–2: 49–66.
Harivaṃśa. Parashuram Lakshman Vaidya (ed.) (1969–71) *The Harivaṃśa: being the khila or supplement to the Mahābhārata, for the first time critically edited*, 2 vols, Poona: Bhandarkar Oriental Research Institute.
Harzer, Edeltraud (2005) 'Bhīṣma and the *vrātya* question', in T.S. Rukmani (ed.) *The*

Mahābhārata: what is not here is nowhere else (yannehāsti na tadkvacit), Delhi: Munshiram Manoharlal.

Hawthorne, Sîan (2004) 'Rethinking subjectivity in the gender-oriented study of religions: Kristeva and the "subject-in-process" ', in Ursula King and Tina Beattie (eds) *Gender, Religion and Diversity: cross-cultural perspectives*, London: Continuum.

Hegarty, James M. (2001) 'An apprenticeship in attentiveness: narrative patterning in the *Dyūtaparavan* and the *Nalopākhyāna* of the *Mahābhārata*', *Rocznik Orientalistyczny* 54.1: 33–62.

—— (2004) 'A fire of tongues: narrative patterning in the Sanskrit Mahābhārata', unpublished thesis, University of Manchester.

—— (2006) 'Extracting the *kathā-amṛta* (elixir of story): creation, ritual, sovereignty and textual structure in the Sanskrit Mahābhārata', *Journal of Vaishnava Studies* 14.2: 39–60.

Hejib, Alaka and Young, Katherine K. (1981) '*Klība* on the battlefield: towards a reinterpretation of Arjuna's despondency', *Annals of the Bhandarkar Oriental Research Institute* 61: 235–44.

Held, G.J. (1935) *The Mahābhārata: an ethnological study*, London: Kegan Paul, Trench, Trübner and Co.

Hermans, H.J.M. (2002) 'The dialogical self: one person, different stories', in Yoshihisa Kashima, Margaret Foddy, and Michael J. Platow (eds) *Self and Identity: personal, social, and symbolic*, Mahwah, NJ: Lawrence Ehrlbaum Associates Press.

Hermans, H.J.M. and Kempen, H.J.G. (1993) *The Dialogical Self: meaning as movement*, New York: Academic Press.

Hermans, H.J.M, Kempen, H.J. and van Loon, R.J. (1992) 'The dialogical self: beyond individualism and rationalism', *American Psychologist* 47.1: 23–33.

Hermans, H.J.M., Rijks, T.I. and Kempen, H.J.G. (1993) 'Imaginal dialogues in the self: theory and method', *Journal of Personality* 61.2: 207–36.

Hill, Peter (2001) *Fate, Predestination and Human Action in the Mahābhārata: a study in the history of ideas*, New Delhi: Munshiram Manoharlal.

Hiltebeitel, Alf (1976) *The Ritual of Battle: Krishna in the Mahābhārata*, Ithaca, NY, and London: Cornell University Press. Reprinted Albany: State University of New York Press, 1990; Delhi: Motilal Banarsidass, 1991.

—— (1977) 'Nahuṣa in the skies: a human king of heaven', *History of Religions* 16.4: 329–50.

—— (1980a) 'Draupadī's garments', *Indo-Iranian Journal* 22.2: 97–112.

—— (1980b) 'Śiva, the Goddess, and the disguises of the Pāṇḍavas and Draupadī', *History of Religions* 20.1–2: 147–74.

—— (1980–1) 'Sītā *vibhūṣitā*: the jewels for her journey', *Indologica Taurinensia* 8–9: 193–200.

—— (1981) 'Draupadī's hair', *Puruṣārtha* 5: 179–214.

—— (1982) 'Brothers, friends, and charioteers: parallel episodes in the Irish and Indian epics', in Edgar C. Polomé (ed.) *Homage to Georges Dumézil*, Washington DC: Institute for the Study of Man.

—— (1984) 'The two Kṛṣṇas on one chariot: Upaniṣadic imagery and epic mythology', *History of Religions* 24.1: 1–26.

—— (1988) *The Cult of Draupadī*, vol. 1, *Mythologies: from Gingee to Kurukṣetra*, Chicago, IL, and London: University of Chicago Press.

—— (1991a) *The Cult of Draupadī*, vol. 2, *On Hindu Ritual and the Goddess*, Chicago, IL, and London: University of Chicago Press.

—— (1991b) 'Two Kṛṣṇas, three Kṛṣṇas, four Kṛṣṇas, more Kṛṣṇas: dark interactions in the *Mahābhārata*', in Arvind Sharma (ed.) *Essays on the Mahābhārata*, Leiden: Brill.

—— (1994) 'Epic studies: classical Hinduism in the *Mahābhārata* and *Rāmāyaṇa*', *Annals of the Bhandarkar Oriental Research Institute* 74: 1–62.

—— (1998) 'Hair like snakes and mustached brides: crossed gender in an Indian folk cult', in Alf Hiltebeitel and Barbara D. Miller (eds) *Hair: its power and meaning in Asian cultures*, Albany: State University of New York Press.

—— (1999a) *Rethinking India's Oral and Classical Epics: Draupadī among Rajputs, Muslims, and Dalits*, Chicago, IL, and London: University of Chicago Press.

—— (1999b) 'Reconsidering Bhṛguisation', in Mary Brockington and Peter Schreiner (eds) *Composing a Tradition: concepts, techniques and relationships*, Zagreb: Croatian Academy of Sciences and Arts.

—— (1999c) 'Fathers of the bride, fathers of Satī: myths, rites, and scholarly practices', *Thamyris* 6.1: 65–94.

—— (2000) 'Draupadi's question', in Alf Hiltebeitel and Kathleen Erndl (eds) *Is the Goddess a Feminist? The politics of South Asian goddesses*, Sheffield: Sheffield Academic Press.

—— (2001a) *Rethinking the Mahābhārata: a reader's guide to the education of the dharma king*, Chicago, IL, and London: University of Chicago Press.

—— (2001b) 'Bhīṣma's sources', in Klaus Karttunen and Petteri Koskikallio (eds) *Vidyārṇavavandanam: essays in honor of Asko Parpola* (= *Studia Orientalia* 94), Helsinki: Finnish Oriental Society.

—— (2004a) 'Role, role model, and function: the Sanskrit epic warrior in comparison and theory', in Jacqueline Suthren Hirst and Lynn Thomas (eds) *Playing for Real: Hindu role models, religion, and gender*, New Delhi: Oxford University Press.

—— (2004b) 'More rethinking the *Mahābhārata*: toward a politics of bhakti', *Indo-Iranian Journal* 47.3–4: 203–27.

—— (2005a) 'Not without subtales: telling laws and truths in the Sanskrit epics', *Journal of Indian Philosophy* 33.4: 455–511.

—— (2005b) 'Buddhism and the *Mahābhārata*: boundary dynamics in textual practice', in Federico Squarcini (ed.) *Boundaries, Dynamics and Construction of Traditions in South Asia*, Florence: Firenze University Press/Munshiram Manoharlal.

—— (2005c) 'On reading Fitzgerald's Vyāsa', *Journal of the American Oriental Society* 125.2: 241–61.

—— (2006) 'Aśvaghoṣa's *Buddhacarita*: the first known close and critical reading of the Brahmanical Sanskrit epics', *Journal of Indian Philosophy* 34.3: 229–86.

—— (in press) 'Authorial paths through the two Sanskrit epics, via the *Rāmopākhyāna*', in Robert P. Goldman and Muneo Tokunaga (eds) *Proceedings of the Twelfth World Sanskrit Conference, Helsinki, 2003 (epic panels)*, Delhi: Motilal Banarsidass.

Hiltebeitel, Alf and Kloetzli, Randy (2004) 'Time', in Sushil Mittal and Gene R. Thursby (eds) *The Hindu World*, London and New York: Routledge.

Hirst, Jacqueline (1998) 'Myth and history', in Paul Bowen (ed.) *Themes and Issues in Hinduism*, London: Cassell.

Hofmann, Hasso (1974) *Repräsentation: Studien zur Wort- und Begriffsgeschichte von der Antike bis ins 19. Jahrhundert*, Berlin: Duncker and Humblot.

Hopkins, Edward Washburn (1969) *Epic Mythology*, New York: Biblo and Tannen. First published Strassburg, 1915.

Horner, I.B. (1999) 'Women under primitive Buddhism: laywomen and almswomen', in Kumkum Roy (ed.) *Women in Early Indian Societies*, New Delhi: Manohar.

Houben, Jan E.M. (2000) 'The ritual pragmatics of a Vedic hymn: the "riddle hymn" and the Pravargya ritual', *Journal of the American Oriental Society* 120.4: 499–536.

Huberman, Eric A. (1996) 'A note on the multi-centred imagination of the *Mahābhārata*', *Journal of Vaishnava Studies* 4.3: 151–60.

Hudson, D. Dennis (1996) 'Arjuna's sin: thoughts on the *Bhagavad-gītā* in its epic context', *Journal of Vaishnava Studies* 4.3: 65–84.

—— (2001) 'The "barley-corn" pattern of *Bhagavad-gītā* 12–16', *Journal of Vaishnava Studies* 9.2: 181–94.

Hudson, Emily T. (2005) 'Heaven's riddles or the hell trick: theodicy and narrative strategies in the *Mahābhārata*', in T.S. Rukmani (ed.) *The Mahābhārata: what is not here is nowhere else (yannehāsti na tadkvacit)*, New Delhi: Munshiram Manoharlal.

—— (2006) 'Disorienting *dharma*: ethics and the poetics of suffering in the *Mahābhārata*', unpublished thesis, Emory University.

Hughes, Mary Alice (1992) 'Epic women: east and west – a study with special reference to *The Mahabharata* and Gaelic heroic literature', *Journal of the Asiatic Society of Bengal* (4th series) 34.1–2: 33–96 (pt 1); 34.3–4: 1–106 (pt 2).

Hynes, William J. and Doty, William G. (eds) (1993) *Mythical Trickster Figures*, Tuscaloosa: University of Alabama Press.

Indradeva, Shrirama (1966) 'Correspondence between woman and nature in Indian thought', *Philosophy East and West* 16: 161–8.

Irigaray, Luce (1985) *This Sex which is Not One*, tr. Catherine Porter, Ithaca, NY: Cornell University Press.

Jacobsen, Knut A. (1996) 'The female pole of the Godhead in Tantrism and the *prakṛti* of Sāṃkhya', *Numen* 43.1: 56–81.

—— (1999) *Prakṛti in Sāṃkhya-Yoga: material principle, religious experience, ethical implications*, New York: Peter Lang.

—— (2005) '*Puruṣa* is different from everything: metaphors of difference in the *Mahābhārata*', paper presented at the *Epic Constructions* conference, SOAS, London, July 2005.

Jamison, Stephanie W. (1994) 'Draupadī on the walls of Troy: *Iliad* 3 from an Indic perspective', *Classical Antiquity* 13.1: 5–16.

—— (1996) *Sacrificed Wife / Sacrificer's Wife: women, ritual, and hospitality in ancient India*, New York and Oxford: Oxford University Press.

—— (1998) 'Rhinoceros toes, *Manu* V.17–18, and the development of the dharma system', *Journal of the American Oriental Society* 118.2: 249–56.

—— (1999) 'Penelope and the pigs: Indic perspectives on the *Odyssey*', *Classical Antiquity* 18.2: 227–72.

—— (2002) 'Giver or given? Some marriages in Kālidāsa', in Laurie L. Patton (ed.) *Jewels of Authority: women and textual tradition in Hindu India*, New York: Oxford University Press.

Jarow, E.H. Rick (1999) 'The letter of the law and the discourse of power: Karṇa and controversy in the *Mahābhārata*', *Journal of Vaishnava Studies* 8.1: 59–76.

Težić, Mislav (1986) 'Textual layers of the *Bhagavadgītā* as traces of Indian cultural history', in Wolfgang Morgenroth (ed.) *Sanskrit and World Culture: proceedings of the Fourth World Sanskrit Conference, Weimar, 1979*, Berlin: Akademie Verlag.

Johnson, Oliver A. (ed.) (1978) *Ethics: selections from classical and contemporary writers*, 4th edn, New York: Holt, Rinehart and Winston.

Johnson, William J. (ed. and tr.) (1998) *The Sauptikaparvan of the Mahābhārata: the massacre at night*, Oxford: Oxford University Press.

—— (tr.) (2005) *Mahābhārata*, book 3, *The Forest*, vol. 4, New York: New York University Press / John and Jennifer Clay Foundation.

Jones, W.T., Sontag, Frederick, Beckner, Morton O. and Fogelin, Robert J. (1977) *Approaches to Ethics: representative selections from classical times to the present*, 3rd edn, New York: McGraw-Hill Book Co.

Joshi, N.P. (1979) *Iconography of Balarāma*, New Delhi: Abhinav Publications.

Kakar, Sudhir (1978) *The Inner World: a psycho-analytic study of childhood and society in India*, Delhi: Oxford University Press.

Kāmasūtra. Gosvamī Dāmodar Shastri (ed.) (1929) *The Kāmasūtra by Srī Vātsyāyana Muni, with the Commentary Jayamangala of Yashodhar*, Benares: Chowkhamba Sanskrit Series Office (Kāshi Sanskrit Series). For English translation, see Doniger and Kakar 2003.

Kane, Pandurang Vaman (1968–77) *History of Dharmaśāstra (ancient and mediaeval religious and civil law)*, 2nd edn, Poona: Bhandarkar Oriental Research Institute.

Kangle, R.P. (1986) *The Kauṭilīya Arthaśāstra* (pts 1–2, text and translation), Delhi: Motilal Banarsidass.

Kantorowicz, Ernst H. (1957) *The King's Two Bodies: a study in mediaeval political theology*, Princeton, NJ: Princeton University Press.

Karve, Irawati (1969) *Yuganta: the end of an epoch*, tr. Irawati Karve, Poona: Deshmukh Prakashan. Reprinted New Delhi: Sangam Press, 1974; Bombay: Disha Books / Orient Longman, 1990.

Kaṭha Upaniṣad. See Olivelle 1998.

Kauṣītaki Brāhmaṇa. E.R. Sreekrishna Sarma (ed.) (1968), Wiesbaden (Verzeichnis der orientalischen Handschriften in Deutschland).

Kauṣītaki Upaniṣad. See Olivelle 1998.

Keith, Arthur Berriedale (1914) *The Veda of the Black Yajus School entitled Taittirīya Saṃhitā*, Cambridge, MA: Harvard University Press.

Kelkar, Meena (2003) 'Man-woman relationship in Indian philosophy', in Meena Kelkar and Deepti Gangavane (eds) *Feminism in Search of an Identity: the Indian context*, Jaipur and New Delhi: Rawat Publications. First published in *Indian Philosophical Quarterly*, 1999.

Khandelwal, Meena (2004) *Women in Ochre Robes: gendering Hindu renunciation*, Albany: State University of New York Press.

Kinjawadekar, Ramachandrashastri (ed.) (1929–36) *The Mahābhāratam with the Bhārata Bhāwadeepa Commentary of Nīlakaṇṭha*, 7 vols (incl. *Harivaṃśa*), Poona: Citrashala Press. Reprinted New Delhi: Oriental Reprint Books, 1979.

Kirfel, Willibald (1927) *Das Purāṇa Pañcalakṣaṇa: Versuch einer Textgeschichte*, Leiden: Brill.

Kiruṣṇappiḷḷai (1980) *Patiṉeṭṭāmpōr Nāṭakam*, Madras: Irattiṉa Nāyakar and Sons.

Klaes, Norbert (1975) *Conscience and Consciousness: ethical problems of Mahabharata*, Bangalore: Dharmaram College.

Koskikallio, Petteri (1995) 'Epic descriptions of the horse sacrifice', in Cezary Galewicz *et al.* (eds) *International Conference on Sanskrit and Related Studies, September 23–26, 1993: proceedings*, Cracow: Enigma.

—— (ed.) (2005) *Epics, Khilas, and Purāṇas: continuities and ruptures*, Zagreb: Croatian Academy of Sciences and Arts.

Krishan, Y. (1989) 'The meaning of the *puruṣārthas* in the *Mahābhārata*', in B.K. Matilal (ed.) *Moral Dilemmas in the Mahābhārata*, Shimla: Indian Institute of Advanced Study / Motilal Banarsidass.

Kristeva, Julia (1984) *Revolution in Poetic Language*, tr. Margaret Waller, New York: Columbia University Press.

Kuiper, F.B.J. (1962) 'The three strides of Viṣṇu', in Ernest Bender (ed.) *Indological Studies in Honor of W. Norman Brown*, New Haven, CT: American Oriental Society; reprinted in Kuiper 1983.

—— (1970) 'Cosmogony and conception – a query', *History of Religions* 10.2: 91–138; reprinted in Kuiper 1983.

—— (1975) 'The basic concept of Vedic religion', *History of Religions* 15.2: 107–20; reprinted in Kuiper 1983.

—— (1979) *Varuṇa and Vidūṣaka: on the origin of the Sanskrit drama*, Amsterdam: North Holland Publishing Co.

—— (1983) *Ancient Indian Cosmogony*, ed. J. Irwin, Delhi: Vikas.

Kulke, Hermann and Rothermund, Dietmar (1998) *A History of India*, 3rd edn, London: Routledge. First published 1986.

Kūrma Purāṇa. Anand Swarup Gupta (ed.) (1971) Varanasi: All India Kashiraj Trust.

Kurtz, Stanley N. (1992) *All the Mothers Are One*, New York: Columbia University Press.

Kuznetsova, Irina (2006) '*Karmayoga* as sacrifice: tracing the continuity of ideas from the Vedas to the Mahābhārata', *Journal of Vaishnava Studies* 14.2: 115–27.

Lacan, Jacques (1977) *Écrits: a selection*, tr. Alan Sheridan, New York: W.W. Norton & Co.

—— (1982). See Mitchell and Rose (eds) (1982).

—— (1993) *The Seminar*, book 3, *The Psychoses, 1955–1956*, ed. Jacques-Alain Miller, tr. Russell Grigg, London: Routledge.

Laine, James W. (1981) 'The creation account in Manusmṛti', *Annals of the Bhandarkar Oriental Research Institute* 62: 157–68.

Larrington, Carolyne (tr.) (1996) *The Poetic Edda*, Oxford: Oxford University Press.

Lath, Mukund (1990) 'The concept of *ānṛśaṃsya* in the *Mahābhārata*', in R.N. Dandekar (ed.) *The Mahābhārata Revisited*, New Delhi: Sahitya Akademi.

Leslie, I. Julia (1986) '*Strīsvabhāva*: the inherent nature of women', in N.J. Allen *et al.* (eds) *Oxford University Papers on India*, vol. 1, pt 1, New Delhi: Oxford University Press.

—— (1989) *The Perfect Wife: the orthodox Hindu woman according to the Strīdharmapaddhati of Tryambakayajvan*, Delhi: Oxford University Press.

—— (ed.) (1991) *Roles and Rituals for Hindu Women*, London: Pinter.

—— (ed.) (1996) *Myth and Mythmaking: continuous evolution in Indian tradition*, Richmond: Curzon.

—— (1998) 'A bird bereaved: the identity and significance of Vālmīki's *krauñca*', *Journal of Indian Philosophy* 26.5: 455–87.

Leslie, Julia and McGee, Mary (eds) (2000) *Invented Identities: the interplay of gender, religion and politics in India*, New Delhi: Oxford University Press.

Lévi-Strauss, Claude (1955) 'The structural study of myth', *Journal of American Folklore* 78, no. 270: 428–44; reprinted in Lévi-Strauss 1968.

—— (1968) *Structural Anthropology*, New York: Doubleday and Co.

Lidova, Natalia (2002–3) 'Indramahotsava in late Vedic and early epic traditions', *Journal of the Asiatic Society of Mumbai* 77–8: 85–108.

Lindtner, C. (1995) '*Lokasaṃgraha*, Buddhism and *buddhiyoga* in the *Gītā*', in Satya Pal Narang (ed.) *Modern Evaluation of the Mahābhārata: Prof. R.K. Sharma felicitation volume*, Delhi: Nag.

Linke, Uli (1989) 'Women, androgynes, and models of creation in Norse mythology', *Journal of Psychohistory* 16.3: 231–62.

Lothspeich, Pamela (2006) 'Avenging the violation of Draupadi (and *Bhārata Mātā*) in Badrinātha Bhaṭṭa's *Kuru-vana-dahana*', *Journal of Vaishnava Studies* 14.2: 129–45.

Lubotsky, Alexander (1997) *A Ṛgvedic Word Concordance*, 2 vols, New Haven, CT: American Oriental Society.

Luhmann, Niklas (1998) *Gesellschaftsstruktur und Semantik: Studien zur Wissens-soziologie der modernen Gesellschaft*, vol. 1, Frankfurt: Suhrkamp.

Luper, Steven and Brown, Curtis (1999) *The Moral Life*, 2nd edn, Fort Worth, TX: Harcourt Brace College Publishers.

Lutgendorf, Philip (1991) *The Life of a Text: performing the Rāmcaritmānas of Tulsidas*, Berkeley: University of California Press.

Macdonell, A.A. (1974) *Vedic Mythology*, Delhi: Motilal Banarsidass. First published Strassburg: Trübner, 1897.

McGee, Mary (2002) 'Ritual rights: the gender implications of *adhikāra*', in Laurie L. Patton (ed.) *Jewels of Authority: women and textual tradition in Hindu India*, New York: Oxford University Press.

McGrath, Kevin (2004) *The Sanskrit Hero: Karṇa in epic Mahābhārata*, Leiden: Brill.

Magnone, Paolo (2000) 'Floodlighting the deluge: traditions in comparison', in Piotr Balcerowicz and Marek Mejor (eds) *On the Understanding of Other Cultures*, Warsaw: Instytut Orientalistyczny, Uniwersytet Warszawski.

—— (2003) 'Patterns of *tejas* in the epics', paper presented at the Twelfth World Sanskrit Conference, Helsinki, July 2003.

Mahābhārata. See Vishnu S. Sukthankar *et al.* (eds) 1933–66.

Malamoud, Charles (1989) 'Un dieu védique: le Courroux', in *Cuire le Monde: rite et pensée dans l'Inde ancienne*, Paris: Éditions la Decouverte.

Malinar, Angelika (1996) *Rājavidyā: Das königliche Wissen um Herrschaft und Verzicht. Studien zur Bhagavadgītā*, Wiesbaden: Harrassowitz.

—— (2005) 'Blindheit und Sehen in der Erzählung des Mahābhārata', in A. Luther (ed.) *Odyssee-Rezeptionen*, Frankfurt: Verlag Antike.

Mallison, Françoise (1979) 'A note on holiness allowed to women: pativratā and satī', in J.P. Sinha (ed.) *Ludwik Sternbach Felicitation Volume*, vol. 2, Lucknow: Akhila Bharatiya Sanskrit Parishad.

Mānava Dharmaśāstra. Patrick Olivelle (ed. and tr.) with the editorial assistance of Suman Olivelle (2005) *Manu's Code of Law: a critical edition and translation of the Mānava-Dharmaśāstra*, New York: Oxford University Press.

Mangels, Annette (1994) *Zur Erzähltechnik im Mahābhārata*, Hamburg: Kovac.

Mani, Vettam (1979) *Purāṇic Encyclopaedia*, Delhi: Motilal Banarsidass. First English edition 1975.

Matchett, Freda (1996) 'The *Harivaṃśa*: supplement to the *Mahābhārata* and independent text', *Journal of Vaishnava Studies* 4.3: 139–50.

Matilal, Bimal Krishna (1991) 'Kṛṣṇa: in defence of a devious divinity', in Arvind Sharma (ed.) *Essays on the Mahābhārata*, Leiden: Brill.

—— (2002) 'Dharma and rationality', in Jonardon Ganeri (ed.) *Ethics and Epics: philosophy, culture, and religion. The collected essays of Bimal Krishna Matilal*, New Delhi: Oxford University Press.

Mauss, Marcel (1990) *The Gift: the form and reason for exchange in archaic societies*, tr. W.D. Halls, London: Routledge. First published in French, Paris, 1925.

Mehendale, M.A. (1984) 'Nemesis and some *Mahābhārata* episodes', in S.D. Joshi (ed.) *Amṛtadhārā: Professor R.N. Dandekar felicitation volume*, Delhi: Ajanta.

—— (1995a) *Reflections on the Mahābhārata War*, Shimla: Indian Institute of Advanced Study.

—— (1995b) 'Is there only one version of the game of dice in the *Mahābhārata*?', in Satya Pal Narang (ed.) *Modern Evaluation of the Mahābhārata: Prof. R.K. Sharma felicitation volume*, Delhi: Nag.

—— (2001) 'Interpolations in the *Mahābhārata*', *Annals of the Bhandarkar Oriental Research Institute* 82: 193–212.

Mehta, J.L. (1990) 'Dvaipāyana, poet of being and becoming', in R.N. Dandekar (ed.) *The Mahābhārata Revisited*, New Delhi: Sahitya Akademi.

Mehta, M. (1973) 'The problem of the double introduction to the *Mahābhārata*', *Journal of the American Oriental Society* 93.4: 547–50.

Meiland, Justin (tr.) (2005) *Mahābhārata*, book 9, *Śalya*, vol. 1, New York: New York University Press / John and Jennifer Clay Foundation.

Menski, Werner F. (2005) *Hindu Law: beyond tradition and modernity*, Oxford: Oxford University Press. First published 2003.

Meyer, Johann Jakob (1930) *Sexual Life in Ancient India: a study in the comparative history of Indian culture*, tr. unknown, London: Routledge. First published as *Das Weib im altindischen Epos*, Leipzig: Verlag von Wilhelm Heims, 1915.

Miller, Barbara Stoler (1991) 'Contending narratives: the political life of the Indian epics', *Journal of Asian Studies* 50.4: 783–92.

Millet, Kate (1972) *Sexual Politics*, London: Abacus.

Minkowski, Christopher Z. (1989) 'Janamejaya's *sattra* and ritual structure', *Journal of the American Oriental Society* 109.3: 401–20.

—— (1991) 'Snakes, *sattra*s and the *Mahābhārata*', in Arvind Sharma (ed.) *Essays on the Mahābhārata*, Leiden: Brill.

—— (2001) 'The interrupted sacrifice and the Sanskrit epics', *Journal of Indian Philosophy* 29.1–2: 169–86.

Mitchell, Juliet and Rose, Jacqueline (eds) (1982) *Feminine Sexuality: Jacques Lacan and the École Freudienne*, tr. Jacqueline Rose, New York: W.W. Norton / Pantheon Books.

Mitchell, Stephen A. and Black, Margaret J. (1995) *Freud and Beyond: a history of modern psychoanalytic thought*, New York: Basic Books.

Monier-Williams, Monier (1964) *A Sanskrit–English Dictionary, etymologically and philologically arranged, with special reference to cognate Indo-European languages*, Oxford: Clarendon Press. First published 1899.

Moorthy, K. Krishna (1990) 'Socio-cultural milieu of the *Mahābhārata*', in R.N. Dandekar (ed.) *The Mahābhārata Revisited*, New Delhi: Sahitya Akademi.

More, Sadanand (1995) *Kṛṣṇa: the man and his mission. An enquiry into the rationale of inter-relationship between Kṛṣṇa's life, mission and philosophy*, Pune: Gaaj Prakashan.

Morson, Gary Saul (1994) *Narrative and Freedom: the shadows of time*, New Haven, CT: Yale University Press.

Moya, Paula L. (1996) 'Postmodernism, realism, and the politics of identity: Cherrie, Moraga, and Chicana feminism', in C.T. Mohanty and M. Jacqui Alexander (eds) *Feminist Genealogies, Colonial Legacies, and Democratic Futures*, New York: Routledge.

Muṇḍaka Upaniṣad. See Olivelle 1998.

Nāgānanda. Mādhava Candra Ghoṣa (ed.) (1991) *The Recensions of the Nāgānanda by Harṣadeva*, vol. 1, *The North Indian Recension*, with a general introduction by Michael Hahn, New Delhi: Aditya Prakashan.

Ñāṇamoli, Bhikku (tr.) (1975) *The Path of Purification (Visuddhimagga) by Bhadantācariya Buddhaghosa*, Kandy: Buddhist Publication Society.

Nanda, Serena (1990) *Neither Man nor Woman: the hijras of India*, Belmont, CA: Wadsworth.

Narang, Satya Pal (ed.) (1995) *Modern Evaluation of the Mahābhārata: Prof. R.K. Sharma felicitation volume*, Delhi: Nag.

Natarajan, Kanchana (2001) 'Gendering of early Indian philosophy: a study of *Samkhyakarika*', *Economic and Political Weekly*, April 28: 1398–404.

Nicholas, Ralph (1995) 'The effectiveness of the Hindu sacrament (*saṃskāra*): caste, marriage, and divorce in Bengali culture', in Lindsey Harlan and Paul B. Courtright (eds) *From the Margins of Hindu Marriage: essays on gender, religion, and culture*, New York: Oxford University Press.

Nīlakaṇṭha. See Kinjawadekar.

Norman, K.R. (1985) *The Rhinoceros Horn and Other Early Buddhist Poems: the group of discourses (Sutta Nipāta)*, London: Pali Text Society.

Oberlies, Thomas (1988) 'Die Śvetāśvatara-Upaniṣad: eine Studie ihrer Gotteslehre (Studien zu den "mittleren" Upaniṣads I)', *Wiener Zeitschrift für die Kunde Südasiens* 32: 35–62.

—— (1995) 'Arjunas Himmelreise und die Tīrthayātrā der Pāṇḍavas. Zur Struktur des Tīrthayātrāparvan des Mahābhārata', *Acta Orientalia* (Copenhagen) 56: 106–24.

—— (1997) 'Die Textgeschichte der Śvetadvīpa-Episode des *Nārāyaṇīya* (Mbh. 12.321–326)', in Peter Schreiner (ed.) *Nārāyaṇīya-Studien*, Wiesbaden: Harrassowitz.

—— (1999) *Die Religion des Ṛgveda*, vol. 2, *Kompositionsanalyse der Soma-Hymnen*, Vienna: De Nobili Research Library.

—— (2003) *A Grammar of Epic Sanskrit*, New York: Walter de Gruyter.

Obeyesekere, Gananath (1990) *The Work of Culture: symbolic transformation in psychoanalysis and anthropology*, Chicago, IL: University of Chicago Press.

O'Flaherty, Wendy Doniger (1973) *Asceticism and Eroticism in the Mythology of Śiva*, London: Oxford University Press.

—— (1980) *Women, Androgynes, and Other Mythical Beasts*, Chicago, IL, and London: University of Chicago Press.

—— (tr.) (1981) *The Rig Veda: an anthology*, London: Penguin.
—— (1984) *Dreams, Illusion, and Other Realities*, Chicago, IL, and London: University of Chicago Press.
O'Flaherty, Wendy Doniger: see also Doniger, Wendy.
Olivelle, Patrick (ed. and tr.) (1977) *Vāsudevāśrama Yatidharmaprakāśa: a treatise on world renunciation*, part 2, Vienna: De Nobili Research Library.
—— (1978) 'Ritual suicide and the rite of renunciation', *Wiener Zeitschrift für die Kunde Südasiens* 22: 19–44.
—— (1993) *The Āśrama System: the history and hermeneutics of a religious institution*, New York: Oxford University Press.
—— (tr.) (1996) *Upaniṣads*, New York: Oxford University Press.
—— (1997) 'Amṛtā: women and Indian technologies of immortality', *Journal of Indian Philosophy* 25.5: 427–49.
—— (tr.) (1998) *The Early Upaniṣads: annotated text and translation*, New York: Oxford University Press.
—— (tr.) (1999) *Dharmasūtras: the law codes of ancient India*, New York: Oxford University Press.
—— (tr.) (2000) *Dharmasūtras: the law codes of Āpastamba, Gautama, Baudhāyana, and Vasiṣṭha. Annotated text and translation*, Delhi: Motilal Banarsidass.
—— (ed. and tr.) (2004) *The Law Code of Manu*, New York: Oxford University Press.
Pai, Anant (ed.) and Kadam, D. (illustr.) (1989) *Mahābhārata*, 42 Amar Chitra Katha comic books, Bombay: India Book House Pvt. Reprinted in 3 vols, 2005.
Pande, G.C. (1990) 'The socio-cultural milieu of the *Mahābhārata*: an age of change', in R.N. Dandekar (ed.) *The Mahābhārata Revisited*, New Delhi: Sahitya Akademi.
Parkhill, Thomas (1995) *The Forest Setting in Hindu Epics: princes, sages, demons*, Lewiston, NY: Mellen University Press.
Parpola, Asko (1984) 'On the Jaiminīya and Vādhūla traditions of South India and the Pāṇḍu/Pāṇḍava problem', *Studia Orientalia* 55: 3–42.
—— (2002) 'Πανδαίη and Sītā: on the historical background of the Sanskrit epics', *Journal of the American Oriental Society* 122.2: 361–73.
Parrott, Rodney J. (1986) 'The problem of the Sāṃkhya *tattvas* as both cosmic and psychological phenomena', *Journal of Indian Philosophy* 14.1: 55–77.
—— (1990) 'The worth of the world in classical Sāṃkhya', *Annals of the Bhandarkar Oriental Research Institute* 71: 83–108.
Patton, Laurie L. (2002a) 'Introduction', in Laurie L. Patton (ed.) *Jewels of Authority: women and textual tradition in Hindu India*, New York: Oxford University Press.
—— (2002b) 'Mantras and miscarriage: controlling birth in the late Vedic period', in Laurie L. Patton (ed.) *Jewels of Authority: women and textual tradition in Hindu India*, New York: Oxford University Press.
—— (2004) ' "When the fire goes out, the wife shall fast": notes on women's agency in the *Aśvalāyana Gṛhya Sūtra*', in Maitreyee Deshpande (ed.) *Problems in Sanskrit and Vedic Literature*, Delhi: New Indian Book Centre.
Pelissero, Alberto (2002) 'A sexual masquerade: Arjuna as a eunuch in the *Mahābhārata*', in Alessandro Monti (ed.) *Hindu Masculinities Across the Ages: updating the past*, Turin: L'Harmattan Italia.
Penner, Hans H. (1965–6) 'Cosmogony as myth in the Vishnu Purāṇa', *History of Religions* 5: 283–99.

Phaedrus. Harold North Fowler (tr.) (1943) *Plato I: Euthyphro, Apology, Crito, Phaedo, Phaedrus*, London: William Heinemann (Loeb Classical Library; first published 1914).

Piantelli, Mario (2002) 'King Janaka as a male chauvinistic pig in the *Mahābhārata*', in Alessandro Monti (ed.) *Hindu Masculinities Across the Ages: updating the past*, Turin: L'Harmattan Italia.

Piatigorsky, Alexander (1993) *Mythological Deliberations: lectures on the phenomenology of myth*, ed. Audrey Cantlie, London: School of Oriental and African Studies, University of London.

Pintchman, Tracy (1998) 'Gender complementarity and gender hierarchy in Purāṇic accounts of creation', *Journal of the American Academy of Religion* 66.2: 257–82.

—— (2007) 'Lovesick *gopī* or woman's best friend? The mythic *sakhi* and ritual friendships among women in Benares', in Tracy Pintchman (ed.) *Women's Lives, Women's Rituals in the Hindu Tradition*, New York: Oxford University Press.

Porter, Roy and Teich, Mikulas (eds) (1994) *Sexual Knowledge, Sexual Science: the history of attitudes to sexuality*, Cambridge: Cambridge University Press.

Proudfoot, I. (1979) 'Interpreting *Mahābhārata* episodes as sources for the history of ideas', *Annals of the Bhandarkar Oriental Research Institute* 60: 41–63.

Radin, Paul (1972) *The Trickster: a study in American Indian mythology, with commentaries by Karl Kerényi and C.G. Jung*, New York: Schocken Books.

Ramankutty, P.V. (1999) *Curse as a Motif in the Mahābhārata*, Delhi: Nag.

Ramanujan, A.K. (1989) 'Where mirrors are windows: toward an anthology of reflections', *History of Religions* 28.3: 187–216.

—— (1991) 'Repetition in the *Mahābhārata*', in Arvind Sharma (ed.) *Essays on the Mahābhārata*, Leiden: Brill.

Rāmāyaṇa. G.H. Bhatt, U.P. Shah *et al.* (eds) (1960–75) *The Vālmīki-Rāmāyaṇa Critically Edited for the First Time*, 7 vols, Baroda: Oriental Institute.

Rees, Alwyn and Rees, Brinley (1961) *Celtic Heritage: ancient tradition in Ireland and Wales*, London: Thames and Hudson.

Reich, Tamar C. (1998) 'A battlefield of a text: inner textual interpretation in the Sanskrit *Mahābhārata*', unpublished thesis, University of Chicago.

—— (2001) 'Sacrificial violence and textual battles: inner textual interpretation in the Sanskrit *Mahābhārata*', *History of Religions* 41.2: 142–69.

—— (2005a) 'The critic of ritual as ritual reviler in the Āśvamedhikaparvan', in T.S. Rukmani (ed.) *The Mahābhārata: what is not here is nowhere else (yannehāsti na tadkvacit)*, Delhi: Munshiram Manoharlal.

—— (2005b) 'Violence, sacrifice and debate in the *Mahābhārata*', paper presented at the *Epic Constructions* conference, SOAS, London, July 2005.

Renou, Louis (1979) *L'Inde Fondamentale: études d'indianisme réunies et présentées par Charles Malamoud*, Paris: Hermann.

Ṛgveda. N.S. Sontakke *et al.* (eds) (1933–51) *Ṛgveda-Saṁhitā with the Commentary of Sāyaṇāchārya*, 5 vols, Poona: Vaidika Saṁśodhana Maṇḍala.

Rígsþula. See Dronke 1997; Larrington 1996.

Rocher, Ludo (1979) 'The Sūtras and Śāstras on the eight types of marriage', in J.P. Sinha (ed.) *Ludwik Sternbach Felicitation Volume*, vol. 1, Lucknow: Akhila Bharatiya Sanskrit Parishad.

—— (1986) *The Purāṇas*, Wiesbaden: Harrassowitz.

Roebuck, Valerie (tr.) (2003) *The Upaniṣads*, London: Penguin. First published by Penguin Books India, 2000.

Róheim, Géza (1952) 'Culture hero and trickster in North American mythology', in Sol Tax (ed.) *Indian Tribes of Aboriginal America: selected papers of the Twenty-Ninth International Congress of Americanists*, Chicago, IL: University of Chicago Press.

Rose, Jacqueline (1982) 'Introduction – II', in Juliet Mitchell and Jacqueline Rose (eds) *Feminine Sexuality: Jacques Lacan and the École Freudienne*, New York: W.W. Norton / Pantheon Books.

Roy, Kumkum (1996) 'Vedic cosmogonies: conceiving/controlling creation', in R. Champakalakshmi and S. Gopal (eds) *Tradition, Dissent and Ideology: essays in honour of Romila Thapar*, Delhi: Oxford University Press.

Rubin, Gayle (1996) 'The traffic in women: notes on the "political economy" of sex', in Joan Wallach Scott (ed.) *Feminism and History*, Oxford: Oxford University Press.

Saklani, Atul and Negi, Rajpal Singh (2005) 'The living legend of Rāja Duryodhana: socio-historical constructions on *Mahābhārata* in Himalayan society', in T.S. Rukmani (ed.) *The Mahābhārata: what is not here is nowhere else (yannehāsti na tadkvacit)*, Delhi: Munshiram Manoharlal.

Sāmba Purāṇa. See von Stietencron 1966.

Sāmkhyakārikā. See Gerald J. Larson (1969) *Classical Sāṃkhya: an interpretation of its history and meaning*, Delhi: Motilal Banarsidass, pp. 257–82; Burley 2007, pp. 163–79.

Sangari, Kumkum and Chakravarti, Uma (eds) (1999) *From Myths to Markets: essays on gender*, New Delhi: Manohar.

Sanyal, Apurba Kumar (2006) 'The wonder that is the Mahabharata', *Bulletin of the Ramakrishna Mission Institute of Culture* 57.4: 195–9.

Śatapatha Brāhmaṇa. Albrecht Weber (ed.) (1924) *The Çatapatha-Brāhmaṇa in the Mādhyandina-Çākhā, with extracts from the commentaries of Sāyaṇa, Harisvāmin and Dvivedaganga*, Leipzig (first published Berlin, 1855). For English translation, see Julius Eggeling (tr.) (1963) *The Śatapatha-Brāhmaṇa According to the Text of the Mādhyandina School*, 5 vols, Delhi: Motilal Banarsidass (first published Oxford: Clarendon, 1882–1900).

Sax, William S. (1997) 'Fathers, sons, and rhinoceroses: masculinity and violence in the *pāṇḍav līlā*', *Journal of the American Oriental Society* 117.2: 278–93.

—— (2002) *Dancing the Self: personhood and performance in the pāṇḍav līlā of Garhwal*, New York: Oxford University Press.

Scharf, Peter (2003) *Rāmopākhyāna – the story of Rāma in the Mahābhārata. An independent-study reader in Sanskrit*, London: RoutledgeCurzon.

Scheftelowitz, J. (1929) *Die Zeit als Schicksalsgottheit in der indischen und iranischen Religion*, Stuttgart: Kohlhammer.

Schmidt, Hanns-Peter (1987) *Some Women's Rites and Rights in the Veda*, Poona: Bhandarkar Oriental Research Institute.

Schmidt, Richard (1922) *Beiträge zur indischen Erotik: das Liebensleben des Sanskritvolkes, nach den Quellen dargestellt*, 3rd edn, Berlin: Hermann Barsdorf.

Schreiner, Peter (1988) 'Yoga – lebenshilfe oder sterbetechnik?', *Umwelt & Gesundheit* (Köln) 3–4: 12–18.

—— (ed.) (1997) *Nārāyaṇīya-Studien*, Wiesbaden: Harrassowitz.

—— (1999a) 'What comes first (in the *Mahābhārata*): Sāṃkhya or Yoga?', *Asiatische Studien / Études Asiatiques* 53.3: 755–77.

—— (1999b) 'Fire – its literary perception in the *Mahābhārata*', in Maya Burger and Peter Schreiner (eds) *The Perception of the Elements in the Hindu Traditions*, Bern: Peter Lang.

Scott, Erica (2001) 'Composing as a person: gender, identity, and student writing', *Women in Literacy and Life Assembly* 10: 17–22.

Selvanayagam, I. (1992) 'Aśoka and Arjuna as counterfigures standing on the field of *dharma*: a historical-hermeneutical perspective', *History of Religions* 32: 59–75.

Shah, Shalini (1995) *The Making of Womanhood: gender relations in the Mahābhārata*, New Delhi: Manohar.

—— (2002) 'Sexual politics and the cult of the mother goddess in the *Mahābhārata*', in Nilima Chitgopekar (ed) *Invoking Goddesses: gender politics in Indian religion*, New Delhi: Har-Anand.

Shankar, S. (1994) 'The thumb of Ekalavya: postcolonial studies and the "third world" scholar in a neocolonial world', *World Literature Today* 68.3: 479–87.

Sharma, Arvind (2000) 'Of *śūdras*, *sūtas* and *ślokas*: why is the *Mahābhārata* preeminently in the *anuṣṭubh* metre?', *Indo-Iranian Journal* 43.3: 225–78.

Shulman, David Dean (1991) 'Towards a historical poetics of the Sanskrit epics', *International Folklore Review* 8: 9–17; reprinted in *The Wisdom of Poets: studies in Tamil, Telugu, and Sanskrit* (2001), New Delhi: Oxford University Press.

—— (1992) '*Devana* and *daiva*', in A.W. van den Hoek, D.H.A. Kolff and M.S. Oort (eds) *Ritual, State and History in South Asia: essays in honour of J.C. Heesterman*, Leiden: Brill.

—— (1993) *The Hungry God: Hindu tales of filicide and devotion*, Chicago, IL, and London: University of Chicago Press. Reprinted 2002.

—— (1994) 'On being human in the Sanskrit epic: the riddle of Nala', *Journal of Indian Philosophy* 22.1: 1–29.

—— (1996) 'The Yakṣa's questions', in G. Hasan-Rokem and D. Shulman (eds) *Untying the Knot: on riddles and other enigmatic modes*, New York: Oxford University Press.

von Simson, Georg (1984) 'The mythic background of the Mahābhārata', *Indologica Taurinensia* 12: 191–223.

—— (1986) 'Ṛśyaśṛṅga: Ursprung und Hintergrund', in Eivind Kahrs (ed.) *Kalyāṇamitrārāgaṇam: essays in honour of Nils Simonsson*, Oslo: Norwegian University Press / Institute for Comparative Research in Human Culture.

—— (1992) 'Gaṇeśa and Vṛtra', in H.S. Prasad (ed.) *Philosophy, Grammar and Indology: essays in honour of Professor Gustav Roth*, Delhi: Indian Books Centre.

—— (1994) 'Die zeitmythische Struktur des Mahābhārata', in Reinhard Sternemann (ed.) *Bopp-Symposium 1992 der Humboldt-Universität zu Berlin*, Heidelberg: Universitätsverlag C. Winter.

—— (1999) 'Narrated time and its relation to the supposed year myth in the *Mahābhārata*', in Mary Brockington and Peter Schreiner (eds) *Composing a Tradition: concepts, techniques and relationships*, Zagreb: Croatian Academy of Sciences and Arts.

—— (2000a) 'A propos *jīvan-mukta* in the *Mahābhārata*: the case of Yudhiṣṭhira', in Ryutaro Tsuchida and Albrecht Wezler (eds) *Harānandalaharī: volume in honour of Professor Minoru Hara on his seventieth birthday*, Reinbek: Dr Inge Wezler / Verlag für Orientalistische Fachpublikationen.

—— (2000b) 'Interpreting Vedic myth: the story of Indra and Kutsa', *Indologica Taurinensia* 17–18 (1991–2): 333–42.

—— (2005) 'The Nalopākhyāna as a calendar myth', in Petteri Koskikallio (ed.) *Epics, Khilas, and Purāṇas: continuities and ruptures*, Zagreb: Croatian Academy of Sciences and Arts.

—— (forthcoming) 'The lunar character of Balarāma/Saṃkarṣaṇa', in Petteri Koskikallio (ed.) *Parallels and Comparisons*, Zagreb: Croatian Academy of Sciences and Arts.

Singh, K.S. (ed.) (1993) *The Mahābhārata in the Tribal and Folk Traditions of India*, Shimla: Indian Institute of Advanced Study / New Delhi: Anthropological Survey of India.

Singh, Sarva Daman (1988) *Polyandry in Ancient India*, Delhi: Motilal Banarsidass.

Sinha, Braj M. (1991) '*Arthaśāstra* categories in the *Mahābhārata*: from *daṇḍanīti* to *rājadharma*', in Arvind Sharma (ed.) *Essays on the Mahābhārata*, Leiden: Brill.

Sircar, D.C. (1971) *Studies in the Religious Life of Ancient and Medieval India*, Delhi: Motilal Banarsidass.

Śiva Purāṇa. Pāṇḍeya Rāmateja (ed.) (*saṃvat* 2020, = 1963 CE) Kāśī: Paṇḍita-Pustakālaya. For other editions, see the notes accompanying the references in the text.

Skanda Purāṇa. Skandamahāpurāṇam (2003), Varanasi: Chowkhamba Sanskrit Series Office (Chowkhamba Sanskrit Series).

Slaje, Walter (2000a) 'Towards a history of the *jīvanmukti* concept: the *Mokṣadharma* in the *Mahābhārata*', in Ryutaro Tsuchida and Albrecht Wezler (eds) *Harānandalaharī: volume in honour of Professor Minoru Hara on his seventieth birthday*, Reinbek: Dr Inge Wezler / Verlag für Orientalistische Fachpublikationen.

—— (2000b) 'Liberation from intentionality and involvement: on the concept of *jīvanmukti* according to the *Mokṣopāya*', *Journal of Indian Philosophy* 28.2: 171–94.

Smith, Brian K. (1989) *Reflections on Resemblance, Ritual, and Religion*, New York: Oxford University Press.

—— (1994) *Classifying the Universe: the ancient Indian varṇa system and the origins of caste*, New York: Oxford University Press.

Smith, John D. (1992) 'The hero as gifted man: the story of Nala', in Christopher Shackle and Rupert Snell (eds) *The Indian Narrative: perspectives and patterns*, Wiesbaden: Harrassowitz.

—— (ed.) (1999a) *Mahābhārata* (e-text), Pune: Bhandarkar Oriental Research Institute (http://bombay.indology.info/mahabharata/statement.html).

—— (1999b) 'Winged words revisited: diction and meaning in Indian epic', *Bulletin of the School of Oriental and African Studies* 62: 267–305.

Smith, Mary Carroll (1991) 'Epic parthenogenesis', in Arvind Sharma (ed.) *Essays on the Mahābhārata*, Leiden: Brill.

Smith, William L. (1986) 'Explaining the inexplicable: uses of the curse in Rāma literature', in Eivind Kahrs (ed.) *Kalyāṇamitrārāgaṇam: essays in honour of Nils Simonsson*, Oslo: Norwegian University Press / Institute for Comparative Research in Human Culture.

Söhnen-Thieme, Renate (1999) 'On the composition of the *Dyūtaparvan* of the *Mahābhārata*', in Mary Brockington and Peter Schreiner (eds) *Composing a Tradition: concepts, techniques and relationships*, Zagreb: Croatian Academy of Sciences and Arts.

—— (2005) 'Buddhist tales in the *Mahābhārata*?', paper presented at the Fourth

Dubrovnik International Conference on the Sanskrit Epics and Purāṇas, September 2005.

Solli, Brit (2002) *Seid: myter, sjamanisme og kjønn i vikingenes tid*, Oslo: Pax Forlag.

Sörensen, Sören (1963) *An Index to the Names in the Mahābhārata, with short explanations and a concordance to the Bombay and Calcutta editions and P.C. Roy's translation*, Delhi: Motilal Banarsidass. First published 1904.

Spratt, Philip (1966) *Hindu Culture and Personality: a psycho-analytic study*, Bombay: P.C. Manaktalas and Sons Private Ltd.

Stein, Wolfgang (1993) *Der Kulturheros-Trickster der Winnebago und seine Stellung zu vergleichbaren Gestalten in den oralen Traditionen nordamerikanischer Indianer: eine Kritik an der Kulturheros-Trickster-Konzeption Paul Radins*, Bonn: Holos.

von Stietencron, Heinrich (1966) *Indische Sonnenpriester: Sāmba und die Śākadvīpīya-Brāhmaṇa*, Wiesbaden: Harrassowitz.

Stokes, Bryan (2004) *Adam's Curse: a future without man*, New York: W.W. Norton.

Strong, John S. (1983) *The Legend of King Aśoka: a study and translation of the Aśokāvadāna*, Princeton, NJ: Princeton University Press.

Sukthankar, Vishnu S. (ed.) (1933) *The Ādiparvan: being the first book of the Mahābhārata, the great epic of India*, 2 parts, Poona: Bhandarkar Oriental Research Institute. Vol. 1 of Sukthankar *et al.* (eds) 1933–66.

—— (1957) *On the Meaning of the Mahābhārata*, Bombay: Asiatic Society of Bombay.

Sukthankar, Vishnu S., Belvalkar, Sripad Krishna, Vaidya, Parashuram Lakshman *et al.* (eds) (1933–66) *The Mahābhārata for the First Time Critically Edited*, 19 vols, Poona: Bhandarkar Oriental Research Institute.

Sullivan, Bruce M. (1990) *Kṛṣṇa Dvaipāyaṇa Vyāsa and the Mahābhārata: a new interpretation*, Leiden: Brill; reprinted as *Seer of the Fifth Veda: Kṛṣṇa Dvaipāyana Vyāsa in the Mahābhārata* (1999), Delhi: Motilal Banarsidass.

—— (2006) 'The ideology of self-willed death in the epic *Mahābhārata*', *Journal of Vaishnava Studies* 14.2: 61–79.

Sullivan, Bruce M. and Unni, N.P. (1995) *The Sun God's Daughter and King Saṃvaraṇa: 'Tapatī-Saṃvaraṇam' and the Kūṭiyāṭṭam drama tradition*, Delhi: Nag.

—— (2001) *The Wedding of Arjuna and Subhadrā: the Kūṭiyāṭṭam drama 'Subhadrā-Dhanañjaya'*, Delhi: Nag.

Sutherland, Gail Hinich (1990) '*Bīja* (seed) and *kṣetra* (field): male surrogacy or *niyoga* in the *Mahābhārata*', *Contributions to Indian Sociology* (new series) 24.1: 77–103.

Sutherland, Sally J.M. (1989) 'Sītā and Draupadī: aggressive behavior and female role-models in the Sanskrit epics', *Journal of the American Oriental Society* 109.1: 63–79.

—— (1992) 'Seduction, counter seduction, and sexual role models: bedroom politics and the Indian epics', *Journal of Indian Philosophy* 20.2: 243–51.

Sutherland Goldman, Sally J. (2000) 'Speaking gender: *vāc* and the Vedic construction of the feminine', in Julia Leslie and Mary McGee (eds) *Invented Identities: the interplay of gender, religion and politics in India*, New Delhi: Oxford University Press.

Sutton, Nicholas (1997) 'Aśoka and Yudhiṣṭhira: a historical setting for the ideological tensions of the *Mahābhārata*?', *Religion* 27.4: 333–41.

—— (1999) 'An exposition of early Sāṁkhya, a rejection of the *Bhagavad-Gītā* and a critique of the role of women in Hindu society: the *Sulabhā-Janaka-Saṁvāda*', *Annals of the Bhandarkar Oriental Research Institute* 80: 53–65.

—— (2000) *Religious Doctrines in the Mahābhārata*, Delhi: Motilal Banarsidass.
—— (2005) 'What is *dharma*? Ethical tensions within the *Mahābhārata*', in T.S. Rukmani (ed.) *The Mahābhārata: what is not here is nowhere else (yannehāsti na tadkvacit)*, Delhi: Munshiram Manoharlal.

Śvetāśvatara Upaniṣad. See Olivelle 1998.

Swanson, Christina (1999) 'Narrative temporality and the aspect of time in Franz Kafka's short fiction', unpublished thesis, University of California, Irvine.

Szczurek, Przemysław (2002) 'Some remarks on the so-called epic layer of the *Bhagavadgītā*', in Mary Brockington (ed.) *Stages and Transitions: temporal and historical frameworks in epic and purāṇic literature*, Zagreb: Croatian Academy of Sciences and Arts.
—— (2005a) '*Dharmarāja* and *Dhammarāja*: remarks on Yudhiṣṭhira's dilemmas', paper presented at the Fourth Dubrovnik International Conference on the Sanskrit Epics and Purāṇas, September 2005.
—— (2005b) 'Bhakti interpolations and additions in the *Bhagavadgītā*', in Petteri Koskikallio (ed.) *Epics, Khilas, and Purāṇas: continuities and ruptures*, Zagreb: Croatian Academy of Sciences and Arts.

Taittirīya Saṃhitā. E. Roer, E.B. Cowell and M. Nyāyaratna (eds) (1860–99) *The Sanhitā of the Black Yajur Veda, with the commentary of Mādhava Āchārya*, 6 vols, Calcutta (Bibliotheca Indica). For English translation, see A.B. Keith (tr.) (1914) *The Veda of the Black Yajus School entitled Taittiriya Sanhita*, 2 vols, Cambridge, MA: Harvard University Press.

Thapar, Romila (1961) *Aśoka and the Decline of the Mauryas*, Oxford: Oxford University Press.
—— (1976) ['*Mahābhārata*: myth and reality'], in S.P. Gupta and K.S. Ramachandran (eds) *Mahābhārata: myth and reality – differing views*, Delhi: Agam Prakashan.
—— (1986) 'Society and historical consciousness: the Itihāsa-Purāṇa tradition', in S. Bhattacarya and R. Thapar (eds) *Situating Indian History: for Sarvepalli Gopal*, Delhi: Oxford University Press; reprinted in *Cultural Pasts: essays in early Indian history* (2000), New Delhi: Oxford University Press.
—— (2002) *Early India: from the origins to AD 1300*, London: Allen Lane.

Thomas, Lynn (2006a) 'Disappearing dragons and Russian dolls: unpacking the *Vṛtrahatya* in the *Āraṇyakaparva*', *Journal of Vaishnava Studies* 14.2: 9–38.
—— (2006b) 'From the ocean bed to the rule of heaven: a comparison of the two main epic accounts of the *vṛtrahatya*', paper presented at the Thirteenth World Sanskrit Conference, Edinburgh, July 2006.

Tieken, Herman (2004) 'The Mahābhārata after the great battle', *Wiener Zeitschrift für die Kunde Südasiens* 48: 5–46.

Todorov, Tvetzan (1988) *Bakhtin: the dialogical principle*, tr. W. Godzich, Minneapolis, MN: University of Minneapolis Press.

Tokunaga, Munco (2005) 'Vedic exegesis and epic poetry: a note on *atrāpy udāharanti*', paper presented at the Fourth Dubrovnik International Conference on the Sanskrit Epics and Purāṇas, September 2005.

Trawick, Margaret (1990) *Notes on Love in a Tamil Family*, Berkeley: University of California Press.

Triṣaṣṭiśalākāpuruṣacaritra. See Helen M. Johnson (tr.) (1931–62) *Triṣaṣṭiśalākāpuruṣacaritra, or The Lives of Sixty-Three Illustrious Persons by Ācārya Śrī Hemacandra*, 6 vols, Baroda: Oriental Institute.

Tschannerl, Volker (1992) *Das Lachen in der altindischen Literatur*, Frankfurt: Lang.

Tubb, Gary (2002) 'Numbers that matter', *Journal of Vaishnava Studies* 11.1: 147–52.

Vanita, Ruth (2000) 'Introduction: ancient Indian materials', in Ruth Vanita and Saleem Kidwai (eds) *Same-Sex Love in India: readings from literature and history*, Basingstoke: Macmillan.

—— (2003) 'The self is not gendered: Sulabha's debate with King Janaka', *National Women's Studies Association Journal* 15.2: 76–93.

Varenne, Jean (1977–8) 'Agni's role in the Ṛgvedic cosmogonic myth', *Annals of the Bhandarkar Oriental Research Institute* 58–9: 375–86.

Vāsiṣṭha Dharmasūtra. See Olivelle 2000.

Vassilkov, Yaroslav (1995) 'The *Mahābhārata*'s typological definition reconsidered', *Indo-Iranian Journal* 38.3: 249–56.

—— (1999) '*Kālavāda* (the doctrine of cyclical time) in the Mahābhārata and the concept of heroic didactics', in Mary Brockington and Peter Schreiner (eds) *Composing a Tradition: concepts, techniques and relationships*, Zagreb: Croatian Academy of Sciences and Arts.

—— (2001) 'The *Mahābhārata* similes and their significance for comparative epic studies', *Rocznik Orientalistyczny* 54.1: 13–31.

—— (2002) 'Indian practice of pilgrimage and the growth of the *Mahābhārata* in the light of new epigraphical sources', in Mary Brockington (ed.) *Stages and Transitions: temporal and historical frameworks in epic and purāṇic literature*, Zagreb: Croatian Academy of Sciences and Arts.

van der Veer, Peter (1999) 'Monumental texts: the Critical Edition of India's national heritage', in Daud Ali (ed.) *Invoking the Past: the uses of history in South Asia*, New Delhi: Oxford University Press.

Viṣṇu Purāṇa. M.M. Pathak (ed.) (1997, 1999), vols 1–2, Vadodara: Oriental Institute. For English translation, see Horace Hayman Wilson (tr.) (1961) *The Vishṇu Purāṇa: a system of Hindu mythology and tradition*, Calcutta: Punthi Pustak (first published 1840).

Weinberger-Thomas, Catherine (1999) *Ashes of Immortality: widow-burning in India*, Chicago, IL: University of Chicago Press.

Wenzel, Horst (1990) 'Repräsentation und schöner Schein am Hof und in der höfischen Literatur', in Hedda Ragotsky and Horst Wenzel (eds) *Höfische Repräsentation: Das Zeremoniell und Zeichen*, Tübingen: Niemeyer.

—— (2003) 'Rittertum und Gender-Trouble im höfischen Roman (Erec) und in der Märendichtung (Beringer)', in Claudia Benthien and Inge Stephan (eds) *Männlichkeit als Maskerade: Kulturelle Inszenierungen vom Mittelalter bis zur Gegenwart*, Köln: Böhlau.

West, Emily Blanchard (2005–6) 'An Indic reflex of the Homeric *Cyclopeia*', *The Classical Journal* 101.2: 125–60.

Whitaker, Jarrod L. (2000) 'Divine weapons and *tejas* in the two Indian epics', *Indo-Iranian Journal* 43.2: 87–113.

—— (2002) 'How the gods kill: the *Nārāyaṇa astra* episode, the death of Rāvaṇa, and the principles of *tejas* in the Indian epics', *Journal of Indian Philosophy* 30.4: 403–30.

White, David Gordon (1989) 'Dogs die', *History of Religions* 28: 282–303.

Whitney, William Dwight (1960) *Sanskrit Grammar*, Cambridge, MA: Harvard University Press. First published 1889.

Witzel, Michael (1987) 'On the origin of the literary device of the "frame story" in old Indian literature', in Harry Falk (ed.) *Hinduismus und Buddhismus: festschrift für Ulrich Schneider*, Freiburg: Hedwig Falk.

Woods, Julian F. (2001) *Destiny and Human Initiative in the Mahābhārata*, Albany: State University of New York Press.

Yocum, Glenn (1977) 'The Goddess in a Tamil Śaiva devotional text, Māṇikkavācakar's *Tiruvācakam*', *Journal of the American Academy of Religion* 45.1.

Zaehner, Robert C. (1962) *Hinduism*, Oxford: Oxford University Press.

Zapperi, Roberto (1991) *The Pregnant Man*, tr. Brian Williams, 4th edn, New York: Harwood Academic Publishers. First published in Italian, Cosenza: Lerici, 1979.

Zwilling, Leonard and Sweet, Michael J. (2000) 'The evolution of third-sex constructs in ancient India: a study in ambiguity', in Julia Leslie and Mary McGee (eds) *Invented Identities: the interplay of gender, religion and politics in India*, New Delhi: Oxford University Press.

INDEX

14524445R00197

Printed in Poland
by Amazon Fulfillment
Poland Sp. z o.o., Wrocław